Israel on Trial

How International Law is Being Misused to Delegitimize the State of Israel

Matthijs de Blois and Andrew Tucker

Israel on Trial

How International Law is Being Misused to Delegitimize the State of Israel

Publisher:

The Hague Initiative for International Cooperation

Korte Middelwijkstraat 13
3764 DB Soest
The Netherlands

www.thinc.info

Authors: Matthijs de Blois, Andrew Tucker

All maps are taken from 'The Routledge Atlas of the Arab-Israeli Conflict' by Sir Martin Gilbert, © 2012 - Routledge, reproduced by permission of Taylor & Francis Books, UK. www.martingilbert.com

Cover design and layout: Anat Hod
Cover image: Marja de Blois – Nijburg

ISBN 978-90-828681-0-4

THE HAGUE INITIATIVE
for INTERNATIONAL CO-OPERATION

An initiative to study the relationship between Israel and the nations, in order to promote international peace and security, friendly relations amongst nations, and peaceful resolution of disputes based on the principles of justice and international law.

"The law, history and politics of the Israel-Palestine dispute is immensely complex. ...Context is usually important in legal determinations.... I find the 'history' as recounted by the court ...neither balanced nor satisfactory."

—Judge Higgins, Separate Opinion, 2004 ICJ

"Fidelity to law is the essence of peace, and the only practical rule for making a just and lasting peace."

—Eugene V. Rostow, Former Dean of Yale Law School and Distinguished Fellow at the United States Institute of Peace

"For false words are not only evil in themselves, but they infect the soul with evil."

—Plato, Phaedo

"The Arab Heads of State have agreed to unite their political efforts at the international and diplomatic level to eliminate the effects of the aggression and to ensure the withdrawal of the aggressive Israeli forces from the Arab lands which have been occupied since the aggression of June 5. This will be done within the framework of the main principles by which the Arab States abide, namely, no peace with Israel, no recognition of Israel, no negotiations with it, and insistence on the rights of the Palestinian people in their own country."

—The Khartoum Resolution, issued by eight Arab states after the Six-Day War, September 1967

"Palestine's admission to the United Nations would pave the way for the internationalization of the conflict as a legal matter, not only a political one. It would also pave the way for us to pursue claims against Israel at the United Nations, human rights treaty bodies and the International Court of Justice. ... We call on all friendly, peace-loving nations to join us in realizing our national aspirations by recognizing the State of Palestine on the 1967 border and by supporting its admission to the United Nations. Only if the international community keeps the promise it made to us six decades ago, and ensures that a just resolution for Palestinian refugees is put into effect, can there be a future of hope and dignity for our people."

—"The Long Overdue Palestinian State," Op-ed, by Mahmoud Abbas, Chairman of the Palestine Liberation Organization and President of the Palestinian National Authority, published in The New York Times, 16 May 2011

"Our right to the Land of Israel does not stem from the Mandate and the Balfour Declaration. It precedes those. The Bible is our mandate... I can state in the name of the Jewish People: The Bible is our mandate, the Bible that was written by us in our Hebrew language, and in this land itself, is our mandate. Our historical right has existed since our beginnings as the Jewish People, and the Balfour Declaration and the Mandate recognize and confirm that right."

—David Ben-Gurion: Testimony to the
Peel Royal Commission, Notes of Evidence taken
on Thursday, 7 January 1937

"I believe that each people, anywhere, has a right to live in their peaceful nation. I believe the Palestinians and the Israelis have the right to have their own land. But we have to have a peace agreement to assure the stability for everyone and to have normal relations."

—Saudi Crown Prince Muhammad bin Salman,
Jerusalem Post, 4 April 2018

Table of Contents

Acronyms

AIV (Dutch Advisory Council on International Affairs)

BDS (Boycott, Divestment, and Sanctions Movement)

CEIRPP (United Nations Committee on the Exercise of the Inalienable Rights of the Palestinian People)

CEDAW (Convention on the Elimination of all Forms of Discrimination against Women)

COGAT (Coordinator of Government Activities in the Territories)

CSDP (Common Security and Defence Policy)

DOP (Declaration of Principles on Interim Self-Government Arrangements)

EAD (Euro-Arab Dialogue)

EC (European Council)

ECOSOC (United Nations Economic and Social Council)

ECSC (European Coal and Steel Community)

EEC (European Economic Community)

EU (European Union)

FGC (Fourth Geneva Convention)

GA (United Nations General Assembly)

Hague Convention IV (The Hague Convention (IV) Respecting the Laws and Customs of War on Land (1907))

Hebron Protocol (Protocol concerning the redeployment in Hebron)

Interim Agreement on the West Bank and the Gaza Strip (Oslo II or Interim Agreement)

ICC (International Criminal Court)

ICJ (International Court of Justice)

ICCPR (International Covenant on Civil and Political Rights)

ICRC (International Committee of the Red Cross)

ICERD (International Convention on the Elimination of All Forms of Racial Discrimination)

ICESCR (International Covenant on Economic, Social and Cultural Rights)

IDF (Israeli Defense Forces)

IHH (Foundation for Human Rights, Freedoms and Humanitarian Relief)

IHL (International Humanitarian Law)

LAW (Palestinian Committee for the Protection of Human Rights and the Environment)

LOIAC (Law of International Armed Conflict)

MAG (Military Advocate General)

MIFTAH (Palestinian Initiative for the Promotion of Global Dialogue and Democracy)

NAM (Non-Aligned Movement)

NGOs (Non-governmental organizations)

OCHA (United Nations Office for the Coordination of Humanitarian Affairs)

OIC (Organization of Islamic Cooperation)

OPT (Occupied Palestinian Territories)

PA (Palestinian Authority)

PCIJ (Permanent Court of International Justice)

PFLP (Popular Front for the Liberation of Palestine)

PLA (Palestinian Liberation Army)

PLO (Palestine Liberation Organization)

PNC (Palestinian National Council)

SANGOCO (the South African NGO Committee)

SC (United Nations Security Council)

The Arab League (League of Arab States)

UDHR (Universal Declaration of Human Rights)

UN (United Nations)

UNCRC (UN Convention on the Rights of the Child)

UNDOF (UN Disengagement Observer Force)

UNDPR (Special Unit on Palestinian Rights in the United Nations Secretariat, or the Division for Palestinian Rights)

UNEF (UN Emergency Force)

UNESCO (UN Educational, Scientific and Cultural Organization)

UNHRC (UN Human Rights Council)

UNIFIL (UN Interim Force In Lebanon)

UNRWA (UN Relief and Works Agency for Palestine Refugees)

UNSC (UN Security Council)

UNSCOP (UN Special Committee on Palestine)

WCAR (UN World Conference Against Racism)

WEOG (Western European and Others Group)

WZO (World Zionist Organization)

Acknowledgments

This project started out as an expanded English-language version of Matthijs de Blois's book, written in Dutch, "Israel – een staat ter discussie." In its essence, the project was an attempt to assess the persuasiveness of the legal analysis of the International Court of Justice (ICJ) in the 2004 Wall Advisory Opinion.

We took the comment of ICJ Judge Higgins in her Separate Opinion in the Wall case as an invitation: "The law, history and politics of the Israel-Palestine dispute is immensely complex. ...Context is usually important in legal determinations.... I find the 'history' as recounted by the court ... neither balanced nor satisfactory."

Indeed, the ICJ's complete lack of historical consciousness is alarming to say the least, as is its apparent disregard for the enormous contribution of the Jewish State to the well-being of its citizens and its neighbors, and the dilemma's facing the State of Israel in its struggle to respect human rights while also fighting against terrorism.

This project was given extra focus and urgency following the adoption by the United Nations (UN) Security Council of Resolution 2334 in December 2016. Suddenly, we realized that this is no longer a mere academic exercise. The legal paradigm reflected in that resolution, and the 2004 Wall Advisory Opinion, has so far dismally failed to produce a peaceful resolution of the Israel/Palestine conflict. Worse, the line of thinking in Resolution 2334 could even be read as justifying a prohibition on Jews from living in the Old City of Jerusalem, Judea and Samaria—places deeply connected with Jewish history, culture and religion.

Does international law justify or require this approach?

In undertaking this task, our intention has been two-fold. First, we wanted to understand and describe the way international law is used (and misused) within the UN system. Uncovering the "behind the scenes" realities of the UN system required us to consider the way international law deals with the distinction between law and politics, between the use and misuse of law.

Second, we wanted to determine the extent to which the legal statements in Resolution 2334 and the ICJ's analysis in the 2004 Wall Advisory Opinion are correct, as a matter of law. In doing so, we have not sought to create new insights or propound new approaches to international law; on the contrary, we have simply tried to draw together the many contributions of eminent lawyers and tribunals over many decades that touch on the issues raised by Resolution 2334 and the 2004 Wall Advisory Opinion, and which did not seem to find their way into the deliberations leading up to the formulation of those instruments.

We fully acknowledge that advocating a legal analysis based on respect for historical events may not have mainstream support, and that the just and peaceful resolution of disputes in general—and the Israel/Palestine conflict in particular—requires the legalities of past events to be balanced with more recent legal and factual realities. Nevertheless, we believe that justice will never be done unless those historical realities are respected and their legal significance properly understood. Respect for the human rights of Palestinian Arabs (and all others living in Israel/Palestine) must also give adequate legal recognition to the fundamental justice of the return of the Jewish people to the land over the last two centuries from persecution, neglect and numerous attempts at ethnic cleansing in the diaspora—not only in Europe, but also in the Middle East.

We have chosen a number of Sir Martin Gilbert's maps from The Routledge Atlas of the Arab-Israeli Conflict to illustrate and clarify the text. They are very accurate and contain valuable background information enabling the reader to comprehend more of the context.

We are grateful to the many people who have contributed towards this publication over the last few years.

A special thanks to our research assistants: Faith Collins, Robbert van de Bovenkamp, Jeannette Gabay-Schoonderwoerd, Mikayla Brier-Mills and Matthew Thorn.

We are grateful for the legal insights of all those who participated in The Hague Seminar in the Peace Palace in June 2017, in which we grappled with the many legal complexities arising out of UN Resolution 2334. (The results of that Seminar are found in the "The Hague Statement of Jurists on the Israel-Palestine Conflict", available at www.thinc.info).

With masterful skill and tact, our thinc. colleague, Pieter Hoogendoorn, has managed the process of turning a rough manuscript into a publishable book under a tight deadline.

Tomas Sandell (European Coalition for Israel) has provided many strategic insights over the years.

Alan Stephens has encouraged us to present our case without favor or fear and has helped us steer away from too many unnecessary legal minefields.

Gijs Cremer Eindhoven (Chairman of The Hague Initiative for International Cooperation) has encouraged us and strengthened us in our conviction that this is a worthwhile project despite the many challenges and setbacks.

Avi Bell, Johannes Gerloff, Yitzhak Sokoloff and Chaim Even Zohar read parts of the manuscript and gave us the benefits of their insights and suggestions.

Peter Schregardus did a brilliant job editing the footnotes and compiling the bibliography.

Special thanks to Rachel Segal for proofreading and Anat Hod for the layout and design.

Last but not least—our deepest appreciation to our wives, Marja and Marianne, who have tolerated the many days of our absence from domestic duties, and without whom this would never have been possible.

All responsibility for defects or shortcomings in the manuscript remains ours alone.

INTRODUCTION

Israel on Trial

Introduction: Israel on Trial

The Israel/Palestine conflict is perhaps the most complex, dynamic and ancient dispute in the international arena today. For millennia, this tiny sliver of land that lies strategically at the meeting point of Europe, Asia and Africa, and later became known as "Palestine," has been the focus of the three monotheistic religions of Judaism, Christianity and Islam, and has captured the attention of world empires. For the last 100 years, Jewish and Arab leaders as well as the political leaders of most other nations in the world, together with armies of international lawyers, diplomats, policy advisers and many others, have proposed ideas and developed plans designed to produce peace in the region. When Israeli Prime Minister Yitzhak Rabin and Palestine Liberation Organization (PLO) Chairman Yasser Arafat shook hands on the White House lawn in 1993, most believed the "Oslo Agreements" would pave the way for peace. And yet, today, resolution of the dispute seems as far away as ever. Worse, the region seems to be on the cusp of conflict.

The depth and intensity of the emotions aroused by this piece of land were demonstrated by the events of early December 2017. Normally, a decision to establish an embassy in the capital city of another nation would pass unnoticed. Yet, the announcement by US President Donald Trump on 6 December 2017 of his decision to recognize the city of Jerusalem as the capital of the State of Israel, and to move the US embassy in Israel from Tel Aviv to Jerusalem, provoked a veritable explosion of international outrage. Even accepting that Jerusalem has always attracted disproportionate attention, the reaction was extreme. Palestinian leaders immediately called for "three days of rage." Referring to Jerusalem as "the eternal capital of the State of Palestine," Palestinian Authority (PA) President Mahmoud Abbas rejected the claims of the US as a serious peace broker. One Al Jazeera commentator even referred to the decision as "a declaration of war against the Palestinian people and their rights, and against the international community and its commitment to international law and to a two-state solution." The Organization of Islamic Cooperation (OIC) immediately called an emergency meeting under leadership of Turkey's

President, Tayyip Erdogan, to denounce the decision as "null and void" and a "serious violation of international law."[1] The European Union (EU) High Representative for Foreign Affairs and Security Policy, Federica Mogherini, expressed serious concern about the decision by the American President.[2] Within days, the United Nations (UN) General Assembly, claiming the announcement represented a serious threat to "international peace and security," responded to the US decision by adopting during its Tenth Emergency Special Session a resolution condemning decisions by states to place their diplomatic missions in Jerusalem, and reiterating the claims that Jerusalem has a "specific status" and that Israel's administration of the city is a violation of international law.

President Trump's decision was remarkable not only for the extremity of the response it triggered, but also for the banality of its content. He simply effectuated a decision taken by the US Congress in 1995, under the Democratic President Bill Clinton, and did not in any way change either the situation on the ground in Jerusalem or the status of the city under Israeli or international law. President Trump even left open the question of whether the US Embassy would be located in West or East Jerusalem. The sole fact that he recognized Jerusalem as capital of Israel was apparently enough to turn the diplomatic world upside down.

The Israel/Palestine conflict has become the most important item on the agenda of the UN. This is demonstrated by the fact that in December 2017 the UN General Assembly adopted 251 resolutions in its regular sessions. *Five* resolutions addressed a small selection of the most blatant breaches of human rights on earth—Russia/Ukraine, Syria, the Islamic Republic of Iran, the Democratic Republic of Korea, and Myanmar—regions where thousands have been slaughtered and millions have become refugees. In contrast, *twelve* resolutions were passed condemning Israel's occupation of the Palestinian Territories. And in its only Emergency Special Session (devoted solely to the Israel/Palestine conflict—apparently the only threat to global peace), it adopted Resolution A/RES/ES-10/19—the only time in the history of the UN that a decision by one Member State to recognize a particular city as the capital of another Member State has been condemned.

Singling Out the Israel/Palestine Dispute in the UN

In fact, ever since the establishment of the UN in 1945 and the creation of the State of Israel in 1948, the Israel/Palestine conflict has

1. See: https://www.dailysabah.com/diplomacy/2017/12/13/oic-declares-east-jerusalem-capital-of-palestine-urges-us-to-withdraw-from-peace-process.

2. See: https://eeas.europa.eu/headquarters/headquarters-homepage/37001/s.

absorbed a vastly disproportionate amount of the UN's attention and resources. The state of Israel has been treated much less favorably than other UN member states:

- Israel is the only member of the UN that (until recently) has not been eligible for representation in the Security Council.
- Jerusalem is the only city in the world over which the UN claims to have a special jurisdiction, and Israel is the only country that is denied the right to declare a particular city as its capital.
- More resolutions in the UN General Assembly and Security Council are devoted to criticizing Israel than any other state. Outgoing US Ambassador Samantha Power admitted in December 2016 that Israel has been the subject of inordinate discrimination in the UN General Assembly, which in 2016 passed 18 resolutions directed against Israel. UN Secretary-General Ban Ki-Moon confirmed this in his final speech in late 2016 by saying that the UN has a "disproportionate volume of resolutions, reports and conferences criticizing Israel," and that "in many cases, rather than helping the Palestinian cause, this reality has hampered the ability of the UN to fulfill its role effectively."
- More institutions and projects have been established within the UN devoted to the Palestinian cause than to any other people claiming the right to self-determination. "Palestine" is the only nation to which the UN Member States demand its statehood and contribute annually hundreds of millions of dollars.
- The Israel/Palestine conflict is the only conflict in the world in relation to which the UN seeks to impose a particular solution as satisfying the legitimate interests of all parties—notwithstanding the objections of one of those parties.
- Israel is the object of disproportionate criticism by UN Human Rights institutions. Thirty percent of the resolutions concerning specific states adopted by the UN Human Rights Commission in the 40 years of its existence were against Israel. Israel is the only country that warrants a dedicated place on the agenda of the UN Human Rights Council. Current US Ambassador to the UN, Nikki Haley, criticized the UN Human Rights Council (UNHRC) for what she believes is a biased approach. In an opinion piece for the Washington Post, she said that "the council must end its practice of wrongly singling out Israel for criticism. When the council passes more than 70 resolutions against Israel, a country with a strong human rights record, and just seven resolutions against Iran, a country with an abysmal human rights record, you know something is seriously wrong," she wrote.
- A number of leading specialists in the field of international law ardently

promote the view that Israel is one of the world's foremost infringers of international law. An army of current and former prominent politicians and theologians spare no effort to publicize the view in the media that Israel is guilty of serious breaches of international law, and even that Israel and its leaders should be prosecuted for war crimes. Prominent non-governmental organizations (NGOs), such as Amnesty International and Human Rights Watch, devote proportionally more attention to alleged human rights offenses in Israel and the Palestinian territories than any other nation.

- The UN has facilitated NGOs to promote the cause of the Palestinians and condemn Israel for breaches of international law. Many of these NGOs receive significant amounts of funding from nations whose foreign policy objectives are fundamentally in conflict with those of the Jewish State of Israel.
- The UN General Assembly created a special regime for "Palestinian refugees" who are the only refugees in the world with a so-called "right of return," and Israel is the only nation in the world that is alleged to be under an obligation to re-accept the descendants of refugees that fled from its territories in a time of conflict.
- The Palestinian leadership—supported by many UN Member States—has actively sought to "internationalize the conflict as a legal matter" in the UN institutions and related organizations, like UNESCO and the International Criminal Court (ICC), in order to achieve the declared aim of creating an internationally recognized "State of Palestine" with East Jerusalem as its capital.

The "Two-State Solution"

The main thrust of the resolutions adopted by UN bodies is the notion that the Israeli "occupation" must be ended, in order to ensure the creation and functioning of a Palestinian state in fulfillment of the "inalienable rights" of the Palestinian people, who are considered the rightful owners of the land. Every day, media around the world report on the use of international law in these resolutions, which is often repeated by national governments, courts and multilateral institutions like the EU, to criticize Israeli "occupation" and "settlements" as "dangerously imperilling the viability of the two-state solution" and an "obstacle to global peace."

The two-state solution, involving the creation of a State of Palestine adjacent to Israel, may indeed be a solution to the conflict, and it may even be the only solution that all parties will accept. In fact, Israel has, in one way or another since 1967, seriously entertained the idea of Palestinian autonomy; since 2009, commitment to the two-state solution is official policy of the government of the State of Israel. However, as Prime Minister Benjamin Netanyahu stated in his Bar Ilan speech in 2009, Israel's commitment to the creation of a Palestinian state is not unconditional. Specifically, Israel will only accept a Palestinian state if it is demilitarized, and if it accepts Israel as the Jewish State.

Neither of these conditions appears in the various UN resolutions. Moreover, these resolutions do not speak of the two-state solution as a *political option*, rather they increasingly refer to it as a *legal requirement* imposing *legal obligations* on the State of Israel and other states. Most recently, in December 2016, the UN Security Council (with the US abstaining—the last diplomatic initiative of outgoing President Barack Obama and Secretary of State John Kerry) adopted Resolution 2334 in which the Security Council effectively laid down the terms upon which Israel is obliged to accept the "two-state solution."

Resolution 2334 was drafted by Egypt, which initially was prepared at Israel's request to have the vote postponed. However, at the request of New Zealand, Senegal, Malaysia and Venezuela, it was put to the vote and adopted by an overwhelming majority in the Security Council, with only an abstention of the US.[3] The Resolution has been a major influence on the way many states formulate their foreign policy in relation to Israel/ Palestine. Only a few weeks after the adoption of UNSC 2334, on 15 January 2017, around 70 nations met in Paris, at a "Peace Summit" hosted by French President François Hollande, to discuss and issue a resolution on the Israel/Palestine conflict. In their closing statement, the participating nations—which included most European and many other "Western" nations—"reiterated that a negotiated two-state solution should meet the legitimate aspirations of both sides, including the Palestinians' right to statehood and sovereignty, fully end the occupation that began in 1967, satisfy Israel's security needs and resolve all permanent status issues on the basis of United Nations Security Council resolutions 242 (1967) and 338 (1973), and also recalled relevant Security Council resolutions."[4]

Resolution 2334 uses very strong legal language ("legitimate aspirations," "rights to statehood and sovereignty," "condemns," etc.) and attributes great importance to UN resolutions. The Security Council:

- referred to "the obligation of Israel, the occupying Power, to abide

3 *The Guardian*, 23 December 2016.

4 Emphasis added. The full Statement can be accessed at: http://www.haaretz.com/israel-news/1.765207.

scrupulously by its *legal obligations and responsibilities* under the Fourth Geneva Convention relative to the Protection of Civilian Persons in Time of War, of 12 August 1949";

- condemned "all measures aimed at altering the demographic composition, character and status of the Palestinian Territory occupied since 1967, including East Jerusalem, including, *inter alia,* the construction and expansion of settlements, transfer of Israeli settlers, confiscation of land, demolition of homes and displacement of Palestinian civilians, *in violation of international humanitarian law and relevant resolutions*";
- recalled "the *obligation under the Quartet Roadmap,* endorsed by its resolution 1515 (2003) for a freeze by Israel of all settlement activity";
- reaffirmed "that the establishment by Israel of settlements in the Palestinian territory occupied since 1967, including East Jerusalem, has *no legal validity and constitutes a flagrant violation under international law,*" and demanded that Israel "immediately and completely cease all settlement activities" in these territories and "fully respect all of its *legal obligations in this regard*";
- denied any "recogni[tion to] changes to the 4 June 1967 lines, including with regard to Jerusalem, other than those agreed by the parties through negotiation"; and
- called upon all states "to distinguish, in their relevant dealings, between the territory of the State of Israel and the territories occupied since 1967."

These statements repeat claims made in many different UN resolutions over the last 45 years. Nevertheless, Resolution 2334 is very significant because it was the first time the Security Council has issued a resolution in such strong and comprehensive terms. In support of these statements concerning international law, the Security Council referred to the 2004 Advisory Opinion of the International Court of Justice (ICJ) on "The Legal Consequences of the Construction of a Wall in the Occupied Palestinian Territory" (the Wall Advisory Opinion).

Resolution 2334 and the Wall Advisory Opinion can be considered as the most authoritative statements to date on the legal status of Israel and the two-state solution. Essentially, this "Mandatory Two-State Solution Paradigm" says that Israel has no legal claim whatsoever to the territories now known as the "Occupied Palestinian Territories" (comprising East Jerusalem, the West Bank and Gaza). The creation of a Palestinian state based on the "4 June borders" is seen as the only possible solution to satisfy the Palestinian claims. Any action taken by Israel that threatens that outcome is seen as an infringement of international law. Israeli "settlements" in these territories are illegal (and, implicitly, should be removed). Israel is obliged to cooperate with the creation of the State of Palestine, based on the "4 June 1967 lines," and all other states are responsible to ensure that Israel meets these obligations.

This is remarkable when one considers that in 1922—less than 100 years ago—the universal opinion of states (as expressed in the League of Nations) was that Jerusalem and all the territories that are now normally referred to as "occupied territories" were in principle to be reserved for the establishment of a Jewish homeland. In other words, at that time, there was overwhelming international consensus that international law supported all of Palestine becoming a Jewish national homeland (provided the civil and religious rights of minorities are protected). Granted, from the 1930s onwards, the world community explored dividing this territory west of the Jordan River—which was simply known as Palestine—into two separate states (one for the Jews, the other for the Arabs). But apart from a number of Arab/Islamic states, at no time prior to the early 1970s did other states consider the mere existence of Jews in the Old City of Jerusalem and the West Bank as illegal under international law, or the creation of a Palestinian Arab state as mandatory as a matter of law.

In what way has international law—or perceptions of international law—changed in the last hundred years to justify this apparent 180-degree turnaround? What, in international legal terms, is going on? And does international law really require the creation of a Palestinian State on the terms set out by the UN—even though that formula has so far failed to produce a peaceful resolution of the dispute?

International Legal Issues

The "Mandatory Two-State Solution Paradigm" set out in Resolution 2334 reflects the development of five inter-related sets of ideas in recent decades in relation to the application of international law to the Israel/Palestine conflict:

- The first set of ideas concerns the status and identity of Israel as a Jewish state. The Jewish State of Israel—a state in which the Jewish people give expression to their own identity as a nation—was almost universally welcomed in 1948, but it has since become widely perceived as an apartheid, racist, discriminatory and colonial enterprise. "Zionism" (the Jewish longing to return to the Promised Land) has come to be seen as illegitimate, because it was established, and continues to exist, at the expense of the indigenous Arab population. The Mandate for Palestine was a colonialist initiative of European powers imposed at the expense of the indigenous population. The Jews ethnically cleansed Palestine of the Arab population (or at least intended to do so) in the conflict of 1947/49 and have continued to do so since.

- The second group of ideas focuses on the status of the land, and notions of territorial sovereignty. The West Bank and Gaza have somehow come to be seen as "belonging" to the Palestinians. Israel is illegally occupying "Palestinian land" which it took in 1967. Israel is accused of building settlements in order to effect "creeping annexation" of the territories captured in 1967. All Jewish settlements in Jerusalem and the West Bank outside the Green Line are illegal, because they have been built on "Palestinian land," and Israel's refusal to remove them is an obstacle to peace. In fact, some (including the PLO) regard the territory of Israel itself as belonging to the Palestinians.
- The third group of ideas looks at the conflict from the perspective of the human rights of the non-Jewish Palestinians, who are regarded as the truly indigenous people and now simply referred to as "Palestinians." Israel is infringing and obstructing "Palestinian human rights"—especially the right of the "Palestinian people" to self-determination and political independence. This line of argument was originally focused on challenging Israel's presence in the so-called "occupied territories" but has extended to undermine the legitimacy of the State of Israel as such.
- Fourth, "Palestine" is seen as belonging to the indigenous Arab population, which should be recognized as the original inhabitants and rightful owners of the land. The Palestinian refugee problem was caused by the establishment of the State of Israel, and the refugees have a right to return to Israel. Some argue that the State of Palestine exists, or should exist, next to Israel. Others argue that the Jewish State of Israel, like the apartheid regime in South Africa, should be dismantled and replaced by a unified state of "Palestine" encompassing all of the territories known as Israel, the West Bank, the Gaza Strip (also referred to as Gaza) and the Golan Heights.
- Finally, there is the question of the conduct of Israel's leaders and armed forces in the context of military conflict. Israel, it is said, has been guilty of war crimes since 1973, in particular the illegitimate use of force in the conflicts in Lebanon in 1982 and 2006 and in Gaza in 2008/9, 2012 and 2014, and the Flotilla incident in 2010.

It is the purpose of this book to examine the way international law has developed in each of these areas in the last 100 years. Before doing so, in Part I, we examine the nature of international law and the international legal system, and specifically the role of the UN and the position of Israel within UN institutions. This is necessary, in order to explain the significance (or lack of it) of decisions by UN institutions in relation to the various legal issues under consideration.

Part II looks at the Jewish State of Israel—the historical, political and legal background to its creation in May 1948, its character as a "state" under international law, and the question of the "legitimacy" of the State of Israel as a Jewish and democratic state. Part III examines notions of territorial sovereignty, and their application to Israel/Palestine. This will include consideration of the relevance of the law of belligerent occupation to territorial claims. In Part IV, we look at the application of international human rights law as it pertains to Israel. Part V examines the Palestinian Arab claim to self-determination, including the question of whether a State of Palestine exists. Finally, Part VI looks at the application of international humanitarian law to the State of Israel and its conflict with the Palestinian Arabs and its Arab neighbors.

In most chapters, we commence with a quotation from the ICJ Wall Advisory Opinion, or one of the Separate Opinions or Declarations of the individual judges.

It is our contention that the UN system has been deliberately used by the Palestinian Arab leadership—in partnership with various blocks of nations—to undermine the legitimacy of the State of Israel, and thereby to bring about not only the creation of a separate State of Palestine, but ultimately also the destruction of the Jewish State of Israel. This misuse has resulted in distorted and discriminaroty application of international law, as reflected particularly in the ICJ Wall Advisory Opinion and UN Security Council Resolution 2334.

That is a bold claim, and while at first glance it may appear to be opposed to the interests of the Palestinian Arab people, we believe that is not the case. We do not defend the *status quo* in the West Bank and Gaza Strip. In June 1967, Israel took control of the Sinai, East Jerusalem, the West Bank, the Gaza Strip and Golan Heights. Since then it has withdrawn completely from the Sinai and Gaza. East Jerusalem is considered by Israel to be part of its undivided capital and is administered as part of the municipality of Jerusalem. The residents of the remaining "occupied" territories, many of them living in UNRWA "refugee" camps, have become stateless. The political process initiated by the Oslo Agreements, intended to lead to a full resolution of the conflict, has ground to a standstill, and there is at present no prospect that negotiations will resume. The Gaza Strip, under the yoke of Hamas, is a time bomb waiting to explode. There is a lack of sound government in the Palestinian territories. The Palestinian Arabs in the West Bank are forced to live in a no-man's land where they neither enjoy the benefits of an effective government nor the prospects of developing a prosperous society. Conflicts involving acts of terror and the use of force in Gaza, the West Bank and on the northern border with Lebanon have cost many lives, most of them Palestinian Arabs.

Clearly, some solution needs to be found to resolve this situation. An autonomous State of Palestine may indeed be the most desirable solution. But that is a far cry from saying that such a state must—as a matter of law—be created on terms determined by the UN.

Our contention is that various political solutions are possible under international law. But an assessment of all available political options must proceed from a sound evaluation of the legal issues. We argue that the analysis of these issues should start with examining the identity, scope and status of the State of Israel, because statehood, and the sovereign equality of states, remains the fundamental principle underlying the international legal order. If (as we shall argue) a Jewish State of Israel came into existence in 1948, then—being a state—it is under international law entitled to the same rights and subject to the same obligations as any other state.

Some of the most important conclusions of our study are:

a. The State of Israel is a legitimate sovereign state, and has the right to exist as a sovereign state, enjoying the same rights to political independence, territorial inviolability and freedom from aggression as all other states.

b. Israel is under no obligation to withdraw from the "occupied territories" or remove Israeli settlements, for the simple reason it is not an "occupying power" within the meaning of the Hague Rules and Fourth Geneva Convention; and even if it were, international law does not require the abandonment of occupation without a peace treaty.

c. The territories known as "Occupied Palestinian Territories" do not "belong" to the Palestinians; on the contrary, the State of Israel has a very strong claim to territorial sovereignty over the city of Jerusalem, and has a claim to territorial sovereignty over the West Bank equal or superior to that of any other state or legal entity, including the PLO.

d. The creation of a State of Palestine may (or may not) be a desirable political solution, but it is not required under international law, and Israel is under no obligation to facilitate or accept an adjacent Palestinian state that is unwilling or unable to protect Israel's rights to secure borders, political independence and territorial integrity.

e. Conversely, the Palestinians should not be encouraged or allowed to develop autonomously unless they demonstrate that they are both able and willing—as a political entity—to comply with the most fundamental UN Charter principles, such as the obligation to respect other states, the prohibition of force and the requirement of friendly relations.

f. The UN and its Member States have no jurisdiction to determine the borders between the State of Israel and its neighbors, and in any event, insisting on the borders referred to in Resolution 2334 (the "4 June 1967 lines") arguably infringes Israel's rights under international law.

g. Third party states are under no obligation to enforce the two-state solution or facilitate the creation of the State of Palestine; on the contrary, to do so without Israel's consent constitutes a fundamental infringement of Israel's rights.

h. There are significant instances of breaches of human rights in the West Bank. But Israel cannot be held liable for the treatment of Palestinian Arabs in these territories, to the extent to which it is not in control. Both Israel and the Palestinian Arab leadership face many dilemmas in dealing with the current situation. International law does not pre-determine the ways in which Palestinian autonomy should be realized. That is a matter to be determined by the State of Israel in negotiation with the Palestinian Arab people.

i. As a sovereign state, Israel is entitled to defend itself against terrorism and other acts of force, and international humanitarian law should not be applied more onerously to Israel than to other states in equivalent situations.

In this light, it will be apparent that the dispute in question is not simply a dispute between Israel and the Palestinian Arab people. At its deepest, in our view, it is a dispute between the State of Israel and all those who deny it the right to exist as a sovereign state with secure borders and free from threats of annihilation.

Terminology

Finally, a note on language. The use of words plays a crucial role in any discussion or analysis of the Israel/Palestine conflict. Names and titles are used by all sides to make and support their underlying claims. It is now almost impossible to use any specific terminology without suggesting acquiescence in the underlying meaning. For the sake of consistency and simplicity, we have chosen to use the following terms in this book:

"Palestine" – one of the recurring themes throughout this study, and indicative of the way perceptions have changed in the course of the last century, is the use of the term "Palestine." Up until the mid-20th century, "Palestine" referred to a territory, not a political entity. It simply meant the whole of the area covered by the British Mandate—including all of what is today recognized as the State of Israel, plus Gaza and the West Bank and even the territory covered by Jordan. All inhabitants of Palestine—Jews and non-Jews—were referred to as "Palestinians." Today, in contrast, the name "Palestinian" is used in the media and by political leaders and international organizations, and even international jurists (including judges of the International Court of Justice) to refer exclusively to the non-Jewish, Arab-speaking inhabitants of the land—with the implication that they alone are the rightful owners of (part of) the land. Unless otherwise indicated, we use the term "Palestine" in this book to refer to the geographical territory west of the Jordan River covered by the Mandate for Palestine (i.e., not including the territory of the Kingdom of Jordan).

"West Bank" – we use the term "West Bank" to refer to all of the territory west of the Jordan River that was controlled by Jordan between August 1949 and June 1967. Use of this term does not imply acknowledgement of Jordan's territorial claims over this territory, nor the territorial claims of the PLO or others since 1967.

"East Jerusalem" – is used to refer to that part of the city of Jerusalem that fell under Jordanian control following the 1949 Armistice Agreement between Israel and Jordan. As will be seen, the use of the term "east" is a misnomer because the area controlled by Jordan in this period encompassed not only the eastern but also the northern and southern parts of the city.

"Palestinian Arabs" – refers to non-Jews living in the territory of Palestine. As will be seen, the word "Arab" is misleading: many "Palestinian Arabs" are not Arabs in the ethnic sense. Examples are Druze, Bedouins and Aramean Christians. As "Palestine" in the territorial sense encompasses the whole area west of the Jordan River, many Palestinian Arabs live in the State of Israel, and most of those who do so are Israeli citizens (approximately 20 percent of Israeli citizens are Palestinian Arabs). Some Palestinian Arabs, like those living in East Jerusalem, have Jordanian nationality but have Israeli rights of residency and carry Israeli identity cards.

"Israel proper" – is used to refer to the territory that was controlled by the State of Israel prior to the Six-Day War in June 1967. This is a term of convenience. In using it, as we will make clear, we do not mean to imply that the territories over which Israel gained control in June 1967 do not belong to the State of Israel.

PART I

Israel and International Law

1. What Is International Law?

"The Court will now determine the rules and principles of international law which are relevant in assessing the legality of the measures taken by Israel. Such rules and principles can be found in the United Nations Charter and certain other treaties, in customary international law and in the relevant resolutions adopted pursuant to the Charter by the General Assembly and the Security Council."

Advisory Opinion (paragraph 86)[5]

"The Court, however, does not function in a void. It is the principal judicial organ of the United Nations and has to carry out its function and responsibility within the wider political context. It cannot be expected to present a legal opinion on the request of a political organ without taking full account of the context in which the request was made."

Judge Kooijmans, Separate Opinion (paragraph 12)[6]

1.1 Introduction

International law (also called "public international law" or the "law of nations") is traditionally defined as the set of rules generally accepted as governing the way states (or nations) act and relate to each other.[7] In one sense, public international law has been in existence ever since peoples or nations entered into relations with each other. One of the earliest recorded examples is a binding treaty between the Nation of Israel and the Gibeonites, found in the Hebrew Bible.[8] Classical antiquity saw the Ancient Greek nation-states develop a set of rules to

5. *Legal Consequences of the Construction of a Wall in the Occupied Palestinian Territory,* Advisory Opinion, 2004 I.C.J. Reports, pp. 136-203 (9 July 2004), at p. 171.

6. *Ibid.,* separate opinion of Judge Kooijmans, at p. 223.

7. "Public" international law is to be distinguished from "private" international law, which is the field of international law that regulates the interaction between national systems of law.

8. *Joshua* 9. See Grintz (1966).

govern their interaction. Subsequently, the Roman Empire developed *jus gentium* based on principles of fairness and natural law, which governed the interaction between Roman citizens and foreigners.

International law in its current form, however, was birthed in the 17th century. With the break-up of the Holy Roman Empire, a myriad of principalities, kingdoms, and nations fought for legitimacy and power in Europe. These empires gradually asserted authority over the people living within their jurisdiction and entered relations with the nations around them. They formed governments, raised taxes, built armies and fought wars. International trade increased, and new territories were explored. Wars broke out, and new alliances were formed. In the 17th century, Spain and the Dutch Republic were embroiled in the 80-year "Dutch War of Independence" and the Thirty Years' War that engulfed a large part of the continent of Europe. Many questions started to arise: Are these empires subject to any generally recognized rules or norms in times of peace and war? Are there limits to what they can or cannot do? Who decides what these rules are? Who enforces them?

In 1625, Dutch theologian and jurist Hugo Grotius published *The Law of War and Peace*, in which he argued that sovereign states are subject to the rule of law.[9] Grotius identified three kinds of law: natural law (derived from our human nature), divine law (those derived from the relationship between nations and God), and the law that states themselves create (treaties and custom).[10] Grotius emphasized a rationalist perspective: Law consists of certain values, which are derived from essential human reason. The two important principles that developed from this are: "promises must be kept," and "harming others requires restitution."

In 1648, the Peace of Westphalia confirmed the principle of state sovereignty as the cornerstone of international law and relations.[11] The essence of what is known as "Westphalian Sovereignty" is that each sovereign state is (1) equal and (2) has exclusive jurisdiction over its territory and domestic affairs. This means that states are not to interfere in the internal domestic affairs of another state. The principles contained in the Westphalian treaties provided the legal framework for the world

9. Hugo Grotius *De jure belli ac pacis* (*The law of war and peace*), first published in Paris (1625).

10. *Ibid.*, I.I.9-17.

11. The Peace of Westphalia was a series of separate arrangements made in 1648 between 235 official envoys representing hundreds of European Catholic and Protestant polities in two Westphalian towns: Münster and Osnabrück. These arrangements introduced a new system of international relations that brought to an end the Thirty Years War, which had its roots in the Catholic/Protestant conflict but had become a political upheaval that embroiled the whole continent of Western and Central Europe.

order that has governed the existence and expansion of European nations in the succeeding centuries.[12]

Some 150 years later, Europe underwent another political crisis with the French Revolution and the rise of Napoleon. This resulted in the Congress of Vienna (1814), which was "the closest that Europe has come to universal governance since the collapse of Charlemagne's empire."[13] "The subtle equilibrium" achieved in Vienna gradually fell apart in the course of the 19th century, and by 1914 all of Europe was at war. The unprecedented destruction of human lives and national economies in World War I birthed a desire to create a new international order, which would prevent war and produce international peace and security. This endeavor resulted in the creation of the League of Nations in 1920 and the establishment of a Permanent Court of International Justice housed in the Peace Palace in The Hague in 1922. Yet, only two decades later, the whole world was again engulfed by a war that cost 60 million lives—more than all preceding wars together. The atrocities of World War II exposed the weaknesses of the League of Nations system, which was replaced by the United Nations and its related institutions in 1945. The desire for greater international cooperation as a means to avoid conflict also led to the creation of the European Coal and Steel Community (ECSC) in 1951, which has since developed into the European Union (EU) now comprising 28 Member States. The United Nations (UN) became the new platform for the achievement of global peace and security.

International Law in the 20th Century

In the modern era of globalization, multiculturalism and multilateralism, the Westphalian concept of state sovereignty has been the subject of much criticism. With economies, financial and communications systems, and legal institutions becoming more and more interrelated and interdependent, states are under increasing pressure to give up parts of their traditional

12. Kissinger (2014), p. 27. Kissinger emphasizes that the significance of the Peace of Westphalia is the concept of state sovereignty that enabled the competing participants to settle their conflict based not on military strength but on mutual respect between competing and different political powers. "The genius of this system, and the reason it spread across the world, was that its provisions were procedural, not substantive. If a state would accept these basic requirements, it could be recognized as an international citizen able to maintain its own culture, politics, religion, and internal policies, shielded by the international system from outside intervention. The idea of imperial or religious unity - the operating premise of Europe's and most other regions' historical orders - had implied that in theory only one center of power could be fully legitimate. The Westphalian concept took multiplicity as its starting point and drew a variety of multiple societies, each accepted as a reality, into a common search for order."

13. *Ibid.*, at pp. 61-62.

sovereignty. It is even arguable that the Westphalian notion of state sovereignty never really gained ground in many parts of the world, such as Latin America and Africa, where "weak states" often shared power with violent and non-violent non-state actors.[14] In recent decades, those who argue for a new post-Westphalian world order based on humanity, integration and inclusiveness have criticized the concept of state sovereignty as outdated, irrelevant, exclusive and anachronistic.[15]

Perhaps the most important development over the past century has been the creation and exponential rise of international human rights norms since WWII. Human rights law places individuals, rather than states, at the center stage of the international legal system. The modern law of human rights owes its existence in large part to the efforts in the 1940's of Polish Jewish international scholar Hirsch Lauterpacht, who became Professor of International Law at Cambridge University, and strongly influenced the Nuremberg trials of Nazi war criminals the first trials of individuals for crimes against humanity. Lauterpacht's revolutionary approach sought to extend international law beyond states to protect individuals. He stated that international law "should be functionally oriented towards both the establishment of peace between nations and the protection of fundamental human rights."[16] This approach constituted nothing less than a revolution under international law. The extent to which international law is directed to protecting individual rights (as opposed to, and sometimes in conflict with, the rights and obligations of states) remains to this day a hotly contested issue on which many international lawyers disagree. Another major development in the 20th century was the creation of the crime of genocide, which focuses on the destruction of peoples (rather than individuals). The law of genocide was pioneered by Raphael Lemkin, another Jewish scholar, who was born and raised in the same area as Lauterpacht, an area ethnically cleansed of Jews in the years leading up to WWII and during the Nazi occupation.[17]

It is a bitter irony that the law and language of "human rights," "crimes

---

14. See, e.g., Williams (2008): http://www.isn.ethz.ch/Digital-Library/Publications/Detail/?id=93880 (visited: 30 October 2015).

15. For example, in his speech entitled 'Securing Peace in Europe', former NATO Director-General Dr. Javier Solana argued in 1998 that "humanity and democracy - two principles essentially irrelevant to the original Westphalian order - can serve as guideposts in crafting a new international order, better adapted to the security realities, and challenges, of today's Europe." (http://www.nato.int/docu/speech/1998/s981112a.htm).

16. Lauterpacht, Hersch (1946), at p. 51 (emphasis added).

17. See the fascinating study by Philippe Sands on the development of international human rights law and the law of genocide during and after WWII: Sands (2016).

against humanity" and "genocide," which owe so much to the pioneering work of eminent Jewish legal scholars like Lauterpacht and Lemkin in the 1940's and 1950's to redress the horrors of the Holocaust, which resulted in the mass murder of six million Jews, are being used today to single out the Jewish people and attack their right to exist as a nation within secure borders in Palestine. That is particularly poignant when one considers that, had the Jewish homeland in Palestine been established in the form that was required by the League of Nations under the Mandate for Palestine, the destruction of Jewish lives and culture could have been largely avoided.

Notwithstanding the growth of human rights and international criminal law, however, there is no doubt that state sovereignty and the founding principle of state sovereign equality is still—albeit perhaps in modified form—the core concept underpinning the UN system[18] and remains "the scaffolding of international order such as it now exists."[19] That is, in any event, the basis upon which this study proceeds. Indeed, we argue that the many UN resolutions and other diplomatic initiatives criticizing Israel place a one-sided emphasis on the human rights of the Palestinian Arabs (and also because they often exclude the rights of other ethnic and religious groups in Palestine, such as Aramean Christians, Bedouins and Druze). There is no doubt these rights are important, and also no doubt that there are breaches of those rights. But the obsession with Palestinian human rights since the early 1970's has reached disproportionate levels, while the territorial, national and human rights of the Jewish people have been all but ignored. What is needed is a discourse that gives adequate space to, and achieves a fair balance of, all of these elements. That, in a nutshell, is the object of international law, and is the purpose of this study.

1.2 The Sovereign Equality of States

Like all well-functioning legal systems, the international legal system is (or should be) based on the rule of law, which is universally recognized as the cornerstone of all democratic systems and "the central pillar of every free society."[20] The concept of the rule of law developed from the English doctrine that "all men are equal before the law" and has been defined by the UN Secretary-General as:

18. UN Charter, art. 2, para.1. states that "the Organization is based on the principle of the sovereign equality of all its Members".

19. Kissinger (2014), at p. 27.

20. See G. Rose, 'Lawfare', Australia/Israel & Jewish Affairs Council, AIJAC, 29 March 2011: http://www.aijac.org.au/news/article/essay-lawfare (visited: 28 January 2016).

> **"[A] principle of governance in which all persons, institutions and entities, public and private, including the State itself, are accountable to laws that are publicly promulgated, equally enforced and independently adjudicated, and which are consistent with international human rights norms and standards. It requires, as well, measures to ensure adherence to the principles of supremacy of law, equality before the law, accountability to the law, fairness in the application of the law, separation of powers, participation in decision-making, legal certainty, avoidance of arbitrariness and procedural and legal transparency."[21]**

In the context of national legal systems, the idea of the rule of law is reflected in the concept of the separation of powers, whereby the state entrusts the creation, application and enforcement of law to various governmental branches: the legislature, the judiciary, and the executive (*trias politica*).[22] The separation of powers between those institutions provide for checks and balances, which guarantee the equality of individuals before the law and ensure protection of individuals against excessive use or abuse of power by any one arm of government.

In the context of international law (where there is no higher legal authority than states), the concept of the rule of law is reflected in the principle of equality of states. The principle of the "rule of law" is firmly embedded in the preamble of the UN Charter, which states that the aim of the UN is "to establish conditions under which justice and respect for the obligations arising from the treaties and other sources of international law can be maintained."[23] Moreover, the UN has recognized that "the rule of law applies to all states equally, and to international organizations, including the United Nations and its principal organs, and that the respect for and promotion of the rule of law and justice should guide all of their activities and accord predictability and legitimacy to their actions,"[24] which demonstrates the indivisible connection between the rule of law and the principle of sovereign equality of states.

---

21. Report of the Secretary-General, *The Rule of Law and transitional justice in conflict and post-conflict societies*, S/2004/616, 23 August 2004, p. 4.

22. The idea of 'Trias Politica' (the separation of powers) was introduced by Charles Montesquieu in his life work De l'esprit des lois, published in 1748.

23. Preamble to the UN Charter; the rule of law also finds a central place in the preamble of the Universal Declaration of Human Rights: "whereas it is essential, if man is not to be compelled to have recourse, as a last resort, to rebellion against tyranny and oppression, that human rights should be protected by the rule of law."

24. UN G.A. Res. 67/1, para 2 (24 September 2012). According to the International Law Commission, "the rule of law requires States, international organizations and other international entities to conduct their affairs with full deference to law." (See: Report of the International Law Commission, Sixtieth session, 5 May – 8 August 2008, p. 351).

The Westphalian concept of "sovereign equality of states" requires states to implement the basic principles of the rule of law in their dealings with each other—such as transparency, fairness, effectiveness, non-discrimination, accountability and access to justice for all. The conceptual understanding and the implementation of the rule of law on the international level differs from its national counterpart in one important respect: The components of the *trias politica* (legislature, executive and judiciary) do not have a comparable equivalent at the international level. The international legal order does not have a legislature. It does not include independent courts having the jurisdiction to strike down legislation that exceeds the jurisdiction of the legislature, or to protect legal subjects (i.e., states) against unlawful exercise of power by the executive. And it does not have an executive empowered to implement the law under the authority of the legislature and subject to the control of the judiciary. This is still the general norm and remains true—even if sometimes organs of international organizations are invested with executive powers in a specific field (such as the European Commission and, in specific cases, the UN Security Council). This means that there are very few checks and balances to the misuse of power in the international legal order.

The principle of the sovereign equality of states is therefore the only real bulwark against the abuse of power. According to the International Court of Justice, the principle of sovereign equality in Paragraph 2(1) of the UN Charter is "one of the fundamental principles of the international legal order."[25] At the San Francisco Conference, which resulted in the creation of the UN Charter, sovereign equality was said to include the following elements: (1) that states are juridically equal; (2) that each state enjoys the rights inherent in full sovereignty; (3) that the personality of the state is respected, as well as its territorial integrity and political independence; and (4) that the state should, under international order, comply faithfully with its international duties and obligations.[26]

To say that states are "juridically equal," is to say that all members of the international community stand before the law on equal terms despite their *de facto* inequalities (power, size, population) and law must not differentiate between them.[27] This means that no discrimination should occur in the way international normativity is applied to states:

25. Jurisdictional Immunities of the State (Ger. v. It.: Greece intervening), Judgment, 3 February 2012, para 57.

26. The Report of the Rapporteur of Committee I to Commission I, Doc. 944, I/1/34 (I), *Documents of the United Nations Conference on International Organization*, San Francisco, 1945, Vol. VI, p. 457.

27. Kooijmans (1964), p. 101.

"[A]ll States which come within the scope of a rule of law must be treated equally in the application of that rule to them. There must, in other words, be uniformity of application of international law and no discrimination between States in their subjection to rules of law which in principle apply to them."[28] Hence, it is said that non-discrimination is a "general rule inherent in the sovereign equality of States."[29]

The application of the legal principle of equality of states in the UN system can be found in the "one state, one vote" rule and the system of "equality of votes" (equal weight of votes) in numerous UN bodies. Other "implied consequences" are expressed in the principle of participation, meaning that any UN member has a right to participate in the General Assembly on an equal footing with other states, the principle of "equitable geographical representation" or regional representation as is found in the regional group system of the UN, and the subordination of equal states to the jurisdiction of the International Court of Justice.[30] We explore the issue of discrimination further in Chapter 3.

1.3 Subjects of International Law

1.3.1 States

International law is created by, and is primarily applicable to, "states." In the 20th century, there has been an explosion in the creation of nation states. At the end of World War II in 1945, 51 recognized states became UN Members. Today, there are 193 UN Members States. Many of these new states have been created as a result of the decolonization process in the decades after World War II.

What is a state? The traditional definition of statehood is given in the Montevideo Convention of 1933,[31] which states that in order for an entity to qualify as a state under international law, it must meet each of four criteria:

- ***A permanent population:*** There is no minimum requirement for the number of persons, but the population of the claimed state must be non-transient.

---

28. Watts (1993), at p. 31. The ILC found the principle of non-discrimination to be a "general rule inherent in the sovereign equality of State." *Yearbook of the International Law Commission* (YBILC), 1961, Vol. II, at p. 128.

29. YBILC, 1961, Vol. II, at p. 128.

30. Sir Robert Jennings, Opinion regarding the exclusion of Israel from the United Nations Regional Group System, 4 November 1999, pp. 20-24.

31. Montevideo Convention on the Rights and Duties of States, 1933.

- ***A defined territory*:** It does not matter how big or small that territory is,[32] but he territory must be coherent.[33] The fact that a substantial part of the borders of the territory are disputed does not necessarily prevent the existence of a state.[34]
- ***An effective government*:** There must be an "effective government" over that population in the relevant territory.[35] This is perhaps the most important of all the requirements. The authority must be both effective and in a position to exercise its authority independently of any other state.[36]
- ***Capacity to enter into relation with other state:*** This criterion requires the existence of an effective and independent government capable of interacting with other governments.[37] Some argue that this criterion is an aspect of the third criterion or that the capacity to enter into relations with other states is not a condition but a result of statehood.[38]

The Montevideo criteria have been modified by further developments in international law.[39] This has led to the rise of additional criteria for statehood, including the notion of state independence.[40] According to Professor James Crawford, "the requirement that a putative State have an effective government might be regarded as central to its claim to statehood," and is the basis for the other criterion of independence. In fact, the requirements of "government" and "independence" "may be regarded

---

32. For example, the Vatican City has a surface area of only 44 hectares but is universally considered to be a state under international law.

33. Crawford (2006), p. 52.

34. *Ibid.* As we will see in Chapter 2, Israel was established and existed as a state under international law in 1948 (and continues to exist today) notwithstanding the fact that disputes with her neighbors over some of her borders had not been resolved.

35. See Crawford (2006). This aspect is especially important when considering whether or not 'Palestine' exists as a separate state under international law. Crawford's conclusion (in 2006, at p. 447)) was that this is not the case, mainly because in his view the Palestinians lack an effective, independent government, and due to uncertainties about the constitution of such a state. Moreover, it is very doubtful whether 'independence' has a meaning separate from the notion of an 'effective government.'

36. See Crawford (2006), p. 437.

37. Crawford (1977), at p. 119.

38. Crawford (2006), pp. 61-62.

39. Crawford (1990), p. 310.

40. Crawford (1979) describes two elements of state independence: "the existence of an organized community on a particular territory, exclusively or substantially exercising self-governing power, and secondly, the absence of the exercise of another state, and the right of another state to exercise, self-governing powers over the whole of that territory."

as different aspects of the requirement of effective separate control."[41] He explains that there are two elements of state independence: "the existence of an organized community on a particular territory, exclusively or substantially exercising self-governing power, and secondly, the absence of the exercise of another state, and the right of another state to exercise, self-governing powers over the whole of that territory."[42]

This is reflected, for example, in the conditions that are listed in the European Guidelines dealing with the recognition of the successor states of former Yugoslavia.[43]

The question arises: Does the legitimacy or existence of states depend on their recognition by other states? In the case of Israel—was it created by, or does its legitimacy depend upon, the fact that it was recognized by most other states after the declaration of independence on 14 May 1948? And in the case of "Palestine" —is the official "recognition" of "Palestine" by over 100 other states effective to bring the "State of Palestine" into existence?

"Recognition is a statement by an international legal person as to the status in international law of another real or alleged international legal person or of the validity of a particular factual situation."[44] There are two basic theories regarding recognition. The *constitutive* theory says that an entity receives legal validity as result of its recognition by other states. According to this theory, a state is created through the actions of other states; without recognition, an entity cannot constitute a state, and is not able to enjoy the rights and obligations of statehood under international law. The *declaratory* theory, on the other hand, asserts that an entity can acquire the status of statehood on its own, and the recognition of the other states would only prove to be a mere acceptance of this situation. State practice today tends to lean more toward the declaratory theory.[45] While recognition by other states may be important evidence of the existence of another state, it is not conclusive of the existence of that entity as a

---

41. Crawford (2006), p. 55.

42. *Ibid.*, pp. 82-89 and 437.

43. Declaration of the European Council on the 'Guidelines on the Recognition of New States in Eastern Europe and in the Soviet Union', 16 December 1991. Under these Guidelines a candidate state needs to ensure: "respect for the Charter of the United Nations (...) the rule of law, democracy and human rights (...) guarantees for the rights of ethnic and national groups and minorities (...) commitment to settle by agreement, including where appropriate by recourse to arbitration, all questions concerning State succession and regional disputes." The Guidelines also mention that recognition will be withheld in the event an entity comes into being through aggression.

44. Shaw (2008), p. 445.

45. *Ibid.*, p. 447.

state. States do not have the capacity to confer any rights or obligations upon another entity by recognizing it.[46] As Professor Crawford notes, "[A]n entity is not a State because it is recognized; it is recognized because it is a State."[47] Nor is membership at the UN a criterion for statehood.[48]

The UN is not vested with the authority to create or recognize a newly declared state. The question of whether or not an entity is a "state" is a matter of both law and fact to be determined on a case-by-case basis, through the application of the general principles governing the existence of statehood, as expressed in the Montevideo Convention.[49]

Application of these principles to the State of Israel means that its existence as a state does not derive from the fact that it has been recognized by other states or even from its admission as UN Member State in 1949. Nor was the State of Israel created by means of the General Assembly's 1947 Partition Plan. (The legal foundations of the State of Israel are discussed further in Chapter 6.) Application of this principle to the "State of Palestine" is discussed in Chapter 18.

1.3.2 International Organizations

Since the 19th century, many international organizations have developed. They are by now important actors on the international stage. Arguably, the most important multilateral organization on the international legal stage is the UN. We will focus on this organization in more detail below, because of its relevance for the discussion on the position the State of Israel under international law. An international organization can be defined as a permanent institution, established by virtue of a treaty concluded by states, for the realization of specific purposes. International organizations established by states should be distinguished from so-called private organizations, which have been established by private individuals. Only the former qualifies as a legal person under international law.

46. *Ibid.*

47. Crawford (2006), p. 93. As will be discussed in more detail later, the fact that many states have recognized 'Palestine' does not mean that 'Palestine' is a state under international law.

48. Under Article 4 of the UN Charter only "states" may become members of the UN. This may mean that the admission of an entity as a UN member is evidence of the fact that it is a state, but this cannot be conclusive because UN membership is not a legal criterion of statehood. Of course this is a very important issue in considering whether 'Palestine' is a state within the meaning of international law. See further Chapter 18 *infra*.

49. In deciding whether or not to admit a newly-declared state as a member of the UN, the Security Council must decide whether or not that entity qualifies as a "state" within the meaning of the UN Charter. The Council's decision will be important evidence as to whether or not that entity is in fact a state. But it is not conclusive.

1.3.3 "Peoples"

"Peoples" can be subjects of international law.[50] What constitutes a "people" is not entirely clear, due to the lack of a generally accepted definition.[51] A clear example appears in Article 80 of the UN Charter, which provides that the rights of states and *peoples* under the League of Nations mandate system should be respected—pending the entry into force of trusteeship treaties under the new system of the UN. Another well-known example is found in the principle of the self-determination of peoples in Article 1 of the International Covenant on Civil and Political Rights.[52]

1.3.4 Individuals

Although public international law primarily applies to states, modern practice demonstrates that individuals have become increasingly recognized as participants and subjects of international law.[53] In the post 1945-era, individuals were granted numerous rights, as states adopted various treaties and implemented these subsequently in their national legal order, resulting in obligations on states to respect the rights of individuals within their jurisdiction.[54] The rise of individual obligations in international law[55] means, for example, that individuals can be liable for certain offenses and punished for these crimes by international courts and tribunals.[56]

---

50. The authority of the UN Charter was even founded, not upon States, but upon peoples. As the opening words of the Charter state: "We the peoples of the United Nations determined..."

51. There have been many attempts to define "peoples." A group of experts from UNESCO defined it as a group of persons who regard themselves as a people, and who enjoy some or all of the following common features: a) a common historical tradition; b) racial or ethnic identity; c) cultural homogeneity; d) affinity; e) linguistic unity; f) religious or ideological territorial connection; and g) common economic life (in: 'Final Report and Recommendations of an International Meeting of Experts on the Further Study of the Concept of the Right of People for UNESCO', 22 February 1990, SHS-89/CONF.602/7, pp. 7-8).

52. See further discussion of this subject in Parts II and V of this book.

53. Shaw (2008), p. 258.

54. Examples of international human rights treaties are: the Universal Declaration of Human Rights (1948); the International Covenant on Civil and Political Rights (1966); the International Covenant on Economic, Socials and Cultural Rights (1966); the Convention Against the Torture and Other Cruel, Inhuman or Degrading Treatment or Punishment (1984); the Convention on the Elimination of All Forms of Discrimination against Women (1979); and the Convention on the Rights of the Child (1989).

55. Shaw (2008), at p. 39.

56. Individual responsibility has been confirmed with offences such as: aggression, genocide, war crimes, crimes against humanity, crimes against UN and associated personnel, piracy, torture or inhuman treatment and the extensive destruction and appropriation of property (see the Draft Code of Crimes Against the Peace and Security of Mankind, adopted by the International Law Commission in 1991). (See further, e.g., the Statute of the ICC).

1.4 Sources of International Law

When considering the role of international law in relation to any particular situation or dispute, we must answer the following questions: What law is applicable? Where do we find international law? How do we recognize it? And, who decides what international law is, and how it applies in any particular situation?

Being based on the sovereign equality of states, international law essentially comprises norms or rules that are generally accepted as binding by states. This includes treaty rules that have been expressly entered into by states as a voluntary limitation of their sovereignty, norms which are recognized by the states as part of customary law, and fundamental principles that are part of the legal framework of every civilized nation.

Jus Cogens

Some of these norms are also accepted and recognized by the international community of states as peremptory norms of general international law, from which no derogation is permitted and which can only be changed by a norm of general international law that has the same status.[57] Examples of such norms include international crimes such as slavery, torture, genocide and wars of aggression.[58] These norms have the quality of "*jus cogens*" (Latin for "compelling law").

According to the Statute of the International Court of Justice, which is generally considered to be authoritative, there are four sources of international law:

1. International treaties and conventions;
2. International custom, as evidence of a general practice accepted as law;
3. The general principles of law recognized by civilized nations; and
4. Judicial decisions and the writings of highly qualified publicists, which can be referred to as "subsidiary means for the determination of the rules of law."[59]

This enumeration is not exhaustive. In particular, decisions of international organizations have not been included despite their significant role in international law today. As international organizations are based on

57. Vienna Convention on the Law of Treaties , art. 53.

58. Czapliński (2006).

59. Statute of the ICJ, art. 38. Article 38 is widely regarded as an authoritative statement of the sources of international law; see: Brownlie (2001), p. 3; Shaw (2003), p. 66.

powers included in the founding treaty of the organization, it is arguable that they qualify as part of treaty law.

1.4.1 International Treaties and Conventions

Sovereign states and international organizations can make agreements between themselves. Normally referred to as "treaties," agreements between states, between states and international organizations, or between international organizations themselves, can give rise to legal obligations.[60] Often there are many different parties to a treaty. A treaty is the result of negotiations. This is a political process of negotiations and concessions which is ultimately expressed in treaty provisions and is open to future interpretation by the respective parties.

Once the parties have reached agreement on the text, the representatives of the parties sign the treaty. Signature however does not necessarily bind a state; a treaty is often only binding once it has been ratified by each signatory state, according to its own internal processes (often this requires adoption of the treaty by the Parliament), or the state involved has formally acceded to the treaty or in some other way indicated that it regards the treaty as binding and effective.[61] Normally, provisions are included in the treaty stating how and when the treaty becomes effective (many multilateral treaties only become effective once a certain number of the parties have ratified the treaty).

Examples of treaties that affect the territorial status of Jerusalem and the West Bank are the League of Nations, the Mandate for Palestine, the Oslo Agreements and the Peace Treaty between Israel and Jordan.

1.4.2 International Customary Law

The second category of international law is unwritten and known as international customary law.[62] It plays an important role in the international legal order. Some international customs are later codified in treaties. Once a state has ratified such a treaty, the contents of the treaty are considered treaty law for that state. States that have not ratified a treaty continue to be bound by the customary rule. There are two criteria for determining whether a particular custom or practice qualifies as law. First, there must be a general (widely, though not necessarily universal) and

60. Treaties are also often referred to as conventions, treaties, statutes, charters, or protocols.

61. See, e.g., Vienna Convention on the Law of Treaties (1980), Part II: Conclusion and Entry into Force of Treaties.

62. See Brierly (1963), p. 61; Brownlie (1990), pp. 4-11.

consistent practice of states. Secondly, states must recognize the rule as being obligatory—i.e., imposing on them an obligation required by, or consistent with, prevailing international law (*"opinio iuris").*

1.4.3 General Principles of Law

"General principles of law recognized by civilized nations"[63] include principles that have been developed over the course of time in the legal systems of civil societies. Some of these principles are applicable in the context of the Israel/Palestine conflict, such as:

- ***The Principle of Estoppel***
  This is the principle that a state is precluded from denying or asserting anything to the contrary of that which it has previously accepted or asserted as being truthful or legally binding.[64] It is connected with the concepts of *good faith* and *consistency*. For example, a state that openly accepts the validity of a treaty with another state cannot later deny the validity of that treaty in a dispute with that state.[65]
- ***The Principle of Res Judicata***
  The principle of *res judicata* ("issues that have been decided*")* means that matters that have been finally resolved or determined by a court or tribunal[66] cannot be raised again by one of the parties in the same court or even in a different court.[67] This rule is intended to prevent injustice and the waste of resources.
- ***The Principles of Good Faith and Pacta Sunt Servanda***
  The principle of *pacta sunt servanda* ("agreements must be performed") is a principle of good faith whereby "every treaty in force is binding upon the parties to it and must be performed by them in good faith."[68]
- ***The Principle of "Acquired Legal Rights"***
  Under the principle of acquired legal rights, the rights of individuals are not affected by a change in sovereignty.[69] Rather, such rights continue to exist after succession and can be enforced against the

63. Statute of the ICJ, art. 38, para 1.

64. Brownlie (1990), pp. 640-642.

65. See, e.g., Arbitral Award by the King of Spain (Honduras v. Nicaragua.), Judgment, 1960 I.C.J. Reports, pp. 192-218 (18 November 1960), at p. 213.

66. Shaw (2008), p. 1053.

67. See, e.g., Effect of Awards of Compensation Made by the UN Administrative Tribunal, Advisory Opinion, 1954 I.C.J. Reports, p. 53 (13 July 1954).

68. See Vienna Convention on the Law of Treaties, art. 26.

69. Permanent Court of International Justice, *German interests in Polish Upper Silesia*, Series A, No. 7, 42, 1926.

successor state.[70] This principle is reflected in article 80 of the UN Charter, which provides for the preservation of rights under the pre-existing League of Nations Mandate system, pending the entry into force of trusteeship agreements in the new UN framework.[71]

- ***The Principle of "Uti Possidetis Juris"***
  The principle of *uti possidetis juris* ("as you possess under law") presumptively determines the boundaries of states emerging out of colonies or Mandates.[72] It functions as a safeguard for the territorial integrity and sovereignty of newly independent states. The principle ensures the "respect of intangibility of frontiers."[73] Its application constitutes an upgrade of "former administrative delimitations, established during the colonial period, to international frontiers."[74] This means in the practice of states that their "borders, on the day of their independence, constitute a tangible reality."[75]

1.4.4 Judicial Decisions and the Writings of Highly Qualified Publicists

Judicial decisions and the writings of highly qualified publicists are a "subsidiary means for the determination of rules of law."[76] The most important examples of judicial decisions are the decisions of the International Court of Justice. Decisions of national courts (such as the Israeli Supreme Court) are also a potential source of support of international law. Caution needs to be used in extracting general principles of law from individual judicial decisions; case law is more compelling when there is a coherent body of such law on an issue. The persuasive writing of highly qualified publicists includes the work of authors like Grotius, Vattel, Bynkershoek, Oppenheim, Lauterpacht, Brownlie, Shaw and Crawford.

---

70. Shaw (2014), p. 725.

71. UN Charter, art. 80. This will be discussed in detail in Chapter 2.

72. There is extensive literature about this principle. See in particular Ratner (1996); Shaw (1997); Bell & Kontorovich (2016). The principle of *Uti Possidetis Juris* and its application to Israel/Palestine is discussed further in Section 9.5 below.

73. Case concerning the frontier dispute (*Burkina Faso/Republic of Mali*), Judgment, 1986 I.C.J. Reports, pp. 554-652 (22 December 1986), at p. 565.

74. *Ibid.*, p. 566.

75. Organization of African Unity, Resolutions adopted by the first ordinary session of heads of state and government held in Cairo, UAR, from 17 to 21 July 1964, Res. 16(1) - See: http://www.au.int/en/sites/default/files/ASSEMBLY_EN_17_21_JULY_1964_ASSEMBLY_HEADS_STATE_GOVERNMENT_FIRST_ORDINARY_SESSION.pdf (visited: 19 October 2015). The application of this principle will be discussed in Chapter 8.

76. Statute of the ICJ, art. 38(1)(d).

1.4.5 Decisions of International Organizations

Decisions of international organizations may constitute a source of international law, when made by organs of those organizations within the scope of their authority, provided and only to the extent to which the treaty by which the organization has been established explicitly provides that such decisions are to be binding.[77] For example, the UN Charter empowers the Security Council to make binding decisions within the framework of Chapter VII of the Charter. Organs of the EU, more specifically the European Parliament and Council in cooperation, produce numerous Regulations (which are binding instruments, more or less similar to national legislation) and Directives (which require implementaton in national law).

1.5 When is International Law Binding?

It is important to emphasize that statements by international institutions concerning international law are not "binding" in the same sense as under national law. This is true even of the "highest" international court–the International Court of Justice. Absent the consent of states, the international legal system does not have any binding machinery or system for determining what rules may be applicable in a given situation, and how disputes between international actors are to be resolved. As one of the foremost authorities on international law has stated: "Decisions of the International Court, unanimously supported resolutions of the General Assembly of the United Nations concerning matters of law, and important multilateral treaties concerned to codify or develop rules of international law, are all lacking the quality to bind states generally in the same way that Acts of Parliament bind the people of the United Kingdom."[78]

These questions are extremely relevant in relation to the Israel/Palestine dispute. As we shall argue, many of the rules that are often said to be applicable to the case of Israel/Palestine are arguably not intended to be binding.

Furthermore, statements by the UN General Assembly or other UN institutions about the application of international law–that the law of belligerent occupation applies in East Jerusalem, and that it forbids Israel from facilitating or allowing its citizens to live there, etc.–no matter how often repeated, do not in and of themselves either create binding

77. Cassese (2005), p. 183.

78. Brownlie (1990), pp. 1-2.

obligations or constitute indisputable evidence of the existence of such a rule.

It is important to distinguish between norms which are legally binding and those which are politically significant but not legally binding. Because the UN General Assembly and Security Council are primarily political institutions, which do not have the power or authority to make or execute laws, resolutions issued by them—even if expressed in normative terms such as "must," "should," etc.—are primarily of a political nature.

Whether obligations are intended to be directive or only recommendatory depends on their terms and context and the intention of the drafters. States and non-state actors have long found it useful to draw a clear distinction between those norms which are intended to be binding and enforceable—pursuant to the rules of international law, such as treaty provisions—and those which are not.[79] This fundamental distinction is sometimes referred to as the difference between "soft" law and "hard" law.[80] Soft law includes "normative provisions contained in non-binding texts,"[81] which may be contained in a wide spectrum, from resolutions or recommendations all the way to fully political positions.[82] Although such provisions may have some political consequences, soft law by its nature is not legally binding or enforceable.[83] As one commentator notes:

> **"Many international lawyers consider 'soft law' to be a misnomer because it has no binding authority as is. Although it may express noble aspirations, and may, over time, become recognized as reflecting customary international law, or even stimulate sovereign states to promulgate or negotiate legislation or conventions, by definition 'soft law' lacks authority to bind states."[84]**

---

79. Abbott & Snidal (2000), p. 421.

80. *Ibid.*, pp. 421-422.

81. Shelton (ed. 2000), p. 292.

82. Guzman & Meyer (2010), p. 173.

83. Examples of soft law instruments are: informal exchanges of promises, votes in international organizations, agreements on principles, solemn declarations and statements of intention.

84. Weiner (2005). See further on the distinction between soft law and hard law: the references cited by Weiner; the review of Shelton (2000), in: *American Journal of International Law*, Vol. 95 (2001), p. 709; Judgment of the Permanent Court of International Justice in S.S. Lotus (France v. Turkey), 1927 PCIJ (Ser A) No. 10, p. 18; Hart (1958), at pp. 606-615; Kelsen (1967); Brownlie (1988).

2. The United Nations

> "The Court first recalls that, pursuant to Article 2, paragraph 4, of the United Nations Charter; 'All Members shall refrain in their international relations from the threat or use of force against the territorial integrity or political independence of any State, or in any manner inconsistent with the Purposes of the United Nations.'"
>
> Advisory Opinion (paragraph 87)[85]

The United Nations (UN) was established in 1945 following the Allied victory of World War II. It was part of a completely new symmetry in which the international order that would ensure the creation and maintenance of international peace and security for all peoples.[86] Most states in the world are now UN Members. There are currently 193 UN Member States.[87] Israel was accepted as a UN Member State on 11 May 1949.[88]

2.1 The United Nations – Values and Aims

The UN Charter has been referred to as "the constitutional framework of international law today"[89] and is widely considered an authoritative treaty for the universal community as a whole.[90] It was drafted at the San Francisco Conference on 26 June 1945 and codifies important principles of international law.[91] Some of the norms in the UN Charter enjoy *jus cogens* status, which means they create binding obligations for the organization,

85. *Legal Consequences of the Construction of a Wall in the Occupied Palestinian Territory,* Advisory Opinion, 2004 I.C.J. Reports, pp. 136-203 (9 July 2004), at p. 171.

86. Preamble to the UN Charter.

87. http://www.un.org/en/members/ (visited: 15 January 2016).

88. http://www.un.org/en/members/growth.shtml (visited: 15 January 2016).

89. Waldock (1962), p. 20.

90. Verdross & Simma (1984), pp. vii-viii.

91. Zemanek (1997), p. 47.

its members, and even non-members.[92] Moreover, the obligations under the UN Charter prevail over other international obligations in the event of a conflict between the two.[93]

The UN Charter is built on the idea of international peace and security. Given the fact that many of the drafters of the UN Charter and leading international lawyers of the time were Jewish, it is perhaps not unsurprising that the language, goals and objectives of the UN Charter are reminiscent of the values of the Hebrew Bible. As one commentator has stated:

> **"[T]he aims and purposes of the UN, as espoused in the Charter, were in fact identical with those lofty principles which had been proclaimed by the prophets of Israel in Jerusalem some twenty-eight hundred years ago, to wit, the equality and brotherhood of man, the intrinsic value and dignity of the human being, social justice, general disarmament and eternal peace among nations."[94]**

In recognition of this vision, the following verse from the Prophet Isaiah 2:4 was inscribed on the wall in what is now the Ralph Bunke Park opposite the UN Headquarters in New York:

> **"They shall beat their swords into plowshares, and their spears into pruning hooks; nation shall not lift up sword against nation, neither shall they learn war any more."[95]**

The values of the UN are found in the Preamble of the UN Charter, which state that the peoples of the UN proclaim that they are determined "to save succeeding generations from the scourge of war... to reaffirm faith in fundamental human rights... to establish conditions under which justice and respect for the obligations arising from treaties and other sources of international law can be maintained, and ... "[96] To achieve these ends they vow to combine their efforts to accomplish the following aims:

---

92. Military and Paramilitary Activities in and Against Nicaragua (Nicaragua v. United States of America), Jurisdiction of the Court and Admissibility of the Application, 1984 I.C.J. Reports, para 73 (26 November 1984). (Principles that are part of customary international law, which also find their place in the United Nations Charter, are mentioned by the Court in this case: the non-use of force, non-intervention, respect for independence and territorial integrity of states). Article 2(6) reads: "The Organization shall ensure that States which are not Members of the United Nations act in accordance with these Principles so far as may be necessary for the maintenance of international peace and security."

93. UN Charter, art. 103.

94. Blum (1998).

95. *Isaiah* 2:4.

96. Preamble to the UN Charter.

- "to practice tolerance and live together in peace with one another as good neighbors;
- to unite our strength to maintain international peace and security;
- to ensure, by the acceptance of principles and the institution of methods, that armed force shall not be used, save in the common interest; and
- to employ international machinery for the promotion of the economic and social advancement of all peoples."[97]

Some argue that the values and aims set out in the Preamble of the UN Charter are of more ideological ("soft law") than legal ("hard law") in character.[98] However, the technical committee of the San Francisco Conference stated that all the provisions of the UN Charter are to be considered "indivisible as in any other legal instrument"[99] and "equally valid and operative."[100] This supports the view that the broad ideas contained in the Preamble have the same legally binding character as the operative provisions of the UN Charter.[101] This may be an overstatement, but there is no doubt the overarching values and aims set out in the Preamble of the UN Charter have a normative character. Not only Israel and the Palestinians but also third states that seek to play a role in the resolution of the Israel/Palestine conflict are therefore required to comply with the UN values. As we describe later, in our view, the diplomatic emphasis on the 1949 Armistice Lines as the *de facto* border of Israel, the insistence on the creation of a State of Palestine, and disproportionate attention within the UN to the Israel/Palestine dispute arguably conflict with these fundamental UN values and principles.

2.2 The Purposes and Principles of the UN Charter

The *Purposes* of the UN are set out in Article 1 of the UN Charter. In summary, these are:

- to maintain international peace and security;
- to develop friendly relations among nations;

97. *Ibid.*

98. Kelsen (2000), p. 9.

99. UNCIO (United Nations Conference on International Organization), Report of the Rapporteur of Committee I to Commission, Doc. 944, I/1/34 (I), *Documents of the United Nations Conference on International Organization*, San Francisco, 1945;.see Kelsen (2000), p. 11 (footnote 3)., Vol. VI, p. 457.

100. *Ibid.*

101. *Ibid.*

- to achieve international cooperation in solving international problems of an economic, social, cultural, or humanitarian nature, and in promoting respect for human rights; and
- to be a center for harmonizing the actions of nations in the attainment of these common ends.

The *Principles* for the UN are set out in Article 2 of the UN Charter. Almost all of these principles have achieved the status of *jus cogens* (peremptory international law). They include:

- the sovereign equality of all Members States;
- the obligation to fulfill in good faith the obligations assumed by the Members States;
- the duty to settle their international disputes by peaceful means, and to refrain in their international relations from the threat or use of force against the territorial integrity or political independence of any state;
- UN Member States are bound to give the UN their assistance in any action made in accordance with the UN Charter. The UN itself shall ensure that non-Member States act in accordance with these Principles, so far as may be necessary for the maintenance of international peace and security; and
- Finally, Article 2 provides that nothing contained in the UN Charter shall authorize the UN to intervene in matters which are within the domestic jurisdiction of any state.

A number of these purposes and principles are especially relevant to the Israel/Palestine dispute:

Friendly Relations Among Nations

General Assembly Resolution 2625 (XXV) "Declaration on Principles of International Law concerning Friendly Relations and Co-operation among States in accordance with the Charter of the United Nations" suggests that the essential components of friendly relations are the duty of states: [102]

- to refrain from the threat or use of force against the territorial integrity or political independence of a state;
- to settle international disputes by peaceful means;
- not to intervene in the affairs of any other state;
- to cooperate with one another in accordance with the UN Charter;

102. UN G.A. Res. 2625 (XXV), Declaration on Principles of International Law concerning Friendly Relations and Co-operation among States in accordance with the Charter of the United Nations (24 October 1970).

- to respect the equal rights and self-determination of peoples;
- to respect the sovereign equality of states;[103]
- to fulfil in good faith the obligations of States under the UN Charter.

We will elaborate briefly on some aspects.

"Refrain from the Threat or Use of Force against the Territorial Integrity and Political Independence of any state."

The prohibition of the threat or use of force is directly linked with Article 1(1) of the UN Charter and is considered "the cornerstone of the peace in the UN Charter."[104] This obligation is addressed to UN Member States and is extended to non-members as result of its status as customary law.[105] The provision establishes a regime under which the use of force is prohibited. The UN Charter allows for only two exceptions: the use of the right of self-defense (Article 51) and collective measures made under Chapter VII. In addition, there is a third—albeit disputed—exception of humanitarian intervention. The principle of non-aggression is further developed in the Friendly Relations Declaration, which states: "Every state has the duty to refrain from organizing, instigating, assisting or participating in acts of civil strife or terrorist acts in another State or acquiescing in organized activities within its territory directed towards the commission of such acts."[106]

The principles of "territorial integrity" and "political independence" are inherent in statehood and have been qualified by the International Court of Justice (ICJ) as "an important part of the international legal order."[107] While there are those today who would challenge this view, as a matter of law it is difficult to discern any weakening of the principle.[108] The concept of territorial integrity is expounded upon in a number of declarations of the UN General Assembly, including the Friendly Relations Declaration

103. Goodrich (ed.) (1970), The principle of equal rights, as mentioned here, corresponds with the second phrase of the preamble of the UN Charter.

104. Waldock (1952), p. 492.

105. Simma et al. (2002), p. 112.

106. UN G.A. Res. 2625 (XXV), Declaration on Principles of International Law concerning Friendly Relations and Co-operation among States in Accordance with the Charter of the United Nations (24 October 1970).

107. International Court of Justice, Accordance with international law of the Unilateral Declaration of Independence of Kosovo, Advisory Opinion, 2010 I.C.J. Reports, para. 80 (2010).

108. For example, it was concern for territorial integrity and the stability of borders that led the Organization of African Unity (now the African Union) to insist upon the maintenance of the colonial borders as at independence. Indeed, international law still affords a central place to the principle of territorial integrity. See Wood (n.d.): http://pesd.princeton.edu/?q=node/271 (visited: 8 September 2017).

and the Definition of Aggression.[109] The words "against the territorial integrity and political independence of any state" were inserted into Article 2(4) of the UN Charter "in order to emphasize the importance of not infringing on territorial integrity and political independence; and they cannot be interpreted (as is occasionally suggested) as limiting the non-use of force principle embodied in the Charter."[110]

The right of States to territorial integrity and political independence is reflected for example in Security Council Resolutions 242 and 338, which recommend negotiation of peace based on "[t]ermination of all claims or states of belligerency and respect for and acknowledgement of the sovereignty, territorial integrity and political independence of every state in the area and their right to live in peace within secure and recognized boundaries free from threats or acts of force."

Peaceful Settlement of Disputes

Article 2(3) corresponds to Article 1(1) as it encourages UN Member States to maintain peace internationally and it establishes an obligation for Member States to settle their disputes by means that are peaceful.[111] In view of the judgment in the Nicaragua case, the principle has obtained the status of customary law, making the obligation that derives from article 2(3) also binding on non-Member States.[112]

Respect for the Equal Rights and Self-Determination of Peoples

The obligation on states to respect the "equal rights and self-determination of peoples" was further elaborated in General Assembly Resolution 1514 (XV).[113] Within a colonial context, the application of this principle amounts to the entitlement of a people to sovereign statehood. In the context of peoples in existing states, however, "self-determination is transmuted into a principle relating to the internal governance of

---

109. UN G.A. Res. 2625 (XXV), Declaration on Principles of International Law concerning Friendly Relations and Co-operation among States in accordance with the Charter of the United Nations (24 October 1970); UN G.A. Res. 3314 (XXIX), Definition of Aggression (14 December 1974).

110. Wood (n.d.): http://pesd.princeton.edu/?q=node/271 (visited: 8 September 2017).

111. A list of means that are considered to be peaceful can be found in article 33(1) of the Charter. This non-exhaustive list of means for peaceful settlement can be divided into two categories: means that are non-compulsory and those that are compulsory. The first group includes means such as negotiation, enquiry, mediation and conciliation; the second group makes mention of arbitration, judicial settlement, resort to regional agencies or arrangements.

112. Military and Paramilitary Activities in and Against Nicaragua (Nicaragua v United States), 1986 I.C.J. Reports, p. 290, Merits (26 June 1986).

113. UN G.A. Res. 1514 (XV), Declaration on the granting of independence to colonial countries and peoples (14 December 1960).

independent states"[114] and is interpreted as a right of peoples to minority protection within an existing state.[115] The practice of the international community illustrates that the principle of self-determination is to be applied within the framework of existing independent states and not in a way as to harm the rights of states.[116] And so, in the present post-colonial world, the right to self-determination of a people is subordinate to the principle of sovereign equality of states. We will explore this later when discussing the "two-state solution" and the claimed the right of the Palestinian people to self-determination. In our view, since the establishment of the UN in 1945, the consistent rejection of Israel's rights to territorial integrity and political independence by the Arab States and the Palestinian Arab leaders amounts to no less than an assault on the principle of "friendly relations." The consequent use of force by Arab nations and Palestinian Arabs against Israel cannot be justified by reference to the right to self-determination.

2.3 Organs of the United Nations

The most important organs of the UN are the General Assembly, the Security Council, the Economic and Social Council, the UN Secretariat and the International Court of Justice (ICJ).[117]

2.3.1 The UN General Assembly

The General Assembly functions as the UN's forum for discussion of world politics. All 193 Members States are equally allowed to participate in the Assembly and its sessions.[118] They come together during an annual

114. Shaw (1997), at p. 124.

115. Yugoslavia Arbitration Commission, Opinions on Questions Arising from the Dissolution of Yugoslavia, Opinion No. 2, 11 January 1992, 31 I.L.M 1497. In light of the atrocities committed against the Kosovo population, the international community called for self-autonomy and self-administration for Kosovo.

116. *Ibid.*,. para 2. The 1970 Declaration on Principles of International Law Concerning Friendly Relations (see note 102) states that "nothing in the section of self-determination shall be construed as authorizing or encouraging the dismembering or impairing of the territorial integrity of states." As explained by Shaw: "The principle of self-determination, applies beyond the colonial context, within the territorial framework of independent states. It cannot be utilized as a legal tool for the dismantling of sovereign states." (Shaw [1998], para 122). UN S.C. Res. 541 on the situation in Cyprus, UNDoc. S/RES/541 (18 November 1983), and UN S.C. Res. 1244 on the situation in Kosovo, UNDoc. S/RES/1244 (10 June 1999). Part V elaborates on the right to self-determination in respect of the Palestinian Arabs.

117. UN Charter, art. 7.

118. UN Charter, art. 9(1).

meeting to establish the organization's policy.[119] The General Assembly is a political organ. Under its functions and powers, the General Assembly may discuss matters,[120] initiate studies,[121] receive and consider reports,[122] and request the ICJ to give an advisory opinion on a legal question.[123] The General Assembly furthermore may make recommendations in various fields of the competences of the UN.[124] Moreover, the General Assembly is empowered to establish subsidiary organs in order to assist it in carrying out its functions.[125] An example of such an organ is the Human Rights Council, comprised of representatives of 47 Member States, entrusted with monitoring the compliance of UN Member States with their human rights obligations. The General Assembly is generally considered not to be a legislative body, but a parliamentary advisory body.[126] One could say the General Assembly is the ears and hands of the UN, though not its executive hands.[127] Functioning as a "debating chamber" or "forum for the exchange of ideas and the discussion of international problems,"[128] its power to make decisions is restricted to the admission of new Member States, voting procedure, and apportionment of the annual budget.[129] Outside the scope of these (internal) matters,[130] its resolutions lack the power to create obligations that are legally binding for Member States.[131]

2.3.2 The UN Security Council

There are 15 Members of the UN Security Council; five permanent Members[132] (China, France, Russia, United Kingdom and United States

---

119. UN Charter, art. 20.

120. UN Charter, arts. 10 and 11(b).

121. UN Charter, art. 13.

122. UN Charter, art. 15.

123. UN Charter, art. 96(a).

124. UN Charter, art. 15.

125. UN Charter, art. 22.

126. Shaw (2008), p. 115.

127. Goodrich & Hambo (1946), p. 95.

128. Shaw (2008), p. 1212.

129. For all matters concerned with the internal functioning of the Organization, see UN Charter, arts. 4, 17 and 18.

130. See Brownlie (2001), p. 14 and pp. 699-700. General Assembly's resolutions and deliberations may however constitute evidence of customary law.

131. Shaw (2008), p. 115; Öberg (2006), p. 883. See also ICJ, South West Africa Cases, Judgment, 1966 I.C.J. Reports, p. 98 (18 July 1966).

132. UN Charter. art.23. The Russian Federation is the successor to the USSR, which is still mentioned in Article 23.

of America), and ten non-permanent Members.[133] The non-permanent Members are elected for a period of two years by the General Assembly. In theory, each UN Member is entitled to be a non-permanent Member of the Security Council. In practice, however, Israel is the only country that has consistently been excluded from Membership on the Security Council.[134]

The primary task of the Security Council is the maintenance of international peace and security. According to Article 24(1), "In order to ensure prompt and effective action by the United Nations, its Members confer on the Security Council primary responsibility for the maintenance of international peace and security, and agree that in carrying out its duties under this responsibility the Security Council acts on their behalf." To maintain international peace and security, the Security Council has power to act in two situations:

- In the case of a dispute that is likely to endanger international peace and security, the Security Council can "recommend" appropriate procedures for the settlement of the dispute by peaceful means.[135]
- In the event the Security Council determines that there is an actual threat to the peace, breach of the peace, or act of aggression, the Security Council can make recommendations, decisions, or take such action as it deems necessary or desirable to maintain or restore peace and security.[136] This can include military measures against an offending state ("peace enforcement").[137]

In addition, the Security Council has developed peacekeeping activities as an instrument to maintain international peace and security. UN Peacekeeping forces operate under the UN flag in areas of conflict with the consent of the conflicting parties.[138] In the context of Israel, the most important peacekeeping operations are the UNDOF forces in the Golan Heights (since 1974) and UNIFIL in Lebanon (since 1978).[139]

Only decisions made under Chapter VII of the UN Charter ("Action

133. *Ibid.*

134. This may change soon. On 3 October 2013, Israel announced its plans to run for a Security Council seat in 2019-2020 (see: http://www.reuters.com/assets/print?aid=USBRE99213020131003). Elections for a seat in the Security Council will take place during the 72nd Session of the General Assembly in 2018.

135. UN Charter, arts. 33 and 36.

136. This is the 'collective security' mechanism under Chapter VII of the Charter.

137. UN Charter, arts. 41 and 42.

138. UN peacekeeping missions are deployed on the basis of mandates issued by the UN Security Council.

139. UNDOF was established by UN S.C. Res. 350, UNDoc S/RES/350 (31 May 1974) and UNIFIL by UN S.C. Res. 425, UNDoc. S/RES/425 (19 March 1978).

with Respect to Threats to the Peace, Breaches of Peace and Acts of Aggression") are considered to be binding. Member States agree to "accept and carry out the decisions of the Security Council in accordance with the Charter."[140] It is important to emphasize that the Security Council is not a law-making body; the functions assigned to it are more of a political nature.[141] Regarding non-procedural matters, decisions of the Security Council require the unanimous vote of all the permanent Members.[142] Thus, each permanent Member has a veto right. The reason for this is that when it comes to maintaining international peace and security, a binding decision that is not supported by all of the most powerful countries in the world carries very little weight. The permanent members to the Security Council often use their veto power and their right to abstain. The United States has often used its veto power in relation to proposed resolutions directed against Israel.[143] UN Security Council Resolution 2334 was an exception to this practice.

2.3.3 The UN Secretariat

The Secretary-General, who is the chief administrative officer of the UN, heads the Secretariat.[144] The Secretary-General has significant political influence. Under the UN Charter, the Secretary-General has the power to bring forth important initiatives and may draw the attention of the Security Council to any matter which "in his opinion may threaten the maintenance of international peace and security."[145]

2.3.4 The International Court of Justice (ICJ)

The ICJ is "the principle judicial organ of the United Nations." Located in the Peace Palace in The Hague, Netherlands, the ICJ is the successor to the Permanent Court of International Justice (PCIJ), which was established by the Covenant of the League of Nations and was dissolved in 1946. Fifteen justices sit on the ICJ panel, each of whom are appointed by the General

---

140. UN Charter, art. 25.

141. Military and Paramilitary Activities in and against Nicaragua (*Nicaragua v. United States of America*), Jurisdiction and Admissibility, Judgment, 1984 I.C.J. Reports, pp. 434-435 (27 June 1984).

142. UN Charter, art. 27(3). Add explanatory parenthetical (e.g. a decision to use force against a state that is guilty of acts of aggression).

143. For example, on 18 February 2011, the United States vetoed a draft resolution in the Security Council, which would have described "that all Israeli settlement activities in the Occupied Palestinian Territory, including East Jerusalem, are illegal." (Draft Resolution S/2011/24).

144. UN Charter, art. 97.

145. UN Charter, art. 99.

Assembly and the Security Council for a period of nine years.[146] Judges must be persons of high moral character, and they must either possess the qualifications required in their respective countries for appointment to the highest judicial offices or be lawyers of recognized competence in international law.[147] The ICJ may not include more than one national of the same Member State.[148] It must represent the main forms of civilization and the principal legal systems of the world.[149]

The ICJ has only two roles. First, it settles disputes of a legal nature that are submitted by states (contentious cases). Only states are entitled to submit a case to the ICJ; this right is not granted to individuals, international organizations, or other entities.[150] Second, it gives advisory opinions on legal questions at the request of the organs of the UN (or specialized agencies authorized to make such a request).[151]

Although the ICJ is sometimes referred to as the "World Court,"[152] it has a much more limited role than a court of appeal in a national jurisdiction. The ICJ only has jurisdiction in *contentious* cases if all of the states involved in the dispute consent to the ICJ's jurisdiction. A state cannot be compelled to submit to the jurisdiction of the ICJ.[153] Once the ICJ does have jurisdiction, each state that is a party to the proceeding is bound to comply with the ICJ's decision.[154] In the event one party does not comply with the ICJ's decision, the other party is entitled to take the matter to the Security Council, which may take measures to enforce the ICJ's judgment.[155]

The ICJ's *advisory jurisdiction* means that the General Assembly, the Security Council, and other UN organs can ask the ICJ to give an advisory opinion on a specific legal issue.[156] Such decisions of the ICJ, as the name suggests, are advisory only; they are not binding on the UN organ

---

146. Statute of the ICJ], art. 3, para 1.

147. Statute of the ICJ, art. 2.

148. Statute of the ICJ, art. 3.

149. Statute of the ICJ, art. 9.

150. Statute of the ICJ, arts 34(1) and 36(1).

151. Statute of the ICJ, arts 38(1) and 65-68. Explanatory parenthetical for the first portion of the sentence– in accordance with international law.

152. http://www.un.org/Overview/uninbrief/icj.shtml (visited 21 January 2016).

153. Statute of the ICJ, art. 36.

154. UN Charter, art. 94. Article 59 of the Statute of the ICJ provides that "[T]he decision of the Court has no binding force except between the parties and in respect of that particular case."

155. UN Charter, art. 94(2).

156. Statute of the ICJ, art. 65.

or any state that may be involved or the subject of the opinion.[157] Both in contentious cases and in the framework of its advisory jurisdiction, the judges vote on the matters decided.[158] The judges' votes on different sections of the decision are a matter of public record.[159] Each judge is entitled to issue a separate concurring or dissenting opinion.[160]

The ICJ's mandate is to give advice on and to settle disputes presented to it. The ICJ is forbidden from "legislating," meaning that judgments are made entirely on the existing law. [161] Article 59 stipulates that decisions of the ICJ are not binding upon parties, except for those of the dispute.[162] Lawyers, politicians, and advisers should see judgments and advisory opinions of the ICJ as important statements on the law as it stands in respect to specific international problems. Article 38(1) of the Statute notes that judicial decisions may be a subsidiary means for the determination of rules of law.[163] But they are not in and of themselves binding. The Wall Advisory Opinion is an example of this.[164]

---

157. Statute of the ICJ, arts 59 and 65-68. Interpretation of Peace Treaties with Bulgaria, Hungary and Romania, First Phase Advisory Opinion, ICJ Reports 1950, 71.

158. Statute of the ICJ, art. 56.

159. *Ibid.*

160. Statute of the ICJ, art. 57.

161. Legality of the Use or Threat of Nuclear Weapons, Advisory Opinion, 1996 I.C.J. Reports, p. 18 (8 July 1996); see Brownlie (2001). Also made clear by the Statute of the ICJ in art. 59.

162. Statute of the ICJ, art. 59.

163. Statute of the ICJ, art. 38.

164. *Legal Consequences of the Construction of a Wall in the Occupied Palestinian Territory,* Advisory Opinion, 2004 I.C.J. Reports, p. 136.

3. The Use and Misuse of Law against Israel

> "Decades of political maneuverings have created a disproportionate volume of resolutions, reports and conferences criticizing Israel. In many cases, rather than helping the Palestinian cause, this reality has hampered the ability of the UN to fulfill its role effectively."
>
> Ban Ki-moon, Former Secretary-General of the United Nations[165]

3.1 "Lawfare" – The Discriminatory Use of Law

The deliberate use of law and legal systems as a strategy to achieve military or political objectives is sometimes referred to as "lawfare."[166] It involves:

> "[T]he use of the law as a weapon of war or, more specifically, the abuse of Western laws and judicial systems to achieve strategic military or political ends. It consists of the *negative* manipulation of international and national human rights laws to accomplish purposes other than, or contrary to, those for which they were originally enacted. Lawfare is also evident in the manipulation of domestic legal systems (by state and non-state parties) to implement laws inconsistent *with general principles of liberal democracy*. The principles underlying lawfare are also present in glaring failures to apply human rights law and in the *disproportionate and biased* application of the law."[167]

In other words, "lawfare" is about the *illegitimate, misplaced, discriminaroty or unfair use* of law. The distinction between the legitimate and illegitimate use of law is a fine but crucial one. "A purely instrumental view deprives law of any internal moral integrity: law becomes an empty

165. Ziri (2016): http://www.jpost.com/Israel-News/UN-chief-urges-Israeli-lawmakers-to-reconsider-settlement-bill-475617.

166. Council of Foreign Relations, 'Lawfare, the latest in Assymetries', 18 March, 2003: http://www.cfr.org/defense-and-security/lawfare-latest-asymmetries/p5772.

167. Goldstein (n.d.) (emphasis added): http://www.thelawfareproject.org/what-is-lawfare.html.

vessel that can be used to do anything, no matter how reprehensible."[168] Whereas the essence of a system of legality is marked by the quality of being rule-bound,[169] in a system where the law is no longer strictly followed and applied but, instead, instrumentally used to achieve political ends, the stability, certainty and predictability of the legal system is threatened.

A good example is in relation to international humanitarian law (the law of war). The deliberate application and enforcement of international law is critically important in the implementation of the rule of law and protecting human rights against excessive use of power. In combat situations, the international law of armed conflict provides the necessary institutional framework for achieving an appropriate balance between the actions of governments in pursuing legitimate military objectives, on the one hand, and the protection of combative and civilian lives on the other. But international humanitarian law is often misused by those who object to the right of states to use force in self-defense. It is arguable, for example, that some NGOs claiming pacifist agendas misuse the law of armed conflict to influence decision-makers in Western nations in order to impede conventional warfare from being carried out in a legitimate way to protect the interests of sovereign states.[170]

The Arab nations and the Palestinian Arab leaders have made no secret of their intention to use the international legal system to achieve their goal of the return of Palestinian Arab refugees and Palestinian statehood based on the "4 June 1967 lines." As President of the Palestinian Authority and Chairman of the Palestine Liberation Organization (PLO), Mahmoud Abbas, stated in 2009:

> **"Palestine's admission to the United Nations would pave the way for the internationalization of the conflict as a legal matter, not only a political one. It would also pave the way for us to pursue claims against Israel at the United Nations, human rights treaty bodies and the International Court of Justice. ...We call on all friendly, peace-loving nations to join us in realizing our national aspirations by recognizing the State of Palestine on the 1967 border and by supporting its admission to the United Nations. Only if the international community keeps the promise it made to us six decades ago, and ensures that a just resolution for Palestinian refugees is put into effect, can there be a future of hope and dignity for our people."[171]**

168. Tamanaha (2007), p. 505.

169. *Ibid.*, p. 486.

170. See: Dunlop (2001). See also: Susskind (2010) (www.americanthinker.com/2010); Dunlop (2011).

171. 'The Long Overdue Palestinian State', Op-ed, by Mahmoud Abbas, Chairman of the Palestine Liberation Organization and President of the Palestinian National Authority, published in *The New York Times*, 16 May 2011.

3.2 Lawfare against Israel in the UN General Assembly

Since the late 1960's, the political nature of the UN General Assembly has enabled states that are militarily hostile to Israel to generate support for resolutions critical of Israeli policy or condemning Israeli actions. Each Member State of the UN has a single vote in the General Assembly.[172] Resolutions on important issues—including recommendations concerning international peace and security—require a two-thirds majority of the Member States present and voting.[173] According to Rules of Procedure of the General Assembly, "members present and voting" refers to members casting an affirmative or negative vote. Members which abstain from voting are considered as not voting.[174] In practice, this means that a state or group of states that is able to consistently gather a bare majority of present and voting members is in a position to push through resolutions that do not have the support of more than half of the total number of Member States.

The UN currently has 193 Member States. It had 51 Member States at its inception in 1945. By 1967, this number had more than doubled to 123 UN Member States; and by 1980, there were 154 Member States—largely as a result of the decolonization process in Africa and Asia during the 1960s and 1970s. Many of these post-colonialist UN Member States became members of the Non-Aligned Movement (NAM), an informal alliance of nations that started in the early 1960s in response to the Cold War, colonialism and Western dominance.[175] Representing over two-thirds of the total number of UN states and 55 percent of the world population, the members of the NAM have been extremely critical of the US and Israel.

Although Israel has been a member of the UN since 1949, it has been excluded from the regional geographical groups which control appointments to UN posts, form common policy and provide a platform for coordinated voting. Despite being geographically located in Asia, 23 of the 53 Asian Group Member States are members of the Organization of Islamic Conference (OIC), which has actively blocked Israel from

172. UN Charter, art. 18(1).

173. UN Charter, art. 18(2).

174. UN General Assembly Rules of Procedure, Rule 86 [126].

175. The NAM is an informal alliance of nations. With 120 members, the NAM currently represents over two-thirds of the total number of UN states and 55 percent of the world population. The members of the NAM (mostly African, Latin American and Asian nations) have tended to be extremely critical of the United States and Israel, and supportive of the Palestinian cause. It is indicative that the 16th annual summit of the NAM was held in Tehran in 2012.

membership. Exclusion from the geographical groups means that during its 65-year history Israel—until recently—has not been eligible for election as a non-permanent member of the UN Security Council.[176] Israel's position improved in 2000 when it became a full member of the Western European and Others Group (WEOG) on a temporary basis (subject to renewal) in WEOG's headquarters in the US, thereby enabling it to put forward candidates for election to various UN bodies. In 2004, Israel obtained a permanent renewal to its membership in WEOG's headquarters in the US, while remaining an observer at the UN offices in Geneva, Nairobi, Rome and Vienna. On 14 June 2005 Dan Gillerman, on recommendation of the WEOG, was elected to the position of Vice-President of the 60th UN General Assembly. (The last Israeli to hold this position was UN envoy Abba Eban in 1952). On 1 December 2013, Israel was invited to become a "temporary full member" of the WEOG in Geneva. In June 2016, Israeli Permanent Representative to the UN Danny Danon was appointed Chair of the Sixth Committee (Legal)—the first time an Israeli has been appointed to head a UN General Assembly permanent committee.[177]

Anti-Israel Resolutions

The UN General Assembly started to produce resolutions critical of Israel and promoting the political aspirations of the Palestinian Arabs after the General Assembly on 14 October 1974 invited the PLO to participate in deliberations of the General Assembly as representative of the Palestinian people. On 13 November 1974, Arafat addressed the UN General Assembly—the first time a non-state representative addressed the General Assembly—in his famous "olive branch and freedom-fighter's gun" speech.[178] Then, on 22 November 1974, two very significant resolutions were adopted. In each case, almost half of the UN Member States either abstained from voting or voted against the resolution. Resolution 3236 (XXIX) "reaffirm[ed] the inalienable rights of the Palestinian people in Palestine, including (a) the right to self-determination without external interference and (b) the right to national independence and sovereignty,"

176. UN General Assembly Rules of Procedure, Rule 143.

177. *The Times of Israel*, 13 June 2016.

178. Arafat's appearance at the UN General Assembly 29nd Session was the result of the efforts of a group of Arab and African states that had sent a letter to the United Nations on 11 September 1974 in which they requested the Secretary General to include the 'Question of Palestine' on the agenda of the G.A.'s 29th Session. Seeing the item included on the agenda, the bloc of Arab and African states (backed by some communist and Asian states) moved on to sponsor the text of Resolution 3210, which invited the Palestine Liberation Organization to the session of the General Assembly. See: http://www.un.org/en/ga/62/plenary/palestine/bkg.shtml (visited: 2 November 2015).

and also "reaffirm[ed] the inalienable right of the Palestinians to return to their homes and property from which they have been displaced and uprooted."[179] In Resolution 3237 (XXIX) the General Assembly invited the PLO to participate as "observer" in all sessions and work of the General Assembly as well as conferences organized under the auspices of the General Assembly.[180] The anti-Israel ball was set rolling.

In 1974, what was previously referred to as the "Israeli-Arab" conflict became known as the "Israeli-Palestinian" conflict. The PLO was firmly accepted as a participant within the UN, and the "question of Palestine" became a fixed item on the agenda of the General Assembly. The position of the PLO was further institutionalized the following year, when the UN Committee on the Exercise of the Inalienable Rights of the Palestinian People (CEIRPP) was established by the General Assembly on 10 November 1975.[181]

The stream of "Israel-critical" resolutions reached a zenith with the infamous "Zionism = Racism" resolution 3379 in 1975.[182] This highly politicized Resolution was sponsored by 25 predominantly Arab and or Islamic states[183] and was further supported by 47 nations (primarily China, the Soviet bloc nations and many African nations), resulting in a narrow majority of only 72 states of, in total, 144 UN Member States.[184] Thirty-five states (including most Western/democratic nations) voted against the Resolution, 32 states abstained, and five states were simply not present. Thus, less than half of the total number of UN Member States voted in favor of this resolution. The resolution demonstrated the capacity of the Arab States to form alliances with other groupings within the UN system. US Permanent Representative to the UN at the time, Jeane Kirkpatrick, later wrote with regard to the Resolution, that it:

179. UN G.A. Res. 3236 (XXIX) (22 November 1974). The text of the Resolution was sponsored by a bloc of Arab and African states (see: UN Yearbook 1974, Chapter X, on Questions relating to the Middle East, p. 224). The voting record of the Resolution shows an Arab/Africa/Asia/Communist bloc of 89 countries that voted in favor, a European and South American bloc that abstained and eight countries that rejected it (see: UN Yearbook 1974, Chapter X, on Questions relating to the Middle East, p. 226).

180. UN G.A. Res. 3237 (XXIX) (22 November 1974). The text of the Resolution was sponsored by a bloc of Arab and African states (see: UN Yearbook 1974, Chapter X, on Questions relating to the Middle East, p. 225). The voting record of the Resolution shows an Arab/Africa/Asia/Communist bloc of 95 countries that voted in favor and a few European and South American countries that voted in opposition to it (see: UN Yearbook 1974, Chapter X, on Questions relating to the Middle East, p. 227).

181. This was done under UN G.A. Res. 3376 (XXX) (10 November 1975).

182. *Ibid.*

183. See the discussion of this resolution in Chapter 5 (Human rights).

184. In 1975 there were 144 UN Member States.

> **"[S]ymbolizes the alliance of the African and Arab blocs inside of the United Nations with regard to all questions concerning the Middle East. That alliance, although not written on paper, clearly stipulates that African nations will vote against Israel on questions involving the Middle East, and Arabs will vote with Africans on all matters concerning South Africa. That alliance plus the Soviet bloc, which can always be counted on to join a vendetta, provides the famous automatic majority available for all resolutions against Israel. Together, these provide the stable structural base for anti-Israel actions inside the UN body."[185]**

Ideas similar to those behind Resolution 3379 were expressed at the UN World Conference Against Racism held in Durban, South Africa in 2001 (WCAR). "Both in 1975 and in 2001 the Palestinians, in cooperation with external sponsors and with the support of a group of African and Islamic countries, launched such initiatives. In the first case, the Soviet Union was the major mover, and, in the second, Iran."[186]

Attended by over 1500 NGOs, the major participants in the WCAR included MIFTAH (The Palestinian Initiative for the Promotion of Global Dialogue and Democracy, an NGO established by Hanan Ashwari, an important Palestinian politician and spokeswoman of the PLO), and the Palestinian Committee for the Protection of Human Rights and the Environment, (also known as LAW), which had received over $1 million from the Ford Foundation, funds from the European Union and over 30 additional sponsors. They played a central role in steering committees, workshops, and related activities, based on the theme "that Israel was an apartheid state." Major allies, such as the South African NGO Committee (SANGOCO), helped to promote this agenda and codified much of the language that was the basis for the final declaration.[187] WCAR was preceded by four Regional Conferences whose task was to draft a composite Declaration against Racism and a Plan of Action. Israel was excluded by the Iranian government from the last of these regional conferences in Teheran. At these conferences, Israel was depicted as a "criminal" state and perpetrator of war crimes, crimes against humanity and genocide, against which the Palestinians have a right to "armed struggle" and "resistance." "The clarion call was clear: just as the struggle against racism in the 20th century required the dismantling of South Africa as an apartheid state, so the struggle against racism in the 21st century

---

185. Jeane Kirkpatrick, 'Bracing for the truth', adapted from a speech delivered to the State Department on 10 December 1984, CZA/S110/48, cited by Fishman (2011), at p. 82.

186. Fishman (2011), at p. 75.

187. Steinberg (2006): http://www.ngo-monitor.org/article/_the_centrality_of_ngos_in_the_durban_strategy.

requires the dismantling of Israel as an apartheid state."[188] The NGO Forum Declaration and Programme of Action explicitly called for the use of legal processes to advance the political war against Israel.[189] WCAR thus formed the basis of the modern Boycott, Divestment, and Sanctions (BDS) Movement, the stated purpose of which is—adopting the South African model—to bring about not only the withdrawal of Israeli military forces from the "occupied territories," but the dismantling of Israel as an expression of the right to self-determination of the Jewish people.[190]

In his last speech to the Security Council before retiring as Secretary-General in 2016, Ban Ki-Moon admitted the strong anti-Israel bias in the UN. "Decades of political maneuverings have created a disproportionate volume of resolutions, reports and conferences criticizing Israel," Ban said. "In many cases, rather than helping the Palestinian cause, this reality has hampered the ability of the UN to fulfill its role effectively."[191]

3.3 Lawfare against Israel in Other UN Institutions

A further example of the "instrumentalization of law" is found in the practice of the United Nations Human Rights Council (UNHRC), the principal intergovernmental body that is "responsible for strengthening the promotion and protection of human rights around the globe and for addressing situations of human rights violations and making recommendations on them."[192] General Assembly Resolution 60/251 of 15 March 2006, establishing the Human Rights Council states, "...that all human rights must be treated in a fair and equal manner, on the same footing and with the same emphasis..." and "...the work of the Council shall be guided by the principles of universality, impartiality, objectivity and non-selectivity, constructive international dialogue and cooperation..."[193] and equal application of the law will eventually suffer and the rule of law will corrode. The UNHRC has failed abysmally to live up to its charter. Since

188. Cotler (2009). Herzberg, Anne (2010) describes and analyses the role of Non-Governmental Organisations (NGO's) in "lawfare" against Israel since 2001 by initiating civil and criminal cases against Israeli officials for "war crimes" through expansion of universal jurisdiction statutes. The report also documents the financial support of these NGO's by the EU and several EU member states.

189. See generally on the Durban Conference: Steinberg (2006).

190. Barghouti (2011). See also Fishman (2011).

191. http://www.jpost.com/Israel-News/UN-chief-urges-Israeli-lawmakers-to-reconsider-settlement-bill-475617 (visited: 1 March 2017).

192. See: http://www.ohchr.org/EN/HRBodies/HRC/Pages/AboutCouncil.aspx (visited: 27 April 2017).

193. See: https://www.change.org/p/in-response-to-un-anti-israel-bias-declaration-against-un-anti-israel-bias (visited: 5 May 2017).

its creation in 2006, the UNHRC has issued over 100 resolutions, over which half have focused on Israel.[194]

Such "disproportionate volume of resolutions"[195] is also displayed in the number of UN Security Council resolutions. Almost 10 percent of UN Security Council Resolutions since 1946 address the Arab-Israeli conflict.[196]

Another example of unequal treatment is the constant criticism of Israel as "occupying power." In a recent study, Prof. Kontorovich concludes that Israeli settlement activity has been criticized by UN bodies for violating article 49(6) Fourth Geneva Convention,[197] while similar critique is applied by "*no* international actor or body" on other settlement contexts where there is (state-sponsored) migration of persons into the occupied territory.[198] It is remarkable that the International Criminal Court Prosecutor has commenced a preliminary examination of Israeli settlement activities but has not taken any such steps in relation to *other* alleged settlement contexts that fall within its jurisdiction. These instances, where international actors are not treated equally before the law and where the records show such unequal outcome, point out the fact that "the international rule of law is not operating."[199]

In addition to the UN institutions, in several of the UN Specialized Agencies, especially UNESCO, we find international law being used by Member States to promote a particular political agenda, including the establishment of an Arab state of Palestine (with "East Jerusalem" as its

194. Kittrie (2016), p. 37.

195. In his last address to the UN Security Council, departing Secretary-General Ban Ki-Moon stated that "[d]ecades of political maneuverings have created a disproportionate volume of resolutions, reports and conferences criticizing Israel," and "in many cases, rather than helping the Palestinian cause, this reality has hampered the ability of the UN to fulfill its role effectively." See: http://www.jpost.com/Israel-News/UN-chief-urges-Israeli-lawmakers-to-reconsider-settlement-bill-475617 (visited: 12 May 2017).

196. For a list of Security Council Resolutions on the Arab-Israeli Conflict from 1946 to 23 December 2016, see: https://en.wikipedia.org/wiki/List_of_the_UN_resolutions_concerning_Israel_and_Palestine (visited 12 May 2017). Prior to 1990 this percentage of Israel-related resolutions by the UN Security Council amounted up to 23 percent, see: Gruenberg (2009), at. p. 494.

197. Article 49(6) states that an "Occupying Power shall not deport or transfer parts of its own civilian population into the territory it occupies."

198. Kontorovich (2017), p. 66. Kontorovich used for his study nine settlement contexts: East-Timor, Western Sahara, Northern Cyprus, Syria/Lebanon, Vietnam/Cambodia, Armenia/Azerbaijan (Nagorno-Karabakh), Russia-Georgia (Abkhazia) & Ukraine (Crimea), and the Baltic States (Estonia, Latvia and Lithuania). It appeared that in none of these cases the Occupying Power received from the international community the condemnation of violating art. 49(6), while the migration of people into occupied territory appeared as "a near-ubiquitous feature of extended belligerent occupation."

199. McCorquodale (2016), at p. 69.

capital) through denial of the historical connection of the Jewish people with the land. We will discuss UNESCO in more detail in chapter 14 (in connection with the Holy Places in Jerusalem).

3.4 Role of Islamic Nations and Europe in the UN

The UN works in close cooperation with two Islamic multilateral organizations: the Organization of Islamic Conference (OIC) and the League of Arab States (Arab League). In 1975, the UN General Assembly decided to invite the OIC to participate in the sessions and the work of the General Assembly and of its subsidiary organs in the capacity of observer.[200] Regular general meetings have identified priority areas of cooperation between the UN and OIC, and there are periodic high-level meetings between the Secretary-General of the UN and the Secretary-General of the OIC, as well as between senior secretariat officials of the two organizations, and the UN encourages their participation in important meetings of the two organizations.[201]

Similarly, the UN works in close cooperation with the Arab League and its Member States. In 1984, for example, the UN General Assembly noted "the vital importance for the countries members of the League of Arab States of achieving a just, comprehensive and durable solution to the Middle East conflict and the question of Palestine, the core of the conflict." Referring to a "framework of co-operation between the United Nations and the League of Arab States in certain priority sectors" and "the need for closer co-operation between the United Nations system and the League of Arab States and its specialized organizations in realizing the goals and objectives set forth in the Strategy for Joint Arab Economic Development adopted by the Eleventh Arab Summit Conference, held at Amman from 25 to 27 November 1980," the General Assembly requested the Secretary-General to "strengthen co-operation with the General Secretariat of the League of Arab States for the purpose of implementing United Nations resolutions relating to the question of Palestine and the situation in the Middle East in order to achieve a just, comprehensive and durable solution to the Middle East conflict and the question of Palestine, the core of the conflict."[202]

---

200. UN G.A. Res. 3369 (XXX) of 10 October 1975.

201. See: A/RES/55/9 (12 December 2000), 'Cooperation between the United Nations and the Organization of the Islamic Conference' and A/RES/57/42 (21 November 2002).

202. A/RES/39/9 (8 November 1984), 'Cooperation between the United Nations and the League of Arab States'.

3.4.1 The League of Arab States (Arab League)

The Arab League is a regional organization that was founded in 1945. Through Resolution 477, it received permanent observer status to the UN on 1 November 1950. The Arab League asserts influence within the UN by submitting reports to the General Assembly and the Security Council, which often results in the initiation of meetings or the draft of UN Resolutions. In the context of issues relating to the Israeli-Palestinian conflict, the Arab League is often invited to participate in Security Council or General Assembly discussions.[203] The Arab League is also a member of the Committee on the Inalienable Rights of the Palestinian People.

The Arab League offered to be the vehicle through which the Palestine Liberation Organization (PLO) would be created. In 1964, the leaders of Arab League gathered for a summit in Cairo at which they agreed to organize the Palestinian people to enable them to play their part in the liberation of their country. In follow-up to this summit, the first Palestinian National Council was convened in Jerusalem, which drafted the Palestinian National Covenant and established the PLO.

The Charter of the Arab League, also known as the Pact of the League of Arab States, stipulates that the Member States of the Arab League support recognition of "Palestine (State of)," which it understands to be an Arab state that was recognized by the League of Nations in 1922. This suggests that the State of Palestine, which the Arab League strives to see established comprises all the territory of the Mandate for Palestine:

> **"Even though Palestine was not able to control her own destiny, it was on the basis of the recognition of her independence that the Covenant of the League of Nations determined a system of government for her. Her existence and her independence among the nations can, therefore, no more be questioned *de jure* than the independence of any of the other Arab States. [...] Therefore, the States signatory to the Pact of the Arab League consider that in view of Palestine's special circumstances, the Council of the League should designate an Arab delegate from Palestine to participate in its work until this country enjoys actual independence."[204]**

It is not surprising, then, that the Arab League Member States,[205] meeting in Khartoum after the Six-Day War in June 1967, categorically

203. For example in 1980, on the status of Jerusalem, the Security Council invited the League of Arab States to its meetings. See: http://cdn.un.org/unyearbook/yun/chapter_pdf/1980YUN/1980_P1_SEC1_CH12.pdf page 400 (visited: 11 November 2015).

204. Pact of the League of Arab States (22 March 1945), Annex on Palestine.

205. Egypt, Syria, Jordan, Lebanon, Iraq, Algeria, Kuwait and Sudan.

denied the right of Israel to exist and rejected the principles and processes described in Resolution 242:

> **"The Arab Heads of State have agreed to unite their political efforts at the international and diplomatic level to eliminate the effects of the aggression and to ensure the withdrawal of the aggressive Israeli forces from the Arab lands which have been occupied since the aggression of June 5. This will be done within *the framework of the main principles by which the Arab States abide, namely, no peace with Israel, no recognition of Israel, no negotiations with it, and insistence on the rights of the Palestinian people in their own country.*"**

Six years later—on the holiest day of the Jewish year (Yom Kippur), Saturday 6 October 1973—Egypt and Syria (later joined by Jordan) launched yet another concerted military attack against Israel, this time using advanced weapons supplied from the Soviet Union and Western Europe. Their official goal was to liberate the territories that Israel had conquered in 1967. But the rhetoric of then-Syrian President, Hafez al-Assad, and other Arab leaders before and during the war indicated that the Arabs were prepared to cross the 1949 cease-fire lines.[206] Responding to Arab threats of oil boycotts, most European nations closed their airspace and NATO bases to American aircraft preventing them flying much-needed supplies to Israel. The Arabs failed in their attempt, and Israel took control of even more territory.

Following their military failure in 1973, the PLO and the Arab nations renewed their campaign, as expressed in the Khartoum Declaration, to "unite their political efforts" to achieve what in essence were military goals: namely, "to ensure the withdrawal of the aggressive Israeli forces from the Arab lands which have been occupied since the aggression of June 5."[207] They did this by gradually mobilizing a majority of states in the UN General Assembly to issue a stream of resolutions during the 1970's and 1980's. At the Arab League Summit in Rabat in October 1974, the Arab nations officially recognized the PLO as the "sole legitimate representative of the Palestinian people." This was followed almost immediately by the General Assembly's recognition of the PLO as "sole legitimate representative" of the Palestinian people.

The Arab League was behind resolutions rejecting Israel's unification of Jerusalem, demanding Israel's full withdrawal from the "occupied territories,"

206. On 16 October 1973, at the height of the war, Assad declared: "Our forces will continue to pursue the enemy and strike at him until we restore our positions in our occupied land, After that, we will continue until we liberate the whole land."

207. Khartoum Declaration,, September 1967.

insisting on recognition of "inalienable Palestinian rights to self-determination" and their "right to return," and condemning Zionism as a form of racism.

The Khartoum Declaration suggests that these demands were part of a strategy to achieve a larger goal, namely rejection of the existence of the Jewish State of Israel as a legitimate state. It is illustrative that in the 19 years that Egypt and Jordan occupied Gaza and the West Bank, respectively, no resolutions were adopted in the General Assembly either demanding Egypt or Jordan's withdrawal from those territories or the recognizing the rights of the Palestinians.

In the resolutions of the UN Security Council and General Assembly, as well as the reports of other UN bodies, reference is often made to the Arab Peace Initiative[208] that was initiated by the Arab League and calls *inter alia* upon the complete withdrawal by Israel from occupied territories and the right of return for Palestinians.

3.4.2 The Organization of Islamic Cooperation (OIC)

The OIC[209] was established in 1969 and is based in Jeddah (Saudi Arabia). Today it brings together 56 states,[210] as well as the "State of Palestine." Most of OIC's Member States are officially Islamic states or have a Muslim majority, although some of its members, such as Uganda and Cameroon, have only a Muslim minority. Some other states with a significant Muslim minority, such as Russia and Thailand, have Observer status in the OIC. The OIC has the status of a Permanent Observer within the UN.

The OIC is modeled on the UN organizational structure. The OIC is an explicitly Islamic institution, as although some existing members do not have a Muslim majority, under the OIC Charter only states with a "Muslim-majority" may join.[211] The OIC Charter[212] (adopted in 2008 "in the name of Allah") states that the OIC's purpose is, inter alia, to revitalize Islam's pioneering role in the world, achieve an Islamic Common Market,

---

208. See: http://www.jcpa.org/text/Arab-Peace-Initiative.pdf (visited: 11 November 2015).

209. In 2011 the Organization of Islamic Conference was renamed as the Organization of Islamic Cooperation. See: http://www.oic-oci.org (visited: 8 September 2017).

210. Afghanistan, Albania, Algeria, Azerbaijan, Bahrain, Bangladesh, Benin, Brunei, Burkina Faso, Cameroon, Chad, Comoros, Cote d'Ivoire, Djibouti, Egypt, Gabon, Gambia, Guinea Bissau, Guinea, Guyana, Indonesia, Iran, Iraq, Ivory Coast, Jordan, Kazakhstan, Kuwait, Kyrgyzstan, Lebanon, Libya, Malaysia, Maldives, Mali, Mauritania, Morocco, Mozambique, Niger, Nigeria, Oman, Pakistan, Qatar, Saudi Arabia, Senegal, Sierra Leone, Somalia, Sudan, Suriname, Syria, Tajikistan, Turkmenistan, Togo, Tunisia, Turkey, Uganda, United Arab Emirates, Uzbekistan, Yemen.

211. OIC Charter, art. 3(2).

212. See: http://www.oic-oci.org/oicv2/page/?p_id=53&p_ref=27&lan=en (visited: 17 July 2015).

promote noble Islamic values, inculcate Islamic values in children and youth, promote the unity and solidarity among Muslim peoples, and defend the universality of the Islamic religion.[213] The overriding importance of the "Ummah" (the collective community of Islamic nations) is reflected throughout the OIC Charter.

The Palestinian Permanent Representative to the OIC signed the new OIC Charter on 18 November 2008. Article 1(8) of the OIC Charter states specifically that one of the objectives of the OIC is "to support the struggle of the Palestinian people to exercise their right to self-determination and establish their sovereign state with Al-Quds Al-Sharif as its capital, while safeguarding its historic and Islamic character as well as the Holy places therein."[214] The importance of Jerusalem (Al-Quds) and "Palestine" is reflected in the fact that the City of Al-Quds is intended to become the headquarters of the OIC (taking over from the current headquarters, Jedda) once Al-Quds has been "liberated."[215] The "Al Quds Committee" is one of only four Standing Committees of the OIC, while one of the posts of Assistant Secretary General shall be devoted to "the cause of Al-Quds Al-Sharif and Palestine" for which the "State of Palestine" has the sole right to designate a candidate.[216]

3.4.3 The Influence of the OIC and the Arab League in Relation to Israel/Palestine Issues

The OIC and Arab League have been instrumental since their inception in sponsoring and facilitating numerous UN General Assembly and Security Council resolutions every year opposing Israel's presence in the "post-1967 territories" as illegal, condemning alleged breaches of human rights by Israel against Palestinians, and supporting Palestinian rights to statehood.[217] For example, the UN General Assembly adopted each year between 1993 and 2016 many reports of the Special Committee to Investigate Israeli Practices Affecting the Human Rights of the Palestinian People and Other Arabs of the Occupied Territories. *All* of these Resolutions were introduced and sponsored by OIC and Arab League Member States,

213. OIC Charter, preamble.

214. OIC Charter, art. 1(8).

215. OIC Charter, art. 21.

216. OIC Charter, art. 11(1)(i).

217. See the adoption of Resolution 476 (1980) in which the Security Council expressed its concerns regarding the steps that where taken by the Israeli government to declare Jerusalem as the capital of Israel. This Resolution, followed by a call for withdrawal of diplomatic missions from Jerusalem in Resolution 478, came after Pakistan called on behalf of the OIC for an immediate meeting of the Security Council.

showing that the OIC and the Arab League were instrumental—directly or indirectly—in the creation of these resolutions.[218]

3.4.4 The Euro-Arab Dialogue (EAD)

The European Union (EU) and before it came into existence, the EEC, has played a significant role in the delegitimization of Israel since the 1970's. The common policy of the EU and its Member States with respect to Israel is essentially based on two objectives. On the one hand, Europe promotes ever closer economic and political cooperation between the EU and Israel, founded on common values and mutual economic interests. On the other hand, the EU institutions are committed to the notion that peace and security is to be achieved in the region through the creation of a "viable Palestinian state."

According to the EU Foreign Affairs Council, international law requires both the EU and Israel to ensure the creation of a Palestinian state, because[219]:

- International humanitarian law—including the Fourth Geneva Convention—applies in the "Occupied Palestinian territory";
- Israeli settlements are illegal, "irrespective of recent decisions by the government of Israel";
- All of Area C "belongs" in principle to the future Palestinian State—"it is its main land reserve";
- Israel is under a legal obligation to ensure the viability of a two-state solution. In fact, international law prohibits Israel from taking any steps which may prejudice the creation of a viable Palestinian state or which "threaten to make a two-state solution impossible";
- In addition, Israel is under a positive obligation to work together with the Palestinian Authoritiy (PA) to improve the social and economic living conditions of the Palestinian population in Area C. Building permit procedures must be simplified. Palestinians must have guaranteed access to water. Palestinian master plans must be approved quickly, and the PA must be given "more access and control" over Area C;
- The Palestinian state must—under international law—be based on the pre-1967 borders unless the PLO agrees otherwise. "The EU reiterates that it will not recognize any changes to the pre-1967 borders including with regard to Jerusalem, other than those agreed by the parties"; and
- Jerusalem must be divided (in accordance with the "pre-1967 borders") and become the capital of both Israel and the new Palestinian State.

---

218. See Appendixes.

219. See the conclusions of the EU Foreign Affairs Council on the Middle East Process, May 2012, July 2014 and January 2016. Cf. Appendixes.

The EU's commitment to ensuring Palestinian statehood, based on its perception of international law, is summarized in this statement of the EU Foreign Affairs Council in 2009:

> **"The EU stands ready to further develop its bilateral relations with the Palestinian Authority reflecting shared interests, including in the framework of the European Neighbourhood Policy. Recalling the Berlin Declaration, the Council also reiterates its support for negotiations leading to Palestinian statehood, all efforts and steps to that end and its readiness, when appropriate, to recognize a Palestinian state. It will continue to assist Palestinian state-building, including through its CSDP missions and within the Quartet. The EU fully supports the implementation of the Palestinian Authority's Government Plan 'Palestine, Ending the Occupation, Establishing the State' as an important contribution to this end, and will work for enhanced international support for this plan."[220]**

Accordingly, since the 1970's, the EU (EEC) and its Member States have been, by far, the largest donor to the PA, investing in total over €8 billion in the peace process.[221]

The roots of this EU common policy were laid in late 1973. In the late 1960's and early 1970's, the West was being confronted by a wave of Palestinian terrorism and the Arab oil boycott—a strategy implemented as a result of the Arab failure in the Yom Kippur war, and designed to force the international community to back the Arabs' claims.[222] In response to these developments, on 6 November 1973, the nine countries of the European Economic Community (EEC)[223] issued a Declaration on the Middle East[224] that, for the first time, articulated a common European Middle East policy. This was based on three assertions, each of which represented a reversal of what had until then been generally understood

220. http://eeas.europa.eu/enp/pdf/2015/joint-communication_en.pdf (visited: 2 April 2015). CSDP refers to the Common Security and Defence Policy.

221. According to the website of the European External Action Service (EEAS), "The EU is the largest donor to the Palestinians. In recent years, the combined contribution of the European Commission and EU Member States has reached €1 billion per year." (See:: https://eeas.europa.eu/headquarters/headquarters-homepage/337/middle-east-peace-process_en).

222. As one Arab leader later declared: "The Arab-Israeli conflict and the oil problem are not only related but inseparable. Had it not been for the said conflict the oil weapon would not have been unleashed." Dr. Ibrahim A. Obaid (Saudi Arabia director general of Ministry of Petroleum and Mineral Resources and Arab delegate to the EAD), 'Political Preconditions for Cooperation with Western Europe' (statement at a meeting of EAD experts in Amsterdam, 1975).

223. In early 1973, the United Kingdom, Denmark and Ireland had joined the EEC. 'EEC' refers to the European Economic Community, which has since been incorporated in the EU.

224. For this declaration on the Middle East, see: https://www.cvce.eu/content/publication/1999/1/1/a08b36bc-6d29-475c-aadb-0f71c59dbc3e/publishable_en.pdf.

to be the position under international law:

1. The Member States of the EEC emphasized "the inadmissibility of the acquisition of territory by force"—implicitly referring to Israel's control over the post-1967 territories. In so doing, they took this legal principle of the "inadmissibility of acquiring territory by force" out of context, and ignored the fact that Israel acquired control over the territories in 1967 as a result of a defensive war.
2. Israel must "end the territorial occupation which it has maintained since the conflict of 1967." Effectively, this was a demand for Israel to withdraw to the armistice lines of 1949. In so doing, the EEC adopted the French/Arab interpretation of UN Security Council resolution 242, and elevated the 1949 armistice lines to international borders—which they were not.
3. According to the EEC, the "legitimate rights of the Palestinians" must be included in any definition of peace for the Middle East. This was a complete innovation. Resolution 242 did not refer at all to the Palestinian people; on the contrary, it imposed obligations on the Arab nations.

Not surprisingly, the EEC's declaration was immediately greeted with approval by the Arab States who, meeting on 28 November 1973 in Algiers for the Sixth Summit of the Arab Conference, welcomed the "first manifestations of a better understanding of the Arab cause by the states of Western Europe."[225] President Georges Pompidou of France responded swiftly by calling an EEC summit in Copenhagen on 15 December 1973, at which four Arab foreign ministers were invited to present the Arab conditions for European-Arab cooperation. This was the birth of the Euro-Arab Dialogue (EAD).

The November 1973 Declaration on the Middle East itself was the culmination of developments from the mid-1960's in several European nations to strengthen ties with the Arab/Islamic world, and to develop what has since been referred to as the "Palestinianization" of European policy towards the Middle East.[226] France was the main, but not the only, force behind this development. As early as 1967, President Charles de Gaulle of France publicly condemned Israel's foreign policy and announced France's cooperation with the Arab world as "the fundamental basis of our foreign policy."[227] France developed close economic and political ties

---

225. http://www.jewishvirtuallibrary.org/declaration-of-the-arab-summit-conference-at-algiers-november-1973.

226. Bat Ye'or (2011), p. 28.

227. Bat Ye'or (2005), p. 44.

with Muammar al-Qadaffi of Libya and leaders of the other Arab nations, and from 1973 consistently voted in favor of Arab League resolutions condemning Israel. From 1969, France even began to explore with Libya the idea of an EAD. Historian Bat Ye'or has painstakingly documented the pivotal role played by the OIC in the establishment of the EAD in 1974 and the succeeding decades.[228]

The EAD was officially launched at a series of high-level meetings between the EEC and Arab League in Paris in July/August 1974. Representatives and experts from Arab and European nations then met for the first meeting of the EAD in Cairo in June 1975. They expressed the general principles and objectives of the EAD as follows[229]:

> "The Euro-Arab Dialogue is the fruit of a common political desire which emerged at the highest level and which aims to establish special relationships between two groups. ...The two parties are mindful that the Dialogue had originated in their exchanges at the end of 1973, and, particularly, the declaration made by the nine States members of the European Community, 6 November 1973, concerning the situation in the Middle East as well as the declaration addressed to the Western European countries by the 6th Summit conference of Arab countries in Algiers on 28 November 1973."

Bat Ye'or concludes:[230] "It is clear, therefore, that the basis for the Dialogue was the endorsement by the EEC of Arab policy concerning Israel, in accordance with the Algiers declaration. ...The EAD from its inception thus emphasized that the many aspects of the Euro-Arab *entente* depended entirely on the EEC's adherence to Arab anti-Israeli policy: the Arabs would dictate the criteria for peace, stability, security and justice."

The EEC's commitment to ensure the realization of Palestinian statehood was taken a step further in June 1977, when the European Council (EC) issued a declaration stating that "a solution to the conflict in the Middle East will be possible only if the legitimate right of the Palestinian people to give effective expression to its national identity is translated into fact, which would take into account the need for a homeland for the Palestinian people..." Subsequently, in the Venice Declaration of 13 June 1980—considered the European response to the American-brokered Camp David Accords—the heads of state and foreign ministers of the nine EEC

---

228. See in particular: Bat Ye'or (2005) and (2011).

229. Joint memorandum issued in Cairo in June 1975 by European and Arab representatives, reproduced in: Bourrinet (1979), pp. 296-306.

230. Bat Ye'or (2005), pp. 67-68.

members proposed a "special role" for the Europeans in an international endeavor to achieve a comprehensive Arab-Israeli settlement. The Venice Declaration went beyond previous European statements in that it called for self-determination for the Palestinians and articulated a role for the PLO in the negotiations:

> **"A just solution must finally be found to the Palestinian problem, which is not simply one of refugees. The Palestinian people... must be placed in a position, by an appropriate process defined within the framework of the comprehensive peace settlement, to exercise fully its right to self-determination. ...These principles apply to all the parties concerned, and thus to the Palestinian people, and to the PLO, which will have to be associated with the negotiations," (articles 6 and 7).**

The policy declaration also stated that the EC would "not accept any unilateral initiative designed to change the status of Jerusalem" and maintained that "settlements, as well as modifications in population and property in the occupied Arab territories, are *illegal under international law."*[231]

In the late 1980's, Europe more actively promoted the idea of an international conference under the auspices of the UN in the conflict, calling such an international conference "the only formula which would allow the peace process in the region to move forward." The EEC then endorsed the 1991 Madrid Peace Conference and its subsequent negotiating tracks. The EU is currently deeply involved in the multilateral track of this process. Together with the United States, the UN and Russia, the EU is a member of the "Middle East Quartet" and endorses the "performance-based and goal-driven Roadmap for Peace," the central pillar of which is the creation of a viable Palestinian state.

231. Emphasis added.

4. The "Wall Opinion": An Example of Lawfare against Israel?

"I am compelled to vote against the Court's findings on the merits because the Court did not have before it the requisite factual bases for its sweeping findings; it should therefore have declined to hear the case. In reaching this conclusion, I am guided by what the Court said in Western Sahara, where it emphasized that the critical question in determining whether or not to exercise its discretion in acting on an advisory opinion request is 'whether the Court has before it sufficient information and evidence to enable it to arrive at a judicial conclusion upon any disputed questions of fact the determination of which is necessary for it to give an opinion in conditions compatible with its judicial character' (Western Sahara, Advisory Opinion, ICJ Reports 1975, pp. 28-29, para. 46)."

Judge Buergenthal, Declaration, (Paragraph 1)[232]

4.1 Introduction

Discussions of the international legal aspects of the conflict between Israel and Palestine inevitably include references to the Advisory Opinion of the International Court of Justice (ICJ) of 9 July 2004 on the *Legal Consequences of the Construction of a Wall in the Occupied Palestinian Territory."*[233] The ICJ's Advisory Opinion was requested by the General Assembly of the United Nations (UN), which in 2003 sought an answer to the question of the legal consequences of the construction of the wall that was then in the process of being built by Israel in what the General Assembly considered to be "Occupied Palestinian Territory."

This wall was constructed in response to the "Second Intifada" or "Al Aqsa Intifada" that had erupted as a result of the failure of the "slo peace

232. *Legal Consequences of the Construction of a Wall in the Occupied Palestinian Territory,* Advisory Opinion, 2004 I.C.J. Reports, pp. 136-203 (9 July 2004), Declaration of Judge Buergenthal, at p. 240.

233. *Legal Consequences of the Construction of a Wall in the Occupied Palestinian Territory,* Advisory Opinion, 2004 I.C.J. Reports, pp. 136-203 (9 July 2004).

process and the collapse of the Israeli-Palestinian Camp David summit in 2000. Some argue that the outbreak of violence was triggered by the controversial visit by the (then) Israeli opposition leader Ariel Sharon to the Temple Mount on 28 September 2000. Others argue that Palestine Liberation Organization (PLO) Chairman Yasser Arafat launched the intifada when he abandoned the Camp David summit. Whatever the proximate cause, in the subsequent years, hundreds of Israelis and Palestinians were killed. Construction of this structure totaling some 700km in length was commenced in late 2000.

Israel has consistently defended the barrier as a necessary response to Palestinian terrorism and is justified by its right to self-determination under international law. The PLO and others, on the contrary, argue that the barrier is in fact intended to effectively annex "Palestinian land" in the guise of security.

In its Wall Advisory Opinion, the ICJ concluded that Israel's construction of the barrier was contrary to international law, and that Israel was obliged to cease its construction, to dismantle the wall, and make reparation for the damage caused by its construction. According to the ICJ, all (other) states are under an obligation not to recognize the illegal situation resulting from the construction of the wall and not to aid or assist the maintaining of the situation. Furthermore, the States Parties to the Fourth Geneva Convention (1949) have an additional obligation to ensure compliance by Israel with international humanitarian law as embodied in that Convention. According to the ICJ, the UN itself and specifically the General Assembly and the Security Council "should consider what further action is required to bring to an end the illegal situation resulting from the construction of the wall and the associated regime."

The ICJ Wall Advisory Opinion has formed a watershed in the application and—perhaps even more importantly—*perceptions about* the application of international law in relation to the Israel/Palestine conflict. It has been extremely influential at many layers of the international community: not only at the political level of the UN, but also within the framework of other multilateral institutions such as the European Union. In the UN, the General Assembly responded to the ICJ's Advisory Opinion by adopting a Resolution in which it called upon Israel to comply with the legal obligations which the ICJ had mentioned and likewise called upon the UN Member States to do the same.[234]

Since 2004, the ICJ's Advisory Opinion has been consistently referred

234. A/RES/ES-10/15 of 2 August 2004.

to in the plethora of General Assembly resolutions condemning Israel. It is also frequently relied upon by subsidiary UN organs. Resolutions of the UN Economic and Social Council [235] and the universal periodic reviews of the Human Rights Council both make frequent references to the ICJ Advisory Opinion.[236] The Special Rapporteur on the situation of Human Rights in the "Occupied Palestinian Territories" , Richard Falk, devoted a whole chapter to the ICJ Advisory Opinion in his Report of 2014.[237] The ICJ Advisory Opinion is also explicitly referred to—for the first time in the Security Council—in recent UN Security Council Resolution 2334.

The ICJ Advisory Opinion has also become an important weapon in the hands of the Boycott, Divestment and Sanctions movement (BDS) that was launched by Palestinian civil society one year after the ICJ Advisory Opinion (in 2005) and whose campaign is supported and amplified by thousands of NGOs around the world. In their efforts to convince companies to put an end to their trade and investment relations with Israeli entities located, or with connections, in the "Occupied Palestinian Territories," and to convince governments to implement sanctions against Israel until it withdraws from "the territories occupied since 1967," these NGOs refer frequently to international law and specifically to the ICJ Advisory Opinion in their activities and reports.[238]

The ICJ Advisory Opinion is also frequently and consistently relied upon by national governments, opinion-makers and even academics as "conclusive evidence" that Israel is "occupying" the West Bank, including East Jerusalem, that the security barrier is "illegal," and that Israel's annexation of East Jerusalem and all Israeli settlements in the West Bank are "illegal." For example, in April 2013, the Dutch Advisory Council on International Affairs (AIV)—a purportedly independent, official advice organ to the Dutch Ministry of Foreign Affairs—issued an advice to the Dutch Government in which it stated: "In this connection, the AIV has taken as its reference point the Advisory Opinion issued by the International Court of Justice in 2004. Though this Opinion was initially issued in response to questions about the legality of Israel's construction of the 'wall' (much of it on Palestinian territory), the opinion of the Court encompasses almost all legal issues associated with the conflict. The Court also considered the

---

235. ECOSOC 2005/51 of 25 July 2005.

236. A/HRC/25/15 (19 December 2013), and A/HRC/10/76, (8 January 2009).

237. A/HRC/25/67, *Report of the Special Rapporteur on the situation of human rights in the Palestinian territories occupied since 1967, Richard Falk*, 13 January 2014.

238. 'Trading Away Peace, How Europe helps sustain illegal Israeli settlements', October 2012, pp. 13 and 15 (this report to the European Union was produced by 22 European NGOs).

Israeli settlements on the West Bank of the Jordan in its deliberations. It concluded that Israel's settlement policy violates international law. The violations concern the Palestinian people's right to self-determination, the freedom of movement of all the inhabitants of the "occupied territories" and the right to work, health care and education. The Court also believes that the barrier and the settlements violate the Fourth Geneva Convention (relative to the Protection of Civilian Persons in Time of War) and Security Council resolutions on the matter, because they are helping to change the demographic profile of the occupied territories. There can be no doubt as to the applicability of the Convention in these territories."[239]

4.2 **Background to the Wall Advisory Opinion**

On 8 December 2003 the General Assembly, acting in accordance with Article 96 (1) of the UN Charter, requested the ICJ to issue an Advisory Opinion on the following question:

> **"What are the legal consequences arising from the construction of the wall being built by Israel, the Occupying Power, in the Occupied Palestinian Territory, including in and around East Jerusalem, as described in the report of the Secretary-General, considering the rules and principles of international law, including the Fourth Geneva Convention of 1949, and relevant Security Council and General Assembly resolutions?"[240]**

The request for the Advisory Opinion emerged in the context of the General Assembly's Tenth Emergency Special Session. That session commenced in 1997, following Arab claims that Israeli settlements in "Occupied East Jerusalem and the rest of the 'Occupied Palestinian Territory' were illegal"[241]—long before the wall was even conceived of. That, in itself, is enough to show that the real issue which the General Assembly wanted the ICJ to resolve was the existence of "settlements"—and not the wall as such.

The driving forces behind these Special Sessions and the drafting of the December 2003 Resolution were the Arab League, the Non-Alignment Movement (NAM), the Organization of Islamic Conference (OIC) and UN Permanent Observer Palestine. As we have observed, all of these entities are well-known for their aggressive criticism of Israel, their refusal to accept the existence of Israel as a Jewish state, and their rejection of the

---

239. Advisory Council on International Affairs, *Between words and deeds. Prospects for a sustainable peace in the Middle East,* no. 83, March 2013, p. 44.

240. General Assembly, Tenth Emergency Session, UNDoc. A/RES/ES-10/14 (8 December 2003).

241. *Ibid.*

right of Israeli citizens to live in the "Occupied Palestinian Territories."[242] In fact, a number of the Member States of the Arab League and the OIC do not even acknowledge the *existence* of the State of Israel, let alone the *legality* of its actions.

As a result of their efforts and at the request of the UN General Assembly,[243] the Secretary-General produced a Report in which he observed that Israel's construction of the wall constituted "a deeply counterproductive act"[244] and then moved the General Assembly to adopt the Resolution in which it formulated its request for an Advisory Opinion.

Of the 191 UN Member States then in existence, only 92 Member States voted in favor of the Resolution. Eight voted against, and a massive 74 Member States abstained from voting.[245] The resolution was thus adopted by less than half of all UN Member States in existence at that time.[246] The majority of votes in favor of the resolution were cast by Muslim-majority

---

242. UN Yearbook, 2003, Middle East, pp. 472, 476 and 480-481.

243. G.A. UNDoc. A/RES/ES-10/13 (27 October 2003), in which the General Assembly demanded that "Israel stop and reverse the construction of the wall in the Occupied Palestinian Territory" and requested the Secretary-General to report on compliance with the present resolution periodically.

244. G.A. UNDoc. A/ES-10/248 (24 November 2003), para 7. In its Advisory Opinion, the Court *inter alia* relied on the information presented by this Report.

245. The voting record for UN G.A. Res. 10/14, UNDoc A/RES/ES-10/14 is as follows: *In Favor:* Algeria, Antigua and Barbuda, Argentina, Armenia, Azerbaijan, Bahamas, Bahrain, Bangladesh, Barbados, Belarus, Belize, Benin, Bhutan, Botswana, Brazil, Brunei, Darussalam, Burkina Faso, Cambodia, Cape Verde, Central African Republic, Chad, China, Comoros, Côte d'Ivoire, Cuba, Democratic People's Republic of Korea, Djibouti, Egypt, Gambia, Ghana, Grenada, Guinea, Guinea-Bissau, Guyana, Haiti, India, Indonesia, Iran, Jamaica, Jordan, Kazakhstan, Kenya, Kuwait, Kyrgyzstan, Lao People's Democratic Republic, Lebanon, Lesotho, Libyan Arab Jamahiriya, Malaysia, Maldives, Mali, Mauritania, Mauritius, Mexico, Mongolia, Morocco, Mozambique, Myanmar, Namibia, Nepal, Niger, Nigeria, Oman, Pakistan, Panama, Qatar, Saint Lucia, Saint Vincent, Grenadines, Saudi Arabia, Senegal, Sierra Leone, Somalia, South Africa, Sri Lanka, Sudan, Suriname, Swaziland, Syrian Arab Republic, Timor Leste, Togo, Trinidad and Tobago, Tunisia, Turkey, Turkmenistan, United Arab Emirates, United Republic of Tanzania, Vietnam, Yemen, Zambia, Zimbabwe. Against: Australia, Ethiopia, Israel, Marshall Islands, Micronesia, Nauru, Palau, United States. Abstaining: Albania, Andorra, Austria, Belgium, Bolivia, Bosnia and Herzegovina, Bulgaria, Burundi, Cameroon, Canada, Chile, Colombia, Costa Rica, Croatia, Cyprus, Czech Republic, Denmark, Dominican Republic, Ecuador, Estonia, Fiji, Finland, France, Georgia, Germany, Greece, Guatemala, Honduras, Hungary, Iceland, Ireland, Italy, Japan, Latvia, Liechtenstein, Lithuania, Luxembourg, Malta, Monaco, the Netherlands, New Zealand, Nicaragua, Norway, Papua New Guinea, Paraguay, Peru, Philippines, Poland, Portugal, Republic of Korea, Republic of Moldova, Romania, Russian Federation, Samoa, San Marino, Serbia and Montenegro, Singapore, Slovakia, Slovenia, Solomon Islands, Spain, Sweden, Switzerland, Tajikistan, Thailand, The former Yugoslav Republic of Macedonia, Tonga, Uganda, Ukraine, United Kingdom, Uruguay, Uzbekistan, Vanuatu, Venezuela.

246. Most resolutions of the General Assembly require a simple majority of members "present and voting" (UN Charter, art.18). In 2003 there were 191 UN Member States.

Member States. No Western or European Member States voted in favor of the Resolution.[247]

The General Assembly's formulation of the question contained a number of factual and legal presumptions. As a result, one of the ICJ Judges (Judge Kooijmans) expressed in his separate opinion that the formulated question was "far from being 'legally neutral.'"[248] For example, the use of the pejorative term "wall" was used to describe a construction that in fact contains many different parts and in many sections does not resemble a wall but can arguably better be described as a "fence" or "barrier." Moreover, the General Assembly referred to the territories administered by Israel since June 1967 as "Occupied Palestinian Territory, including in and around East Jerusalem" and Israel as "Occupying Power." The term "Occupied" implies that these territories are "occupied" within the meaning of international law. The word "Palestinian" implies that in some sense these territories belong to "the Palestinians." As we will see, the legal grounds for these claims are highly debatable.

Having received the request for an Advisory Opinion, the ICJ notified all UN Member States that they had six weeks within which to make submissions. The date 23 February 2004 was set down as for commencement of hearing of oral statements and comments. Palestine, the Arab League and the OIC were given special permission to make written and oral statements even though they are not UN Member States. Written statements were submitted by 44 Member States plus the EU, the UN, the Arab League and the OIC. From 23-25 February 2004, the ICJ heard oral statements made by Palestine, South Africa, Algeria, Saudi Arabia, Bangladesh, Belize, Cuba, Indonesia, Jordan, Madagascar, Malaysia, Senegal, Sudan, the League of Arab States and the OIC—all of them openly hostile towards Israel.

"Palestine" was the first party to be heard. In contrast to all other parties (which were represented by one or at most two lawyers), "Palestine" was represented by a team of four professors of international law, including the leading professors of public international law at the time at the Universities of Cambridge and Oxford (Professors James Crawford and Vaughan Lowe respectively). Israel was effectively compelled to counter a barrage of factual and legal claims put by an army of international lawyers representing a number of UN Member States that deny its existence, two multi-lateral institutions that are dominated by states which deny

---

247. This balance of power has been a common feature of the hundreds of proposed General Assembly resolutions since the 1970's which condemn or criticize Israel.

248. *Legal Consequences of the Construction of a Wall in the Occupied Palestinian Territory,* Advisory Opinion, 2004 I.C.J. Reports, pp. 136-203 (9 July 2004), Separate Opinion Judge Kooijmans, at p. 227.

Israel's right to exist as a Jewish state, and Palestine, whose national charter commits it to the destruction of Israel as a Jewish state. Within the period of only two months, and on the basis of factual evidence and legal arguments that were not put to the test of cross-examination, the ICJ decided to investigate and make conclusions on matters that have proven too difficult for the brightest of legal minds over the past 100 years.

Israel took a strategic decision not to enter into a substantive discussion of the security fence before the ICJ, but rather to deny the court's jurisdiction. In a detailed 130-page document, it set out the reasons why it believes that the ICJ did not have jurisdiction in the matter, and why, even if had, it should exercise its discretion to decline to hear the case. Israel raised two main concerns about the request for the ICJ's Advisory Opinion: first, the request was totally silent on the reason for the fence (Palestinian terrorism), and second, compliance with the request was likely to frustrate the Roadmap process.[249]

Fourteen of the 15 judges rejected Israel's submissions and voted in favor of complying with the General Assembly's request, and in their opinion, essentially condemned Israel's construction of the wall. Only the American Judge Buergenthal, in a separate Declaration,[250] dissociated himself from the ICJ Advisory Opinion as a whole.

The ICJ Advisory Opinion relied heavily on information that was submitted by the findings of the (then) Special Rapporteur of the Commission on Human Rights, John Dugard, concerning the situation of "human rights in the Palestinian territories occupied by Israel since 1967."[251] Dugard not only provided factual information about the construction of the wall and the socio-economic impact thereof on the Palestinian people, he also offered his own legal interpretation of these facts.[252] As a result, as we shall later demonstrate, the factual underpinning of the ICJ Advisory Opinion was both inadequate and untested, and the legal reasoning of the ICJ Advisory Opinion was politically biased and one-sided.[253] In short, the ICJ allowed itself to become part of a political process.

---

249. For a summary of Israel's submissions. see: https://unispal.un.org/DPA/DPR/unispal.nsf/0/C43A1490073AAB9985256E5100752639 (visited: 8 September 2017).

250. *Legal Consequences of the Construction of a Wall in the Occupied Palestinian Territory*, Advisory Opinion, 2004 I.C.J. Reports, pp. 136-203 (9 July 2004), Declaration Judge Buergenthal,, at pp. 240-245.

251. E/CN.4/2004/6.

252. The Written Statement of the Government of Israel was filed with the Registry on 30 January 2004. See also: Blois, de (2015), p. 109. The Special Rapporteur himself leaned in his findings on the input of non-governmental organisations.

253. Blois, de (2015), pp. 109-110.

4.3 The Procedure

A number of issues arose in the procedure, which dealt with the question of whether the ICJ had the competence (jurisdiction) to deal with the UN General Assembly's request. We will examine four of these issues.

4.3.1 The UN General Assembly Did Not Have Competence

Resolution ES-10/14—by which the General Assembly requested the ICJ to give an Advisory Opinion—was adopted during the Tenth Emergency Special Session. It had been submitted by Israel in its written statement on the jurisdiction of the ICJ that the General Assembly acted *ultra vires* (beyond power) by adopting the Resolution requesting an advisory opinion of the ICJ.[254] The background of this contention is that the Charter of the UN explicitly in Article 12 (1) prioritizes the powers of the Security Council over those of the General Assembly: "While the Security Council is exercising in respect of any dispute or situation the functions assigned to it in the present Charter, the General Assembly shall not make any recommendation with regard to that dispute or situation unless the Security Council so requests." Early in the history of the UN, when the exercise of the functions of the Security Council in the field of international peace and security was paralyzed because of the veto power its permanent members, the General Assembly adopted the "Uniting for Peace Resolution"[255] allowing it to make recommendations to Member States in the event of a threat to the peace, breach of the peace, or act of aggression. This Uniting for Peace Resolution was the basis of the Tenth Emergency Special Session, because the Security Council, as a result of the negative votes of the USA, failed to adopt two resolutions on Israeli settlements. This Session was convened by the General Assembly for the first time on 7 March 1997, and reconvened since then 11 times, including on 8 December 2003, the day it adopted UN Resolution ES-10/14.

Israel argued that a draft resolution with the request for an Advisory Opinion on the legal consequences of the wall was never brought before the Security Council, so a deadlock in the Security Council on this issue could not be assumed. Furthermore, it argued that the conditions for application of the Uniting for Peace Resolution had not been fulfilled, because the Security Council was actively exercising its responsibilities in connection with the Israeli-Palestinian conflict. In fact, it had adopted

254. Written Statement of the Government of Israel on Jurisdiction and Propriety, 30 January 2004.

255. UN G.A. Res. 377 (V), 'Uniting for Peace' (3 November 1950).

unanimously a resolution[256] endorsing a diplomatic initiative—called the *Roadmap*—only 19 days before the General Assembly adopted its resolution with the request for the ICJ Advisory Opinion. Israel also submitted that the "rolling character" of the Tenth Emergency Special Session, was at odds with the emergency situation presupposed by the Uniting for Peace Resolution. Finally, it pointed out the fact that it was convened at the same time the General Assembly was in regular session. Notwithstanding the weight and seriousness of these arguments, the ICJ was not persuaded.[257] It endorsed the evolutionist interpretation of Article 12 of the Charter towards a more lenient view of the relationship between the General Assembly and the Security Council. It accepted the impossibility of the adoption of a resolution in the Security Council on the wall (not including a request for an advisory opinion) due to a negative vote of a Permanent Member, as sufficient reason for the use of the Uniting for Peace resolution. Therefore, the adoption of the resolution with the request was seen as being within the competence of the General Assembly.

4.3.2 Israel's Non-Consent to the International Court of Justice's Jurisdiction

In its submission, Israel argued that the ICJ had no jurisdiction over the matter described in the General Assembly's request, and that if the ICJ were to proceed to adjudicate this matter, it would be breaching the principle that the ICJ only has jurisdiction to hear a contentious case when all the parties consent.[258]

As discussed in Chapter 2, the ICJ only has jurisdiction in *contentious* cases if all of the states involved in the dispute consent to the ICJ's jurisdiction; states cannot be compelled to submit to the jurisdiction of the ICJ.[259]

The ICJ's *advisory jurisdiction*, on the other hand, means that the General Assembly, the Security Council, and other UN organs can ask the ICJ to give an advisory opinion on a specific legal issue.[260] Such decisions of the ICJ, as the name suggests, are advisory only; while highly important,

256. UN S.C. Res.1515, UNDoc S/RES/1515 (19 November 2003).

257. *Legal Consequences of the Construction of a Wall in the Occupied Palestinian Territory*, Advisory Opinion, 2004 I.C.J. Reports, pp. 136-203 (9 July 2004), at pp. 148-152.

258. A State's consent is considered as an essential requirement in the fairness of proceedings within the international legal order.

259. Statute of the ICJ, art. 36.

260. Statute of the ICJ, art. 65.

they are not binding as such on either the UN organ or any state that may be involved or the subject of the opinion.[261]

Israel's argument that this was in substance a contentious case between Israel and Palestine was dismissed by the ICJ, which noted "that the lack of consent to the Court's contentious jurisdiction by interested States did not have bearing on its jurisdiction to give an advisory opinion."[262] This is a most astonishing statement by the ICJ, given that the questions the ICJ was being asked to consider went to the heart of the issues identified in the Oslo Agreements as matters for negotiation between Israel and the PLO. By reasoning this way, the ICJ completely ignored the background to the case, especially the fact that it arose out of the Tenth Emergency Session which was concerned with Israeli settlements and not the construction of the wall. Further, the ICJ also contradicted its own reasoning in previous similar cases, such as the *Western Sahara Advisory Opinion*, in which the ICJ had determined that "[i]n certain circumstances [...] the lack of consent of an interested State may render the giving of an advisory opinion incompatible with the Court's judicial character. An instance of this would be when the circumstances disclose that to give a reply would have the effect of circumventing the principle that a state is not obliged to allow its disputes to be submitted to judicial settlement without its consent."[263]

4.3.3 Participation of "Palestine"

Another preliminary issue that was raised before the ICJ was the invitation to Palestine to participate in the proceedings, as a result of which Palestine was effectively equated with Member States of the UN. The ICJ supported this decision by mentioning that "the General Assembly had granted Palestine a special status of observer and that the latter was co-sponsor of the draft resolution requesting the advisory opinion."[264] However, this would seem to be in conflict with the reasoning of Article 66 of the Statute of the Court, which implies that only UN Member States and international

261. Statute of the ICJ, arts 59 and 65-68. *Interpretation of Peace Treaties with Bulgaria, Hungary and Romania, First Phase, Advisory Opinion*, 1950 I.C.J. Reports, p. 71.

262. *Legal Consequences of the Construction of a Wall in the Occupied Palestinian Territory*, Advisory Opinion, 2004 I.C.J. Reports, pp. 136-203 (9 July 2004), at pp. 157-158.

263. *Ibid.*, p. 158; see also the condition of consent as outlined by the Permanent Court of International Justice in its Advisory Opinion: "no State without its consent [should] be compelled to submit its dispute (...) to any pacific settlement", in: *Status of Eastern Carelia* (Advisory Opinion), PCIJ Series B, No 5 (1923).

264. *Legal Consequences of the Construction of a Wall in the Occupied Palestinian Territory*, Advisory Opinion, 2004 I.C.J. Reports, pp. 136-203 (9 July 2004), at p. 141.

organizations are entitled to present written or oral statements before the ICJ in proceedings related to its advisory jurisdiction.[265]

4.3.4 Composition of the Court

The procedure also gave rise to a dispute with regard to the composition of the ICJ. Article 17(2) was invoked in response to the participation of the Egyptian Judge Elaraby as member of the ICJ.[266] Judge Elaraby was described by the government of Israel as "a Member of the Court who has played a leading role in recent years in the very Emergency Special Session from which the advisory opinion request has now emerged."[267] Other doubts with regard to his impartiality came from comments by Judge Elaraby in an interview that he made in an Egyptian newspaper only two months prior to his appointment to the ICJ, in which he had accused Israel of grave violations of humanitarian law and qualified its occupation of Palestinian territory as in violation with international law.[268] According to dissenting ICJ Judge Buergenthal, these remarks created "an appearance of bias" that would require the ICJ to "preclude [his] participation in the proceedings."[269] However, the invocation of Article 17(2) was quite simply dismissed by the ICJ, which concluded that the advisory question had not been at issue in the Emergency Special Session until Judge Elaraby had ceased to participate, and that the judge furthermore had not expressed his opinion in the interview with regard to legal consequences of the construction of the wall. This aspect of the ICJ's reasoning is extremely weak. The court ignored the fact that it should avoid not only actual bias but also the "appearance" of bias.

---

265. Statute of the ICJ, art. 66.

266. Article 17(2) reads: "No member may participate in the decision of any case in which he has previously taken part as agent, counsel, or advocate for one of the parties, or as a member of a national or international court, or of a commission of inquiry, or in any other capacity."

267. *Legal Consequences of the Construction of a Wall in the Occupied Palestinian Territory*, Order of 30 January 2004, I.C.J. Reports 2004, p. 3. Judge Elaraby had participated in these Special Sessions as a representative of the Egyptian government.

268. *Legal Consequences of the Construction of a Wall in the Occupied Palestinian Territory*, Order of 30 January 2004, Dissenting Opinion of Judge Buergenthal, 2004 I.C.J. Reports, p. 8.

269. *Ibid.*, p. 10. In paragraph 11 of his opinion Judge Buergenthal explains that reading the comments by Judge Elaraby as falling out of reach of article 17 (2) would be "neither legally justified nor (...) wise judicial policy.": *Ibid.*, p. 9.

4.4 The Court's Advisory Opinion: The Main Substantive Findings

In light of the ICJ's acknowledgement that the question of the wall was part of a much larger matter, it is clear that the ICJ "went beyond solely assessing the legal consequences of the construction of the wall."[270] It asserted its discretionary use of power, in what some would call an overreach, to present its findings on contentious issues, some of which were not directly related to the question concerning the wall:

- the status of the "occupied" territories;
- the applicability of international treaties to the territories;
- the status of the "Palestinian people";
- the status of the Israeli "settlements" in these territories;
- the alleged violations by Israel of international humanitarian and human rights law in the territories; and
- Israel's right to self-defense under the UN Charter.

In the subsequent chapters, we will appraise these substantive aspects of the ICJ Advisory Opinion in more detail. This analysis will show that in many respects, the ICJ uncritically adopted what might be called "the Palestinian historical narrative" and legal reasoning. In doing so, the ICJ not only failed to take Israel's legitimate legal rights into account, it undermined the principle of sovereign equality of UN Member States, one of the most fundamental principles of the UN Charter.

4.4.1 Status of the "Occupied Palestinian Territories"

The ICJ briefly analyzes the status of the territories "situated between the Green Line and the former eastern boundary of Palestine under the Mandate."[271] In one short paragraph, it purported to describe almost 100 years of history from the Mandate period up to the agreements that Israel signed with the PLO in 1993. The remaining part of the analysis was used by the ICJ to discuss relevant UN resolutions, since the date dealing with the status of the territories.[272] In line with the reasoning of these documents, the ICJ then came to the conclusion that the territories were "occupied territories in which Israel had the status of occupying Power."[273]

270. *Legal Consequences of the Construction of a Wall in the Occupied Palestinian Territory*, Advisory Opinion, 2004 I.C.J. Reports, pp. 136-203 (9 July 2004), at p. 160.

271. *Ibid.*, p. 78.

272. As will be discussed more thoroughly in Part II, clarity of the status of the territories is determined by the text of the Mandate and the San Remo Resolution.

273. *Legal Consequences of the Construction of a Wall in the Occupied Palestinian Territory*, Advisory Opinion, 2004 I.C.J. Reports, pp. 136-203 (9 July 2004), at p. 167.

4.4.2 Applicability of International Treaties to the Territories

The ICJ then considered the applicability of several international treaties to the territories: the Fourth Geneva Convention, the International Covenant on Civil and Political Rights (ICCPR), the International Covenant on Economic, Social and Cultural Rights (ICESCR), and the Convention on the Rights of the Child. With regard to the first, the ICJ considered "that the Fourth Geneva Convention is applicable in any occupied territory in the event of an armed conflict... and is applicable in the Palestinian territories."[274] Subsequently, the ICJ considered that the human rights conventions are also applicable in respect of acts committed by Israel in the exercise of its jurisdiction "outside" of its own territory.[275]

4.4.3 Israeli "Settlements" in the Territories

It is arguable that the ICJ used biased language when it considered the legal status of "Israeli settlements in the occupied Palestinian territory,"[276] determining that the "wall's sinuous route has been traced in such a way to include within that area a great majority of these Israeli settlements."[277] In the ICJ's view, the presence of these "settlements in the territories" infringes on the Fourth Geneva Convention's prohibition to "deport transfer parts of [an Occupying Power's] own civilian population into the territory it occupies."[278] The ICJ then reasoned that "since 1977, Israel has conducted a policy and developed practices involving the establishment of settlements in the Occupied Palestinian Territory."[279] The ICJ comes to the remarkable conclusion that all of these settlements have been established in breach of international law.[280]

4.4.4 Israel's Violation of the Palestinian Right to Self-Determination

The ICJ considered the claimed right to self-determination of the Palestinian people and held that the existence of a "Palestinian people is no longer in issue"[281] and that recognition of the right to self-determination

---

274. *Ibid.*, p. 177. The Court refers hereby to the armed conflict that arose in 1967 between two High Contracting Parties, Israel and Jordan.

275. *Ibid.*, pp. 180-181.

276. *Ibid*, p. 183.

277. *Ibid.*

278. Article 49(6) of the Fourth Geneva Convention.

279. *Legal Consequences of the Construction of a Wall in the Occupied Palestinian Territory,* Advisory Opinion, 2004 I.C.J. Reports, pp. 136-203 (9 July 2004), at p. 183.

280. *Ibid.*, p. 184.

281. *Ibid.*, pp. 182-183.

is one of their "legitimate rights."[282] Subsequently, the ICJ concluded that Israel has violated this right to self-determination, because of the construction of the wall and the compulsory eviction of a significant number of Palestinian people from certain areas.[283]

4.4.5 Israel's Violation of Human Rights Law

Having determined in its view that the ICCPR and ICESC are applicable to the territories that Israel occupies, the ICJ considered that the construction of the wall constitutes breaches of a number of obligations under these treaties. Leaning heavily on the findings of UN Reports (especially the Report of the Special Rapporteur of the Commission on Human Rights, John Dugard, on the situations of human rights in the Palestinian territories occupied by Israel since 1967), the ICJ came to the conclusion that the construction of the wall impedes the liberty of movement under ICCPR and the right to work, to health, to education, and to an adequate standard of living under the ICESCR.[284]

4.4.6 Israel's Right to Self-Defense

The ICJ dismissed Israel's submission that "the fence is a measure wholly consistent with the right of States to self-defence enshrined in Article 51 of the Charter."[285] It does so by referring to the text of Article 51, which states, "[N]othing in the present Charter shall impair the inherent right of individual or collective self-defence if an armed attack occurs against a member of the United Nations. ...The Court stated that Israel's right to self-defence does not apply here, since the attacks against it have not come from a foreign state."[286] The ICJ's reasoning could be questioned, given that Article 51 only refers to "armed attacks" and does not specify that such attacks must come from a foreign state.

---

282. *Ibid.*

283. *Ibid.*, pp. 184 and 191.

284. E/CN.4/2004/6 (8 September 2003) and A/58/311 (22 August 2003).

285. *Legal Consequences of the Construction of a Wall in the Occupied Palestinian Territory,* Advisory Opinion, 2004 I.C.J. Reports, pp. 136-203 (9 July 2004), at p. 194. From September 2000 to December 2003 more than 900 victims were counted as result of Palestinian terror (see: http://www.mfa.gov.il/mfa/foreignpolicy/terrorism/palestinian/pages/saving%20lives-%20israel-s%20 anti- terrorist%20fence%20-%20answ.aspx, visited: 26 January 2016). When the building of the wall was completed, the number of succeeded attacks went down from 73 (September 2000 – July 2003) to three (August 2003 – July 2004): see: http://www.securityfence.mod.gov.il/Pages/ENG/news.htm (visited: 26 January 2016).

286. *Legal Consequences of the Construction of a Wall in the Occupied Palestinian Territory,* Advisory Opinion, 2004 I.C.J. Reports, pp. 136-203 (9 July 2004), at p. 194. See for further discussion of self-defense: Chapter 20 in this book.

4.4.7 The Legal Consequences of the Violation of International Law: for Israel and Other States

In assessing the consequences of the violations by Israel (of its obligations under international law—that are allegedly caused by the construction of the wall), the ICJ made a distinction between legal consequences that arise for Israel and those that arise for other UN Member States. As for Israel, the ICJ determined: (1) Israel must comply with the obligation to respect the Palestinian right to self-determination;[287] (2) Israel is obliged to cease the construction of the wall, and (3) it must dismantle those parts of the wall that are situated in what is called the "Occupied Palestinian Territories" including East-Jerusalem and repeal legislative action with regard to the wall;[288] (4) Israel is obliged to provide compensation for damage to all the natural or legal persons concerned;[289] and (5) Israel is obliged to either return the land it has seized from any natural or legal person for purposes of construction of the wall in the "Occupied Palestinian Territories" or compensate these persons.[290] In considering the legal consequences for other states, the ICJ held that the obligations violated by Israel include "obligations that are of the concern of all states" (*erga omnes* obligations).[291] For this reason, all states are under the obligation not to recognize the situation resulting from the construction of the wall, are not to render assistance in maintaining the situation created hereby, must see that violation of Palestinian right to self-determination is brought to an end, and are to ensure Israel's compliance with international humanitarian law.

4.5 Shortcomings of the 2004 ICJ Wall Advisory Opinion

The ICJ's Advisory Opinion can be criticized on a number of grounds. We address its findings on various substantive issues in more depth in the subsequent chapters of this book. Here, we will refer briefly to some aspects that directly affect the legal authoritativeness of the Advisory Opinion.[292]

287. *Legal Consequences of the Construction of a Wall in the Occupied Palestinian Territory*, Advisory Opinion, 2004 I.C.J. Reports, pp. 136-203 (9 July 2004), at. p. 197.

288. *Ibid.*, pp. 197-198.

289. *Ibid.*, p. 198.

290. *Ibid.*.

291. *Ibid.*, p. 199.

292. These criticisms concur with those in: Blois, de (2015).

4.5.1 This Was a Contentious Judgment in Disguise

The central presupposition of international adjudication is, according to Article 36 of the Statute of the ICJ, that contentious issues can be adjudicated by the ICJ only if its jurisdiction has been accepted by both parties. This is because the sovereign equality of UN Member States is the cornerstone of the international legal order (Article 2 (1) UN Charter. It is rather obvious that the substance of the request of the ICJ Advisory Opinion was immediately related to a conflict of a contentious nature between Israel and the Palestinian Arabs. It was also clear that Israel did not consent, while Palestine, not being a state, could not even consent. The court itself had stated in its previous *Western Sahara Advisory Opinion* that "[i]n certain circumstances... the lack of consent of an interested State may render the giving of an advisory opinion incompatible with the Court's judicial character. An instance of this would be when the circumstances disclose that to give a reply would have the effect of circumventing the principle that a state is not obliged to allow its disputes to be submitted to judicial settlement without its consent."[293] Notwithstanding this, the ICJ decided to give the Advisory Opinion. However, the arguments to do so are not impressive. The ICJ acknowledges that Israel and Palestine "have expressed radically divergent views on the legal consequences of Israel's construction of the wall," but that, according to the ICJ, was not sufficient to qualify the issue as being contentious, because, "[d]ifferences of views... on legal issues have existed in practically every advisory proceeding."[294] That is not very convincing. As Judge Owada observed in his Separate Opinion: "It is undeniable that there is in this case an underlying legal controversy or a dispute between the parties directly involved in this situation (...)."[295] On this basis, the ICJ should have refrained from giving an opinion.

4.5.2 Lack of Historical Context

Secondly, the ICJ Advisory Opinion illustrates an alarming lack of historical consciousness in respect of the development of the State of Israel and its conflict with the Palestinian Arabs. With a characteristic English understatement, Judge Rosalyn Higgins expressed a similar concern in her Separate Opinion: "I find the 'history' as recounted by the

---

293. I.C.J. Reports 2004, p. 158.

294. *Ibid.* Here the Court is quoting itself from the *Legal Consequences for States of the Continued Presence of South Africa in Namibia (South West Africa) notwithstanding Security Council Resolution 276 (1970)*, Advisory Opinion, 1971 I.C.J. Reports, p. 24.

295. I.C.J. Reports 2004, p. 264.

Court (...) neither balanced nor satisfactory."[296] The imbalance is illustrated by the selective attention paid to the Mandate for Palestine. In general terms, the ICJ mentions the objectives of the Mandate system, namely the interest of the inhabitants of the territory, and of humanity in general, thereby quoting from its *International Status of South West Africa Advisory Opinion*.[297] It did not mention the background and the unique character of the Mandate for Palestine, as recognized in its central Article 2, which obliges the mandatory power to secure the establishment of a National Home for the Jewish people in Palestine.[298] Different from all the other mandates, the Mandate for Palestine concerned a population part of which was not established in the territory and it included therefore a right to establishment of Jewish settlers in the territory (Article 6).[299] It was the recognition of a "sacred trust of civilization" in respect of a people which had been for many centuries the victim of persecution and even from time to time endangered by attempts to annihilation in all parts of the world. The Preamble of the Mandate recognized the historical connection of the Jewish people with Palestine and the grounds for reconstituting their national home there. All this should have informed observations of the ICJ on the issues of "borders" and "Israeli settlements" and the Palestinian right to self-determination, but it did not. It only quoted Article 13 of the Mandate on the status of Holy Places.[300] The ICJ ignored in a sense the "birth certificate" of the State of Israel and gave the impression that the position of the State of Israel was not to be taken seriously. The ICJ seems tacitly to agree to a revision of the history and legal significance of the Mandate for Palestine, which has been presented for example in the writings of John Quigley, who defends the thesis that the State of Palestine indeed derives its legitimacy from the Mandate for Palestine, but then as a state for Palestinian Arabs.[301] In short, the ICJ could be criticized for

---

296. I.C.J. Reports 2004, p. 211.

297. I.C.J. Reports 2004, p. 165; *International Status of South West Africa,* Advisory Opinion, 1950 I.C.J. Reports 1950, pp. 131 and 132.

298. "The Mandatory shall be responsible for placing the country under such political, administrative and economic conditions as will secure the establishment of the Jewish national home, as laid down in the preamble, and the development of self-governing institutions, and also for safeguarding the civil and religious rights of all the inhabitants of Palestine, irrespective of race and religion." See also: Blois, de (2016).

299. "The Administration of Palestine, while ensuring that the rights and position of other sections of the population are not prejudiced, shall facilitate Jewish immigration under suitable conditions and shall encourage, in co-operation with the Jewish agency referred to in Article 4, close settlement by Jews on the land, including State lands and waste lands not required for public purposes."

300. I.C.J. Reports 2004, p. 188.

301. See, inter alia, Quigley (2012).

not paying any attention to the central obligations and rights under the Mandate, which, as we will see, are absolutely vital to an understanding of the character and territorial scope of the State of Israel, and are still relevant in legal terms having regard to the preservation of the rights of peoples under the mandate-system in Article 80 of the UN Charter.[302]

4.5.3 Weak Factual Underpinning

The main point of criticism of the only dissenting ICJ judge, Judge Buergenthal, in his Declaration was that "The Court did not have before it the requisite factual bases for its sweeping findings."[303] Also, the Israel Supreme Court, in the first judgment in which it had the possibility to take into account the ICJ Advisory Opinion, expressed its view that the ICJ based its findings on insufficient evidence, especially where Israel's security interests were at stake.[304] This criticism refers both to the available information before the ICJ, as well as to the way the ICJ substantiated its findings based on that evidence.

The ICJ based its findings primarily on information comprised in UN Reports, such as a preparatory report by the Secretary-General[305] and reports by two Special UN Rapporteurs.[306] These Rapporteurs did not restrict themselves to findings of fact, but sometimes also felt free to come up with far-reaching interpretations of these facts. John Dugard, for example, qualified the construction of the security barrier as an act of unlawful (*de facto*) annexation,[307] a qualification which was reproduced by the ICJ.[308] In short, there was one-sidedness in the material before the ICJ. It has to be noted that Israel decided not to take part in the oral proceedings before the ICJ, while "Palestine" did. Apart from the question of whether the Israeli decision was a wise one, it should not have been

---

302. See on this, for example, Feinberg (1974), at pp. 405 and 419-420; Rostow (1993), pp. 10 and 15; Grief (2008), pp. 255-257. See further Chapter 5.

303. I.C.J. Reports 2004, p. 240.

304. Israel Supreme Court Sitting as the High Court of Justice [12 September 2004; 31 March 2005; 21 June 2005], Case HCJ 7957/04, Ma'arabe v. The Prime Minister of Israel, in: Israel Supreme Court, *Judgments of the Israel Supreme Court: Fighting Terrorism within the Law*, Vol. 2 (2004-2005), pp. 62-149, at. pp. 107-109.

305. A/ES-10/248.

306. Report of the Special Rapporteur of the Commission on Human Rights, John Dugard, on the situation of human rights in the Palestinian territories occupied by Israel since 1967, submitted in accordance with Commission resolution 1993/2A, E/CN.4/2004/6; 'The right to food', Report by the Special Rapporteur, Jean Ziegler. Addendum: Mission to the Occupied Palestinian territories, E/CN.4/2004/10/Add.2.

307. E/CN.4/2004/6, para 6-16.

308. I.C.J. Reports 2004, p. 184.

a reason for the ICJ not to examine Israel's security interests in a way which might be expected of a court. Judge Owada expressed comparable concerns in his Separate Opinion: "What seems to be wanting (...) is material explaining the Israeli side of the picture (...)."[309]

The application of humanitarian law and human rights law required the court to balance the fundamental rights of Palestinians with the right of the State of Israel to protect the security of its citizens against terrorist attacks. However, in the ICJ Advisory Opinion, we find the following pattern. The violations of the rights of the Palestinians are held to be established on the basis of the available information in the UN reports. On the other hand, the security interests of Israel are mentioned only briefly and without a thorough analysis, followed by the conclusion that: "On the material before it, the Court is not convinced that [for example] the destructions carried out (...) were rendered absolutely necessary by military operations."[310] It is not explained *why* the ICJ was not convinced. It belongs, however, to the judicial function not only to examine the available material but also to explain why it came to a conclusion, in other words to give its reasons. This was also stressed by Judge Owada: "The Court (...) should be extremely careful not only in ensuring the objective fairness in the result, but in seeing to it that the Court is seen to maintain fairness throughout the proceedings (...)." [311]

4.5.4 Lack of Objective Fairness

There are serious reasons to doubt whether, using Judge Owada's words, the objective fairness in the result has been met in this case. There is an impression that the genuine threats to the State of Israel and its citizens which led to the decision to build the security fence were not taken sufficiently seriously by the ICJ. Take for example its widely criticized decision on the right to self-defense under Article 51 of the UN Charter, invoked by Israel in connection with the security barrier to protect its citizens from attacks by terrorists.[312] The ICJ quotes this provision and concludes immediately: "Article 51 (...) *thus* recognizes the existence of an inherent right of self-defence in case of armed attack by one State against another State."[313] Noting that Israel does not claim that the attacks are imputable

309. I.C.J. Reports 2004, p. 268.

310. In the case of the alleged interference with Article 53 of the Hague Regulations of 1907, see: I.C.J. Reports 2004, p. 192.

311. I.C.J. Reports 2004, p. 269.

312. See among many other articles Wedgwood (2005) and Murphy (2005).

313. I.C.J. Reports 2004, p. 194 (emphasis added).

to another UN Member State it concludes that Article 51 is not applicable. This conclusion is not warranted by the wording of this provision, which does not refer to the source of an attack, nor by the case from which the modern doctrine of self-defense originated, the *Caroline* case, which was about an attack by rebels.[314] The reasoning of the ICJ (or more correctly the lack of reasoning) on this point brought Judge Higgins to, maybe, her fiercest criticism in her very critical Separate Opinion, formulated in a way that makes her support of the Opinion a mystery. She also pointed at a serious inconsistency in the ICJ's reasoning; "(...) Palestine cannot be sufficiently an international entity to be invited to these proceedings, and to benefit from humanitarian law, but not sufficiently an international entity for the prohibition of armed attack on others to be applicable. This is formalism of an uneven-handed sort."[315] Not only this inconsistency but also the superficiality of the reasoning on the central issue of self-defense raises serious doubts as to the fairness of the Court's opinion. The security barrier was an answer to the Second Intifada, with its frequent suicide attacks purposely aimed at many innocent Israeli citizens. It was a relatively peaceful and effective means to counter these attacks; it is clear that other forms of deterrence will not work in case of suicide bombers. Buergenthal rightly observed that the attacks on Israel "are never really seriously examined by the Court, and the dossier provided [to] the Court by the United Nations on which the Court to a large extent bases its findings barely touches on that subject."[316] We have to conclude that the scant attention of the security interests of Israel, and the other aspects addressed above, cast doubt on the authoritativeness of the ICJ Advisory Opinion with respect to certain legal aspects of the conflict between Israel and the Palestinians.

314. Dixon & McCorquodale (2000), pp. 561-562.

315. I.C.J. Reports 2004, p. 215.

316. I.C.J. Reports 2004, p. 241.

PART II

The State of Israel

5. Self-Determination of the Jewish People in Historical Perspective

> **"The law, history and politics of the Israel-Palestine dispute is immensely complex. ...Context is usually important in legal determinations.... I find the 'history' as recounted by the court ...neither balanced nor satisfactory."**
>
> Judge Higgins, Separate Opinion (Paragraph 16)[317]

5.1 Introduction

The State of Israel was established in May 1948, upon the issuance of the Israeli Declaration of Independence. This declaration referred to the Jewish State of Israel as a "national rebirth in its own country." Whether or not, as a matter of international law, the State of Israel existed on that date depends on whether it satisfied the legal criteria for statehood, to which we have earlier referred. We will answer that question in Chapter 7. In the meantime, however, it is appropriate to reflect on the historical connection between the Jewish people and the land leading up to the creation of the State in 1948. This connection is often ignored, misrepresented, or misunderstood when the legal status of Israel is discussed. The impression is created that Palestine was a land that "belonged" to an Arab people called "Palestinians," and that it was "invaded" by the Jewish people and "colonized" by the British, in much the same way as Australia was invaded and colonized by the British Empire in the 18th-19th centuries at the expense of Australian aboriginals.[318]

---

317. I.C.J. Reports 2004, p. 211.

318. This line of reasoning reflects the increased recognition of aboriginal rights during the course of the 20th century. A good example of this is the case of aboriginal peoples in Australia. For many decades, it was considered that Australia was "terra nullius" when the British established colonies in the 18th and 19th centuries, as a result of which all the laws of England applied to these new colonies. More recently, however, the High Court of Australia recognized the pre-existing "native rights" of the Aboriginal peoples with respect to the land, as a result of which pre-existing customary laws present at the time of "settlement" survived the reception of English law to the extent not modified or excluded by subsequent inconsistent laws and acts of the sovereign power. (See: *Mabo and others v Queensland (No.2)* [1992] HCA 23 (1992) 175 CLR 1).

When considering the "status" of the territories regained by Israel in 1967, the ICJ completely ignores the relationship between the Jewish people and these territories. Instead, the court adopts without further explanation the term "Occupied Palestinian Territories." It is remarkable that the court made not one single reference to the Jewish people, or their historical connection with the land, and apart from the fleeting statement that "Palestine was part of the Ottoman Empire" it did not mention at all the history of the territories prior to 1918. As Judge Rosalyn Higgins noted in her separate opinion, "[T]he history as recounted by the Court [was] neither balanced nor satisfactory."[319] That is not a light criticism.

In an effort to remedy this defect, this chapter examines the historical context that led to the creation of the Jewish State of Israel. Special consideration will be given to the unique and continuous connection between the Jews and the land over a period of more than two millennia, leading up to the Mandate for Palestine, and the modern right of the Jewish people to self-determination. Furthermore, the implications of this right, as expressed in the present State of Israel as a Jewish and democratic state will be elaborated.

5.2 The Self-Determination of Peoples

The international legal principle of "the right of peoples to self-determination" developed around the end of WWI, in the context of the Allied victory over the German and Ottoman Empires, and the subsequent creation of the League of Nations as a new international legal order based on justice and security and not just the balance of powers. Woodrow Wilson made a speech setting out Fourteen Points, which he regarded as the only basis for enduring peace. These included the need for openness and transparency in international diplomacy (a response to the secret deals that characterized French, British and Russian diplomacy leading up to and including WWI, such as the Sykes-Picot agreement), and the principle of "a free, open-minded, and absolutely impartial adjustment of all colonial claims based upon a strict observance of the principle that in determining all such questions of sovereignty the interests of the populations concerned must have equal weight with the equitable government whose title is to be determined."[320] The substance of parts of these points found their way into the Covenant of the League of Nations.

There is no doubt that the right of peoples to self-determination existed

319. I.C.J. Reports 2004, p. 211.

320. Principle V (see: http://avalon.law.yale.edu/20th_century/wilson14.asp).

by the time the Jewish people declared the creation of the State of Israel in 1948, and that it is now a part of customary international law. The United Nations (UN) Charter states that one of the purposes of the UN is: "[t]o develop friendly relations among nations based on respect for *the principle of equal rights and self-determination of peoples*, and to take other appropriate measures to strengthen universal peace." [emphasis added].[321] This right was further described in the International Covenants on Civil and Political Rights (ICCPR) adopted in 1960 and on Economic, Social and Cultural Rights (ICESCR) adopted in 1966. Article 1(1) common to both Covenants recognizes the right of all peoples to self-determination as including the right to "freely determine their political status and freely pursue their economic, social and cultural development" and the right to manage and dispose of their own resources, and they have a negative right not to be deprived of its means of subsistence.[322] States' Parties to the Covenants, including those who are still responsible for non-self-governing and trust territories (colonies), shall promote and respect the rights of peoples to self-determination.[323] Many of the states in the world have been created in reliance on the principle of self-determination. Between 1946 and 1960 alone, the peoples of 37 nations, exercising their right to self-determination, freed themselves from colonial status or emerged from mandates, trusts, protectorates or similar regimes in Asia, Africa, and the Middle East and established independent states that are currently fully recognized as such under international law.

While the right to self-determination undoubtedly exists, however, its content is notoriously uncertain. Under international law the subjects of the right to self-determination are "peoples" (sometimes referred to as "nations"). In order to define what is a "people," various objective and subjective criteria have emerged during the course of the last century as the principle of self-determination has developed as a principle of international law. Broadly speaking, the main objective criterion is that the people must have a distinct historical, cultural, religious and linguistic identity.[324] The first question is therefore: Is there a "Jewish people" having a common history, culture, language, and religion? The subjective criterion requires that this people possess the political will to become an

321. UN Charter, art. 1(2).

322. ICCPR and ICESCR, art. 1(2).

323. *Ibid.*, art. 1(3).

324. See, e.g., Summers (2013). See also Veerman (1977), pp. 55-61. Similar criteria are mentioned in the Final Report and Recommendations of the International Meeting of Experts on further study of the concept of the rights of peoples, in the framework of UNESCO, Paris, 27-30 November 1989, SHS-89/CONF.602/7, pp. 7-8. See also Bassiouni (1971), at pp. 31-32.

independent nation. The second question is therefore: Have the Jewish people expressed an intentional desire to determine for themselves their political future?

5.3 Objective Criterion: Historical Identity of the Jewish People

5.3.1 2100 BCE – 135 CE

The history of the Jewish people began its development that ultimately led to the establishment of the modern State of Israel about 4000 years ago.[325] Abraham arrived in the area today known as Israel, or Palestine, in about 2100 BCE, having journeyed from his birthplace Ur in Babylonia (modern day Iraq). The Hebrew Bible tells us that Abraham believed that God promised to give his descendants the land shown to him. His grandson Jacob (later renamed "Israel") became father of 12 sons, each of whom became the head of a tribe of the nation of Israel. As a consequence of famine, Jacob and his descendants fled to Egypt, where they lived for 400 years and for a considerable period suffered under the oppression of the Pharaohs, who subjected them to slavery. The deliverance from this house of bondage and the journey of the people under the leadership of Moses to the land promised to their fathers is the central historical experience that was vital for the nation building of the people of Israel. During this *exodus* from Egypt, the people received the *Torah*, the divine law, at Mount Sinai. Under the leadership of Moses's successor, Joshua, the people settled in the land currently known as the West Bank. Initially, leaders, who were called judges, ruled them. Later on, a kingdom was established. The most famous of the Kings, David, succeeded in conquering Jerusalem, which from then on (about 1000 BCE) became the political center of the country. Under David's son, Solomon, the (First) Temple was built on Mount Moriah (probably today's Temple Mount), making Jerusalem also the religious center. After Solomon's death, the kingdom was divided into a northern part called Israel and a southern part called Judah (or Judea). The inhabitants of the northern kingdom were defeated, and many were deported in 722 BCE by the Assyrians, while the Judeans (of the southern kingdom) were brought into captivity in Babylon, circa 586 BCE, when Nebuchadnezzar II destroyed the City of Jerusalem and the Temple. A remnant of the exiled Judeans returned in 537 BCE to the

325. The primary sources for this historical account are the texts of the Hebrew Bible (*Tenach*), the Christian Old Testament. There is no reason to doubt the historical accuracy of these accounts. See further on the history of the Jewish people *inter alia* the following treatises: Whiston (transl.) (1987); Milman (1939); Eban (1968); Eisenberg (1970); Bruce (1963); Gilbert (1978).

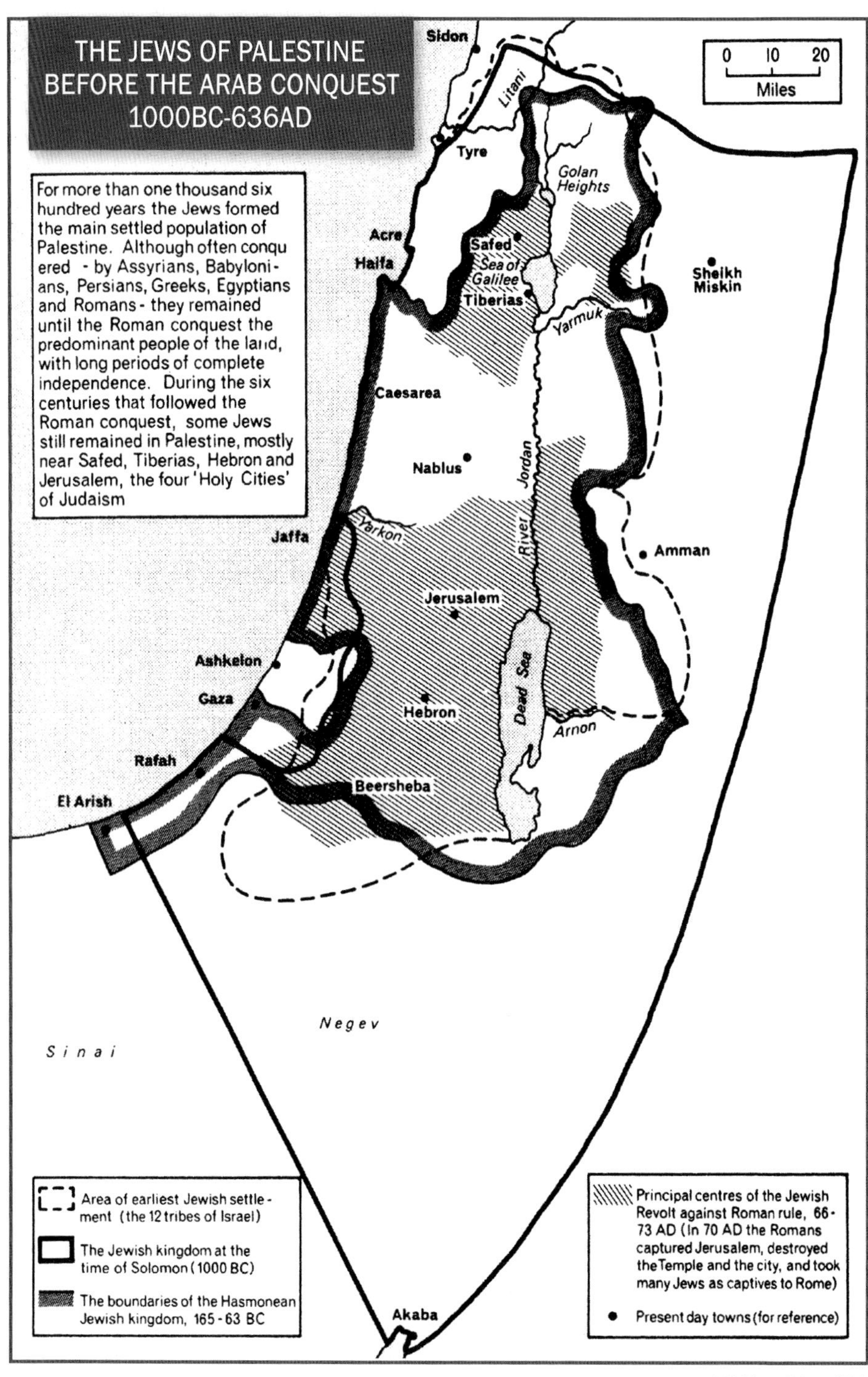
THE JEWS OF PALESTINE
BEFORE THE ARAB CONQUEST
1000BC-636AD
For more than one thousand six hundred years the Jews formed the main settled population of Palestine. Although often conquered - by Assyrians, Babylonians, Persians, Greeks, Egyptians and Romans - they remained until the Roman conquest the predominant people of the land, with long periods of complete independence. During the six centuries that followed the Roman conquest, some Jews still remained in Palestine, mostly near Safed, Tiberias, Hebron and Jerusalem, the four 'Holy Cities' of Judaism
0 10 20
Miles
Sidon
Litani
Tyre
Golan Heights
Acre
Haifa
Safed
Sea of Galilee
Tiberias
Yarmuk
Sheikh Miskin
Caesarea
Nablus
Jordan
River
Yarkon
Jaffa
Amman
Jerusalem
Ashkelon
Gaza
Hebron
Dead Sea
Arnon
Rafah
Beersheba
El Arish
Negev
Sinai
Akaba
Area of earliest Jewish settlement (the 12 tribes of Israel)
The Jewish kingdom at the time of Solomon (1000 BC)
The boundaries of the Hasmonean Jewish kingdom, 165 - 63 BC
Principal centres of the Jewish Revolt against Roman rule, 66-73 AD (In 70 AD the Romans captured Jerusalem, destroyed the Temple and the city, and took many Jews as captives to Rome)
Present day towns (for reference)

land of Israel and the City of Jerusalem with the approval of the Persian King Cyrus. Jerusalem was rebuilt, and the Second Temple was built. When the Persian Empire was conquered by Alexander the Great, the people and the land came under the rule of the Hellenistic rulers—first Alexander and then his successors among whom his empire was divided (initially the Ptolemies and later the Seleucids). Among the latter was King Antiochus IV Epiphanes, who desecrated the Temple and tried to suppress the Jewish religion. Under the leadership of Judas Maccabeus, the Jewish people rose up against their oppressors (167-166 BCE). They succeeded in purifying the Temple again, which is celebrated every year during *Hanukkah.*[326] Twenty-five years later, the independence of the Jews was recognized under the rule of the Hasmonian dynasty.

In 63 BCE, Roman rule was established. Over a century later, in 66 CE, the Jews rose up against the Romans. In 70 CE, Titus, the son of the Roman Emperor Vespasian, and his army besieged Jerusalem and destroyed the Second Temple. According to the contemporary historian Josephus, more than one million Jews were killed.[327] Most of the survivors fled the country and were dispersed throughout the Roman Empire and beyond.[328] A small Jewish community remained in the land of Israel. A second uprising under Bar Kokhba (Bar Kosiba) was defeated in 135 CE, and Judea was renamed *Syria Palaestina* by Roman Emperor Hadrian. The name "Palaestina" is derived from a Latinised corruption of the Greek name Philistia—the land of the Philistines—illustrating Hadrian's goal to sever all Jewish connection to the Land of Israel.[329]

5.3.2 135 CE - 1850 CE

From 135 CE to 1917, the area of "Palaestina" was part of a larger area of the Middle East.[330] Various ethnic, religious and national groups moved in and out of the region during this time—including Jews, Christians and Muslims (of many different nationalities), Arabs, Bedouins, and Turks. Palaestina came under successive foreign rulers: Romans (135 to 324), Byzantines (324 to 638), Arabs (638 to 1099), Crusaders (1099 to 1291), Mamluks (1265 to 1516), and Ottomans (Turks) (1516 to 1917). Each

326. See the Apocryphical Books of the Maccabeans. On Hanukkah, see: Roth & Wigoder (1975), pp. 840-841.

327. *The Wars of the Jews,* Book 6, Chapter 9.3; Whiston (transl.) (1987), p. 749.

328. Gilbert (1978), pp. 3-12.

329. Gilbert (1978), p. 6; Keller (1966), p. 91.

330. See for a general overview: Milman (1939); Eban (1968); Eisenberg (1963); Gilbert (1978); Peters (1984); Lewis (1995).

successive conqueror allowed or promoted immigration from a variety of countries and nationalities.[331]

Following the defeat of the Jews in 135 CE, Palestine was not a distinct political entity, but was part of the larger region controlled by the Romans, including modern-day Syria, Jordan, Egypt and the Arabian Peninsula. It was the crossroads of many different cultures, religions, ethnic groups and economic interests. The historian Kiernan remarks, "Under this *Pax Romana*, in which indigenous political distinctions were blurred and different national economies were integrated, the region prospered."[332] The population of Palestine was made up of many different ethnic and nation groups; Kiernan describes this period as "the largest-scale assimilation among the local populations yet seen in the Middle East."[333] During the six centuries following the Roman conquest of Judea and the suppression of the last Jewish uprising, Jews were scattered throughout the Middle East and beyond. Many Jews and Christians found refuge in Arabia, where they established settlements and spread Aramaic and Hellenistic culture. During the seventh century, however, Muslims decimated many of the Jewish and Christian populations in Arabia. Sweeping northward from the Arabian Peninsula through the Middle East and into southern Europe and central Asia, Arab Muslims conquered Jerusalem in 637 CE. At this time, several hundred thousand Jews were living in Palestine, and they remained one of the population groups in this geographical area.[334] In the subsequent centuries, they suffered varying misfortunes under their various occupiers, and the composition, size and location of the Jewish population varied considerably. The Jews lived mostly near Safed, Tiberias, Hebron and Jerusalem—the four "Holy Cities" of Judaism.[335] As to their position Gilbert wrote:

> **"From 637 to 1099 the Arabs sometimes ill-treated and were sometimes tolerant towards their Jewish subjects. From 1099 to 1291 the Christian Crusaders mercilessly persecuted and slaughtered the Jews of Palestine. The Mamluks (Muslims) who ousted the Crusaders in 1291, and ruled until 1516, at times encouraged Jewish settlement, and many Jews came to Palestine to escape from Christian persecution in Europe. After 1517, under the Ottoman Turks, the Jews of Europe continued to seek refuge in Palestine from Christian persecution and expulsion, despite spasmodic ill-treatment by their Muslim rulers."[336]**

331. Peters (1984), pp .151-157.
332. Kiernan (1978), p. 91.
333. *Ibid.*
334. See Karsh (2010), p. 9, citing Gil (1992).
335. Gilbert (2005), p. 1.
336. *Ibid.*, p. 2.

In the meantime, Jews in Europe were being persecuted, resulting in the mass expulsions of Jews from Britain (1290), France (1394), and Spain (1492). This led to an increase of the Jewish population in Palestine, where they were not always allowed to live in peace. A pilgrim from Bohemia in the late 15th century wrote:

> **"There are not many Christians, but there are many Jews, and these the Moslems persecute in various ways ... The Moslems know that the Jews think and even say that this is the Holy Land which has been promised to them and that those Jews who dwell there are regarded as holy by Jews elsewhere, because, in spite of all the troubles and sorrows inflicted on them by the Moslems, they refuse to leave the Land."[337]**

Under Ottoman (Turkish) rule, the region of Palestine was a sub-district (*vilayet)* of the region of Syria ruled from Constantinople (Istanbul). One of the most stable and constant groups living in Palestine throughout the period of Ottoman-Turkish rule was the Jewish people.

5.4 Zionism: The Political Will of the Jewish People to Become an Independent Polity

By the mid-19th century, the population in the land west of the Jordan River was, as before, a heterogeneous mix of many different nationalities, ethnic groups, and religions. According to Morris, in 1881—before the Zionist immigration—there were about 450,000 Arabs (90 percent Muslim, 10 percent Christian) and 27,000 Jews in Palestine.[338] Peters points to the fact that the notion "Arabs" in this connection does not refer to a homogeneous people, but to a variety of ethnic groups, including Arabs *per se*, Turks, Circassians, Algerians Egyptians, Druze, Kurds and Bosnians, most of whom had come from other places over the course of the preceding centuries.[339] The Jews were thus one of many different ethnic groups living in the land. The majority of Jews worldwide lived outside Palestine. In this Diaspora, the voices of the prophets of Israel who foretold the return to their ancestral homeland were never silenced, and the desire to return has always been in the heart of the Jewish people—as it was said in the Pesach liturgy: "Next year in Jerusalem..." In the 19th century, there was a growing sense of urgency to return to the land of their fathers. The Zionist movement in its varieties (religious and

---

337. Quoted from the pilgrim's book *Journey to Jerusalem* (published in 1491), by Gilbert (1978), p. 19.

338. Morris (2008), p. 2.

339. Peters (1984), p. 196. See also: Luke & Keith-Roach (1922).

secular, cultural and political) began to emerge in several parts of the Western world.[340] The chief aim for many in the Zionist movement was the establishment of a Jewish state in Palestine, which they considered to be the Promised Land. The most notable leader of this movement was Theodor Herzl who, in 1896, published his book "The Jewish State" outlining his vision of a reconstituted Jewish state.[341] The creation of the World Zionist Organization (WZO) in 1897, which held its first congress in Basel, with Herzl as President, gave an enormous impetus to political Zionism. In Basel, the WZO adopted the basic program of Zionism, with the following opening phrase: "The aim of Zionism is to create for the Jewish people a home in Palestine secured by public law."[342] The echo of this proclamation can be heard in the Balfour Declaration of 1917, which will be discussed later.

Jews started returning to the Holy Land in larger numbers towards the end of the 19th century, mainly in response to growing anti-Semitism and persecution in Europe. It is common to distinguish six currents of *aliyah* (from the Hebrew word for "ascent," meaning in this connection the return to Eretz Yisrael—the Land of Israel) in the period before World War II.[343] The First Aliyah (1882-1903) refers to the groups of immigrants who fled the pogroms in Russia and Romania and also to those Jews who fled from Yemen. Immigrants who participated in this First Aliyah founded agricultural settlements, which contributed to the development of the land. Other immigrants followed these pioneers during the Second Aliyah (1904-1914), escaping from the pogroms in Russia in 1903 and 1905. This brought many people to Israel who wanted to build a society according to socialist ideals. These ideals took form in the construction of communities *(kibbutzim)*, the first of which was established in Deganyah. During World War I, however, groups of Jews who were not Ottoman subjects either fled Palestine or were deported by Turkish authorities.[344] This led to a temporary drop in the Jewish population. After the war, many Jews returned or immigrated for the first time to Palestine. The Third Aliyah (1919-1923) was stimulated partly by the Balfour Declaration (1917) and partly by pogroms in the years of the Russian Civil War and the war

340. See, in general, Laqueur (1978) and Gilbert (1978).

341. Herzl (1896). Herzl left open the possibility that this Jewish state could be established outside Palestine. For various reasons, this option was later dismissed: see Gilbert (1999), p. 14.

342. Roth & Wigoder (1975), p. 247.

343. Roth & Wigoder (1975), pp.71-74; Laqueur (1978); Gilbert (1999), pp. 3-169; Shamir & Shavit (1987), pp. 134-135, 140-141, and 148-149. There is some variation in the literature as to the years demarcating the consecutive aliyahs.

344. Gilbert (1978), p. 82; Peters (1984), p. 215.

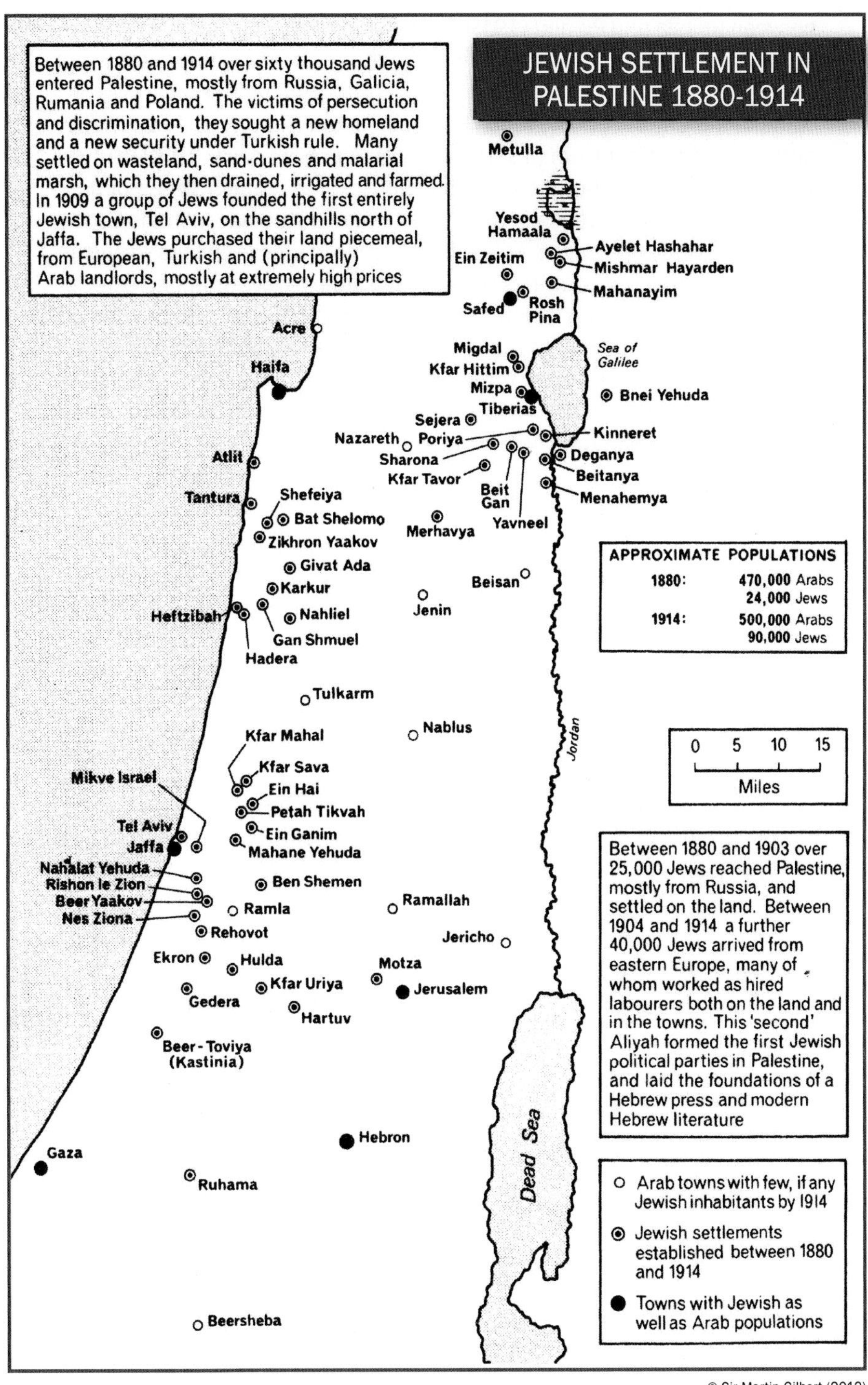
JEWISH SETTLEMENT IN PALESTINE 1880-1914
Between 1880 and 1914 over sixty thousand Jews entered Palestine, mostly from Russia, Galicia, Rumania and Poland. The victims of persecution and discrimination, they sought a new homeland and a new security under Turkish rule. Many settled on wasteland, sand-dunes and malarial marsh, which they then drained, irrigated and farmed. In 1909 a group of Jews founded the first entirely Jewish town, Tel Aviv, on the sandhills north of Jaffa. The Jews purchased their land piecemeal, from European, Turkish and (principally) Arab landlords, mostly at extremely high prices
Metulla
Yesod Hamaala
Ayelet Hashahar
Ein Zeitim
Mishmar Hayarden
Mahanayim
Safed
Rosh Pina
Acre
Haifa
Migdal
Kfar Hittim
Mizpa
Tiberias
Sea of Galilee
Bnei Yehuda
Sejera
Nazareth
Poriya
Kinneret
Sharona
Deganya
Kfar Tavor
Beitanya
Beit Gan
Menahemya
Atlit
Tantura
Shefeiya
Bat Shelomo
Zikhron Yaakov
Merhavya
Yavneel
Givat Ada
Karkur
Beisan
Jenin
Heftzibah
Nahliel
Gan Shmuel
Hadera
APPROXIMATE POPULATIONS
1880: 470,000 Arabs
24,000 Jews
1914: 500,000 Arabs
90,000 Jews
Tulkarm
Kfar Mahal
Nablus
Jordan
0 5 10 15
Miles
Kfar Sava
Mikve Israel
Ein Hai
Petah Tikvah
Tel Aviv
Ein Ganim
Jaffa
Mahane Yehuda
Nahalat Yehuda
Rishon le Zion
Ben Shemen
Beer Yaakov
Ramla
Ramallah
Nes Ziona
Rehovot
Jericho
Ekron
Hulda
Motza
Kfar Uriya
Jerusalem
Gedera
Hartuv
Beer-Toviya (Kastinia)
Between 1880 and 1903 over 25,000 Jews reached Palestine, mostly from Russia, and settled on the land. Between 1904 and 1914 a further 40,000 Jews arrived from eastern Europe, many of whom worked as hired labourers both on the land and in the towns. This 'second' Aliyah formed the first Jewish political parties in Palestine, and laid the foundations of a Hebrew press and modern Hebrew literature
Dead Sea
Hebron
Gaza
Ruhama
Arab towns with few, if any Jewish inhabitants by 1914
Jewish settlements established between 1880 and 1914
Towns with Jewish as well as Arab populations
Beersheba

between Russia and Poland (1919-1920). During the Fourth Aliyah (1924-1931), in the British Mandate period, the urban-social middle class was strengthened, mainly by Jews who fled fiscal restrictions in Poland. Many came to the City of Tel Aviv, which had been established on the coast just north of the ancient town of Jaffa in 1909. The Fifth Aliya (1932-1940) was in response to the rise of Nazism in Germany, which was a direct threat to the very existence of the Jews. It made a safe haven in the Land of Israel of vital importance. This was all the more urgent because Jewish immigration to other countries was only possible to a very limited extent. The heavy restrictions of the British immigration policy prevented many Jews from entry into the Mandate Palestine. A number of immigrants succeeded to "illegally" enter the land. The brutal anti-Semitism in Europe brought Jews to Palestine in the Sixth Aliyah (1941-1947), but due to the harsh policies of the British government, many of those who succeeded to escape from the Nazis perished before they could reach the shores of the land of their forefathers. Immediately after the establishment of the State of Israel in 1948, the limitations on the immigration of Jews were lifted. The Declaration of the Establishment of the State of Israel (14 May 1948) proclaims: "The State of Israel will be open for Jewish immigration and for the Ingathering of the Exiles." In the succeeding decade, hundreds of thousands fled many Arab countries, which had introduced anti-Jewish policies and practices.[345] In the next chapter, the legal steps leading to the Declaration of the Establishment of the State of Israel will be discussed.

345. Meron (1995), pp. 47-55.

6. The Balfour Declaration, San Remo Resolution and Mandate for Palestine

"At the end of the First World War, a class 'A' Mandate for Palestine was entrusted to Great Britain by the League of Nations (...)"

Advisory Opinion (Paragraph 70)[346]

6.1 Introduction

As World War I drew to a close and the collapse of the Ottoman Turkish Empire approached, it was incumbent on the Allied Powers to make arrangements on the future of parts of this Empire, including Palestine. As with the Allied Powers, the Zionist leaders were plainly interested in the future of Palestine; since 1897, they had been seeking the support of influential states—including the United Kingdom—for the ideal formulated in the Basel Program "to create for the Jewish people a home in Palestine secured by public law."[347] After much internal debate and consultations with Zionist leaders, on 31 October 1917 (the same day that the Allies freed Beersheba, opening the way for the liberation of Jerusalem a few weeks later), the British government decided to declare its support for the re-establishment of a Jewish national homeland in what was then known as Palestine. This commitment was later incorporated in the San Remo Resolution, agreed upon by the Allied Powers on 25 April 1920, and in the Mandate for Palestine, adopted by the Council of the League of Nations on 24 July 1922.

6.2 The Balfour Declaration

The Balfour Declaration was contained in a letter, dated 2 November 1917, from the British Minister of Foreign Affairs Arthur James Balfour,

346. I.C.J. Reports 2004, p. 165.

347. Roth & Wigoder (1975), p.247.

on behalf of the British Cabinet, to Lord Rothschild, as representative of the Jewish community.[348] It stated:

> **"His Majesty's Government view with favour the establishment in Palestine of a national home for the Jewish people, and will use their best endeavours to facilitate the achievement of this object, it being clearly understood that nothing shall be done which may prejudice the civil and religious rights of existing non-Jewish communities in Palestine, or the rights and political status enjoyed by Jews in any other country."**

Balfour, Prime Minister Lloyd George, and other senior British government figures were—on the basis of their belief in the Bible—sympathetic towards the Zionist desire for the Jewish people to return to the land of their forefathers.[349] Not all British politicians shared their enthusiasm, however; it is clear that important political considerations also played a significant role in the creation of the Balfour Declaration. With the impending collapse of the Ottoman Empire in sight, Britain was engaged in intensive discussions with the other powers, especially France, Italy and Russia, regarding the potential division of the Ottoman Empire. All of these nations were anxious to maximize their influence and protect their interests in the region. It was a period of great unrest; much was at stake. Britain desired to gain the support of Jews in Russia and America.[350] France declared its support for the restoration of the Jewish homeland in the land from which it had been evicted so many centuries ago.[351] This implied that France did not want to implement the—initially secret—Sykes-Picot agreement, concluded in 1916 between Britain and France, by which they had divided their spheres of influence in the Levant, including the establishment of an international condominium, shared by Britain, France and Russia, in respect of part of Palestine. This condominium would have included a significant part of the historical land of Israel: an area including Tiberias, Jerusalem, Jericho, Bethlehem, Hebron, Gaza, Jaffa and Tel Aviv.[352]

The Balfour Declaration was a unilateral and explicit statement by Britain to promote the achievement of a Jewish national home in Palestine. Such a declaration is primarily a political document and is not binding as

348. Laqueur (1978), pp. 181-205; Gilbert (1999), pp. 34-35. See also Schneer (2010), pp. 75-86.

349. See, e.g., Weizmann (1983), p. 183; Tuchmann (1982), pp.311-324. See also Morris (2008), p. 10.

350. Gilbert (1978), pp. 92-108; Schneer (2010), for instance p. 366.

351. Letter from the French Minister for Foreign Affairs Cambon to the Zionist leader Sokolow, who had been sent by the British Government to Paris to raise support for the Zionist cause. See Laqueur (1978), p. 192.

352. Laqueur (1978), pp. 190-192; Gilbert (1978), pp. 89-91; Schneer (2010), pp. 75-86.

a matter of law. Nevertheless, it is not without legal significance, given the fundamental principle of good faith, which is applicable to all states.[353] The British government arguably failed to fulfill the commitment they had taken upon themselves in the Balfour Declaration, having regard to the poor implementation of their obligations under the Mandate for Palestine to establish a national home for the Jewish people in Palestine.[354] We will elaborate on that below. More importantly, however, the League of Nations ultimately adopted the Balfour Declaration in the Mandate for Palestine. Because of this, the Balfour Declaration plays a central role in the matrix of historical and legal developments leading to the creation of the State of Israel in May 1948.

6.3 Promises to the Arabs: The McMahon–Hussein Correspondence

It is often claimed that the British made conflicting promises to the Arabs, which were subsequently not honored. Some have argued that as a result, the Balfour Declaration and subsequent Mandate for Palestine are not decisive.[355] There is no doubt that Britain made differing and ambiguous promises to various Arab leaders during this period. In particular, between 14 July 1915 and 30 January 1916, the Sharif of Mecca, Hussein bin Ali, and Sir Henry McMahon, British High Commissioner in Egypt, exchanged a series of letters concerning the future political status of the lands under the Ottoman Empire. The Arabs agreed to revolt against the Turks in alliance with Britain; and in return, the British agreed to recognize Arab independence.[356] Yet, McMahon explicitly clarified that Palestine was never included in his nor Britain's intent when promising Arab independence. McMahon wrote to the Colonial Office, seven years after the exchange of letters: "It was as fully my intention to exclude Palestine, as it was to exclude the more northern part of Syria."[357] Again, in 1937, he declared, "I feel it my duty to state, and I do so definitely and emphatically, that it

353. See Permanent Court of International Justice (the forerunner of the ICJ) in the East Greenland Case (1933), Publications of the Court, Series A/B, No. 53, p. 71. A more recent example is the judgment of the ICJ in the Nuclear Tests Case, 1974 ICJ Reports 253.

354. See Gilbert (1978), pp.109-309; Feinberg (1974), p. 68.

355. See, e.g., Shlaim (2005), pp. 251-270, and Nutting (1972).

356. See on this, in general, Schneer (2010), pp. 64-74.

357. Quoted by Gilbert (1978), p. 87.

was not intended by me in giving the pledge to King Hussein to include Palestine in the area in which Arab independence was promised."[358]

6.4 The Allied Occupation of the Middle East, the Paris Peace Conference, the League of Nations and the Treaty of Versailles

A little more than a month after the Balfour Declaration was issued, on 11 December 1917, British military forces led by General Edmund Allenby entered Jerusalem, which had been abandoned by the Turks two days earlier.[359] The British immediately placed the City of Jerusalem under military control. The whole of Palestine came under British control in September 1918, upon the defeat of the Ottoman Empire. Martial law was imposed, until the British Civil Administration was established in July 1920 in anticipation of the Mandate for Palestine, based on Article 22 of the Covenant of the League of Nations.

The League of Nations was established under the Covenant of the League of Nations, which was drafted and adopted during the Paris Peace Conference and subsequently incorporated into the Treaty of Versailles on 28 June 1919. Largely inspired by US President Woodrow Wilson and his famous Fourteen Points, the objective of the League of Nations was to create an international legal structure enabling political cooperation and maintenance of peace following the World War I.[360] In order to do so, the Allies needed to determine the status of the territories covered by the defeated German and Ottoman Empires. In the so-called "Smuts Resolution" (named after the South African General Jan Christiaan Smuts, member of the British delegation at the Peace Conference in Paris) it was stated, "...because of the historic misgovernment by the Turks of subject peoples and the terrible massacres of Armenians and others in recent years, the Allied and Associated Powers are agreed that Armenia, Syria,

358. Report of a Committee set up to consider certain correspondence between Sir Henry McMahon (His Majesty's High Commissioner in Egypt) and the Sharif of Mecca in 1915 and 1916, March 1939, London, Printed and published by His Majesty's Stationery Office: https://unispal.un.org/DPA/DPR/unispal.nsf/0/4C4F7515DC39195185256CF7006F878C (visited: 9 September 2017).

359. Gilbert (1978), p. 111.

360. Point Twelve of Wilson's Fourteen Points held that: "The Turkish portion of the present Ottoman Empire should be assured a secure sovereignty, but the other nationalities which are now under Turkish rule should be assured an undoubted security of life and an absolutely unmolested opportunity of autonomous development,(...)."

Mesopotamia, *and Kurdestan*, Palestine and Arabia must be completely severed from the Turkish Empire..."[361]

6.5 The League of Nations Mandate System

These considerations ultimately resulted in Article 22 of the Covenant of the League of Nations, which established a system of Mandates applicable to the former German colonies and the territories that had been part of the collapsed Ottoman Turkish Empire. The Mandate system was intended to prepare these territories for self-government in view of the welfare and development of the peoples of the territory and the protection of the rights of these peoples.[362] For each Mandate, a Mandatory—the government of a State—was appointed to act as a trustee, representing the conscience of the civilized world.[363]

Article 22 of the Covenant of the League of Nations created three classes of Mandates, which became known as Class A, B, and C Mandates.[364] "Class A Mandates related to communities formerly belonging to the Turkish (Ottoman) Empire. Class B Mandates were created for certain peoples in Central Africa, while Class C Mandates concerned South-West Africa and certain South Pacific Islands. The character of the various mandates varied according to the stage of development of the people, the geographical situation and the economic conditions of the territory and similar circumstances. Class A Mandates most closely approximated self-government. The Covenant the League of Nations refers to Class A Mandates as follows:

> **"Certain communities formerly belonging to the Turkish Empire have reached a stage of development where their *existence as independent nations* can be provisionally recognized subject to the rendering of administrative advice and assistance by a Mandatory until such time as they are able to stand alone. The wishes of these communities must be a principal consideration in the selection of the Mandatory."[365]**

361. See for the full text Miller (1928), Vol. I, p. 109 (emphasis in the original, indicating an amendment). Also cited by Grief (2008), p. 68. General Jan Christiaan Smuts was the South African Prime Minister and Minister without portfolio on Lloyd George's War Cabinet.

362. South West Africa Cases (Preliminary Objections), 1962 I.C.J. Reports, p. 329.

363. Bentwich (1921-22), pp. 48-56.

364. League of Nations, The Mandates System, *Series of League of Nations Publications* VI.A.MANDATES 1945. VI.A.1, Geneva 1945, LoN/1945.VI.A.1.

365. Covenant of the League of Nations, art. 22, para 4 (emphasis added).

The Mandates should be seen as an application of the principle of the right of peoples to self-determination.[366] The Mandates were international agreements having the character of a treaty or convention.[367] As the International Court of Justice (ICJ) has stated, citing the Covenant of the League of Nations, the Mandates were created "in the interest of the inhabitants of the territory, and of humanity in general, as an international institution with an international object—a sacred trust of civilization."[368] Essential principles of the Mandate system that were listed by the ICJ were the non-annexation of territory and the well-being and development of peoples concerned.[369] The ultimate objective was the "self-determination and independence of the peoples concerned."[370]

While the League of Nations considered the Palestine Mandate to be a Class A Mandate, as it concerned a former part of the Turkish Empire, it also recognized its "very special character" resulting from "a number of provisions designed to apply the policy defined in the "Balfour Declaration."'[371]

In addition, it is important to note that under Article 20 of the Covenant of the League of Nations, the 42 countries that comprised the League in 1922 "solemnly undertake that they will not hereafter enter into any engagements inconsistent with the terms [of this Covenant]." Of the 63 nations that at various times were parties to the Covenant, almost all have since 1973 fundamentally breached this commitment by voting in favor of UN resolutions that (as we will later explain) directly conflict with the terms of the Palestine Mandate.

---

366. See section 5.2 above.

367. South West Africa Cases (Preliminary Objections), 1962 I.C.J. Reports, p. 330.

368. *International Status of South West Africa*, Advisory Opinion, 1950 I.C.J. Reports, p. 132 (11 July 1950).

369. *Ibid.*, p. 131.

370. *Legal Consequences for States of the Continued Presence of South Africa in Namibia (South West Africa) notwithstanding Security Council Resolution 276 (1970),* Advisory Opinion, 1971 I.C.J Reports, p. 31.

371. League of Nations, The Mandates System, *Series of League of Nations Publications* VI.A.MANDATES 1945. VI.A.1, Geneva 1945, LoN/1945.VI.A.1.

6.6 The San Remo Resolution

The Supreme Council of the Principal Allied and Associated Powers[372] (Britain, France, Italy, Japan and the USA[373]) convened in San Remo in April of 1920. The purpose of this meeting was to deliberate on the future of the territories which had been captured from the Ottoman Empire at the end of the World War I. As victors, the Allies had gained, in conformity with the standards of international law applicable at that time, extensive rights and powers over these territories.[374] The San Remo Conference was an extension of the Paris Peace Conference, held the previous year in Paris. Because the question of the Turkish Ottoman territories had not been adequately dealt with in Paris, it was necessary to convene another meeting of the Principal Allied Powers. Having met in London on 12 February 1920, they reconvened at San Remo in Italy on 18 April 1920, where the Allies decided pursuant to Article 22 of the Covenant of the League of Nations to create three Class A Mandates for the former Ottoman territories: Palestine, Syria and Mesopotamia (later Iraq). On 25 April 1920, the Supreme Council adopted the following Resolution:

It was agreed:

a. "To accept the terms of the mandates article as given below with reference to Palestine, on the understanding that there was inserted in the process-verbal an understanding by the mandatory powers that this would not involve the surrender of the rights hitherto enjoyed by the non-Jewish communities in Palestine; this undertaking did not refer to the question of religious protectorate of France, which had been settled earlier in the previous afternoon by the undertaking given by the French Government that they recognized this protectorate as being at and end.
b. That the terms of the mandates article should be as follows: The High Contracting Parties agree that Syria and Mesopotamia shall, in accordance with the fourth paragraph of article 22, Part I (Covenant of the League of Nations) be provisionally recognized as independent States, subject to the rendering of administrative advice and assistance

372. Being an Associated Power, the USA was present as an observer at the San Remo conference; it did not, like the other four - Britain, France, Italy and Japan - belong to the Principal Allied Powers. The USA only joined the First World War in April 1917. See Gauthier (2007), and Wallace (2012).

373. President Woodrow Wilson attended the Paris Peace Conference on behalf of the USA. A Democrat, Wilson excluded the Republicans from participation in this conference. Later, when the Republicans gained a majority in the Senate, they refused to endorse many of the commitments made by Wilson in Paris. Thus, for example, the USA never became a member of the League of Nations.

374. "[T]he actual territories concerned except where they have attained self-government or independence."

by a mandatory until such time as they are able to stand alone. The boundaries of the said States will be determined, and the selection of the mandatories made, by the Principle Allied Powers. The High Contracting Parties agree to entrust, by application of such provisions of article 22, the administration of Palestine, within such boundaries as may be determined by the Principal Allied Powers, to a mandatory, to be selected by the said powers. The Mandatory will be responsible for putting into effect the declaration originally made on 8th [2nd] November, 1917, by the British Government, and adopted by the other Supreme Council, in favour of the establishment in Palestine of a national home for the Jewish people, it being clearly understood that nothing shall be done which may prejudice the civil and religious rights of existing non-Jewish communities in Palestine, or the rights and political status enjoyed by Jews in any other country."[375]

Britain was appointed the Mandatory Power for the Palestine and Mesopotamia Mandates, and France for the Syria Mandate.

6.7 The Treaties of Sèvres and Lausanne

In August 1920, the Allies entered into the Treaty of Sèvres with Turkey, setting out the terms for partitioning of the Ottoman Empire. The parties recognized the establishment of a national home for the Jewish people in Palestine and contained a reference to the Balfour Declaration that had been adopted in San Remo.[376] However, due to the rise of the nationalist movement, the demise of the Ottoman Empire, and the establishment of the Republic of Turkey in 1922 under Mustafa Kemal Atatürk, Turkey never ratified the Treaty of Sèvres, which was therefore annulled and replaced by the Treaty of Lausanne on 24 July 1923 between the British Empire, Italy, Greece, Japan, Romania, the Serb-Croat-Slovene State, and the new Republic of Turkey. The Treaty of Lausanne provided for the recognition of the Republic of Turkey and the establishment of its borders. In Article 16, Turkey renounced all rights and titles with respect to the former Ottoman territories outside Turkey's newly established borders: "The future of these territories being settled or to be settled by the parties concerned."[377] Territories referred to included Palestine, which was by then under British control and over which in the meantime the Mandate for Palestine had been created by the League of Nations.

375. *Documents on British Foreign Policy, 1919-1939*, Vol. VIII, pp. 176-177.

376. See Treaty of Sèvres, art. 95.

377. See Treaty of Lausanne, art. 16.

6.8 The Mandate for Palestine

6.8.1 General

The Council of the League of Nations adopted the Mandate for Palestine on 24 July 1922; and, it entered into force on 29 September 1923.[378] The Mandate for Palestine was conferred on His Britannic Majesty. The Preamble to the Mandate refers to the Balfour Declaration and states that "recognition has thereby been given to the historical connection of the Jewish people with Palestine and to the grounds for reconstituting their national home in that country." This gives international legal effect to both the close relationship which the Jewish people have had with the land from Biblical times, as well as to the urgency for granting them a national home arising from the centuries of persecution in the Diaspora. By incorporating the terms of the Balfour Declaration, the Mandate for Palestine recognized the accepted right of the Jewish people to *reconstitute* their national home in Palestine. The national home that had existed in Biblical times was to be restored. This shows the unique character of the Mandate for Palestine, when compared with the other Mandates, such as the Mandates for Mesopotamia (Iraq) and Syria, which created rights for the population already living in the mandate territory. In contrast to those Mandates, the Jews were, at the time the Mandate for Palestine was created, still a minority in Palestine, and most of the beneficiaries of the Mandate for Palestine—the Jewish people—were living *outside* the Mandate area.[379] This unique character was completely ignored by the ICJ in its Wall Advisory Opinion (2004).[380] The objectives of the Mandate for Palestine, with its unique character, could only be effectuated by making it possible for Jews to return to the land of their forefathers. The Mandate for Palestine was intended to benefit the worldwide Jewish people, and not just those Jews living in Palestine at that time. This is reflected in the obligations which the Mandate for Palestine imposes on the Mandatory as stated in Article 6:

> "The Administration of Palestine, while ensuring that the rights and position of other sections of the population are not prejudiced, shall facilitate Jewish immigration under suitable conditions and shall encourage, in co-operation with the Jewish agency referred to in article 4, close

---

378. Resolution of the Council of the League of Nations adopted during the Twenty-Third Meeting (Private) of the Council on September 29th 1923, *League of Nations Official Journal*, Vol. 4, Issue 11, 1355 (November 1923).

379. Bentwich (1921-22), at p. 51. See also: Blois, de(2016).

380. See also Chapter 4.

> **settlement by Jews on the land, including State lands and waste lands not required for public purposes."**

In 1947, in its Report to the General Assembly of the UN, the UN Special Committee on Palestine (UNSCOP) explicitly recognized this provision, together with Article 2 and 4 as one of the major obligations under the Mandate for Palestine.[381]

Article 2, the central provision of the Mandate, states:

> **"The Mandatory shall be responsible for placing the country under such political, administrative and economic conditions as will secure the establishment of the Jewish national home, as laid down in the preamble, and the development of self-governing institutions, and also for safeguarding the civil and religious rights of all the inhabitants of Palestine, irrespective of race and religion."**

The core of this obligation is the securing of the establishment of the Jewish national home. To achieve this, the Mandate for Palestine includes provisions for self-governance by the Jewish people. According to Article 4, a Jewish Agency is recognized as a public body that is to cooperate with the Mandatory and to advise it in matters connected with the realization of the Jewish national home and the interests of the Jewish population in Palestine. Article 6 provides for a right of settlement for Jews in the Mandate territory, as we have already underlined.

Article 7 states:

> **"The Administration of Palestine shall be responsible for enacting a nationality law. There shall be included in this law provisions framed so as to facilitate the acquisition of Palestinian citizenship by Jews who take up their permanent residence in Palestine."**

This clearly presupposes the immigration of Jews, who may acquire Palestinian citizenship. No mention is made of granting Palestinian citizenship to non-Jewish immigrants. At this point a side comment can be made on the notion of Palestinian citizenship, anticipating the discussion of Palestinian rights to self-determination in Part V. From the time of Emperor Hadrian (135 CE) until 1948, the Jewish homeland was referred to as Palestine. In 1908, the World Zionist Organization established a Palestine office in Jaffa; the Palestine Symphony Orchestra was a Jewish orchestra; the Palestine Post was today's Jerusalem Post—a Jewish

381. A/364, 3 September 1947, United Nations Special Committee on Palestine; Report to the General Assembly, Volume 1, Lake Success, New York, 1947.

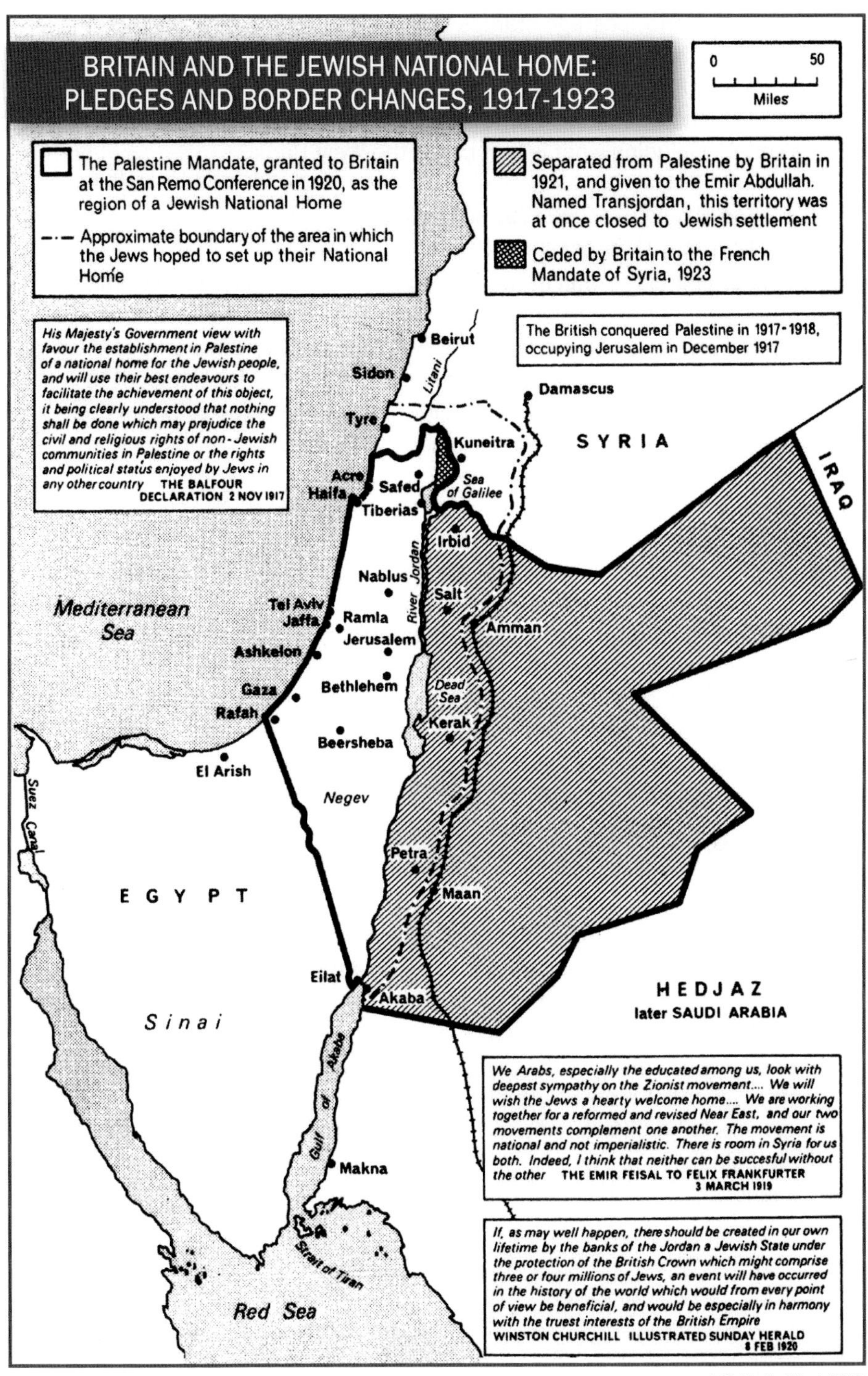
BRITAIN AND THE JEWISH NATIONAL HOME:
PLEDGES AND BORDER CHANGES, 1917-1923
0 50
Miles
The Palestine Mandate, granted to Britain at the San Remo Conference in 1920, as the region of a Jewish National Home
Approximate boundary of the area in which the Jews hoped to set up their National Home
Separated from Palestine by Britain in 1921, and given to the Emir Abdullah. Named Transjordan, this territory was at once closed to Jewish settlement
Ceded by Britain to the French Mandate of Syria, 1923
His Majesty's Government view with favour the establishment in Palestine of a national home for the Jewish people, and will use their best endeavours to facilitate the achievement of this object, it being clearly understood that nothing shall be done which may prejudice the civil and religious rights of non-Jewish communities in Palestine or the rights and political status enjoyed by Jews in any other country THE BALFOUR DECLARATION 2 NOV 1917
The British conquered Palestine in 1917-1918, occupying Jerusalem in December 1917
Beirut
Sidon
Litani
Damascus
Tyre
Kuneitra
SYRIA
IRAQ
Acre
Haifa
Safed
Sea of Galilee
Tiberias
Irbid
Nablus
River Jordan
Salt
Mediterranean Sea
Tel Aviv
Jaffa
Ramla
Jerusalem
Amman
Ashkelon
Gaza
Bethlehem
Dead Sea
Rafah
Kerak
Beersheba
El Arish
Suez Canal
Negev
Petra
EGYPT
Maan
Eilat
Akaba
HEDJAZ
later SAUDI ARABIA
Sinai
Gulf of Akaba
We Arabs, especially the educated among us, look with deepest sympathy on the Zionist movement.... We will wish the Jews a hearty welcome home.... We are working together for a reformed and revised Near East, and our two movements complement one another. The movement is national and not imperialistic. There is room in Syria for us both. Indeed, I think that neither can be succesful without the other THE EMIR FEISAL TO FELIX FRANKFURTER 3 MARCH 1919
Makna
Strait of Tiran
Red Sea
If, as may well happen, there should be created in our own lifetime by the banks of the Jordan a Jewish State under the protection of the British Crown which might comprise three or four millions of Jews, an event will have occurred in the history of the world which would from every point of view be beneficial, and would be especially in harmony with the truest interests of the British Empire WINSTON CHURCHILL ILLUSTRATED SUNDAY HERALD 8 FEB 1920

newspaper; and, postage stamps were issued bearing the inscription Palestine-El–El represented *Eretz Israel* (the Land of Israel). Under the Mandate for Palestine, a Jew in Palestine was by definition "a Palestinian," and he or she was entitled by law to settle in any part of the territory of Palestine, including what is now called the West Bank.

6.8.2 The Mandate for Palestine and Article 22 of the Covenant of the League of Nations

In the first paragraph of the preamble of the Mandate for Palestine, it is stated that the Principal Allied Powers have agreed, for the purpose of giving effect to the provisions of Article 22 of the Covenant of the League of Nations, to entrust to a Mandatory the administration of the territory of Palestine. It has been suggested by some, especially by those with sympathies for the self-determination of Palestinian Arabs, that the terms of the Mandate for Palestine are at odds with Article 22, especially its fourth paragraph, which refers to the Class A Mandates concerning the former parts of the Turkish Empire. It is argued that the reference in this paragraph to the wishes of the communities concerned as a prime criterion in the selection, was ignored by making Great Britain the Mandatory without the consent of the Palestinian Arabs. Furthermore, the powers entrusted to the Mandatory in the Mandate for Palestine do not fit the terms of the Class A Mandates ("advice and assistance"); the extensive powers of the British were more like those of the Class B Mandates. Finally, it is seen as a problem that the Mandate included numerous commitments to establish a Jewish national home, while at the time the indigenous Arab population was almost 90 percent of the total number of inhabitants.[382] Similar concerns were expressed even before the Mandate entered into force.

In response, it is important to underline the unique character of the Mandate for Palestine, in the same vein as the letter from the British Colonial Office to the Palestine Arab Delegation of the first of March 1922. It held that the Principal Allied Powers "were well advised in applying to Palestine a somewhat different interpretation of paragraph 4, Article 22 of the Covenant than was applied to the neighboring countries of Iraq and Syria." The different interpretation, as it was called, was motivated by the pledge made by the British government to the Jewish people.[383] Stoyanovski observed in his seminal work on the Mandate for Palestine

382. See, e.g., Dajani (1997-1998), at pp. 34-35.

383. *Palestine. Correspondence with the Palestine Arab Delegation and the Zionist Organisation. Presented by Command of His Majesty. June 1922. London, Published by HMSO 1922.* Cmd. 1700.

that: "[T]he Jewish people as a whole may be considered (...) as forming virtually part of the population of Palestine. The Mandate system has been applied to Palestine not merely on account of the inability of its present population to stand alone, as is the case with other mandated territories, but also, and perhaps chiefly, on account of the fact that the people whose connection with Palestine has been recognized is still outside its boundaries. The Mandatory power thus appears (...) as a kind of a provisional administrator of the interest of an absent people.(...) the mandatory has assumed an obligation not towards the actual but the virtual population of Palestine."[384] From that perspective it is possible to understand the Mandate for Palestine as being in harmony with the purposes of the Mandate system as formulated in Article 22 of the Covenant of the League of Nations. That was, of course, the opinion of the Council of the League of Nations, that according to the eighth paragraph of Article 22 had the authority to define the terms of the Mandate for Palestine.[385] Also the Permanent Court of International Justice accepted the Mandate for Palestine as legally binding in its judgment of 30 August 1924 in the *Mavrommatis* case.[386] The focus of the objectives of the Mandate system in respect of Palestine was the development towards independence of the Jewish people.

6.8.3 San Remo, the Mandate for Palestine and the Rights and Interests of Non-Jewish Inhabitants

The fact that the Mandate for Palestine was intended to create a Jewish homeland in Palestine does not mean that the political ambitions and interests of Arabs and other non-Jewish inhabitants of the Ottoman Empire were ignored. As World War I evolved, and then as the Allied Powers grappled in the Paris Peace Conference with the complex question of how to manage their victory in WWI, there was extensive dialogue and contact between the various Principal Allied Powers, the diverse Zionist organizations and representatives, Arab nationalist leaders, and the local Palestinian Arab leaders. During this period, many different proposals and ideas were expressed concerning the future status of the peoples and territories of the former Ottoman empire. In all of this, it was clear to all that there was a tension between the Zionist aspirations

---

384. Stoyanovsky (1928), pp. 41-42.

385. Covenant of the League of Nations, art. 22(8): "The degree of authority, control, or administration to be exercised by the Mandatory shall, if not previously agreed upon by the Members of the League, be explicitly defined in each case by the Council." This provision is paraphrased in the Preamble of the Mandate. Cf. also Crawford (2011), pp. 428-430.

386. *Mavrommatis Palestine Concessions (Greece v. U.K.)*, 1924 P.C.I.J. (Ser. B), No 3 (1924).

for a Jewish homeland, the Arab nationalist aspirations as represented by Emir Feisal, and the aspirations of the Palestinian Arab leaders, who had expressed their opposition to the creation of the Jewish homeland in no uncertain terms.

In this context, the Mandate for Palestine is based on the Mandate system created pursuant to the Treaty of Versailles—"the most far-reaching and comprehensive settlement ever effected in any international dispute... in the aftermath of the greatest clash of arms between nations ever waged on this earth."[387] As far as the Middle East was concerned, the Mandate system expressly intended and achieved not only the creation of the Jewish homeland but also the foundation of several new Arab nation-states in the former Turkish territories. Just as the State of Israel, the modern states of Syria, Transjordan (later Jordan) and Iraq (Mesopotamia) all owe their legal and historical foundation to the mandate system of the League of Nations.

As far as Palestine was concerned, the creation of the Jewish homeland was, given the extraordinary connection of the Jewish people with Palestine, and the outbreak of anti-Jewish sentiment in Europe, considered a just and equitable outcome—provided the civil and religious rights of the non-Jewish inhabitants of Palestine were protected. Following the Balfour Declaration, both the San Remo Resolution and the Mandate for Palestine included provisions intended to protect the rights and interests of the non-Jewish communities in Palestine. The idea was to create a Jewish national home *in* Palestine, a territory in which established residents who did not belong to the Jewish community would continue to live. This resulted in Article 2, the central provision in the Mandate on the establishment of the Jewish national home, which explicitly requires the safeguarding of the civil and religious rights of all the inhabitants of Palestine, irrespective of race and religion. Their rights are also addressed in the provisions that impose the duty on the Mandatory to ensure the protection of the holy places and religious buildings and sites, freedom of conscience, race, religion and worship, and the celebration of holy days.[388]

Further, in anticipation of discussion concerning the territories in Part III, it is important to note that the Mandate for Palestine territory extended initially to the eastern borders of the present Kingdom of Jordan, on which territory eventually both a Jewish and an Arab state were created.

---

387. Lloyd George (1938), p. 17, cited by Gauthier (2007), p. 334.

388. Articles 13, 14, 15, and 23.

6.8.4 Jewish National Home

The framers of the Mandate for Palestine cited the Balfour Declaration, which refers to a national home rather than a state. The UNSCOP report in 1947 suggests that this was a compromise resulting from different views within the British Cabinet regarding the establishment of a Jewish state.[389] Whether or not a Jewish state would be established would depend on the efforts of the Jewish people. For those involved in the creation of the Balfour Declaration, it was clear from the beginning that the ultimate goal of the Mandate for Palestine was to enable the creation of a Jewish state. Lord Balfour declared three months after the issue of the Declaration: "My personal hope is that the Jews will make good in Palestine and eventually found a Jewish State."[390] He also stated that the goal was to bring the national status of the Jews in line with that of other races, by giving them what all other nations possess: a land to live in and a national home.[391] This refers to the recognition of national aspirations that were to result in an independent state. Article 22 of the Covenant of the League of Nations recognizes the former Turkish communities as "independent nations" almost capable of "standing alone"—which shows they were intended to result in independent political entities having distinct legal personality. In a conversation with Chaim Weizmann in 1921, Balfour and Prime Minister Lloyd George declared that they both had intended the ultimate creation of a Jewish state.[392] Comments by other members of the British government reflect the same opinion.[393] The South African Prime Minister and one time member of the Imperial War Cabinet, Jan Christiaan Smuts, told an audience at Johannesburg in November 1919, "You will see a great Jewish State rising there once more."[394] Colonial Secretary Ormsby Gore confirmed in 1937 that the Balfour Declaration and the British Mandate for Palestine were binding documents, and that their binding character was to remain until replaced by an independent Jewish State.[395] It should be noted in this connection that the system of Mandates established by the League of Nations was intended as a temporary regime in preparation for the independence of peoples, who were, at the time the Mandate was created, not yet

---

389. See UNSCOP, para 76, based on the 1936 Peel Commission Report.

390. Quoted by Morris (2008), p. 10,

391. See the Foreword of Lord Balfour in Sokolow (1919), p. xxxiii, as quoted by Stoyanofsky (1928), p. 70.

392. Gilbert (2007), p. 71.

393. *Ibid.*

394. Quoted by Gilbert (1978), p. 127.

395. See Feinberg (1974), at p. 69.

sufficiently developed to govern themselves. The idea of the Mandate system as the preparatory phase to independence fitted the optimistic ideas of the American President Woodrow Wilson on self-determination.[396] A commission created by Wilson to elaborate his Fourteen Points in 1919 expressed its favor for the establishment of a Jewish state:

> **"If the Jews, being given full opportunity, make it such. It was the cradle and home of their vital race, which has made large spiritual contributions to mankind, and is the only land in which they can find hope to find a home of their own, they being in this last respect unique among significant peoples."[397]**

The positive American attitude towards the idea of self-determination of the Jewish people prevailed also under President Wilson's successor. On 21 September 1922, the American Congress passed a resolution, signed by President Warren G. Harding, giving explicit support to the establishment of a Jewish national homeland in Palestine.[398] American support of the Mandate for Palestine was further emphasized in a treaty, concluded in 1924, on the Mandate for Palestine between the U.S. and the United Kingdom.[399]

6.8.5 Implementation of the Mandate: 1922–1948

The Mandate for Palestine had been adopted on 24 July 1922 and officially entered into force on 29 September 1923. The Mandate for Palestine entrusted the British government with full powers of legislation and administration.[400] It had these powers until the withdrawal of British troops and termination of the exercise of their authority under the Mandate at midnight on 14 May 1948. The British civil administration of Palestine was, in accordance with the San Remo Resolution, already installed some years before the official entry into force of the Mandate for Palestine, as of 1 July 1920.[401] The Palestine Order in Council and its subsequent amendments regulated the internal administration.[402] Under Article 22 of the Covenant of the League of Nations, the Permanent Mandates Commission of the League of Nations supervised Britain's observance of the Mandate for Palestine.

396. See also Veerman (1977), p. 151.

397. Feinberg (1974), at p. 431.

398. See Grief (2008), pp. 198-199.

399. American-British Palestine Mandate Convention of December 3, 1924, Treaty Series No. 728.

400. Mandate for Palestine, art. 1.

401. Grief (2008), p. 125.

402. The Palestine Order in Council of 10 August 1922.

The years of British rule during the Mandate period were characterized by conflict, turmoil, and controversy. From the beginning, the administration of the Mandate for Palestine was fraught with difficulties. Large parts of the Arab population resented the creation of a Jewish homeland. This led to vociferous protests and political actions, such as strikes, as means to force the British administration to follow a policy which was more pro-Arab. Many actions were also directed against the Jewish population. This often resulted in violence directed against them, and many were killed. These actions were led or inspired by the Grand Mufti of Jerusalem, Haj Amin al Husseini. He had been appointed in 1921 by the first British High Commissioner in Palestine, in the hope that Al Husseini as Grand Mufti would exert a moderating influence. The opposite was the result. Al Husseini was very likely one of the instigators of the riots in Hebron in 1929, leading to the slaughter of the local Jewish population.[403] He was the leading anti-Zionist Arab leader throughout the Mandate period and later developed an alliance with Hitler. He remained influential in the region until his death in exile in 1972. Pressure from the Arabs within and outside Palestine, as well as from influential Muslim leaders in the British Empire (from British India) on the British government to refrain from implementing its obligations to establish a Jewish national home in Palestine was not without effect. Such violence led to a growing resistance of the British Cabinet and the British Parliament to comply with its obligations under the Mandate for Palestine.

The succeeding decades saw a gradual retreat of the British Government from its obligations under the Mandate for Palestine, especially concerning Jewish immigration. This development is expressed in the three White Papers on the Mandate for Palestine published in 1922, 1930 and 1939.[404] The immigration of Jews to Palestine was subjected to severe restrictions. Even the rise to power of Nazism in Germany and their anti-Jewish policies, which, already anticipated the "final solution," failed to bring about a positive change to British policies. On the contrary, Britain seemed more inclined to cater to the Arab's desire to curtail Jewish immigration. In 1939, the third White Paper was approved and adopted by a majority of the members of the British Parliament. It imposed severe restrictions by limiting Jewish immigration for the following five years to 75,000 and after that subjecting any immigration to approval of the Arabs.[405] Winston Churchill, who voted

---

403. Gilbert (1978), pp. 151-153.

404. Known as the Churchill White Paper (1922), the Passfield White Paper (1930), and the MacDonald White Paper (1939), after the responsible Colonial Secretary. See also: Blois, de (2016).

405. British White Paper of 1939, Yale Law School, The Avalon Project Documents in Law, History and Diplomacy, (http://avalon.law.yale.edu/20th_century/brwh1939.asp). See also Gilbert (1978).

against the White Paper, called its proposals, "a violation of the pledge... [and an] abandonment of the Balfour Declaration."[406] The British policy also led to criticism of the Permanent Mandates Commission of the League of Nations, which saw Palestine as the main place of refuge for persecuted Jews from Germany, Romania, and Poland.[407] As the Dutch member of the Permanent Mandates Commission, Baron Van Asbeck, observed, "The emphasis has been shifted from the Jews to the Arabs."[408] The Permanent Mandates Commission concluded that the 1939 White Paper was not in accordance with the interpretation of the Mandate for Palestine that it had always followed. A majority of four members of the Permanent Mandates Commission did not feel able to state that the White Paper was in conformity with the Mandate for Palestine, having regard to its terms and the intentions of its authors. A minority of three concluded that the existing circumstances would justify the policy of the White Paper.[409] The severe restrictions on immigration of Jews in Palestine led to numerous, at times successful, attempts by desperate refugees to enter the territory of Palestine illegally. Even the systematic mass murder of Jews following the Wannsee Conference in Berlin in January 1942 brought initially no change in the British policies. In the last part of the summer of 1943, there was an adaptation of the policy, in order to facilitate immigration by those who succeeded in reaching Turkey, but it came too late for most victims.[410] At least six million Jews had been murdered in the *Shoah*.[411] The end of the war did not bring the relief for the surviving Jews which might have been expected. Again, thousands of Jews were refused entrance to the Promised Land, and, at times, they were even forced to return from the harbor of Haifa to camps in Europe.[412]

406. Gilbert (1978), p. 230.

407. *Ibid.*, p. 195.

408. League of Nations Permanent Mandates Commission Minutes of the Thirty-Sixth Session (Geneva, 8-29 June 1939), Fourteenth Meeting (https://unispal.un.org/DPA/DPR/unispal.nsf/0/D54DB2B34342AE5D052565E9004F24DF), p. 52.

409. Permanent Mandates Commission of the League of Nations Report, 29 June 1939, A. Palestine: Observations on the policy laid down in the White Paper of May 1939, paragraphs 9-15 (http://www.mideastwed.org/league_mandates_report_1939.htm). See also Grief (2008), p. 208.

410. Gilbert (1978), pp. 258-271.

411. *Ibid.*, p. 270.

412. *Ibid.*, pp. 272-309, in particular pp. 301-302.

6.9 The UN Partition Plan 1947 – Resolution 181

In 1947, the British administration finally announced its intention to terminate Britain's responsibilities under the Mandate for Palestine. They did not put any procedures in place to ensure an orderly transition. As we have seen already, no Trusteeship regime was ever established under the UN Charter, which in the meantime had replaced the League of Nations. The United Kingdom simply requested the UN General Assembly to put Palestine on its agenda and to make recommendations with regard to the future administration of Palestine. A UN Special Committee on Palestine (UNSCOP) was set up and its work resulted in Resolution 181(II).[413] On 29 November 1947, UNSCOP's proposal was adopted by the General Assembly: 33 votes in favor, 13 against, and 10 abstentions. In this resolution, the General Assembly made a non-binding recommendation to implement a "Partition Plan" for Palestine. This plan envisioned the creation of two states—one Jewish and the other Arab—while Jerusalem was to be "internationalized." In addition, an Economic Union of Palestine was to be created, uniting the two states and the city of Jerusalem. The territory allocated to the Jewish State under the Partition Plan encompassed only a very small part of the territory originally covered by the Mandate for Palestine, and therefore was arguably not in conformity with the Mandate's obligation to ensure the "establishment of a Jewish national home in Palestine." Under enormous pressure to find an immediate solution for the (approximately) 150,000 European Jewish survivors of the *Shoah*, the Jewish Agency accepted the Partition Plan, under the proviso that it would be accepted by the Arabs.[414] The Arabs immediately rejected the Partition Plan, arguing that the General Assembly was not authorized to make such a recommendation and that it was in breach of the rights of the Arab residents of Palestine to determine their own political future.[415] The reason for this rejection appeared to be that the Arabs did not accept the presence of a Jewish state on what they considered to be Arab territory, which had been under Islamic dominion. The adoption of the Resolution in the UN led to a wave of anti-Jewish violence not only in the territory of Palestine, but also in the Arab world. This only underlined the urgent need for a Jewish homeland, not only for the European survivors of the *Shoah*, but also for many Jews in other parts of the world.

---

413. See the Report of UNSCOP to the G.A.: UNDoc. A/364 (3 September 1947).

414. Grief (2008), pp. 154-155.

415. See generally: Stahn-Don (2017): http://www.thinc.info/wp-content/uploads/2017/11/TheMandateforPalestine-Defining-Jewish-Sovereignty-under-International-Law2-thinc-website.pdf.

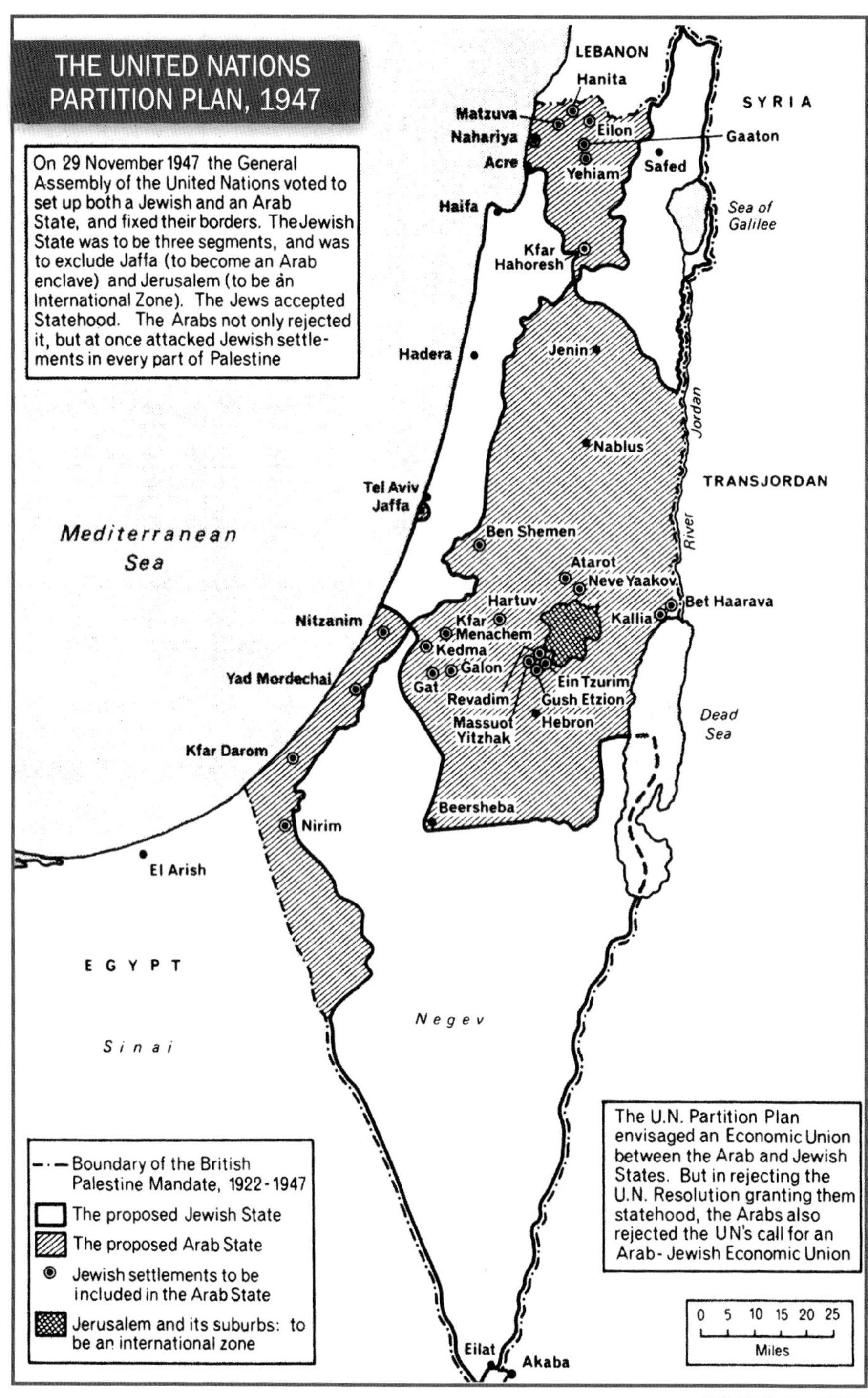
THE UNITED NATIONS PARTITION PLAN, 1947
On 29 November 1947 the General Assembly of the United Nations voted to set up both a Jewish and an Arab State, and fixed their borders. The Jewish State was to be three segments, and was to exclude Jaffa (to become an Arab enclave) and Jerusalem (to be an International Zone). The Jews accepted Statehood. The Arabs not only rejected it, but at once attacked Jewish settlements in every part of Palestine
LEBANON
Hanita
SYRIA
Matzuva
Eilon
Nahariya
Gaaton
Acre
Yehiam
Safed
Haifa
Sea of Galilee
Kfar Hahoresh
Hadera
Jenin
Jordan
Nablus
TRANSJORDAN
Tel Aviv
Jaffa
River
Mediterranean Sea
Ben Shemen
Atarot
Neve Yaakov
Hartuv
Bet Haarava
Nitzanim
Kfar Menachem
Kallia
Kedma
Galon
Yad Mordechai
Gat
Ein Tzurim
Revadim
Gush Etzion
Massuot Yitzhak
Hebron
Dead Sea
Kfar Darom
Beersheba
Nirim
El Arish
EGYPT
Negev
Sinai
Boundary of the British Palestine Mandate, 1922-1947
The proposed Jewish State
The proposed Arab State
Jewish settlements to be included in the Arab State
Jerusalem and its suburbs: to be an international zone
The U.N. Partition Plan envisaged an Economic Union between the Arab and Jewish States. But in rejecting the U.N. Resolution granting them statehood, the Arabs also rejected the UN's call for an Arab-Jewish Economic Union
0 5 10 15 20 25
Miles
Eilat
Akaba

7. A Jewish and Democratic State

" (...) on 14 May 1948, Israel proclaimed its independence on the strength of the General Assembly resolution."

Advisory Opinion (Paragraph 71)[416]

7.1 Introduction

In the preceding chapter, we dealt with the collapse of the British Mandate regime and the Arab rejection of the UN Partition Plan, which included the establishment of a Jewish state. In the months following 29 November 1947, the conflict between Jews and Arabs intensified. The British—frustrated and now determined to withdraw from Palestine—hardly intervened. The situation turned into a full-fledged armed conflict between Jews and Arabs.[417] And, just hours before British forces departed, the State of Israel was proclaimed. In this chapter, we will discuss the Israeli Declaration of Independence, which refers to Israel as a Jewish and democratic state. Is it possible for a state to be both Jewish and democratic?

7.2 Declaration of the Establishment of the State of Israel

In the Tel Aviv Museum on Rothschild Boulevard in the afternoon of 14 May 1948, only hours before the Mandate for Palestine was due to end and the last remaining British forces were to leave Palestine, David Ben Gurion declared the establishment of the State of Israel.[418] He proclaimed the Declaration of the Establishment of the State of Israel (the Declaration of Independence) before Rabbi Fischmann recited the *Shehecheyanu*

416. I.C.J. Reports 2004, pp. 165-166.

417. Morris (2008).

418. Ben-Gurion (1972), pp. 79-82.

blessing.[419] Then, those members of the Provisional State Council (the temporary legislature) who were present signed the Declaration. The national anthem, the *Hatikvah,* was sung. This solemn occasion was of tremendous importance to the Jewish people, which now, for the first time since the defeat of Bar Kokhba in 135 CE, succeeded in establishing an independent state. Golda Mabovitch Meyerson—later known as Golda Meir, who was to become Prime Minister of Israel—wrote: "The long exile was over. From this day on we would no longer live on sufferance in the land of our forefathers. Now we were a nation like other nations, masters—for the first time in centuries—of our own destiny."[420]

The celebrations were short-lived. The five Arab States of Egypt, Syria, Lebanon, Transjordan, and Iraq launched a full army attack on the newly established State of Israel on the following morning—15 May 1948.[421] A week before the attack, Azzam Pasha, the Secretary-General of the Arab League, declared: "It does not matter how many [Jews] there are. We will sweep them into the sea."[422] Ahmed Shukeiry, later founding chairman of the Palestine Liberation Organization (PLO), formulated the war aim as "the elimination of the Jewish State."[423] Fortunately, this did not come to pass. By 20 July 1949, with the signing of the last Armistice Agreement (with Syria), the conflict formally came to an end. Four Armistice Agreements were concluded between Israel and its Arab neighbors. The conflict had lasted eight months, and the casualties were high for all parties involved. Jordanian forces had occupied important parts of Judea and Samaria, and the Old City of Jerusalem. All Jewish residents were killed or evicted; many synagogues and other important places in the Jewish Quarter were destroyed. Also, another part of the original Mandate territory was occupied: the Gaza Strip (Gaza), with Egypt as the occupying power.

The proclamation of the establishment of the State of Israel in the solemn Declaration of Independence on 14 May 1948 was the ultimate expression of the self-determination of the Jewish people in *Eretz Israel*.[424]

---

419. The *Shehecheyanu* blessing can be translated as follows: "Blessed are You, LORD our God, King of the Universe, who has given us life, sustained us, and brought us to this time", in: Sacks (2009), p. 880.

420. Quoted by number: Gilbert (1978).

421. Morris (2008), pp. 75-179. It has to be remarked that the Transjordanian Arab Legion, the army most feared by the Jews, was commanded by a British officer, Glubb, and included another 50 to75 British officers and non-commissioned officers.

422. Morris (2008), p. 187.

423. *Ibid.*

424. The Land of Israel.

It constituted a legitimate exercise of the right to self-determination under international law. The Declaration of Independence refers to *Eretz Israel* as the birthplace of the Jewish people, where their spiritual, religious and political identity was shaped. It refers to the Dispersion, but also to the fact that the hope to return to their land had never faded away. Israel's Declaration of Independence recalls the Zionist movement and Theodor Herzl. Both the Balfour Declaration and the Mandate for Palestine are mentioned. The text evokes the Holocaust (*Shoah*) as the catastrophe that demonstrated the urgency of the re-establishment of the Jewish State in *Eretz Israel*. Referring to the Partition Resolution, the Declaration of Independence states that the recognition by the UN of the right of the Jewish people is irrevocable. That is, most likely, the background of the quote at the beginning of this chapter, that "Israel proclaimed its independence on the strength of the General Assembly resolution." As we will demonstrate, there are more convincing legal arguments for the legitimacy of the State of Israel than this non-binding Resolution. The full text of the Declaration of the Establishment of the State of Israel is included in the Appendixes.

7.3 When Did the State of Israel Come into Existence?

The State of Israel entered the international scene on 14 May 1948. At that moment, it became clear that Israel satisfied the criteria of statehood, namely:

1. it existed within a territory (though only part of the original Mandate territory; part of the boundaries of this new state were as yet undefined);[425]
2. this territory was inhabited by a population (both Jewish and non-Jewish); and
3. the territory and population were governed by an effective government that had been established since 1920 under the Mandate for Palestine; during the War of Independence, this government prepared for independence, and on 14 May 1948, it came into effect as the governing authority over the newly established State of Israel.

In our view, therefore, Israel qualified as a state under international law on 14 May 1948, or soon afterwards, even though, at that time, the fledgling state was embroiled in an existential conflict with its neighbors and with a significant part of its own Arab population, which refused to recognize its existence.[426]

---

425. In Part III we will discuss this issue further.

426. Cf., e.g., Brownlie (1990), pp. 72-79.

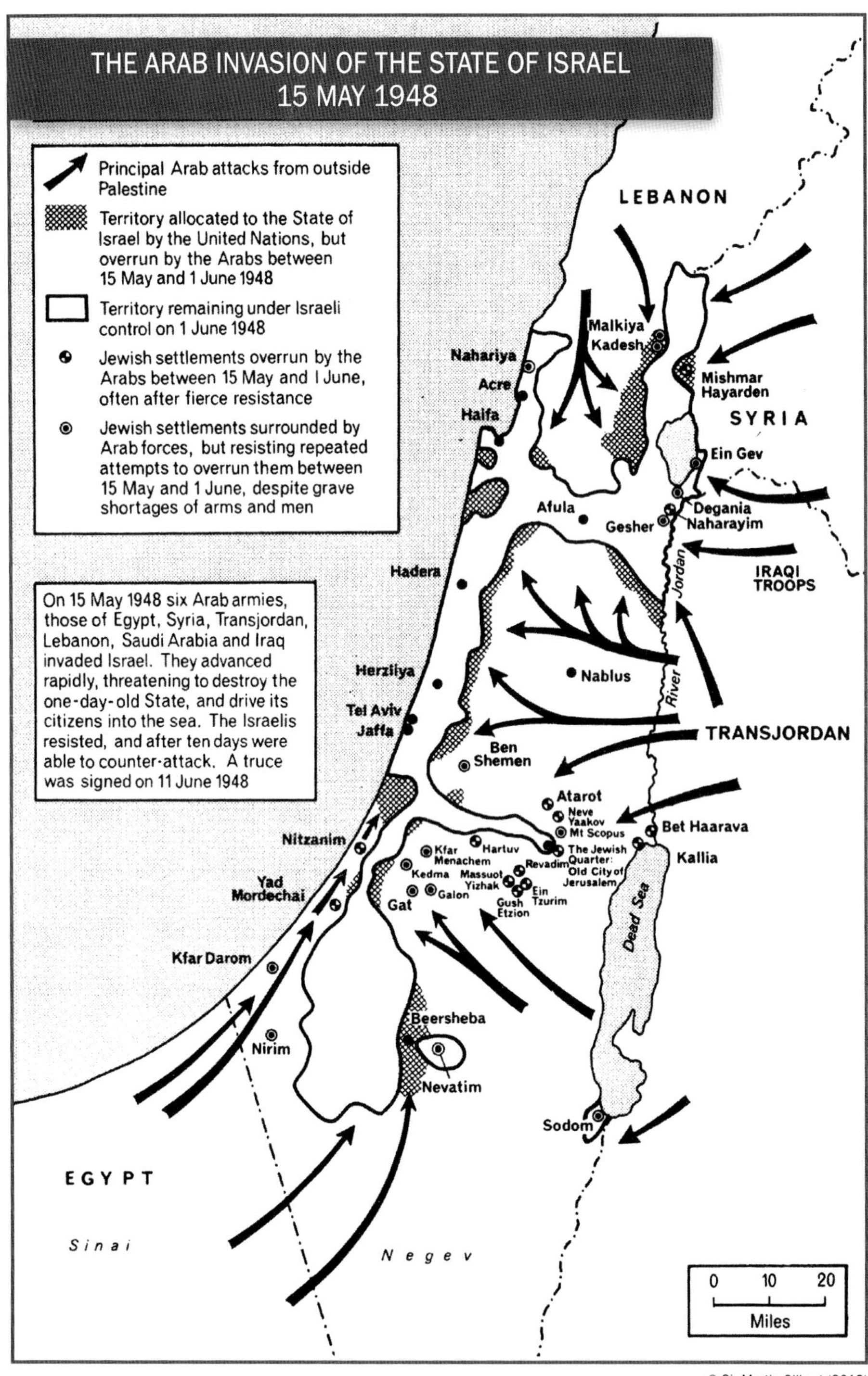
THE ARAB INVASION OF THE STATE OF ISRAEL
15 MAY 1948
Principal Arab attacks from outside Palestine
Territory allocated to the State of Israel by the United Nations, but overrun by the Arabs between 15 May and 1 June 1948
Territory remaining under Israeli control on 1 June 1948
Jewish settlements overrun by the Arabs between 15 May and I June, often after fierce resistance
Jewish settlements surrounded by Arab forces, but resisting repeated attempts to overrun them between 15 May and 1 June, despite grave shortages of arms and men
On 15 May 1948 six Arab armies, those of Egypt, Syria, Transjordan, Lebanon, Saudi Arabia and Iraq invaded Israel. They advanced rapidly, threatening to destroy the one-day-old State, and drive its citizens into the sea. The Israelis resisted, and after ten days were able to counter-attack. A truce was signed on 11 June 1948
LEBANON
SYRIA
IRAQI TROOPS
TRANSJORDAN
EGYPT
Sinai
Negev
Malkiya
Kadesh
Nahariya
Acre
Haifa
Mishmar Hayarden
Ein Gev
Degania
Naharayim
Gesher
Afula
Hadera
Jordan
River
Nablus
Herzliya
Tel Aviv
Jaffa
Ben Shemen
Atarot
Neve Yaakov
Mt Scopus
The Jewish Quarter: Old City of Jerusalem
Bet Haarava
Kallia
Dead Sea
Nitzanim
Kfar Menachem
Hartuv
Revadim
Kedma
Massuot Yizhak
Ein Tzurim
Galon
Gush Etzion
Gat
Yad Mordechai
Kfar Darom
Beersheba
Nirim
Nevatim
Sodom
0 10 20
Miles

Many members of the international community recognized the new State of Israel without reservation. It was recognized by the United States immediately, and by the USSR three days later. Thereafter, Israel was recognized by many other nations, and admitted as a UN Member State in 1949.[427]

7.4 Israel – A Jewish State

7.4.1 Connection between the Jewish People and the Land

The term "Jewish" in the context of the State of Israel refers in the first instance to the connection between the Jewish people and the Land. The Declaration of Independence refers to "the establishment of a Jewish State in *Eretz Israel*, to be known as the State of Israel." The name "Israel" itself refers to the Biblical history of the Jewish nation in the Land. The term *Eretz Israel*, which is used in the Declaration of Independence, refers to the land that was the locus of the nation of the Jewish people under King David and his successors. The Declaration of Independence, which, in the absence of a written constitution, is the basic charter of the State of Israel, refers repeatedly to the historical, spiritual, religious, and political connection of the Jewish people to the Land. This aspect of the Jewish character of Israel is perhaps most significantly reflected in the Israeli Law of Return (1950), pursuant to which all Jews worldwide have a right to return to the Land and receive Israeli citizenship. According to David Ben Gurion, this law—the basis of which was already laid in the Mandate for Palestine—represents the heart of the Jewish State.[428] In recent years, several (controversial) proposals have been made to enact the Jewish character of Israel even more strongly in its legislation. On 7 May 2017, the Ministerial Committee for Legislation voted in favor of a bill: "Basic Law: Israel as the Nation State of the Jewish people." It passed the preliminary reading in the Knesset on 10 May 2017. If it also successfully passes the next stages of the legislative procedure, it may become law in 2018.[429]

7.4.2 The Jewish Population

The Jewish nature of Israel refers also to the cultural, religious, spiritual, legal, and ethical identity of the Jewish nation that makes it so unique. The Jewish people form the majority of the population.[430] Israel currently has

427. UN G.A. Res.273 (III), *Admission of Israel to Membership in the United Nations* (11 May 1949).

428. Altschul (2002).

429. *The Times of Israel*, 10 May 2017.

430. Vital Statistics: Latest Population Statistics for Israel (updated: March 2014): http://www.jewishvirtuallibrary.org/latest-population-statistics-for-israel (visited: 9 September 2017).

approximately eight million citizens, of whom six million are Jews.[431] The Jewish citizens of Israel bring with them a vast diversity of ethnic backgrounds. Approximately, 73 percent of Israeli Jews are Israeli-born. (*Sabras*).[432] Additionally, there are immigrants from Europe, the Americas, Asia, and Africa (including the Arab World). About 1.1 million citizens of Israel have immigrated from the former Soviet Union.[433] Of these, 300,000 are not considered Jewish by the Orthodox Rabbinate, but are eligible for Israeli citizenship under the Law of Return.[434] Jews from Western, Central and Eastern Europe and their Israeli-born descendants, are known as *Ashkenazi* Jews. *Sephardi* Jews are those originating from Spain and Portugal and their descendants. Finally, there is the group of *Mizrahi* or Oriental Jews, who came from Arab and/or Muslim countries in the Middle East and Northern Africa and their descendants.[435] Israeli Jews vary widely in their religious views and practices. Since 1999, there has been a tendency towards more religiosity.[436] In 2011, a study by the Israel Central Bureau of Statistics showed that nine percent of the Jews in Israel qualified themselves as *Haredim*, which is often defined as ultra-orthodox, 10 percent as non-*Haredi* orthodox, 15 percent as traditional religious, 23 percent as traditional, and 43 percent as secular, most of whom observe some Jewish traditions. A poll taken in 2013 shows that between 500,000 and 600,000 of the traditional and secular Jews have affinity with Conservative and Reform streams of Judaism. So too is there a community of about 20,000 "Messianic" Jews.[437] According to a survey, released in 2012, about 80 percent of Israeli Jews believe that God exists.[438]

7.4.3 Official Symbols

Israel's Declaration of Independence mentions that Israel will be "based on freedom, justice and peace as envisaged by the prophets of Israel." This is a clear reference to the Hebrew Bible (*Tanakh*), which includes the

---

431. *Ibid.*

432. CIDI (2014). p. 20.

433. Cohen et al. (2011), at p. 9.

434. Yakobson (2010).

435. Zoher (ed.) (2005).

436. The Israel Democracy Institute &and AVI CHAI Israel Foundation, *A Portrait of Israeli Jews. Beliefs, Observance, and Values of Israeli Jews, 2009,* The Israel Democracy Institute Publications 2012 (see Bibliography, under Arian (2012); note: Asher Arian was the team leader of the survey project).

437. US Department of State, International Religious Freedom Report for 2013, 'Israel and the Occupied Territories', Section I, Religious Demography: https://www.state.gov/j/drl/rls/irf/2013religiousfreedom/#wrapper (visited: 20 April 2018).

438. Arian (2012).

writings of the prophets of Israel. In light of this, it is not surprising that the official symbols of Israel reflect aspects of the Jewish religion. The symbol of Israel is the seven-armed lamp, the *Menorah*, from the Temple in Jerusalem. The national flag of Israel is one of the most outspoken expressions of Jewish nationhood. The Israeli flag, designed at the end of the 19th century, is full of symbolism. It recalls the *Tallit*, the Jewish prayer shawl, which is white with blue stripes. The symbol in its center represents the *Magen David* (Shield or Star of David), which has been a Jewish symbol for hundreds of years.[439] The national anthem of Israel is the *Hatikvah* (English: "The Hope").[440] The text is derived from a poem by Naphtali Herz Imber, a Romanian-Jewish poet. Israeli law recognizes the *Shabbat* as the weekly day of rest, and nine official holidays during the year—among them the national Day of Independence, and the most important Jewish feasts and prayer days: *Rosh Hashana*, *Yom Kippur*, *Sukkot*, *Pesach* and *Shavuot*. All citizens are required to observe the National Day of Independence, while non-Jews are free to disregard the other national holidays.

7.4.4 **The Legal System**

Regarding the legal system, Israeli law is to a large extent secular.[441] However, family law in Israel incorporates large parts of Jewish religious law relating to the marriage of Jews, as interpreted by the rabbinical courts.[442] Islamic or Christian religious law governs the relevant issues concerning family law of other religious groups. In the Foundations of Law Statute, there is a very general reference to what may be interpreted as Jewish religious law as a supplementary source of law.[443] It provides: "Where the court, faced with a legal question requiring decision, finds no answer to it in statute law or case-law or by analogy, it shall decide it in the light of the principles of freedom, justice, equity, and peace of Israel's heritage."[444]

7.4.5 **Citizenship of Israel**

The identity of a state is also reflected in its nationality law. Under the Israeli Nationality Law, there are four ways in which Israeli citizenship

439. Reagan (n.d.).

440. Martin (1999), p. 7.

441. See for a general overview: Barak (2002).

442. See Rabbinical Courts Jurisdiction (Marriage and Divorce) Law 1953. See further, *inter alia*, Blois, de (2011), pp. 207-233.

443. Foundations of Law Statute (1980).

444. Foundations of Law Statute (1980), Section 1. See also Friedell (2009).

can be attained.[445] Citizenship based on the Law of Return is central to maintaining the Jewish character of the State of Israel, and it is the most important area of discussion in this topic. In addition, non-Jews and Jews have equal rights to citizenship based on residence in the land prior to the entry into force of the Israel's Nationality Law of 1952. Citizenship is also extended to children born of Israeli citizens. Finally, there is a possibility of naturalization of non-Jews. Acquiring nationality through naturalization is far harder than through the Law of Return.

7.4.6 **Right of Return**

The Jewish character of Israel and, in a sense, its *raison d'être* is reflected in the right to become a citizen through the right of return. Israel's Declaration of Independence proclaims: "[T]he state of Israel will be open for Jewish immigration and for the Ingathering of the Exiles." This principle has been elaborated in the Law of Return of 1950.[446] Israel's Nationality Law 1952 provides that every person qualifying as an *oleh* under the Law of Return shall become an Israeli national.[447] An *oleh* (plural: *olim*) is a Jew immigrating to the land of Israel. An amendment to the Law of Return in the 1970's introduced in a definition of the term "Jew": "A person who was born of a Jewish mother or has become converted to Judaism and who is not a member of another religion."[448] It established that the spouse of a Jew, the children of a Jew and their spouses, and the grandchildren of a Jew and their spouses would also be covered under the Law of Return and thus eligible for an *oleh* certificate, provided that the Jew on behalf of whom they request the certificate did not practice a religion other than Judaism willingly (he or she may, however, be a non-observant Jew).[449] This extended definition of those eligible for becoming an Israeli national under the Law of Return is wider than the definition of who is a Jew in the *halakhah,* that is the Jewish religious law.[450] This is, however, understandable against the background of the anti-Semitic Nazi legislation. The Nazi Nuremberg Race Laws of 1935 used also a definition

445. Nationality Law No. 32, 5712-1952, passed by the Israeli Knesset on 1 April 1952, Section 1.

446. See, inter alia, Gavison (2010).

447. Nationality Law No. 32, 5712-1952, passed by the Israeli Knesset on 1 April 1952, Section 2.

448. Law of Return (1970's amendment), section 4B.

449. *Ibid.*, section 4A.

450. According to Jewish Law (*halakhah*) a Jew is a person who was born of a Jewish mother or has become converted to Judaism. In a sense the Law of Return is also narrower than the *Halacha*, according to which conversion to another religion does not imply that a Jew ceases to be Jewish. See Yakobson (2010), at p. 237.

of Jew, which is wider than the *halakhic* definition and even introduced the concept of *Mischlinge* (partial Jews) in various degrees.[451]

Israeli citizenship for *olim* who qualify for nationality under the Law of Return is acquired on the moment of arrival in Israel. The Law of Return and the Nationality Law therefore draw a distinction between Jews and non-Jews. Non-Jews cannot apply for citizenship based on nationality under the Law of Return; therefore, acquiring Israeli citizenship is much harder for non-Jews than for Jews. It is arguable that this distinction is a justifiable and natural expression of the legitimate right of the Jewish people to determine their cultural identity. David Ben Gurion remarked that the right of settlement of Jews in the State of Israel "is inherent in every Jew by virtue of his being a Jew." In addition, he observed that this right of settlement "preceded the State of Israel; it is that which built the State."[452] The right of return reflects the condition of the Jewish people. Once established as a nation-state, Jews have been dispersed for centuries in different countries around the world; yet, they have retained their Jewish national identity and connection with the land. The acquisition of nationality because of someone's ethnic identity is, incidentally, not unique for Israel. There are a number of other examples, such as the possibility for people of Greek origin to acquire Greek Nationality or the Law of the Republic of Armenia on Citizenship of the Republic of Armenia, which provides for a privileged position for people of Armenian origin when it comes to the acquisition of nationality.[453] Similarly, the Jewish people can be compared with the Greek and Armenian people, who were also dispersed and returned to their original land. The right of return may grant Jews favored status in respect of the capacity to become Israeli citizens, but once they become Israeli citizens they are in no more privileged a position than non-Jewish Israeli citizens.

451. See on this in general: Friedländer (1998), pp. 145-176.

452. Both quotes in: Gilbert (1999), p. 270.

453. See the following fragments of Article 15.2 of the Code of Greek Citizenship (2004): "People of Greek descent may acquire Greek citizenship provided there are no 'restrictive' conditions, as mentioned in sub-paragraph b, paragraph 1, of article 5 of this law, according to a decision issued by the Secretary General of the Prefecture, which must also be published in the Government's Gazette. (....) To establish the status of the person of Greek descent, the above committee interviews the interested party and evaluates the presented evidence proving said status."; and of Article 13 of the Law of the Republic of Armenia on Citizenship of the Republic of Armenia: "A person who is not an RA Citizen may be granted RA Citizenship without being subject to the conditions set forth in points 1) and 2) of the first part of this article, if he/she: (...) 3) is Armenian by origin (is of Armenian ancestry) (...)."

7.4.7 Racism and Apartheid?

Sometimes these expressions of Jewish national identity are regarded as racist or as evidence that Israel is an apartheid-state. The word "Apartheid" refers to the legal order based on racial supremacy, which prevailed in South Africa up to 1994. Sometimes, these unjustified and absurd claims are related to such national symbols as the flag, the anthem and state holidays.[454] Generally speaking, the allegations are limited to the nationality law. Also, in that case, the comparison is not valid. As was explained above, the Law of Return is an expression of the right to self-determination of the Jewish people, especially in respect of its cultural identity, as recognized in international law. In the context of naturalization laws, a system that gives preference to those who have historical links to the state concerned is, as has been explained, moreover not unique to Israel. This has so far not been a reason to disqualify these states concerned as being racist. So too, this allegation is unfounded in respect of Israel.[455]

It is inherent in the right to self-determination that the people concerned are entitled to determine their own cultural identity. Denial of the legitimate existence of the Jewish nation, such as in the Palestinian National Charter (1968), should be categorically condemned as an infringement of existing international law. The Jewish people have the same rights as any other people in this respect. They are entitled to express their Jewishness in the laws, institutions, customs, and practices of their nation. In the existing states of the world today, we see a wide variety of modalities regarding the relationship between religion and state. Apparently, the international community has no problem with explicitly Islamic states, such as Saudi Arabia, and official Christian states, like the United Kingdom, which recognizes the Anglican Church as the State Church. Some other states, like France, are explicitly secular. It is generally accepted that these identities do not at all exclude that all citizens enjoy equal religious, civil and political rights, although in some Islamic states, Muslims have a preference when it comes to human rights. These rights are recognized in the Israeli legal order *for all citizens*, irrespective of their religion. As in any state, in practice, they are, from time to time, infringed upon. An independent judiciary examines these infringements. The criticism of Israel as a Jewish state reflects a preference for either a secular state, in which religion is banished to the private sphere; or an Islamic state, in which Islam is the dominant religion and Judaism by definition has a *dhimmi* status. However, international law does not impose a specific

454. Glaser (2003).

455. The apartheid allegation is discussed in more detail in Chapter 16.

regime on the relation between religion and state. In fact it can be argued that the denial of the right of the Jewish people to self-determination in the form of a Jewish state reflects a modern form of anti-Semitism.[456]

7.5 Israel – A Democratic State

Israel is both a Jewish and a democratic state; it is neither a monarchy, nor a theocracy. Despite its Jewishness (or, some would argue, precisely *because* of its Jewishness), Israel is a modern democratic state that fully embodies the rule of law. Consider the following:

7.5.1 Fundamental Rights

The Declaration of the Establishment of the State of Israel (Declaration of Independence) asserts that the State of Israel will:

> **"[F]oster the development of the country for the benefit of all its inhabitants; it will be based on freedom, justice and peace as envisaged by the prophets of Israel; it will ensure complete equality of social and political rights to all its inhabitants irrespective of religion, race or sex; it will guarantee freedom of religion, conscience, language and culture."[457]**

The protection of human rights in Israel is not only proclaimed by the Declaration of Independence but also guaranteed in a series of "Basic Laws," which have been enacted since 1948. This fundamental legislation, according to the Israel Supreme Court, has a higher status than normal legislation.[458] These Basic Laws have a function comparable to written constitutions in other states.[459]

7.5.2 Legislature

Israel is a parliamentary democracy. The Parliament (Knesset) comprises 120 members elected on the basis of the principle of proportional representation. As a result, there are many different political parties represented in the Knesset that represent a wide variety of political, social, ethical, and religious opinions. Since 1948, there have always

---

456. As Martin Luther King already commented in the 1960's. See Cotler (2009), p. 5.

457. Like a number of other western democracies (such as the United Kingdom and New Zealand), Israel does not have a written constitution. In its absence, the Declaration constitutes the de facto charter of the State of Israel.

458. See Israel Supreme Court's statement on this issue (16 September 2013) in the cases of: Adam and others v. The Knesset and others (7146/12); Doe and others v. Ministry of Interior and others (1192/13); Tahangas and others v. Ministry of Interior (1247/13).

459. The protection of fundamental civil rights in Israeli law is addressed in more detail in Chapter 15.

been Arab and Druze members of the Knesset. In 2012, there were 15 non-Jewish members of the Knesset.[460]

7.5.3 Independent Judiciary

Israel recognizes and enforces the rule of law, which is reflected in the separation of powers between the legislature, executive, and judiciary. There is an independent judiciary in Israel.[461] The highest judicial body, the Supreme Court of Israel, is amongst the most well-respected appeal courts in the world.[462] The Supreme Court protects the individual civil and political rights of the citizens of Israel, and often criticizes the executive arm of government.

7.5.4 Military Service

Israeli men are required to do three years of military service from the age of 18 and serve one month every year thereafter until they are 50. Women must serve for two years. Israeli Druze must serve in the army; however, Israeli Arabs are exempted from military duty and are not required to perform any compensating civilian service. Since some of the surrounding Arab states are the avowed enemies of Israel and dedicated to its destruction (Israel has peace agreements with only Egypt and Jordan), this exemption is granted by the Israeli government to its Arab citizens, so as to spare them conflicts of loyalty and conscience. However, Israeli Arabs may voluntarily join the army.

460. *The Jerusalem Post*, 2 December 2012.

461. Barak (2002).

462. Dershowitz (2015).

PART III

Territorial Sovereignty and Boundaries

8. Historical Background of the Territorial Issues

> "The territorial boundaries of the Mandate for Palestine were laid down by various instruments, in particular on the eastern border by a British memorandum of 16 September 1922 and an Anglo-Transjordanian Treaty of 20 February 1928."
>
> Advisory Opinion (Paragraph 70)[463]

8.1 Introduction

In this Part, we examine questions related to the territorial status of the territory of Israel/Palestine. As we have earlier described, the centuries after the Israelites defeated the local tribes in Canaan in about 1500 BCE right up to 135 CE, the Jews were the most significant group of people living in Judea and Samaria—the area now commonly called East Jerusalem and the West Bank.[464] For hundreds of years, all of this area was part of the sovereign Kingdoms of Israel and Judah. For 1900 years after the destruction by the Romans of the Second Temple in 70 C., and the overthrow of the Jewish uprising and destruction of Jerusalem in 135 CE and until the Mandate for Palestine entered force in 1922, the territories comprising Jerusalem and the area of the West Bank were an indistinguishable portion of successive foreign-controlled empires. Throughout this period, there was a small but continual Jewish presence in the West Bank: mainly in cities such as Hebron and Bethlehem. Most of the West Bank was, by virtue of its rugged topographical character, sparsely populated. At no time prior to 1948 was the area devoid of Jews. Under the Mandate for Palestine, the term "Palestine" referred to the territory covered by the Mandate, and all residents of that territory (not

463. I.C.J. Reports 2004, p. 165.

464. The term 'West Bank' was adopted by Jordan in 1950 in order to erase the ancient Biblical geographical names 'Judea' and 'Samaria'. It had never been used before 1950, and this area was never recognized as an independent or separate territory prior to 1950. Israel officially refers to this area as Ezor Yehuda VeShomron ("The Judea and Samaria Area").

just Arabs) were "Palestinians." East Jerusalem and the West Bank were indivisibly part of this greater whole.

8.2 From the Palestine Mandate to the Six-Day War

The Mandate for Palestine comprised—after the separation of Transjordan in 1922—all of the area, with its western border being the Mediterranean Sea, and eastern border the Jordan River, and a line extending south from the Dead Sea to the Red Sea near Aqaba. In the Mandate period (from 1922 to the establishment of the state of Israel in 1948), the British divided the Mandate for Palestine territory into different districts for different purposes. Further geographical restrictions on Jewish settlement were imposed by the 1939 White Paper. The final reshuffling was in 1945, when the British re-divided Palestine into six districts and 16 sub-districts.[465] Throughout the Mandate for Palestine period, there was no difference in legal terms between the territory covered by what is Israel today and the West Bank: the whole of the territory west of the Jordan River was unequivocally part of the territory covered by the Mandate for Palestine. Under Article 6 of the Mandate for Palestine, Jews were to be encouraged and enabled to settle in any part of the Mandate territory. However, while Jerusalem was predominantly Jewish, relatively few Jews lived in other parts of the West Bank in the Mandate for Palestine period. This reflected British policy to concentrate Jewish immigration in the western and northern parts of mandate Palestine.

Despite the cease-fires negotiated with its enemies in 1949, during the period 1949-1967 Israel was still in a state of war with its Arab neighbors. Jordan, Syria, Egypt, and Lebanon—supported by Iraq and Saudi Arabia—did not give up their attitude of belligerent opposition to the existence of the infant Jewish nation. Tensions escalated when, in a provocative blockade of the Gulf of Akaba in 1955, Egypt cut off Israel's trade routes to Africa and Asia. This led to the Suez crisis and Israel's Sinai Campaign in which it captured the Sinai and Gaza. Israel withdrew in March 1957 under international pressure, and UN peacekeeping forces were installed in Gaza, Sharm el-Sheik and along the Sinai border, and Egypt continued to refuse to allow Israel access to the Suez Canal.

Britain and France gradually lost influence in the region after 1957. Though replaced to some extent by the increased presence of the United Nations (UN) (in Sinai/Gaza and later the Golan Heights) and upgraded involvement of the United States, it was the Soviet Union that became the

465. Bell & Kontorovich (2016).

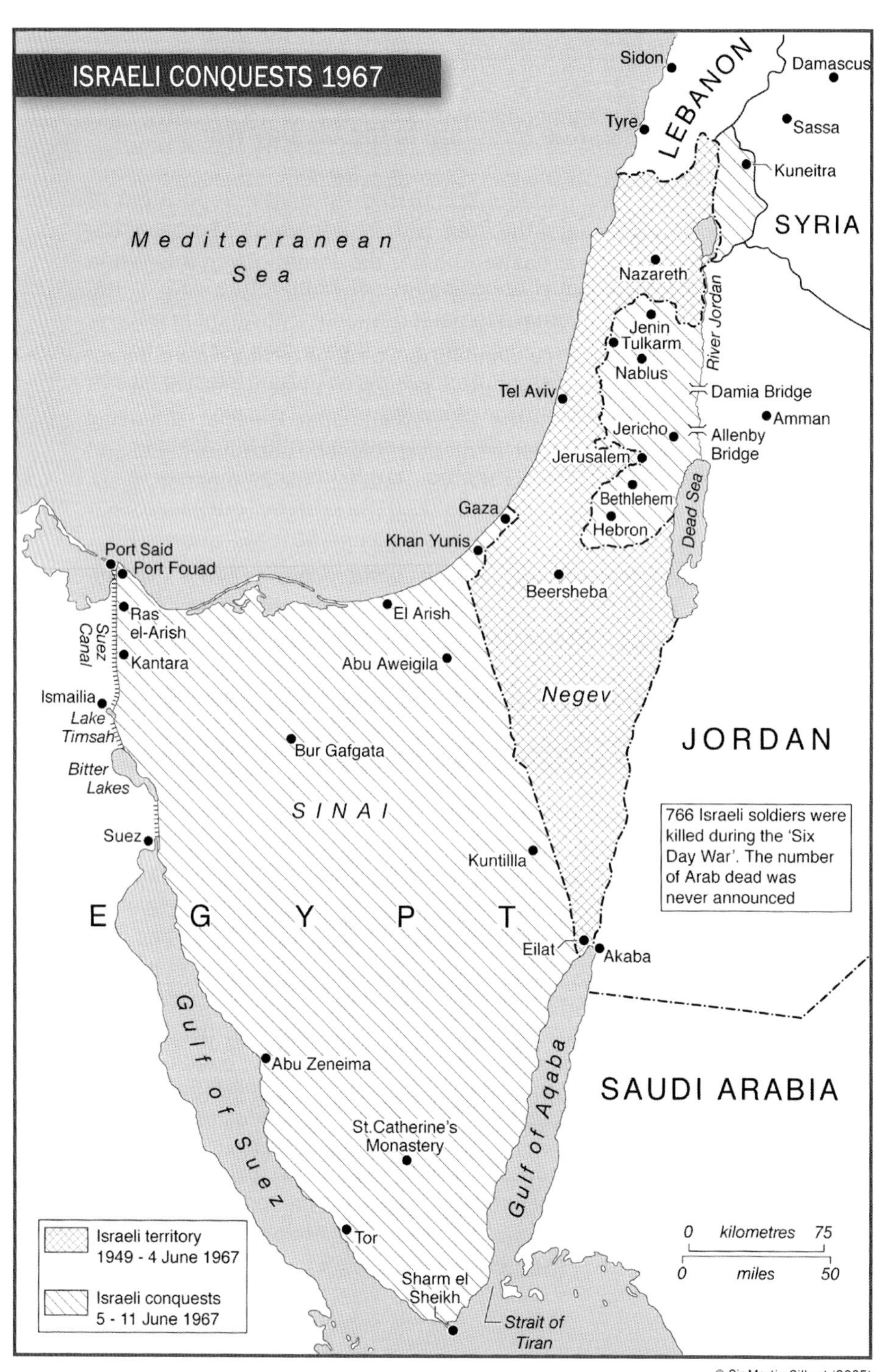
ISRAELI CONQUESTS 1967
Sidon
LEBANON
Damascus
Sassa
Tyre
Kuneitra
SYRIA
Mediterranean Sea
Nazareth
River Jordan
Jenin
Tulkarm
Nablus
Tel Aviv
Damia Bridge
Amman
Jericho
Allenby Bridge
Jerusalem
Bethlehem
Hebron
Dead Sea
Gaza
Khan Yunis
Port Said
Port Fouad
Beersheba
El Arish
Ras el-Arish
Suez Canal
Kantara
Abu Aweigila
Ismailia
Lake Timsah
Negev
Bur Gafgata
JORDAN
Bitter Lakes
SINAI
Suez
Kuntillla
766 Israeli soldiers were killed during the 'Six Day War'. The number of Arab dead was never announced
E G Y P T
Eilat
Akaba
Gulf of Suez
Gulf of Aqaba
Abu Zeneima
SAUDI ARABIA
St.Catherine's Monastery
Tor
Israeli territory 1949 - 4 June 1967
Israeli conquests 5 - 11 June 1967
Sharm el Sheikh
Strait of Tiran
0 kilometres 75
0 miles 50

region's dominant force. Between 1965 and 1973, for example, the Soviet Union—determined to consolidate its influence over the Mediterranean and Middle East—provided arms worth over US$8.7 billion to the Arab states (Egypt, Syria, Iraq, Algeria, Libya, Sudan, South Yemen). These arms, which were supplied via states like Czechoslovakia and paid with petro-dollars, were intended to be used in the ongoing struggle against Zionism.[466]

Israel was constantly on the alert for potential invasion by its Arab neighbor states. But it was also fighting another war. From 1950 onwards, terrorist groups in Gaza, Sinai and Jordan launched systematic raids into Israel, sponsored and supported by Egypt, Jordan, Syria, Lebanon and Saudi Arabia.[467] Between 1951 and 1955, Arab terrorists killed 967 Israelis.[468] "In an attempt to halt terrorist activity, the Israeli Government organized a series of raids, first against villages sheltering terrorists (up to 1953), then against regular terrorist and Egyptian military units."[469]

In April 1967, Syria—having entered into a defense treaty with Egypt—escalated its shelling of villages in northern Israel.[470] Israel responded by shooting down six Syrian MiG fighters. Syrian armed infiltrations of Israel increased. The Soviet Union actively encouraged Syria and Egyptian aggression. In May 1967, Egyptian President Gamal Abdel Nasser spoke openly of war, declaring that "the battle will be a general one, and our basic objective will be to destroy Israel."[471] On 16 May 1967, Egypt ordered the UN to partially withdraw its peacekeepers from the Negev and Sinai, where the UN Emergency Forces (UNEF) had been stationed since 1956. UN Secretary General U Thant refused. Nasser was not to be deterred. On 18 May 1967, Egypt responded to U Thant's refusal by demanding full UNEF withdrawal. By that time, Nasser had assembled 80,000 soldiers and 550 tanks on Israel's southern border. U Thant gave in; he ordered the UNEF to withdraw and decided to fly to Cairo to negotiate with Nasser. But before he arrived, Nasser ordered the closure of the Straits of Tiran, thereby blocking Israel shipping access to its most important ports. Israel rightly considered this to be an act of war.

---

466. Gilbert (2002), pp. 60 and 82.

467. *Ibid.*, p. 58.

468. *Ibid.*, p. 58.'Arabian' rather than 'Palestinian'.

469. *Ibid.*, p. 59.

470. A detailed analysis of the complex events leading up to the Six Day War is provided in Oren (2002). See also Gold (2004), pp. 91-99.

471. In a speech to Arab Trade Unionists on 26 May 1967. See Laqueur & Schueftan (eds.) (2016), p. 99.

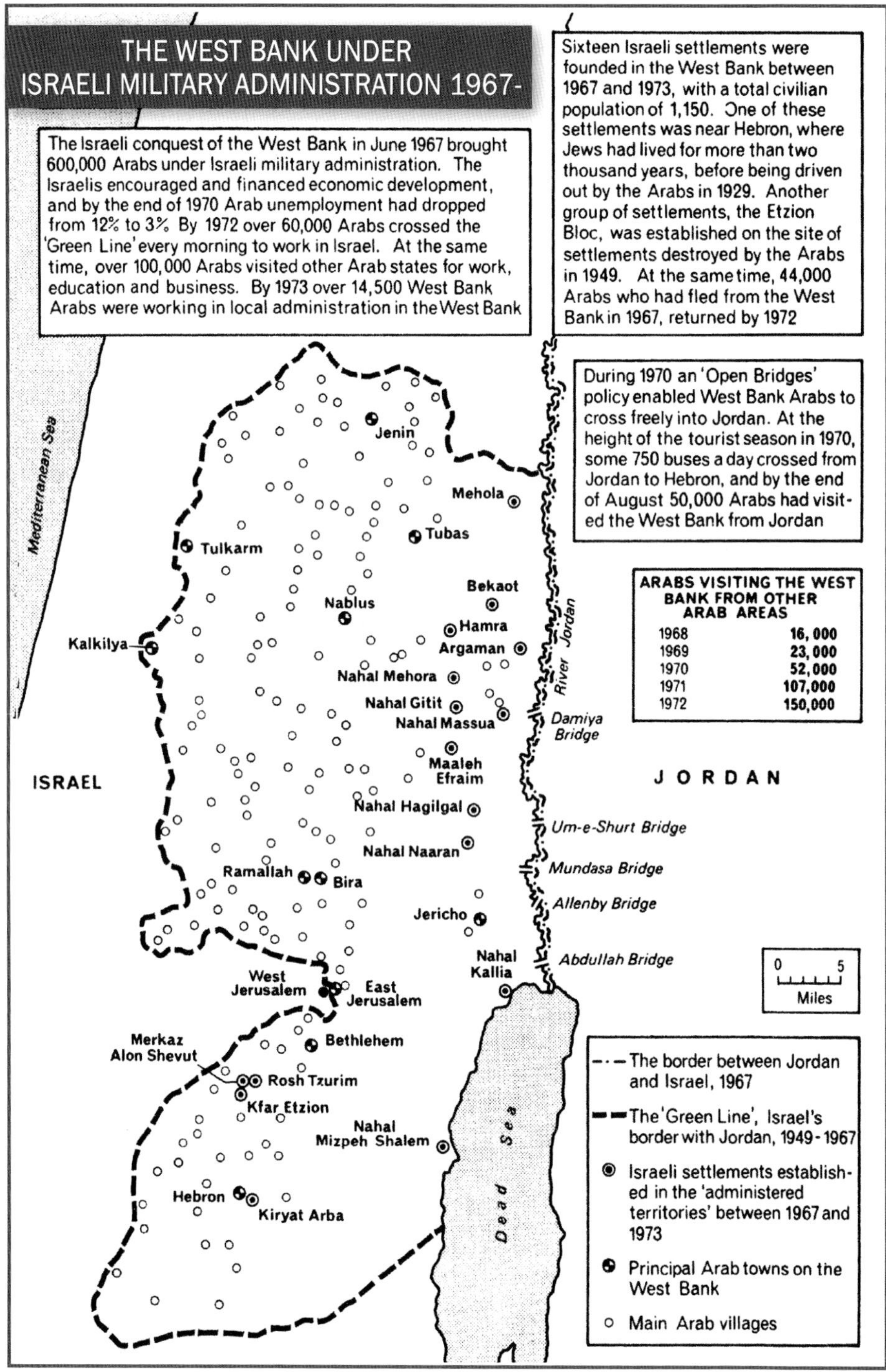
THE WEST BANK UNDER ISRAELI MILITARY ADMINISTRATION 1967-
The Israeli conquest of the West Bank in June 1967 brought 600,000 Arabs under Israeli military administration. The Israelis encouraged and financed economic development, and by the end of 1970 Arab unemployment had dropped from 12% to 3%. By 1972 over 60,000 Arabs crossed the 'Green Line' every morning to work in Israel. At the same time, over 100,000 Arabs visited other Arab states for work, education and business. By 1973 over 14,500 West Bank Arabs were working in local administration in the West Bank
Sixteen Israeli settlements were founded in the West Bank between 1967 and 1973, with a total civilian population of 1,150. One of these settlements was near Hebron, where Jews had lived for more than two thousand years, before being driven out by the Arabs in 1929. Another group of settlements, the Etzion Bloc, was established on the site of settlements destroyed by the Arabs in 1949. At the same time, 44,000 Arabs who had fled from the West Bank in 1967, returned by 1972
During 1970 an 'Open Bridges' policy enabled West Bank Arabs to cross freely into Jordan. At the height of the tourist season in 1970, some 750 buses a day crossed from Jordan to Hebron, and by the end of August 50,000 Arabs had visited the West Bank from Jordan
ARABS VISITING THE WEST BANK FROM OTHER ARAB AREAS
1968 16,000
1969 23,000
1970 52,000
1971 107,000
1972 150,000
Mediterranean Sea
Jenin
Mehola
Tubas
Tulkarm
Bekaot
Nablus
Hamra
Kalkilya
Argaman
Nahal Mehora
Nahal Gitit
Nahal Massua
River Jordan
Damiya Bridge
Maaleh Efraim
ISRAEL
JORDAN
Nahal Hagilgal
Um-e-Shurt Bridge
Nahal Naaran
Ramallah
Bira
Mundasa Bridge
Allenby Bridge
Jericho
Nahal Kallia
Abdullah Bridge
West Jerusalem
East Jerusalem
0 5 Miles
Bethlehem
Merkaz Alon Shevut
Rosh Tzurim
Kfar Etzion
Nahal Mizpeh Shalem
Dead Sea
Hebron
Kiryat Arba
The border between Jordan and Israel, 1967
The 'Green Line', Israel's border with Jordan, 1949-1967
Israeli settlements established in the 'administered territories' between 1967 and 1973
Principal Arab towns on the West Bank
Main Arab villages

During this period, Syria amassed its armies on the Golan Heights. In early June 1967, Jordan's King Hussein agreed to place his troops under Egyptian command, and to allow neighboring States to move their troops into Jordan, in readiness for an attack on Israel from the east, via the Jordanian-occupied West Bank. Accordingly, both Egypt and Iraq stationed massive troops in Jordan. By early June, over 250,000 troops, 2,000 tanks and 700 front-line aircraft stood ready to attack Israel.

Now surrounded, Israel decided to launch a pre-emptive strike. On the morning of 5 June 1967, Israel aircraft headed for Egypt's airfields, where they destroyed the Egyptian air force on the ground. At the same time, Israel passed on a message to Jordan: If Jordan would maintain the 1949 Armistice Lines, Israel would not attack Jordan. Jordan ignored this request and attacked Israel from the east. The result was a full-fledged war—involving Israel, Egypt, Jordan, Syria and Iraq—lasting six days and costing the lives of over 10,000 men, the vast majority of them Egyptian. Between 175,000 and 250,000 Palestinian Arabs fled the West Bank for Jordan, "many of them second-time refugees who were once again billeted in wretched camps."[472]

Not only did Israel survive this war, but in the course of only six days, it took control of over 67,000 km^2 of territory that had been under Arab control for the last 19 years: the Sinai desert, Gaza Strip, Golan Heights, and the West Bank (including the Old City of Jerusalem).

Israel did not enter the conflict with the intention to seize control of these territories.[473] But in the aftermath of the war, Israel was faced with a dilemma: to give up control of these territories or not, and if so under what conditions. Opinions varied within the Israeli Cabinet. On 19 June 1967, following a fierce debate, the Cabinet took a secret decision to exchange the Sinai Peninsula and Golan Heights for peace with Egypt and Syria, and to retain control over the Gaza Strip (Gaza). A consensus was reached to retain Jerusalem under Israeli sovereignty; no decision, however, could be reached on the future of the West Bank.[474]

In the subsequent months and years, Israeli policy regarding the West Bank remained ambivalent. The leadership was essentially divided into the "politicians" who favored the exchange of territories for peace, and the "security men" who, "for strategic and ideological reasons, insisted

472. Oren (2002), p. 306.

473. *Ibid.*, pp. 311-312.

474. *Ibid.*

on keeping most of the territories."[475] The latter argued that the previous effective "boundaries" between Israel and its neighbors—created by the 1949 Armistice Lines—were unsustainable. Former Israeli Foreign Minister Abba Eban even said the 1949 Lines "have a memory of Auschwitz."[476] Prime Minister Levi Eshkol sought to find a balance between the political and security concerns, arguing for demilitarized zones and IDF outposts, while negotiating peace treaties with Jordan, Egypt and Syria based on territorial concessions, resettling of Palestinian Arab refugees and the achievement of Palestinian self-rule. The Palestinians were divided, however, while Nasser (Egypt) and Hussein (Jordan) refused to contemplate peace based on anything less than the full return of all the territories now occupied by Israel. Some of the Jews who settled in Jerusalem and other communities in the Judean and Samarian hills after June 1967 were returning to properties which they (or their forebears) had owned prior to their displacement by the Jordanian and Egyptian armies in 1948. Examples of this are Hebron and Gush Etzion.

475. *Ibid.*, p. 314.

476. *Der Spiegel*, 5 November 1969.

9. Territorial Sovereignty and Boundaries

> **"Palestine was part of the Ottoman Empire. At the end of the First World War, a class 'A' Mandate for Palestine was entrusted to Great Britain by the League of Nations, pursuant to paragraph 4 of Article 22 of the Covenant, which provided that:**
> **'Certain communities, formerly belonging to the Turkish Empire have reached a stage of development where their existence as independent nations can be provisionally recognized subject to the rendering of administrative advice and assistance by a Mandatory until such time as they are able to stand alone.'"**

Advisory Opinion (Paragraph 70)[477]

> **"The international legal status of the Palestinian Territory (...) merits a more comprehensive treatment. (...) The point of departure (...) is the League of Nations Mandate (...)'**

Judge El Araby, Separate Opinion,(Paragraph 2.1)[478]

9.1 Introduction

When Israel unexpectedly took control over East Jerusalem and the West Bank in early June 1967, and the Six-Day War came to an end, the question arose: To whom did East Jerusalem and the West Bank belong? Was Israel entitled to annex these territories, on the basis that they belonged to the State of Israel? Or did they belong to Jordan, which had occupied them for 19 years? Or did they belong to the Palestinian Arabs, which constituted the main part of the population of these territories?

This is perhaps the most fundamental issue to be determined when considering the competing claims of Israel and the Palestine Liberation Organization (PLO) to these territories. International law comprises a number of principles that are essential to take into account when determining

477. I.C.J. Reports 2004, p. 165.

478. I.C.J. Reports 2004, p. 249.

this question. Yet, surprisingly, both the International Court of Justice (ICJ) in the Wall Advisory Opinion, and the United Nations (UN) Security Council in Resolution 2334, simply assume that these territories in 1967 somehow "belonged" to the Palestinian Arabs. This assumption is implicit, for example, in the use of the word "Palestinian" in the term "Occupied Palestinian Territories." The ICJ and the Security Council fail to provide any legal or factual arguments to support this claim. This failure is the root of much confusion in the diplomatic and public debates concerning the status of East Jerusalem and the West Bank.

9.2 Territorial Sovereignty and Integrity

Territorial Sovereignty

International law distinguishes between state sovereignty and territorial sovereignty. The first concerns the legal competence of a state to exercise its rights, liberties and powers in a specific territory, and the latter deals with the right of a state to a specific territory to the exclusion of other states. Territorial sovereignty is also described as "the fullest rights over territory known to law."[479] Public international law provides us with an approach to the question of what party holds territorial sovereignty over a territory by means of the legal concept of "title." The concept of title relates to the factual and legal conditions under which a territory is deemed to belong to one particular authority.[480] The notion of "title" thus comprehends both those facts that may create a sovereign right, and the actual source of those rights.

Under international law, there are essentially four types of territorial status: territorial sovereignty; a special type of regime such as that applicable under Mandates and Trusts; *terra nullius* (land that is not owned by any state); and *terra communis* (land governed by a special regime, such as the high seas).[481] The notion of territorial sovereignty under international law is analogous with the concepts of "ownership" and "title" under municipal law. Like ownership and title, sovereignty implies a bundle of rights to govern, administer and dispose of territory.[482]

Territorial sovereignty is thus a function of state sovereignty. This means that only states can possess and exercise territorial sovereignty.

479. Brierly (1963), p. 162.

480. Tams & Sloan (eds.), (2013), p. 154.

481. Brownlie (1990), p. 127.

482. *Ibid.*, pp. 108-109.

If—as we later argue—Palestine has not (yet) attained status as a state, this would seem to nullify any claims by Palestine to territorial sovereignty.

Inadmissibility of the Use of Force to Gain Territory

The traditional view is that there are five ways in which a state can obtain territorial sovereignty: occupation, accretion, cession, conquest and prescription.[483] Today, international law does not allow sovereignty to be acquired by force: The use or threat of force by states to settle disputes or otherwise effect territorial gain is illegal.[484] This means that the territorial gains of Egypt (Gaza and Sinai) and Jordan (East Jerusalem and the West Bank) during the 1947-1949 War of Independence were illegal and ineffective, as they resulted from the use of force by these and other states against the fledgling State of Israel in May 1948. Similarly, if—as we will argue—the Six-Day War was from Israel's perspective a defensive war, the principle that the use of force to gain territory is illegal means that none of the aggressive states could have acquired title to any of these territories in those conflicts.

Israel did not obtain sovereignty as a result of victory in the June 1967 war. But neither did the conflict affect any pre-existing title that Israel may have had over those territories. Further, because it was acting defensively, Israel is entitled to retain control (possession) of these territories pending the reaching of a binding peace treaty settling the dispute. Whether or not Israel had title with respect to East Jerusalem and the West Bank upon its creation as a state in May 1948 or upon its gaining control of those territories in June 1967 must be determined by the application of general principles of international law relating to territorial sovereignty applicable at that time.

"Territorial Integrity"

The State of Israel, like every other state, has a right to territorial integrity, and other states and international actors are obliged to respect this right. The principle of territorial integrity refers to the right to existence of a state within a given territory, the borders of which are well-defined and recognized by international law.[485] The notion can be divided into

483. *Ibid.*, p.131.

484. See UN Charter, art. 2(4) and the following quote from the Declaration on Principles of International Law concerning Friendly Relations and Co-operation among States in accordance with the Charter of the United Nations (Annex UN G.A. Res. 2625 (XXV)): "[T]he territory of a State shall not be the object of acquisition by another State resulting from the threat or use of force. No territorial acquisition resulting from the threat or use of force shall be recognized as legal." See further: Shaw (2008), pp. 500-502.

485. El Ouali (2012), p. 8.

material and non-material elements.[486] The material element covers the "physical and demographic resources that lie within the territory (land, sea and air space) and are delimited by the State's frontiers."[487] This brings forth the idea that territorial limits of a sovereign state cannot be altered against the will of the state and the protection of these limits exists as an international responsibility. The non-material element of territorial integrity understands the territory as the exclusive zone in which the political independence of a state can find its expression and where foreign governments may not—as a matter of principle—interfere.[488]

Determination of Territorial Boundaries

For the most part, territorial boundaries are settled by routine diplomatic negotiations between the respective territorial sovereigns of which the outcomes are subsequently reflected in (boundary) treaties. Another method for the determination of boundaries is the submission of disputes to international adjudication; states may resort to third-party negotiation or may by special agreement or compromise appoint an ad hoc court or arbitration.[489] If states accept the jurisdiction of the ICJ, for example, they can also submit their case before the ICJ whose decision will be binding upon the parties and "for all practical purposes upon all states in the absence of maintained protest."[490] Subsequently, in the determination of the boundaries, these international judicial actors will frequently apply general principles of law such as the rights of states to territorial integrity, *uti possidetis juris*, acquiescence and estoppel as well as take into account geographical, ethnographical and economic factors.

Israel's borders with Egypt and Jordan have been determined in agreement by means of the Peace Treaties with those nations. In the case of the PLO, the question of the boundary between Israel and the Palestinian entity (whether it be a state or other entity) is the subject of negotiation pursuant to the terms of the Oslo Accords. In the process of negotiations, no doubt the international law principle of territorial integrity will play an important role. Similarly, the United Nations, the European Union and any third state or international organization that seeks to involve itself in these negotiations are bound to respect the rights of all states in the region—including the State of Israel—to territorial integrity.

486. *Encyclopedia of Public International Law* (1987), p. 481.

487. *Ibid.*

488. Marxsen (2015), p. 10.

489. Prescott & Triggs (2008), p. 140.

490. Shaw (2008), p. 497.

Relationship between Territorial Sovereignty and Humanitarian Law

It is often argued (and seems to be implied by the ICJ in the Wall Advisory Opinion) that the fact that Israel "occupied" these territories in June 1967 somehow means it is not entitled to claim sovereignty over them. The ICJ uses the term "occupation," without further explanation, to infer that Israel took control of territory that did not belong to Israel. However, this is to confuse two very different areas of law. The law concerning territorial sovereignty is concerned with sovereign title (ownership), not with the conduct of the sovereign power or the rights of individuals living in that territory. The law of belligerent occupation is concerned with the conduct of the power that controls the territory and the rights of civilians on those territories—and not with the question who "owns" those territories.

The fact that Israel may have become an "occupying power" as a matter of either law of fact after the Six-Day War does not affect the question of who "owned" East Jerusalem and the West Bank at the outset of the Six-Day War, or the ongoing claims of any of the relevant parties to territorial sovereignty. The principles of international law concerning sovereignty and title to territory operate independently from international human rights and humanitarian law. It is perfectly possible that a state that, in the course of defensive war, takes control of territory claimed by its neighbor, may simultaneously have a legally valid claim to such territory, based on prior events, while at the same time becoming an "occupying power" within the meaning of the law of belligerent occupation. In the case of Israel, this means that—assuming Israel has not subsequently waived its rights or transferred sovereignty to another party—the finding that Israel is an "occupying power" with respect to East Jerusalem and the West Bank, and/or that the Palestinian Arabs have a legitimate claim to autonomy (self-government) within those territories, and/or that individual Arabs or Jews may have individual human rights (such as the right to worship) do not prejudice Israel's underlying claims to sovereignty over those territories based on events prior to 1967.

The Rule of Inter-Temporality

Questions of territorial sovereignty and title based on past events must be determined according to the law applicable at the time of the relevant events. According to Brownlie, "the fact is that in many instances the rights of parties to a dispute derive from legally significant acts, or a treaty concluded, very long ago." [491] The legal relevance of such acts is to be

491. Brownlie (1990), p. 129; Fitzmaurice (1953), pp. 5-8.

determined on the basis of the rules of international law applicable at the time. This means that in order to determine the legal status of Jerusalem and the West Bank, it is necessary to go back to all the successive events that could have affected the territorial status of those territories. The key dates and events that possibly could have created or affected sovereignty over these territories prior to 1967 were:

- The decision of the Principal Allied Powers at San Remo in April 1920
- The creation of the Mandate for Palestine by the League of Nations in 1922
- Turkey's relinquishment of the territory of Palestine under the Treaty of Lausanne in 1923
- The UN General Assembly's Partition Plan in November 1947
- The termination of the Mandate for Palestine and the creation of the State of Israel in May 1948
- The War of Independence and the subsequent belligerent occupation of East Jerusalem and the West Bank by Jordan in 1949
- The Armistice Agreement between Israel and Jordan in 1949

The legal significance of each of those events must be examined by application of the relevant rules of international law at the time of such event.

9.3 What Was the Territorial Sovereign Status of East Jerusalem and the West Bank in June 1967?

Applying the above principles, let us seek to answer the question: Which state or international actor (if any) possessed territorial sovereignty with respect to East Jerusalem and the West Bank in June 1967?

While the law and practice of states in relation to territorial sovereignty and title to land is extremely complex, and subject to change over time as circumstances develop, and the application of these rules to Israel/Palestine is made even more difficult by the complex history of these territories, nevertheless, there is no doubt that international law throws light on the question of the status of East Jerusalem and the West Bank. It is therefore quite remarkable that the ICJ devoted very little attention in the Wall Advisory Opinion to the question of the status under international law of the territories that were described as "Occupied Palestinian Territories," either at the date upon which the State of Israel came into existence in 1948 or at the commencement of the Six-Day War in 1967. The answer to that question would have brought clarity to the question of the status of those territories when Israel gained control over them in June 1967. Instead, the ICJ limited its analysis to examination of the question whether international humanitarian and human rights law are applicable in these territories—especially the applicability of the Fourth Geneva Convention 1949 to these territories.

This was no doubt the result of the fact that the framing of the UN General Assembly's request, and the submissions made to the ICJ, focused only on those issues. Israel's potential "ownership" or "sovereignty" with respect to these territories was simply not submitted to the ICJ, and therefore was not discussed by the ICJ. Israel itself did not address the question of the sovereign status of these territories in its own submissions, which purposefully did not deal with the substantive issues but were limited to questions related to the ICJ's jurisdiction. Other states had no interest to make submissions about Israel's possible sovereignty over those territories prior to 1967. As a result, apart from one short paragraph describing the Mandate for Palestine, the ICJ virtually ignored the question of "ownership" of the land prior to 1967, and came to the conclusion that the Fourth Geneva Convention is applicable regardless of whether these territories "belonged" to the State of Israel or any other particular state.

9.3.1 Sovereign Title Created, Transferred or Recognized by the San Remo Resolution and the Mandate for Palestine

As the ICJ stated in the Wall Advisory Opinion, Palestine "was part of the Ottoman Empire" for 400 years until the end of WWI. But this statement says nothing about the sovereign territorial status of Palestine prior to or after the collapse of that Empire.

It can be argued that the Jewish people received title from the Principal Allied and Associated Powers, which through their victory in the War (and later the terms of the Treaty of Lausanne) obtained sovereign title to the ex-Turkish territories. In his extensive study of Sovereignty over the Old City of Jerusalem, Gauthier observes: "Although the Principal Allied and Associated Powers did not immediately acquire full sovereignty rights, they possessed most of the rights and attributes normally associated with the concept of sovereignty under international law."[492] Gauthier, relying on Professor Brownlie's analysis of the disposition of the German territories, argues that, because the Principal Allied and Associated Powers had (under international law at that time) the "power of dispossession," the decision of the Allied Powers as expressed in the San Remo Resolution was in and of itself effective to transfer title to the beneficiaries of the proposed Mandate system—the Jewish people. He also argues that "[s]ince the ex-Turkish territories were treated by the Principal Allied Powers

492. Gauthier (2007), p. 334.

basically in the same way as the ex-German territories, it is arguable that similar 'reversionary interests' were still possessed by the Principal Allied Powers in respect to Palestine after the Paris Peace Conference,"[493]

There can be no doubt that the "national home" for the Jewish people that is referred to in the San Remo Resolution and later in the Mandate for Palestine was intended to include East Jerusalem and the West Bank. In the preamble to the Mandate for Palestine, the members of the League of Nations give their recognition to "the historical connection of the Jewish people with Palestine." There can be no doubt that, owing to the close relationship of the Jews with Jerusalem, Judea and Samaria, this Jewish national home was intended to encompass Jerusalem and the West Bank at the very least. This is because the Principal Allied Powers gave recognition to the right of the Jewish people to self-determination based on the historic connection of the Jewish people to the land where their forefathers had previously lived. The Old City of Jerusalem and the area known to the Jewish people as "Judea" and "Samaria" are at the heart of this historical connection, going back as far as 2100 BCE.[494]

US President Woodrow Wilson stated that "the Allied Powers, with the full concurrence of their own Government and people [were] agreed that in Palestine should be laid the foundations of a Jewish Commonwealth."[495] And although these Allied Powers did not intend the immediate establishment of this Jewish State, it was clearly understood by the leaders of the Allied Powers that its reconstruction was, as was already formulated by the British War Cabinet in 1917, "*a matter of gradual development* in accordance with the ordinary laws of political evolution."[496]

9.3.2 Territorial Sovereignty over Palestine during the Mandate Period

Even if the San Remo Resolution and Mandate for Palestine were effective to confer on the Jewish people, in recognition of their right to self-determination in Palestine, certain sovereign rights with respect to the territory of Palestine, the question arises: Where was sovereignty before the Jewish people were able to fully exercise this right? Where was territorial sovereignty over Palestine located during the Mandate period? This question has been the subject of much debate. Basically, four lines of argument have been advanced.

---

493. *Ibid.*, p. 335.

494. See Chapter 5.

495. Andrews (1931), p. 360.

496. War Cabinet minutes, 31 October 1917 (emphasis added).

A first line of argument is based on the view that territorial sovereignty during the Mandate for Palestine period remained with the Jewish people, being the recipients of the transfer of title under the San Remo Resolution, even though they did not obtain full control of these territories until much later. Grief explains this by arguing that the Jewish People acquired *de jure* (legal) but not *de facto* (actual) title in 1920.[497] *De facto* (actual) title was conferred on Britain as Mandatory, which had the responsibility to facilitate the creation of a Jewish homeland in Palestine. Although title (sovereignty) was ultimately intended for the Jewish People once they reached self-determination, Britain in the meantime "exercised the attributes of sovereignty, particularly the power of enacting legislation, except as limited by the terms of the Mandate." Britain thus held sovereignty "in abeyance for the Jewish People until Palestine could be developed as an independent Jewish State, a process that required as much time as it would take to enable the Jews to become a majority in Palestine through immigration and their recognized right of return."[498] Upon its creation in 1948, the State of Israel—being an expression of the Jewish people's self-determination—inherited the rights previously conferred on "the Jewish people." The result of this reasoning is that when Israel took possession of East Jerusalem and the West Bank in June 1967, it was taking physical possession of territory that—as a matter of law—already belonged to Israel.

Second, there are scholars who argue that "sovereignty was in abeyance" during the period of the British rule under the Mandate for Palestine until the independence of the State of Israel. In his Separate Opinion attached to the Advisory Opinion in the South West Africa case in 1950, Judge McNair implies that the objective of the Mandate system is eventually the emergence of sovereign states: "Sovereignty over a Mandated Territory is in abeyance; if and when the inhabitants of a Territory obtain recognition as an independent State (...) sovereignty will revive and vest in the new State."[499] Stahn describes the Mandate system as a "special type of foreign

497. Grief (2008), pp. 136-147, argues that although Israel did not enjoy de facto (actual) sovereignty - effective control - over the whole Mandate territory at this moment (as the UNSCOP report of 1947 shows, the Jewish administration exercised control only over the "western" and "northern" parts of the country), Israel continued to maintain de jure (legal) sovereignty over the whole territory of the Mandate, as factual restrictions do not infringe on legal title itself. The International Court of Justice has confirmed this line of reasoning in other cases by arguing that legal title is accorded with pre-eminence over effective possession as a basis of sovereignty (Frontier Dispute (Burkina Faso. V. Mali), Judgment, I.C.J. 1986, 23 (22 December 1986), and Frontier Dispute (Benin. V. Niger), Judgment, I.C.J. 2005, 47 (12 July 2005).

498. Grief (2008), p. 137.

499. *International Status of South West Africa,* Advisory Opinion, 1950 I.C.J. Reports, p. 150 (11 July 1950).

administration under which states exercised non-sovereign powers over (not yet sovereign) people as agents of the League."[500] Consequently and in view of this theory, Mandate territories did not become part of another state and did also not fall under the sovereignty of supervising international organizations.[501]

The third theory is that sovereignty rested with the League of Nations and the Mandatory jointly.[502] In support of this theory, Lauterpacht argues that through the establishment of the Mandate for Palestine, "a tacit transfer by the Principal Powers to the League of Nations"[503] took place and that by this transfer, the League of Nations derived its sovereignty over Palestine.

A fourth theory is that the Principal Allied Powers retained sovereignty over Palestine during the Mandate period. As result of the Treaty of Lausanne, Turkey had renounced its sovereignty claims over the territory of Palestine in favor of the Principal Allied Powers. Another indication for this view would be that the Allied Powers had agreed that the determination of the boundaries of Palestine would rest with them.[504] And, these Powers only restricted their obtained sovereignty by entrusting the administration of the territory of Palestine to a Mandatory.

9.3.3 Continuation of the Territorial Rights of Israel and the Jewish People after 1948

By the late 1930s, the League of Nations had become dysfunctional, and it was finally dissolved in July 1946. It was in effect replaced by the UN, which came into existence in 1945. This brought to an end the system of Mandates under the League of Nations, and the role and responsibilities of the League and the Permanent Mandate Commission in relation to the existing Mandates. The dissolution of the League of Nations did not—and could not—terminate the rights and obligations under the Mandate for Palestine itself, nor the pre-existing rights of the Jewish people or the obligations of the United Kingdom as Mandatory, because these had originally been conferred by the Allied Powers, not the League.[505]

The principle of estoppel arguably prohibits the Allied Powers of World

---

500. Stahn (2008), p. 88.

501. Wilde (2008), p. 167.

502. Lauterpacht, Hersch (1977 a), p. 68.

503. *Ibid.*

504. Preamble to the San Remo Resolution and Preamble to the Mandate for Palestine.

505. See Gauthier (2004), p. 561.

War I (The United Kingdom, Italy, France and Japan) from denying the validity of the rights which they granted to the Jewish people in the context of the Covenant of the League of Nations, as expressed in the San Remo Resolution, and which were consummated in the Mandate for Palestine.[506] The same principle applies to all states that were members of the Council of the League of Nations that adopted the Mandate for Palestine in 1922. It can be applied also to the Central Powers of World War I, who recognized the Mandate system, as well as to all Member States of the League.[507]

The UN was entitled to assume certain responsibilities of the League of Nations with respect to the Mandate system and existing Mandates. But it did not–and could not–take over the role of Britain as Mandatory. The UN and its Member States should, according to Article 80 of the UN Charter, respect the rights of the Jewish people and other peoples under the Mandates. It states:

> **"Except as may be agreed upon in individual trusteeship agreements, made under Articles 77, 79, and 81, placing each territory under the trusteeship system, and until such agreements have been concluded, nothing in this Chapter shall be construed in or of itself to alter in any manner the rights whatsoever of any states or any peoples or the terms of existing international instruments to which Members of the United Nations may respectively be parties."**

This provision constitutes part of the transitional arrangements from the system of Mandates under the League of Nations to the system of the UN Charter. No attempt was made to place Palestine under the Trusteeship system, and a Trusteeship Agreement for Palestine was never created.[508] Resolution 181 (II) adopted by the General Assembly (GA) on 29 November 1947, was a non-binding decision by the General Assembly with recommendations on the future of the Mandate territory; it was *not* a Trusteeship Agreement. Such an Agreement is a treaty to be agreed upon by the states directly concerned, including the mandatory power.[509] In Resolution 181 (II) there is a reference to the Trusteeship Council (a supervisory organ established by the UN Charter) as an authority which is involved in the proposed special international regime for the City of

506. Grief (2008), pp.175-222.

507. *Ibid.*, pp. 216-217.

508. After 1949 it was no longer possible to subject the territory of Palestine to the UN Trusteeship system, as Israel had by then become a recognized State and a Member of the United Nations: see UN Charter, art 78.

509. UN Charter, art. 79.

Jerusalem, but this does not make the Resolution the equivalent of a Trusteeship Agreement. The Trusteeship Council itself made this clear in December 1947: "Although the General Assembly of the United Nations vested the Trusteeship Council with power to define, to constitute and to administer the international regime of the City of Jerusalem, it is obvious that the City is not a trust territory..."[510]

Article 80 of the UN Charter is extremely important. The fact that it is often referred to as the "Palestine Article" or the "Palestine Clause" reflects the fact that it was drafted with the rights of the Jewish people under the Mandate for Palestine in mind.[511] From the drafting history, it is clear that a Jewish delegation present at the San Francisco Conference in 1945 intended to protect the right of settlement of the Jewish people guaranteed by the Mandate.[512] It was successful in having the word *peoples* included in the text, which was missing in the original draft. All participants in the discussions of the draft knew that the term *peoples* referred to the Jewish people in Palestine.[513] By including this term, the drafters of the UN Charter explicitly observed the general principle of law requiring respect for acquired legal rights.[514]

The ICJ has also underlined the relevance of the rights bestowed by a Mandate on the people concerned. The ICJ argued in 1950 for the continuing relevance of the obligations and rights under a Mandate as follows:

> **"Their *raison d' être* and original object remain. Since their fulfillment did not depend on the existence of the League of Nations, they could not be brought to an end merely because this supervisory organ ceased to exist. Nor could the right of the population to have the Territory administered in accordance with these rules depend thereon. This view is confirmed by Article 80, paragraph 1, of the Charter, which maintains the rights of States and peoples and the terms of existing international instrument until the territories in question are placed under the Trusteeship System."[515]**

In an Advisory Opinion in 1971, the ICJ again emphasized the continuing relevance of the rights of a people under a Mandate after the dissolution

---

510. Quoted by Stahn (2008), p. 101 (footnote 48).

511. Grief (2008), p. 257. See also: Lauterpacht, Hersch (1977 b), at p. 108.

512. See Rostow (1993), pp. 10 and 15; Gold (2007), p. 131; Auerbach (2012): http://www.nysun.com/foreign/how-bezion-netanyahu-helped-put-in-the-un/87809/.

513. Grief (2008), p. 257; Rostow (1993), p. 10.

514. See on general principles of law as a source of law Chapter 1.

515. *International Status of South-West Africa Case*, Advisory Opinion, 1950 I.C.J. Reports, pp. 128, 133 (11 July 1950).

of the League of Nations.[516] Unfortunately, the ICJ did not follow these precedents when the issue of the relevance of the Mandate for Palestine for the rights of settlement of the Jewish people was at stake in the Wall Advisory Opinion in 2004.[517]

9.4 The "Uti Possidetis Juris" Principle and Its Application to Israel/Palestine

9.4.1 General

Some authors argue that upon its establishment in May 1948, the borders of the State of Israel were determined by the international legal principle known as "*uti possidetis juris.*"[518] According to Bell and Kontorovich, this principle is decisive in the determination of the borders and scope of territorial sovereignty of the State of Israel both upon its establishment in 1948, and today.[519] Surprisingly, little attention has been given to this doctrine in the debates about the Israel/Palestine conflict and the territorial scope of the State of Israel. Yet, "Israel's independence would appear to fall squarely within the bounds of circumstances that trigger the rule of *uti possidetis juris*. Applying the rule would appear to dictate that Israel's borders are those of the Palestine Mandate that preceded it, except where otherwise agreed upon by Israel and its relevant neighbor." [520]

Uti possidetis juris is one of the main principles of customary international law intended to ensure stability, certainty and continuity in the demarcation of boundaries. It "clarifies and determines the territorial boundaries of newly emerging states by providing that states emerging from decolonization shall presumptively inherit the colonial administrative borders that they held at the time of independence."[521] In effect, the principle of *uti possidetis juris* transforms the colonial and administrative lines existing at the moment of the birth of the new State into national borders. The principle "applies to the State as it is [at the moment of independence], i.e. to the 'photograph' of the territorial situation then

516. *Legal Consequences for States of the Continued Presence of South Africa in Namibia (South West Africa) notwithstanding Security Council Resolution 276 (1970)*, Advisory Opinion, 1971 I.C.J. Reports, pp. 33-38 (21 June 1971).

517. *Legal Consequences of the Construction of a Wall in the Occupied Palestinian Territory*, Advisory Opinion, 2004 I.C.J. Reports, pp. 136-203 (9 July 2004).

518. Bell & Kontorovich (2016).

519. Professor Malcolm Shaw reviews the content, background and modern application of this legal principle: see Shaw (1997).

520. Bell & Kontorovich (2016), at p. 637.

521. Ratner (1996).

existing."[522] According to Brownlie,[523] application of the principle of *uti possidetis juris* to determine the borders of post-colonial states is not mandatory, but it "is in accordance with good policy."

This principle has been applied to determine the borders and thus also the scope of territorial sovereignty of almost all new states that have emerged in the last century. *Uti possidetis juris* has determined the borders of states emerging from the de-colonialization process in Latin America (e.g. El Salvador, Honduras, Nicaragua, Argentina, Chile and Brazil), Africa (e.g. Benin, Nigeria, Mali, Burkina Faso, Togo, Ghana, Cameroon, Namibia, Uganda, Ruanda, Burundi, Eritrea, Ethiopia, Tunisia and Libya), Asia (e.g. Cambodia/Thailand) and the Pacific region (e.g. New Guinea, Samoa, Nauru and East Timor). More recently, it has also been used to determine the borders of the states emerging from the dissolution of the Soviet Union (e.g. Russia/Ukraine), Czechoslovakia (Czech and Slovak Republics), and former Yugoslavia (e.g. Serbia, Croatia). It is the principle upon which the borders of many states in the Middle East that emerged from the post-WWI Mandate system have been determined and are universally recognized: e.g. Syria, Lebanon, Iraq and Jordan. It was on the basis of this principle that the international community intervened after Iraq's attack on Kuwait in 1990 and the Iraq/Kuwait border was subsequently established by the UN-appointed border demarcation Commission along the Mandatory Lines. More recently, it is the principle upon which the international community almost universally objected to Russia's unilateral intervention in the Crimea.

9.4.2 What Were the Administrative Boundaries of Palestine under the Mandate?

The San Remo Resolution and the Mandate for Palestine did not specifically define the borders of the Mandate territory of Palestine as these were to be fixed by the Principal Allied Powers.[524] In the years following the San Remo Resolution of 1920, the Principal Allied Powers proceeded in fixing the boundaries of Palestine. The first determination of the northern boundary came by the British-French boundary agreement of 1920, which determined that the Mandate for Palestine was to include the Golan Heights.[525] The boundary line between "the Greater Lebanon and

522. The ICJ in the *Frontier Dispute* (Burkina Faso v Mali), I.C.J. Reports 1986, pp. 554 ff., at p 568.

523. Brownlie (1990), p. 135.

524. Mandate for Palestine, preamble.

525. See: The Franco-British [Boundary] Convention of December 23, 1920, art 1. See also: Marshall (ed.) (2002), p. 35.

Syria on the one side and Palestine on the other side" was demarcated more specifically in 1922 and received effect on 7 March 1923.[526] Under this agreement, however, the Golan Heights were referred to as falling under the Mandate for Syria.[527]

In the first instance the Principal Allied Powers had agreed that the territory of Palestine was to include the territories lying between the Jordan River and the eastern boundary of Palestine (also known as "Transjordan"). However, eventually the eastern boundary of Palestine was determined by the Palestine Order-in-Council, which was then communicated by way of a note to the Council of the League of Nations in September 1922. In Article 2 of this note, it was formulated that the provisions of "the Mandate for Palestine are not applicable to the territory known as Trans-Jordan, which comprises all territory lying to the east of a line drawn from a point two miles west of the town of Akaba on the Gulf of that name up the centre of the Wadi Araba, Dead Sea and River Jordan to its junction with the River Yarmuk: thence up the centre of that river to the Syrian Frontier."[528] The British government could take this step under Article 25 of the Mandate, provided the Council of the League of Nations would consent. On 16 September 1922, just two months after the adoption of the Mandate for Palestine, the Council of the League of Nations approved the decision of the British government to withhold the application of the provisions of the Mandate to these territories and to accept their full responsibility as Mandatory for Transjordan.[529] This was confirmed in an Anglo-Transjordanian Treaty of 20 February 1928.

The southern boundary between Palestine and Egypt was established by a boundary agreement between the British and the Ottomans in 1906.

---

526. Agreement between His Majesty's Government and the French Government respecting the Boundary Line between Syria and Palestine from the Mediterranean to El-Hamme, *Treaty Series*, No. 13 (7 March 1923).

527. The transfer of the Golan Heights to France is arguably in breach of the original intention of the Mandate for Palestine; pursuant to the Mandate's article 5 no Palestine territory was to be transferred to or placed under the control of a foreign power. The Golan Heights became a part of Syria upon Syria's independence in April 1946.

528. Note by the Secretary-General Relating to its Application to the Territory known as Transjordan under the provisions of Article 25, December 1922. Subsequently, the Israel-Jordan Peace Treaty in 1994 determined the international boundary between Israel and Jordan "with reference to the boundary definition under the Mandate [for Palestine]."

529. Article 25 of the Mandate for Palestine and article 3 of the 'Memorandum by the British Representative' to the Mandate for Palestine.

This line served only as an "administrative separating line"[530] between Egypt and Palestine and did not have the status of an international boundary.[531]

9.4.3 The Application of the Principle of "uti possidetis juris" to the Palestine Mandate

The administrative borders of Palestine at the time of Israel's independence in 1948 were thus the boundaries of the Mandate as they had been demarcated by the parties in these various boundary agreements. *Uti possidetis juris* operates to change these administrative borders into international boundaries upon the moment of independence of the State of Israel on 14 May 1948. As a consequence of the application of this principle, the entire Mandate territory became the territory of the newly independent state.[532] As a matter of fact and law, application of this principle means that at the moment of its birth on 14 May 1948, the State of Israel automatically obtained territorial sovereignty over the territories within the boundaries of the Mandate as applicable at that date.

Israel's peace treaties with neighboring states to date—with Egypt[533] and Jordan[534]—appear to confirm and reinforce the application of the principle of *uti possidetis juris*. In clear terms, both treaties explicitly ratify the borders between Israel and its neighbors based on the boundaries of the British Mandate for Palestine.

9.4.4 Some Objections against Israeli Sovereignty over the Territories

The argument could be put forth that the State of Israel did not have effective control over East Jerusalem and the West Bank at the moment of its independence; consequently, it could not be considered to have sovereignty over them. However, this view should be rejected, since the relevant legal question is not which territories where physically controlled

---

530. This term was deliberately chosen, in order to distinguish it from a boundary line with an international or quasi-international character. See: Kliot (1995), p. 7.

531. Biger (2004), p. 80. The Israel-Egypt Peace Treaty of March 1979 subsequently transformed the 1906 line into an international boundary.

532. Land, Island and Maritime Frontier Dispute (El Salvador/Honduras, Nicaragua intervening), 1992 I.C.J. Reports, 351, 42 (11 September 1992) - the Court noted here that one of the purposes of *uti possidetis juris* is to avoid that there is a territory without a sovereign (*terra nullius*).

533. Treaty of Peace art. 2, Egypt-Isr., Mar. 26, 1979, reprinted in: 18 I.L.M. 362 (1979) ("The permanent boundary between Egypt and Israel is the recognized international boundary between Egypt and the former mandated territory of Palestine...").

534. Treaty of Peace Between The State of Israel and The Hashemite Kingdom of Jordan, art. 3, Isr.-Jordan, Oct. 26, 1994, 34 I.L.M. 43 (1995) ("The international boundary between Israel and Jordan is delimited with reference to the boundary definition under the Mandate.").

in the 1947-1949 conflict, but what the administrative boundaries were of the Mandate as carried out by Britain acting as Mandatory Power.

Another objection to Israeli sovereignty over these territories would be on the basis of the claim to the right to self-determination of other groups inhabiting the territory during the period of the Mandate. However, the Mandate for Palestine was unique in the sense that it recognized the pre-existing historical connection and the right to self-determination of the Jewish people—even though at that time they represented only a minority of the inhabitants of Palestine. The Mandate explicitly gave preference to the Jewish people; it protected the civil and religious rights of other people groups living in the territory but denied them territorial rights.[535]

9.5 The Legal Significance of the 1947 UN "Partition Plan"

It is often argued that the boundaries of the State of Israel were determined by the Partition Plan proposed by the UN General Assembly in November 1947. This plan envisaged an economic union between two contiguous states—one Jewish and one Arab—with Jerusalem to be brought under an international regime. The Jewish State was to be constituted in three segments and excluded Jaffa (which would become an Arab enclave). Although accepted reluctantly by the Jewish Agency, the Partition Plan was immediately and categorically rejected by the Arabs.

The boundaries proposed under the 1947 UN Partition Plan have no significance under international law. In the first place, the Partition Plan was a non-binding proposal only. In any event, the Partition Plan was categorically rejected by the Arabs, including the Arab population of Palestine, and was never implemented. Application of the legal principles such as *estoppel* would suggest that the Palestinian Arabs cannot now claim any benefit from the proposal which they then rejected.

9.6 The "Green Line" – the 1949 Armistice Lines

The War of Independence broke out when the Arabs initiated violent resistance to the Partition Plan in November 1947. It entered a new phase when five neighboring Arab states attacked Israel immediately upon its creation on 14 May 1948, and came to an end when hostilities ceased and Armistice Agreements were signed in early/mid 1949 with Egypt (24 February 1949), Lebanon (23 March 1949), Jordan (3 April 1949),

535. See further discussion in Chapter 6.

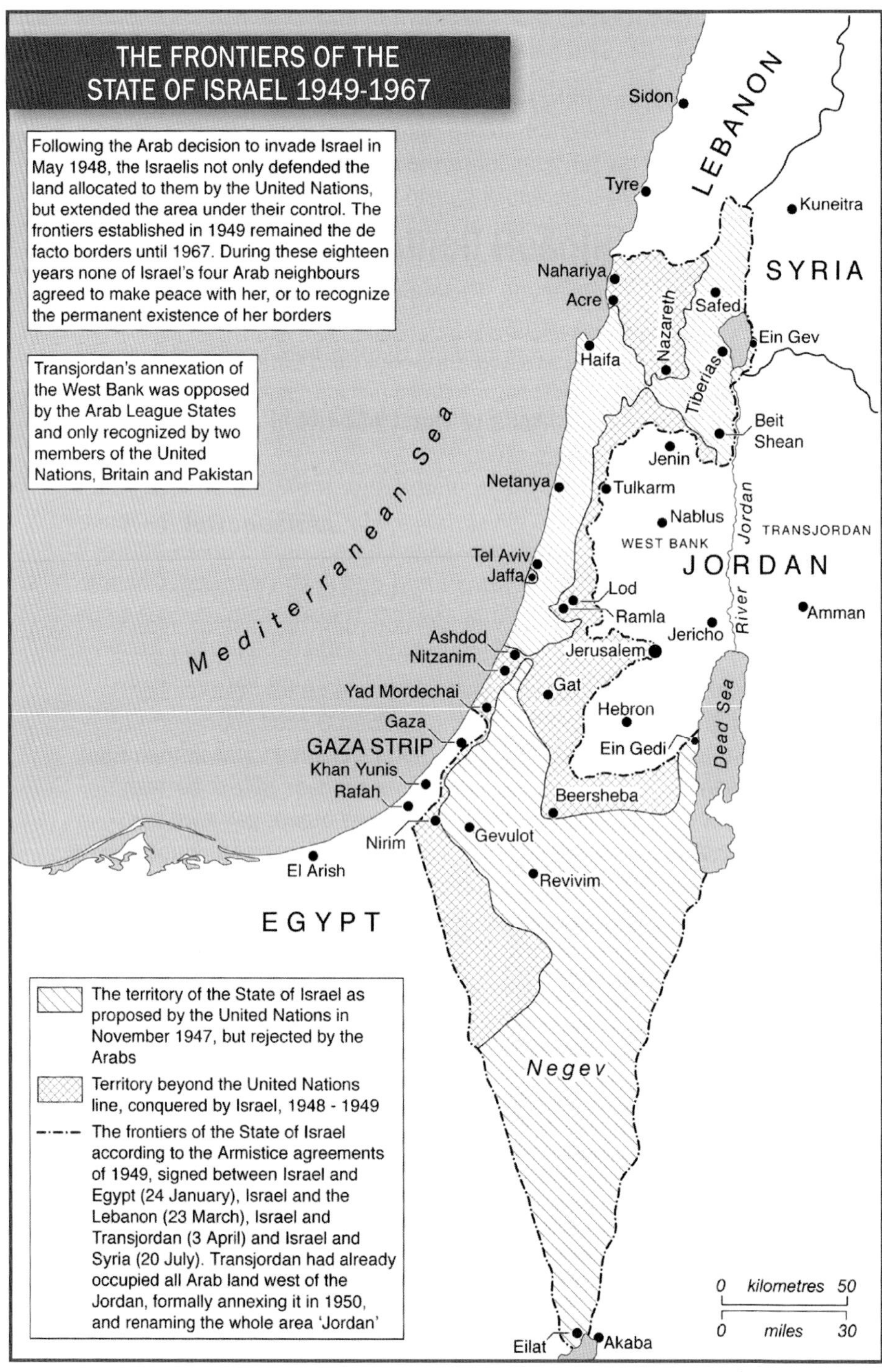
THE FRONTIERS OF THE
STATE OF ISRAEL 1949-1967
Following the Arab decision to invade Israel in May 1948, the Israelis not only defended the land allocated to them by the United Nations, but extended the area under their control. The frontiers established in 1949 remained the de facto borders until 1967. During these eighteen years none of Israel's four Arab neighbours agreed to make peace with her, or to recognize the permanent existence of her borders
Transjordan's annexation of the West Bank was opposed by the Arab League States and only recognized by two members of the United Nations, Britain and Pakistan
Mediterranean Sea
LEBANON
Sidon
Tyre
Kuneitra
SYRIA
Nahariya
Acre
Nazareth
Safed
Ein Gev
Haifa
Tiberias
Beit Shean
Jenin
Netanya
Tulkarm
Nablus
River Jordan
TRANSJORDAN
WEST BANK
JORDAN
Tel Aviv
Jaffa
Lod
Ramla
Amman
Jericho
Ashdod
Nitzanim
Jerusalem
Gat
Yad Mordechai
Hebron
Gaza
GAZA STRIP
Ein Gedi
Dead Sea
Khan Yunis
Rafah
Beersheba
Nirim
Gevulot
El Arish
Revivim
EGYPT
Negev
The territory of the State of Israel as proposed by the United Nations in November 1947, but rejected by the Arabs
Territory beyond the United Nations line, conquered by Israel, 1948 - 1949
The frontiers of the State of Israel according to the Armistice agreements of 1949, signed between Israel and Egypt (24 January), Israel and the Lebanon (23 March), Israel and Transjordan (3 April) and Israel and Syria (20 July). Transjordan had already occupied all Arab land west of the Jordan, formally annexing it in 1950, and renaming the whole area 'Jordan'
0 kilometres 50
0 miles 30
Eilat
Akaba

and Syria (20 July 1949).[536] The result was that, although Israel gained control of more territory than had been contemplated by the Partition Plan, it still did not control a significant part of the territory west of the Jordan River, which was included in the Mandate for Palestine.

The boundaries described in the Armistice Agreements—often referred to as the "Green Line"— were cease-fire lines only.[537] They were not intended to (and could not) affect the underlying status (sovereignty) of the territories concerned. They were not intended to constitute permanent international borders. Article 2 of the Armistice Agreement between Israel and Transjordan, for example, states that "no provision in this agreement shall in any way prejudice the rights, claims and positions of either party hereto in the ultimate peaceful settlement of the Palestine question."

Egypt took control of the Gaza Strip (but did not annex it), while Jordanian and Iraqi forces occupied Judea, Samaria and East Jerusalem (including the Old City). Jordan subsequently annexed Judea and Samaria. This purported annexation was only officially recognized by three other states (the UK, Iraq and Pakistan—and the latter did not recognize Jordan's annexation of East Jerusalem), and was rejected by the Arab League. Arab residents of the West Bank were subsequently granted Jordanian citizenship,[538] and the area became known as "the West Bank of the Hashemite Kingdom of Jordan" in 1950. Jordan's annexation of the West Bank was clearly in breach of international law, the area having been obtained by force following an act of aggression, and therefore having no effect on the sovereignty of the State of Israel over these territories upon its independence in 1948.

9.7 The Golan Heights

The Golan Heights were originally intended to be part of the Mandate for Palestine, but when they were finally excluded in 1922, the area

536. The armistice with Iraq was covered by the Armistice Agreement with Jordan.

537. The cease-fire boundaries agreed under these Armistice Agreements have come to be known as the Green Line, because of the color of the ink used when the lines were being drawn during the negotiations.

538. In 1988 (Israel in the meantime having gained control over the West Bank), Jordan relinquished its claim to the area, ceding its territorial claims to the PLO and eventually stripping 'West Bank' Palestinians of Jordanian citizenship.

was recognized as falling under the Mandate for Syria.[539] The Golan Heights thus arguably became a part of Syria upon its independence in April 1946.

Between 1948 and 1967, the Golan Heights were controlled by Syria, which consistently exploited them as a vantage point from which to attack Jewish kibbutzim in the Galilee region. In June 1967, Israeli forces captured the Golan Heights, and Israeli military law was subsequently applied to the region.

Following the 1973 Yom Kippur War, Israel agreed to return about five percent of the territory to Syrian civilian control. A de-militarized zone was created, which extends eastward from the cease-fire lines and today remains under the military control of UN peacekeeping forces.

Construction of Israeli settlements began in the remainder of the territory held by Israel, which was governed under military administration until 1981, when Israel passed the Golan Heights Law extending Israeli law and administration throughout the territory. This move was condemned by the UN Security Council in Resolution 497, according to which, "the Israeli decision to impose its laws, jurisdiction and administration in the occupied Syrian Golan Heights is null and void and without international legal effect."

Assuming the validity of the 1922 UK/France agreement, the fact that the Golan Heights became part of the territory of Syria means that they arguably belonged to the territory of another state when Israel took control of them in 1967. As a result, the international law of belligerent occupation (in particular the Fourth Geneva Convention) is likely to apply to the Golan Heights. For the reasons set out above, however, this does not render the occupation "illegal" nor does it definitely determine the sovereign status of the Golan Heights or prohibit Israeli settlement as such.

Israel asserts its right to retain the Golan Heights, citing the text of UN Resolution 242. From time to time, Israel and Syria have considered negotiations on the Golan Heights. In the present situation there seems to be no prospect of an agreement.

539. Agreement between His Majesty's Government and the French Government respecting the Boundary Line between Syria and Palestine from the Mediterranean to El Hamme, *Treaty Series*, No. 13 (March 1923). This Agreement is arguably in breach of the Mandate for Palestine; pursuant to article 5 of the Mandate no Palestine territory was to be transferred to or placed under the control of a foreign power.

10. Security Council Resolution 242

> **"Illegal actions and unilateral decisions have been taken on all sides, whereas, in the Court's view, this tragic situation can be brought to an end only through implementation in good faith of all the Security Council resolutions, in particular resolutions 242 (1967) and 338 (1973)."**
>
> Advisory Opinion (Paragraph 162)[540]

10.1 Introduction

Following the Six-Day War, the situation in the Middle East was the subject of heated international debate. The United Nations (UN) General Assembly referred the issue to the Security Council. After lengthy discussion, the final draft for a Security Council resolution was presented by British Ambassador Lord Caradon on 22 November 1967 and was adopted unanimously by the Security Council on the same day. This resolution referred to a number of provisions and principles that, it was hoped, would lead to a negotiated settlement of the conflict. Resolution 242 was to become the cornerstone of Middle East diplomatic efforts in the coming decades. The full text of Resolution 242 can be found in the Appendixes.

Resolution 242 is often incorrectly cited in support of the claims that Israeli settlements in the West Bank are illegal, and that Israel is required to withdraw all Israeli citizens and military personnel from all of the West Bank. On the contrary, Resolution 242 does not render the occupation illegal, nor does it require Israel to withdraw from all of the territories gained in 1967.

"A right to live in peace within secure and recognized boundaries"

United States President Lyndon B. Johnson pronounced in his speech on 19 June 1967 five principles that he believed were essential components of any UN settlement of the Middle East. Referring to the fifth of these principles, he remarked that: "The crisis [in the Middle East] underlines the

---

540. I.C.J. Reports 2004, pp. 200-201.

importance of respect for political independence and territorial integrity of all the states of the area. We reaffirmed that principle at the height of this crisis. We reaffirm it again today on behalf of all." He continued by stating that "this principle can be effective in the Middle East only on the basis of peace between the parties. The nations of the region have had only fragile and violated truce lines for 20 years. What they now need are recognized boundaries and other arrangements that will give them security against terror, destruction, and war. Further, there just must be adequate recognition of the special interest of three great religions in the holy places of Jerusalem."[541]

At the negotiation table of the Security Council, this last principle was incorporated in a draft resolution of the United States which stated "that the fulfilment of the above Charter principles requires the achievement of a state of just and lasting peace in the Middle East embracing (...) the right of every State in the area to sovereign existence, territorial integrity, political independence, secure and recognized boundaries, and freedom from the threat or use of force (...)."[542] Lord Caradon, the British ambassador to the Security Council, subsequently used this last wording of the United States' draft resolution and inserted it in his draft resolution that would later be adopted as Resolution 242.

Does "secure and recognized boundaries" mean the existing armistice lines of 1949 (pre-5 June 1967 lines) or refer to new boundaries to be negotiated?

The reference to secure and recognized boundaries suggests that the agreement needs to come to pass between Israel and the states of the area concerned. This wording therefore was not intended to refer to the armistice lines of 1949, as it was said that these lines did not answer the description of "secure and recognized boundaries" and that a return to these lines would not bring peace.

Resolution 242 Refers to "States"

By referring to "the States concerned" and (on several occasions) to "every State in the area," the language of UN Security Council Resolution 242 clearly suggests that the Security Council is directing its recommendations solely to the states that were involved in the conflict.[543] The resolution

541. Address of US President Johnson at the State Department's Foreign Policy Conference for Educators, 19 June 1967.

542. USA draft resolution S/8229, submitted on 7 November 1967.

543. UN S.C. Res. 242, para 3.

makes no mention of "peoples," and specifically did not refer to "Palestine" or Palestinian Arabs, which were neither a recognized people nor a state at the moment of the resolution's adoption. Further, by referring to "the grave situation in the Middle East," the resolution recognized that the conflict was not a conflict between Israel and Palestinian Arabs about territory, but a much wider conflict involving many states. The resolution addressed not only Israel and the states that were Israel's immediate neighbors, but also "every State in the area"[544] affected by the conflict—including Iraq.

10.2 Legal Status of Resolution 242

Resolution 242 is an example of "soft law." It was not based on Chapter VII of the UN Charter (which enables the Security Council to make binding resolutions) but on article 36 of the UN Charter, which only empowers the Security Council to make "recommendations."[545] The effective part of Resolution 242 is the decision (in paragraph 3) to request the UN Secretary-General to appoint a Special Representative to work with the states concerned (Israel, Egypt, Jordan, Syria) "in order to promote agreement and assist efforts to achieve a peaceful and accepted settlement in accordance with the provisions and principles of this resolution." This affirms that the objective and purpose of the resolution is to facilitate negotiations with a view to achievement of an agreed settlement based on principles of international law. The "provisions and principles" referred to in Resolution 242 were intended to form the framework of those negotiations. It is an agreed, negotiated settlement that was the intended outcome. Resolution 242 does not envisage or intend the imposition of a solution on the parties without their consent.

10.3 "Inadmissibility of the Acquisition of Territory by War"

Resolution 242 refers in its preamble to the "inadmissibility of the acquisition of territory by war." The UN Charter obliges states to "refrain in their international relations from the threat or use of force against the territorial integrity or political independence of any state," (article 2(4)

544. *Ibid.*, preamble.

545. As the UN Secretary-General has stated, "[a] resolution not based on Chapter VII is non-binding. For your information, Security Council Resolution 242 (1967) is not based on Chapter VII of the Charter", UN Press Release SG/SM/4718, 11, of 19 March 1992, and the clarification, DPI of 20 March 1992, cited by Lapidoth (2011), at p. 87.

UN Charter).[546] International law forbids any state from using force in an attempt to exercise sovereignty within the territory of another state. As Jennings writes, "No rule is clearer than the precept that no state may lawfully attempt to exercise its sovereignty within the territory of another ... unlawful force is that which is employed against the 'territorial integrity' of another State ..."[547]

But the UN Charter does not prohibit the use of force as such, nor does it prohibit states from controlling and administering territory that has been obtained through the use of force. The UN Charter in particular makes a clear distinction between aggressive and defensive uses of force. Article 51 of the UN Charter explicitly recognizes "the inherent right of individual or collective self-defence if an armed attack occurs against a Member of the United Nations, until the Security Council has taken measures necessary to maintain international peace and security." Under international law, a state that has been the victim of aggression is entitled to remain in control of territory that has been lawfully occupied in the course of self-defense "pending negotiation of a peace treaty."[548]

Historians have demonstrated that Israel was acting in self-defense in the Six-Day War.[549] This was also the general understanding at the time, demonstrated by the fact that the US and other members of the Security Council opposed Soviet attempts to deny that Israel was acting in self-defense.[550]

Israel's military conquest of territories in June 1967 could not *ipso facto* confer territorial rights on Israel. But equally, Israel was entitled to use force against those states that attacked it (or threatened to attack it), and to remain in control of those territories gained as a result of its successful defense.

Reference to the "inadmissibility of the acquisition of territory by war" in Resolution 242 was directed not only towards Israel, but equally towards the other parties to the 1967 conflict: including Egypt and Jordan. The West Bank and Gaza were both part of the Mandate for Palestine

---

546. The Council emphasized that "all Member States in their acceptance of the Charter of the United Nations have undertaken a commitment to act in accordance with Article 2 of the Charter."

547. Jennings (1963), p. 2.

548. Lacey (ed.) (2004), p. 7. (emphasis added). See also the excellent article by Professor Ruth Lapidoth (Lapidoth, 2011), in particular the sources cited under notes 15-18, supporting the conclusion that "[a]s an act of self-defence, this military occupation was and continues to be legitimate, until a peace settlement can be reached and permanent borders agreed upon."

549. See. e.g., Oren (2002); Gold (2004).

550. See Gold (2004), pp. 91-110.

territory and were taken by force by Jordan and Egypt respectively in 1948. Gaza was occupied by Egypt, and East Jerusalem and the West Bank (Judea and Samaria) were invaded (and later illegally annexed) by Jordan. These areas were "re-conquered" by Israel in June 1967, whilst fighting a defensive war against those same countries, as well as others. As former International Court of Justice (ICJ) President Stephen Schwebel has noted, the principle of the "inadmissability of acquisition of territory by war" must be seen in light of the general principle of international law that rights cannot be obtained through injustice ("ex iniuria non oritur"). This means that, under international law, neither Egypt nor Jordan obtained any legitimate territorial rights in (respectively) Gaza and the West Bank as a result of their aggressive invasion of these territories in May 1948.

Indeed, according to Schwebel, the fact alone that Israel was acting defensively confers on it better title to the captured territories than the title of its aggressors. "[W]here the prior holder of territory had seized that territory unlawfully, the state which subsequently takes that territory in the lawful exercise of self-defence has, against that prior holder, better title."[551] This means that Israel's title to territories which it conquered in 1967 (especially Gaza, East Jerusalem and the West Bank) is stronger than any title that could be claimed by either Egypt (Gaza) or Jordan (East Jerusalem and the West Bank).[552]

10.4 Principles for a "Just and Lasting Peace"

Resolution 242 states that the establishment of just and lasting peace in the Middle East "should include" the application of two "principles" set out in paragraph (1). Each principle is of equal importance, and both of these principles need to be considered and applied:

i. "Withdrawal of Israel armed forces from territories occupied in the recent conflict;
ii. Termination of all claims or states of belligerency and respect for and acknowledgment of the sovereignty, territorial integrity and political independence of every State in the area and their right to live in peace within secure and recognized boundaries free from threats or acts of force."

---

551. Schwebel (1994), p. 523.

552. The point is now moot as far as Egypt and Jordan are concerned. Under its Peace Treaty with Israel (1979), in which the Sinai was returned to Egypt, Egypt withdrew any claim it may have had to the Gaza Strip. Under the Peace Treaty between Jordan and Israel (1994), Jordan effectively withdrew its claims with respect to the West Bank (including Jerusalem).

These principles are mutually conditional. The Security Council was very careful to state that Israel is not obliged to withdraw its armed forces if there was not an equal commitment from the other states to cease all belligerent claims and activities (which would include not only acts of terrorism or other acts of warfare, but also verbal expressions of hostility) and respect the sovereignty, territorial integrity and political independence of Israel.

Principle 1: "Withdrawal of Israeli armed forces from territories occupied in the recent conflict."

The words *"withdrawal of Israeli armed forces from territories occupied in the recent conflict"* were chosen very carefully and were the subject of extensive and intensive discussion. The Security Council did not intend to require Israel to withdraw all of its forces from all of these territories. The (official) English-language text of Resolution 242 explicitly and intentionally omitted the definite article "the," and instead referred only to "territories." Some confusion has arisen due to the fact that the French version calls for "retrait des forces armées israeliennes des territoires occupés lors du récent conflit." The Arab states and the PLO have subsequently argued that the French text ("des territoires") requires Israeli withdrawal from "all the" territories occupied in June 1967. This is a difficult argument to sustain. The French text was a translation of the original English-language text of Resolution 242. [553] The English text is unambiguous. The omission of the word "the" in the English text of the resolution as proposed by Lord Caradon was deliberate and intentional.

This is clear when we consider the context of Resolution 242. The Security Council recognized that the 1949 Armistice Lines were neither legally binding nor secure boundaries. The U.S. Ambassador to the UN in 1967, Arthur Goldberg, in 1973 observed that the resolution's omission of a call for total withdrawal demonstrated a recognition that "Israel's prior frontiers had proven to be notably insecure." The Soviet delegate to the UN, Vasily Kuznetsov, who fought against the final text, also conceded that the resolution gave Israel the right to "withdraw its forces only to those lines

553. According to Lapidoth, "it seems there was no other way to translate the provision into French: 'When the French text appeared, the British and American Governments raised the matter at once with the United Nations Secretariat, and with the French Government, to be told that the French language offered no other solution for the problem (...) [N]one of the people involved could think of a more accurate translation...". (Lapidoth [2011], p. 90 and footnote 26). See Rostow (1975), at p. 285. See also Rosenne (1971), at p. 363.

it considers appropriate."[554] Lord Caradon—the British UN Ambassador at the time and the principle drafter of Resolution 242, who introduced it to the Security Council, stated unequivocally in 1974 that "[i]t would have been wrong to demand that Israel return to its positions of June 4, 1967, because those positions were undesirable and artificial." Eugene V. Rostow[555] summed up the legal effect of Resolution 242 as follows:

> **"Resolution 242 ... calls on the parties to make peace and allows Israel to administer the territories it occupied in 1967 'until a just and lasting peace in the Middle East' is achieved. When such a peace is made, Israel is required to withdraw its armed forces 'from territories' it occupied during the Six Day War—not from 'the' territories, nor from 'all' the territories, but from some of the territories, which included the Sinai Desert, the West Bank, the Golan Heights, East Jerusalem and the Gaza Strip."**

Resolution 242 built on the text of the Armistice Agreements of 1949, which provided [see Article II.2] that the Armistice Demarcation Lines separating the military forces were "not to be construed in any sense as political or territorial boundaries," and that "no provision" of the Armistice Agreements "shall in any way prejudice the right, claim, and positions" of the parties "in the ultimate peaceful settlement of the Palestine problem."[556]

Israel has withdrawn its armed forces from most of the territories occupied as a result of the Six-Day War. In making peace with Egypt in 1979, Israel withdrew from the entire Sinai, though for security it depended on patrolled demilitarization in the huge area of the desert rather than on territorial change. In 2005, Israel voluntarily withdrew all its citizens and armed forces from the Gaza Strip (Gaza), and since 1993 Israel has withdrawn its armed forces and civilians from significant parts of the West Bank pursuant to the Oslo Agreements. As a result, more than 90 percent of the territories Israel occupied in June 1967 are now under Arab sovereignty or control. It is hardly surprising that some Israelis take the view that such transfers fulfil the territorial requirements of Resolution 242, no matter how widely they are construed.

Resolution 242 says nothing about territorial sovereignty, and "leaves the issue of dividing the occupied areas between Israel and its neighbors entirely to the agreement of the parties in accordance with the principles it

---

554. Cited by Wallace (2012).

555. Rostow (1991). Rostow was Undersecretary of State for Political Affairs between 1966 and 1969 and one of the drafters of Resolution 242.

556. Article II.2 of the Hashemite Jordan Kingdom - Israel: General Armistice Agreement, 3 April 1949.

sets out. It was, however, negotiated with full realization that the problem of establishing a "secure and recognized boundary" between Israel and Jordan would be the thorniest issue of the peace-making process."[557]

Specifically, Resolution 242 intentionally did not require Israel to withdraw from Jerusalem. As Arthur Goldberg (the Security Council's US Representative during the course of the discussions preceding the adoption of Resolution 242) has subsequently recorded, "I never described Jerusalem as an occupied area.... Resolution 242 does not refer to Jerusalem in any way whatsoever, and this omission was deliberate."[558]

Further, it is important to note that the principle of Israeli "withdrawal" in Resolution 242 is limited to Israel's "armed forces," and does not apply to civilians living in the relevant territories. It cannot therefore be argued that Resolution 242 prohibits the construction of settlements by Israeli citizens.

Goldberg stated: "To seek withdrawal without secure and recognized boundaries ... would be just as fruitless as to seek secure and recognized boundaries without withdrawal. Historically, there have never been secure or recognized boundaries in the area. Neither the armistice lines of 1949 nor the cease-fire lines of 1967 have answered that description... such boundaries have yet to be agreed upon. An agreement on that point is an absolute essential to a just and lasting peace just as withdrawal is..."[559]

On 10 September 1968, President Johnson stated that "[w]e are not the ones to say where other nations should draw lines between them that will assure each the greatest security. It is clear, however, that a return to the situation of 4 June 1967 will not bring peace. There must be secure and there must be recognized borders. Some such lines must be agreed to by the neighbours involved."

US Assistant Secretary of State Joseph Sisco stated that "[t]hat Resolution did not say 'withdrawal to the pre-June 5 lines.' The Resolution said that the parties must negotiate to achieve agreement on the so-called final secure and recognized borders. In other words, the question of the final borders is a matter of negotiations between the parties."[560]

Finally, it is extremely important to note that Resolution 242 explicitly recognizes that, in order to guarantee the territorial inviolability and political

557. Rostow (1991).

558. Gold (2004), p. 174.

559. S/PV. 1377 of 15 November 1967, para 65.

560. NBC 'Meet the Press', 12 July 1970.

independence of every state in the area, withdrawal of Israel's armed forces will not be sufficient. Other measures including "the establishment of demilitarized zones" will need to be agreed and implemented.

Principle 2: "Termination of all claims or states of belligerency and respect for and acknowledgment of the sovereignty, territorial integrity and political independence of every State in the area and their right to live in peace within secure and recognized boundaries free from threats or acts of force."

Just as important as withdrawal of Israeli armed forces was the principle that all states must acknowledge Israel's existence and its right to sovereignty and political independence, and for them to terminate their hostility towards Israel. The fact that Egypt, Syria and Jordan attacked Israel only six years later, in October 1973, proves that they definitely did not comply with the terms of Resolution 242. While Egypt and Jordan have subsequently entered into peace treaties with Israel, Syria has never abandoned its declaration of war against Israel. In this light, it is the height of hypocrisy that Syria, time and again, both sponsors (through its membership of the Organization of Islamic Conference (OIC) and the League of Arab States (Arab League)) and votes in favor of UN resolutions demanding termination of Israel's occupation of the West Bank and East Jerusalem.

Finally, because the Security Council refers to "the grave situation in the Middle East" and directs its recommendations to "every State in the area," Resolution 242 is equally applicable to other Arab states that maintain an ongoing attitude of hostility towards Israel, denying its legitimacy and threatening its annihilation. The formula of Resolution 242 means that—unless and until such threats are terminated—Israel can be under no obligation to withdraw its armed forces from East Jerusalem and the West Bank.

10.5 Security Council Resolution 338 (1973)

Security Council Resolution 338, issued after the Yom Kippur war in October 1973, "calls upon the parties concerned to start immediately after the cease-fire the implementation of Security Council resolution 242 (1967) in all its parts" and "decides that, immediately and concurrently with the cease-fire, negotiations start between the parties concerned under appropriate auspices aimed at establishing a just and durable peace in the Middle East."

The fact that the Security Council expressly calls for the parties to negotiate with each other (under "appropriate auspices") confirms that Resolution 242 was intended to lay a framework of recommended principles within which the parties to the conflict should negotiate a settlement of their dispute. In other words, Resolution 338 confirms that Resolution 242 was not intended to lay down binding rules to override or replace negotiations, but rather to facilitate negotiations between Israel and its hostile neighbors with a view to achieving peace treaties in which the parties would agree to cease all hostilities and Israel would be guaranteed "secure and recognized boundaries."

11. International Law of Belligerent Occupation

"The territories situated between the Green Line ... and the former eastern boundary of Palestine under the Mandate were occupied by Israel in 1967 during the armed conflict between Israel and Jordan. Under customary international law, these were therefore occupied territories in which Israel had the status of occupying Power. Subsequent events in these territories ... have done nothing to alter this situation. All these territories (including East Jerusalem) remain occupied territories and Israel has continued to have the status of occupying Power."

Advisory Opinion,(Paragraph 78)[561]

"In view of the foregoing, the Court considers that the Fourth Geneva Convention is applicable in any occupied territory in the event of an armed conflict arising between two or more High Contracting Parties. Israel and Jordan were parties to that Convention when the 1967 armed conflict broke out. The Court accordingly finds that that Convention is applicable in the Palestinian territories which before the conflict lay to the east of the Green Line and which, during that conflict, were occupied by Israel, there being no need for any enquiry into the precise prior status of those territories."

Advisory Opinion (Paragraph 101)[562]

11.1 Introduction

After the Six-Day War, Israel introduced a military administration in the newly controlled territories of East Jerusalem and the West Bank that had been controlled by Jordan. Following the 1978 Camp David Accords with Egypt, in 1981, Israel created a Civil Administration for the West Bank and Gaza Strip (also referred to as Gaza), which is part of the Coordinator of Government Activities in the Territories (COGAT) under the

561. I.C.J. Reports 2004, p. 167.

562. I.C.J. Reports 2004, p. 177.

Israeli Ministry of Defense. The Civil Administration has the responsibility to "run all regional civil matters, ... for the wellbeing and for the sake of [local] population, and with the purpose of providing and operating the public services, considering the need to maintain a proper governance and public order."[563]

There are three main issues that need to be considered in relation to the application of the law of belligerent occupation to the territories administered by Israel since 1967:

1. Does the international law of belligerent occupation, as embodied in the Fourth Geneva Convention, apply as a matter of law to the territories controlled by Israel since June 1967?
2. Does this law apply to territories from which Israel has withdrawn effective control (e.g. Gaza and the areas transferred to the Palestinian Authority under Oslo II)?
3. To the extent that it applies, what conduct or activities does the law of belligerent occupation mandate, and what does it prohibit, more specifically in respect of the settlements?

In this chapter, the first two questions are addressed. The third (settlements) will be discussed in Chapter 13.

11.2 Foundations and Scope of the International Law of Belligerent Occupation

The law of belligerent occupation is a branch of the *ius in bello*, which is part of the Law of International Armed Conflict (LOIAC) or International Humanitarian Law (IHL). The evolution of the international law of occupation in the 19th and 20th centuries reflected a number of more fundamental trends in this period: the rejection of colonialism, the principle that states can no longer be allowed to use force to acquire territory belonging to others, and the increased focus (especially after WWII) on the protection of civilians in times of war. In essence, the law of occupation means that any state which legitimately takes control of neighboring territory belonging to another state as a result of war or conflict is required to administer that territory temporarily: until the conflict has been terminated and a peace treaty has been negotiated. In the meantime, the "occupier" is subject to certain strict obligations that are primarily directed at protecting the civil population in that territory.

563. Military Order No. 947.

Articles 42 and 43 of the Hague Regulations , which are annexed to the Hague Convention respecting the Laws and Customs of War on Land, 1907 (Hague Convention IV)—now seen as the expression of international customary law—describe occupation and the powers of the occupant in the following way:

- ***Article 42:*** *"Territory is considered occupied when it is actually placed under the authority of the hostile army. The occupation extends only to the territory where such authority has been established and can be exercised."*
- ***Article 43:*** *"The authority of the legitimate power having in fact passed into the hands of the occupant, the latter shall take all the measures in his power to restore, and ensure, as far as possible, public order and safety, while respecting, unless absolutely prevented, the laws in force in the country."*

These articles assume that the area concerned is under the control of a hostile power. They seem to assume that the relevant territory was previously under the control of a "legitimate power": in other words, another sovereign state. The idea that the occupant should respect as much as possible the laws in force in the country presumes that the territory will eventually be returned to the prior sovereign. Oppenheim stated: "As the occupant actually exercises authority, and the legitimate Government is prevented from exercising its authority, the occupant acquires a temporary right of administration over the territory and its inhabitants; and all legitimate steps he takes in the exercise of this right must be recognized by the legitimate Government after the occupation has ceased."[564]

The customary law of occupation, as reflected in The Hague Conventions, was supplemented by the Geneva Conventions (1949) drafted in the aftermath of WWII. The horrendous atrocities committed by Nazi Germany, Imperial Japan and the Axis powers in WWII demonstrated the weakness and limitations of the law of belligerent occupation as it then existed. The Fourth Geneva Convention concerns the protection of civilian persons in time of war.[565] Two Additional Protocols to the Geneva Conventions were adopted in 1977.

The law applicable in armed conflict as embodied in the Hague Convention IV and the Geneva Conventions has become part of international customary

564. Lauterpacht, Hersch (ed.) (1952), pp. 436-437.

565. See for the background and purposes of the Fourth Geneva Convention the following text published by the International Committee of the Red Cross (ICRC): http://www.icrc.org/ihl/INTRO/380 (visited: 9 September 2017).

law. All states (including Israel) have expressed their consent to be bound by the Fourth Geneva Convention. Breaches of the principles contained in the conventions were subsequently placed within the competence of international criminal tribunals, including the International Criminal Tribunal for the former Yugoslavia (ICTY) (Articles 2 and 3 of the Updated Statute of the ICTY) and the International Criminal Court (ICC) (Article 8 of the Statute of the ICC).

International law does not prohibit a state from occupying land that has been legitimately taken in self-defense during a conflict. It does not require the withdrawal of civilian or military personnel, it simply regulates the conduct of the occupying power during such occupation. As former International Court of Justice (ICJ) president and leading international lawyer Prof. Rosalyn Higgins has stated, "[T]here is nothing in either the Charter or general international law which leads one to suppose that military occupation pending a peace treaty is illegal."[566]

11.3 The Law of Belligerent Occupation and Territorial Sovereignty

Through their loose use of the terms "occupation" and "Palestinian Territories," the ICJ in 2004 and the Security Council in 2016 create the impression that the land occupied by Israel since 1967 somehow belongs to the Palestinian Arabs, and that Israel's "occupation" is, in and of itself, illegal. As previously explained, this perception is incorrect. It is extremely important to note that not only does the law of belligerent occupation not render the occupation illegal, it does not affect the underlying or pre-existing status of the territories concerned. This means that, even if the law of belligerent occupation applies to East Jerusalem and the West Bank (which we doubt—see below), this does not in any way affect the pre-existing sovereign territorial rights and interests of Israel and the Jewish people or any other party with respect thereto.[567]

11.4 Does the Fourth Geneva Convention Apply to "East Jerusalem" and the West Bank?

Article 2 of the Fourth Geneva Convention provides:

> **"In addition to the provisions which shall be implemented in peacetime, the present Convention shall apply to all cases of declared war or any**

566. Higgins (1970), at p. 8.

567. See, e.g., Cuyckens (2015), pp. 69-74 and the authorities cited therein.

> other armed conflict which may arise between two or more of the High Contracting Parties, even if the state of war is not recognized by one of them.
>
> The Convention shall also apply to all cases of partial or total occupation of the *territory of a High Contracting Party*, even if the said occupation meets with no armed resistance.
>
> Although one of the Powers in conflict may not be a party to the present Convention, the Powers who are parties thereto shall remain bound by it in their consensual relations. They shall furthermore be bound by the Convention in relation to the said Power, if the latter accepts and applies the provisions thereof."[568]

Article 2 of the Fourth Geneva Convention is rather ambiguous. The core issue is whether the notion of "occupation" in the Fourth Geneva Convention is limited to situations where one state takes control of territory belonging to another "High Contracting Party," or whether it applies to any situation of conflict in which one state takes control of a population that was previously controlled by the enemy (whether or not the ousted enemy had a legitimate claim to the territory).

Most take the latter view. The UN General Assembly has expressed in Resolution 58/292 of 17 May 2004, what is now apparently the commonly accepted opinion that "Israel, the occupying Power, has only the duties and obligations of an occupying Power under the Geneva Convention relative to the Protection of Civilian Persons in Time of War, of 12 August 1949 and the Regulations annexed to the Hague Convention respecting the Laws and Customs of War on Land, of 1907." Similarly, in 1999 and 2001, a conference of the High Contracting Parties to the Fourth Geneva Convention decided that the Convention did apply in the "Occupied Palestinian Territory," including Jerusalem.[569] In 2004, the ICJ considered the matter in its Advisory Opinion. However, the ICJ did not even consider the argument that one of the underlying purposes of the customary law of occupation is to protect the position of the "ousted sovereign." Instead, the ICJ, limiting itself to an interpretation of Article 2 of the Fourth Geneva Convention, accepted the Palestinians' contentions that the first paragraph of Article 2 of the Fourth Geneva Convention should be read widely to mean that the Fourth Geneva Convention is applicable in all cases of "armed conflict" and the resulting military developments,

---

568. Emphasis added.

569. United Nations (2002). *Yearbook of the United Nations, 2000*. United Nations Publications. pp. 421, 437. See for 2001: https://www.icrc.org/eng/resources/documents/misc/5fldpj.htm#1, para 12 (visited: 13 November 2015).

including occupation, and that the second paragraph of that provision (which refers specifically to "the territory of a High Contracting Party") should not be read as narrowing that wide application. There are good reasons, however, to criticize these views.

No "ousted sovereign" in East Jerusalem, Gaza or the West Bank

As noted, Jordan illegally controlled East Jerusalem and the West Bank between 1949 and 1967, having acquired control as a result of an illegal act of aggression. Its subsequent purported annexation of this territory was not sufficient to give it rights over this territory. In other words, Jordan had no sovereign title with respect to East Jerusalem and the West Bank between 1948 and 1967. The contrary view has been expressed by Dinstein, who concludes that in 1967 Jordan was the "displaced sovereign" of these territories.[570]

The view that Jordan obtained sovereignty over the West Bank in 1948 is not convincing. Jordan's occupation of the West Bank was not based on any pre-existing claim to sovereignty and it did not confer any sovereignty on Jordan. Further, its physical occupation was the result of its aggression against Israel and the Jewish people. The principle of the prohibition of acquisition of territories by force would seem to apply to this situation. In any event, Jordan's purported "annexation" in 1950 was acknowledged as lawful by only three states (Pakistan, Iraq and the United Kingdom) and rejected by all other states. As a result, when Israel defeated the Jordanian forces and regained control of this territory in June 1967, it was not a question of Israel occupying "the territory *of a High Contracting Party*" [i.e. another state]. The late Professor Julius Stone has expressed this as follows:[571]

> **"[B]ut the Convention itself does not by its terms apply to these territories. For, under Article 2, the Convention applies 'to cases of ... occupation of the territory of a High Contracting Party, by another such Party.' Insofar as the West Bank at present held by Israel does not belong to any other State, the Convention would not seem to apply to it at all. This is a technical, though rather decisive, legal point."**

This is more than a technical point. It goes to the heart of the legal doctrine of occupation as established under The Hague Conventions. The Fourth Geneva Convention may have changed the focus of the law of occupation by giving greater attention to the rights of the population of the

570. Dinstein (2009), p. 15.

571. Lacey (ed.) (2004), p. 14 (emphasis added).

occupied territory, but it did not change the notion of "occupation" itself. The law of occupation makes no sense, and has no application, in our submission, when there is no sovereign power that is "ousted" from the territory. As Benvenisti has stated: "The foundation upon which the entire law of occupation is based is the principle of inalienability of sovereignty through the actual or threatened use of force... From the principle of inalienability of sovereignty over a territory spring the constraints that international law imposes on the occupant."[572] The purpose of the law of belligerent occupation is not only to protect civilians as against the occupying army, it is also to "safeguard the reversionary rights of the ousted sovereign".[573] In situations (like the West Bank and Gaza) where there was no "ousted sovereign," there can accordingly be no question of "occupation" in the sense of international law.[574]

The Israeli government takes the position that—in the absence of an ousted prior sovereign—the Fourth Geneva Convention does not apply to the territories controlled since 1967. Israel distinguished (and continues to distinguish) between *de jure* (legal) and *de facto* (practical) application of the Fourth Geneva Convention to the Territories. In other words, Israel denies that the law of belligerent occupation applies *as a matter of law* to the territories but has decided voluntarily to apply the humanitarian provisions of those laws to them *as a matter of fact*.

As the question of sovereignty (ownership) over these territories remains the subject of dispute between Israel and the Palestinian Arabs, as represented by the Palestine Liberation Organization (PLO), it would in our view be more accurate to speak of "disputed" rather than "occupied" territories.

An additional question is whether the Fourth Geneva Convention applies since the 1994 Peace Treaty between Jordan and Israel in which Jordan "waived" its claim to the West Bank in favor of the Palestinians: who did not then constitute a state party to the Fourth Geneva Convention. The argument would appear to be a strong one, that because the law of belligerent occupation is intended to regulate affairs between States until a peace treaty is signed, Israel's occupation of East Jerusalem and

---

572. Benvenisti (1993), pp. 5-6. See also: Avinoam (2009).

573. Blum (1968), at p. 293.

574. See also Judgment of the International Criminal Tribunal for the Former Yugoslavia, *The Prosecutor v. Naletillic & Martinovic*, 31 March 2003, which states that the international law of belligerent occupation requires that "the occupying power must be in a position to substitute its own authority for that of the occupied authorities, which must have been rendered incapable of functioning publicly," and "the enemy's forces have surrendered, been defeated or withdrawn."

the West Bank (if such existed) terminated upon the signing of the Israel-Jordan Peace Treaty in 1994.

Further, as the Geneva Conventions apply with respect to occupation as between states, they could have no application between Israel and the Palestinian Arabs, either before or after 1994.[575] Some argue that the fact that the Palestinians are not yet formally a state is immaterial. Dinstein, for example, argues that the third paragraph of article 2 of the Fourth Geneva Convention covers this situation:

> **"Although one of the Powers in conflict may not be a party to the present Convention, the Powers who are parties thereto shall remain bound by it in their consensual relations. They shall furthermore be bound by the Convention in relation to the said Power, if the latter accepts and applies the provisions thereof."**

In our view, this argument should be rejected. Article 2 of the Fourth Geneva Convention only applies to "Powers," which implies statehood. As the PLO is not a state, it cannot claim the benefit of the Fourth Geneva Convention. (This is notwithstanding the recent purported accession by "Palestine" to the Geneva Conventions - see chapter 18).

11.5 Does the Fourth Geneva Convention Apply to Territories from Which Israel has Withdrawn? The Case of Gaza

As was shown, there are good reasons to say that *de jure* the Fourth Geneva Convention is not applicable in the West Bank and the Gaza Strip. But even assuming that this would be the case the question arises, what is the legal status of the Gaza Strip, from which Israel withdrew its troops and citizens in 2005?

The Gaza Strip was part of the British Mandate territory. Egypt took control of the Gaza Strip in 1948 and occupied it until it was ousted in 1967. An "all-Palestine Government" was established by the Arab League in the Egyptian-occupied territory of Gaza in September 1948. This was an attempt to limit the power of Transjordan in Palestine and was finally dismantled in 1959. In the period 1948-67, Egypt administered the Gaza Strip as a controlled territory with a military governor. Residents of Gaza were not offered Egyptian citizenship but received assistance from the United Nations Relief and Works Agency for Palestine Refugees

575. See: https://www.icrc.org/applic/ihl/ihl.nsf/States.xsp?xp_viewStates=XPages_NORMStatesParties&xp_treatySelected =380. Since April 2014 Palestine is considered a State Party to the Fourth Geneva Convention.

(UNRWA). Approximately 200,000 Palestinian Arabs poured into the Gaza Strip as a result of the June 1967 conflict, causing a sharp decline in living standards. Today, approximately 1.6 million Palestinian Arabs live in the Gaza Strip, of which approximately 1 million are UNRWA-registered refugees. The annual GDP of the Gaza Strip is around $700 million, the vast majority of which is financed by the EU, United States, UN Agencies and other donors.

Israel withdrew its military presence and removed all Israeli settlers from the Gaza Strip in 2005. Nine thousand Israelis, mostly living in Gush Katif, were forcibly removed. Today, not one single Jew lives in the Gaza Strip. Extreme Islamic party Hamas took over all control of the Gaza Strip in 2007, claiming to represent the Palestinian people. There has been an ongoing conflict between Hamas and Fatah. Between 2006 and 2007 alone, more than 600 Palestinians were killed in the fighting between Hamas and Fatah.

Despite its withdrawal in 2005, Israel has continued to exercise significant influence over the Gaza Strip:

- Israel is the main supplier of electricity and fuel;
- From 2006, Israel implemented restrictions on the movement of goods to Gaza, and from 2008 a sea blockade; and
- Israel controls the air space and territorial waters.

It should be realized that the Gaza Strip forms an enormous security threat to Israel. Not only does the Hamas leadership refuse to cooperate with Israel, it advocates the destruction of the Jewish state of Israel and its replacement by an Islamic state covering all of historic Palestine, by means of *jihad* against Israel and its citizens.[576] Since the Second Intifada in 2000, Israel has been subject to the building of tunnels for terrorist purposes, and constant rocket attacks and bombings of Israeli border localities by Palestinian guerrillas from the Gaza Strip, especially

---

576. The Preamble of the Hamas Covenant (1988) reads: "Israel will exist and will continue to exist until Islam will obliterate it, just as it obliterated others before it. (...)." Article 6 reads: "The Islamic Resistance Movement (...) strives to raise the banner of Allah over every inch of Palestine." Article 15 reads: "The day that enemies usurp part of Moslem land, Jihad becomes the individual duty of every Moslem. In the face of Jew's usurpation, it is compulsory that the banner of Jihad be raised." In 2017 a new version of the Hamas Covenant was published. The terminology has been adapted. The 'enemy' is now often called the 'Zionist project' or the 'Zionist entity'. The overall political goals seem to be the same, although formulations are confusing. For example, in Article 18 it is said that "[t]he establishment of Israel is entirely illegal...". It envisages "the full and complete liberation of Palestine, from the river to the sea," while adding at the same time a vague formula that could be seen as an acceptance of a state along the lines of 4 July 1967 (Article 20). It also declares "[r]esisting the occupation with all means and methods a legitimate right." (Article 25).

by Hamas and Jihad Islamic movements. The constant attacks on Israeli citizens and military culminated in Israel's invasion of the Gaza Strip in December 2008 (*Operation Cast Lead*), in 2012 (*Operation Pillar of Cloud*) and in 2014 (*Operation Protective Edge*).

Despite the fact that Israel has no military or civilian presence within the Gaza Strip, the EU, the International Committee of the Red Cross (ICRC), UN organs and many NGOs maintain the view that Israel is still "occupying" the Gaza Strip and thus continues to be bound by the law of belligerent occupation including the Fourth Geneva Convention.[577] According to Juan-Pedro Schaerer, ICRC Head of Delegation, Israel and the Occupied Territories:

> "[W]hile it cannot be said that the Gaza Strip is a 'classic' situation of occupation, Israel has not entirely relinquished its effective control over the Strip... This reflects a *functional approach* to the law of occupation (...) In simplified terms it means that to the extent that an occupying power retains control of key functions and authorities in the occupied territory it also remains bound by the relevant provisions of the law of occupation. (...)."[578]

The Israeli Supreme Court takes a different approach and denies that Israel is bound by the law of belligerent occupation in the Gaza Strip. According to the Supreme Court, while Gaza may be economically dependent on Israel (e.g. Gaza relies almost wholly on electricity supplies from Israel), the obligations of Israel towards the civilian population of Gaza derive from the general law relating to the state of armed conflict between Israel and Hamas: not the law of occupation. As Israel has no "effective control over what takes place in the territory" or capability to restore order in the Gaza Strip, it cannot be held responsible for complying with the law of belligerent occupation.[579]

The official position of the ICRC in relation to Gaza appears to conflict with the views expressed by a committee of experts organized by the ICRC itself. That committee concluded that it is "difficult to sustain" the view that the law of occupation continues to apply in Gaza, given "the

577. The European Commission's 2013 Guidelines on EU Funding of the settlements (2013/C 205/05) are expressed to apply to all the "territories occupied by Israel since June 1967" – including the Gaza Strip. See also UN S.C. Res. 1860 (2009) and ICRC's President, Peter Maurer: Maurer (2012), at. p. 1508.

578. http://www.algemeiner.com/2013/10/10/the-red-cross-displays-blatant-anti-israel-bias/ (visited: 13 November 2015).

579. High Court of Justice, Verdict in the case of *Jaber al-Basyuni Ahmad et al.* v. *The Prime Minister and the Minister of Defence*, Case No. HCJ 9132/07, 12, Session of 27 January 2008.

traditional rules about occupation with their strong emphasis on the factual basis of a continuing presence on the ground."[580]

The question whether Israel is legally "occupying" Gaza has significant consequences. As we have seen, the law of belligerent occupation imposes onerous responsibilities on the occupying power to protect the well-being of the local civilian population. If Israel is indeed the "occupying power" of Gaza from a legal perspective, then the residents of Gaza become "protected persons," and Israel is required to ensure "public order and safety" in the Gaza Strip. Given the hostility of Hamas, that is an impossible requirement.

The law of belligerent occupation is unclear in many respects, and the factual situation in the Gaza Strip is extremely complex, to say the least. It is inadvisable to draw hard conclusions. What can be said is that there are two cumulative conditions for the existence of belligerent occupation: (i) the establishment of authority by the occupying power as a matter of fact; and (ii) the ability of the occupying power to exercise that authority. In other words, "belligerent occupation pertains only to that area in which the Occupying Power is *actually* exercising its authority and is *capable* of doing so."[581] Although Israel continues to have a major influence on Gaza, it is difficult to see how Israel could be in a position to fulfill those criteria given the fact that Hamas—and not Israel—has effective control over the people of Gaza.

580. 'The Termination of Military Occupations' – Preliminary comments by Prof. Adam Roberts (http://www.icrc.org/eng/assets/files/publications/icrc-002-4094.pdf)

581. Dinstein (2009), p. 42, para 96 (emphasis added).

12. The Oslo Agreements

"(...) a number of agreements have been signed since 1993 between Israel and the Palestine Liberation Organization imposing various obligations on each party."

Advisory Opinion (Paragraph 77)[582]

12.1 Introduction

Ever since the encouragement of peace negotiations in United Nations (UN) Security Council Resolution 242 (1967), there have been attempts to initiate negotiations on the territories that came under Israeli control in 1967.[583] They were successful in respect of the Sinai, when the Camp David negotiations in 1978 resulted in an agreement that was formalized in the peace treaty with Egypt of 26 March 1979. Further developments had to wait for the Madrid Conference of October 1991, which was co-sponsored by the United States and the USSR, and which started a complex process of bilateral and multilateral peace negotiations. Regional working groups were established dealing with complex regional issues, such as water, environment, arms controls, refugees and economic development. Parallel to these regional discussions, Israel entered into bilateral negotiations with Syria, Lebanon, Jordan and the Palestinians, with a view to achieving peace treaties. In October 1994, Israel and Jordan entered into a Peace Treaty. Negotiations with Lebanon and Syria have since stalled.

Since 1993, Israel has entered into a series of agreements known as "the Oslo Agreements" (owing to the role played by Norway in those negotiations) with the Palestine Liberation Organization (PLO), resulting in a complex set of arrangements for the governance of the West Bank.

582. I.C.J. Reports 2004, p. 167.

583. See for a general overview, e.g., Turnberg (2017).

12.2 The Oslo Agreements

The most important of these agreements are:

- Declaration of Principles on Interim Self-Government Arrangements (DOP) (1993)
- Agreement on the Gaza Strip and the Jericho Area (Gaza-Jericho Agreement) (1994)
- Interim Agreement on the West Bank and the Gaza Strip (Oslo II or Interim Agreement) (1995)
- Protocol concerning the redeployment in Hebron (Hebron Protocol) (1995)
- Wye River Memorandum (1998)
- Sharm El-Sheikh Memorandum (1999)
- Agreement on Movement and Access (2005)

The DOP was signed on 13 September 1993 at a ceremony in Washington by the Israeli Prime Minister Yitzkak Rabin and PLO Chairman Yasser Arafat, and witnessed by the United States and Russian Federation. The DOP contains 17 operative provisions, and four annexes. "Agreed Minutes" are included as an integral part of the DOP, amplifying several provisions. The DOP is supplemented by an exchange of letters, dated 9 September 1993, which confirm the recognition by the PLO of Israel's right to exist, the renunciation of terrorism, an undertaking to amend the Palestinian National Charter, and the recognition by Israel of the PLO as the representative of the Palestinian people. According to the DOP, the ultimate goal of the parties is to "put an end to decades of confrontation and conflict and to live in peaceful coexistence, mutual security and dignity" and to "achieve a just, lasting and comprehensive peace settlement and historic reconciliation." The DOP does not impose a specific outcome. Rather, it contains an agreed set of principles to guide the negotiating process via an "agreed framework for the interim period"[584] towards "permanent status" arrangements.

The Gaza-Jericho Agreement (1994) provided for the institution of the Palestinian Authority (PA). Following the partial withdrawal from Gaza and Jericho in 1994, the Interim Agreement (Oslo II) was signed in Washington on 28 September 1995. Oslo II was witnessed by the European Union, as well as the United States, the Russian Federation and Norway. It

584. The interim period of five years was based on the interim period incorporated in the 1978 Camp David Accords between Israel and Egypt.

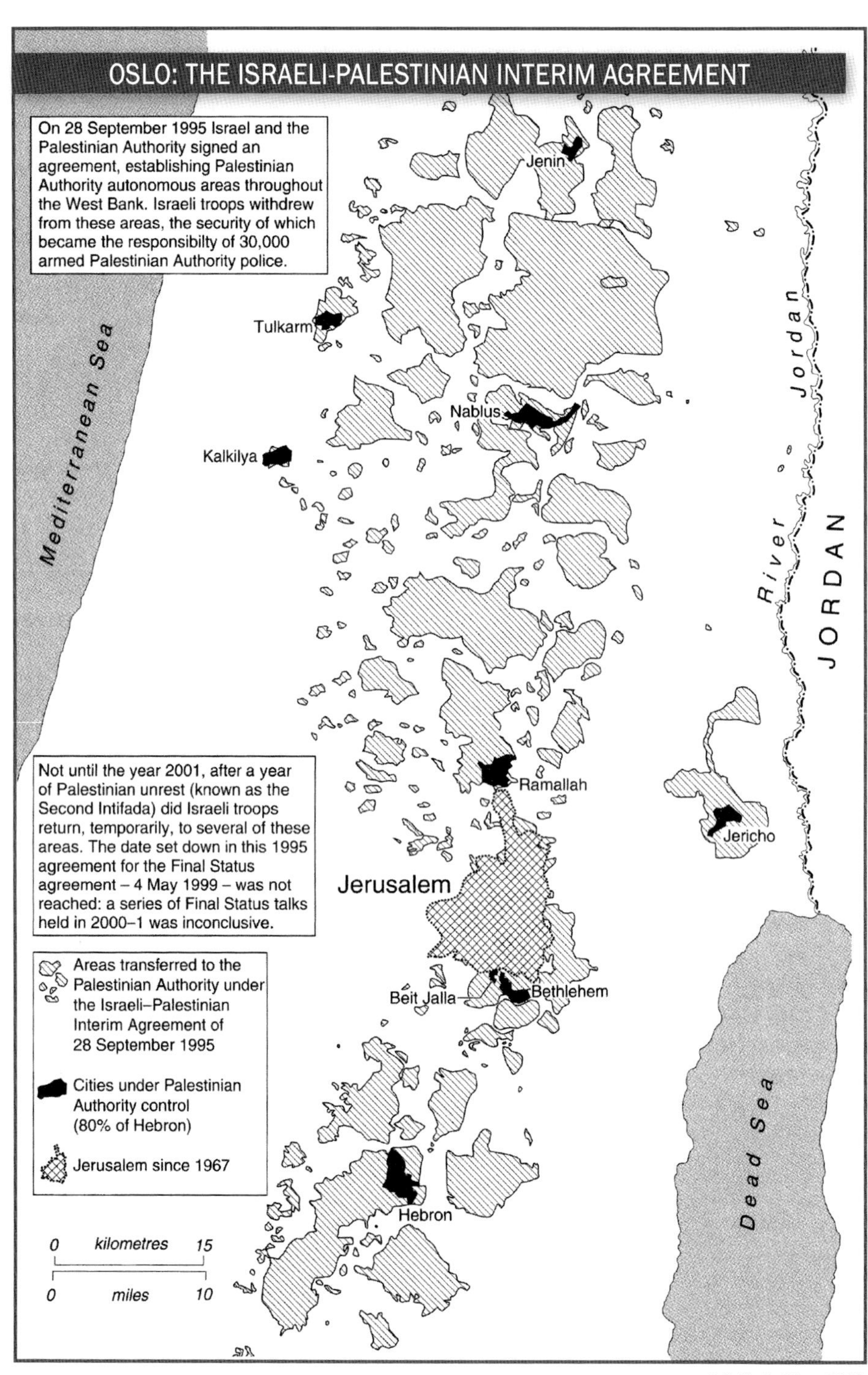
OSLO: THE ISRAELI-PALESTINIAN INTERIM AGREEMENT
On 28 September 1995 Israel and the Palestinian Authority signed an agreement, establishing Palestinian Authority autonomous areas throughout the West Bank. Israeli troops withdrew from these areas, the security of which became the responsibilty of 30,000 armed Palestinian Authority police.
Jenin
Tulkarm
Mediterranean Sea
Nablus
Kalkilya
River Jordan
JORDAN
Ramallah
Jericho
Not until the year 2001, after a year of Palestinian unrest (known as the Second Intifada) did Israeli troops return, temporarily, to several of these areas. The date set down in this 1995 agreement for the Final Status agreement – 4 May 1999 – was not reached: a series of Final Status talks held in 2000–1 was inconclusive.
Jerusalem
Areas transferred to the Palestinian Authority under the Israeli–Palestinian Interim Agreement of 28 September 1995
Cities under Palestinian Authority control (80% of Hebron)
Jerusalem since 1967
Beit Jalla
Bethlehem
Dead Sea
Hebron
0 kilometres 15
0 miles 10

is a complex document of more than 300 pages and seven annexes. Under this agreement, elections were to be carried out to establish the Palestinian Legislative Council. The West Bank was divided into three administrative areas:

- **Area A:** covers approximately three percent of the territory of the West Bank and includes all of the major Arab cities (Nablus, Jenin, Tulkarem, Qalqilya, Ramallah, Bethlehem, Jericho and most of Hebron). There are no Israeli settlements and no Jews living in this Area, which is forbidden to Israeli citizens. Full civil and security control has been transferred to the PA.
- **Area B:** covers approximately 23 percent of the West Bank and includes about 400 Arab villages. Civil control has been transferred to the PA. Security is controlled by the PA and Israel jointly.
- **Area C:** covers approx. 72-74 percent of the West Bank. Israel retains full civil and security control over Area C. Subject to the matters negotiated as part of the final status negotiations, Area C was to be gradually transferred to PA jurisdiction.

12.3 Legal Effect of the Oslo Agreements

Under the Oslo Agreements, Israel retains all powers and responsibilities that are not explicitly transferred to the Palestinian Legislative Council. In Area C, no powers have yet been transferred to the Palestinian Legislative Council. Although civil control has been handed over to the Palestinian authorities in Areas A and B, internal security control in Area A, and the Israeli Civil Administration has been dissolved in Areas A and B, Israel retains responsibility in areas A, B and C for essential matters such as external security and external relations throughout the whole of the West Bank. From an Israeli point of view, the nature of the regime established under the Oslo Agreements throughout the West Bank is "that of a Palestinian autonomy under the supreme authority of the Israeli military government."[585]

Although the interim period has expired, and no final status agreement has been reached, the Interim Agreement (Oslo II) is still valid and binding on the parties. The complex arrangements made under the Oslo Agreements seem to have resulted in a special legal regime (*lex specialis)* in relation to the West Bank territories. They limit the scope of the Palestinian Arab right to self-determination, just as they impose limitations on Israel's

585. Singer (1995), at p. 8. See also Malanczuk (1996).

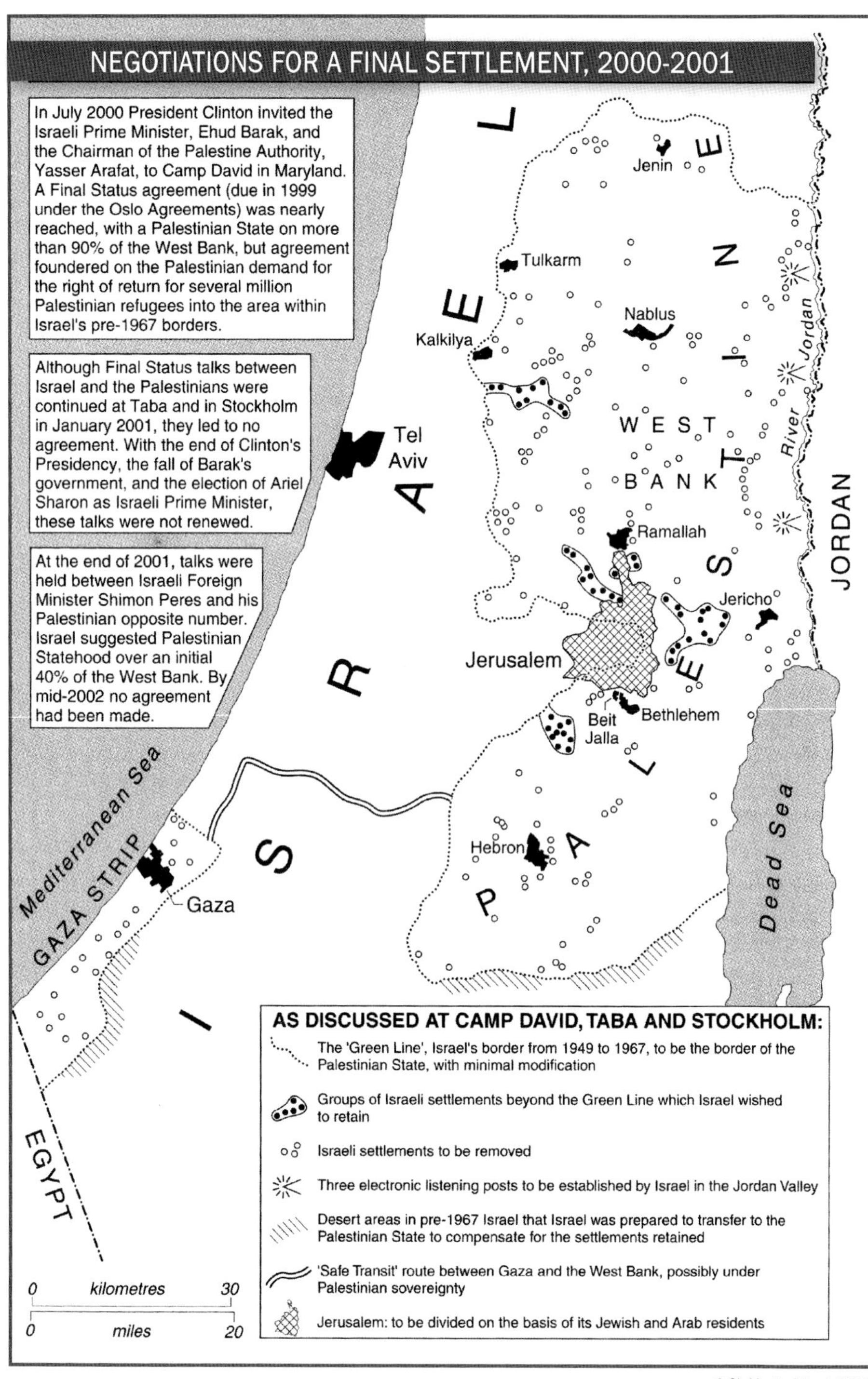
NEGOTIATIONS FOR A FINAL SETTLEMENT, 2000-2001
In July 2000 President Clinton invited the Israeli Prime Minister, Ehud Barak, and the Chairman of the Palestine Authority, Yasser Arafat, to Camp David in Maryland. A Final Status agreement (due in 1999 under the Oslo Agreements) was nearly reached, with a Palestinian State on more than 90% of the West Bank, but agreement foundered on the Palestinian demand for the right of return for several million Palestinian refugees into the area within Israel's pre-1967 borders.
Although Final Status talks between Israel and the Palestinians were continued at Taba and in Stockholm in January 2001, they led to no agreement. With the end of Clinton's Presidency, the fall of Barak's government, and the election of Ariel Sharon as Israeli Prime Minister, these talks were not renewed.
At the end of 2001, talks were held between Israeli Foreign Minister Shimon Peres and his Palestinian opposite number. Israel suggested Palestinian Statehood over an initial 40% of the West Bank. By mid-2002 no agreement had been made.
ISRAEL
PALESTINE
WEST BANK
Jenin
Tulkarm
Nablus
Kalkilya
Tel Aviv
Ramallah
Jericho
Jerusalem
Beit Jalla
Bethlehem
Hebron
Gaza
GAZA STRIP
Mediterranean Sea
River Jordan
JORDAN
Dead Sea
EGYPT
0 kilometres 30
0 miles 20
AS DISCUSSED AT CAMP DAVID, TABA AND STOCKHOLM:
The 'Green Line', Israel's border from 1949 to 1967, to be the border of the Palestinian State, with minimal modification
Groups of Israeli settlements beyond the Green Line which Israel wished to retain
Israeli settlements to be removed
Three electronic listening posts to be established by Israel in the Jordan Valley
Desert areas in pre-1967 Israel that Israel was prepared to transfer to the Palestinian State to compensate for the settlements retained
'Safe Transit' route between Gaza and the West Bank, possibly under Palestinian sovereignty
Jerusalem: to be divided on the basis of its Jewish and Arab residents

exercise of territorial sovereignty and right to political independence. As instruments of international law,[586] they impose mutual rights and obligations, limiting the application of general principles of law.

It is not entirely clear to what extent the Oslo Agreements affect Israel's claim to sovereignty over the West Bank.[587] Given that Israel retains all "residual" powers not explicitly transferred to the Palestinian Legislative Council, it would seem that—pending final agreement—even in respect of Areas A and B, the Oslo Arrangements do not affect the underlying territorial sovereignty. In respect of Area C, there can be no doubt that the Oslo Agreements do not compromise Israel's claims to territorial sovereignty.

The Interim Agreement (Oslo II) prohibits both parties from initiating "any step that will change the status of the West Bank and the Gaza Strip pending the outcome of the permanent status negotiations."[588] The question arises whether the construction of settlements in Jerusalem or other parts of the West Bank constitutes a "step" that "change the status of the West Bank pending the outcome of permanent status negotiations." It is difficult to see how that could be the case. The question of the settlements is one of those issues explicitly reserved for permanent status negotiations, together with "Jerusalem, refugees, security arrangements, borders, relations and cooperation with other neighbours and other issues of common interest."[589] Pending successful negotiation on those issues, Israel retains full power and responsibility within Area C (including Jerusalem). This includes zoning and planning responsibilities. As demonstrated in the Camp David negotiations in 2000, Israel has repeatedly indicated that, as part of a final agreement, it is willing to give up control over large parts of the West Bank that include Israeli settlements.

By explicitly incorporating UN Security Council Resolutions 242 and 338 into the DOP and Interim Agreement (Oslo II), Israel and the Palestinians recognize that any outcome of the negotiations must comply with the criteria set out in those resolutions. Specifically, they recognize that Israel is not required to withdraw from all of the "post-1967" territories.

---

586. There is much discussion about the exact nature of these documents. Notwithstanding the fact that the PLO is not a State, it seems to be generally accepted that these agreements are governed by international law and are binding on the parties.

587. As described above, Israel considers it still has a "claim to sovereignty" over the West Bank, and that this area is not de jure "occupied territory" in the sense of het Fourth Geneva Convention. See Singer (1994), at p. 276.

588. Article XXXI(7) of the Interim Agreement.

589. Article V(3) of the DOP.

Further, all states in the region have a responsibility not to endanger the territorial integrity or political independence of Israel (or any other state in the region, for that matter).[590] Given the relationship between the PLO and the Arab League, this would include an obligation on the Arab League states to ensure that the PLO terminates terrorism and other acts of hostility towards Israel.

590. See Becker (1998), at pp. 347-352.

13. Are Israeli "Settlements" Illegal?

"As a result of the planned route, nearly 320,000 Israeli settlers (of whom 178,000 are in East Jerusalem) would be living in the area between the Green Line and the wall."

Advisory Opinion (Paragraph 84)[591]

"The Court concludes that the Israeli settlements in the Occupied Palestinian territory (including East Jerusalem) have been established in breach of international law."

Advisory Opinion (Paragraph 121)[592]

13.1 Introduction

Critics of Israel qualify Israeli settlements in East Jerusalem and the West Bank territories as *the* major stumbling block for peace between Israel and the Palestinian Arabs, and therefore for peace in the Middle East. United Nations (UN) Security Council Resolution 2334 (2016) expressed in the preamble the view that "continuing Israeli settlement activities are dangerously imperiling the viability of the two-State solution based on the 1967 lines." In its first operative paragraph, the Security Council declared that the establishment of settlements "has no legal validity and [that it] constitutes a flagrant violation under international law..."

The word "settlement" is not defined by the Security Council. While attention is often directed to the building of houses, what it is apparently intended to refer to is not so much the physical infrastructure as the Israeli citizens living as communities in East Jerusalem and the West Bank. By the end of 2015, over half a million Israelis—594,000—lived in the West Bank and East Jerusalem: approximately 386,000 Israelis

---

591. I.C.J. Reports 2004, p. 170.

592. I.C.J. Reports 2004, p. 184.

in Area C of the West Bank, and 208,000 in East Jerusalem.[593] Israeli policy and practice concerning the zoning, planning and construction of settlements in the West Bank has gone through many phases. Over the years, many different policies have been developed, some of them more "expansionist" than others. Particularly since the late 1970s, official Israeli policy has explicitly stimulated Israelis to build, live and work in the "occupied" territories.

The physical constructions supporting or enabling Israelis to live in these territories range in character from farming communities and frontier villages to urban suburbs and neighborhoods. Besides "east" Jerusalem, the largest "settlements" are the cities of Modi'in, Illit, Ma'ale Adumim, Beitar Illit and Ariel, having populations ranging between 18,000 and 55,500. The infrastructure supporting these communities includes not only industrial constructions and domestic homes and public buildings, but also roads and other infrastructure necessary to support and connect these communities.[594] Criticism of settlements also extends to the fact that some of the roads connecting settlements with one another and with Israel-proper are restricted to use by Israeli-registered vehicles (of both Jews and Arabs), i.e. for security reasons, non-Israeli-registered vehicles are prohibited from using many of these roads.

Three administrative mechanisms have been used by Israel since 1967 to allow or facilitate the construction of settlements in the West Bank:

1. Requisition of land for "military needs." This was the primary mechanism used in the period 1967-1979 to enable settlements to be built. A relatively small number of the Israeli settlements existing today in the West Bank were originally built on land that was seized by the Israeli military commander from Palestinian land owners. It would seem

593. A/HRC/34/39 of 16 March 2017, 'Israeli settlements in the Occupied Palestinian Territory, including East Jerusalem, and the occupied Syrian Golan', Report of the Secretary General, p. 4, para 11. Approximately 4.5 million Palestinians live in the disputed territories – 2.8 million Palestinians in the West Bank (including "East Jerusalem") and 1.7 million in the Gaza Strip. See, Palestinian Central Bureau for Statistics, 'Palestinians at the end of 2013' (http://www.pcbs.gov.ps/post.aspx?lang=en&ItemID=996, visited: 20 April 2018).

594. The UN Human Rights Council fact-finding Mission to investigate Israeli settlements in the OPT uses the following expansive definition of 'settlement': "For the purpose of its work, the Mission understands 'Israeli Settlements', hereinafter 'settlements', to encompass all physical and non-physical structures and processes that constitute, enable and support the establishment, expansion and maintenance of Israeli residential communities beyond the 1949 Green Line in the OPT. The Mission does not differentiate between 'settlements', 'settlement blocs', 'outposts' or any other structures that have been erected, established, expanded and/or appropriated or any land or natural resources appropriated." This definition is so astonishingly broad, and would seem to go well beyond the concept of 'transfer of population' in Article 49(6) of the FGC.

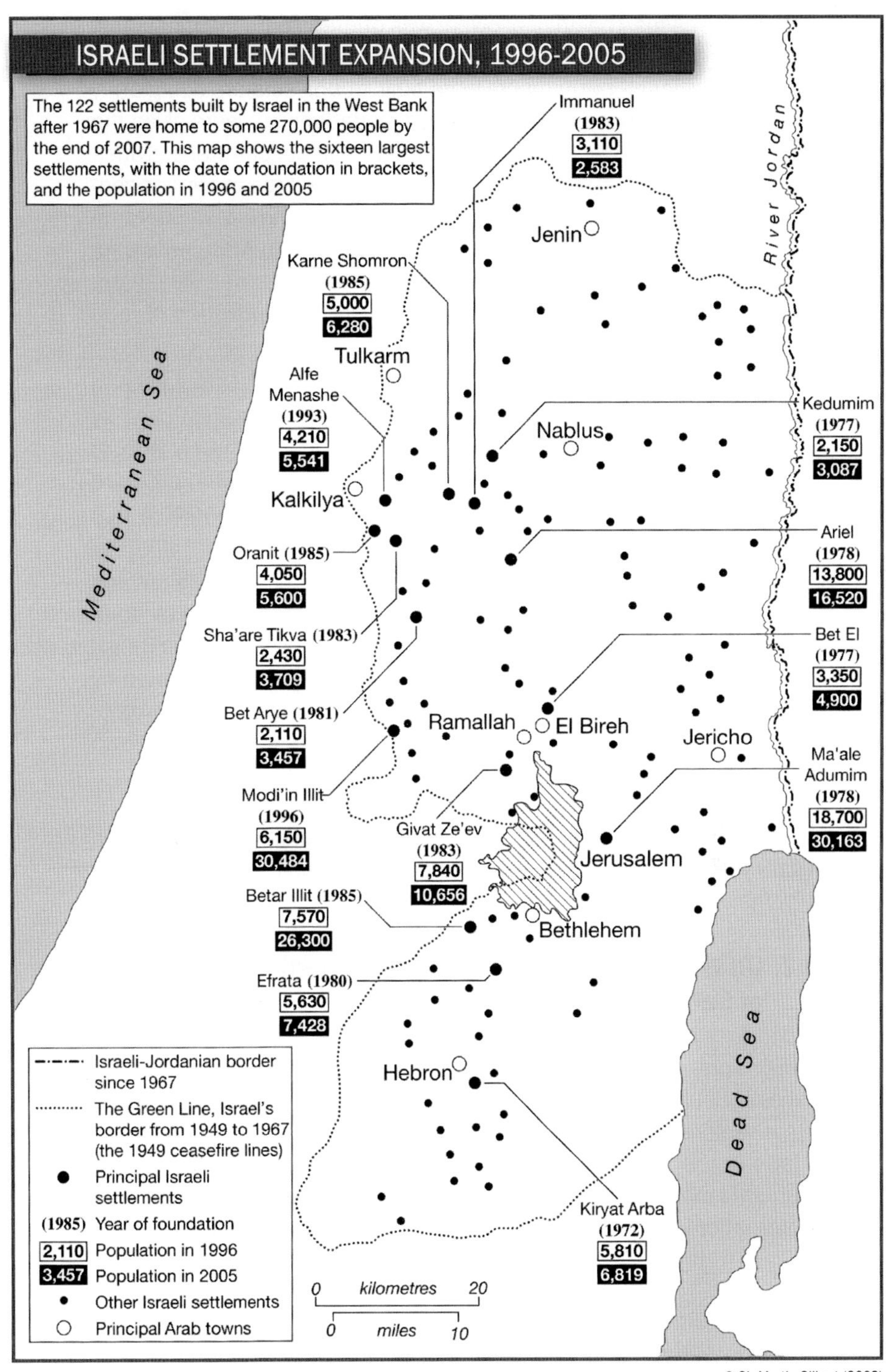
ISRAELI SETTLEMENT EXPANSION, 1996-2005
The 122 settlements built by Israel in the West Bank after 1967 were home to some 270,000 people by the end of 2007. This map shows the sixteen largest settlements, with the date of foundation in brackets, and the population in 1996 and 2005
Immanuel (1983) 3,110 2,583
River Jordan
Jenin
Karne Shomron (1985) 5,000 6,280
Mediterranean Sea
Tulkarm
Alfe Menashe (1993) 4,210 5,541
Kedumim (1977) 2,150 3,087
Nablus
Kalkilya
Ariel (1978) 13,800 16,520
Oranit (1985) 4,050 5,600
Sha'are Tikva (1983) 2,430 3,709
Bet El (1977) 3,350 4,900
Bet Arye (1981) 2,110 3,457
Ramallah
El Bireh
Jericho
Ma'ale Adumim (1978) 18,700 30,163
Modi'in Illit (1996) 6,150 30,484
Givat Ze'ev (1983) 7,840 10,656
Jerusalem
Betar Illit (1985) 7,570 26,300
Bethlehem
Efrata (1980) 5,630 7,428
Dead Sea
Hebron
Kiryat Arba (1972) 5,810 6,819
Israeli-Jordanian border since 1967
The Green Line, Israel's border from 1949 to 1967 (the 1949 ceasefire lines)
Principal Israeli settlements
(1985) Year of foundation
2,110 Population in 1996
3,457 Population in 2005
Other Israeli settlements
Principal Arab towns
0 kilometres 20
0 miles 10

that in all cases, the original owner was offered compensation. Most of the first settlements built after 1967 were military outposts. In addition, "Nahal" settlements were built: Young soldiers doing army service were housed in military accommodations but were given the opportunity to engage (on a part-time basis) in agricultural activities. Most of these Nahal settlements have subsequently been "civilianized." Following the *Elon Moreh* case in 1997, in which the Israeli Supreme Court held that the seizure of private property from Arab owners for the purposes of building Israeli civilian settlements was illegal, the Israeli military government has abandoned the requisition of land and started to allocate public lands.[595]

2. Declaration by Israel of land as "state land," under the Ottoman Land Law of 1858. This has been the primary legal mechanism used by Israel to authorize settlements since 1979. "Approximately 90% of the settlements [in the West Bank] are established on land declared 'state land'."[596] Most, but not all, of the settlements in Israel today that have been built on "state land" were built with official Israeli approval.
3. Private transfers of land. Some settlements have been built on land that was purchased and transferred pursuant to private transactions. Some of this land has been owned by Jews since the days of the British Mandate or even the Ottoman Empire, and illegally confiscated by Jordan in 1949-1967. An example is the Gush Etzion bloc. In other cases, land has been purchased from "absentee landlords": Arab landowners resident in other countries.

Palestinian Arabs claiming that land has been appropriated or acquired illegally are entitled to take proceedings in the Israeli courts. There are many instances of such proceedings.

13.2 On What Basis Could the Establishment of Settlements Be Said to Be Illegal?

In Chapter 6, we argued that Israeli settlements are legitimate based on the continuing relevance of the Mandate for Palestine, especially Article 6, that required the Mandatory Power to enable the "close settlement" of Jews in the Mandate territory. Here, we will address the common arguments made for the claim that the settlements are illegal according to international law. Those who claim that the settlements are illegal do

595. See Dinstein (2009), p. 245.

596. Albeck (1985), 'Lands in Judea and Samaria', cited in B'Tselem (2002), p. 51.

so on the basis of one or more of three claims:

a. Settlements are forbidden by article 49(6) of the Fourth Geneva Convention;
b. Settlements are illegal because they constitute "creeping annexation";
c. Settlements are illegal because they infringe on the human rights of Palestinians, including the right to freedom of movement and the right to a contiguous state.

The International Court of Justice (ICJ) in its Wall Advisory Opinion seemed to base its conclusion that Israeli settlements are illegal on all of these grounds.

13.3 The Prohibition on Deportation or Transfer of the Occupier's Civilian Population into Occupied Territories

The primary basis on which "Israeli settlements" are said to be illegal is the sixth paragraph of article 49 of the Fourth Geneva Convention. This provides:

> **"The Occupying Power shall not deport or transfer parts of its own civilian population into the territory it occupies."**

Article 49(6) was intended to apply to large-scale *forced transfers or deportations* of population groups. Paragraph (6) must be interpreted in the context of the whole of article 49. All of the preceding paragraphs of article 49 are explicitly stated only to apply to forced transfers of population. As Ambassador Morris Abram—a member of the US staff at the Nuremburg Tribunal and later involved in the drafting of the Fourth Geneva Convention—has stated, the convention "was not designed to cover situations like the Israeli settlements in the occupied territories, but rather the forcible transfer, deportation or resettlement of large numbers of people."[597]

Further, according to the International Committee of the Red Cross (ICRC),[598] which is responsible for implementing the Fourth Geneva Convention, article 49(6) only applies to deportations carried out with

---

597. Ambassador Abram in discussion with Arab ambassadors in Geneva, February 1990, cited by Baker (2011 c), footnote 9.

598. International Committee of the Red Cross, Convention (IV) relative to the Protection of Civilian Persons in Time of War, Geneva, 12 August 1949, Commentary - Art. 49.

a specific reason or intention: namely political, racial or colonial. While we should not place too much emphasis on this statement—the ICRC's commentary is not binding, and these words do not appear in the text of the Fourth Geneva Convention itself—nevertheless, we cannot ignore the fact that those who drafted Article 49(6) of the Convention apparently had a specific kind of "deportation" in mind. They were concerned to prevent states from misusing their own populations in order to suppress the population of the occupied territory. As Prof. Eugene V. Rostow has stated, in order for state encouragement of population transfers into the occupied territory to qualify as illegal, there must be some "atrocious purpose." According to the ICRC, article 49(6) "is intended to prevent a practice adopted during the Second World War by certain Powers, which transferred portions of their own population to occupied territory for political and racial reasons or in order, as they claimed, to colonize those territories. Such transfers worsened the economic situation of the native population and endangered their separate existence."[599] The ICRC was referring to the practice adopted by Nazi Germany and the Soviet Russian regimes (and their allies) to forcibly deport or transfer massive population groups into areas they had conquered during the war. In total, over 40 million people were subject to such "forced migration" during and after WWII, including 15 million Germans, 5 million Soviet citizens, and millions of Poles, Ukrainians and Hungarians. To quote Professor Julius Stone:[600]

> **"It is clear that in the drafting history, Article 49 as a whole was directed against the heinous practice of the Nazi regime during the Nazi occupation of Europe in World War II of forcibly transporting populations of which it wished to rid itself, into or out of occupied territories for the purpose of liquidating them with minimum disturbance of its metropolitan territory, or to provide slave labor or for other inhumane purposes. The genocidal objectives, of which Article 49 was concerned to prevent future repetitions against other peoples, were in part conceived by the Nazi authorities as a means of ridding their Nazi occupant's metropolitan territory of Jews: of making it, in Nazi terminology, *judenrein*. Such practices were, of course, prominent among the offences tried by war crimes tribunals after World War II. Article 49 (6) was drafted to prevent the impairment of the economic situation or racial integrity of the native population of the occupied territory and the inhuman treatment of its own population."**

That the word "transfer" is limited to direct coercion on the part of the occupying power of the person who is being transferred, is also supported

599. See ICRC Commentary to the Fourth Geneva Convention, edited by Jean S. Pictet (1958) at pp. 3-9 for a discussion of the background and drafting of the Convention.

600. Lacey (ed.) (2004), pp. 14-15.

by the fact that the drafters of the Rome Statute of the Criminal Court in 2002 felt it necessary to insert the words "directly or indirectly" in the equivalent provision,[601] in what has been called "a snub to Israel."[602]

13.3.1 Has Israel "Deported" or "Transferred" Parts of Its Population into East Jerusalem and the West Bank Since 1967?

With the exception of military outposts, most if not all of Israeli citizens who have moved into these areas since 1967 have done so voluntarily: While they may have received government assistance, they have not been "induced," "coerced" or "forced" to do so by the Israeli government.

Even if one, for the sake of argument, would concede that article 49(6) of the Fourth Geneva Convention prohibits voluntary settlement that is actually assisted or facilitated by the occupying power, whether financially or otherwise, this may apply to many of settlements, but it is by no means true of all settlements. Some settlements have been financed and constructed without any government support. Many have been built on private land owned by Jews prior to 1948 (in some cases prior to the British Mandate for Palestine), or purchased since 1967 for full market value, without government support. We would concur with the more nuanced approach of Professor Dinstein that "[w]hen settlers act entirely in their own initiative, when they do not arrogate for themselves land belonging to others or expropriated from its rightful owners, and when they do not benefit from any overt or covert government inducement neither the letter nor the spirit of Article 49 (sixth paragraph) comes into play."[603]

The claim that all Israeli settlements amount to illegal transfers of population, and the suggestion that Israel is under an obligation to remove them, is a gross distortion of both the letter and the spirit of this provision. As Professor Julius Stone has stated so eloquently: "[I]rony would thus be pushed to the absurdity of claiming that Article 49(6), designed to prevent repetition of Nazi-type genocidal policies of rendering Nazi metropolitan territories *judenrein*, has now come to mean that Judea and Samaria (the West Bank) must be made *judenrein* and must be so maintained, if necessary by the use of force by the government of Israel against its own inhabitants."[604]

---

601. Article 8(2)(b)(viii) of the Rome Statute defines as a war crime the "transfer, directly or indirectly, by the Occupying Power of parts of its own civilian population into the territory it occupies."

602. Cryer (2005), p. 274.

603. Dinstein (2009), p. 241.

604. Lacey (ed.) (2004), p. 15. See also Baker (2011 b), at p. 70.

It is important to understand the far-reaching implications of the ICJ's conclusion that all Israeli settlements in the West Bank and East Jerusalem have been established in breach of international law. That broadly formulated conclusion, together with the fact that "settlement" is not defined by the ICJ (and potentially refers to any Israeli residing in these territories and any activity relating thereto), coupled with the obligation on other states "not to recognize such illegalities" and on the UN itself to bring such illegalities to an end,[605] potentially lays the foundation for the use of diplomatic and perhaps even military measures to compel Israel to remove all of its citizens from these territories. This approach is reflected in paragraph 9 of UN Security Council Resolution 2334, in which the Council:

> "*Urges in this regard* the intensification and acceleration of international and regional diplomatic efforts and support aimed at achieving, without delay a comprehensive, just and lasting peace in the Middle East on the basis of the relevant United Nations resolutions, the Madrid terms of reference, including the principle of land for peace, the Arab Peace Initiative and the Quartet Roadmap and an end to the Israeli occupation that began in 1967; and *underscores* in this regard the importance of the ongoing efforts to advance the Arab Peace Initiative, the initiative of France for the convening of an international peace conference, the recent efforts of the Quartet, as well as the efforts of Egypt and the Russian Federation."

This conclusion is alarming, and extremely dangerous, if nothing else because it effectively denies any Jewish Israeli citizen the right to live in territories to which his ancestors have incontrovertibly had a unique and close connection, and which are so very important to his religion as a Jew. It is setting up the justification of a scenario in which this most Jewish of all territories in the world—and, with the exception of those territories currently incorporated in the State of Israel, the last area in the Middle East in which Jews can freely live—is to be forcibly cleansed of Jews.

13.4 The "Creeping Annexation" Argument

Some critics of the settlements claim that Israel has facilitated the construction of settlements in order to extend its sovereign territorial borders, by means of practices and policies of "creeping expropriation" or "*de facto* annexation" in the West Bank. John Dugard, for example, qualified the construction of the security barrier as an act of unlawful (*de*

605. See paragraphs 159 and 160 of the Opinion.

facto) annexation,[606] a qualification which was reproduced by the ICJ, as is clear from the following quotation:

> **"The Court considers that the construction of the wall and its associated regime create a 'fait accompli' on the ground that could well become permanent, in which case, and notwithstanding the formal characterization of the wall by Israel, it would be tantamount to *de facto* annexation."** [607]

In Resolution 2334, the UN Security Council picked up on this argument by condemning "all measures aimed at altering the demographic composition, character and status of the Palestinian Territory occupied since 1967, including East Jerusalem, including, *inter alia*, the construction and expansion of settlements, transfer of Israeli settlers, confiscation of land, demolition of homes and displacement of Palestinian civilians, in violation of international humanitarian law and relevant resolutions."

Inevitably, private and public statements by Israeli leaders can be quoted to support the claim that Israel has deliberately sought to "annex" the West Bank. And of course, although the word "annexation" is not used, there is no doubt that since 1967 Israel has applied full Israeli administration and law to East Jerusalem. Such statements probably reflect the widely held opinion in Israel that the Jewish people have an equal if not superior entitlement to the territories occupied since 1967, based on their historical connection with the land, and the official Israeli view that these are not legally "occupied" territories in the sense of the Fourth Geneva Convention. As we have seen, this view is not unfounded. International law does not prohibit Israel from asserting its claims to territorial sovereignty over East Jerusalem and the West Bank. The fact remains, however that Israel has demonstrated on many occasions that it is willing to give up territorial claims to most of the land on which settlements have been built since 1967. Israel has even evicted thousands of settlers from the territories occupied since 1967 (the entire settlement communities in Sinai and the Gaza Strip, and several settlements in the West Bank).

Further, the underlying suggestion in the "creeping annexation" claim is that Israel is deporting Palestinian Arabs from East Jerusalem and the West Bank in order to "alter the status" of these territories. There is no doubt that the housing of several hundreds and perhaps even thousands of Palestinian Arabs is being affected by Israel both in Israel-proper and in

---

606. E/CN.4/2004/6, paragraphs 6-16.

607. I.C.J. Reports 2004, p. 184.

Area C of the West Bank. According to the UN Office for the Coordination of Humanitarian Affairs (OCHA):[608]

> **"Thousands of Palestinians throughout the occupied Palestinian territory have been forcibly displaced or are at risk of forced displacement, which has immediate and longer-term physical, socio-economic and psycho-social impacts on Palestinian families, particularly on children. In the West Bank, displacement is primarily driven by occupation-related policies, including the inability to obtain building permits and related demolitions, residency status issues and the impact of the barrier."**

There is no evidence, however, as far as we are aware, that Israel is systematically displacing Arabs with the intention of altering the demographic character of the West Bank. House evictions and demolitions have only occurred as punishment for terrorism or in relation to established breaches of Israeli law, planning requirements or security. Further, Palestinian Arabs—even those that are not Israeli citizens—have a right to compensation in the event of confiscation of property, and full access to the Israeli legal system to enforce their rights. [609]

Finally, even if there is some truth in the claims that Israel's policies have the effect of altering the demographic character in East Jerusalem and Area C, we would note that house demolitions and forcible removal of Palestinian Arabs do not in any way alter the legal status of these territories. Whether or not Israel or the PLO have a valid claim to territorial sovereignty over these territories depends not on the current demographic composition of these territories, or the conduct of Israel in relation to individual Palestinian Arabs, the legal significance of events prior to June 1967.

Finally, it should be noted that the challenges of managing different ethnic, religious and national groups within one geographical area is bound to raise difficulties. Systems are bound to be imperfect, and particular

608. See on the website of the Office for the Coordination of Humanitarian Affairs: https://www.ochaopt.org/theme/displacement.

609. Freedom House reported in 2017: "According to the UN Office for the Coordination of Humanitarian Affairs (UNOCHA), 1,093 Palestinian-owned structures in the West Bank, including East Jerusalem, were demolished or seized during the year, nearly double the number for 2015, with a comparative monthly average of 91 versus 46. More than 1,600 Palestinians were displaced as a result of these demolitions or seizures. A fraction of such demolitions are conducted to punish families of Palestinians accused of perpetrating violence against Israelis or in the course of military operations. Israel cited a lack of Israeli-issued building permits for the majority of demolitions and seizures, which occurred in East Jerusalem and in Area C, the portion of the West Bank under its direct administrative and security control." See: https://freedomhouse.org/report/freedom-world/2017/west-bank (visited: 12 March 2018).

groups are bound to claim that their rights have been insufficiently respected. This challenge is not in itself a consequence of the "occupation," nor is it unique to East Jerusalem and the West Bank. A good example is the case of the Bedouins in the Negev and Galilee regions in Israel. Discussions have been going on in Israel for years about how to respect the legitimate interests of this semi-nomadic group while also managing the development of the State of Israel. So far, a suitable arrangement has yet to be found, and there are troubling discrepancies in social standards, but there is at least an open and transparent process. In the meantime, Bedouins are participating fully in Israeli society—many serve in the Israeli army (IDF), and some reach high positions in Israeli society.

To conclude: Instead of being a case of gross breach of human rights, the standards applied by the State of Israel—both within Israel proper as well as East Jerusalem and the West Bank—in giving recognition to the interests of different ethnic and religious groups while at the same time managing economic and social development and fighting terrorism are among the highest in the world.[610] According to Freedom House, respect for the human rights of minorities in Israel and Area C of the West Bank far exceeds that of neighboring states, such as Syria, Jordan, Lebanon and Egypt—who paradoxically tend to be the most outspoken critics of Israel. It also far exceeds the human rights record of the PA in Areas A and B of the West Bank, where there is no stable and effective governing authority, and there are massive breaches of civil liberties and freedom of speech, movement and religion.[611]

13.5 Settlements as Infringement on Palestinian Human Rights

There is no doubt that the freedoms of some Palestinians are detrimentally affected by some settlements. But as far as we are aware, no evidence has been adduced to show that Israel's settlement policies *as a whole* have had the purpose or effect of worsening the economic situation of the Palestinian Arabs. It is also difficult to see how the existence of Jewish settlements could be said to endanger the separate existence

610. In 2017, Freedom House summarized human rights compliance in Israel as follows: "Israel is a multiparty democracy with strong and independent institutions that guarantee political rights and civil liberties for most of the population. Although the judiciary is active in protecting minority rights, the ruling elite has traditionally discriminated against the Arab and, to a lesser degree, the ultra-Orthodox and Ethiopian minorities." See: https://freedomhouse.org/report/freedom-world/2017/israel (visited: 12 March 2018).

611. See: https://freedomhouse.org/report/freedom-world/2017/west-bank (visited: 12 March 2018).

of the Palestinian Arab people or impair their economic situation. On the contrary, many Palestinian Arabs benefit greatly by some of the settlements. Thousands of Palestinian Arabs are employed by enterprises owned by Israeli citizens and situated in the West Bank. Israeli investment in natural resources and infrastructure development also provides direct and indirect benefits to the Palestinian Arab population in these territories.

There is also no conclusive evidence that the mere presence of Israeli citizens in East Jerusalem and the West Bank is preventing Palestinian Arabs from enjoying self-determination—even if that right is considered to include a right to statehood. Israel has demonstrated under several governments that it is willing to remove certain settlements as part of an overall peace agreement.

Finally, even if the territories (or any part of them) would become part of a Palestinian State or autonomous entity, that does not mean that Jews living there should leave. As one commentator has stated: "[I]n principle, there should be a symmetry between Israel and its neighbors. Israel has a large Arab minority that enjoys civil rights within it. Why shouldn't Jews be allowed to live in neighboring Arab countries?"[612]

13.6 Discriminatory Application of the "Transfer" Allegation

There are many examples of alleged belligerent occupation in the world—territories where, in the context of military conflict, one state has taken control over territory belonging (or claimed to belong) to another sovereign power. In many of these cases, the "occupying power" has deliberately moved parts of its population into the occupied territory. In a recent study entitled "*Unsettled: A Global Study of Settlements in Occupied Territories,*"[613] Professor Eugene Kontorovich examined nine such settlement contexts, each of which is commonly understood to constitute "occupation" within the meaning of the international law of belligerent occupation: East-Timor, Western Sahara, Northern Cyprus, Syria/Lebanon, Vietnam/Cambodia, Armenia/Azerbijan (Nagorno-Karabak), Russia-Georgia (Abkhazia) & Ukraine (Crimea), the Baltic States (Estonia, Latvia and Lithuania). Kontorovich concluded that in none of these cases has the alleged Occupying Power received from the international community condemnation for violation of article 49(6) of the Fourth Geneva Convention. This is remarkable, given that the migration of residents of the occupying

612. Gavison (1996).

613. Kontorovitch (2017), p. 66.

power into occupied territory appeared as "a near-ubiquitous feature of extended belligerent occupation."

Israel is the only state since WWII that has been consistently condemned in UN resolutions for occupying territory and transferring its population into "occupied" territories and threatened with measures to remove those populations. This disproportionate attention to Israel cannot be explained on purely legal grounds, given the existence of other glaring examples of population transfers into occupied territories (for example Turkey's movement of its citizens into Northern Cyprus), with massive breaches of human rights. In light of the complexity of the Israel/Palestine case, and the objective legal and factual strength of the Israeli claim to sovereignty over East Jerusalem and the West Bank, in comparison with many of the other cases of occupation, this constant criticism of Israel constitutes a blatantly discriminatory and unfair application of international law—suggesting that the purpose of the constant criticism of Israel's "settlement policies" is not driven by concern for the sanctity of law, or the needs of justice, but by extraneous political and military objectives.

13.7 Relevance of the Oslo Agreements to the Status of Israeli Settlements

Finally, a note must be made on the relevance of the Oslo Agreements to the issue of the settlements. Under Article V(3) of the DOP, the issue of the settlements is subject to the permanent status negotiations. This means first that the parties accept that they are not by definition illegal. Moreover, this postpones a definitive conclusion as to the legal position of the settlements until a final agreement has been reached. In any event, there is no reason why Israeli settlers who are legitimately living on lands or properties in the West Bank should be seen as impeding a final status agreement regarding these territories. Once a comprehensive peace agreement has been reached, some Israeli settlers may (depending on the terms of that agreement) have to either dismantle their homes or choose to live under the new regime.

14. Jerusalem

"From 1967 onwards, Israel took a number of measures in these territories aimed at changing the status of the City of Jerusalem."

Advisory Opinion (Paragraph 75)[614]

14.1 Introduction

For the Jewish people, the Old City of Jerusalem is an essential and inexorable part of their identity as Jews. Jerusalem is where the Temple was built and rebuilt. It is where the Kings of Israel reigned. It is where they believe the Messiah will come. Since the destruction of Jerusalem in 70 CE, Jews worldwide have been praying daily to return to Jerusalem. This city expresses the essence of the Jewish people; it represents their past, their present and their future as a people. Despite the destruction of the Second Temple in 70 CE and the mass slaughter and eviction of Jews in 135 CE, Jews have always had a significant presence in East Jerusalem. Jerusalem has always had a mixed population, and it has never been an Arab city. In 1881, Jews constituted 52 percent of the population of Jerusalem. In 1914, Jews constituted 42 percent of the population of Jerusalem, which by then had extended beyond the Old City walls. In 1948, there were 100,000 Jews in the whole of Jerusalem, and 65,000 Arabs. In June 1993, official records show a Jewish majority in East Jerusalem: 155,000 Jews and 150,000 Palestinians. At the end of 2008, the population of East Jerusalem was 456,300, comprising 60 percent of Jerusalem's residents. Of these, 195,500 (43 percent) were Jews (comprising 40 percent of the Jewish population of Jerusalem as a whole), and 260,800 (57 percent) were Muslim (comprising 98 percent of the Muslim population of Jerusalem).

The Palestinians claim East Jerusalem (*Al-Quds* in Arabic) as the capital of their state. The term "East Jerusalem" is used to refer to that part of the

614. I.C.J. Reports 2004, p. 166.

city which is east, north and south of the 1949 Green Line, including the Old City of Jerusalem. The Green Line effectively runs through the heart of Jerusalem, cutting off the Old City from so-called "West" Jerusalem. The Old City is the heart of Jerusalem, where Jews, Muslims, Christians, and others have lived side by side for centuries. It comprises the Temple Mount and the Western Wall, as well as the Jewish, Christian, Armenian and Muslim Quarters, and includes many places of historical and religious significance for Christians, Muslims and Jews worldwide. Until about 1860, Jerusalem *was* limited to the Old City. As Jewish immigration increased, the city gradually developed beyond the Old City walls after that date.

14.2 History

The history of Jerusalem is complex, and it is certainly not possible to do it justice here. Suffice to say that in the 18 centuries between 135 CE and the fall of the Ottoman Turkish Empire in 1917, Jerusalem was controlled by a series of foreign powers and kingdoms: Romans, Byzantines, Arabs, Crusaders, Mamluks and Ottomans.[615] Each empire had a different perspective on the importance and significance of Jerusalem. But, with the exception of the Crusaders' Latin Kingdom of Jerusalem (1099-1291), at no time was Jerusalem the capital of any of those empires. Under the Ottoman Empire (1517-1918), Jerusalem was home to Jews and non-Jews. During these four centuries, the Jewish residents of Jerusalem went through various fortunes, depending on the Ottoman leadership of the time. In the 16th and 17th centuries, one of the lowest periods in its history, Jerusalem counted only 10,000 inhabitants.[616] In the mid-1800s, Palestine (and Jerusalem in particular) started attracting more and more international attention as the European powers (especially Britain, France, Germany and Russia) sought to extend their influence in the area and awaited the collapse of the Ottoman Empire (the "Sick Old Man"). Between 1918 and 1920, Jerusalem was under British military occupation, as was all Palestine. Anticipating the Mandate for Palestine entering into force, British occupation in 1920 was replaced by a civil administration. From 1923 to 1948, Jerusalem was part of the Mandate for Palestine, which made no specific mention of Jerusalem.

In June 1948, the Old City of Jerusalem was captured by the Arab Legion of Transjordan (led by British General John Glubb and heavily supported by the British) and remained under Jordanian control until

---

615. See Chapter 5. See also: Karsh (2010), p. 8.

616. Gauthier (2007), p. 215.

the Six-Day War in 1967. The Armistice Agreement with Jordan in 1949 drew the cease-fire line (the Green Line) through the middle of Jerusalem, effectively dividing West Jerusalem from the Old City and East Jerusalem. The Armistice Agreement between Israel and Jordan did not give Jordan sovereignty over this territory; on the contrary it explicitly left the question of the legal status of this territory open.[617] In April 1950, following elections in Jordan and the West Bank, the Jordanian parliament officially annexed the West Bank, including East Jerusalem and the Old City, proclaiming them to be part of the Kingdom of Jordan. Military occupation was replaced by Jordanian administration in these territories. The move was immediately rejected by the League of Arab States, which threatened to expel Jordan from the League. The only states to officially recognize Jordan's annexation of the West Bank were Iraq, Pakistan and Great Britain. Jordanian King Abdullah's claims to Jerusalem and the West Bank were not only rejected by the Arab League and the international community, they were bitterly opposed by the Grand Mufti of Jerusalem, Haj Amin El Husseini, who attempted to establish his own government over all of Palestine. This attempt failed, and in late 1948 Husseini fled to Egypt.

The status of Jerusalem remained controversial. For over a year after the cessation of hostilities in early 1949, discussion within the international community raged, most parties remaining committed to the "internationalization" of Jerusalem as contemplated in the 1947 Partition Plan. No consensus was reached about what this internationalization should consist of. The Vatican[618] and others insisted on *territorial* internationalization of the Old City, whereby the Old City would become legally unique, a *corpus separatum*. Others, such as the United States,[619] while not recognizing Israel's or Jordan's claims to sovereignty, favored *functional* internationalization of Jerusalem. The United States submitted proposals granting a significant level of administrative autonomy over the Old City for Israel and Jordan.

In December 1949, the United Nations (UN) General Assembly adopted Resolution 303 (IV), which contemplated the establishment of an international regime over the Jerusalem area, and called for the Trusteeship Council to draft a statute for Jerusalem. A draft resolution along these lines was presented to the General Assembly in December 1950, but it

617. See article II(2) of the Agreement: "... no provision of this Agreement shall in any way prejudice the rights, claims and positions of either Party hereto in the ultimate peaceful settlement of the Palestine question, the provisions of this Agreement being dictated exclusively by military considerations."

618. Gauthier (2007), pp. 635-636.

619. See Slonim (1984), p. 192, quoted by Gauthier (2007), p. 634 (footnote 2548).

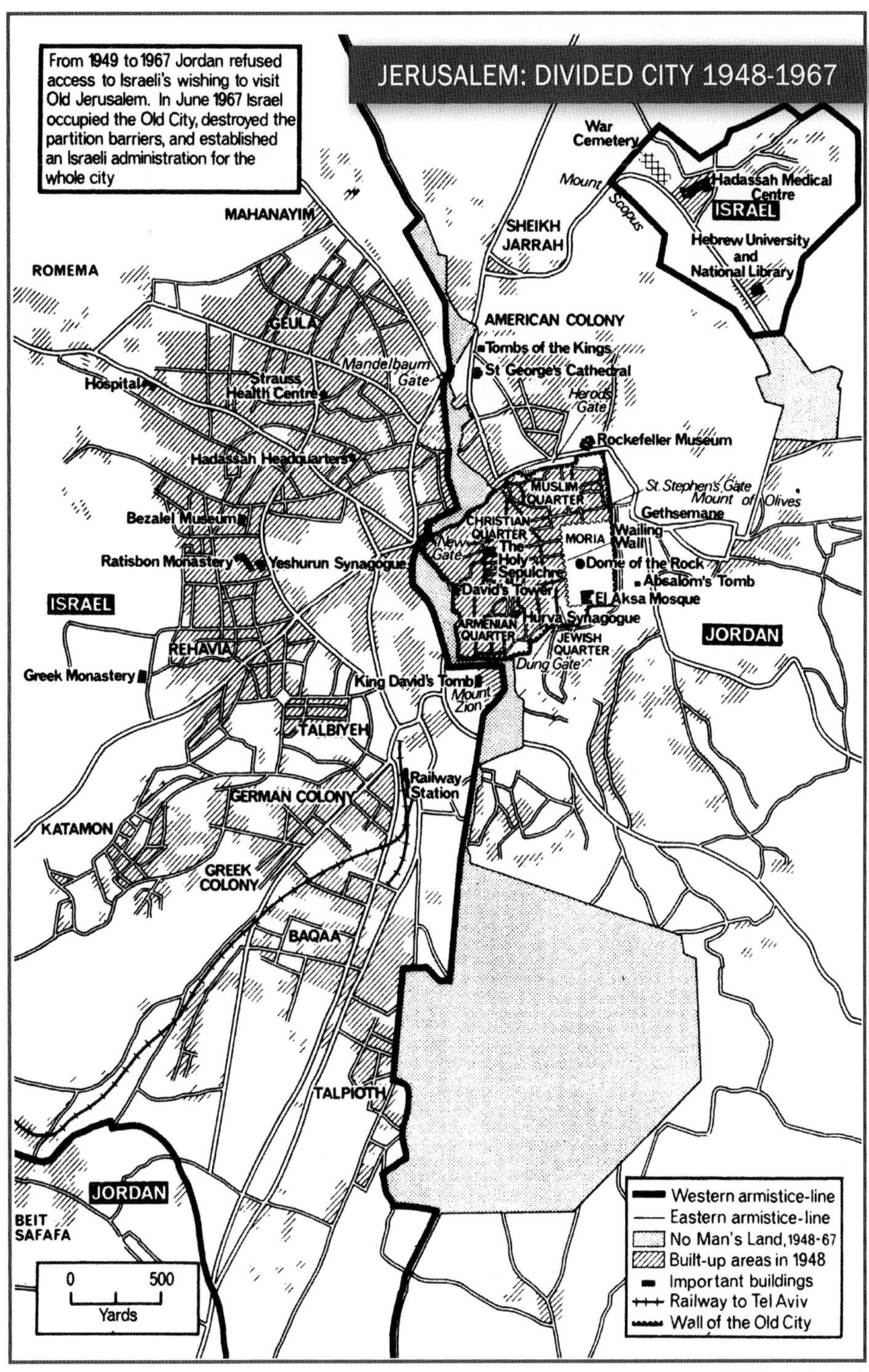
JERUSALEM: DIVIDED CITY 1948-1967
From 1949 to 1967 Jordan refused access to Israeli's wishing to visit Old Jerusalem. In June 1967 Israel occupied the Old City, destroyed the partition barriers, and established an Israeli administration for the whole city
War Cemetery
Mount Scopus
Hadassah Medical Centre
ISRAEL
Hebrew University and National Library
MAHANAYIM
SHEIKH JARRAH
ROMEMA
GEULA
AMERICAN COLONY
Tombs of the Kings
Mandelbaum Gate
St George's Cathedral
Hospital
Strauss Health Centre
Herods Gate
Rockefeller Museum
Hadassah Headquarters
MUSLIM QUARTER
St. Stephen's Gate
Mount of Olives
Gethsemane
Bezalel Museum
CHRISTIAN QUARTER
New Gate
The Holy Sepulchre
MORIA
Wailing Wall
Ratisbon Monastery
Yeshurun Synagogue
Dome of the Rock
Absalom's Tomb
David's Tower
El Aksa Mosque
ISRAEL
ARMENIAN QUARTER
Hurva Synagogue
JEWISH QUARTER
JORDAN
REHAVIA
Dung Gate
Greek Monastery
King David's Tomb
Mount Zion
TALBIYEH
Railway Station
GERMAN COLONY
KATAMON
GREEK COLONY
BAQAA
TALPIOTH
JORDAN
BEIT SAFAFA
0 500
Yards
Western armistice-line
Eastern armistice-line
No Man's Land, 1948-67
Built-up areas in 1948
Important buildings
Railway to Tel Aviv
Wall of the Old City

proved impossible to find a two-thirds majority supporting the proposal. Gradually it became clear that the UN was unable to create an international regime for Jerusalem, whether territorial, administrative or functional. The whole idea was abandoned in early 1952, when Resolution 512 (VI) was adopted, urging Jordan and Israel to "take appropriate steps" to resolve their differences. No more reference was made to internationalization of Jerusalem, and the whole idea of establishing a *corpus separatum* for Jerusalem was thereafter "allowed quietly to drop."[620]

Israel's Declaration of Independence did not contain any reference to Jerusalem. In fact, although referring to the Partition Plan in support for its right to independence, the declaration does not specifically mention borders at all. Israel, although agreeing to stop fighting in April 1949, refused to acknowledge the legality of Jordanian occupation of East Jerusalem and the West Bank, and immediately asserted sovereignty over Jerusalem. In December 1949, the Israeli Cabinet decided that Jerusalem would be the capital of Israel, and on 26 December 1949, Israel's Knesset held its first session in West Jerusalem. In January 1950, the Knesset declared Jerusalem to be the capital of Israel.[621]

Israeli forces ousted Jordanian forces from East Jerusalem and the West Bank in the Six-Day War ending on 10 June 1967. Israel immediately took steps to assume administrative control and apply Israeli law (with certain amendments) in the whole of Jerusalem.

14.3 The Legal Status of Jerusalem

14.3.1 The Aftermath of the Six-Day War

A series of laws passed by Israel's Knesset in late June 1967 authorized the Minister of the Interior to enlarge the boundaries of the city of Jerusalem and apply Israeli law to those enlarged boundaries.[622] Not many states or other international actors today seriously dispute Israel's sovereignty over the territories under its control following the cease-fire agreement with Jordan in 1949. But what was the legal status of the area outside the Green Line—especially the Old City of Jerusalem and the West Bank—in the 19-year period of Jordanian occupation between May 1948 and June 1967? This issue is critical, because it will determine the question of sovereignty after 10 June 1967. There are three possible views under international law:

---

620. Lauterpacht, Elihu (1968), p. 36.

621. Gilbert (1996), pp. 243-244.

622. Jerusalem Basic Law was passed on 28th June 1967.

- Jordan obtained sovereignty over these territories;
- A legal vacuum was created following the termination of the Mandate for Palestine in those territories; the question then is whether Israel was entitled to fill this vacuum in 1967 when it asserted sovereignty over Jerusalem.
- The rights and obligations created under the Mandate for Palestine continued with respect to the whole Mandate territory after 14 May 1948.

As explained in previous pages, the third option is to be preferred. However, UN Resolutions since 1967 have consistently condemned Israel's exercise of control over East Jerusalem (including the Old City) as in breach of international law. On 4 July 1967 the General Assembly (GA)—presented with a Pakistani draft on the situation in Jerusalem[623]—adopted Resolution 2253 (ES-V) declaring that the General Assembly, "deeply concerned at the situation prevailing in Jerusalem as a result of the measures taken by Israel to change the status of the City,

- considers that these measures are invalid,
- calls upon Israel to rescind all measures already taken and to desist forthwith from any action which would alter the status of Jerusalem,
- *Requests* the Secretary-General to report to the General Assembly and the Security Council on the situation and on the implementation of the present resolution not later than one week from its adoption."

Ten days later, on 14 July 1967, Resolution 2254 (ES-V) was adopted along similar lines:

> **"Having received the report submitted by the Secretary-General, taking note with the deepest regret and concern of the non-compliance by Israel with resolution 2253 (ES-V), the General Assembly reiterates its call to Israel in that resolution to rescind all measures already taken and to desist forthwith from taking any action which would alter the status of Jerusalem."**

The Security Council followed suit less than a year later, on 21 May 1968, with Resolution 252 (1968), in which it:

> **"2. *Considers* that all legislative and administrative measures and actions taken by Israel, including expropriation of land and properties thereon, which tend to change the legal status of Jerusalem are invalid and cannot change that status; and**

623. The Resolution was adopted by a vote of 99 in favor, none against, 20 abstentions, and 3 absent.

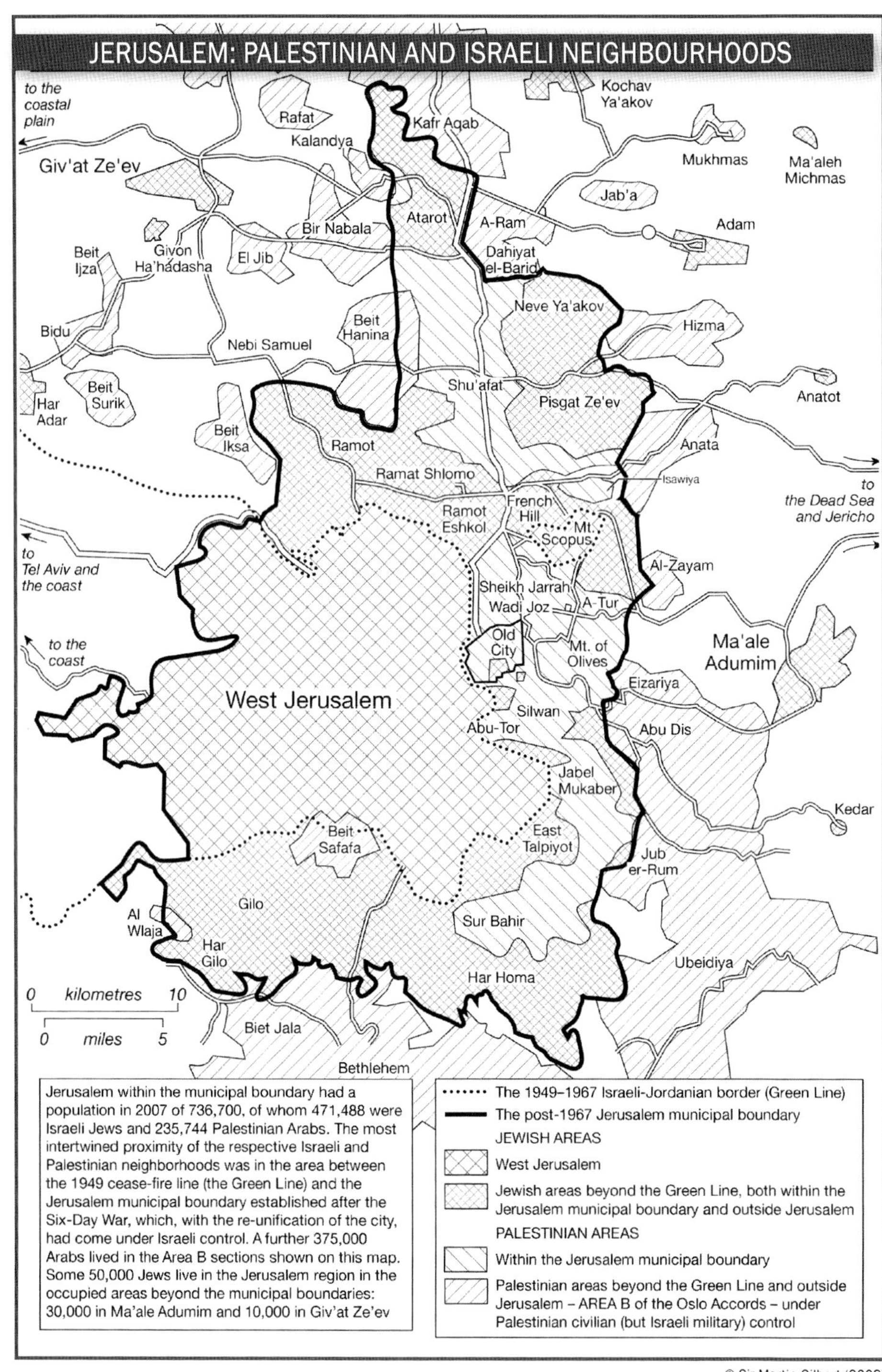
JERUSALEM: PALESTINIAN AND ISRAELI NEIGHBOURHOODS
to the coastal plain
Giv'at Ze'ev
Rafat
Kalandya
Kafr Aqab
Kochav Ya'akov
Mukhmas
Ma'aleh Michmas
Jab'a
Adam
Bir Nabala
Atarot
A-Ram
Dahiyat el-Barid
Beit Ijza
Givon Ha'hadasha
El Jib
Neve Ya'akov
Hizma
Bidu
Beit Hanina
Nebi Samuel
Beit Surik
Har Adar
Shu'afat
Pisgat Ze'ev
Anatot
Beit Iksa
Ramot
Anata
Ramat Shlomo
Isawiya
to the Dead Sea and Jericho
French Hill
Ramot Eshkol
Mt. Scopus
to Tel Aviv and the coast
Al-Zayam
Sheikh Jarrah
Wadi Joz
A-Tur
to the coast
Old City
Mt. of Olives
Ma'ale Adumim
Eizariya
West Jerusalem
Silwan
Abu-Tor
Abu Dis
Jabel Mukaber
Kedar
Beit Safafa
East Talpiyot
Jub er-Rum
Gilo
Al Wlaja
Sur Bahir
Har Gilo
Ubeidiya
Har Homa
0 kilometres 10
0 miles 5
Biet Jala
Bethlehem
Jerusalem within the municipal boundary had a population in 2007 of 736,700, of whom 471,488 were Israeli Jews and 235,744 Palestinian Arabs. The most intertwined proximity of the respective Israeli and Palestinian neighborhoods was in the area between the 1949 cease-fire line (the Green Line) and the Jerusalem municipal boundary established after the Six-Day War, which, with the re-unification of the city, had come under Israeli control. A further 375,000 Arabs lived in the Area B sections shown on this map. Some 50,000 Jews live in the Jerusalem region in the occupied areas beyond the municipal boundaries: 30,000 in Ma'ale Adumim and 10,000 in Giv'at Ze'ev
The 1949–1967 Israeli-Jordanian border (Green Line)
The post-1967 Jerusalem municipal boundary
JEWISH AREAS
West Jerusalem
Jewish areas beyond the Green Line, both within the Jerusalem municipal boundary and outside Jerusalem
PALESTINIAN AREAS
Within the Jerusalem municipal boundary
Palestinian areas beyond the Green Line and outside Jerusalem – AREA B of the Oslo Accords – under Palestinian civilian (but Israeli military) control

> 3. *Urgently calls* upon Israel to rescind all such measures already taken and to desist forthwith from taking any further action which tends to change the status of Jerusalem;..."

This Resolution was adopted with 13 votes in favor; of the Permanent Representatives, Canada and the United States abstained.

About a year later, on 3 July 1969, the Security Council used even stronger language in a similar resolution on Jerusalem. In this Resolution 267 (1969) the Security Council said that it:

> "3. Censures in the strongest terms all measures taken to change the status of the City of Jerusalem;..."

This time the Resolution was adopted unanimously.

In November 1967, the Security Council adopted Resolution 242. It is significant, from a legal perspective, that Resolution 242 does not specifically refer to Jerusalem.

14.3.2 Basic Law: Jerusalem the Capital of Israel (5740-1980)

On 30 July 1980, the Knesset passed a law (known as the "Basic Law: Jerusalem the Capital of Israel (5740-1980)") establishing Jerusalem as the "undivided capital" of Israel. The 1980 Basic Law was met with much international criticism. Even before its enactment, the law was condemned by the UN Security Council in Resolutions 476 of 30 June 1980 (adopted at the instigation of Pakistan) and 478 of 20 August 1980.[624] This last Resolution asserted that the Basic Law is in contravention of international law and that it does not prevent the continuing application of the Fourth Geneva Convention to the Palestinian and other Arab territories occupied since June 1967. The Basic Law and all other measures which seek to alter the status of Jerusalem were declared to be null and void and considered to be a serious obstruction to achieving a comprehensive, just and lasting peace in the Middle East. Resolution 478 called for all states with diplomatic missions in Jerusalem to withdraw and relocate those missions. Most nations with embassies in Jerusalem relocated their embassies to Tel Aviv following the adoption of Resolution 478. Following the withdrawals of Costa Rica and El Salvador in August 2006, no country maintains its embassy in Jerusalem, although Paraguay and Bolivia have theirs in nearby Jerusalem suburb Mevasseret Zion.

---

624. The United States abstained from voting on UN S.C. Resolutions 476 and 478 in 1980.

Recently however, there are signs of a new approach. On 6 December 2017, US President Donald Trump announced his Administration's intention to move the US Embassy from Tel Aviv to Jerusalem,[625] by implementing the Jerusalem Embassy Act, which the American Congress with overwhelming majorities in both the House and Senate had enacted in 1995.[626] President Trump decided to no longer use the possibility of postponing the implementation of this Act, as his predecessors used to do. Guatemala has also announced its intention to move its embassy in Israel to Jerusalem.[627]

Like the UN, also the European Union has condemned Israel's "annexation" of the Old City and East Jerusalem as illegal[628] and refuses to acknowledge Israeli claims to sovereignty over East Jerusalem. The Council of the EU held:

> **"The EU reiterates that it will not recognize any changes to the pre-1967 borders including with regard to Jerusalem, other than those agreed by the parties."[629]**

The Council of the EU has its own ideas on Jerusalem as a Capital: "The EU reiterates that a way must be found through negotiations to resolve the status of Jerusalem as the future capital of two states. Until then, the EU calls for an equitable provision of resources and investment to the city's population." [630]

More recently, the Basic Law on Jerusalem has again become a stone of contention within the UN. On 30 November 2017, the UN General Assembly adopted a resolution on Jerusalem (A/RES/72/15) with the votes of 151 Member States in favor, including all Members of the EU. Only six UN Member States voted against: Canada, Micronesia, Israel, Marshall Islands, Nauru and the US. There were nine abstentions. The

---

625. https://globalnews.ca/news/3900657/donald-trump-full-speech-u-s-.

626. Jerusalem Embassy Act of 1995, Public Law 104-45, 8 November 1995, 109 Stat. 398.

627. *The New York Times*, 24 December 2017.

628. In March 2009, a confidential 'EU Heads of Mission Report on East Jerusalem' was published, in which the Israeli government was accused of "actively pursuing the illegal annexation" of East Jerusalem. The report stated: "Israeli facts in the ground – including new settlements, construction of the barrier, discriminatory housing policies, house demolitions, restrictive permit regime and continued closure of Palestinian institutions – increase Jewish Israeli presence in East Jerusalem, weaken the Palestinian community in the city, impede Palestinian urban development and separate East Jerusalem from the rest of the West Bank: see McCarthy (2009).

629. Council of the EU, Press Release 9110/12, 14 May 2012.

630. *Ibid.*

second preambular paragraph of the Resolution refers explicitly to the Basic Law on Jerusalem and the proclamation of Jerusalem as the capital of Israel as measures that are null and void. Less than a month later, on 21 December 2017, the UN General Assembly once more adopted a resolution on Jerusalem (A/RES/ES-10/19), in response to the US declaration of 6 December 2017.

It is significant that the resolution of 21 December 2017 was adopted during a meeting of the Tenth Emergency Special Session.[631] This means that the announcement by the US president was seen as an emergency situation, threatening international peace and security. Unlike the earlier resolution, Resolution A/RES/ES-10/19 was adopted with the votes of only 128 UN Member States in favor, including 22 of the Members of the EU. Six EU states abstained. Only nine UN Member States voted against: Guatemala, Honduras, Israel, Marshall Islands, Micronesia, Nauru, Palau, Togo and the US. There were 35 abstentions, while 21 UN Member States were not present. The General Assembly expressed "its deep regret at the recent decisions concerning the status of Jerusalem." This no doubt refers to the status of Jerusalem as the capital of Israel. It should be underlined, first of all, that the US President did not take a decision on the status of Jerusalem. The State of Israel, as a sovereign state, had decided on the status of Jerusalem and declared Jerusalem to be its capital, in 1949/1950 and again in 1980. The American president simply recognized the sovereign decisions of Israel. And Israel was fully entitled to take these decisions. As we have explained, Jerusalem as a whole was part of the territory under the Mandate for Palestine, destined as the location of the Jewish national home.

In its Resolution of 21 December 2017, the General Assembly "calls upon all States to refrain from the establishment of diplomatic missions in the Holy City of Jerusalem, pursuant to Security Council (SC) resolution 478 (1980)." This non-binding Security Council resolution is apparently the main basis of the request of the General Assembly. Indeed, there is no binding rule of international law that could support the call of the General Assembly. The basic principle of international law concerning the establishment of diplomatic relations between states and of permanent

631. This Session on the 'Illegal Israeli actions in Occupied East Jerusalem and the rest of the Occupied Palestinian Territory' was convened for the first time in 1997 (!) and met for the last time in 2009. Emergency special sessions have been made possible by UN G.A. Res. 377 (V) (1950) ('Uniting for Peace') as a possibility for the General Assembly to bypass the Security Council (SC) in cases of threats of world peace when decision-making in the SC is blocked by one of its permanent members. Apparently it was assumed that this was at issue here. The adoption of a similar resolution of the SC on Jerusalem was vetoed by the USA on 18 December 2017.

diplomatic missions is, according to Article 2 of the Vienna Convention on Diplomatic Relations (1961), the mutual consent between the states concerned. Article 21 obliges the receiving state to facilitate acquisition of premises or assist in obtaining accommodation in some other way. It is clear that the Israeli government fully agrees with the American decision, so there are no legal impediments for relocation of the embassy to Jerusalem. According to the UN Charter, the General Assembly has no powers at all to interfere with the sovereign decisions of both the sending and the receiving state on the location of an embassy. On the contrary, it should respect the principle of the sovereign equality of its Member States pursuant to Article 2 (1) of the UN Charter. Apparently, the General Assembly feels free to single out one of the UN Member States and subject it to criticism for the choice of its capital. There is no example of similar treatment of another Member State about such a choice. The approach of the General Assembly is one of the numerous examples within UN practice of singling out the Jewish State and subjecting it to special standards. It is the international equivalent of the many abject examples in history of the special treatment of Jews in national legal orders; in other words: anti-Semitism.

14.3.3 Jerusalem in the Oslo Agreements and the Israeli-Jordanian Peace Treaty

It is worthwhile to reflect for a moment on the status of Jerusalem in the instruments that can be seen as the outcome of peace negotiations between Israel and its Arab neighbors after the Madrid Conference in 1991. This resulted in 1993 in the agreement on the Declaration of Principles on Interim Self-Government Arrangements, which is the first of a set of agreements generally referred to as the Oslo Agreements. In addition, Israel and Jordan concluded a peace treaty in 1994. Under Oslo I, it is explicitly agreed that the status of Jerusalem is to be included in the parties' final negotiations. Article V (3) provides: "It is understood that these negotiations shall cover remaining issues, including: Jerusalem, refugees, settlements, security arrangements, borders, relations and cooperation with other neighbors, and other issues of common interest." No doubt negotiations on the issue of Jerusalem will be difficult. It is important to underline that, contrary to common assumptions, in these negotiations the position of Israel is not that of a state that has occupied the City of Jerusalem, which it may control only temporarily in conformity with the international law on belligerent occupation. As has been explained before, Israel has full sovereign rights over Jerusalem.

Notwithstanding the Oslo Agreements, which reserved the question of the status of Jerusalem for the final negotiations, the "President of the State of Palestine" issued on 5 October 2002 a "Capital Law of 2002, which declares 'Holy Jerusalem' to be the capital of the State of Palestine" (Article 1). This Act imitates to some extent the Israeli Basic Law on Jerusalem. It appoints this city as the seat of the three powers of government: legislative, executive and judiciary (Article 1). It proclaims Palestinian sovereignty over the holy sites and makes the Palestinian state responsible for ensuring freedom of worship and practice of "all religious rituals" (Article 2). It provides for a special installment of the annual budget for Jerusalem (Article 3). It declares legislation or agreement diminishing Palestinian rights in Jerusalem to be null and void (Article 4). It also has an entrenchment provision: The Law can only be amended or annulled by a two-thirds majority of the members of the Palestinian Legislative Council (Article 5). It has to be noted that, contrary to the Israeli Basic Law, the Palestinian claim in this Act, has no clear legal foundation. Moreover, it is clear that the assumed Palestinian sovereignty is not restricted to just a part of Jerusalem but extends to the whole of the city. It ignores completely the position of the State of Israel. Significantly, this Palestinian Arab law has not attracted any censure in the international community.

We now add a few words on the Peace Treaty entered into between Israel and Jordan in 1994. In this agreement, we find a reference to Jerusalem. It is not about Jordanian sovereignty claims, which were already relinquished in 1988. It is about holy places. It is agreed that Israel "respects the present special role of Hashemite Kingdom of Jordan in Muslim Holy Shrines in Jerusalem. When negotiations on the permanent status [of the West Bank and Gaza] will take place, Israel will give high priority to the Jordanian historic role in these shrines ..." (Article 9 (2)).[632] This arrangement is not without complexities, which was illustrated by the aftermath of the terror attack on the Temple Mount in July 2017, in which two Israeli (Druze) police officers were killed. Israeli Prime Minister Benjamin Netanyahu spoke with the Jordanian King Abdullah II, who condemned the murder, but criticized the introduction by Israel of security measures—metal detectors—to control access to the Temple Mount. At the end of the day, although these security measures were hardly exceptional, Israel gave in to international pressure and removed the detectors.[633]

---

632. See Lapidoth (1996), at. pp 30-31; Gold (2007), p. 176.

633. See: jewishnews.com/2017/o7/25/Israeli-cabinet-decides-to-remove-metal-detectors-from-the-temple-mount/

14.4 Governance of the "Holy Places" in Jerusalem

The holy places in Jerusalem and Hebron were the subject of special conflict and attention during the Ottoman Empire. In 1852, responding to the conflicting claims of the Russians and French, the Ottoman government published the first of a series of *firmans,* which purported to regulate access to and use of the holy sites by the various church denominations. These *firmans* became known as the "status quo" and were recognized and adopted by the European powers in the Treaty of Paris following the Crimean War (1856) and Treaty of Berlin (1878).[634] When the Mandate for Palestine came into place in 1922, the Mandatory was obliged to respect existing rights and ensure free access to the Holy Places. The Mandatory had no right to "interfere with the fabric or the management of purely sacred Moslim shrines, the immunities of which are guaranteed" (Article 13). Under Jordanian rule (1948-1967), no obligations or requirement were in place to protect Jewish and Christian holy sites in Jerusalem. All Jewish synagogues were destroyed, and cemeteries were desecrated. The claims of the Vatican and other Christian denominations to churches in Jerusalem were basically respected. When Israel recaptured the Old City and the West Bank in June 1967, it fully appreciated the importance of respecting Muslim and Christian claims to their holy places. Specific agreements are in place between Israel and the Holy See and other Christian institutions regarding Christian holy sites in Jerusalem such as the Church of the Holy Sepulchre in Jerusalem and the Church of the Nativity in Bethlehem.[635] Despite all criticisms and allegations of infringing international law, Israel continues to maintain the policy that "Jerusalem must remain the united capital of Israel with continued religious freedom for all faiths."[636]

The Temple Mount

The most important and contentious site—at least from Jewish and Muslim perspectives—is the Temple Mount, *Har HaBayit* (Hebrew) or *Al-Haram al-Sharif* (Arabic), encompassing on the west side the Western Wall (*Kotel*) and, on top of the plateau, the Dome of the Rock and the Al-Aqsa Mosque. The Temple Mount has a prominent place in Jewish history as the location of the Binding of Isaac, and of the First and Second Temples.

634. Treaty of Peace between the State of Israel and the Kingdom of Jordan, art. 9. See also Lapidoth (1995), at p. 663.

635. Fundamental Agreement between The Holy See and The State of Israel, 30 December 1993, reprinted in: 33 I.L.M. 153 (1994).

636. Prime Minister Netanyahu, speech at Bar Ilan University, 2009.

It is an important place for Christianity, as Jesus called the Temple his "Father's house," while in Islam it is associated with the ascension of Muhammed.

One week after the end of the Six-Day War, Moshe Dayan handed over control over the Temple Mount to the Muslims and ordered that the Haram al-Sharif (the Arabic name of the Temple Mount) be open to all Muslims throughout Israel. Since 1967, the holy places in Israel have been subject to the Protection of Holy Places Law 5727-1967 enacted on 27 June 1967, which provides that the country's holy places shall be protected from desecration and other violations and from anything likely to violate the freedom of access by the various religions to places sacred to them, or their feelings with regard to those places.[637] Under this law, administration of non-religious affairs in Jerusalem was effectively placed under Israeli control, while administration of religious affairs was shared between Jewish, Christian and Muslim authorities. The administration of the Haram al-Sharif and other Muslim holy sites was in 1967 placed under the authority of the Islamic Waqf by Israel. The Waqf currently controls the day-to-day administration, including guards supervising the entrance to the Haram al-Sharif. Under this authority, Muslims have daily access to the Haram al-Sharif and can freely worship there. Yet, the Waqf has restricted the rights of Jews and other non-Muslims by limiting the rights of access and the freedom to worship on the Haram al-Sharif; while Muslims have unrestricted access, non-Muslims are only allowed to visit the place at fixed times, they cannot enter the al-Aqsa mosque and they are not allowed to pray on the Haram al-Sharif.[638]

Israel also acknowledges the special position of Jordan in relation to the Muslim Holy Places in Jerusalem. In the Peace Treaty entered into between Israel and Jordan in 1994, it is agreed that Israel "respects the present special role of Hashemite Kingdom of Jordan in Muslim Holy Shrines in Jerusalem. When negotiations on the permanent status [of the West Bank and Gaza] will take place, Israel will give high priority to the Jordanian historic role in these shrines ..." (Article 9 (2)).[6391]

Recently, the Palestine Liberation Organization and Palestinian Authority (PLO/PA) and Jordan have taken steps to further restrict access to the

637. For the Protection of Holy Places Law 1967, see: http://www.mfa.gov.il/mfa/foreignpolicy/mfadocuments/yearbook1/pages/14%20protection%20of%20holy%20places%20law.aspx (visited: 12 November 2015).

638. http://mfa.gov.il/MFA/ForeignPolicy/Issues/Pages/Jerusalem-Temple-Mount-12-Nov-2014.aspx (visited: 12 November 2015).

639. See Lapidoth (1996), pp. 30-31; Gold (2007), p. 176.

Temple Mount by Jews. According to an agreement[640] executed on 31 March 2013, between King Abdullah II of Jordan and the PLO/PA, the PLO/PA affirms recognition by the Palestinian Arabs of the Hashemite King as custodian of the Islamic Holy Places in Jerusalem.[641] The agreement also purports to recognize Palestinian self-determination and sovereignty over the land where the Islamic holy places are situated. This agreement "affirms that all Muslims, now and forever, may travel to and from the Islamic holy sites and worship there, in conformity with the freedom of worship." The Waqf and its properties are to be administered "in accordance with the laws of the Hashemite Kingdom of Jordan." These arrangements contain no guarantees whatsoever that Jews or Christians will continue to have access to their holy places connected with the Temple Mount. On the contrary, they therefore show that access will be limited to Muslims.[642]

A matter of deep concern, finally, is the position of the UN Educational, Scientific and Cultural Organization (UNESCO) with respect to the Temple Mount. During its 197th session on 21 October 2015, the Executive Board of UNESCO adopted a Decision in which it condemned Israel for restricting Muslims' freedom of worship and access to the Al-Aqsa Mosque/Al-Haram Al Sharif.[643] It did so again during its 200th session in Paris on 18 October 2016.[644] In these Decisions, as well as in a Decision of its World Heritage Committee of 26 October 2016,[645] the Jewish and Christian relationship to the Temple Mount is systematically ignored. Both texts refer only to the site according to its Islamic name in Arabic (*Al-Haram Al-Sharif)* combined with the Arabic name for the Islamic house of worship, the *Al-Aqsa Mosque*. In both texts, it is called a Muslim holy site. The importance for the Jewish faith of the Temple Mount, which is located on the site of both the First and Second Temples, is not mentioned. It seems that UNESCO endorses the recent Palestinian attempts to erase the Biblical history from Jerusalem, the city so essential to the Jewish faith. It is difficult to believe that an international organization dealing with issues of *education, science* and *culture* is prepared to contribute to the falsification of history. We should not forget that by blaming UNESCO,

---

640. http://jordanembassyus.org/news/jordanian-palestinian-agreement-jointly-defend-al-masjid-al-aqsa (visited: 11 September 2017).

641. In his capacity as descendant of the Sharif Hussein bin Ali of Mecca, who was Caliph of Islam for several months in 1924.

642. For more information about this agreement, see: Lapidoth (2013).

643. UNESCO Executive Board, 197 EX/SR.1.

644. UNESCO Executive Board, 200 EX/25; 200 EX/26.

645. UNESCO World Heritage Committee, 40 COM 7A.13.

we in fact criticize many of its Member States; it is the Member States of UNESCO that voted to support these decisions that bear the responsibility for these decisions.

The General Assembly in its Resolution of 30 November 2017 (A/RES/72/15) also addresses the status of the Temple Mount, without using these words or the Hebrew equivalent *Har HaBayit*. Instead, the General Assembly only calls the place by its Arab name *Haram al-Sharif*. In doing so, the General Assembly follows the example of UNESCO institutions to ignore the prominent place in Jewish history of the Temple Mount. Also, the General Assembly seems to accept the false new Palestinian narrative, which purposely wants to erase the relationship between the Jewish people and the land of Israel and Jerusalem. It is rather cynical to read in the fourth operative paragraph of the concerns of the General Assembly about the status quo at the holy places of Jerusalem, having regard to the fact that history has shown that only under Israeli sovereignty have the free access to the holy places of Judaism, Christianity and Islam been guaranteed, as well as the freedom of religion in general. This is in contrast to many of the sponsors and supporters of the General Assembly Resolution which do not respect the freedom of religion in their own countries.

PART IV

Israel and Human Rights

15. Israel and Human Rights Law

"On 3 October 1991 Israel ratified both the International Covenant on Economic, Social and Cultural Rights (...) and the International Covenant on Civil and Political Rights (...)"

Advisory Opinion (Paragraph 103)[646]

15.1 Introduction

Critics of Israel who cite international law often argue that Israel is breaching human rights that are guaranteed under international treaties and agreements as well as in national Israeli law. It is important that we consider these human rights in more detail. Basic human rights–also known as rights of man, or constitutional rights–form an essential part of the national legal system of many states (including Israel). However, the protection of human rights is not just a question of domestic law. States often voluntarily enter into treaties in which they undertake obligations to respect the rights of individuals and groups within their own legal system. The beneficiaries of these rights are often entitled to enforce the state's compliance with these obligations.

15.2 International Human Rights Law

Prior to the World War II, international law was basically restricted to the rights and obligations between states (and other international actors), and did not concern itself with the way citizens are treated by their governments *within* a state. The expansive growth of human rights law since then constitutes perhaps the most significant development in international law in the last century. One of the triggers of this development was the Universal Declaration of Human Rights.

646. I.C.J. Reports 2004, p. 177.

15.2.1 The Universal Declaration of Human Rights

The Universal Declaration of Human Rights (UDHR) was adopted by the United Nations (UN) General Assembly on 10 December 1948, which none of the participating states voted against and from which only eight states abstained (the Soviet Union and its socialist allies, South Africa and Saudi Arabia). Although the UDHR is not in itself a binding legal document, it has been the inspiration for many subsequent binding treaties. The UDHR and the treaties based on it must be seen in the context of the global consequences of Nazi terrorism, culminating in the horrors of the *Shoah*. Interestingly, one of the drafters of the UDHR, the French Jewish jurist René Samuel Cassin, drew a parallel between basic human rights and the Ten Commandments.[647] Article 1 of the UDHR provides, that "all human beings are born free and equal in dignity and rights. They are endowed with reason and conscience and should act towards one another in a spirit of brotherhood." This lofty statement is a prelude to the concrete human rights defined in the UDHR. Most of the rights provided for in the UDHR are classical human rights, which seek to protect the freedom of the individual against unjustified encroachment by the state. Such rights are often referred to as civil or political rights. Examples are the right to life, freedom and security of the person, prohibition on slavery, torture or cruel, inhuman or degrading treatment or punishment, the right to equality before the law and the right to equal protection against any discrimination, the right to a fair and public hearing by an independent and impartial tribunal, the right to freedom of movement and residence within the borders of each state, the rights to own property, the right to freedom of thought, conscience and religion, and the right to freedom of opinion and expression.[648] In addition, the UDHR contains a number of so-called social, cultural and economic rights, guaranteeing the basic conditions necessary for human endeavor and development. Such rights often require the state to take active steps. Examples are: the rights to social security, work and favorable work conditions, a reasonable standard of living, and education.[649]

The UDHR was proclaimed according to its Preamble "as a common standard of achievement for all peoples and all nations." Virtually all states in the world will at least pay lip service to the UDHR, though common ground on human rights in different parts of in the world and more specifically between Israel and its Islamic counterparts is not guaranteed.

---

647. Cassin (1971).

648. Universal Declaration of Human Rights (hereafter: UDHR) arts 3, 4, 5, 7, 10, 13, 17, 18.

649. UDHR, arts 22, 23, 25, 26.

For example, the Cairo Declaration on Human Rights in Islam, adopted on 5 August 1990 by the Nineteenth Islamic Conference of Foreign Ministers, contains many rights we also find in the UDHR. However, it also provides for some qualifications, such as: "All the rights and freedoms stipulated in this Declaration are subject to the Islamic *Shari'ah,*" and "[t]he Islamic Shari'ah is the only source of reference for the explanation or clarification of any of the articles of this Declaration."[650] Additionally, in the preamble to the Arab Charter on Human Rights (2004)—a treaty included in the framework of the Arab League—we find in the same paragraph a rejection of Zionism *and* an affirmation of the principles of the UDHR *and* a reference to the Cairo Declaration:

> "Rejecting all forms of racism and Zionism, which constitute a violation of human rights and a threat to international peace and security, recognizing the close link that exists between human rights and international peace and security, reaffirming the principles of the Charter of the United Nations, the Universal Declaration of Human Rights and the provisions of the International Covenant on Civil and Political Rights and the International Covenant on Economic, Social and Cultural Rights, and having regard to the Cairo Declaration on Human Rights in Islam, The States parties to the Charter have agreed as follows..."

This should be kept in mind when we proceed with our discussion of human rights.

15.2.2 International Human Rights Treaties

The basic rights expressed in the UDHR have been elaborated in more detailed provisions of numerous international human rights treaties created under the auspices of the UN and other international organizations. Israel is party to most of these treaties. The most important of these are the International Covenant on Civil and Political Rights (ICCPR)[651] and the International Covenant on Economic, Social and Cultural Rights (ICESCR).[652] Other international human rights treaties to which Israel is a party include the UN Convention against Torture and Other Cruel, Inhuman or Degrading Treatment or Punishment (1984), the International Convention on the Elimination of All Forms of Racial Discrimination (ICERD, 1966), the Convention on the Elimination of all Forms of Discrimination

650. Cairo Declaration on Human Rights in Islam, arts 24 and 25.

651. The ICCPR was adopted by the UN General Assembly on 16 December 1966, and came into force on 23 March 1976.

652. The ICESCR was adopted by the UN General Assembly on 16 December 1966, and came into in force on 3 January 1976.

against Women (CEDAW, 1979) and the UN Convention on the Rights of the Child (UNCRC, 1989).[653]

15.2.3 Application of International Human Rights Law in National Legal Systems

All of these international treaties are of immense importance for individuals and groups within nation-states. States that enter into these treaties are obliged to ensure that the rights which they guarantee (in the international treaties) are adequately reflected in domestic laws and procedures, but they are free to determine the way in which they implement these obligations in their own legal systems. Accordingly, they can be either implemented in specific laws, which reflect local conditions, or the treaties themselves can be declared to have direct application in the national law, in which case citizens can request an appropriate court to apply the terms of the treaty directly.

Israel has a legal system strongly influenced by the English common law tradition (a heritage of Britain's influence as mandatory under the Mandate for Palestine), and under many common law systems international treaties cannot be applied directly in national courts. An individual cannot simply go to a court in a common law country like the UK or Israel and file a suit against the state for breach of its obligations under human rights treaties. On the other hand, Israeli law is based on the human rights principles contained in the various human rights treaties to which Israel is a party, and the judges in Israel refer to these treaties where necessary in interpreting and applying Israeli national law. In doing so, they assume that the Knesset intends to comply with Israel's obligations under international law when drafting national legislation (*presumption of compatibility*). [654]

15.3 Human Rights Norms in Israeli National Law

Although Israel does not have a written constitution, Israel's legal system is one of the most advanced in the world when it comes to guaranteeing human rights. The country's Declaration of Independence states:

> **"THE STATE OF ISRAEL will be open for Jewish immigration and for the Ingathering of the Exiles; it will foster the development of the country for the benefit of all its inhabitants; it will be based on freedom, justice and peace as envisaged by the prophets of Israel; it will ensure complete equality of social and political rights to all its inhabitants irrespective of**

653. Israel's Arab neighbors Egypt, Jordan, Lebanon, and Syria have all ratified these conventions.

654. See Einhorn (2011).

religion, race or sex; it will guarantee freedom of religion, conscience, language, education and culture; it will safeguard the Holy Places of all religions; and it will be faithful to the principles of the Charter of the United Nations."[655]

The Declaration of Independence also contains a commitment to treat all citizens of Israel—Jewish and non-Jewish—equally:

"WE APPEAL—in the very midst of the onslaught launched against us now for months—to the Arab inhabitants of the State of Israel to preserve peace and participate in the upbuilding of the State on the basis of full and equal citizenship and due representation in all its provisional and permanent institutions."[656]

The protection of human rights in Israel is furthermore guaranteed in a series of "Basic Laws" which have been enacted since 1948: fundamental legislation that has a higher status than normal legislation. The Basic Law on Human Dignity and Liberty, states:

"Fundamental human rights in Israel are founded upon recognition of the value of the human being, the sanctity of human life, and the principle that all persons are free; these rights shall be upheld in the spirit of the principles set forth in the Declaration of the Establishment of the State of Israel."[657]

The Law goes on to establish the following rights. Note that these rights apply to all persons in Israel, regardless of race, sex or religion:

"1. The purpose of this Basic Law is to protect human dignity and liberty, in order to establish in a Basic Law the values of the State of Israel as Jewish and democratic state.
2. There shall be no violation of the life, body or dignity of any person as such.
3. There shall be no violation of the property of a person.
4. All persons are entitled to protection of their life, body and dignity.
5. There shall be no deprivation or restriction of the liberty of a person by imprisonment, arrest, extradition or otherwise.
6. (a) All persons are free to leave Israel.
   (b) Every Israel national has the right of entry into Israel from abroad.
7. (a) All persons have the right to privacy and to intimacy.
   (b) There shall be no entry into the private premises of a person who has not consented thereto.

655. The Declaration of Independence of 14 May 1948.

656. *Ibid.*

657. The Basic Law of 17 March 1992 on Human Dignity and Liberty.

(c) **No search shall be conducted on the private premises of a person, nor in the body or personal effects.**
(d) **There shall be no violation of the confidentiality of conversation, or of the writings or records of a person."**

Fundamental human rights can also be derived from the case law of the Israeli Supreme Court, which adopts a liberal attitude in defining the right for respect of human dignity. In that respect, the legal structure in Israel guarantees freedom of religion, freedom of expression and the right to equal treatment. The practical application of such basic human rights is also reflected in a myriad of ordinary laws. Such rights are worthless if they cannot be enforced. The rights of individuals are protected by independent courts, headed by the Supreme Court: one of the most respected high courts of appeal in the world, which often makes statements critical of the government practice and policy. [658]

Under Israeli law, the Supreme Court of Israel, sitting as the High Court of Justice, exercises extensive powers of *judicial review*. That means, in the first place, that executive acts of government institutions are subject to judicial scrutiny. There are many examples of decisions of the government (inter alia in respect of the security barrier) that have been quashed by the Supreme Court on the ground that they conflict with the law.[659] A more recent development is that the Supreme Court also examines legislation adopted by the Knesset in the light of human rights as established in Israeli Basic Laws. For example, the Supreme Court annulled a provision of the Law on the Prevention of Infiltration.[660] The power of judicial review of legislation is based on section 8 of the Basic Law: Human Dignity and Liberty, which affirms: "There shall be no violation of rights under this Basic Law except by a law befitting the values of the State of Israel, enacted for a proper purpose, and to an extent no greater than is required."[661] However, the extension of the judicial review to legislation is a controversial issue in Israel[662] and we note with concern the recent proposals to limit the judicial review jurisdiction of the Supreme Court.

658. See Dershowitz (2003), p. 183.

659. HCJ 2056/04 Beit Sourik Village Council v. 1. The Government of Israel; 2. Commander of the IDF Forces in the West Bank, in: *Judgments of the Israel Supreme Court: Fighting Terrorism within the Law*, Vol. 2 (2004-2005), pp. 7-61.

660. Israeli Supreme Court on 16 September 2013.

661. Basic Law on Human Dignity and Liberty, section 8.

662. See, e.g., Posner (2010).

15.4 Is International Human Rights Law Applicable in the Disputed Territories?

There is considerable debate on the law on the protection of individuals and groups in the disputed territories. Is it international human rights law, humanitarian law (that is, the law applicable in armed conflicts), or both?[663] Several issues are involved here. First, whether both sets of legal norms can be applicable in situations of armed conflict. Secondly, assuming that both sets of norms are applicable, the question arises whether human rights law applies to the conduct of a state extra-territorially, i.e. outside its borders. Finally, as to the disputed territories, which laws apply to Areas A and B where significant powers have been transferred to the Palestinian Authority (PA) pursuant to the Oslo Agreements?

The government of Israel is of the opinion that humanitarian law should be applied in the disputed territories, while human rights law is applicable to the relationship between the State of Israel and its inhabitants in the undisputed territory of Israel.[664] It is difficult to apply both bodies of law simultaneously. A strong argument for this position is the very different background of the two sets of norms. Humanitarian law has been developed over a long period of time, since the 19th century, to limit the atrocities of war. It provides a set of detailed and complex rules for the protection of combatants and non-combatants within a framework that balances humanitarian and legitimate military interests. Human rights law, on the other hand, is the international equivalent of national constitutional rights. The greater part of it only emerged after the World War II. It includes rather abstract, sometimes high-sounding principles on the protection of the freedom, equality and social welfare of the citizens. In general, they also include broadly formulated restriction clauses, in order to protect other general interests or the rights of other human beings. As compared with humanitarian law, human rights law lacks a detailed framework for the balancing of individual rights with broader public interests. That means that the interpreters of this law have a considerable discretion to decide what is and what is not a violation of human rights.

Israel's position that both sets of norms cannot be simultaneously applicable is only shared by the US.[665] International supervisory human rights bodies as well as the International Court of Justice (ICJ) assume

663. See on humanitarian law Chapter 20.

664. CCPR/C/ISR/2001/2, p. 3.

665. Hampson (2008), at para 5. See also Feinstein (2005).

that in situations of armed conflict, both sets of norms apply.[666] In the Wall Advisory Opinion, the ICJ assumes that human rights law is applicable in situations of armed conflict in principle, subject to the possibility for state parties to derogate explicitly from their human rights obligations in times of a national emergency.[667] Further, the ICJ states that humanitarian law is a *lex specialis* of human rights law.[668] This means that, in the event humanitarian law provides for a more specific set of rules on, say, the protection of life in connection with other legitimate interests (e.g. military necessity), these more specific rules should prevail. As was rightly submitted by the Turkel Commission in its report on the Maritime incident of 31 May 2010 (the flotilla incident), the legitimacy of the Israeli naval blockade should be determined by the international humanitarian law concerning maritime warfare and not by human rights provisions on the freedom of movement.[669]

The second issue is the extraterritorial application of human rights law. The position of Israel is that its human rights obligations are only relevant for the internal situation in the State of Israel. Therefore, they should not be held against Israel in connection with its activities in the disputed territories. However, this approach is strongly criticized. In general, the liability of a state under human rights law extends to all territories in which it exercises jurisdiction, which may not be limited to its national territories. This is exemplified by the judgments of the European Court of Human Rights on the military activities of the UK in Iraq.[670] Furthermore, in its 2004 Advisory Opinion, the ICJ concluded that Israel's policies in the Territories should be assessed under international human rights law, although a literal reading of the ICCPR could have resulted in another approach. The ICJ held:

> **"The scope of application of the International Covenant on Civil and Political Rights is defined by Article 2, paragraph 1, thereof, which provides: 'Each State Party to the present Covenant undertakes to respect and to ensure to all individuals within its territory and subject to its jurisdiction the rights recognized in the present Covenant, without distinction of any kind, such as race, colour, sex, language, religion, political or other**

666. See, e.g., Schabas (2007).

667. *Legal Consequences of the Construction of a Wall in the Occupied Palestinian Territory*, Advisory Opinion, 2004 I.C.J. Reports 2004, pp. 136-203 (9 July 2004), at p. 178.

668. *Ibid.*

669. The Public Commission to Examine the Maritime Incident of 31 May 2010 (The Turkel Commission), January 2011, pp. 102-104.

670. Al-Skeini v. United Kingdom, App. No. 55721/07, 53 Eur.H.R.Rep. 589 (2011). See on this case: Miko (2013).

> opinion, national or social origin, property, birth or other status.' This provision can be interpreted as covering only individuals who are both present within a State's territory and subject to that State's jurisdiction. It can also be construed as covering both individuals present within a State's territory and those outside that territory but subject to that State's jurisdiction. The Court will thus seek to determine the meaning to be given to this text. The Court would observe that, while the jurisdiction of States is primarily territorial, it may sometimes be exercised outside the national territory. Considering the object and purpose of the International Covenant on Civil and Political Rights, it would seem natural that, even when such is the case, States Parties to the Covenant should be bound to comply with its provisions. The constant practice of the Human Rights Committee is consistent with this... The *travaux préparatoires* of the Covenant confirm the Committee's interpretation... Israel took the position that 'the Covenant and similar instruments did not apply directly to the current situation in the occupied territories'... In conclusion, the Court considers that the International Covenant on Civil and Political Rights is applicable in respect of acts done by a State in the exercise of its jurisdiction outside its own territory."[671]

There is, finally, the specific complication that under the Oslo Agreements parts of the powers of the Israeli government have been transferred to the PA. More specifically, according to the Israeli-Palestinian Interim Agreement of 1995, important powers in the civil sphere have been transferred to the PA, including issues concerning civil and political rights.[672] Israel no longer has any control within Area A and limited control in Area B. The Oslo Agreements explicitly require the PA to exercise their powers and responsibilities in the areas which came under their control "with due regard to internationally-accepted norms and principles of human rights and the rule of law."[673] To the extent to which jurisdiction has been transferred to the PA, it would seem absurd to hold Israel liable for human rights violations by Palestinian institutions against their own people. It appears this point was not brought to the ICJ's attention.

671. *Legal Consequences of the Construction of a Wall in the Occupied Palestinian Territory*, Advisory Opinion, 2004 I.C.J. Reports 2004, pp. 136-203 (9 July 2004), at pp. 179-180.

672. The Israeli-Palestinian Interim Agreement on the West Bank and the Gaza Strip (1995) divides the West Bank into Areas A, B and C.

673. The Israeli-Palestinian Interim Agreement on the West Bank and the Gaza Strip (1995), art. XIX.

15.5 International Human Rights Organs

15.5.1 General

Israel is almost constantly under the microscope when it comes to its compliance with international human rights norms. Being a member state of the UN and party to its various human rights treaties, Israel should expect to be scrutinized. The amount of attention paid to Israel is far out of proportion, however, especially when we consider the appalling human rights records of other countries, including Israel's closest neighbors.

There are many different bodies that are responsible for monitoring how well states comply with their obligations under the various human rights treaties. Some of these are *political* bodies—i.e. made up of representatives of UN Member States, who meet together, to investigate and report on human rights compliance by other Member States. In addition, there are a number of—according to the relevant treaty provisions—*independent* international supervisory bodies, which monitor human rights compliance by the States Parties to human rights treaties. These bodies are composed of independent experts. An example is the Human Rights Committee established under the International Covenant on Civil and Political Rights (ICCPR).

The most important political entity responsible for monitoring human rights was the former UN Commission on Human Rights (UNCHR). The way the UNCHR operated meant that Member States that themselves were guilty of gross human rights offenses were able to dominate the Commission's decision-making processes. In 2003, for example, Libya (then still under the ruthless dictatorship of Colonel Muammar Gaddafi) was Chair of the UNCHR! The People's Republic of China—which also does not have an unblemished human rights record, to say the least—was consistently able to prevent negative resolutions from being adopted concerning its own human rights compliance. On the other hand, it was always possible to find a majority willing to support resolutions condemning Israel for human rights abuses. In 2005, half of the resolutions adopted by the UNCHR concerned Israel. Earlier, in 2002, Anne Bayefsky wrote that "commission members seek to avoid directly criticizing states with human rights problems, frequently by focusing on Israel, a state that, according to analysis of summary records, has for over 30 years occupied 15 percent of commission time and has been the subject of a third of country-specific resolutions."[674]

674. Bayefsky (2002). At that time Anne Bayefsky was professor of international law at York University in Toronto.

The UNCHR's criticism of Israel was based on an expansionist view of the rights of the Palestinian people in the disputed territories, which rights Israel was said to be breaching. According to the UNCHR, these fundamental rights not only imposed obligations and restrictions on Israel, they also justified active Palestinian resistance to the "occupation." On 15 April 2002, during the Second Intifada, the UNCHR approved a resolution affirming the "legitimate right of the Palestinian people to resist the Israeli occupation in order to free its land and be able to exercise its right of self-determination."[675] In so doing, the Palestinian people were declared as "fulfilling its mission, one of the goals and purposes of the United Nations."[676] Of the 53-member commission, 40 countries voted yes, five voted no, and seven abstained. The resolution was widely reported as condoning resistance to Israel by "all available means, including armed struggle," although the resolution itself does not contain those words.[677] Alfred Moses, a former US ambassador to the UNCHR and now chairman of the monitoring group UN Watch, said, "A vote in favor of this resolution is a vote for Palestinian terrorism."[678] In a letter to the UNCHR on 15 November 2002, following an attack by Palestinians on Israelis in the town of Hebron, Nabil Ramlawi, the permanent observer for Palestine at the UN, appealed to the resolution as justification for the attack.[679]

The UNCHR gradually lost its credibility with both governments and NGOs. Criticism of the UNCHR reached its zenith in 2006 when the UN General Assembly voted overwhelmingly to dismantle the UNCHR and replace it with a new body—the UN Human Rights Council (UNHRC). The UNHRC is made up of 47 members—all UN Member States—who are elected by the General Assembly. In electing the UNHRC members, the General Assembly must take into account "the contribution of the candidates to the promotion and protection of human rights, as well as their voluntary pledges and commitments made thereto."[680] It was hoped that the new UNHRC would be more balanced and credible than the previous UNCHR was. It is doubtful whether this is the case. In the first six months of its operation, the only state that the Council criticized was

675. UN Commission on Human Rights, Resolution 2002/8, UN Doc. E/CN.4/RES/2002/8, 15 April 2002.

676. *Ibid.*

677. See, e.g., 'Question of the Violation of Human Rights in the Occupied Arab Territories, Including Palestine', Commission on Human Rights, Fifty-eighth session, Agenda item 8. E/CN.4/2002/L.16 (9 April 2002).

678. Edwards (2002).

679. Morgan (2004), at pp. 539-540.

680. A/Res/60/251, para 8, adopted on 15 March 2006.

Israel. That was in the period of appalling human rights abuses in Darfur, Congo, North Korea, and Zimbabwe. In the subsequent years, the UNHRC has condemned Israel repeatedly. In 2007, when an independent NGO (UN Watch) representative raised his concerns about the imbalanced criticism of Israel, he was confronted with the angry response of the UNHRC Chairman, the Ambassador of Mexico.[681] In short, the UNHRC seems to be following the example set by its predecessor.

15.5.2 UNHRC Rapporteurs

That can also be seen in the choice of Special Rapporteurs. The UNHRC has by now identified 37 human rights "themes" and 14 countries deserving special attention. Special Rapporteurs are appointed to investigate and report on the compliance with human rights in relation to each of those themes and countries. The Council has appointed dedicated Special Rapporteurs to report on human rights abuses in the following countries Belarus, Cambodia, Central African Republic, Côte d'Ivoire, Haiti, North-Korea, Iran, Mali, Myanmar, Somalia, Sudan, Syria, and the "Palestinian territories occupied since 1967." Among the Special Rapporteurs for the "Occupied Palestinian Territories," there are notable examples of experts who in their reports gave expression to one-sided, excessive and unjustified criticism of Israel. The Dutch-based South African Professor of international law, John Dugard, consistently compared the policies of Israel with the apartheid regime in South Africa.[682] He called on the government of Israel to recognize Hamas as a legitimate participant in the Palestinian government: notwithstanding the fact that Hamas regularly and openly calls for the destruction of the Jewish state of Israel.[683]

Dugard's six-year term expired in 2008; after which, American professor Richard Falk replaced him. Falk came to the position as an outspoken critic of Israel, especially its conduct in the territories. For example, he had served with Dugard on a UNCHR inquiry on the Palestinian occupied territories, which recognized the Palestinians' right to resistance of the occupation. Furthermore, Falk authored a published article in which he compared Israel's treatment of the population of the Gaza Strip (Gaza) with Nazi policies in the 1930s and 1940s. The sentiments expressed in that article reflect an underlying perspective that Israel intends to

---

681. Fendel (2007), p. 7.

682. Statement by John Dugard, Special Rapporteur on the situation of human rights in the Occupied Palestinian Territory: https://www.adalah.org/uploads/oldfiles/newsletter/eng/oct07/dugard-oct07.pdf (visited: 11 September 2017).

683. See: *The Jerusalem Post*, 29 May 2007.

exterminate the Palestinians in Gaza and perhaps elsewhere, on a scale that can be compared with the massacre of more than six million Jews across Europe in the Holocaust:

> "There is little doubt that the Nazi Holocaust was as close to unconditional evil as has been revealed throughout the entire bloody history of the human species. Its massiveness, unconcealed genocidal intent, and reliance on the mentality and instruments of modernity give its enactment in the death camps of Europe a special status in our moral imagination... Is it an irresponsible overstatement to associate the treatment of Palestinians with this criminalized Nazi record of collective atrocity? I think not. The recent developments in Gaza are especially disturbing because they express so vividly *a deliberate intention on the part of Israel and its allies to subject an entire human community to life-endangering conditions of utmost cruelty.* The suggestion that this pattern of conduct is *a holocaust-in-the-making* represents a rather desperate appeal to the governments of the world and to international public opinion to act urgently to prevent these current *genocidal tendencies* from culminating in a collective tragedy."[684]

In his final report, Falk again uses misleading and pejorative language in respect of Israeli policies, using terms such as annexation, colonial ambitions, apartheid, and ethnic cleansing.[685] There is no sign of an intention to take the rights, interests and concerns of Israel and its citizens seriously. The Special Rapporteur violated the basic principle of fairness required of an "impartial" international expert in the performance of his task.

In June 2014, the Indonesian diplomat Makarim Wibisono succeeded Richard Falk as Special Rapporteur. He resigned 4 January 2016, because he was refused access to the Palestinian territories by Israel. The resignation has become effective as of the 31 March 2016. On 24 March 2016, the UNHRC appointed the Canadian law professor, Michael Lynk, as his successor. According to UN Watch, he has record of bias against Israel. He has, for example promoted the Israel Apartheid Week. The information does not give hope that he will bring an end to the one-sidedness of his predecessors. [686] On 19 October 2016, he published his first report, including the recommendation that "the Government of Israel bring a complete end to the almost 50 years of occupation of the Palestinian territories

---

684. Falk (2007) (emphasis added): https://www.tni.org/my/node/9132 (visited: 11 September 2017).

685. A/HRC/25/67, *Report of the Special Rapporteur on the situation of human rights in the Palestinian territories occupied since 1967, Richard Falk*, 13 January 2014.

686. http://www.unwatch.org/un-nominates-anti-israeli-professor-6-year.

occupied since 1967."[687] The Special Rapporteur has recently written a Report which elaborates on this point. [688] This Report was submitted to the General Assembly, with the clear objective to heighten the pressure of the "international community" on Israel considerably. It is not without reason that the *Jerusalem Post* headlined: "Special Rapporteur calls for making Israel a 'pariah state.'"[689] The Rapporteur's intention is to put Israel in the same position as South Africa at the time of the Apartheid regime. South Africa has been the object of severe economic sanctions and international isolation. Lynk observes that Israel's occupation of the Palestinian territory is the longest-running military occupation in the modern world. He notes that so far Israel was seen by the international community as the lawful occupant, albeit that it was criticized for violations of the international law of occupation. Lynk now takes it a step further by claiming that the occupation as such has become illegal. In order to substantiate this claim, he takes as his starting point the central importance of fundamental rights and, more specifically, the right to self-determination in international law. Based on that, he develops a fourfold test to decide if belligerent occupation remains lawful. At all four points—summarized by the key words: "no annexation," "temporariness," "the best interest of the people" and "administration of the territory in good faith"—Israel fails to comply with the standard developed by the Special Rapporteur, bringing him to the conclusion that the occupation is illegal. This determination serves in his view several far-reaching purposes. First, it would encourage member states to prevent or discourage national entities to invest in or sustain the occupation. It also may encourage national and international courts to apply the laws to prevent or discourage involvement with the occupation. In the third place, it would invite the international community to review its cooperation with Israel, as long as it continues with its occupation. Fourthly, it would create a solid precedent for judging other occupations of long duration. It would, finally, "confirm the moral importance of upholding the international rule of law when aiding the besieged and the vulnerable."[690]

The Special Rapporteur recommends the General Assembly to consider the advantages to ask for an advisory opinion from the ICJ on the question of the legality of the occupation. It is not an exaggeration to assume that this Report may trigger a further isolation of Israel in the international community.

687. A/71/554, quotation from p. 25.

688. Report of 23 October 2017, A/72/43106.

689. *The Jerusalem Post*, 27 October 2017.

690. A/72/43106, para 65, p. 22.

15.5.3 Assessment by the UNHRC

On 18 June 2007, in its very first year of operation, the UNHRC decided to make the question of human rights in the "Occupied Palestinian Territories" a fixed agenda item—an action only taken in relation to Israel. One might be forgiven for thinking that there would have been more reason to place countries like North Korea, Saudi Arabia or Sudan permanently on the agenda—states with demonstrated serious human rights abuses—but this has not occurred, demonstrating the relative ease with which a political majority to criticize Israel can be obtained.

When the UNHRC was established, a new system of universal periodical assessment (Universal Periodic Review—UPR) was introduced. Every four years, the Council assesses the human rights compliance of every UN member state. This is done on the basis of information supplied by the state itself, information obtained in the context of other UN monitoring procedures, and information supplied by NGOs. A Working Group—comprising representatives of three UNHRC Member States—is established to draft a report based on this information. The result is that, in effect, states which are themselves guilty of gross human rights infringements (far worse than those of Israel), like Saudi Arabia, Cuba, and Venezuela, may be involved in drafting reports critical of Israel's human rights record. In 2013, the Working Group in respect of Israel's report consisted of Maldives, Sierra Leone, and Venezuela. In 2018, the team was composed of the UK, Mongolia and Rwanda.

The strong anti-Israel bias of the UNHRC was also exemplified in its Report on the Gaza conflict in 2009 and the report of its fact-finding mission to investigate the human rights implications of the Israeli settlements.[691] The refusal to provide Israel with a fair treatment led to a suspension of the cooperation of Israel with the UNHRC in 2012. In his letter to the UNHRC President, the Israeli Ambassador Aharon Leshno Yaar explained:

> **"This decision was reached in light of the ongoing, unrelenting singling out of Israel in the Human Rights Council, which has been persistent since its inception in 2006, continued through the review process, and exists to this day. The Council and the Office of the High Commissioner for Human Rights, respectively, have become a political tool and a**

691. A/HRC/12/48, Report of the United Nations Fact Finding Mission on the Gaza Conflict (23 September 2009); A/HRC/22/63, Report of the independent international fact-finding mission to investigate the implications of the Israeli settlements on the civil, political, economic, social and cultural rights of the Palestinian people throughout the Occupied Palestinian Territory, including East-Jerusalem (7 February 2013).

convenient platform, cynically used to advance certain political aims, to bash and demonize Israel."[692]

15.5.4 Committee on the Exercise of the Inalienable Rights of the Palestinian People (CEIRPP)

The Committee on the Exercise of the Inalienable Rights of the Palestinian People (CEIRPP) deserves special attention within the framework of the UN institutions that are engaged in the assessment of Israeli policies in the field of human rights. The CEIRPP was established by Resolution 3376 in 1975[693] under the mandate of recommending a program of implementation to the UN General Assembly that would enable the Palestinian people to exercise their inalienable rights to self-determination without external interference.[694] Originally, the CEIRPP was to exercise this mandate by submitting its reports and recommendations to the Security Council in 1976, which would subsequently realize the rights of the Palestinians. The Security Council however vetoed the submission in 1976, making the General Assembly the body that would from then on receive annual reports and recommendations from the Committee.[695]

Among the 14 committees within the UN system, the CEIRPP is the only UN organ devoted to a specific people group: the "Palestinian people." The CEIRPP owes its existence to the cooperation of 55 states[696] that

692. blog.unwatch.org/index.php/2012/05/15/letter-to-un-israel-tells-head-of-rights-council-its -suspending-all-ties.

693. UN G.A. Res. 3376 (XXX) was adopted on the same day as the 'Zionism is Racism' resolution 3379 (XXX).

694. UN G.A. Res. 3376 (XXX). The CEIPPR exercises this mandate under the position in principle that the permanent settlement of the Question of Palestine could only be achieved through the ending of the occupation, establishing a Palestinian state and granting the right of return to Palestinians. See: http://www.un.org/depts/dpa/qpal/docs/Committee/2014/AnnualReport/English.pdf (visited: 10 November 2015).

695. The General Assembly shows on a yearly basis the same response to these submissions: it exercises its appreciation to the Committee; notes that the Committee can make a valuable and positive contribution to the international effort to promote the effective implementation of interim Self-government arrangements; endorses the recommendations in the Committee's report and requests the Secretary-General to circulate the report of the Committee to all the competent UN bodies and urges them to take the necessary action as appropriate. (see e.g.: UN Resolution 48/158 A).

696. Member states that sponsored UN G.A. Res. 3376: Afghanistan, Algeria, Bahrain, Bangladesh, Bulgaria, the Byelorussian SSR, Cambodia, the Congo, Cuba, Cyprus, Czechoslovakia, Dahomey, Democratic Yemen, Egypt, the Gambia, the German Democratic Republic, Guinea, Guinea-Bissau, Hungary, India, Iraq, Jordan, Kuwait, Laos, Lebanon, the Libyan Arab Republic, Madagascar, Malaysia, Maldives, Mali, Malta, Mauritania, Mauritius, Mongolia, Morocco, Mozambique, Oman, Pakistan, Poland, Qatar, Romania, Rwanda, Saudi Arabia, Senegal, Somalia, the Sudan, the Syrian Arab Republic, Tunisia, Uganda, the Ukrainian SSR, the USSR, the United Arab Emirates, the Upper Volta, Yemen and Yugoslavia.

voted to adopt the text of the Resolution 3376 and can be regarded as the institutionalization of the Palestinian item in the UN.[697]

In the years following its establishment, the mandate of the CEIRPP was expanded by the General Assembly. One expansion came through the adoption of Resolution 32/40 in 1977, which created the Special Unit on Palestinian Rights in the United Nations Secretariat (the "Division for Palestinian Rights" or UNDPR); an organ that was entrusted with the primary objective of making a contribution to raise international awareness for the Question of Palestine.[698]

Through Resolution 32/40, three main responsibilities were given to the UNDPR: to assist the work of the CEIRPP by means of preparing studies and publications on the inalienable rights of the Palestinian people and on the relevant resolutions of the General Assembly; to promote maximum publicity for such studies and publications by all appropriate means; and to organize an annual observance of the "International Day of Solidarity with the Palestinian people" on 29 November each year.[699] Over the years, the General Assembly has further expanded the powers of the institution by including the tasks to: organize conferences and seminars,[700] monitor relevant developments,[701] maintain contact with non-governmental organizations,[702] administer a website[703] and to provide for an annual training programme for staff of the Palestinian Authority (PA).[704]

697. In 2015, the CEIPPR was composed of the following Member States: Afghanistan, Belarus, Bolivia (Plurinational State of), Cuba, Cyprus, Ecuador, Guinea, Guyana, India, Indonesia, the Lao People's Democratic Republic, Madagascar, Malaysia, Mali, Malta, Namibia, Nicaragua, Nigeria, Pakistan, Senegal, Sierra Leone, South Africa, Tunisia, Turkey, Ukraine and Venezuela (Bolivarian Republic of). The observers at the Committee meetings are: Algeria, Bangladesh, Bulgaria, China, Egypt, Iraq, Jordan, Kuwait, Lebanon, Libya, Mauritania, Morocco, Niger, Qatar, Saudi Arabia, Sri Lanka, the Syrian Arab Republic, the United Arab Emirates, Viet Nam and Yemen, as well as the State of Palestine, the African Union, the League of Arab States and OIC. See: http://www.refworld.org/docid/564051174.html (visited: 9 November 2015).

698. UN G.A. Res. 69/21.

699. UN G.A. Res. 32/40 B (XXXII). The 29th of November was chosen as reference to the date on which the Partition Plan (Resolution 1981 (II)) was adopted in the General Assembly in 1948.

700. UN G.A. Res. 34/65 D.

701. *Ibid.*

702. UN G.A. Res. 38/58 B.

703. UN G.A. Res. 46/74 B.

704. UN G.A. Res. 53/40.

15.6 New Developments?

In late 2013, Israel resumed its cooperation with the UNHRC. On 29 October 2013, Israel's human rights situation was discussed in the framework of the UNHRC's procedure of Universal Periodic Review. To a certain extent, the isolation of Israel within the UN human rights structures was brought to an end, when in 2013 Israel was admitted to the ranks of the Western European and Others group (WEOG), which includes other non-European states including Canada, Australia, and New Zealand.[705] The WEOG is one of the five regional groups of states that cooperate in the context of the UNHRC. This cooperation extends to substantive human rights issues, but also to the nomination of States for membership of the UNHRC. The membership of this body is divided along the lines of the five regional groups in the world. While Israel geographically belongs to Asia, it has never been admitted to the Asian group, and, consequently, until 2013 it was excluded from the ordinary channels by means of which all UN Member States are able to exert influence in the UNHRC framework. In February 2014, Israel also was admitted to JUSCANZ, a grouping of (Western-oriented, democratic states) within the framework of the UN's General Assembly Third Committee that discusses human rights issues.[706] Moreover, in 2012, an Israeli professor of law joined the Human Rights Committee, the independent body of experts that supervises the implementation of the International Covenant on Civil and Political Rights.[707] Finally, in 2014, the State Parties to the ICCPR unanimously appointed the Israeli UN Ambassador Ron Prosor to chair the elections for members of the Human Rights Committee.[708]

705. Israel Ministry of Foreign Affairs (MFA), 29 November 2013.

706. Israel Ministry of Foreign Affairs (MFA), 11 February 2014.

707. Prof. Yuval Shani of the Hebrew University of Jerusalem.

708. *The Jerusalem Post*, 20 February 2014.

16. Specific Allegations Against Israel Based on International Human Rights Law

"What seems to be wanting (...) is material explaining the Israeli side of the picture, especially in the context of why and how the construction of the wall as it is actually planned and implemented is necessary and appropriate."

Judge Owada, Separate Opinion (Paragraph 22)[709]

16.1 Introduction

When we look at the practice and procedures relating to human rights, we see that Israel is under heavy attack. Most of the criticism of Israel is connected with its identity as a Jewish state. Israel is often accused of discriminating on the basis of race or ethnicity. This criticism usually refers to the alleged discriminatory character of the rules and institutions which are intended to preserve the Jewish character of the state of Israel and the treatment of Palestinian Arabs. A selection of issues will be addressed. First, the issue of discrimination: in the form of allegations that Zionism is to be equated to racism, and that Israel is consequently an Apartheid state. Secondly, the claim that Israel infringes religious freedom will be addressed. Finally, we discuss the accusations that the measures taken by Israel to combat terrorism have infringed Palestinian human rights. We acknowledge that there are many other allegations of infringement of Palestinian Arab human rights by Israel (both within Israel proper and the West Bank), such as land ownership and access to natural resources, which need to be investigated but are outside the scope of this book.

709. I.C.J. Reports 2004, p. 268.

16.2 Discrimination

16.2.1 Resolution 3379 (XXX) – "Zionism is Racism"

A notorious expression of the accusation of discrimination is the claim that Zionism is racism. This was apparently the opinion of the UN General Assembly as formulated in its Resolution 3379 (XXX) passed on 10 November 1975. It literally declared, "Zionism is a form of racism and racial discrimination." As historian Joel Fishman has described, the idea that Zionism is a form of racism originated during the discussions that took place in the UN Sub-Commission on the Prevention of Discrimination and the Protection of Minorities in 1965, which was attempting to draft a Convention on the Elimination of All Forms of Racial Discrimination.[710] An article condemning apartheid as a form of racism along with Nazism and neo-Nazism was unanimously adopted. However, things got complicated when the American representative, mindful of the Holocaust, proposed adding an explicit condemnation of anti-Semitism, which the Soviets immediately countered by submitting an amendment condemning Zionism. Following a bitter debate, all specific references to racism (excepting apartheid) were dropped. As a result, not only was anti-Semitism prevented from being referred to as a form of racism, but the Soviets succeeded in introducing the idea that there is a link between Zionism and Nazism—a concept which the Palestinians and Arab states successfully exploited eleven years later in the UN General Assembly in September 1975, supported by the Soviets and a number of African nations. The support of this idea by African nations was also expressed in the Preamble of the African Charter on Human Rights and Peoples Rights (1981), where the States Parties state that they are conscious of their duty to eliminate not only apartheid, but also Zionism. Although the UN resolution of 1975 was later revoked by the General Assembly in 1991, the line of thinking expressed in resolution 3379 (XXX) provided the psychological foundation upon which the non-governmental players at the "Durban 1" conference in 2001 were able to turn this slogan into a political program, which today is manifested in the BDS (Boycott, Divestment and Sanctions) movement.

The notion that "Zionism is racism" is still a key tenet of the Palestine National Charter and is implicitly embedded in the constitutions of Islamic

710. Fishman (2011).

organizations such as Organization of Islamic Cooperation (OIC).[711] It is also implied in the Arab Charter on Human Rights, where the rejection of "all forms of racism and Zionism" is mentioned in one breath.[712] Is there any truth in this charge? Or is the counter-criticism, leveled by some of Israel's advocates, true—that the "Zionism = Racism" charge is nothing more than a veiled form of anti-Semitism?

16.2.2 Israel Alleged to Be an Apartheid State

A logical implication of the accusation that "Zionism is racism" is the allegation that Israel, the state rooted in Zionism, is an apartheid state.[713] Former Special UN Rapporteur John Dugard made this allegation of apartheid in relation to the occupied territories, in particular referring to the difference in treatment between the Palestinian Arabs and the Jewish "settlers."[714] His successor as Special Rapporteur, Richard Falk, gave expression time and again to the same opinion.[715] This allegation should not be underestimated. The claim that the Jewish state of Israel is a racist or "apartheid" state, and the underlying sentiment that it invokes, is a powerful one that potentially threatens the legitimacy of the state itself. It is politically and economically dangerous, given the precedent of the international campaign against apartheid in South Africa, which included an international boycotting of South Africa. In this context, there are now many organizations that demand the boycotting of Israeli goods

---

711. The preamble to the OIC Charter states that one of the aims of the 57 OIC member states is "to support the struggle of the Palestinian people, who are presently under *foreign occupation*, and to empower them to attain their *inalienable rights, including the right to self-determination*, and to establish their sovereign state with Al-Quds Al-Sharif as its capital, while safeguarding its historic and Islamic character, and the holy places therein." (emphasis added). The OIC makes no distinction between the status of Palestinian Arabs in Israel proper and their status in the Occupied Territories; it therefore supports the view that all Palestinian Arabs - even those in Israel - are under foreign occupation. See also for example Article 22 of the Palestinian National Charter: "Zionism is a political movement organically associated with international imperialism and antagonistic to all action for liberation and to progressive movements in the world. It is racist and fanatic in its nature, aggressive, expansionist and colonial in its aims, and fascist in its methods. Israel is the instrument of the Zionist movement, and geographical base for world imperialism placed strategically in the midst of the Arab homeland to combat the hopes of the Arab nation for liberation, unity and progress...."

712. Preamble of the Arab Charter on Human Rights (2004).

713. Glaser (2003).

714. Statement by John Dugard, Special Rapporteur on the situation of human rights in the Occupied Palestinian Territory: www.adalah.org/newsletter/eng/ovt07/dugard-oct07.pdf. Dugard's comments have led to a study initiated by the South African Human Sciences Research Council, which concludes that Israel is guilty of apartheid. See *Occupation, Colonialism, Apartheid*: www.hsrc.ac.za/Document-3327.p.html. See also: Dugard & Reynolds (2013).

715. A/HRC/25/67, *Report of the Special Rapporteur on the situation of human rights in the Palestinian territories occupied since 1967, Richard Falk*, 13 January 2014.

and services, divestment from Israel, and the implementation of sanctions against Israel (this is known as the BDS movement—boycott, divestment and sanctions). The idea that Israel is an apartheid state has become the favorite slogan of left-wing academics like Noam Chomsky, and influential (former) leaders like Archbishop Desmond Tutu, former US President Jimmy Carter and former Dutch Prime Minister Dries van Agt, whose views have gained considerable ground in Europe.[716] During the United Nations World "Conference against Racism, Racial Discrimination, Xenophobia and Related Intolerance," held in Durban in 2001 ("Durban 1"), the NGO Forum Declaration held: "We declare Israel as a racist, apartheid state in which Israel's brand of apartheid as a crime against humanity has been characterized by separation and segregation, dispossession, restricted land access, denationalization, 'bantustanization' and inhumane acts."[717] The stated purpose of all of these initiatives is to equate Zionism (i.e. the creation and maintenance of a Jewish state) with racism and apartheid, and thereby —following the South African model—to establish the international legal framework to bring about the destruction of the Jewish state of Israel. All of these initiatives—the "Zionism=Racism" resolution in 1975, the 2001 Durban I conference, and the current BDS movement—have been launched by the Palestinian Arab leaders together with their political allies. In 1975, the Palestinians' major ally was the Soviet Union, and in 2001 it was Iran. In addition, there are certain influential NGOs that strongly support the apartheid allegation, which became manifest during the Durban I conference.

16.2.3 What is Apartheid?

The official system of racial segregation in South Africa comprised a legal system of political, social and economic discrimination enforced by the minority white population group against non-European, non-white population groups.[718] Legislation was introduced mainly as from 1948 classifying inhabitants into four: black, white, colored and Indian. Intermarriage was forbidden, and blacks were forbidden from living in white areas. More stringent legislation was introduced and enforced in 1970,

716. Seligson (2010); Carter (2006); Agt, van (2009); Tutu (2014).

717. 'The United Nations World Çonference against Racism, Racial Discrimination, Xenophobia and Related Intolerance' in Durban, South Africa in September 2001, the NGO Forum Declaration (of 3 September 2001), para 162. For the background and context of the Durban 1 conference, see Chapter 7 in this book.

718. See in particular: South Africa Prohibition of Mixed Marriages Act (Act No. 55 of 1949); Immorality Amendment Act (Act No. 21 of 1950); Separate Representation of Voters Act (Act No. 46 of 1951); and South African Group Areas Act (Act No. 41 of 1950).

when non-white political representation was completely abolished; blacks were deprived of their citizenship, legally becoming citizens of homelands called Bantustans: four of which became nominally independent states. The government segregated medical care and public places and provided black people with public services inferior to those of white people.

In the 1960s, the international community started to object to the system of apartheid in South Africa. The struggle against apartheid led to the adoption in 1973 of the International Convention on the Suppression and Punishment of the Crime of Apartheid. In 1977 the (First) Additional Protocol to the Geneva Conventions qualified in Article 85 paragraph 4 (c) practices of apartheid as grave breaches of this Protocol. Apartheid was finally included in the definition of crimes against humanity in Article 7.1 (j) and 2 (h) of the Rome Statute of the International Criminal Court. It defines the crime of apartheid as follows:

> **"The crime of 'apartheid' means inhumane acts of a character similar to those referred to in paragraph 1 [i. e. acts 'committed as part of a *widespread or systematic attack* directed against any civilian population, with knowledge of the attack'], committed in the context of *an institutionalized regime of systematic oppression and domination by one racial group over any other racial group or groups and committed with the intention of maintaining that regime."*[719]**

16.2.4 Is Israel an Apartheid State?

The Jewish State of Israel is most commonly charged with being an apartheid regime for three reasons: (1) the so-called preferential treatment of Jews in the field of immigration under the 1950 Law of Return and its legal consequences in other fields; (2) differential treatment of Jewish settlers as compared to the Palestinian inhabitants of the disputed territories; and (3), the application of the security laws, especially to Palestinians.[720] In addition to this, some writers refer even to the Jewish character of the State of Israel, as symbolized by flag, national anthem and state holidays as evidence of "apartheid."[721] This is an absurd allegation. It would make many states apartheid-states, for example if they observe Christian or Islamic holidays, or in case their flags display crosses or crescents, or if they, like the Netherlands, include Christian elements in their national anthem. Consequently, our analysis will be restricted to the three more common charges mentioned above.

719. Statute of Rome, art. 7. 2 (h) (2002) (emphasis added).

720. See Dugard & Reynolds (2013).

721. Glaser (2003).

As to the first point, it should be reiterated that the Law of Return is a justifiable and natural expression of the legitimate right of the Jewish people to self-determination.[722] It reflects the unusual condition of the Jewish people. Once established as a nation state, Jews have been dispersed for centuries in different countries around the world, yet retaining their Jewish religious, cultural, and national identity and connection with the land of their forefathers. Israel was established to create a safe haven for them in a world that in many respects and in numerous areas was and sometimes still is hostile to them. The Jewishness of the state is a direct result of the fact that the state was borne by virtue of the right of the Jewish people to self-determination. It is inherent in the right of a particular people group to self-determination that the state, which they create, is characterized by the identity of that people. If the people were not allowed to take measures to protect their identity, the right to pursue its cultural development would have no value. It has been remarked, by the way, that the acquisition of nationality because of someone's identity is not unique for Israel. Think of the examples of Greece and Armenia.[723] Further, the right of return may grant Jews favored status in respect of the capacity to become Israeli citizens, but once they become Israeli citizens they are in no more privileged a position than non-Jewish Israeli citizens. The parallel comparison between Israel and South Africa is totally misplaced. The racist laws and practices in South Africa were based on a notion that the whites were superior as a race to the blacks. There are no laws or government practices in Israel based on racial superiority. The population consists of persons of all skin colors; all are travelling in the same buses, walking in the same parks, and enjoying their evenings in the same restaurants. The equality of all peoples is an unchallenged foundation of the Israeli legal system. Jews and non-Jews[724] with Israeli citizenship have the right to vote and to be elected. The Supreme Court currently has and previously had Arab and Druze members and the government currently has and previously had Arab and Druze Cabinet ministers. There are Arab members of the Knesset. Israel has Arab heads of hospital departments, Arab university professors, Arab diplomats in the Foreign Service, and senior Arab police and army officers.[725] It is also interesting to note that members of many other groups, such as Arameans and Armenians, enjoy equal civil and political rights in Israel.

722. See, *inter alia*, Gavison (2010); Ernst (2009).

723. See the discussion in Chapter 7 of this book.

724. Mainly Arabs and Druze.

725. Sabel (2009).

The second allegation refers to the separate legal regimes in the disputed territories with respect to Israeli citizens on the one hand and Palestinian Arab inhabitants on the other. These regimes are indeed different. The Jewish persons residing in East Jerusalem and the West Bank are in general Israeli citizens, or at least qualified to become so according to the Law of Return. The Palestinian Arabs in the disputed territories are in general not Israeli citizens. Arabs residing in Jerusalem are permitted to apply for Israeli citizenship, provided they meet the requirements for naturalization—e.g. swearing allegiance to Israel and renouncing all other citizenships. Most Arabs in East-Jerusalem refuse to accept Israeli citizenship even though they are entitled to it. At the end of 2005, 93 percent of the Arab population of East Jerusalem had permanent residency and five percent had Israeli citizenship. The different legal regimes are due to the nationality of the persons concerned. In many if not all states in the world, nationals and non-nationals are to some extent subject to different legal regimes. In respect of the disputed territories, there is the common understanding that the present situation has to be seen as temporary. The Israeli government and representatives of the Palestinians are involved in a process of negotiations to come to some more definite arrangement. One stage in this process is acknowledgement of the provisions adopted in the framework of the Oslo Agreements, which grants different degrees of autonomy with corresponding legal regimes. All of this has to be seen against the background of the fact that the disputed territories cannot be qualified as being ordinary occupied territories, let alone as territories subject to illegal occupation. Under these circumstances, the differences in legal regimes cannot be qualified as an expression of apartheid being the systematic oppression and domination by one racial group over any other racial group or groups and committed with the intention of maintaining that regime.

Application of the security laws, especially to Palestinians, is seen as a third example of an apartheid policy. Laws and practices which restrict the freedom of Palestinian Arabs—and in some cases they do so drastically—are in general the result of the need to protect Israeli citizens and others from terrorist attacks. In this connection, the existence of separate roads in the disputed territories for Israeli and Palestinian traffic is presented as example of apartheid. This claim ignores the real security threat to Israeli road traffic, which, by the way, also includes cars of Arabs who are Israeli citizens.[726] Unfortunately, the threat of terrorism is still prevalent. Radical movements are today spreading hatred against Jews and the Jewish State

726. *Ibid.*

and sometimes engage in violence—supported by radical Islamist states, including as Iran. Under these circumstances, strong security measures are sometimes necessary to protect lives. Israeli security forces make mistakes and they sometimes violate the relevant legal provisions. In such cases, their behavior is scrutinized by the independent judiciary in Israel, and if necessary those responsible are punished. The situation in the disputed territories cannot be compared to the daily life in the relatively quiet residential areas of Western states where the fierce critics of Israel usually live. Imperfect application of security measures cannot lead to the conclusion that Israel is an apartheid state.

To conclude: There is no good reason to qualify Israel as an apartheid state. Rather, this allegation is part of a hostile campaign against Israel. In the words of Michael Ignatieff: "International law defines 'Apartheid' as a crime against humanity. Labelling Israel as an 'Apartheid' state is not only inaccurate and misleading, it is a deliberate and discriminatory attempt to undermine the legitimacy of the Jewish state itself."[727]

16.3 Freedom of Religion

16.3.1 Introduction

An issue frequently addressed in debates concerning human rights in Israel is the freedom of religion. This may be surprising, considering that Israel is not only the cradle of both Judaism and Christianity (and is considered important by Muslims) but also considering Israel's respect for the freedom of religion, which is unique in the whole of the Middle East. It is telling that Israel is the only country in this region where the Christian population has increased since 1948.[728] Israel is accused of breaching freedom of religion by restricting access to Muslim and Christian sites. An example of the kinds of allegations concerning infringement of human rights and more specifically the freedom of religion is the statement by Morocco in the UN Human Rights Council (UNHRC) demanding that Israel implement "all resolutions adopted by the Council, particularly its resolution 7/18 in which it requested Israel to ... immediately withdraw all legislative and administrative measures aimed at making the occupied East Jerusalem Jewish, including measures that allow archaeological digging around the Aqsa Mosque, the building of a synagogue, the establishment and expansion of settlements and the shutting

727. Ignatieff (2009). Between 2000 and 2005 Michael Ignatieff was Professor of Human Rights Policy at Harvard University.

728. Simmons (2012), p. 249, quoting from the Israeli Central Bureau of Statistics, 2009.

down of Palestinian institutions."[729] The reference to the construction of a synagogue in "East Jerusalem" is particularly interesting. This is undoubtedly a reference to the reconstruction of the *Hurva* Synagogue in the heart of the Jewish Quarter in the Old City of Jerusalem. This synagogue, constructed in 1700, burned down in 1721 and was reconstructed in 1856; it had been totally destroyed by the British-led Jordanian Arab Legion during the War of Independence in 1948. Following the recapture of the Old City by Israel in 1967, the synagogue was meticulously reconstructed and reopened in 2010. One can understand how the *destruction* of a synagogue could qualify as an infringement on the right to freedom of religion, but it is difficult to appreciate how the *construction* of a synagogue could be so regarded.[730] There is no evidence whatsoever that the construction of a synagogue has the effect of restricting the freedom of a Muslim in East Jerusalem to practice his or her religion. The background to this argument by Morocco is not closely related to religious freedom. Rather, it is the allegation that Israel is consistently "making the occupied East Jerusalem Jewish," as if Jews have no right to build constructions or carry out activities having a specifically Jewish character in the city, which for more than 3000 years is of crucial importance to the Jewish faith.

European Union (EU) institutions consistently criticize Israel for restricting the religious freedom and other human rights of Muslims and Christians in Jerusalem. An example is the EU Heads of Mission Report on East Jerusalem issued in March 2014, which alleges that Israeli government policies and actions restrict the freedom of Christians and Muslims, specifically by allowing or facilitating archaeological excavations on "religiously sensitive" sites, particularly near the Temple Mount, restricting the freedom of operation of churches in East Jerusalem, and the access of Christian clergy to the Church of the Holy Sepulchre in the Old City and restricting access by Muslims to the Temple Mount. Concurrently, the report expresses concern about "intensive settler-related activities emphasizing the Jewish character and history of the Old City and its surroundings at the expense of the Christian and Muslim narratives." This seems to imply the application of different yardsticks. From the perspective of the freedom of religion, it can be imagined that the representatives of the EU States are concerned about what they see as *restrictions* on religious freedom of Muslims and Christians. From the same perspective, the concern about the *exercise* of this freedom by Jews (at the Temple Mount) is difficult to

---

729. A/HRC/10/76, p. 7.

730. Meyerowitz-Katz (2013): http://www.aijac.org.au/news/article/israel-refuses-to-participate-in-human-rights.

understand.[731] It seems that the European representatives are ignorant of the undeniable fact that the Temple Mount is of primary importance for Judaism. It can even be feared that EU representatives do not dispute the ridiculous idea that there was not any historical connection between the Temple Mount and the Jews, an idea which nowadays is popular among the Palestinian Arabs.[732]

16.3.2 Freedom of Religion in Israel[733]

In order to put the allegations against Israel concerning religious freedom in perspective, it makes sense to shed some light on the protection of the freedom of religion in Israel. It is clear both from Israel's Declaration of Independence and from the Basic Law of 17 March 1992 on Human Dignity and Liberty that the State of Israel is both a Jewish and democratic state. It is not a purely secular state as is France. Nor is it a state governed by religious law, as is Saudi Arabia. Similar to the Netherlands or Germany, Israel's legal order has a respectful attitude towards all religious expression. This principle is carried into the public sphere. As earlier explained, Israeli law is—to a large extent—secular. In line with other former parts of the Ottoman Empire, only family law in Israel incorporates religious law. That means that questions of marriage and divorce of Jews are decided according to Jewish law. Similar questions of Christians are decided in accordance with the canon law of the various Christian denominations. Finally, Islamic law is applied to these family law issues when the parties are Muslim.[734] Additionally, the Foundations of Law statute (1980) contains a very general reference to what may be interpreted as Jewish religious law serving as a supplementary source of law. The connection between the Jewish and the democratic nature of the state resulted in the recognition of the right to freedom of religion. In the Declaration of Independence, it was already proclaimed that Israel would guarantee freedom of religion, conscience, language, education and culture and that it will safeguard the holy places of all religions. The Basic Law: Human Dignity and Liberty (1992) and the Basic Law: Freedom of Occupation (1994) are interpreted by the Israeli Supreme Court as implying religious freedom. This Court has in several important judgements

---

731. EU HOMS Report on Jerusalem, 18 March 2014 (www.kaapeli./i/...EAST%20JERUSALEM%REPO). The quotation is from para 27.

732. Gold (2007).

733. See Lerner (2007); Ravitch (2009); Shetreet (n.d.): http://www.jewishvirtuallibrary.org/jsource/Society_&_Culture/freedom.html.

734. Cf. Blois, de (2011).

recognized the freedom of religions in the strongest of terms. It held for example in the *Hass v. IDF Commander in West Bank* case, which dealt with the access to the Machpela Cave at Hebron:

> "The freedom of religion is a constitutional basic right of the individual, with a preferred status even in relation to other constitutional rights. It extends to the freedom of the individual to believe and act according to his belief while practising its commandments and customs... The said freedom is related to the exercising of the individual's own identity. Within the limits of said freedom, the desire of the believer to pray at holy sites is recognized. Such recognition is a part of the broad constitutional protection given to the right of access of members of the various religions to their holy sites and the prohibition of offending their feelings in respect of such places (Section 1 of the Protection of Holy Sites Law, 5727-1967). The freedom of religion is regarded as a branch of freedom of expression in the sphere of religious belief."[735]

It can be derived from this quotation that the freedom of religion in Israel not only includes the freedom to believe the tenets of a certain religion but also the freedom to practice a religion and observe religious commandments. This conforms with international standards such as Article 18 of the International Covenant on Civil and Political Rights (ICCPR), which recognizes the freedom to "manifest his religion or belief in worship, observance, practice and teaching." It is also made clear by the Supreme Court that the freedom of religion in Israel extends to all religions: Jewish, Christian, Islamic and other religious groups enjoy the protection of this freedom in Israel. In practice, it is inevitable that members of religious groups may have their rights infringed by other citizens or government restrictions: for this reason, the Israeli legal system is open to hearing all such cases. Despite its weaknesses and deficiencies, there can be no doubt that minority groups in Israel enjoy a level of protection by the Israeli legal system far exceeding that enjoyed by minorities in Islamic countries.

16.4 The International Fight against Terrorism

16.4.1 Alleged Infringements on International Human Right Obligations by the State of Israel

In the international arena, the State of Israel is often accused of violations of international law when adopting restrictive measures to

735. HCJ 10356/02 Hass v. IDF Commander in West Bank (4 March 2004); [2004] Isr SC 58 (3) 443; [2004] IsrLR 53, para 19.

combat terrorism on its territory. These accusations of human rights violations against the State include among others: the construction of the security fence,[736] preventive administrative detention of persons who are suspected of planning terrorist acts, restrictions on the access of suspects to lawyers, the use of certain interrogation methods, the [summary] executions of terrorists without legal proceedings, and the demolition of houses and other buildings in connection with fighting terrorism.

Without prejudice to the substance of these accusations, it should be noticed here that the dealing of a state with terrorism on its territory belongs not to a single case, but should instead be understood in a broader context of the global struggle against international terrorism. Responding to the occurrence of terrorist attacks and also noting in this respect a need to protect the fundamental human rights of individuals,[737] the international community has expressed its utmost determination "to combat by all means threats to international peace and security caused by terrorist acts."[738] The Security Council has in this regard placed great emphasis on the participation of all states[739] in preventing and suppressing terrorist acts and on the incorporation of counter-terrorism measures into states' national legal orders.

16.4.2 Counter-Terrorism and Human Rights

In the context of counter-terrorism, there exists an international obligation for states "to ensure that any measures taken to combat terrorism comply with all their obligations under international law, [meaning they] should adopt such measures in accordance with international law, in particular international human rights law, refugee law, and humanitarian law." The obligations to take effective counter-terrorism measures and to promote human rights are in view of the United Nations "not conflicting goals, but complementary and mutually reinforcing."[740]

736. The International Court of Justice stated that the State of Israel violated arts. 9, 12 and 17 of ICCPR and 6, 7, 10, 11 ,12, 13 and 14 of the ICESCR in the context of the construction of the fence.

737. Office of the UN High Commissioner for Human Rights: HR/Terrorism and Counter-Terrorism, Fact Sheet No. 32, p. 7. In view of the High Commissioner, States have not only a right but also a duty to take effective counter-terrorism measures in order to protect [the fundamental rights of] individuals that are under their jurisdiction from terrorist attacks.

738. UN S.C. Res. 1373 (2001); UN S.C. Res. 1611 (2005).

739. See, e.g., UN S.C. Res. 1377 (2001) which: "[a]ffirms that a sustained, comprehensive approach involving the active participation and collaboration of all Member States of the United Nations, and in accordance with the Charter of the United Nations and international law, is essential to combat the scourge of international terrorism."

740. United Nations Global Counter-Terrorism Strategy (UN G.A. Res. 60/288, annex Plan of Action).

Having regard to both the obligation to fight terrorism and protect human rights, the State of Israel addresses its security concerns and meets its pressing need for timely intelligence, while at the same time it ensures (under Israeli law the safeguards of) an independent judicial review and access to counsel.[741] Additionally it grants also "prompt access to the courts [that does not only extend] to criminal suspects but also to security detainees and unlawful combatants, regardless of nationality, including those seized in territories under military occupation and those captured in battle on foreign soil."[742]

However, despite the obligation to abide by international human rights in combatting international terrorism, human rights conventions specifically contain provisions that allow for human rights to be limited against conflicting rights or interests. The human rights framework provides in this context that "States may legitimately limit the exercise of certain rights, including the right to freedom of expression, the right to freedom of association and assembly, the right to freedom of movement and the right to respect for one's private and family life."[743] Additionally, "as a general matter, given the direct impact of terrorism on fundamental human rights, security and the functioning of various aspects of international and domestic societies, there is no doubt that the prevention and repression of international terrorism is an important objective which can, in principle, permit the limitation of certain rights," subject to the fact that "the imposition of such limitation satisfies various requirements."[744]

One such example of a restriction of a human right is found in the right to freedom of movement protected by Article 12 of the ICCPR.[745] This provision is applicable to the restrictions on the freedom of movement of Palestinian Arabs and others resulting from the erection of the security fence. Paragraph 3 of Article 12 provides in this context:

---

741. *Ibid.*, p. 3. Under Israeli national law, decisions of the executive are subject to judicial review by courts. See Supreme Court of Israel sitting as High Court of Justice 6 September 1999, in the case of Public Committee Against Torture in Israel v. The State of Israel: http://www.derechos.org/human-rights/mena/doc/torture.html (visited: 7 September 2016).

742. Supreme Court of the United States, Lakhdar Boumediene v George W. Bush, Nos. 06-1195 & 06-1196, Brief of Amici Curiae Specialists in Israeli Military Law and Constitutional Law in Support of Petitioners, p. 2.

743. Fact Sheet No. 32 UN High Commissioner for Human Rights, p. 23.

744. *Ibid.*, pp. 24 and 25. A human right must be capable of limitation, the limiting measure must be imposed within the bounds of certain procedural requirements and it must be necessary to achieve a particular counter-terrorism objective.

745. Paragraph 1 provides: "Everyone lawfully within the territory of a State shall, within that territory, have the right to liberty of movement and freedom to choose his residence."

"The above-mentioned rights shall not be subject to any restrictions except those which are provided by law, are necessary to protect national security, public order, public health or morals or the rights and freedoms of others, and are consistent with the other rights recognized in the present Covenant."

The International Court of Justice (ICJ), when considering the legality of Israel's security fence in 2004, failed to take this provision seriously. Without further explanation and ignoring the argument that it had insufficient evidence to enable it to reach this conclusion, the ICJ simply concluded that these conditions were not satisfied (i.e. that the barrier was not necessary to protect the national security or the right or freedoms of others).[746]

16.4.3 Comprehensive Legal Framework Pertaining to Counter-Terrorism

The increase of terrorist incidents worldwide[747] provided for an impulse to the development of a comprehensive legal framework pertaining to combatting international terrorism.[748] In this framework, states are addressed as the legal subjects who can find their acts in counter-terrorism to be governed by certain norms and obligations.

Forty-two legal instruments that pertain to international terrorism[749] establish this international legal regime. Among the international obligations accepted by the State of Israel are the Convention for the Suppression of Unlawful Seizure of Aircraft,[750] the Convention for the Suppression of Unlawful Acts against the Safety of Civil Aviation,[751] the Convention on the Prevention and Punishment of Crimes against Internationally Protected Persons, including Diplomatic Agents, 1973,[752] the Convention on the Physical Protection of Nuclear Material,[753] the International Convention

746. I.C.J. Reports 2004, pp. 193-194.

747. A/70/826, Report of the Secretary-General, Activities of the United Nations system in implementing the United Nations Global Counter-Terrorism Strategy, 12 April 2016, para 8. According to the Global Terrorism Database, terrorist incidents worldwide increased from 2,729 in 2006 to 4,782 in 2010, and to 16,818 in 2014.

748. *Ibid.*, para 19.

749. A/70/211, Report of the Secretary-General, *Measures to Eliminate International Terrorism*, 29 July 2015.

750. Convention for the Suppression of Unlawful Seizure of Aircraft, 1970.

751. Convention for the Suppression of Unlawful Acts against the Safety of Civil Aviation, 1971.

752. Convention on the Prevention and Punishment of Crimes against Internationally Protected Persons, including Diplomatic Agents, 1973.

753. Convention on the Physical Protection of Nuclear Material, 1980.

for the Suppression of Terrorist Bombings[754] and the Amendment to the Convention on the Physical Protection of Nuclear Material, 2005.[755]

Under these instruments, State Parties have an obligation among others: to criminalize and make punishable by domestic law a number of specified acts;[756] to adopt such measures as may be necessary in order to ensure that certain criminal acts are under no means justifiable;[757] to hold persons liable for a number of specified acts; and to extradite perpetrators of a number of specified acts.[758] Moreover, State Parties have an obligation to protect certain facilities and materials within their territory[759] and an obligation to take necessary and effective measures to prohibit and prevent the manufacture of unmarked plastic explosives and prevent the movement thereof in their territory.[760]

16.4.4 Counter-Terrorism Norms Adopted by the Security Council

The Security Council also has become actively involved in the development of the framework regarding international terrorism. In its Resolutions, the Security Council has labelled international terrorism as "one of the most serious threats to peace and security"[761] and defined it as: "certain criminal acts committed with intent to cause death or serious bodily injury, or taking hostages, with the purpose of provoking a state of terror in the population or compelling a government or an international organization to do or abstain from doing an act, which constitute an offence within the anti-terrorist conventions, embody the notion of terrorism."[762] The Security Council has stated that "*all acts* of terrorism irrespective

754. International Convention for the Suppression of Terrorist Bombings, 1997.

755. Amendment to the Convention on the Physical Protection of Nuclear Material, 2005.

756. See, e.g.,: Convention for the Suppression of Unlawful Seizure of Aircraft, 1970, art 2; Convention for the Suppression of Unlawful Acts against the Safety of Civil Aviation, 1971, art. 3; Convention on the Prevention and Punishment of Crimes against Internationally Protected Persons, including Diplomatic Agents, 1973, art. 2(2); and International Convention for the Suppression of Acts of Nuclear Terrorism, 2005, art. 5.

757. "In particular where they are intended or calculated to provoke a state of terror in the general public or in a group of persons or particular persons (...)", see, e.g., International Convention for the Suppression of Terrorist Bombings, 1997, art. 3.

758. See, e.g., Convention for the Suppression of Unlawful Seizure of Aircraft, 1970, art. 6; Convention for the Suppression of Unlawful Acts against the Safety of Civil Aviation, 1971, art. 6; and International Convention for the Suppression of Acts of Nuclear Terrorism, 2005, art. 10(2).

759. Amendment to the Convention on the Physical Protection of Nuclear Material, 2005, art. 2A.

760. Convention on the Marking of Plastic Explosives for the Purpose of Detection, 1991, arts 2 and 3.

761. UN S.C. Res. 1566 (2004).

762. *Ibid.*

of their motivation and by whosoever committed" should in this context be condemned.[763]

16.4.5 The Obligations of UN Member States under Resolutions 1373, 1566 and 1624

The duty on UN Member States to combat terrorism on a national level increased after the attacks on 9/11, in response to which the Security Council adopted Resolution 1373 (2001). Acting under its Chapter VII powers, the Security Council laid down a number of binding obligations for Member States to take measures against international terrorism. That Resolution imposed obligations on Member States to take the necessary steps to prevent the commission of terrorist acts; deny safe haven to those who finance, plan, support, or commit terrorist acts, or provide safe havens; prevent those who finance, plan, facilitate or commit terrorist acts from using their respective territories for those purposes against other Member States or their citizens; prevent the movement of terrorists or terrorist groups by effective border controls; ensure that any person who participates in the financing, planning, preparation or perpetration of terrorist acts or in supporting terrorist acts is brought to justice and ensure that, in addition to any other measures against them, such terrorist acts are established as serious criminal offencss in domestic laws and regulations.[764]

Following Resolution 1373 (2001), the Security Council adopted another two Resolutions that were not adopted under Chapter VII of the UN Charter: Resolutions 1566 (2004) and 1624 (2005). Resolution 1566 (2004) sets out a number of non-binding measures for Member States: "to find, deny safe haven and bring to justice, on the basis of the principle to extradite or prosecute, any person who supports, facilitates, participates or attempts to participate in the financing, planning, preparation or commission of terrorist acts; and prevent and punish criminal acts, including against civilians, committed with the intent to cause death or serious bodily injury, or taking of hostages, with the purpose to provoke a state of terror in the general public."[765] Resolution 1624 subsequently calls upon Member States to adopt such measures as may be necessary and appropriate and in accordance with their obligations under international law to prohibit by

763. *Ibid.* (emphasis added). A position that is highly interesting in the context of claims that "opposition to foreign occupation" should fall outside the scope of terrorism.

764. UN S.C. Res. 1373 (2001). By this Resolution the Counter Terrorism Committee was established that received the task to monitor State compliance with these obligations.

765. UN S.C. Res. 1566 (2004).

law incitement to commit a terrorist act or acts, to prevent such conduct and also to strengthen the security of their international borders.[766]

16.4.6 Definition of "Terrorism" as an International Crime

Despite the fact that the existing normative framework on counter-terrorism stipulates the obligations for states in relation to "terrorism," there is as yet no general definition of the "crime of terrorism" in international law. The Committee and Working Group established in 1996 by the UN General Assembly established have not been able to reach a consensus on the formulation of the definition of terrorism due to opposing views on whether such definition should be applicable to the use of force of states against its own civilians and whether or not it should include the actions of self-determination movements opposing foreign occupation.[767]

Furthermore, the crime of terrorism is not yet included in the Statute of the International Criminal Court (ICC). It is however included in the Statutes of the International Criminal Tribunal for Rwanda and the Special Court for Sierra Leone, that have stipulated in their Statutes that "acts of terrorism" are war crimes over which it has the power to prosecute persons.[768] The International Criminal Tribunal for Former Yugoslavia that has held "acts of violence the primary purpose of which was to spread terror among the civilian population" to amount to a war crime that is punishable under Article 3 of its Statute.[769]

One institution that has made an important contribution to the formulation of a comprehensive definition on the crime of terrorism is the Special Tribunal for Lebanon. The Appeals Chamber of this institution found in 2011 that "existing anti-terrorism treaties, UN Resolutions, and the legislative and judicial practice of states showed the formation of a general *opinio juris* in the international community, accompanied by a practice consistent with such opinion, to the effect that a customary rule of international law regarding the international crime of terrorism, at least

766. UN S.C. Res. 1624 (2005).

767. The Committee and Working Group were established through Resolution 51/210 under the mandate of "further developing a comprehensive legal framework of conventions dealing with terrorism."

768. Statute of the International Tribunal for Rwanda, art. 4(d); Statute of the Special Court for Sierra Leone, art 3(d).

769. See e.g.: International Tribunal for Former Yugoslavia, Prosecutor v. Stanislav Galić, Trial Judgment, 5 December 2003, para 796; International Tribunal for Former Yugoslavia, Prosecutor v. Karadžić,, Judgment, 24 March 2016, para 458.

in time of peace, has indeed emerged."[770] A definition on terrorism would involve in view of the Special Tribunal three key elements:

1. the perpetration of a criminal act (murder, kidnapping, hostage-taking, arson, among others), or threatening such act;
2. the intent to spread fear among the population or directly or indirectly coerce a national or international authority to take some action or refrain from it; and
3. when the act involves a transnational element.[771]

This customary rule of international law would subsequently address itself to international subjects - including rebels and others non-state entities and trigger individual criminal liability. Moreover, it would include not only a legal obligation for states to prevent, repress and prosecute terrorism, but also a right for states to prosecute and repress the crime of terrorism.[772]

Returning to the threats Israel is confronted with on a daily basis from terrorist groups, we see the relevance of this definition. These groups are prepared to commit criminal acts as defined above; they also have the intent to spread fear or try to coerce authorities. Finally, having regard to their weaponry and affiliations, they do represent a transnational element. We can conclude that the measures taken by Israel to combat terrorism, including construction of the security barrier, are not only permissible but also obliged under international law.

770. Special Tribunal for Lebanon, Interlocutory Decision on the Applicable Law: Terrorism, Conspiracy, Homicide, Perpetration, Cumulative Charging, STL-11-01/I, A.Ch., 16 February 2011, para 85. The Appeals Chamber thereby finds support in regional treaties that have defined terrorism as "criminal acts intended to terrorise populations or coerce an authority", General Assembly Resolutions which have insisted that "criminal acts intended or calculated to provoke a state of terror in the general public, a group of persons or particular persons for political purposes are in any circumstance unjustifiable" and in the earlier mentioned definition given in Resolution 1566 of the Security Council.

771. *Ibid.*, para 85.

772. *Ibid.*, para 102. "The customary rule can be held to: (i) impose on any State (as well as other international subjects such as rebels and other non-State entities participating in international dealings) the obligation to refrain from engaging through their officials and agents in acts of terrorism, as defined in the rule; (ii) to impose on any State (and other international subjects and entities endowed with the necessary structures and judicial machinery) the obligation to prevent and repress terrorism, and in particular to prosecute and try persons on its territory or in territory under its control who are allegedly involved in terrorism, as defined in the rule; (iii) to confer on any State (and other international subjects endowed with the necessary structures and judicial machinery) the right to prosecute and repress the crime of terrorism, as defined in the rule, perpetrated on its territory (or in territory under its control) by nationals or foreigners, and an obligation on any other State to refrain from opposing or objecting to such prosecution and repression against their own nationals (unless they are high-level state agents enjoying personal immunities under international law)."

PART V

"Palestine"

17. Palestinian Self-Determination

" ...the Court observes that the existence of a 'Palestinian people' is no longer an issue."

Advisory Opinion (Paragraph 118)[773]

17.1 Introduction

The basic argument underlying the various claims for Palestinian statehood is that the Palestinian Arabs have been denied self-determination ever since the collapse of the Ottoman Empire. The Mandate for Palestine, the 1947 Partition Plan, and all other events leading to the creation of the Jewish State of Israel in 1948 were imposed upon the inhabitants of the land by external powers. It is sometimes argued that the Mandate for Palestine requiring a "Jewish national home" was contrary to Article 22 of the League of Nations Covenant and therefore amounted to a kind of colonialism in the form of Zionist immigration.[774] The modern State of Israel was, in this view, established at the expense of Palestine's real inhabitants' right to self-determination: an injustice which needs to be rectified.

The Palestine Liberation Organization (PLO), purporting to act as the "sole legitimate representative" of "the Palestinian people," has claimed an inalienable right to self-determination and independence, including the right to statehood.[775] It is even claimed that the state of Palestine

773. I.C.J. Reports 2004, pp. 182-183.

774. See. e.g., Cattan (1976), pp. 65-68; Bassiouni (1971), at p. 38.

775. These claims are set out in various documents. See in particular the 1968 Palestinian Charter; the 1998 Declaration of Palestinian Statehood; Annex II (Summary legal position of the Palestinian Liberation Organization) of the Secretary-General's Report on Illegal Israeli Actions in Occupied East Jerusalem and the rest of the Occupied Palestinian territory, A/ES-10/248 (24 November 2003); Application of the State of Palestine for Admission to membership of the United Nations (23 September 2011); and UN G.A. Res. 67/19 'Status of Palestine in the United Nations' (29 November 2012).

already exists as a matter of law.[776] The United Nations (UN) General Assembly advocates Palestinian independence referring to "the right of the Palestinian people to self-determination, including the right to their independent State of Palestine."[777]

Israel is accused of preventing the Palestinian people from realizing their right to full self-determination. In its Wall Advisory Opinion, the International Court of Justice (ICJ) concluded that it is an irrefutable fact that the Palestinian people constitute a people that have a right to self-determination and qualified the construction of the fence as an illegitimate restriction on this right.[778] Judge Rosalyn Higgins issued a separate opinion and was very critical of the IJC's reasoning on this point. She said that the construction of the fence could not be seen as a serious impediment to the Palestinian Arab right to self-determination.[779]

In order to assess the PLO's claims to self-determination under international law, several questions need to be answered:

- First, what is to be understood by the concept of "Palestine"?
- Secondly, who are the beneficiaries of the claimed Palestinian right to self-determination? (i.e. are the Palestinian Arabs a *people* in the sense of the principle of self-determination under international law?)
- Thirdly, to what territory does that right apply? (In the debate on Palestinian self-determination, there is considerable confusion about the territorial scope of the claims of Palestinian Arabs to sovereignty.)
- Fourthly, what does the "right to self-determination" mean in this context? (i.e. does it include a right to statehood or to other forms of autonomy?)
- Finally, how is Palestinian Arab self-determination to be reconciled with the rights of the State of Israel to sovereignty, security and territorial integrity?

---

776. On 25 July 2014, the Minister of Justice of the State of Palestine and the General Prosecutor at the Court of Justice of Gaza filed a 'complaint' with the ICC's Prosecutor (Article 15.1 and 53 of the Statute of the ICC). The document starts with general information on Palestine. It surprisingly bases the Palestinian 'sovereignty' on the Mandate for Palestine of 24 July 1922: State of Palestine - ICC- 25 July 2014.

777. See, e.g., the eighth Preamble to UN G.A. Res. 67/19, 'Status of Palestine in the United Nations', 29 November 2012.

778. I.C.J. Reports 2004, pp. 182-183.

779. I.C.J. Reports 2004, p. 214.

17.2 What is "Palestine"?

After their suppression of the Bar Kokhba uprising (132-135 CE), the Romans renamed the province of Judea as "Palaestina". This was a deliberate reference to the Philistines, intended to erase the Jewish connection to this territory.[780] After 135 CE, a small number of Jewish inhabitants remained in Palestine, mostly in or near Safed, Tiberias, Hebron and Jerusalem—the four "Holy Cities" of Judaism.[781] Arabs arrived in Palestine in significant numbers when Islam swept through the Middle East in the 7th century CE, conquering Jerusalem in 637 CE. Throughout the centuries of successive invading empires (Arabs, Christian Crusaders, Mamelukes), right up to the Turkish Ottoman Empire (1517-1917), the Jews remained one of the population groups in the area, suffering changing fortunes under their various occupiers. Each successive conqueror introduced new and mainly non-Arab immigrants from a wide variety of countries and nationalities to Palestine.[782]

During the Paris Peace conference after WWI, the term "Palestine" was used to refer to the territory that was to house the proposed Jewish national home, in contradistinction to those territories that were to become "Arab" states. This is also reflected in the Agreement of January 1919 between Dr. Chaim Weizmann (President of the World Zionist Organization who represented the Jewish people at the Paris Peace Conference), and Emir Feisal Ibn al-Hussein al-Hashemi (representing the Arab nations). They referred to "the racial kinship and ancient bonds existing between the Arabs and the Jewish people, and realising that the surest means of working out the consummation of their natural aspirations is through the closest possible collaboration in the development of the Arab State and Palestine..."[783] The agreement was subsequently rejected by the Arabs, and for that reason was never executed. The territory of Palestine was, in 1918, home to many different ethnic, cultural, and religious groups. It was for that reason that the Balfour Declaration specifically stated that the establishment of the Jewish national home should respect the "civil and religious rights of the existing non-Jewish communities in Palestine." Under the Mandate for Palestine (1922) the term "Palestine" refers to the *locus* within which the Jewish national home was to be established. Its

---

780. Gilbert'(1978), p. 6. The name "Palestina" was already used by Egyptian and Greek writers as early as the 12th century BCE. See also: Gerloff (2016).

781. See Gilbert (2005), p. 1.

782. Peters (1984), p. 152.

783. See for the text Antonius (1938), pp. 437-439.

Article 7, for example, imposed a duty on the Mandatory power to enact legislation to provide for "the acquisition of Palestinian citizenship by Jews who take up their permanent residence in Palestine." Remarkably, however, the Jews chose not to claim the name Palestine for the Jewish State. In May 1948, the Jewish leadership in Palestine ("Yishuv") decided to call their new state "Israel."[784] By doing so, they could be said in effect to have "abandoned the 'Palestine' trademark."[785] The result was that for more than a decade after the Israeli War of Independence, the term "Palestine" laid more or less in abeyance. It was only later that the local Arab movement started to identify its national interests with the geographical territory of Palestine and adopted the name "Palestine" for themselves, excluding the Jewish residents from that designation.

17.3 Beneficiaries of the Principle of Self-Determination

The concept of the "self-determination" in international law is notoriously complex and uncertain. It may safely be stated that under international law the subjects of the right to self-determination are "peoples" (sometimes referred to as "nations") and that in order to define what is a people, various objective and subjective criteria have emerged during the course of the last century as the principle of self-determination has developed as a principle of international law. Broadly speaking, the main objective criterion is that the people must have a distinct historical, cultural, religious and linguistic identity.[786] The first question is therefore: Do the "Palestinian people" have a common history, culture, language, and religion? The subjective criterion requires that this people possess the political will to become an independent nation. The second question can therefore be stated as: Has the Palestinian people expressed an intentional desire to determine for themselves their political future?

17.4 Objective National Identity

To which historical, cultural, religious and linguistic group(s) does the non-Jewish population of Palestine belong? The claim is sometimes made that the "Palestinians ... descend from the Canaanites and other groups

---

784. The question of which name would be adopted was highly controversial, and was not resolved until the very last minute of the meeting held in Tel Aviv on 14 May 1948. See Gilbert (1999), p. 187.

785. Hertz (2009): www.allenzhertz.com/2009/11/aboriginal-rights-to-israel.html.

786. Cf. Chapter 5. See also, e.g., Summers (2013).

that inhabited Palestine in the second millennium BC."[787] For example, Chief Palestinian negotiator Saeb Erekat has claimed: "I am the proud son of the Canaanites who were there 5,500 years before Joshua bin Nun burned down the town of Jericho."[788] This is unlikely. As has been said before, historical evidence shows that the Canaanites, Philistines and other population groups no longer lived in the region by the time the Romans occupied Palestine. In fact, there is considerable evidence that the ancestors of many who today call themselves "Palestinians" arrived in Palestine within the last 200 years from other countries. Experts have established that Saeb Erekat and his family are not descendants of the Canaanites but are part of the Bedouin Huweitat clan, which originated in the Hejaz area of Saudi Arabia, arrived in Palestine from the south of Jordan, and settled in the village of Abu Dis in the early 20th century.[789]

The evidence shows that at the end of the 19th century: (a) large tracts of Palestine were uninhabited, and (b) to the extent that Palestine was inhabited, it was inhabited by a very diverse, disparate and transient population.[790] In her ground-breaking book *From Time Immemorial*, Joan Peters refutes the claim that the creation of a Jewish state in 1948 "displaced Arabs who had been living in Palestine for centuries." She explains that in the period 1830-1920 (i.e. prior to the Mandate for Palestine), the "Arab" population of Palestine was "small and limited."[791] In the course of the 19th century—a period of great political unrest—the population of Palestine was effectively doubled. This was a result of the immigration of Jews from Eastern Europe, creating trade, employment, health services and infrastructure. The Jews' presence and economic productivity attracted immigrants from the surrounding nations who also settled land.[792] Muslims who immigrated into Palestine in the 20th

787. See e.g. Quigley (2005), p. 68: "Therefore, as of 1880 - the time just before the onset of Zionist immigration - the majority population of Palestine, though Arabized, descended from the Canaanites and other groups that inhabited Palestine in the second millennium B.C." A member of the Jordanian Parliament, Sheikh Mousa Abu Sweilam, has stated that "the Palestinians are the original owners of Palestine." Ahmed Tibi, a member of Israel's Knesset, is quoted in Haaretz newspaper as saying in 2014: "...the Arab citizens of Israel are an indigenous population." See: http://www.haaretz.co.il/magazine/.premium-1.2212485#sthash.bYZwWem3.dpuf.

788. http://www.algemeiner.com/2014/02/02/pa-negotiator-saeb-erekat-claims-family-was-canaanite-in-israel-for-9000-years/ (visited: 11 September 2017).

789. See Baker (2014): http://jcpa.org/article/changing-historical-narrative-saeb-erekats-new-spin/ (visited: 11 September 2017).

790. See generally Dershowitz (2003), pp. 24-28. See also Karsh (2010), pp. 8-10.

791. Peters (1984), p. 245, quoting Dr. Carl Hermann Voss, Chairman of the American Christian Palestine Committee.

792. *Ibid.*, p. 249.

century came from many countries including Egypt, Kurdistan, Turkey, and even Bosnia.[793] Of the approximately 500,000 "Arabs" who were living in Palestine by 1918 (compared with "only 50,000 Jews"), many were not Arab but (for example) Circassians, Egyptians, Druze, Turks, Bosnians, Armenians, and Algerians.[794] Furthermore, their religion was not always Islam, as there were also considerable numbers of Christians and Druze among them. Many of them lived a nomadic existence.

In the Mandate period of 1920-1948, Britain tried to regulate immigration into and emigration from Palestine. Britain severely restricted Jewish immigration into Palestine, which was in breach of the terms of the Mandate for Palestine, requiring Britain to facilitate Jewish immigration and settlement. Britain simultaneously allowed an "uncontrolled influx of illegal Arab immigrants into Palestine from Egypt, Transjordan and Syria," mostly seeking to benefit from the economic growth in Palestine (compared with their home countries) under the Mandate for Palestine.[795]

As a result, of the approximately 700,000 Arabs who were said to have fled Israel-to-be and become refugees in 1948, less than half (according to Peters only a maximum of 343,000) had been "settled" in the area for more than a few decades.[796] In all likelihood, given the mass illegal Arab immigration (which cannot be quantified), the figure is much lower.[797]

All this does not mean that the non-Jewish population was not significant or that Palestine was "a land without a people" in the sense that when the Jewish immigrants arrived in greater numbers in the late 19th and early 20th centuries, nobody was living in the land.[798] On the contrary, prior to the Mandate for Palestine, there were people in Palestine, but they were a plurality of historical, cultural, linguistic and religious groups, one of which was the Jewish people. All in all, this means that a single Palestinian "people" arguably did not exist in the sense of the objective criterion in 1922.

In the succeeding decades, however, the non-Jewish Palestinian population increasingly developed a coherent historical, cultural, religious

---

793. See generally also: Avnery (1982); Karsh (2010).

794. Peters (1984), pp. 245-268.

795. *Ibid.*, p. 232.

796. *Ibid.*, p. 262.

797. Benny Morris speaks of "an indeterminate amount of illegal immigration", See: Morris (2008), p. 15.

798. The Palestinian Declaration of Independence (1988) claims that "it was the Palestinian people, already wounded in its body, that was submitted to yet another type of occupation over which floated the falsehood that 'Palestine was a land without people'."

and linguistic identity, so that by 1988 it is arguable that they existed as a distinct "people" under international law.

17.5 Subjective National Identity

Pan-Arab Nationalism

The self-understanding or "subjective" identity of the non-Jewish population in Palestine as a distinct "people" or "nation" appears only to have arisen long after the collapse of the Ottoman Empire, and to have grown incrementally in the decades after the creation of the State of Israel in 1948.

This is complicated by the fact that the emergence of the Palestinian Arab identity was integrally intertwined with growing pan-Arab nationalism after World War I.

Both prior to the Mandate for Palestine and throughout its existence, the Arab leadership was fully involved in the delicate and intense efforts of the Principle Allied Powers to seek a fair balance between the legitimate interests of both the Jewish people, on the one hand, and the Arab and other peoples of the whole region on the other. In the period 1917-1920, there was much communication between the Allied Powers (especially Great Britain) and Arab leaders. Emir Feisal bin Hussein led the delegation representing the Arab people of the region—including the Palestinian Arabs—at the Paris Peace Conference. It was well-known that there was local Palestinian Arab opposition to the Balfour Declaration and re-creation of the Jewish homeland.[799] The decision to give priority to the interests of the worldwide Jewish community, in preference to those of the local Arab population, did not mean that the local non-Jewish population in Palestine were ignored; on the contrary, the Mandate for Palestine explicitly attempted to deal with this tension by including the requirement that "nothing should be done which might prejudice the civil and religious rights of existing non-

799. For example, in 1919 President Wilson dispatched a commission to the Near East to report on the political situation there. In its report to the Paris Peace Conference in August 1919, the commissioners King and Crane expressed their concern about the conflict between the wishes of the Jewish population for a national homeland and the interests of the non-Jewish population in Palestine: "[I]t is to be remembered that the non-Jewish population of Palestine - nearly 9/10 of the whole - are emphatically against the entire Zionist programme. The tables show that there was no one thing upon which the population of Palestine was more agreed upon than this. To subject a people so minded to unlimited Jewish immigration, and to steady financial and social pressure to surrender the land, would be a gross violation of the principle just quoted, and of the people's rights, though it kept within the forms of law." See: https://unispal.un.org/DPA/DPR/unispal.nsf/0/392AD7EB00902A0C852570C000795153 (visited: 11 September 2017).

Jewish communities in Palestine."[800] This does not mean that this was a formula that was perfect in its equitable distribution of interests, or that it was likely to be successful in practice, but it does mean that the subject was dealt with in the Mandate for Palestine. Moreover, it should be seen in the context of the distribution of rights and interests throughout the region in the aftermath of the collapse of the Turkish Ottoman Empire.

During the Mandate period, there was fierce local Arab opposition to the creation of a Jewish homeland. This appears to have been driven largely by the political elite. Their motivation was not so much the promotion of the interests of a perceived separate, non-Jewish Palestinian people as the rejection of the notion of Jewish nationhood that was expressed in the Mandate for Palestine. Significantly, in the late 1920's and early 1930's, opposition to the Mandate for Palestine was a regional struggle that attracted many Arab nationalist militants from across the Middle East. One of these, Sheikh Izaddin al-Qassam from Syria, established the Black Hand militant group and laid the foundations for the 1936 Arab revolt. Following the assassination of al-Qassam by the British in late 1935, tensions erupted in 1936 resulting in the Arab general strike and general boycott soon deteriorating into violence against the British and the Jews. In the first wave, lasting until early 1937, the Arab gangs were defeated by the British and many Arab leaders were forcibly removed from Mandate Palestine. The revolt led to the establishment of the Peel Commission, which in 1937 proposed partitioning of Palestine. This was rejected by the leaders of the Palestinian Arabs.

The most prominent of the Palestinian Arab leaders was Haj Amin al-Husseini whom the British High Commissioner appointed as the Grand Mufti of Jerusalem (a political and religious leader of the local Palestinian Arab population) in 1921 and as President of the Supreme Muslim Council in 1922. As head of the Arab Higher Committee, he was also the leader of the Palestinian Arab national movement.[801] Husseini did not limit his ambitions and national identity to the geographical territory of Palestine. His radical and violent opposition to the creation of a Jewish state was based not on the view that he was leader of a separate Palestinian people having a right to self-determination in Palestine. Rather, until the end of World War II, he retained the objective in cooperation with Nazi-Germany to create a united Arab state covering all the territory that was then Iraq, Syria, and Palestine—both east and west of the Jordan River.[802] The ordinary

800. See also Chapter 6, section 10 of this book.

801. Morris (2008), p. 13.

802. Wistrich (2010), p. 669.

Palestinian Arabs were not consulted in 1920 or at any time prior to 1948; their own leadership excluded them.[803] Nevertheless, the British tried to appease the Palestinian Arabs' opposition to Jewish nationhood, at the cost of the neglect of the Mandatory Power's obligations towards the Jews. This resulted in many attempts to seek a balance of the competing interests, such as the proposals of the 1939 MacDonald White Paper to create a within 10 years an independent Palestine State in which Arabs and Jews would share government.[804] In 1947, the UN General Assembly proposed the partition of the territory into separate Jewish and Arab states with Jerusalem under an international trusteeship. However, this partition proposal was immediately rejected both by the leadership of the Palestinian Arabs and by the Arab States. The result was the "War of Independence" from 1947-1949.

17.6 The Palestine Liberation Organization (PLO) as Beneficiary of the Palestinian Right to Self-Determination

17.6.1 The Palestine Liberation Organization (PLO)

After Jordan occupied and subsequently annexed the West Bank in 1950, residents of the West Bank were granted Jordanian citizenship. Palestinian political self-identity took a new turn when the PLO was established by 13 Arab nations at the first Arab League summit in Cairo in 1964. The PLO became an embodiment of the claim for self-determination of the Arab residents of Palestine and their descendants. The philosophy, goals, and strategies of the PLO were set out in the Palestinian National Charter, adopted on 28 May 1964 by the Palestinian National Council (PNC). It was revised in July of 1968.

The Palestinian National Charter of 1964 suggests that the Arab residents of Palestine regarded themselves primarily not as members of a separate "Palestinian" nation but as citizens of "the great Arab homeland."[805] The change in the self-perception of the Arab population of Palestine is demonstrated by comparing Article 1 of the 1964 version of the Charter with article 1 of the revised Charter in 1968. Article 1 in the 1964 Charter states: "Palestine is an Arab homeland bound by strong Arab national ties to the rest of the Arab Countries and which together

803. Halwani & Kapitan (2008).

804. The Avalon Project: British White Paper of 1939: http://avalon.law.yale.edu/20th_century/brwh1939.asp (visited: 31 March 2015, 16:58:13).

805. Palestinian National Charter of 1964.

form the great Arab homeland." In 1968, this is changed to "Palestine is the homeland of the Arab Palestinian people; it is an indivisible part of the Arab homeland, and the Palestinian people are an integral part of the Arab nation."

The Palestinian National Charter[806] states in Article 2, "Palestine with its boundaries at the time of the British Mandate is an indivisible regional unit." It refers in Article 4 to "Zionist occupation." Article 3 is central when it comes to the right of self-determination: "The Palestinian Arab people possess the legal right to their homeland and have the right to determine their destiny after achieving the liberation of their country in accordance with their wishes and entirely of their own accord and will." It also implies a right of return for Palestinians not residing in their *homeland*.[807]

The Palestinian National Charter defines Palestinians as the population that was living in Palestine (meaning the whole of the Mandate area) prior to 1947: "The Palestinians are those Arab nationals who, until 1947, normally resided in Palestine regardless of whether they were evicted from it or have stayed there. Anyone born, after that date, of a Palestinian father—whether inside Palestine or outside it—is also a Palestinian."[808] This is the definition that is widely accepted in the international community through the acceptance of the PLO as the sole legitimate representative of the Palestinian People.[809] Article 6 adds: "The Jews who had normally resided in Palestine until the beginning of the Zionist invasion will be considered Palestinians." In other words, Jews who came to reside in "Palestine" after the late 1800s are not considered to be legitimate citizens of Palestine.

After 1967, when it became apparent that Israel's Arab neighbors were unable to remove the sovereign Jewish State, the notion of Palestine as a separate polity having territorial sovereignty entered into international political discourse. This trend took a dramatic momentum in the 1970's with the growing influence of the Organization of Islamic Conference (OIC),[810] the Yom Kippur War of 1973, the subsequent oil crisis, and the

806. Unless otherwise indicated the quotations in this paragraph are from the revised (1968) version.

807. Palestinian National Charter, arts 5, 8, 26.

808. Palestinian National Charter, art. 5.

809. See UN G.A. Res. 67/19 of 4 December 2012, para 2: "without prejudice to the acquired rights, privileges and role of the Palestinian Liberation Organization in the United Nations as the representative of the Palestinian people, in accordance with the relevant resolutions and practice."

810. The Organization of Islamic Conference was established in 1974; in 2011 it was renamed the Organization of Islamic Cooperation.

development of European pro-Arab policies from the mid-1970's onwards.[811]

In 1974, the PNC approved the "Ten Point Program," which was formulated by Fatah's leaders and called for the establishment of a national authority over any piece of captured Palestinian land and the active pursuit of the establishment of a democratic state in Palestine. Considered by some as the first attempt by PLO at a peaceful resolution, the ultimate goal of the Ten Point Program was "completing the liberation of *all Palestinian territory*, and as a step along the road to comprehensive Arab unity."[812]

The PLO's methodologies to achieve peace were not always peaceful. The PLO was an umbrella organization for a diverse range of terrorist groups, most of which were established in the 1960's and 1970's, such as the Palestinian Liberation Army (PLA), Al Fatah (the leading faction, co-founded in 1959 by Yasser Arafat), the Popular Front for the Liberation of Palestine (PFLP), and Black September. All of these groups were united in their common aim to destroy the state of Israel. From the late 1960's until the early 1980's, these PLO-affiliated groups—often in collaboration with other terrorist groups like the German Baader-Meinhof group, the Italian Red Brigade, the IRA and the Japanese Red Army—staged a relentless series of terrorist attacks in Israel, Europe, and Africa, killing hundreds of European, Israeli, African, and US citizens.[813] Israeli diplomatic missions and Jewish institutions around the world were targets of letter bombs, hijackings, sabotage, Molotov-cocktails, kidnappings, assassinations, and other terrorist attacks.

17.6.2 The Proclamation of the State of Palestine in 1988

A strong expression of the claim to self-determination by the Palestinian Arabs was formulated after July of 1988, when King Hussein of Jordan announced the legal and administrative disengagement of Jordan from the West Bank. In November 1988, the PNC met in Algiers and proclaimed "the establishment of the State of Palestine on our Palestinian territory with its capital Holy Jerusalem."[814] This declaration was acknowledged

811. See Bat Ye'or (2005).

812. Political Program adopted at the 12th Session of the Palestinian National Council, Cairo, 8 June 1974. Available online on the website of the Permanent Observer Mission of Palestine to the United Nations. Emphasis added.

813. Some of the most significant terrorist attacks were in West Berlin (1969); Lod Airport, Munich (1972); Entebbe (1976); Palma de Mallorca, Frankfurt (1977); Zurich (1980); Nairobi (1980); Rome (1979 and 1982); Antwerp (1981); Bonn (1982); West Berlin (1982); and Verona (1982).

814. See minutes of the meeting of the Palestinian National Council.

in General Assembly Resolution 43/177 of 15 December 1988 as "in line with General Assembly Resolution 181(II) and in exercise of the inalienable rights of the Palestinian people" and the "need to enable the Palestinian people to exercise their sovereignty over their territory occupied since 1967."[815] In that resolution, the General Assembly also decided "the designation 'Palestine' should be used in place of the designation 'Palestine Liberation Organization' in the United Nations system..."[816] An application for UN membership was not made at that time. In response to the declaration of statehood, PLO Chairman Arafat was invited to address the UN General Assembly in 1988.

17.6.3 Hamas

In 1988, it also became clear that not all Palestinian Arabs were united under the umbrella of the PLO. In that year, Hamas was founded as the Palestinian branch of the Muslim Brotherhood. Hamas is an acronym that stands for The Islamic Resistance Movement. While the PLO is officially secular, Hamas is a radically Islamist organization. Its aim is the disappearance of the State of Israel, which is seen as a historical necessity grounded in the Koran.[817] The organization is blatantly anti-Semitic. Hamas has been (and is), along with other Palestinian groups, involved in terrorism against Israelis. This was particularly serious during the First Intifada, from 1987-1993. Its Covenant (or Charter) (1988) summons to kill Jews.[818]

In 2017, a new version of the Hamas Covenant was published. Although the terminology has been adapted, the overall political goals seem to be the same (although formulations are confusing). The "enemy" is now often called the "Zionist project" or the "Zionist entity." For example, in Article 18 it is said that: "The establishment of Israel is entirely illegal..." It envisages "the full and complete liberation of Palestine, from the river to the sea," while adding at the same time a vague formula that could be seen as an acceptance of a state along the lines of 4 June 1967 (Article 20). It also declares "[r]esisting the occupation with all means and methods a legitimate right" (Article 25).

815. Resolution 43/177 was adopted, with 104 votes in favor, only two against (the USA and Israel), and 36 abstentions.

816. UN G.A. Res. 181(II).

817. Kortenoeven (2007); Wistrich (2010), p. 734.

818. See Hamas' Covenant, art. 7. For an English translation of the text, see: Yale Law School, Lillian Golsman Law Library, The Avalon Project: http://avalon.law.yale.edu/20th_century/hamas.asp (visited: 11 September 2017).

17.6.4 The Oslo Agreements and Their Aftermath

A change of the international political climate after the fall of communism opened the door for new developments, which—at first sight—provided the perspective of peaceful solutions. This was at least the official intention of the participants at the Madrid Conference, held from 30 October through 1 November 1991. US President George Bush and USSR President Michael Gorbachev shared the chairmanship. The Madrid Conference set the stage for negotiations between Israel and representatives of the Palestinian Arabs, who were officially part of the Jordanian delegation. This resulted in 1993 in the agreement on the Declaration of Principles on Interim Self-Government Arrangements, generally referred to as the Oslo Agreements. These agreements were intended to herald a new phase in Palestinian Arab political existence. Although the Oslo Agreements do not explicitly refer to the right to self-determination or statehood, their goal was to grant autonomy to the Palestinian Arab people.[819] Israeli Prime Minister Yitzak Rabin and PLO Chairman Yasser Arafat exchanged letters on the occasion of the adoption of the Declaration of Principles. In those letters, the PLO expressed that it recognized the right of the State of Israel to exist in peace and security and renounced the use of terrorism. The government of Israel declared it recognized the PLO as the representative of the Palestinian people and was prepared to commence negotiations with the PLO within the Middle East peace process. On the basis of the Oslo Agreements, a Palestinian Authority (PA) was created, which under the interim arrangements is endowed with governmental authority of varying degrees in civil an security matters in the A and B areas of both the West Bank and the Gaza Strip (Gaza).[820] In all the ups and downs of the subsequent process of negotiations, the political claim of self-determination of Palestinian Arabs was clear, even if the exclusive embodiment of this claim by the PLO has become to a certain extent questionable due to the "coup" of the Hamas movement in the Gaza Strip in 2006, that brought an end to the exertion of the powers of the PA in the Gaza Strip. There have been several attempts to bring about reconciliation between Fatah, the most important faction of the PLO, and Hamas. The so-called "Unity Government" which was created 2 June 2014 to overcome the rift between the two movements terminated about a year later on 17 June 2015.[821] On 12 October 2017, again an agreement was concluded between Fatah and Hamas, which should

---

819. See Cassese (1993).

820. See also Chapter 12 in this book.

821. *The Times of Israel*, 17 June 2015.

result in the transfer of the governmental powers in Gaza to the PA.[822] So far, the PA only took over the border control at the border crossings at Rafah, Erez and Kerem Shalom. Other aspects of the agreement are so far not implemented, and it has already been concluded that (also) this reconciliation deal is dying a slow death.[823]

Since the start of the Oslo process, the Palestinian claims have been accompanied by outbursts of violence against Israel and its citizens. The First Intifada was followed by a Second Intifada, from 2000-2004. In addition to the many acts of violence, there has been a notable increase in the spread of hatred against the State of Israel and the Jewish population via the media and even in schools, that has remained a prominent part of Palestinian society. This continues to happen not only in the circles of the so-called radical movements, but also in those united under the PLO umbrella, who—because of their official participation in the peace process—have been considered moderate.[824] The future of the Oslo Agreements has become very uncertain. Mahmoud Abbas, the President of the Palestinian Authority, in his address to the UN General Assembly on 30 September 2015, declared that the Palestinians cannot continue to be bound by these agreements.[825] In a speech addressed to the Palestinian Central Council in Ramallah on 14 January 2018, in which he slammed Zionism as a colonial enterprise that has nothing to do with Jewishness, Abbas even said that Israel had killed the Oslo Agreements.[826]

17.6.5 In Conclusion: The Political Claim of Self-Determination

Apart from the doubtful prospects of the Oslo Agreements it can be concluded that, in light of the foregoing, from the 1960's onwards there has been a group of persons who identify themselves as Palestinian Arab people, and who have the political will to become an independent nation. This means that, on the basis of the subjective test, it is arguable that there is, indeed, a Palestinian people having a right to self-determination.

---

822. Asseburg (2017).

823. 'Palestinian reconciliation deal dying a slow death', The Times of Israel, 2 February 2018.

824. Wistrich (2010), pp. 719-727.

825. *The Times of Israel*, 30 September 2015: http://www.timesofisrael.com/full-text-of-abbas-2015-address-to-the-un-general-assembly/ (visited 11 September 2017).

826. *The New York Times*, 14 January 2018 (https://www.nytimes.com/2018/01/14/world/middleeast/abbas/).

17.7 The Territorial Scope of the Palestinian Claims to Self-Determination

The right of self-determination must, by definition, be related to a specific territory. When it comes to the Palestinian territorial claim, there is some confusion. Is the Palestinian claim to self-determination limited to the so-called "Occupied Palestinian Territories" or does it extend to the whole of the territory of Palestine under the Mandate for Palestine?

17.7.1 The Palestinian National Charter: The Whole of the Mandate Territory

There are valid reasons to doubt whether the Palestinian leadership really has limited their claims to the "occupied territories." In this regard, it is important to note that Yassir Arafat's promise to amend the Articles of the Palestinian Charter that are inconsistent with the existence of the State of Israel has never been implemented. Article 1 of the Palestinian National Charter specifically states, "Palestine is the homeland of the Arab Palestinian people..." In Article 2, it becomes clear what their territorial definition of Palestine is in this connection: "Palestine, with its boundaries at the time of the British Mandate, is an indivisible territorial unit." Additionally, the 1964 version of the Palestinian National Charter included a provision stating that the PLO does not exercise territorial sovereignty over the West Bank, the Gaza Strip, or the Himmah area.[827] Its ambitions were clearly focussed on the territory of the State of Israel. This provision did not return in the 1968 version of the Palestinian National Charter which effectively equates "Palestine" with the Mandate territory, including modern-day Israel. The reason for this is the desire to reclaim (liberate) that whole area from which they were supposedly "dispossessed" by the Jews (Zionists). The Charter states that Palestine is a part of "the great Arab homeland" and the PLO was to provide a vehicle for the Arab people to liberate a specific territory which had come under "enemy" control, so that it could be re-incorporated into the wider Arab nation. The fact that the PLO was established before the 1967 Six-Day War proves that the true objectives of the PLO were the liberation not just of the West Bank but also of all of the Mandate area—i.e. including current Israel. Ambassador Blum, the Israeli representative at the UN in 1980 explained that, prior to 1967, the primary goal of the Palestinian people was not to establish a separate state, but to enable the greater Arab nation to destroy Israel's existence as a Jewish nation. This is evidenced by the fact that in the period 1920-

827. Palestinian National Charter, art. 24.

1980, the Palestinian Arabs repeatedly rejected all two-state proposals and instead repeatedly threatened and attacked Israel with military force.[828]

According to Blum, the PLO's claims since 1967 are part of an overall plan to attain control over the whole area of Palestine, including Israel:

> **"For a number of years now the PLO has advocated a programme which is sometimes described by its spokesmen as a two- or three-stage policy. In essence, it aims in its first stage at the establishment of a second Palestinian Arab state anywhere in the territories administered by Israel since 1967. The second stage of the policy is to use this proposed state as a launching pad for the ultimate overthrow of Israel."[829]**

This program was described with complete candour by Farouk Kaddoumi, one of Yasser Arafat's entourage: "There are two [initial] phases to our return: the first phase to the 1967 lines, and the second to the 1948 lines. The third stage is the democratic State of Palestine. So we are fighting for these three stages."[830] Asked by the interviewer if the PLO had become more moderate, Kaddoumi replied: "By moderation we mean we are ready... to establish a State on a part of our territory. In the past we said no, on all of it, immediately, a democratic State of Palestine. Now we say no, this can be implemented in three stages. That is moderation."[831] No such false "moderation" is found in the Hamas Covenant 1988, which proclaims in Article 6 that Hamas "strives to raise the banner of Allah over every inch of Palestine" and in Article 11, it is said "the land of Palestine is an Islamic Waqf consecrated for future Moslem generations until Judgment Day." In the new version of the Hamas Covenant, of 2017, the language is ambiguous. It states in Article 18 that: "The establishment of Israel is entirely illegal and contravenes the inalienable rights of the Palestinian people..." But Article 20 reads as follows: "Hamas believes that no part of the land of Palestine shall be compromised or conceded, irrespective of the causes, the circumstances and the pressures and no matter how long the occupation lasts. Hamas rejects any alternative to the full and complete liberation of Palestine, from the river to the sea. However, without compromising its rejection of the Zionist entity and without

828. In particular, they rejected the Peel Commission proposals in 1937, as well as Resolution 181 (the Partition Plan) in 1947.

829. Israel Ministry of Foreign Affairs, Israel's Foreign Relations Selected Documents, Volume 6: 1979-1980, 108 Statement in the General Assembly by Ambassador Blum, 23 July 1980. See: http://mfa.gov.il/MFA/ForeignPolicy/MFADocuments/Yearbook4/Pages/108%20Statement%20in%20the%20General%20Assembly%20by%20Ambassado.aspx (visited: 11 September 2017).

830. *Newsweek magazine*, 14 March 1977. Quoted in Carol (2015).

831. See also Wistrich (2010), p. 714.

relinquishing any Palestinian rights, Hamas considers the establishment of a fully sovereign and independent Palestinian state, with Jerusalem as its capital along the lines of 4 June 1967, with the return of the refugees and the displaced to their homes from which they were expelled, to be a formula of national consensus." This is again contradicted by what is said in Article 27: "There is no alternative to a fully sovereign Palestinian State on the entire national Palestinian soil, with Jerusalem as its capital." All in all, the text seems rather inconsistent, to say the least. In any case it provides an unrealistic basis for fruitful negotiations on the territorial aspects of the Palestinian self-determination.

17.7.2 The Territorial Scope of the Palestinian "Right to Self-Determination" in Light of General Assembly Resolutions and the Oslo Agreements

According to the UN General Assembly, the Palestinian Arab people is entitled to "territorial sovereignty"[832] over the "Occupied Palestinian Territories"—as they are held to be the legitimate "owners" of these territories, which therefore are often referred to as "the Palestinian territory occupied since 1967."[833] On this view, the Territories "belonged" to the Palestinians in June 1967, and they were "taken illegally" when Israeli forces took control of them in the Six-Day War.[834] The General Assembly has reaffirmed "the right of the Palestinian people to self-determination and to independence in their State of Palestine on the Palestinian territory occupied since 1967."[835]

The Oslo Agreements do not limit the Palestinian claims to the West Bank and Gaza. These territories are explicitly mentioned in Article I of the Declaration of Principles, without defining more precisely the delineation of these areas.[836] The same article refers also to Security Council Resolution 242, which is far from precise when it comes to territory,[837] referring only to withdrawal of Israel from "occupied" territory (not all occupied territories) and to "secure and recognized boundaries."[838]

---

832. See, e.g., A-ES-10/248, Report of Secretary-General prepared pursuant to General Assembly resolution ES-10/13, 24 November 2003, p. 10.

833. See, e.g., UN G.A. Res. 67/19: Status of Palestine in the United Nations A/RES/67/19 (4 December 2012).

834. See, e.g., Quigley (2005), pp. 192-195. Quigley argues also that the use of force by the Palestinians against Israeli administration in the Territories is lawful because a dependent people may lawfully use force to displace a colonizer.

835. UN G.A. Res. 67/19 (4 December 2012).

836. Article I of the Declaration of Principles.

837. Article I of the Declaration of Principles; UN S.C. Res. 242.

838. *Ibid.*

Moreover, the Oslo Agreements are the starting point in a negotiating process, which includes the permanent settlement of territorial issues.

17.7.3 Final Remarks on the Territorial Aspects

To conclude: It would seem that the PLO and Arab States deliberately leave open the possibility of claims to territorial sovereignty over all of "Palestine," including Israel proper. The territorial claims in the Palestinian National Charter simply exclude the existence of the State of Israel in the Middle East. The international community, on the other hand, seems to understand the Palestinian Arab claims to be limited to the "occupied Palestinian territory,"—which also is the starting point of the Oslo Agreements. They are officially aimed at a final settlement of territorial issues.

17.8 Content of the Palestinian Right to Self-Determination

The right to "self-determination" does not automatically entail a right to statehood. Self-determination of a people may also result in different forms of autonomy. As was stated in General Assembly Resolution 2625 (XXV), "The establishment of a sovereign and independent State, the free association or integration with an independent State or the emergence into any other political status freely determined by a people constitute modes of implementing the right of self-determination by that people."[839] This means that there are in principle three options when it comes to the implementation of the Arab Palestinian right to self-determination, as laid out below.

17.8.1 The Establishment of a Sovereign and Independent "State of Palestine"

In the framework of decolonization, the establishment of a sovereign and independent state was the common way of implementation of the right to self-determination. In general, outside this framework, other forms of implementation may be considered more appropriate.[840] The position of the Palestinian Arabs under Israeli rule cannot be compared

839. This resolution adopted in 1970 included the Declaration on Principles of International Law Concerning Friendly Relations and Co-operation among States in Accordance with the Charter of the United Nations.

840. See also Hilpold (2009), defending the thesis that the right to self-determination only grants an uncontested right to statehood to people living under colonial (or foreign) rule.); and Ryngaert & Griffioen (2009), pointing out that also outside the context of decolonization in limited cases secession is justified..

to a relationship between colonial "empire" and a territory overseas, as was explained above. Nevertheless, the Palestinian Charter clearly asserts the right for Palestinian Arabs to their own state. Article 3 refers to the "right to determine their destiny after achieving the liberation of their country in accordance with their wishes and entirely of their own accord and will." Article 9 refers again to the "right to self-determination and sovereignty over [Palestine]." This is confirmed in the State of Palestine Declaration of Independence adopted by the Palestine National Council on 15 of November 1988. In this text, there are references to: the right to independence and the right to sovereignty over territory and homeland. It uses the expression "political independence" and, finally, proclaims "the State of Palestine." In this regard, it is remarkable that the Palestinians in this State of Palestine Declaration, on the one hand deny the legitimacy of the two-state solution proposed by Resolution 181, because it deprived them of the possibility to exercise their right to self-determination over all of Palestine. On the other hand, they also claim that Resolution 181 creates the basis for their right to self-determination and sovereignty: "Yet it is this Resolution that still provides those conditions of international legitimacy that ensure the right of the Palestinian Arab people to sovereignty."[841] This is a logical and legal conundrum, which the Palestinians seem unable to explain. The Palestine Declaration of Independence was acknowledged by the UN General Assembly a month later in Res. 43/177, which affirmed the need to enable the Palestinian people to exercise their sovereignty over their territory occupied since 1967.[842] The idea of a sovereign and independent Palestinian State is also supported by the UN Security Council, which endorsed the so-called Road Map to a Permanent Two-State Solution to the Israeli-Palestine Conflict.[843] This Roadmap was the result of an initiative of the *Quartet*, composed of the US, the EU, Russia and the UN. This two-state solution still dominates the diplomatic discussion. It implies the co-existence of two sovereign states, Israel and Palestine, next to each other. The International Court of Justice (ICJ) seems to also support this approach in its Advisory Opinion, as it felt obliged to draw the attention of the UN General Assembly to the need to encourage the efforts in the framework of the Roadmap to come to "the establishment of a Palestinian state, existing side by side with Israel."[844]

It is relevant that the Oslo Agreements do not refer explicitly to the right to self-determination, nor do they require the negotiations to result

841. http://www.mideastweb.org/plc1988.htm (visited 5 April 2018).

842. UN G.A. Res. 43/177.

843. UN S.C. Res. 1515 (19 November 2003).

844. I.C.J. Reports 2004, p. 201.

in recognized statehood for the Palestinians. The parties to the conflict agreed that all final status issues are to result from negotiations. The position of the Israeli government, as expressed repeatedly by Prime Minister Benjamin Netanyahu to the UN General Assembly, is that they should lead to a demilitarized Palestinian state, which recognizes the Jewish State of Israel.[845]

Is Palestine a State?

Some argue that the Mandate for Palestine created a Palestinian State under international law in 1922.[846] The argument that the Mandate for Palestine established a state in 1922 must be rejected, if for no other reason than that, while the Mandate for Palestine was clearly intended to lead to statehood, the Class A Mandates were established for the very reason that the relevant peoples were not yet ready to be independent.

Has the State of Palestine come into existence since the Palestinian National Charter's Declaration of the establishment of the State of Palestine in 1988? In light of the criteria for statehood under international law,[847] the key question here is whether at any time since 1988 the PLO or Palestinian Authority (PA) can be said to exercise "effective separate control" over relevant territory. We agree with Crawford that the 1988 Declaration was not in itself effective to establish the State of Palestine, and that, in light of the arrangements under the Oslo Agreements—under which the respective powers of the PA and PLO are explicitly limited, and Israel exercises aspects of control and retains ultimate reversionary authority over Areas A, B and C—neither the PA nor the PLO is in a position to exert effective control over any part of East Jerusalem, the West Bank or Gaza Strip independently of other states. "A process of negotiation towards identified and acceptable ends is still, however precariously, in place. That being so, it misrepresents the reality of the situation to claim that one party already has that for which it is striving."[848]

---

845. See for the Transcript of Netanyahu's UN General Assembly Speech of 1 October 2013: http://www.haaretz.com/misc/article- print-page/1.550012?trailingP .See also the full text of Netanyahu's address to the UN General Assembly on 1 October 2015 (http://www.timesofisrael.com/full-text-of-netanyahu-2015-address-t).

846. Professor John Quigley argues that the State of Palestine already existed in 1922 when the international community established the Mandate for Palestine, even though it was not yet independent (he calls it "a state awaiting independence"). "On the statehood issue, what matters is what the international community established, how it conceived Palestine as an entity, and how the states of the international community regarded Palestine. Palestine could have been created as a state even if it was done in a way that violated the rights of the inhabitants." Quigley (2010), p. 79.

847. See Chapter 1, section 3, in this book.

848. Crawford (2006), p. 446.

17.8.2 Free Association or Integration with an Independent State: "Jordan is Palestine"

Free association or integration with an independent state is another way to implement the right of self-determination. This option was raised in 1980, when the then-Israeli UN Ambassador Yehuda Blum argued that the rights of the Palestinian Arabs had already been satisfied in the establishment of the Kingdom of Jordan:

> **"Central to any discussion of the issue before us is the basic fact which I have just mentioned—namely, that two states have been established on the territory of the former Palestine Mandate. One is the Palestinian Arab State of Jordan, which achieved national self-determination, independence and sovereignty in 1946. The other is the Palestinian Jewish State of Israel, which became independent in 1948. Hence, there is no need or justification whatsoever for the establishment of a second Palestinian Arab State..."[849]**

Association with, or integration into, Jordan may be attractive at first sight and seem well-suited to the original Mandate for Palestine as it was perceived after the division in 1923 of the Mandate territory into two parts on either side of the Jordan River: the western part for the establishment of the Jewish national home, and the eastern part for the establishment of an Arab emirate. It also looks similar to the Weizmann-Feisal Agreement of 1919. However, both association and integration would require *inter alia* the cooperation of another sovereign state, the Hashemite Kingdom of Jordan, which is not expected, because of the turbulent history of the relationship between the Palestinian Arabs and Jordan. In 1970, the PLO tried to overthrow King Hussein of Jordan (Black September). As result of the Jordanian counteraction, thousands of fighters and civilians were killed.[850] Furthermore, in the peace treaty agreed by Israel and Jordan (in 1994), the international boundary (which includes the middle of the Jordan and the Yarmuk Rivers) is recognized "without prejudice to the status of any territories that came under Israeli military government control in 1967."[851] This suggests that Jordan is not likely to be interested in an association or integration of the PLO with Jordan.

---

849. Israel Ministry of Foreign Affairs, Israel's Foreign Relations Selected Documents, Volume 6: (1979-1980), 108 Statement in the General Assembly by Ambassador Blum, 23 July 1980. See: http://mfa.gov.il/MFA/ForeignPolicy/MFADocuments/Yearbook4/Pages/108%20Statement%20in%20the%20General%20Assembly%20by%20Ambassado.aspx (visited: 11 September 2017).

850 Gilbert (1999), p. 417.

851. Article 3 (2) of the Treaty of Peace between the State of Israel and the Hashemite Kingdom of Jordan, 26 October 1994.

17.8.3 Any Other Political Status Freely Determined by a People

The third possible way of implementing the right to self-determination is the creating of another political status determined by a people. This may imply some sort of autonomy for the Palestinian Arabs within the State of Israel. Ambassador Blum considered this option, remarking that Israel was entirely prepared to grant the residents of the West Bank complete autonomy, for a transitional period before reaching an agreement on the final status of the areas concerned, in line with the 1978 Camp David framework, which was based on UN Security Council Resolution 242.[852] This same approach underlies the Oslo Agreements, which transferred autonomy to the Palestinian Arabs as a transitional arrangement pending final status negotiations. The Oslo Agreements themselves do not refer to "self-determination" as such.[853] It is arguable that the kind of autonomy referred to by Ambassador Blum in 1980 could still be achieved,[854] as the Oslo Agreements do not require the negotiations to result in recognized statehood for the Palestinians, nor do they envisage or require any other specific form of political autonomy. All final status issues are to result from negotiations. Even the interim arrangements are not to prejudice the scope and content of any final settlement.[855] The UN's fixation on the creation of a Palestinian Arab State is arguably impeding the exploration of other options than the establishment of a Palestinian state alongside the State of Israel.

17.8.4 Final Remarks on the Content of Self-Determination

The foregoing makes it clear that self-determination may be implemented in several forms. Separate independent statehood is just one of these forms and, as such, is not imposed by international law. The Oslo Agreements only provide for interim arrangements, and leave open to the final status

---

852. Israel Ministry of Foreign Affairs, Israel's Foreign Relations Selected Documents, Volume 6 (1979-1980), p, 108 Statement in the General Assembly by Ambassador Blum, 23 July 1980. See: http://mfa.gov.il/MFA/ForeignPolicy/MFADocuments/Yearbook4/Pages/108%20Statement%20in%20the%20General%20Assembly%20by%20Ambassado.aspx (visited: 11 September 2017). See further: GAOR XXXVth Session, Plenary Meetings, 77th Meeting, 1318, paras 108, 112-113, 130-131. See also: Cassese (1995), pp. 235-237.

853. Cassese (1993).

854. Israel Ministry of Foreign Affairs, Israel's Foreign Relations Selected Documents, Volume 6 (1979-1980), p. 108 Statement in the General Assembly by Ambassador Blum, 23 July 1980. See: http://mfa.gov.il/MFA/ForeignPolicy/MFADocuments/Yearbook4/Pages/108%20Statement%20in%20the%20General%20Assembly%20by%20Ambassado.aspx (visited: 11 September 2017). See further: GAOR XXXVth Session, Plenary Meetings, 77th Meeting, 1318, paras 108, 112-113, 130-131. See also Cassese (1995), pp. 235-237.

855. See Article V of the Declaration of Principles and Article XXXI(6) of the Interim Agreement.

negotiations the resolution of the question how Palestinian autonomy should take form after the interim period. The agreements make clear, however, that whatever form is agreed, it must be contained in a peace agreement that will contain sufficient guarantees to protect Israel's legitimate interests, as reflected in Security Council resolutions 242 and 338. This includes the scenario that a State of Palestine comes into existence.

17.9 How is Palestinian Self-Determination to be Reconciled with the Rights of the State of Israel?

Assuming there is a right of Palestinian Arabs to self-determination within (part of) the original Mandate territory of Palestine, the following question must be answered: How can this right accommodate and coexist with the right of self-determination of the Jewish people, from which the State of Israel emerged? It seems that the recognition of both rights together in respect to the same territory leads to insoluble problems. Although Article 1 of both the International Covenants on Civil and Political Rights and the International Covenant on Economic, Social, and Cultural Rights states, "all peoples have the right to self-determination," it cannot be assumed that this right is absolute.[856] This right should be balanced with the fundamental principles of sovereignty and territorial integrity of existing recognized states:

> **"A legal regime that defends the state's right to preserve its territorial boundaries cannot incorporate a principle that grants all peoples within the state the capacity to independently determine their political status. As one author has noted, sovereignty and self-determination, when viewed in the abstract, reflect the fundamental conflict between legitimacy and revolution."[857]**

Accordingly, self-determination is limited to:

> **"[T]he right of the majority within a generally accepted political unit to the exercise of power. In other words, it is necessary to start with stable boundaries and to permit political change within them... [T]o withdraw this proviso would encourage impermissible use of force across state boundaries, an outcome which the United Nations can hardly encourage."[858]**

---

856. Article 1 of the International Covenants on Civil and Political Rights; Art. 1 of the International Covenant on Economic, Social, and Cultural Rights.

857. Becker (1998), at p. 302, quoting Blum (1975), at pp. 510-511.

858. Higgins (1963), p. 104.

Furthermore, outside the context of decolonization, the right to self-determination is still under development. The UN Charter only sanctions expressions of self-determination that advance peaceful relations between states. Arguably it does not sanction self-determination that would either disrupt friendly relations between states or conflict with the right of existing states to sovereign equality, non-intervention, and territorial integrity.

A claim to Palestinian self-determination that denies the existence of Jewish self-determination in Israel would quite simply contravene basic principles of international law.[859] In this respect, the longstanding negation of the Jewish right to self-determination by representatives of the Palestinian Arabs cannot be overlooked. The Palestinian National Charter in both versions (1964 and 1968) reflects the Arab rejection of Jewish claims to nationhood, territoriality, or political independence. In Article 20 of the 1968 Palestinian National Charter, it states, "Claims of historical or religious ties of Jews with Palestine are incompatible with the facts of history and the true conception of what constitutes statehood ... Nor do Jews constitute a single nation with an identity of its own; they are citizens of the states to which they belong." The amendments made to the Palestinian National Charter in 1968 display an even more vehement determination to eradicate Zionism and to implement a Palestinian state in the place of the Jewish nation. It is stated more explicitly that the liberation can only be achieved through armed struggle.[860] Both versions of the Palestinian National Charter speak about occupation, but the 1968 version speaks specifically about "Zionist occupation" and "Imperialist aggression."[861] Both versions of the Palestinian National Charter reject the claims that Jews have historical and religious ties with the territory of Palestine.[862] The 1968 version formulates explicitly as goal of the PLO to not just bring the occupation to an end, but also the existence of Zionism in Palestine itself.[863] Both versions include the requirement of all states to consider Zionism as an illegitimate movement and outlaw its existence and operations.[864] The belief in peaceful coexistence, which was expressed in Article 22 of the 1964 Palestinian National Charter, was deleted from

859. Becker (1998), at p. 344.

860. Palestinian National Charter (1968), art. 9. As said before the references are to the 1968 version, unless indicated otherwise.

861. Palestinian National Charter (1964 and 1968).

862. Palestinian National Charter (1964 and 1968), art. 20.

863. Palestinian National Charter (1968), art. 15.

864. Palestinian National Charter (1964 and 1968), art .23.

the 1968 Palestinian National Charter.[865] Another new phenomenon in the 1968 version is the fact that the Palestine Liberation Organization takes military responsibility for the liberation of Palestine.[866] To conclude: The Palestinian National Charter of 1968 appears to exclude any form of accommodation between the competing Jewish and Arab Palestinian claims to self-determination.

The 1988 Hamas Covenant uses even stronger terms to express its hatred of Jews in general and Zionism in particular.[867] To give a few examples: In Article 7, it refers to "Zionist invaders." In Article 15, it refers to "the Jew's usurpation of Palestine." In Article 32, it claims, "The Zionist plan... is embodied in the 'Protocols of the Elders of Zion,"' thereby referring to the slanderous anti-Semitic publication, used in Russia and Nazi-Germany, yet today still used in the Arab world to stir hatred against Jews. The new version of the Hamas Covenant of May 2017 attempts to present the vision of Hamas in a more "civilized" language. It no longer refers to the Protocols of the Elders of Zion. The hatred of Zionism and Israel is however still a prominent feature of the text. Israel is frequently referred to as the "Zionist entity." The 2017 Hamas Covenant refers in Article 14 to the Zionist project as "a racist, aggressive, colonial and expansionist project," while the "Israeli entity" is called the "plaything of the Zionist project." In Article 15 the Zionist project is qualified as "the enemy of the Arab and Islamic Ummah." In Article 16 it is held that Hamas has a conflict with the Zionist project, but not with the Jews. This makes it very clear that Hamas willfully ignores the essence of Zionism. The same Article blames the Zionists for identifying Judaism and the Jews with "their own colonial project and illegal entity." In Article 17 the view is expressed that the "Jewish problem, anti-Semitism and the persecution of Jews" is linked to European history and not to Arab and Muslim history. Finally, Article 19 states that "[t]here shall be no recognition of the legitimacy of the Zionist entity."

The fact that the text of the Palestinian National Charter and the Hamas Covenant did not provide for any possibility of accommodation of the Palestinian and the Jewish self-determination was realized by those who were involved in the negotiations leading towards the Oslo Agreements (1993). In his letter of 9 September 1993 to Prime Minister Yitzhak Rabin, PLO Chairman Yasser Arafat stated therefore that those articles, which deny Israel's right to exist, are inconsistent with the PLO's new commitments to

865. *Ibid.*, art. 22.

866. Palestinian National Charter (1968), art. 26.

867. See on the Hamas Covenant: Wistrich (2010), pp. 733-739; Kortenoeven (2007), pp. 115-166.

Israel following their mutual recognition and are no longer valid.[868] Arafat promised to ensure that the Palestinian National Council would confirm this decision by making the necessary amendments according to Article 33 of the Palestinian National Charter.[869] Although the will to change the Charter has since been expressed by the Chairman of the Executive Committee of the PLO, who is also President of the Palestinian National Authority and the Palestinian National Council, no clear amendment has so far been made and no amended version of the Palestinian National Charter has since been published. In a written statement submitted on 20 February 2011 by the World Union of Progressive Judaism to the UN Human Rights Council, it was sadly observed: "Despite repeated assurances to amend it, the Palestinian National Charter remains unchanged—calling for Israel's elimination by any military means."[870]

We have to conclude that 1968 version of the Palestinian National Charter and both versions of the Hamas Covenant (1988 and 2017) present a serious obstacle to a solution to the conflict between Israel and the Palestinians. This also underlines the importance of the Israeli calls for the recognition by the Palestinians of Israel as a *Jewish* State as a condition of any settlement. [871] Not changing the Palestinian National Charter will make it very difficult to trust that there is not a secret agenda on the Palestinian side, which eventually seeks to wipe the Jewish State from the map. The Oslo process did not redress the ambiguous and equivocal nature of the public statements from the Palestinian spokespersons, for whom what is said often depends on the audience. A notable example of this was when Yasser Arafat in a Johannesburg mosque—only ten days after the conclusion of the Gaza-Jericho Agreement in 1994—incited a jihad to liberate Jerusalem as a City to be held exclusively Muslim.[872] This does not increase the likelihood of an agreement, which guarantees both the safety and security of the State of Israel and the Palestinian right to self-determination.

---

868. For Yasser Arafat's letter of 9 September 1993 to Prime Minister Rabin, see: http://www.mfa.gov.il/mfa/foreignpolicy/mfadocuments/yearbook9/pages/107%20israel-plo%20mutual%20recognition-%20letters%20and%20spe.aspx.

869. Palestinian National Charter (1968), art. 33.

870. A/HRC/16/NGO/134.

871. In recent years several proposals have been discussed to enact the Jewishness of Israel stronger in its legislation. On 7 May 2017, the Ministerial Committee for Legislation voted in favor of a bill (see: 'Basic Law: Israel as the Nation State of the Jewish people', The Times of Israel, 10 May 2017). It passed the preliminary reading in the Knesset on 10 May 2017(The Times of Israel, 10 May 2017). If it successfully passes also the next stages of the legislative procedure it may become law in 2018.

872. Wistrich (2010), p. 715.

18. The Status of Palestine in International Organizations and International Treaties

> "...taking into account the fact that the General Assembly had granted Palestine a special status of observer and that the latter was co-sponsor of the draft resolution requesting the advisory opinion, Palestine might also submit a written statement...."
>
> Advisory Opinion (Paragraph 4)[873]

18.1 Introduction

Related to the topic of the right to self-determination of the Palestinian Arabs is the question of the membership of Palestine of international organizations, especially of the United Nations (UN). Palestine has, for some time, been a member of international organizations with an ideological or regional character: The Organization of Islamic Cooperation (OIC) (since 1969) and the Arab League (since 1976). A starting point for its appearance on the stage of global international organizations is 1974, when the Palestine Liberation Organization (PLO)—in its role as a liberation movement—was recognized as an observer by the UN General Assembly .

18.2 UN Membership

18.2.1 General Aspects

The PLO and Palestine applied for UN membership on 23 September 2011. The application was submitted to the Secretary-General by Mahmoud Abbas as "President of the State of Palestine" and "Chairman of the Executive Committee of the Palestine Liberation Organization." Article 4(2) of the UN Charter provides that the General Assembly has

873. I.C.J. Reports 2004, p. 141.

the power to determine applications for UN membership, but that it must do so "upon recommendation of the Security Council." This means that, in practice, a state can only become a member of the UN, if the Security Council approves its application. This requires approval (or acquiescence) by at least nine nations—all five Permanent Members of the Security Council (United States, France, United Kingdom, China, and Russia), as well as at least four of the ten non-permanent Members. The Security Council has not yet made a decision in relation to this application. The United States, although a supporter of Palestinian self-determination, has so far refused to recognize "Palestine" as a state. Its policy has been to support negotiations for a comprehensive peace agreement as the sole means for achieving Palestinian self-determination. The United States therefore threatened in September 2011 to veto the PLO's "unilateral" application for UN membership. The required recommendation of the Security Council does not seem attainable under the present circumstances. Should the United States maintain its opposition of full UN membership for Palestine, it is conceivable that Palestine will attempt to "bypass" the Security Council through the use of UN General Assembly Resolution 377—the "Uniting for Peace" Resolution.[874] Given the voting patterns on 29 November 2012, there is little doubt that the required two-thirds majority of Member States would vote to adopt such a resolution.

While UN membership so far has been "a bridge too far," Palestine was successful when it was accepted as a "Non-Member Observer State" at the UN; this status can only be granted by the UN General Assembly. Resolution 67/19, which granted this status, was adopted on 29 November 2012—exactly 65 years after the Resolution 181 (II) (Partition of Palestine) of 29 November 1947—with the votes of 138 States in favor, 9 against and 41 abstentions.[875] Many Western States, such as France, Italy, and

---

874. Adopted in 1950, this resolution provides that "if the Security Council, because of lack of unanimity of the permanent members, fails to exercise its primary responsibility for the maintenance of international peace and security in any case where there appears to be a threat to the peace, breach of the peace, or act of aggression, the General Assembly shall consider the matter immediately with a view to making appropriate recommendations to Members for collective measures, including in the case of a breach of the peace or act of aggression the use of armed force when necessary, to maintain or restore international peace and security." To facilitate prompt action by the General Assembly in the case of a dead-locked Security Council, the resolution created the mechanism of the 'emergency special session' (ESS), which can be called upon the basis of either a procedural vote in the Security Council, or within twenty-four hours of a request by a majority of UN Members being received by the Secretary-General. In procedural votes, the permanent members of the Security Council cannot block the adoption of draft resolutions. Therefore, unlike substantive matters, such resolutions can be adopted without their consent.

875. UN G.A. Res. 67/19; UN G.A. Res. 181 (II).

Sweden voted in favor. The position of Palestine within the United Nations is now comparable to that of the Holy See.

Finally, 10 September 2015 brought the so-called State of Palestine a political victory when the General Assembly adopted—by 119 votes to 8, with 45 abstentions—Resolution 69/320, including the decision that the flags of Non-Member Observer States at the UN shall be raised at Headquarters and UN offices following the flags of the Member States. In its Preamble, the Resolution refers explicitly to the status granted to the State of Palestine on 29 November 2012.[876] The representative of Palestine interpreted the wide support as a reaffirmation of the legitimacy of the national aspirations of the Palestinian people. As a result of the "Flag Resolution," the Palestinian flag was raised at UN Headquarters in New York for the first time during a ceremony on 30 September 2015, in the presence of Palestinian Authority President Abbas.

18.2.2 **Legal Concerns**

This brings us to the legal concerns concerning a full UN Membership of Palestine. Article 4 of the UN Charter limits membership to states, which are peace-loving and prepared to accept the obligations in the UN Charter and are able and willing to carry out those obligations. As we have seen, it is highly questionable whether Palestine constitutes a "State" under international law, mainly because the Palestinian government lacks the final effective control over the territory. Furthermore, it is also highly questionable whether Palestine fulfills the requirement of being "peace-loving." Mr. Abbas stated that the State of Palestine is a peace-loving nation, which is also suggested by the formal adoption of the commitments made by the PLO in the Oslo Agreements, and the existence of seriously peace-loving movements within the Palestinian territories.[877] It should, however, not be overlooked that that significant elements of Palestinian society remain committed to jihad, violence, and terror, while at Palestinian schools children are incited to hatred against Israel and the Jewish people.[878] Even some elements of the PLO leadership openly support the use of violence towards Israel and the Jewish people. The third and fourth legal requirement is the acceptance of the UN Charter obligations and the ability to carry them out. This is highly questionable,

---

876. A/Res/69/320. See for the debate: A/69/PV.102.

877. The application for membership includes an attached Declaration by Mr. Abbas "that the State of Palestine is a peace-loving nation and that it accepts the obligations contained in the Charter of the United Nations and solemnly undertakes to fulfill them."

878. Groiss & Shaked (2017).

not only because of the fact that there is so far not a Palestinian state, but also because of: (1) the weakness of the present Palestinian institutions in the framework of the Palestinian Authority, (2) the fact that the Gaza Strip is no longer under control of the official Palestinian authorities, and (3) the conflict between Fatah and Hamas. It does not seem likely that this conflict is really solved with the agreement between Fatah and Hamas of 12 October 2017.[879]

Along with the UN Charter's Membership requirements, there are other legal concerns with regard to the Oslo Agreements, which prohibit both parties from initiating "any step that will change the status of the West Bank and the Gaza Strip pending the outcome of the permanent status negotiations."[880] This means that any unilateral steps by the PLO to achieve statehood recognition in relation to these territories—by means of admission as a UN Member State or any other international organization—would directly violate the Oslo Agreements. The future status of these territories and the nature of an independent Palestinian entity can only be settled by negotiations reflecting a balance of competing interests. Provided the parties act in good faith, no specific solution to these issues can be imposed without the mutual consent of both Israel and the Palestinian Arab people. Therefore, in our view it is strongly arguable that the actions of the PLO to seek recognition of Palestine within the UN based on the "pre-1967 borders"—including the 2011 Application for Recognition of Palestinian Statehood—are in breach of the Oslo Agreements.

18.3 UNESCO, Treaties and the ICC

On 31 October 2011, Palestine was admitted as a full Member State of UNESCO, the United Nations Organization Educational, Scientific, and Cultural Organization. It received the support of 107 Member States of that Organization—only 14 states voted against and 52 abstained.

Next, the admission of Palestine as a Non-Member Observer State by the General Assembly in 2012 was followed in 2014 by the accession of the State of Palestine to 15 international treaties, in the field of *inter alia* diplomatic relations, human rights, and humanitarian law. This sometimes led to a formal protest of another state party. For example, after the acceptance of the Palestinian accession to the Hague Convention (IV) respecting the Laws and Customs of War on Land and its annex:

879. See para 17.6.4. Cf. Asseburg (2017); and *Times of Israel* (Staff of) (2018).

880. Article XXXI(7) of the Interim Agreement.

Regulations Concerning the Laws and Customs of War on Land (1907), of which the Netherlands is the depository, the Dutch Ministry of Foreign Affairs received a note from the Canadian Embassy, with the observation "that Palestine does not meet the criteria of a state under international law and is not recognized by Canada as a state." Therefore, the treaty "does not enter into force, or have an effect on Canada's treaty relations, with respect to the State of Palestine."[881]

Finally, we mention the accession of Palestine to the Statute of the International Criminal Court on 2 January 2015, which became effective on 1 April 2015.

Again, we would argue that the fact that Palestine is not a state would appear to bring into question the validity of its accession to UNESCO, ICC and other international bodies and treaties.

881. Zie: https://verdragenbank.overheid.nl/nl/Treaty/Details/00319_b#Palestina.

19. Refugees

".. the present Opinion could have reflected in a more satisfactory way the interests at stake for all those living in the region."

Judge Kooijmans, Separate Opinion, (Paragraph 13)[882]

19.1 Introduction

During the course of Israel's War of Independence (1947-1949), somewhere between 400,000 and 750,000 Palestinian Arabs fled the territory of what is now Israel.[883] Approximately 150,000 Arabs remained in Israel at the end of the War of Independence; they were all offered and accepted Israeli citizenship. During the Six-Day War in June 1967, a further 200,000-300,000 Palestinian Arabs—half of whom were refugees who fled from parts of western Palestine in 1947-1948—fled to Jordan.[884] In 1970, the Palestinian Arabs initiated an unsuccessful *coup d'état* on the Jordanian government. In response to the hostilities, the Jordanian government expelled some 50,000 Palestinian Arabs out of the Jordanian territory. In 1991, during the Gulf War, Kuwait expelled a further 300,000-450,000 Palestinians.[885]

The Palestinian Arabs who left the territory that later became Israeli territory at the end of the War of Independence (and their descendants) are now often referred to as "Palestinian refugees." The descendants of the original Palestinian refugees, approximately five million in total, remain

882. I.C.J. Reports 2004, p. 223.

883. There is considerable controversy about the numbers of Palestinian refugees. In June 1948, the Israelis originally estimated the number of refugees who fled their homes at 335,000. When the UN Relief for Palestine Refugees (UNRPR) commenced operations in December 1948, it found 962,643 refugees on its relief rolls. In Palestine Betrayed, Professor Ephraim Karsh reviews the Jewish, British and Arab sources, and concludes that between 583,000 and 609,000 Arabs fled their homes during the 1947-49 war: see Karsh (2010).

884. Bowker (2003), p. 81 ff.

885. BBC News, 30 May 2001.

unintegrated in the West Bank, Gaza, Syria, Lebanon, and Jordan. Many of them are still in United Nations Relief and Works Agency for Palestine Refugees (UNRWA) refugee camps.[886] It is claimed that the Palestinian refugees—and their descendants—have a right to return to Israel and be recognized as citizens. This question is perhaps the largest single issue preventing a negotiated settlement between Israel and the Palestinians. Israel denies the right of return but has repeatedly indicated willingness to provide compensation or other remedies for the Palestinian refugees. The Palestinians' demand that the right of return is a non-negotiable condition of a peace settlement was, arguably, the main reason that Yasser Arafat rejected Israeli Prime Minister Ehud Barak's offer of over 95 percent of the "occupied territories" at Camp David in 2000.[887]

19.2 Jewish Refugees

The Arabs were not the only ones to suffer displacement during the 1947-1949 conflict. During the 1947-1949 War of Independence, thousands of Jews were killed, and tens of thousands of Jews were displaced from their homes in the prospective Arab state and Jerusalem. They were not considered refugees, because they were able to integrate into the new State of Israel. None of them received any form of compensation for their loss of homes and possessions. During the period from 1948 to 2010, approximately 800,000 Jews, who had been living in Muslim countries of the Middle East for centuries, left as a result of anti-Jewish policies: systemic isolation, discrimination, and oppression.[888] Their exodus was partly stimulated by the establishment of the State of Israel, creating a safe haven in which they could find refuge. It has been estimated that these Jews left behind possessions worth more than 600 billion in US

---

886. UNRWA=United Nations Relief and Works Agency for Palestinian Refugees in the Near East.

887. See, e.g., Ross (2004), in particular pp. 650-758.

888. Centre for Israel Documentation and Information (CIDI), 'Tabel Joodse Bevolkingscentra in Arabische Landen, 1948-2010' in 'Katern 3: Vluchtelingen - ontheemde Palestijnen en Arabische Joden'. According to CIDI the countries with the largest amounts of Jewish refugees were: Algeria (140,000 refugees); Egypt (80,000 refugees); Iraq (135,000 refugees); Yemen (45,000 refugees); Morocco (250,000 refugees); Tunisia (50,000 refugees); and Iran (70,000 refugees). There are now very few Jews living in the Islamic countries of the Middle East (see the website of CIDI: www.cidi.nl/). In his book "La fin du judaïsme en terres d'Islam", the historian Shmuel Trigano concludes that between 1920 and 1970 about 900,000 Jews were expelled from Islamic countries. According to Trigano the reason for this exodus was a general policy of isolation of the Jews in the Islamic countries which was implemented through six different methods: denationalization; discrimination by law; isolation and sequestration; economic despoilment; socio-economic discrimination; and pogroms or similar anti-Semitic acts of violence. See also Meron (1995).

dollars.[889] These "Jewish refugees" were absorbed by their host countries and have integrated in Israel, as well as other Western countries like France, Canada, Australia, and the United States.

The fact that the Palestinian refugees were part of a wider refugee problem at the time is also reflected in UN Security Council Resolution 242 (1967), which called for a just settlement of "the refugee problem."[890] As Justice Arthur Goldberg, the United States Chief Delegate to the UN, who was instrumental in drafting the resolution, has pointed out:

> **"A notable omission in 242 is any reference to Palestinians, a Palestinian state on the West Bank or the PLO. The resolution addresses the objective of 'achieving a just settlement of the refugee problem.' This language presumably refers both to Arab and Jewish refugees, for about an equal number of each abandoned their homes as a result of the several wars..."[891]**

19.3 Legal Analysis

From an international legal perspective, there are three relevant issues to be examined. First, who is responsible for the fact that so many Palestinian Arabs fled their homes in 1947-1949? Second, are the non-Jewish Palestinians who left the territory of Israel-to-be in 1947-1949 and their descendants "refugees" within the meaning of international law? Third, do the original Arab "refugees" and/or their descendants have a "right" under international law to return to the territory of Israel, and if so, on what basis and under what conditions?

19.3.1 Causes of the Palestinian "Refugee" Problem

The immediate cause of the Palestinian refugee problem was the conflict, which started when the Arabs rejected the UN Partition Plan in November 1947 and concluded upon the cessation of hostilities and the conclusion of Armistice Agreements with Syria, Iraq, Jordan, and Egypt during the course of 1949. From 29 November 1947—the adoption of the Partition Resolution by the General Assembly at the United Nations—until 14 May 1948, there was a kind of civil war in Mandatory Palestine, in which the Jewish and Arab communities (the latter supported by the Arab Liberation Army) fought for control of the region of Palestine, which was still officially under British control. From 15 May 1948 until mid-1949, there was a full-fledged Arab-Israeli War, which was the consequence of the rejection by

889. See: Lefkovitz (2007); Schwartz (2008); Krieger (2006).

890. UN S.C. Res. 242 (1967).

891. Goldberg (2002).

PALESTINIAN REFUGEES, 1948-2008
Following the 1948 Israeli War of Independence, UNRWA (the United Nations Relief and Works Agency for Palestine Refugees in the Near East) was established by United Nations General Assembly resolution 302 (IV) of 8 December 1949 to carry out direct relief and works programmes for Palestinian refugees. The Agency began operations on 1 May 1950. In the absence of a solution to the Palestinian refugee problem, the General Assembly has repeatedly renewed UNRWA's mandate, most recently extending it to 30 June 2008
In the immediate aftermath of the Second World War, UNRRA (the United Nations Relief and Rehabilitation Administration) – set up on 9 November 1943 – was responsible for more than a million Displaced Persons (Jews and non-Jews) in Europe. By 1952, all of them had been found new homes in countries worldwide. Following the Israeli War of Independence, 840,000 Jews were expelled from Arab and Muslim lands. 580,000 found permanent homes in Israel, others in Britain, Europe and the Americas. Only UNRWA kept its refugees in camps, rather than seeking to integrate them in the host countries, all of which were Muslim and Arab lands. Because of this policy of maintaining them as refugees, the original 725,000 Palestinian refugees are now 4,448,429. In contrast, thanks to UNRRA, the descendants of the DPs of 1945 are all citizens of the countries in which they live
▲ Palestinian refugee camps in 2008, with the numbers registered in each (2007)
Harab (Aleppo) 17,703
Hama 7,578
Homs 13,230
Tripoli
Nahr el-Bared 30,439
Beddawi 15,641
LEBANON
Baalbek
Wavell 7,551
Beirut
Dbayeh 4,002
Mar Elias 612
Shatila 8,212
Burj el-Barajneh 15,484
SYRIA
Sidon
Mieh Mieh 4,473
Ein el-Hilweh 45,004
Damascus
Sbeineh 17,261
Jaramana 3,721
Qabr Essit 19,475
Burj el-Shem ali 18,625
Tyre
El Buss 9,728
Rashidiyeh 25,745
Khan Eshieh 16,108
Khan Danoun 8,500
In 2007 the total numbers of registered UNRWA refugees, both in camps and outside them, was 1,858,362 (Jordan), 408,438 (Lebanon), 442,363 (Syria), 722,302 (West Bank), and 1,016,964 (Gaza), a total of 4,448,429
Golan Heights
Sea of Galilee
Dera'a 9,306
Irbid 24,351
Husn 20,988
Jenin 15,496
Tulkarm 17,455
Nur Shams 8,659
Far'a 7,244
Souf 15,882
Beit Wazzan 6,508
Askar 14,629
Jerash 15,488
Nablus
Balata 21,903
Jabal el-Hussein 29,998
Baqa'a 68,386
WEST
JORDAN
Jalazone 10,390
Zarqa 18,004
Deir Ammar 2,275
Ein el-Sultan 1,723
Salt
Marka 38,425
Amman
Am'ari 8,085
Amman New Camp 50,703
0 kilometres 50
0 miles 30
Kalandia 10,024
Jericho
Shu'fat 10,069
Aqabat Jabr 5,510
Talbieh 871
Aida 4,534
Dheisheh 12,045
Beit Jibrin 2,025
Arroub 9,859
BANK
Hebron
Dead Sea
Fawwar 7,630
Mediterranean Sea
Ash Shati 78,768
Jabalya 106,691
Nuseirat 57,120
Deir el-Balah 19,534
Bureij 28,770
Maghazi 22,266
Khan Younis 63,219
GAZA STRIP
Rafah 95,187
EGYPT
Since 1948, UNRWA has fed, housed, clothed, educated and given health care to the children, grandchildren and great grandchildren of the original 725,000 refugees: in 2007 there were 4,448,429 registered Palestinian refugees in the Middle East. This map shows their camps and the numbers in each camp

Arab States of a Jewish State on "Arab" soil. The Palestinians and other Arabs refer to the conflict—and the creation of the State of Israel—as *al-Nakba* (the catastrophe). They regard it as a catastrophe, because they say they lost territories, which they had occupied for centuries, the Arab/ Palestinian people were displaced, and following their defeat in the war, they failed to achieve their longed-for Arab/Palestinian state. The irony is: Had they followed the example of the Jewish people and accepted the 1947 Partition Plan—as imperfect as it was—there would have been no war, no refugees, no displacement, and there would have been an Arab/ Palestinian state. The whole question of the Arab refugees and the "right of return" would simply not exist.

There is a lot of controversy surrounding the question, whether the Palestinian Arabs voluntarily left the country, or whether they were driven out of the land by Jewish forces. On the one hand, we have the clear opinion of the Israeli Foreign Minister Moshe Shertok, who was speaking about the "flight of the Arabs" and remarked: "Truly astonishing is that the Arabs have disappeared from a whole section of the country." He continued, "This transformation has occurred in the course of a war initiated by the Arabs. Moreover, the Arabs fled; they were not driven out."[892] The "new Israeli historian" Ilan Pappé presents the opposite view in his book "The Ethnic Cleansing of Palestine," in which he claims the Jews ethnically cleansed, conquered, and dispossessed Palestine of the Palestinians in 1948.[893] This view is shared by some left-wing liberal writers[894] and regularly repeated in the media, by NGOs, and in statements by major Church denominations.[895] The truth is probably more complex. Israeli historian Benny Morris concludes that Jews and Arabs must share responsibility for the Palestinian Arab refugee problem.[896] He also remarks, "[T]ransfer or expulsion was never adopted by the Zionist movement or its main political groupings as official policy at any stage of the movement's evolution—not even in the 1948 war."[897] Neither side deliberately caused it by design, but "the Arab leadership inside and outside Palestine helped precipitate the exodus."[898]

892. Quoted in Ben-Gurion (1972), p. 149.

893. Pappé (2006).

894. See, e.g., Chomsky (2012); Finkelstein (1995).

895. See Church of Scotland (2013).

896. Morris (2008).

897. *Ibid.*, p. 407.

898. *Ibid.*

According to Efraim Karsh in a recent study, many factors contributed to the mass Arab exodus during the 1947-1949 conflict.[899] During the first stage, the Jewish community (*Yishuv*) was on the defensive, responding to Palestinian aggression. There was a general breakdown of law and order in Palestine and a total disintegration of Palestinian Arab society.[900] From December 1947 through March 1948, as many as 75,000 Arabs left, expecting to return after the violence ceased. Many of these were afraid of the Grand Mufti Husseini, who ruled in Palestine. There was a mass flight of the large Arab populations from the mainly Jewish-dominated cities and towns, such as Jaffa, Haifa, Tiberias, and Jerusalem. In many cases, they were ordered to leave (or evicted) by the Palestinian militia or the Arab Legion leaders. Haifa, a city with a mixed population in 1947 (70,910 Arabs—Muslims and Christians—and 74,230 Jews) is a good example. During heavy fighting, virtually the whole Arab population of Haifa fled the city. According to Karsh, "there is an overwhelming body of evidence... that... the Jewish authorities went to considerable lengths to convince them to stay."[901] The fact that some Arab leaders called on the Palestinian Arabs to leave their homes was confirmed by former Syrian Prime Minister Khalid al-Azm: "Since 1948 it is we who demanded the return of the refugees to their houses... while it is we who made them leave... We brought disaster upon... Arab refugees, by inviting them and bringing pressure to bear upon them to leave... We have rendered them dispossessed..."[902] Many fled, convinced that they would soon return once the Jewish State had been wiped off the map of the Middle East. Following Jewish victories, fear triggered a mass exodus from Arab towns and villages.[903] Some Arabs were expelled from their homes by Jewish forces for strategic purposes. This was especially the case from early 1948 onwards. The Jews suffered many fatalities and were fighting for their survival against the Palestinian Arabs, who were gaining the upper hand. Most significantly, the Arabs had successfully besieged Jerusalem, threatening the survival of its 100,000 Jewish inhabitants.[904]

In the background, the Member States of the Arab League were preparing to invade Palestine upon the termination of the Mandate. This led the Hagana (the Jewish Defense Force), in mid-March 1948, to adopt a new,

899. Karsh (2010).

900. *Ibid.*, p. 230.

901. *Ibid.*, p. 138.

902. Khaled Al-Azm (1973), Part 1, pp. 386-387, quoted in Dershowitz (2003), p. 84.

903. Karsh (2010), pp. 182-183.

904. *Ibid.*, p. 118.

offensive strategy.[905] Their first priority was to liberate Jerusalem (Operation Nahshon). The overarching goal was defensive: "To secure the territorial integrity of the Jewish state and to defend its borders, as well as the blocs of Jewish settlement and such Jewish population as were outside those boundaries, against regular, semi-regular and guerrilla forces operating from bases outside or inside the Hebrew state." However, this strategy involved strategic destruction of some villages and expulsion of inhabitants, as happened most notably in Lydda and Ramle in July 1948.[906] There were a number of isolated incidents of Jewish-instigated violence, which arguably cannot be defended on strategic or military grounds. The most notable of these was the Deir Yassin tragedy on 9 April 1948.[907] More than any other event, Deir Yassin has been used to convey the impression that the Jews (of Irgun and Lechi) massacred and ethnically cleansed "Palestine" of the Arabs. Yet, the evidence shows that this was an isolated incident. Moreover, the determination of the facts remains controversial. For example, Menachem Begin, who later became Prime Minister of Israel, states that the inhabitants of Deir Yassin were explicitly warned by the Irgun fighters to leave the village before the outbreak of hostilities.[908]

Surprisingly, many ignore a similar massacre by the Arab Legion on the Jewish kibbutz Kfar Etzion on 12 May 1948.[909] At the time, however, the widely exaggerated descriptions of Jewish atrocities, especially the alleged rapes of women that never took place, spread panic across Palestinian society and intensified the ongoing mass flight.[910] It should be concluded that it is at least clear that many Palestinian Arabs who fled during the period of the War of Independence did so voluntarily. Some of them were forced to flee. It is therefore much too simple to declare that the State of Israel is liable—let alone exclusively liable—for finding a solution to the "refugee problem."

---

905. The so-called 'Plan D'.

906. In July 1948, Ben-Gurion ordered the evacuation of the approximately 50,000 Arab civilians from these two cities (many of whom had recently fled from other Arab cities, like Jaffa). They were escorted to neighboring Arab towns. According to Karsh, the mass Arab exodus from Ramle and Lydda in July 1948 was "the first, indeed the only, instance in the war where a substantial urban population was driven out by Jewish or Israeli forces. Small wonder that it was to become the central plank of the Arab claim of premeditated and systematic dispossession. In fact, the exodus emanated from a string of unexpected developments on the ground and was in no way foreseen in military plans for the cities' capture or reflected in the initial phase of the occupation." See: Karsh (2010), p. 216.

907. Morris (2008), pp. 125-128. See also Smelik (2014), pp. 125-131.

908. Begin (1977), pp. 162-165.

909. Morris (2008), pp. 167-171. See also Smelik (2014), pp. 125-131.

910. Karsh (2010), p. 122.

19.3.2 Status of the Palestinian Arab Refugees

The second issue referred to above is: Whether the Palestinian Arabs, who left the territory of Israel-to-be in 1947-1949 and their descendants, qualify as "refugees" within the meaning of international law. The UN Convention relating to the Status of Refugees (1951) defines the term refugees and prescribes the rights of refugees under international law. According to Article 1 of the Convention, a "refugee" is any person who:

> "[O]wing to a *well-founded fear of being persecuted* for reasons of race, religion, nationality, membership of a particular social group or political opinion, is outside the country of his nationality and is unable, or owing to such fear, is unwilling to avail himself of the protection of that country; or who, not having a nationality and being outside the country of his former habitual residence as a result of such events, is unable or, owing to such fear, is unwilling to return to it."[911]

Ruth Lapidoth, emeritus professor of international law at the Hebrew University of Jerusalem, has remarked that under this definition the number of Palestinians that would qualify as refugees would be less than half a million.[912] This is understandable given the fact that many of them chose to flee without being forced to do so. Lapidoth held that Arab states were successful in excluding Palestinians from the definition by introducing Article 1.D in the Convention:

> "This Convention shall not apply to persons who are at present receiving from organs or agencies of the United Nations other than the United Nations High Commissioner for Refugees protection or assistance. When such protection or assistance has ceased for any reason, without the position of such persons being definitively settled in accordance with the relevant resolutions adopted by the General Assembly of the United Nations, these persons shall *ipso facto* be entitled to the benefits of this Convention."

Although the formulation of this provision is general, it was clear from the beginning that it referred to the Palestinians.[913] The UN agency, which without doubt was in the minds of the drafters of Article 1.D, is the United Nations Relief and Works Agency for Palestine Refugees in the Near East (UNRWA), which was established by the General Assembly in December of 1949 and mandated to provide assistance and protection to the Palestine

911. Emphasis added.
912. Lapidoth (2002).
913. See Goodwin-Gill (1983), pp. 56-57; Salahi (2008), at p. 136.

refugees.[914] There is no official definition of the Palestinian refugee in its founding resolution, nor in any other resolution of the General Assembly.[915] In practice, UNRWA considers a Palestine refugee as someone "whose normal place of residence was Palestine during the period June 1, 1946 to May 15, 1948, and who lost both his home and means of livelihood as a result of the 1948 conflict."[916] It is immediately apparent that this is a much broader definition than that adopted under the UN Refugee Convention (1951). Furthermore, UNRWA has wide discretion in applying its Mandate. UNRWA makes its services available not only to all those who meet this refugee definition, but also to descendants of the original refugees. This leads to a continuing increase in the number of Palestinian refugees. Bocco remarks that "the UNRWA definition of a Palestine refugee is an administrative one and does not translate directly into recognition by international law."[917] When the UN Agency started working in 1950, it was responding to the needs of about 750,000 Palestine refugees. Today, approximately five million Palestinian Arabs are considered eligible for UNRWA services. The refugees had not been able to integrate in the countries where they settled, if they would have the desire to do so, which in general is not the case. Apparently, the Arab states concerned want to preserve the *status quo*, which is a major obstacle to reaching an agreement with Israel.

19.3.3 Is There a "Right to Return"?

The third issue referred to above is whether the Arab refugees have the right to return under international law. The Palestinian leadership claims that the descendants of the original Palestinian refugees have a right to return to Israel. This claim is based primarily on UN General Assembly Resolution 194, which was adopted on 11 December 1948 in response to the Arab invasion of Israel.[918] Before our brief analysis of this Resolution, it has to be remarked that this Resolution is not a binding decision under international law.[919] Rather, Resolution 194 was intended to create a framework for achieving a truce between the warring parties (Egypt, Jordan, Syria, Lebanon, Iraq and Israel). Only one paragraph (Paragraph 11) concerns "refugees." It provides as follows:

---

914. The UN established the Relief for Palestine Refugees (UNRPR) in August 1948; this organization was replaced by the UNWRA in December 1948. See A/RES/302 (IV).

915. Lapidoth, (2002).

916. Bocco (2009), at. p. 237.

917. *Ibid.*, at p. 238.

918. UN G.A. Res. 194.

919. Brownlie (1990), pp. 14 and 699.

> "*Resolves* that the refugees wishing to return to their homes and live at peace with their neighbors should be permitted to do so at the earliest practicable date, and that compensation should be paid for the property of those choosing not to return and for loss of or damage to property which, under principles of international law or in equity, should be made good by the Governments or authorities responsible;
>
> "*Instructs* the Conciliation Commission to facilitate the repatriation, resettlement and economic and social rehabilitation of the refugees and the payment of compensation, and to maintain close relations with the Director of the United Nations Relief for Palestine Refugees and, through him, with the appropriate organs and agencies of the United Nations;..."[920]

Paragraph 11 does not guarantee a right to return. It only recommends ("should be permitted to do so") that refugees should be allowed to return. For those not willing to return, compensation "should be paid." The "right" to return is not unconditional; refugees are only to be allowed to return if they are "willing to live in peace with their neighbors." Furthermore, the return is to take place "at the earliest practicable date." The Resolution refers generically to "governments"; there is not a specific obligation imposed on Israel. This suggests that even if the Resolution is read as imposing obligations (*quod non*), these obligations are to be shared equally by all the respective governments. This would mean that those states, who were responsible for creating the refugee problems, should contribute to the solution proportionally. In this regard, Israel has offered on several occasions to contribute compensation to Palestinian refugees.[921] While Paragraph 11 applies to "refugees," it does not specifically refer to "Arab" refugees. The Resolution therefore could in principle also apply to the approximately 800,000 Jewish refugees, who had fled from Arab countries in 1948, provided that they want to return there, which seems unlikely.

A reference is sometimes made to the general rules of international law concerning the return and repatriation of persons to their country of origin, such as Article 12(4) of the International Covenant on Civil and Political Rights, which provides that "no one shall be arbitrarily deprived of the right to enter his own country." It is doubtful whether the return of Palestinian refugees to Israel could be based on this provision, having regard to the fact that they never were Israeli citizens. Moreover, the

920. UN G.A. Res. 194, para 11.

921. For example, at Camp David in 2000 a "now-or-never" offer of compensation was made, which was withdrawn when Arafat rejected Israel's overall proposal. See Ross (2004).

provision concerns an individual right and does not provide for a mass return.[922]

Resolution 194 only prohibits arbitrary deprivation of the right to enter. The refusal as result of negotiations, as foreseen in the Oslo framework—for example—cannot be qualified as arbitrary.

For all of these reasons, we conclude that there is no basis under international law for the Palestinian claim of a "right of return." The refugee issue should be resolved within the framework of the negotiations between the parties. It is not to be expected that the outcome will be a return of all those who qualify as Palestinian refugees under the UNRWA practice. This would be incompatible with the existence of Israel as a Jewish state.

922. Cf. also Weiner (1997), at pp. 40-41.

PART VI

A State at War

20. The Use of Force in International Law: *Jus ad Bellum*

"The Court's formalistic approach to the right to self-defence enables it to avoid addressing the very issues that are at the heart of this case."

Judge Buergenthal, Declaration (Paragraph 6)[923]

20.1 Introduction

From its inception to the present day, the continued existence of the State of Israel has always been under real and immediate threat from external military forces. No other state in the world is under such constant attack and threat of attack from so many different sources.

The proclamation of the State of Israel in 1948 prompted an immediate invasion by five Arab States, which resulted in what Israelis refer to as the War of Independence (1948-1949). During the Sinai Campaign in 1956, Israel was engaged in hostilities with Egypt. It managed to hold its own against Egypt, Jordan, and Syria in the Six-Day War in 1967. The War of Attrition with Egypt from 1967 to 1970 followed shortly after. A surprise attack by a coalition of Arab States led by Egypt and Syria initiated the Yom Kippur War in 1973. The First Lebanon War (1982) was fought not against Lebanon but against Palestine Liberation Organization (PLO) terrorists operating from Lebanon, marking a shift towards engagement in armed conflict with non-state terrorist groups. This became an increasingly prevalent trend during both the First Intifada, which lasted from 1987-1993, and the Second Intifada, which lasted from 2000-2004. In the Second Lebanon War (2006), Israel fought Hezbollah forces in Lebanon. In the Gaza Strip (Gaza), it engaged in operations against Hamas in 2008-2009 (*Operation Cast Lead*). This happened again in 2012 (*Operation Pillar of Cloud*) and in 2014 (*Operation Protective Edge*). During the course of its history, Israel has had to contend not only with "traditional" forms of warfare, but also with guerrilla warfare.

923. I.C.J. Reports 2004, p. 243.

The identification of wars and military operations in the preceding paragraph should not suggest that there was peace in between. Threats of armed attacks and actual violent incidents have been part of day to day life for the State of Israel since its inception. Since 1949, Israel has been—and remains —in a perpetual state of war with both Lebanon and Syria. Israel is the only Member-State of the United Nations (UN) whose fundamental right to exist is denied by certain other members of the UN to this day. The bellicose statements made by Mahmoud Ahmadinejad, the former President of Iran, are an obvious example.[924] His successor, Hasan Rouhani, called, "The Zionist regime... a wound on the body of the Islamic world for years and the wound should be removed."[925] The current conflict in Syria has already resulted in conflict between Israel and Iranian forces in Syria, which seems likely to escalate. Israel must also contend with a permanent threat from non-state "Palestinian" terrorist organizations, like Hamas and Hezbollah, that have been established to destroy Israel. Despite all this, Israel's military actions are widely criticized by members of the international community and by elements within its own society. Principles of international law are frequently invoked in this context.

It is remarkable that criticism has tended to be leveled almost exclusively against Israel's actions, especially in recent years. The actions of the other parties, such as Hezbollah in Lebanon or Hamas in Gaza, are rarely the focus of critical attention.

20.2 Regulation of the Use of Force by International Law

Elimination of the unbridled use of armed force has always been one of the main purposes of international law. In *De Jure Belli ac Pacis (On the Law of War and Peace)* (1625), Dutch jurist Hugo Grotius established the basic principles of both *jus ad bellum* (the right to enter into war) and *jus in bello* (lawful conduct during war—known as international humanitarian law, or the law of armed conflict).[926] Together, as developed and refined over the centuries, these laws of war define the conditions determining whether entry into war is justified and what actions are considered to be justified in relation to the armed forces and civilian population of the opposing side during war.

---

924. He was quoted as having said that "[a]nyone who loves freedom and justice should strive for the annihilation of the Zionist regime in order to pave the way for world justice and freedom." *The Jerusalem Post*, 2 August 2012.

925. *The Independent*, 18 March 2013.

926. Grotius (1925).

20.3 The Right to Enter into War (*Jus ad Bellum*)

History has taught us that when states use force outside their own territory they often do so at the expense of the rights and security of the local population. The two World Wars are appalling examples of this. Hence, the international legal instruments, developed after World War I and especially after the World War II, impose very strict limits on the use of armed force by states. Today, international law forbids the use of force as a general instrument of international political action. Article 2(4) of the UN Charter provides: "All Members shall refrain in their international relations from the threat or use of force against the territorial integrity or political independence of any state..."

The UN Charter identifies only two situations in which the use of force by states is permissible: (a) action taken or authorized by the UN Security Council according to Chapter VII of the UN Charter, and (b) the inherent right of individual or collective self-defense.[927] In addition to these two exceptions, international law recognizes a third situation in which the use of force is considered to be justified (though this is disputed): When the use of armed force is necessary to protect civilians from blatant forms of injustice, such as serious violations of fundamental human rights. This is called humanitarian intervention.[928]

20.4 Use of Force (Authorized) by the UN Security Council

Use of force by, or authorized by, the Security Council is carried out in accordance with the provisions of Chapter VII of the UN Charter, which is concerned with the preservation of international peace and security.[929] The problem here is that the legitimacy of the use of force depends on a highly politicized decision by fifteen Member States of the UN, five of which (the permanent members: The United States, the United Kingdom, France, the Russian Federation and China) have the power to veto any substantive resolution. This can paralyze the Security Council. When the State of Israel was invaded by five Arab States in 1948, the UN did not take action against this aggression, despite the fact that there was clearly due cause. Given the aggressive states were UN Member States, action by the UN to protect the State of Israel would have been appropriate. During the crisis that preceded the Six-Day War in 1967, Israel expected

927. UN Charter, art. 51..

928. See, in general, Holzgrefe & Keohane (eds.) (2003).

929. See, *inter alia*, Shaw (1986), pp. 557-562.

in vain that the UN Secretary-General would do something to delay the withdrawal of UN troops from the Sinai, which was requested by Egypt. The Secretary General, U Thant, did not even convene the Security Council, but immediately acted in compliance with Egypt's demands. The Soviet Union had also made clear that it would veto all proposals for a resolution going against the wishes of Israel's enemies Egypt and Syria.[930]

20.5 **Self-Defense**

20.5.1 **General**

The authors of the UN Charter foresaw that the operation of the UN Security Council would not be sufficient to guarantee the preservation of the peace and security against aggression. Article 51 of the UN Charter allows for a second situation in which the use of force is permissible, namely the right of individual self-defense (by one state) or collective self-defense (by a group of states) against armed attacks. This right is recognized as an "inherent right" of states.[931] Article 51 of the UN Charter thus confirms the pre-existing right of self-defense in customary law. The right of self-defense is firmly enshrined in international law. It is inextricably associated with and, in a broken world, indispensable in safeguarding a state's right to independence. It has traditionally been invoked and exercised not only in response to attacks on states but also in response to attacks by rebels who use foreign territory to stage attacks on the state against which they are rebelling.[932] A point of discussion is whether a so-called *"pre-emptive strike"*—the launching of a surprise attack as a means of averting a serious threat—falls under the terms of Article 51.[933] A pre-emptive strike occurred on 5 June 1967, when Israel launched a decisive attack against the Egyptian Air Force in response to the build-up of a massive threat. Amos Shapira argues that this did indeed fall within the right of self-defense. He points to the nature of the conflict in the Middle East and explains that, given the preceding open threats from the Arab world, the continued existence of the State of Israel was at stake. The superiority and geographical position of the Egyptian arsenal and the fact that Egypt was receiving support from the Soviet Union were factors that he also considered. Finally, he notes the lack of willingness on the part of the international community and especially on the part

930. Gilbert (1999), pp. 367 and 373. See also: Oren (2003).

931. See on the right of self-defense in general, *inter alia*: Shaw (1986), pp. 549-554.

932. O'Connell (1970), p. 316.

933. UN Charter, art. 51.

of the UN Security Council to intervene.[934] At the time, the Soviet Union tried in vain to get the United Nations Security Council and the General Assembly to rule that Israel's attack on the Egyptian Air Force was illegal.[935]

Article 51 imposes strict limits on a state's right to resort to self-defense and stipulates that measures taken by UN Member States in the exercise of the right of self-defense must immediately be reported to the Security Council.[936] Furthermore, the right of self-defense may only be exercised until the Security Council takes steps to maintain international peace and security. The exercise of the right of self-defense must also meet the requirement of proportionality—the means must be in proportion to the end. An example of the application of the right to self-defense is what happened after the attacks by al-Qaeda terrorists on the World Trade Center in New York and the Pentagon in Washington D.C. on 11 September 2001. The United States justified its military actions in response by invoking the right of self-defense. The Security Council authorized this, and in Resolutions 1368 and 1373 (2001) condemned the terrorist attacks and determined that the attacks constituted a threat to international peace and security.[937] Both resolutions refer explicitly to the "inherent right of individual and collective self-defense."[938] The exercise of the right of self-defense by the United States led to armed attacks on targets in Afghanistan that offered protection to the Al-Qaeda terrorist network headed by Osama bin Laden, which was held responsible for the attacks.

20.5.2 The ICJ's Advisory Opinion on the Right to Self-Defense

In the same vein as the United States, Israel invoked the right of self-defense to legitimize the construction of the security barrier referred to earlier, which was built to protect Israeli civilians from continual attack during the Second Intifada, which began in 2000. The barrier is a relatively peaceful means of protecting civilians. Yet, in its Advisory Opinion rendered on 9 July 2004, the International Court of Justice (ICJ) denied Israel the right to invoke the right of self-defense.[939] The ICJ's reasoning and conclusion is highly contentious.[940] The ICJ starts by citing the first sentence of Article

---

934. Shapira (2004), p. 216.

935. Shaw (1986), p. 551.

936. UN Charter, art 51..

937. UN S.C. Res. 1368 and 1373 (2001).

938. *Ibid.*

939. *Legal Consequences of the Construction of a Wall in the Occupied Palestinian Territory* Advisory Opinion, 2004 I.C.J. Reports 2004, pp. 136-203 (9 July 2004).

940. See, *inter alia*, Wedgwood (2005); Murphy (2005); Caplan (2005).

51 of the UN Charter, which reads, "Nothing in the present Charter shall impair the inherent right of individual or collective self-defense if an armed attack occurs against a Member of the United Nations, until the Security Council has taken measures necessary to maintain international peace and security."[941]

Immediately after citing this provision, the ICJ notes that Article 51 of the UN Charter *thus* recognizes the existence of an inherent right of self-defense in the case of armed attack by one state against another state.[942] It then proceeds to advance the argument that Israel does not claim that the attacks against it are imputable to a foreign state.[943] However, Article 51 makes no reference to another state when it comes to the origin of an armed attack against a Member State of the United Nations.[944] In her Separate Opinion, British Judge Rosalyn Higgins points out that there is nothing in the text of Article 51 that justifies the restrictive interpretation adopted by the ICJ.[945] Furthermore, the history of the doctrine of self-defense in international law confirms that the doctrine does not apply exclusively to attacks by another state.[946] The ICJ adds that the attacks against which Israel wishes to defend itself originate from areas that are under its control.[947] This leads the ICJ to conclude that the circumstances of the situation differ from the circumstances that led the Security Council to adopt Resolutions 1368 (2001) and 1373 (2001), which recognized the United States' right to invoke the right of self-defense in accordance with Article 51 of the UN Charter in response to the terrorist attacks on 11 September 2001. This argument is unconvincing. The attacks on the World Trade Center and the Pentagon are similar to the attacks on Israel during the Intifada in that they were not "armed attacks" by another state.[948] They were terrorist acts by a group of individuals operating from American soil, albeit perpetrators with international connections. In her Separate Opinion, Judge Higgins describes it as incomprehensible that an occupying power should lose the right to defend its citizens against attacks originating from that occupied

941. I.C.J. Reports 2004, p. 194.

942. *Ibid.* (emphasis added).

943. *Ibid.*

944. For criticism of the Court's interpretation, see also Werner (2009), p. 516.

945 I.C.J. Reports 2004, p. 215.

946. See the famous *Caroline* case (1837), which concerned an attack by rebels, in: Dixon & McCorquodale (2000), pp. 561-562.

947. I.C.J. Reports 2004, p. 215.

948. UN S.C. Res. 1368 (2001) and 1373 (2001).

area. She criticizes the inconsistency of the ICJ in this connection. It considered "Palestine" enough of an international actor to take part in the written and oral aspects of the procedure followed by the ICJ—which according to the Statute of the International Court of Justice is something that is only accorded to states and international organizations—but not as an international actor with a locus from which attacks can be launched against a state, which has the right to invoke the right of self-defense in response.[949] This is a double standard.

On the basis of the arguments presented and without further substantiation, the ICJ concluded that Israel was not entitled to invoke the right of self-defense.[950] Israel was denied the right to fulfill the most fundamental task of a state—defence of its citizens against force. Even if we were to concur with the ICJ's conclusion that armed attacks must originate from another state—which is not the case—it was incumbent upon the ICJ to consider that the terrorists threatening Israel have connections with (and receive significant support from) states such as Iran and Syria. The ICJ's unsubstantiated assertions can also be questioned on the evidence that the Palestinian Authority (PA) failed to fulfill the task of combating terrorism in the areas under its control, as it agreed to under the Oslo Agreements. Because of this, Israel invoked the right of self-defense against acts of violence initiated from those areas. The ICJ's decision to restrict the right of self-defense to the traditional model of war between states limits the scope of the provision in an irresponsible way and must give not only Israel but also many other states in the world cause for concern: modern warfare is most likely to involve conflict between a state and one or more terrorist groups.

20.5.3 "Legitimate Self-Defense" in Gaza?

Israel's right to invoke the right of self-defense has also been hotly debated in connection with the wars in the Gaza Strip (Gaza) in 2008-2009, 2012, and 2014. There has been a debate on the qualification of the conflict of Israel with the Hamas-regime in Gaza in terms of the law of armed conflict, and whether it is an international or non-international armed conflict.[951] Although Gaza may be not a state properly speaking, it is also arguably no longer an "occupied territory" after the withdrawal of Israeli

949. UN S.C. Res. 1515 (19 November 2003). See also: *Legal Consequences of the Construction of a Wall in the Occupied Palestinian Territory* Advisory Opinion, 2004 I.C.J. Reports 2004, pp. 136-203 (9 July 2004).

950. See: *Legal Consequences of the Construction of a Wall in the Occupied Palestinian Territory* Advisory Opinion, 2004 I.C.J. Reports 2004, pp. 136-203 (9 July 2004).

951. Cf., *inter alia*, Farrant (2013); Guilfoyle (2011); Makowski (2013).

citizens and troops from the territory in August 2005.[952] Notwithstanding the withdrawal, attacks continued. The violence used by Hamas and other Palestinian militant groups from the Gaza Strip targeting Israeli citizens by launching rockets missiles and mortar bombs, entitled Israel to exert its inherent right to self-defense. Israeli citizens frequently had to rush to air-raid shelters and school times were altered to prevent children from being hit. In the "first round" of this war, from 27 December 2008 to 19 January 2009, Israel launched a military incursion into Gaza (Operation Cast Lead) in an attempt to put an end to the almost constant stream of rocket and mortar attacks. There had been about 12,000 attacks between 2000 and 2008, including nearly 3000 rockets and mortar shells in 2008 alone on civilian targets in towns in the south of Israel.[953]

Israel's right to self-defense was supported by some and challenged by others. In a letter to *The Sunday Times*, several well-known experts on international law, including Sir Ian Brownlie and Professor John Quigley, argued that, given the extent and effectiveness of the rocket fire, Israel did not have the right to invoke the right of self-defense.[954] This is bizarre reasoning. How long was Israel supposed to allow its population to live in fear of an enemy that had no intention of respecting even the most elementary rules of the laws of war? Was Israel only allowed to defend itself once the rocket fire was "effective" on a massive scale? Was Israel supposed to wait until the technical quality of the rockets had improved to such an extent that large numbers of victims could no longer be avoided? The authors of the letter condemned the lack of proportionality and necessity: an accusation leveled by many in connection with the hostilities in Gaza. This has gradually become the standard criticism of Israel.[955] This same criticism was also voiced during and after the Second Lebanon War in 2006. Those who invoke the accusation of disproportionality in connection with the hostilities in the Gaza Strip justify their claims by referring to the difference in the number of fatalities: reporters and commentators often compare the thirteen fatalities on the Israeli side with the 1300 fatalities among the inhabitants of Gaza. There is clearly a significant numerical difference, though there is also some dispute as to the actual extent of the consequences of the hostilities. These figures

952. Adopting here for convenience sake the dominant terminology, which has been criticized in this work. See on the legal status of Gaza: Samson (2010).

953. The State of Israel, *The Operation in Gaza 27 December 2008- 18 January 2009. Factual and Legal Aspects,* July 2009, pp. 1-5.

954. *The Sunday Times*, 11 January 2009.

955. See, e.g., the accusations against Israel by Verrijn Stuart (2009), published before the smoke of battle cleared over Gaza.

do not prove lack of proportionality. As Michael Walzer, an expert on the theory of just war, rightly pointed out, proportionality is not a matter of equal numbers of victims on both sides.[956] The military action by the United States in Afghanistan in response to the attacks of September 11th was not disproportionate, even though the number of deaths among Taliban fighters in Afghanistan far exceeded the number of civilian victims in New York. To draw another parallel: In criminal law, the defense of self-defense (the personal equivalent of the right of a state to self-defense) is not solely justified if the person defending himself against attack loses his life in the process. Walzer points out that the criterion of proportionality must be determined on the basis of a consideration of the intended goal and the means used to achieve it with the future also taken into account. It is important to consider the anticipated effect of the actions taken by the opposing side. This involves an assessment of the possible effects of an action in the future, based on the best empirical knowledge currently available. In the case of the military action against Hamas in the Gaza Strip, it was legitimate to take into account the fact that Hamas could be expected to raise its fighting capacity. In this connection we may think of the development of more advanced rockets that would be able to reach Tel Aviv for example. The proportionality of the self-defense therefore should not be measured by the standard of the relatively primitive projectiles used by Hamas and other groups up until that point. All of these factors need to be considered, when an extremist group such as Hamas explicitly aspires to destroy the State of Israel and specifically and purposefully targets Jewish civilians.[957]

956. Walzer (2009 a).

957. See for a more detailed analysis: Walzer (2009 b).

21. The Use of Force in International Law: *Jus in Bello*

> **"The nature of these cross-Green Line attacks and their impact on Israel and its population are never seriously examined by the Court."**
>
> Judge Buergenthal, Declaration (Paragraph 3)[958]

21.1 Introduction

A second aspect of the regulation of the use of force is *jus in bello*: the rules of international law that determine what is permissible in war in terms of the form, extent, and target of the use of force. It is often called international humanitarian law (IHL). In this field of the law, a distinction is traditionally made between the Law of Geneva and the Law of The Hague.[959] The Geneva Conventions—treaties drafted and periodically revised in the Swiss City of Geneva over the period 1864 to 1977—establish the standards of international law for the humanitarian treatment of the victims of war, such as wounded soldiers, prisoners of war, and civilians affected by war, which include those living in occupied areas. The Geneva Conventions are also referred to as the Red Cross Conventions in view of the fact that the International Committee of the Red Cross has been assigned an important role in their implementation. The Hague Conventions govern matters such as the use of weapons and tactics. Much of the content of these treaties forms part of customary international law, which is binding on all nations, including those that did not ratify the treaties. Israel is party to the four conventions negotiated in 1949, sometimes also collectively referred to as the Geneva Conventions. The purpose of the First Geneva Convention is the amelioration of the condition of the wounded in armies in the field. The purpose of the Second Geneva Convention is the amelioration of the condition of wounded members of armed forces at sea. The purpose of the Third Geneva Convention is

958. I.C.J. Reports 2004, p. 241.

959. Shaw (1986), pp. 576-586.

to govern the protection of prisoners of war. The purpose of the Fourth Geneva Convention is for the protection of civilians in times of war. In 1977, two Additional Protocols (I and II)—which, incidentally, were not ratified by Israel—were added to the four Geneva Conventions of 1949. In so far as the 1977 Protocols codify rules of international customary law, they are applied as such by the Israeli Supreme Court.[960] Because of the disputed status of what many refer to as the "occupied territories," Israel contests the formal applicability of the provisions of the Fourth Geneva Convention in the "occupied territories," but since 1967 has agreed to the *de facto* application of its humanitarian provisions in the Territories.[961] Initially, international humanitarian law was applicable between states. As it is applicable to both international and non-international conflicts, it is now generally assumed that non-state actors, such as Hamas and Hezbollah, are also bound by it.[962] In the words of the Appeals Chamber of the Special Court for Sierra Leone, "It is well settled that all parties to an armed conflict, whether states of non-state actors, are bound by international humanitarian law, even though only states may become parties to international treaties."[963]

Israel has been heavily criticized for its failure to comply with international humanitarian law. It would be beyond the scope of our study to discuss all of the aspects involved. We will therefore confine our discussion to the criticism that hinges on two fundamental principles in international humanitarian law: distinction and proportionality.

21.2 Distinction

The principle of distinction stipulates that parties involved in armed conflict must make a distinction between combatants and non-combatants. Thus, they must make a distinction between those who are actively involved in the conflict (generally members of armed forces), and those who are not (generally civilians). Civilians and civilian objects must be protected, and military operations may only be directed against military objectives. Article 48 of Additional Protocol I provides: "To ensure respect for and protection of the civilian population and civilian objects, the Parties to

960. See, e.g., The Supreme Court of Israel sitting as the High Court of Justice, 14 December 2006, *Public Committee against Torture v. Government,* in: Israel Supreme Court, *Judgments of the Israel Supreme Court: Fighting Terrorism within the Law*, Vol. 3 (2006-2009), pp. 85-162, at p. 122.

961. See, *inter alia*, Bar-Yaacov (1990); Lapidoth (1990), at pp. 99-101.

962. See, e.g., Horowitz, Sigal (2011).

963. Prosecutor v. Sam Hinga Norman, Case No. SCSL-2004-14-AR72(E), Decision on Preliminary Motion Based on Lack of Jurisdiction (Child Recruitment), 31 May 2004, para 22.

the conflict shall at all times distinguish between the civilian population and combatants and between civilian objects and military objectives and accordingly shall direct their operations only against military objectives."

Israel is almost constantly accused of violating this principle because of the numbers of civilians who have died during its various conflicts with the (Palestinian) Arabs. First and foremost, it is important to note that there is ample evidence that the Israeli Army accepts and seeks to apply the principle of distinction.[964] The Israeli Defense Forces (IDF) military units have legal advisors who assist commanders with this. It must also be stressed that the nature of the war waged by terrorist organizations, which is essentially a form of guerrilla warfare, makes it extremely complex if not virtually impossible to apply the principle of distinction. The tactics used by terrorist organizations such as Hamas are designed to blur the distinction between combatants and non-combatants as much as possible. Military operations are conducted from civilian locations, such as private homes, schools, hospitals, and mosques. Furthermore, Hamas and Hezbollah are structured in such a way that it is difficult to make a clear distinction between public services provided by "military" organizations and public services provided by "civic" organizations. Article 28 of the Fourth Geneva Convention stipulates that the presence of a person protected by humanitarian law may not be used to render certain points or areas immune from military operations. The ultimate responsibility for the death or injury of civilians who are used as a shield for military activities lies with the party that used the civilians for this purpose. Article 51(7) of Additional Protocol I states:

> **"The presence or movements of the civilian population or individual civilians shall not be used to render certain points or areas immune from military operations, in particular in attempts to shield military objectives from attacks or to shield, favour or impede military operations. The Parties to the conflict shall not direct the movement of the civilian population or individual civilians in order to attempt to shield military objectives from attacks or to shield military operations."**

The feigning of civilian or non-combatant status is also a violation of international humanitarian law, in particular the specific prohibition of perfidious (devious) methods. Article 37(1) of Additional Protocol I states:

> **"It is prohibited to kill, injure or capture an adversary by resort to perfidy. Acts inviting the confidence of an adversary to lead him to believe that he is entitled to, or is obliged to accord, protection under the rules of international law applicable in armed conflict, with intent to betray that**

964. Weiner & Bell (2008); Baruch (2014).

> **confidence, shall constitute perfidy. The following acts are examples of perfidy: (a) the feigning of an intent to negotiate under a flag of truce or of a surrender; (b) the feigning of an incapacitation by wounds or sickness; (c) the feigning of civilian, non-combatant status; and (d) the feigning of protected status by the use of signs, emblems or uniforms of the United Nations or of neutral or other States not Parties to the conflict."**

There is ample evidence that such practices were employed by Israel's enemies in the recent conflicts in Gaza and also earlier in Lebanon.[965] In these kinds of situations, it is virtually impossible for the opposing party, *in this case* Israel, to make a distinction between combatants and non-combatants.

The recent conflicts in Gaza (2008-2009, 2012, and 2014) provide us with examples of the ways and means used by Israel to try to respect the principle of distinction. Before launching a military operation, the IDF goes to considerable lengths to warn the local civilian population by making telephone calls and distributing flyers.[966] Another device, used in the Operation Protective Edge, is *roof knocking*. In the event ordinary warnings remain unheeded, the IDF launches small, non-explosive projectiles at the corner of the roof of a building, to persuade civilians, used as human shields, to leave the building.[967] A former commander of the British forces in Afghanistan, Colonel Richard Kemp, told the Human Rights Council on 16 October 2009, that in his view: "During *Operation Cast Lead*, the Israeli Defense Forces did more to safeguard the rights of civilians in a combat zone than any other army in the history of mankind."[968] On 6 November 2014, U.S. General Dempsey, Chairman of the Joint Chiefs of Staff, made a similar observation in respect of the Operation Protective Edge in 2014. He said that Israel went to "extraordinary lengths" to limit civilian casualties.[969] Unfortunately, there were nevertheless, as may be expected in this type of guerrilla warfare, also many civilian victims during the Gaza operations.

There tend to be significant differences of opinion regarding the actual numbers of civilian and combatant deaths in the Gaza wars. In a report published on 11 February 2009, UN Special Rapporteur Richard Falk claimed that 235 of the 1,434 Palestinian Arab fatalities were combatant

965. See Simmons (2012), pp. 272-283; International Institute for Counter Terrorism, *Operation 'Protective Edge': A Detailed Summary of Events*, ICT Incident and Activists Database: www.ict.org.il/Article/1262/Operation-Protective-Edge-A-Detailed-Summar-of-Events (visited: 11 September 2017).

966. See, e.g., Benjamin (2014).

967. *Ibid.*, at pp. 54-55.

968. Quoted by Alan Dershowitz in: Dershowitz (2011), at p. 123.

969. Quoted by Benjamin (2014), at p. 45.

deaths.[970] Israel counted 1,166 Palestinian Arab victims, 709 of whom were involved in terrorist activities, which meant that there were 295 regrettable civilian deaths.[971] Later, in November 2010, Hamas admitted that between 600 and 700 militants were killed during *Cast Lead*.[972] This figure is consistent with that given by Israel. After the recent *Operation Protective Edge* in 2014, again different numbers of Palestinian casualties were published. According to the UN, there have died 1483 (67 percent) civilians and 722 (33 percent) combatants. The Meir Amit Intelligence and Terrorism Information Center counted 480 (31 percent) civilian, 467 (30 percent) combatant, and 605 (39 percent) unidentified deaths.[973]

21.3 Proportionality

The principle of proportionality is another cornerstone of international humanitarian law and is a criterion to determine whether the exercise of self-defense is justified. The principle of proportionality is part of international customary law and is articulated in Article 51(5)(b) of Additional Protocol I of the Geneva Convention, which prohibits the use of indiscriminate attacks and the use of disproportionate violence. It prohibits: "an attack which may be expected to cause incidental loss of civilian life, injury to civilians, damage to civilian objects, or a combination thereof, which would be excessive in relation to the concrete and direct military advantage anticipated."[974] This provision implies that before undertaking an attack, which may cause harm to civilians or civilian objects, serious consideration of these interests as well as of the military objectives should take place, to prevent a disproportionate action. It is implicit in the provision that the fact that civilians and civilian objects are hit by military action does not automatically mean that the military action is disproportionate. Yet, this consideration must be made during times of war, which generally offer little opportunity for reflective consideration. It is also a consideration made by those responsible in the field and is sometimes subsequently reviewed by a court. Proportionality applies to military operations against combatants. However, it also applies to the effect of the military action in relation to non-combatants; in other words, the *collateral damage* must be proportional to the military advantage the action is intended to achieve.

970. A|HRC/10/20, Human Rights Situation in Palestine and Other Occupied Arab Territories (11 February 2009).

971. See: http://trendsupdates.com/israel-defends-the-number-of-gaza-victims-as-relatively-low/. See also: IDF Operation Cast Lead, Humanitarian Aspects

972. *Haaretz*, 9 November 2010.

973. See: Gazadeathtoll.org/.

974. Geneva Convention, Additional Protocol 1, art. 51(5)(b).

An assessment of the principle of proportionality can be found in the detailed reasoning given by the Israeli Supreme Court for its unanimous ruling on 14 December 2006 on the question as to whether preventive killings of individual terrorists are permissible from a legal point of view.[975] Innocent civilians (bystanders and family members) are sometimes hit during actions such as these. Israel's Supreme Court considered the issue in accordance with the relevant provisions of international humanitarian law and held that terrorists cannot be regarded as combatants in that they do not present themselves openly as combatants fighting on behalf of an organized movement. One of their tactics is *not* to distinguish themselves from civilians. Though terrorists are civilians, they are not entitled to claim protection under the rules that provide for the protection of civilians in view of the fact that they are actively engaged in hostilities. In this context the Supreme Court referred to Israeli law and also to Article 51(3) of Additional Protocol I, which states, "[C]ivilians shall enjoy the protection afforded by this section, unless and for such time as they take a direct part in hostilities."[976] The Court accepted this provision as an expression of the rule of international customary law and analyzed the different aspects of the provision in detail.[977] In its assessment of the proportionality, the Court included a consideration of other non-fatal means of eliminating terrorists and the need to protect innocent bystanders. The Court came to the conclusion that the harming of terrorists, even if this should result in their death, is permissible on the condition that there is no other less harmful means and on the condition that innocent civilians nearby are not harmed in the process.[978] However, failure to meet the latter condition does not always mean that an action is not permissible. If innocent civilians are harmed, the harm must be proportional, and the criterion of proportionality must be determined on the basis of a consideration of the values involved with a balance being sought between the military advantage and the harm caused to the civilians:

---

975. *HCJ The Public Committee Against* Torture *in Israel* (et al.) *v The Government of Israel* (et al.) The Supreme Court sitting as the High Court of Justice [14 December 2006] in: Israel Supreme Court, Judgments of the Israel Supreme Court: Fighting Terrorism within the Law, Vol. 3 (2006-2009), pp. 85-162.

976. Geneva Convention, Additional Protocol I, art. 51(3).

977. *HCJ The Public Committee Against* Torture *in Israel* (et al.) *v The Government of Israel* (et al.) The Supreme Court sitting as the High Court of Justice [14 December 2006] in: Israel Supreme Court, Judgments of the Israel Supreme Court: Fighting Terrorism within the Law, Vol. 3 (2006-2009), pp. 85-162.

978. *Ibid.*

"Targeting these civilians, even if it results in death, is permitted, provided that there is no other less harmful measure and provided that innocent civilians in the vicinity are not harmed. The harm inflicted on them should be proportionate. That proportionality is determined in accordance with an ethical test, which seeks a balance between the military advantage and the harm to civilians."[979]

21.4 The Goldstone Report on Distinction and Proportionality and Its Aftermath

In order to investigate the military operation of Israel in Gaza in 2008-2009, the UN Human Rights Council appointed a Fact-Finding Mission under the chairmanship of the South African Judge Richard Goldstone.[980] It published a report on 25 September 2009.[981] The Human Rights Council endorsed the Report on 16 October 2009.[982] The report was highly critical of the Israeli military operations. It found that the Israeli forces failed to respect the principles of distinction and proportionality and therefore violated international humanitarian law, as well as international human rights law. Perhaps the most serious allegation in the Goldstone Report was the qualification of the operation as a collective punishment of the Gaza population. It held: "While the Israeli government has sought to portray its operations as essentially a response to rocket attacks in the exercise of its right to self-defense, the UN Fact-Finding Mission considers the plan to have been directed, at least in part, at a different target: the people of Gaza as a whole."[983] It continued, "In this respect, the operations were in furtherance of an overall policy aimed at punishing the Gaza population for its resilience and for its apparent support for Hamas, and possibly with the intent of forcing a change in such support."[984] The Goldstone Report referred to deliberate attacks on civilians and observed that attacks were launched with the intention to spread terror among the civilian population.[985] Alan Dershowitz remarked, "These are among the most serious charges ever leveled by a United Nations organization against a member state."[986]

---

979. Para. 60 of the judgment authored by President (Emeritus) A. Barak, p. 148.

980. Other members were Professor Christine Chinkin, Ms. Hina Jilani and Colonel Desmond Travers.

981. A/HRC/12/48, Report of the United Nations Fact-Finding Mission on the Gaza Conflict. See on the Goldstone Report also Simmons (2012), pp. 309-317.

982. A/HRC/RES/S-12/1.

983. Goldstone Report, para 1883.

984. *Ibid.*, para 1884.

985. *Ibid.*, paa. 1921.

986. Dershowitz (2011), at p. 105.

The Goldstone Report was the target of serious criticism. There were well-founded doubts as to the impartiality of some of the members of the Mission. Before the collection and analysis of the evidence, British Member Professor Chinkin asserted that the Israeli action was not self-defense, but a collective punishment of the inhabitants of Gaza.[987] The contents of the Goldstone Report led to fierce criticism. Experts noted a failure to investigate the use by Hamas of civilians as a human shield. Strong doubts have been raised as to the credibility of the Palestinian sources consulted by the UN Fact-Finding Mission. The willingness of the report's drafters to assume evil intentions on the Israeli side was contrasted with the reluctance to do so in respect of the Hamas side.[988] After a thorough analysis of the Goldstone Report, experts held the legal basis of the UN Fact-Finding Mission's findings to be flawed.[989] Judge Richard Goldstone later reconsidered the findings in the Report. He wrote, "If I had known then what I know now, the Goldstone Report would have been a different document."[990] He also said, "While the investigations published by the Israeli military and recognized in the UN committee's report[991] have established the validity of some incidents that we investigated in cases involving individual soldiers, *they also indicate that civilians were not intentionally targeted as a matter of policy.*"[992] This underlines the doubts expressed by many as to the reliability of the findings of the Goldstone Report. His colleagues in the UN Fact-Finding Mission did not share Goldstone's retraction; in their view, there was no justification for a reconsideration of the Report.[993]

In comparison, the Commission of Inquiry on the Gaza conflict, which was appointed by the UN Human Rights Council on 24 July 2014 to investigate the hostilities of that year in the Gaza Strip, is somewhat more balanced.[994] Canadian law professor William Schabas was appointed as chair. Schabas had previously suggested that Israeli Prime Minister

---

987. Quoted by Alan Dershowitz (ibid., p. 103). See also Simmons (2012, p. 310. She was one of the signatories of an Open letter from a number of academic lawyers published in *The Sunday Times* (11 January 2009), where this opinion was expressed.

988. See on these issues: Landes (2011), pp. 45-67 and also Dershowitz (2011), mentioned in note 10.

989. See in Steinberg & Herzberg (2011) the articles of Berkovitz (2011), pp. 182-202; Blank (2011), pp. 203-264; and Bell (2011), pp. 265-275.

990. *The Washington Post*, 2 April 2011.

991. Goldstone refers here to A/HRC/16/24, Report of the Committee of independent experts in international humanitarian and human rights law, established pursuant to Council resolution 13/9, of 18 March 2011.

992. *The Washington Post*, 2 April 2011 (emphasis added).

993. Statement issued by members of the UN Mission on the Gaza War, in: The Guardian, 14 April 2011.

994. A/HRC/RES/S-21/1.

Benjamin Netanyahu and former President Shimon Peres should be investigated for war crimes. In 2012, he did advisory work for the PLO. After a complaint by Israel, Schabas resigned on 2 February 2015. If he had not done so, the commission would not have been able to uphold even the impression of impartiality. The American Justice Mary McGowan Davis succeeded Schabas as chair. The Commission of Inquiry Report was published on 24 June 2015.[995] This report may be criticized on important points. To give an important example: in giving context, the report refers to the "protracted occupation of the West Bank" including East Jerusalem and the Gaza Strip, the blockade of Gaza by Israel,[996] contentious issues addressed earlier in this book,[997] as well as real threats to the security of Israel. However, it systematically ignores the ideology of Hamas, which denies Israel the right to existence and which calls for the killing of Jews,[998] which is arguably the most important aspect of the context of the Gaza conflict.[999] As compared to the Goldstone Report, however, the Commission of Inquiry Report is more critical of Palestinian violence, mentioning also the security threats to Israel.

21.5 Case Study: The Gaza Flotilla Incident

21.5.1 General

The aftermath of the Gaza War in 2008-2009 led to a legal controversy on the so-called Gaza flotilla incident. In this case issues of both *jus ad bellum* and *jus in bello* were at stake. It provoked an avalanche of criticism against the Israeli government and its military forces. During the Gaza-War of 2008-2009, Israel imposed a naval blockade on the Hamas-controlled Gaza Strip.[1000] On 31 May 2010, a group of six vessels tried to break the blockade, with the purpose to put an end to what was called the "siege of Gaza" and to bring humanitarian goods to the Gaza Strip. To prevent this, the Israeli IDF forces captured the vessels and brought them to the Port of Ashdod. In this incident, the activists and the IDF used force. Nine activists sailing on the main ship, the *Mavi Marmara*, were killed; 55 activists and 9 IDF soldiers were wounded. Almost immediately and

995. A/HRC/29/52, Report of the independent commission of inquiry established pursuant to Human Rights Council resolution S-21/1.

996. *Ibid.*, paragraphs 14-19, pp. 5 and 6.

997. See Chapters 5, 7 and 8.

998. See Hamas Covenant 1988, arts 7, 11, 13 and 14.

999. Cf. also David Horowitz, David (2015): http://www.timesofisrael.com/shame-on-you-mary-mcgowan-davis/ (visited: 11 September 2017).

1000. On 3January 2009.

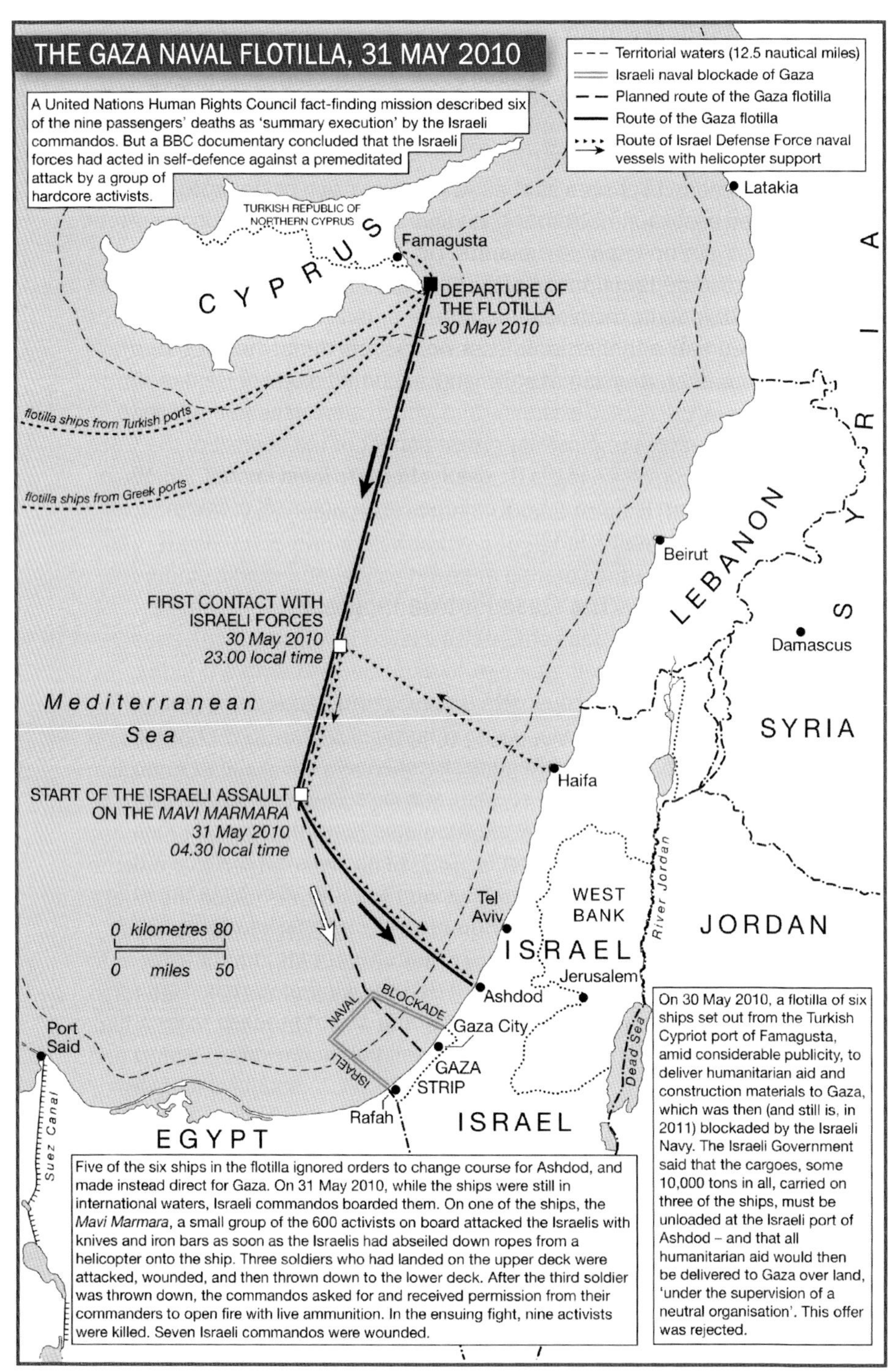
THE GAZA NAVAL FLOTILLA, 31 MAY 2010
Territorial waters (12.5 nautical miles)
Israeli naval blockade of Gaza
Planned route of the Gaza flotilla
Route of the Gaza flotilla
Route of Israel Defense Force naval vessels with helicopter support
A United Nations Human Rights Council fact-finding mission described six of the nine passengers' deaths as 'summary execution' by the Israeli commandos. But a BBC documentary concluded that the Israeli forces had acted in self-defence against a premeditated attack by a group of hardcore activists.
TURKISH REPUBLIC OF NORTHERN CYPRUS
CYPRUS
Famagusta
DEPARTURE OF THE FLOTILLA
30 May 2010
Latakia
flotilla ships from Turkish ports
flotilla ships from Greek ports
FIRST CONTACT WITH ISRAELI FORCES
30 May 2010
23.00 local time
Mediterranean Sea
START OF THE ISRAELI ASSAULT ON THE MAVI MARMARA
31 May 2010
04.30 local time
0 kilometres 80
0 miles 50
Beirut
LEBANON
SYRIA
Damascus
Haifa
Tel Aviv
WEST BANK
River Jordan
JORDAN
ISRAEL
Jerusalem
Ashdod
NAVAL BLOCKADE
ISRAELI
Gaza City
GAZA STRIP
Dead Sea
Port Said
Rafah
ISRAEL
EGYPT
Suez Canal
On 30 May 2010, a flotilla of six ships set out from the Turkish Cypriot port of Famagusta, amid considerable publicity, to deliver humanitarian aid and construction materials to Gaza, which was then (and still is, in 2011) blockaded by the Israeli Navy. The Israeli Government said that the cargoes, some 10,000 tons in all, carried on three of the ships, must be unloaded at the Israeli port of Ashdod – and that all humanitarian aid would then be delivered to Gaza over land, 'under the supervision of a neutral organisation'. This offer was rejected.
Five of the six ships in the flotilla ignored orders to change course for Ashdod, and made instead direct for Gaza. On 31 May 2010, while the ships were still in international waters, Israeli commandos boarded them. On one of the ships, the Mavi Marmara, a small group of the 600 activists on board attacked the Israelis with knives and iron bars as soon as the Israelis had abseiled down ropes from a helicopter onto the ship. Three soldiers who had landed on the upper deck were attacked, wounded, and then thrown down to the lower deck. After the third soldier was thrown down, the commandos asked for and received permission from their commanders to open fire with live ammunition. In the ensuing fight, nine activists were killed. Seven Israeli commandos were wounded.

without further investigation, Israel's actions were condemned by UN Secretary General Ban Ki Moon[1001] and by Richard Falk, the UN Special Rapporteur on the Situation of Human Rights in the "Occupied Palestinian Territories"—who on the day of the action declared that it was a violation of international law.[1002] That conclusion was arguably too quickly drawn. The incident has been investigated by several commissions. established by the Human Rights Council,[1003] the Israeli government (the so-called Turkel Commission, after its chairman, the retired Justice Jacob Turkel[1004]), the Secretary-General of the UN,[1005] and the Turkish government.[1006] Not surprisingly, each of these bodies came to different conclusions. On the basis of the findings of these commissions it can in any case not be concluded that a violation of international law was obvious, as was suggested by Falk.

21.5.2 The Legitimacy of the Blockade

The violence used by Hamas, targeting Israeli citizens from the Gaza Strip by launching rockets, missiles and mortar bombs into Israeli territory, entitled Israel to exert its inherent right to self-defense, which is recognized in Article 51 of the UN Charter.[1007] Within that framework, in principle, a naval blockade may be justified. It was established to prevent the import into Gaza of weapons, ammunition, military supplies, terrorists, and money, which could be used against Israel. It also ensures the prevention of the departure of terrorists, vessels with explosives and other threats from Gaza.

The applicable law of naval warfare is primarily customary law. It has been codified in the San Remo Manual on International Law Applicable to Armed Conflicts at Sea.[1008] There are strong arguments that support the

---

1001. UN News Center, 31 May 2010.

1002. Quoted by Peter Berkowitz (2011 b).

1003. Report of the international fact-finding mission to investigate violations of international law, including international humanitarian and human rights law, resulting from the Israeli attacks on the flotilla of ships carrying humanitarian assistance, A/HRC/15/21, 27 September 2010.

1004. The Public Commission to Examine the Maritime Incident of 31 May 2010. The Turkel Commission, January 2011, Report, part one. See: http://www.pmo.gov.il/SiteCollectionDocuments/turkel_eng_a.pdf (visited: 20 April 2018).

1005. Report of the Secretary-General's Panel of Inquiry on the 31 May 2010 Flottila Incident, September 2011.

1006. Report of the Israeli Attack on the Humanitarian Aid Convoy to Gaza on 31 May 2010, Turkish National Commission of Inquiry, February 2011, Ankara.

1007. UN Charter, art. 51.

1008. International Institute of Humanitarian Law, *San Remo Manual on International Law Applicable to Armed Conflicts at Sea*, 12 June 1994.

conclusion that Israel complied with the legal requirements for a naval blockade.[1009] It is required that such a blockade be declared and notified to the belligerents and to neutral States, specifying its commencement, duration, location, and extent.[1010] Israel did so in a Notice to Mariners, issued on 3 January 2009.[1011] A further requirement is that the blockade should be effective.[1012] This means that a blockade should not be fictitious. Accordingly, all ships that headed for the Gaza Strip were stopped, irrespective of their registration. In so doing, the requirement of impartiality was met.[1013] The flotilla in question was composed of ships flagged in different countries. The main ship, the *Mavi Marmara*, was registered in the Union of the Comores. Other ships were registered in Kiribati, Turkey, Togo, Greece, the USA, and Cambodia. The San Remo Manual also provides that a blockade may not block access to ports and coasts of neutral states, which was not the case when the Israeli forces enforced the blockade.[1014]

A blockade is also prohibited if it has the sole purpose of starving the civilian population or denying other objects essential for survival.[1015] Some of the ships did contain humanitarian supplies; however, this was not the primary purpose of the expedition. It would be very impractical to deliver humanitarian goods to Gaza by sea; because there is not a proper port to handle the delivery of goods. This would only be possible by the transfer of goods from the sea-ships into smaller vessels. The main purpose of the flotilla was to break the blockade and to de-legitimize Israel. In this connection, it is important to notice that the flotilla was led by a Turkish "humanitarian organization" (The Foundation for Human Rights, Freedoms and Humanitarian Relief—IHH); IHH is known as a radical Islamic supporter of Hamas.[1016] In light of these facts, it cannot be held that the Israeli blockade had the purpose to starve the population of Gaza. Although the situation of the people in Gaza under the Hamas regime is far from what an ordinary decent life of the civilian population should entail, Israel has always ensured the provision of basic humanitarian goods, albeit under

1009. See, *inter alia*, Makowski; Farrant (2013); Dershowitz (2010), Berkowitz (2011 b); Benoliel (2011), See for an opposite view: Guilfoyle (2011).

1010. Arts. 93-94 (the Articles mentioned here and in the following passages refer to the San Remo Manual).

1011. Notice to Mariners, issued 3 January 2009.

1012. Art. 95.

1013. Art. 100.

1014. Art. 99.

1015. Art. 102 (a).

1016. Intelligence and Terrorism Information Centre, 26 May 2010.

strict supervision due to realistic security concerns. During the enforcement of the blockade, Israeli naval forces explicitly invited the participants in the flotilla to enter the Ashdod Port in order to deliver the humanitarian goods for the population via the land crossings. In doing so, Israel facilitated the transport of humanitarian supplies into the Gaza Strip.

According to international law, a blockade is also prohibited in the event the damage to the civilian population is excessive in relation to the anticipated military advantage.[1017] This requires balancing the continuing serious threats to the people of Israel from the Gaza Strip and the transfer of humanitarian supplies to its population. A careful and detailed consideration of these aspects in the report of the Turkel Commission leads to the convincing conclusion that the proportionality requirement was met.

21.5.3 Enforcement of the Blockade

Not only the legitimacy of the blockade as such, but also the manner in which it was enforced was the subject of a fierce debate. In order to enforce a blockade, states have the right to capture ships and in case of resistance even to attack them.[1018] The IDF forces intervened on the high seas. Under the law of naval warfare, the capture of vessels is permitted within the area of operations of the warships concerned where that is necessary to make the blockade effective.[1019] In the case of the flotilla, it was very clear that its vessels purposely headed for the Gaza coast in order to break the blockade. Warnings to divert their course were made to no avail. Another issue was the use of violence by the soldiers, as a consequence of which nine activists were killed and 55 activists and 9 IDF soldiers were wounded. The enforcement of a naval blockade should be in conformity with the principles of distinction (between combatants and non-combatants), precaution and proportionality.[1020] A meticulous investigation, into the details of the action wherein the soldiers were threatened by lethal force, led the Turkel Commission to conclude that—in most cases—the use of force was in conformity with the law. In some cases, however, it found itself unable to come to this conclusion due to lack of evidence.

1017. Art. 102(b).

1018. Art. 98.

1019. Art. 146 (f).

1020 Add a supporting citation that defines the principles of distinction.

21.5.4 Referral to the ICC

The legal and political debate regarding the flotilla incident is still ongoing. In this regard, the Union of the Comores, the flag-state of the main vessel, the *Mavi Marmara*, has requested the Prosecutor of the International Criminal Court (ICC) to start an investigation into the incident, in accordance with Article 14 of the Statute of the ICC (referral of a situation by a State Party). The Comores, a State Party to the Statute of the ICC, holds that this court has jurisdiction, because the alleged crimes took place on board a vessel sailing under its flag.[1021] The ICC has received four other communications under Article 15 of the Statute, presumably submitted by NGOs, who want to urge the ICC Prosecutor to initiate proceedings against the officials held responsible for the incident. The Office of the Prosecutor has started a preliminary investigation in order to establish whether the criteria for opening an investigation have been met.[1022] On 6 November 2014, the ICC Prosecutor published a report in conformity with Article 53 (1)(c) of the Statute.[1023] According to this provision, the ICC Prosecutor has to consider *inter alia* whether, taking into account the gravity of the crime and the interest of the victims, there are reasons to believe that an investigation would not serve the interests of justice. In this Report, she concluded, that although the information provided a reasonable basis to believe that war crimes had been committed, the potential case(s) that would likely arise from the investigation would not be of sufficient gravity to justify further action by the ICC. This/these case(s) would therefore be inadmissible pursuant to Article 17(1) d and 53(1)b of the Statute. This was not the end of the involvement of the ICC in the flotilla affair. At the request of the Union of the Comores, the Pre-Trial Camber of the Court reviewed the decision of the ICC Prosecutor. In a majority decision (2 to 1) of the 16th of July 2015, the Chamber requested the ICC Prosecutor to reconsider her decision not to initiate an investigation into the situation.[1024] Subsequently, the ICC Prosecutor appealed the decision. In a majority decision (3 to 2) of 6 November 2015, the Appeals Chamber declared the appeal inadmissible.[1025] In its decision, the Appeals Chamber made the interesting observation that

1021. ICC-01/13-1-Anx2, p. 3.

1022. ICC: The Office of the Prosecutor, *Report on Preliminary Examination Activities 2013*, November 2013, pp. 21-24.

1023. ICC: The Office of the Prosecutor, *Situation on Registered Vessels of Comoros, Greece and Cambodia. Article 53(1) Report,* 6 November 2014.

1024. International Criminal Court, Pre-Trial Camber I, ICC-01/13, 16 July 2015; Judge Kovács dissenting.

1025. International Criminal Court, Appeals Chamber, ICC-01/13 OA, 6 November 2015; Judges Fernandez de Gumendi and Van den Wyngaert dissenting.

"the Prosecutor is obliged to reconsider her decision not to investigate, but [that she] retains ultimate discretion over how to proceed."[1026] On 29 November 2017 the ICC Prosecutor informed the Pre-Trial Chamber of her final decision. She remained of the view that the information did not provide a reasonable basis to proceed with an investigation, because of the absence of a case of sufficient gravity arising from the situation.[1027] That means that the flotilla case is closed.

1026. *Ibid.*, para 59.

1027. ICC: The Office of the Prosecutor, *Report on Preliminary Examination Activities 2017*, 4 December 2017, pp. 68-73.

22. Trial of Israeli and Palestinian Officials for War Crimes?

"Even when the artillery booms and the Muses are silent, law exists and acts and decides what is permitted and what is forbidden, what is legal and what is illegal. And when law exists, courts also exist to adjudicate what is permitted and what is forbidden, what is legal and what is illegal."

Aharon Barak, President of the Israel Supreme Court, in Case H.C. 2161/96, Rabbi Said Sharif v. Military Commander [1028]

22.1 Introduction

After the discussion of the allegations of violations of international humanitarian law, the question arises whether Israeli political and military officials could be prosecuted for war crimes. As previously stated, efforts have been and are being made to bring Israeli officials before the International Criminal Court (ICC) in The Hague. Another possibility that has been suggested is trial by a national court in a country with legislation that provides for such a situation, but that has its own challenges. When discussing these options, we should not forget that the most obvious approach in case of suspicion of war crimes committed by Israeli military or civil officials is prosecution before a national Israeli court. The Israeli system of military justice ensures that transgressions of international humanitarian law, which have been implemented in national Israeli law, will be investigated, prosecuted and tried.

22.2 Trial by the International Criminal Court (ICC)?

22.2.1 General

The ICC was established under the Rome Statute, which entered into force on 1 July 2002. It has jurisdiction over persons suspected of having

1028. Case H.C. 2161/96, Rabbi Said Sharif v. Military Commander, 50 (4) P.D. 485, 491, in: Israel Supreme Court Judgments of the Israel Supreme Court: Fighting Terrorism within the Law, Volume 1, 21.

committed serious war crimes of international significance, as defined in the Statute of the Court. The creation of the ICC is revolutionary in terms of its impact and significance on the development of international law and procedure. There have been and are other international criminal tribunals, but all *ad hoc* in nature. Their jurisdiction was/is limited to a specific conflict. The International Military Tribunal at Nuremberg and the International Criminal Tribunal for the Former Yugoslavia at The Hague are examples. The jurisdiction and procedures of the ICC constitute a new *permanent* international mechanism for implementing criminal justice and, as such, are much broader than any of the other international human rights mechanisms. Perhaps the most significant impact that the ICC has on international law is that its power constitutes a major limitation on national sovereignty. Criminal prosecution traditionally has been the exclusive domain of sovereign states. The states party to the Rome Statute have ceded significant power to the ICC in terms of prosecuting political and military officials for major crimes. The Statute is applicable without any distinction based on official capacity.[1029] Although the ICC is an independent body, NGOs had a major role in the creation of the ICC and continue to exert significant influence (i.e. by submissions to the ICC). This is possible within the framework of Article 15 of the Statute, which allows the ICC Prosecutor to start an investigation *proprio motu* on the basis of information on crimes within the jurisdiction of the ICC. NGOs may be involved in the gathering of evidence in specific cases, and they monitor the work of the ICC.

22.2.2 Crimes

The three main categories of crimes, which are covered by the Rome Statute, are: genocide, crimes against humanity, and war crimes.

- "Genocide" is defined as any act committed with intent to destroy, in whole or in part, a national, ethnical, racial, or religious group, as such. It includes killing members of the group, causing serious bodily or mental harm to members of the group, deliberately inflicting on the group conditions of life calculated to bring about its physical destruction in whole or in part, preventing births within the group, or forcibly transferring children of the group to another group.[1030]
- "Crimes against humanity" are defined as violent acts committed as part of a widespread or systematic attack directed against any civilian population, with knowledge of the attack. They include

1029. Statute of the ICC, art. 27.

1030. *Ibid.*, art. 6.

murder, extermination, enslavement, deportation or forcible transfer of population, imprisonment, torture etc. They also includes "the crime of apartheid" or any "other inhumane acts of a similar character intentionally causing great suffering, or serious injury to body or to mental or physical health."[1031]

- "War crimes" are defined as grave breaches of the Geneva Conventions of 12 August 1949 and other serious violations of the laws and customs applicable in international armed conflict, within the established framework of international law. Under this heading, a whole catalogue of crimes is included in the Statute, among these intentional attacks against the civilian population, pillaging a town, the use of asphyxiating or poisonous gas, and rape.[1032]

22.2.3 **States Parties**

As of 2 November 2017 there were 123 states party to the ICC.[1033] Israel is not a state party. It signed the Statute of the ICC on 31 December 2000 as an indication of its hope that the ICC would remain true to the goals of its founders, but like many other states, Israel has not yet ratified the treaty. In a letter received by the Secretary-General of the UN on 28 August 2002, Israel declared that it did not intend to become a state party.[1034] The main reason was its concern that the ICC was not sufficiently impartial and would be unduly influenced by political parties and concerns, a valid concern given the massive politicization of the UN Human Rights bodies. In particular, Israel fundamentally objected to the inclusion of "the transfer, directly or *indirectly* by the Occupying Power of parts of its own civilian population into the territory it occupies" as a war crime under the Rome Statute.[1035] This provision was added to the Statute at the insistence of the Arab Bloc. It was included and directly intended to refer to the Israeli settlements in the disputed territories, in the hope that the ICC could prosecute those responsible. According to Israel:

> **"This particular offense represents neither a grave breach of the Fourth Geneva Convention, nor does it reflect customary international law. The inclusion of this offense, under the pressure of Arab states, and the**

1031. *Ibid.*, art. 7.

1032. *Ibid.*, art. 8.

1033. According to the information provided by the ICC. Recently Burundi withdrew. Some other African states are reconsidering their membership.

1034. www.amicc.org/ICC/ratifications.

1035. The Rome Statute, art. 8(2)(b)(viii) (emphasis added).

addition of the phrase 'directly or indirectly,' is clearly intended to try to use the court to force the issue of Israeli settlements without the need for negotiation as agreed between the sides."[1036]

Article 8(2)(b)(viii) of the Statute of the ICC goes significantly further than Article 49(6) of the Fourth Geneva Convention, which only states that an Occupying Power "shall not deport or transfer parts of its own civilian population into the territory it occupies." By adding the words "directly or indirectly," the Rome Statute potentially expands the Geneva Convention to cover situations, which were not intended to constitute war crimes. Even apart from this addition, as discussed above, the voluntary establishment of a Jewish community in Judea or Samaria following Israel's victory in the defensive 1967 Six Day War—even if supported or allowed by official Israeli government policy—cannot by any stretch of the imagination be regarded as a war crime which the framers of the Fourth Geneva Convention intended to outlaw.

On 1 April 2015, the Statute of the ICC entered into force for Palestine.[1037] This is the outcome of a remarkable development, which is difficult to reconcile with the concept of statehood under international law. On 22 January 2009, the Minister of Justice of the Government of Palestine declared to accept *ad hoc* the jurisdiction of the Court pursuant to Article 12(3) of the Statute in order to establish the jurisdiction of the ICC in respect of "acts committed on the territory of Palestine since 1 July 2002." This declaration was, however, unsuccessful. The Office of the ICC Prosecutor stated, "It is for the relevant bodies at the United Nations or the Assembly of the States Parties to make a legal determination whether Palestine qualifies as a State for the purpose of acceding to the Rome Statute."[1038]

The next step was the upgrading of "Palestine" within the General Assembly of the UN to the status of a Non-Member Observer State on 29 November 2012.[1039] This did not immediately have an effect on the position of Palestine under the ICC. However, it later became clear that the upgrading indeed paved the way for Palestine to the ICC. The Office of the Prosecutor stated in 2015 that from 29 November 2012, Palestine was able to accept the jurisdiction of the ICC pursuant to Article 12(3) of

1036. See Kohn (2009).

1037. Press Release 1 April 2015, ICC-CPI-20150401-PR1103.

1038. See ICC: The Office of the Prosecutor, Report on Preliminary Examination Activities 2013, November 2013, pp. 53-54.

1039. UN G.A. Res. 67/19, 'Status of Palestine in the United Nations', 4 December 2012, UN Doc. A/RES/67/19.

the Statute.[1040] The ICC Prosecutor apparently agreed with John Dugard on this issue, who in an article published in 2013, had criticized the ICC Prosecutor and her predecessor for not investigating "Palestinian issues."[1041] On 1 January 2015, Palestine accepted the jurisdiction of the ICC in a document handed to the Registrar of the Court.[1042] The next day, Palestine acceded to the Statute of the ICC.[1043] The President of the Assembly of States Parties to the Rome Statute welcomed this on 7 January 2015.[1044] This new legal situation led the Prosecutor of the ICC to start a preliminary examination of the situation in Palestine on 16 January 2015.[1045]

This whole development is a reason for concern. Both the acceptance of the jurisdiction of the ICC pursuant to Article 12(3) of the Statute and accession to the Rome Statute in accordance with Article 125 thereof presupposes the statehood of the actor concerned.[1046] According to the established rules of international law, Palestine is not a state. Although significant powers have been transferred to the Palestinian Authority, given the control exercised by Israel, the Palestinian Authority cannot be considered to have the sovereign authority of an independent state under international law.[1047]

22.2.4 Jurisdiction

Articles 12 and 13 of the Statute determine the jurisdiction the ICC. First, the ICC has jurisdiction in case of suspicion of a crime committed on the *territory* of a state that has accepted the jurisdiction of the ICC (through ratification or *ad hoc*) or on board a vessel or aircraft registered in such a state.[1048] This means that a case may be brought against Israelis, if they are accused of committing a war crime on the territory (or on board a vessel or aircraft) of a state that has accepted the jurisdiction

---

1040. Press Release of 16 January 2015, ICC-OTP-20150116-PR1083.

1041. Dugard (2013), pp. 563-570: the term is used on p. 568.

1042. Press Release of 5 January 2015, ICC-CPI-20150105-PR1080.

1043. January 2, 2015. For Palestine the Statute entered into force on 1 April 2015.

1044. Press Release of 7 January 2015, ICC-ASP-20150107-PR1082.

1045. Press Release of 16 January 2015, ICC-OTP-20150116-PR1083.

1046. Statute of the ICC, arts 12(3) and 125.

1047. See discussion on the question of Palestinian statehood above in Chapter 14. See, e.g., Quigley, J. (2009); http://iccforum.com/media/background/gaza/2009-05-19_Quigley_Memo_on_Palestine_Declaration.pdf (visited: 11 September 2017).

1048. Statute of the ICC, arts 12(2)(a) and 12(3).

of the ICC.[1049] In connection with the recent conflicts, it is important to note that Lebanon and Syria are not parties to the Statute of the ICC. It is more likely that, if the disputed territories are considered to be territory of Palestine, that jurisdiction under this heading concerning alleged crimes of Israelis in these territories may be held to be established, unless the ICC determines that Palestine is not a state according to international law, irrespective of the opinion of political bodies and the Prosecutor on that issue. Furthermore, the jurisdiction of the ICC extends to a person accused of a crime who is a *national* of a State that has accepted the ICC's jurisdiction.[1050] Because Israel has not ratified the Rome Statute, its political and military officials cannot be prosecuted before the ICC. However, the ICC could possibly try a citizen of the State of Israel, who is also a citizen of a State that is a party to the Statute. The Statute also provides for the possibility of an exception to the conditions for jurisdiction elaborated in the preceding lines in a case in which the UN Security Council decides to put a case before the Prosecutor of the ICC in accordance with Chapter VII of the UN Charter.[1051] This Chapter holds that the UN Security Council has the power to maintain peace in the event of a threat to international peace and security.[1052] Should this be the case, the requirement of acceptance of the jurisdiction of the ICC by the state concerned is no longer a precondition.[1053] In this context, Bolivia has asked the UN Security Council to bring the situation in the Gaza Strip before the ICC.[1054] So far, this has been unsuccessful. Nonetheless, there remains a chance—however theoretical—that Israeli politicians or IDF personnel could face prosecution for war crimes or other crimes under the Rome Statute via this avenue. A decision of the Security Council in this connection is subject to the veto power of its permanent members.

22.2.5 Admissibility

Even in cases that fall within the jurisdiction of the ICC, it will not exercise its jurisdiction when the case is inadmissible according to Article 17 of the Statute. As in the case of the Gaza flotilla, this is at stake where the case is not of sufficient gravity to justify further action by the ICC.[1055] A

1049. This is at stake in the referral of the Flotilla incident by the Union of the Comores.

1050. Statute of the ICC, arts 12(2)(b) and 12(3).

1051. *Ibid.*, arts 12 and 13(b).

1052. UN Charter, Chapter VII.

1053. *Ibid.*

1054. GA/10809/Rev.1*.

1055. Statute of the ICC, art 17(1)(d).

case can also be declared inadmissible when it has or is being investigated or prosecuted by a state which has jurisdiction over it, unless the state is unwilling or genuinely unable to carry out the investigation or prosecution.[1056] This demonstrates that the jurisdiction of the ICC is only complementary to the jurisdiction of national courts. The assumption is: in principle, the crimes defined by the Statute will be prosecuted before national judges. Applied to the case of Israel, it seems to be unlikely that a case against Israeli military of political officials would lead to a conviction by the ICC, having regard to the fact that Israel has a well-functioning and independent justice system both in the civil and in the military field.[1057] For example, the Military Advocate General (MAG) investigated many allegations of misconduct by soldiers during *Operation Cast Lead.*[1058] A Committee of independent experts, established by the Human Rights Council in the context of the follow-up of the Goldstone Mission, reported in March of 2011 that more than 400 allegations of misconduct were investigated by Israel. A number of the investigations by the MAG resulted in criminal investigations and prosecutions.[1059] In some cases, soldiers have been convicted.[1060] In contrast, the same committee also observed that what it called the de facto Gaza authorities did not conduct any investigations into the launching of rocket and mortar attacks against Israel.[1061]

22.3 Trial by a National Court outside Israel?

While it seems unlikely that citizens of the State of Israel will be brought to trial before the ICC, it is not inconceivable that they might be put on trial before national courts in states with national war crimes legislation that enshrines the concept of "universal jurisdiction." In other words, states with national courts which have jurisdiction in case of criminal prosecutions, even if there are no national interests involved. International law only authorizes the assertion of universal jurisdiction over the most serious of crimes, which are listed in the Rome Statute. In 1961, the District Court of

1056. *Ibid.*, art. 17(1)(a).

1057. See, *inter alia*, Baruch (2014), at pp. 70-71.

1058. See The State of Israel, *Gaza Operation Investigations. Second Update*, July 2010.

1059. A/HRC/16/24, Report of the Committee of independent experts in international humanitarian and human rights law, established pursuant to Council resolution 13/9, of 18 March 2011, at pp. 6, 17, 21 and 23.

1060. '2 soldiers convicted of using boy as human shield', The Jerusalem Post, 4 October 2010.

1061. A/HRC/16/24, Report of the Committee of independent experts in international humanitarian and human rights law, established pursuant to Council resolution 13/9, of 18 March 2011, at pp. 6, 17, 21 and 23.

Jerusalem cited the universality principle (and the protection principle) as the basis for its jurisdiction, when it sentenced Adolf Eichmann to death for *inter alia* crimes against humanity.[1062] This principle is enshrined in national criminal legislation in a number of countries, such as Belgium. In that country, preparations were made to prosecute the Israeli Prime Minister Ariel Sharon, as well as Amos Yaron, the Director-General of Israel's Defense Ministry, for their alleged involvement in the bloodbath in the Palestinian refugee camps of Sabra and Shatila in Lebanon.[1063] The Belgian *Cour de Cassation* (Supreme Court) ruled in a judgment on 12 February 2003 that Ariel Sharon could not be prosecuted, because of the immunity he enjoyed under international law as Prime Minister of a foreign state. In the case of Yaron, the Belgian Supreme Court ruled that the fact that he was not present in Belgium did not exclude the possibility of prosecution.[1064] The prosecution did not proceed, because Belgian legislation on universal jurisdiction was changed,[1065] which led the Supreme Court to rule in a decision on 24 September 2003 that the case should be withdrawn from Belgian jurisdiction.[1066]

Other attempts have been made to prosecute Israeli officials before national courts. For example, a Spanish court investigated the possibility of trying persons alleged to be responsible for an Israeli air attack on a building in the Gaza Strip in 2002, which was intended to liquidate a Hamas leader and caused the deaths of 14 other people. Seven political and military leaders were alleged to be responsible for the attack. The Spanish Court has since withdrawn the prosecution of this case on the basis that the case is now being investigated in Israel.[1067] However, in November of 2015, a Spanish judge issued an arrest warrant against Prime Minister Netanyahu and seven other former and current Israeli government officials, in connection with the flotilla incident.[1068] Consequently, in theory, they risk arrest, if they set foot on Spanish soil. Due to the rule of international law that provides immunity in respect of national criminal jurisdiction, it is unlikely that politicians in office would

1062. District Court of Jerusalem, 12 December 1961, Criminal case no. 40/61 *(Eichmann).*

1063. Kattan (2004-2005).

1064. Cour de Cassation de Belgique, Arrêt 12 février 2003 [Supreme Court, Judgment 12 February 2003].

1065. Panàkovà (2011), at pp. 61-64.

1066. Cour de Cassation de Belgique, Arrêt 24 septembre 2003 [Supreme Court, Judgment 24 September 2003].

1067. National High Court, Criminal Division, Plenary Session Appeal No.31/09, Ruling No. 1/09, 9 July 2009 (unofficial translation), see: ccrjustice.org/...National%20High%20Court%20-%2

1068. *The Jerusalem Post*, 16 November 2015.

be arrested and prosecuted.[1069] The same immunity does not extend to military officials. In December of 2015, an IDF officer was detained for questioning in Britain, because of allegations that he was involved in war crimes in Gaza. He was only released after intervention by the Foreign Office.[1070] Thus, there are reasons for Israeli politicians and military to be on the alert when visiting certain countries. Nevertheless, there are very few successful examples of the application of the universality principle, which should be confined to very exceptional cases. Whether the country in question has an effective judicial system—capable of prosecuting and convicting members of the armed forces and even politicians found guilty of misconduct—is a relevant factor. In this respect, Israel has a highly sophisticated and rigorous legal system. There are many cases in which members of the Israeli armed forces have had to account for their actions before military courts. In addition, the Israeli Knesset performs an important monitoring function which can lead to an investigation by a parliamentary committee of inquiry, such as the inquiry conducted in connection with the Yom Kippur War and the possible involvement of Ariel Sharon in the Sabra and Shatila massacres.[1071] Israel is an open society where abuses can be exposed. The application of the universality principle is only necessary in situations in which perpetrators of war crimes, crimes against humanity and genocide are otherwise likely to get off scot-free because of an inadequate judicial system. This is not the case in Israel.

Finally, one additional remark has to be made. According to international law, it is not only the universality principle that provides a basis for national jurisdiction regarding acts committed outside the national territory. The passive personality principle and protective principle also allow for the establishment of national jurisdiction in case nationals or national interest are affected outside the territory of the state concerned.[1072] This was an issue in a criminal complaint filed by one of the participants in the Gaza flotilla, Inge Höger, who was a member of the German Parliament (Bundestag) for the extreme left wing party *Die Linke*. She wanted the German Federal Attorney General *(Generalbundesanwalt)* to start criminal proceedings against members

1069. See the Judgment of the ICJ in the Case Concerning the Arrest Warrant of 11 April 2000 (Democratic Republic of the Congo v. Belgium), I.C.J. Reports 2002, p. 3 (14 February 2002).

1070. *The Jerusalem Post*, 13 December 2015.

1071. Gilbert (1998), pp. 509-511.

1072. Akehurst (1975), pp.131-132.

of the IDF.[1073] The Attorney General rejected the complaint and decided not to prosecute, because acts of members of the IDF against her did not qualify as criminal according to German law.

1073. Der Generalbundesanwalt beim Bundesgerichtshof [The Federal Attorney General at the Federal Supreme Court], 30 September 2014. See also: The Jerusalem Post, 29 January 2015.

Executive Summary and Conclusions

Executive Summary and Conclusions

1. Israel on Trial

1.1 This study has been carried out in response to the controversial United Nations (UN) Security Council Resolution 2334 (23 December 2016). It is an attempt to critically assess the interpretation and application of international law in that resolution. As the resolution relies on the Advisory Opinion of the International Court of Justice (ICJ) in the *Wall* case (2004), this book is also a critique of that Opinion. Consequently, it is critical of numerous other resolutions of UN organs in respect of the Israeli/Palestinian conflict that are based a similar approach. Our primary contention is that the ICJ, the UN Security Council and UN General Assembly, and as a result many other institutions, have failed to properly frame the issues requiring solution, and have adopted biased, and in some respects, incorrect interpretations of international law.

1.2 Resolution 2334 and the 2004 ICJ Advisory Opinion advance what we call the "current legal paradigm." This paradigm has four main elements:

a. International peace and security requires the creation of a Palestinian state;
b. This state should be based on the "4 June 1967 borders" as the only possible solution to these competing claims. The UN has jurisdiction to require compliance with these borders;
c. Any action taken by Israel that threatens that outcome is seen as an infringement of international law, and Israel is obliged to cooperate with the creation of the State of Palestine based on the 4 June 1967 lines; and
d. All other states are responsible to ensure that Israel meets these obligations.

1.3 The current legal paradigm relies on a particular interpretation of five inter-related ideas on aspects of international law: statehood, territorial sovereignty, self-determination, human rights and humanitarian law. The understanding of how international law in these fields applies to the case of Israel/Palestine is challenging. One has to take into account a changing world and changing perceptions of international law, combined with the extremely complex historical, political and legal background of these territories and the peoples involved. In our view, the UN Security Council and the ICJ failed to take adequate account of this complex background, and gave insufficient attention to the rights of the Jewish people to self-determination and the status of Israel as a sovereign state enjoying the right to sovereign equality.

1.4 We argue that:

a. Israel has the right to exist as a sovereign state enjoying peace and security as all other states;
b. Israel is under no obligation to withdraw from the "occupied territories" or remove Israeli settlements;
c. the creation of a State of Palestine is not required under international law;
d. even if it were, the UN and its Member States have no jurisdiction to determine the borders between that state and the State of Israel; in any event, the borders mandated in Resolution 2334 (the "4 June 1967 lines") infringe on Israel's rights under international law; and
e. third states are under no obligation to enforce the "two-state solution" or facilitate the creation of the State of Palestine; on the contrary, to do so in the terms of Resolution 2334 constitutes a fundamental infringement of Israel's rights.

1.5 A fundamental review of the current legal paradigm is urgent and important for two main reasons:

a. The discriminatory interpretation and application of international law to the Israel/Palestine conflict is not only unfair to Israel, it is producing perverse results and impeding a negotiated solution; and
b. The "instrumental" use of international law to achieve political or military goals conflicts with the idea of an international legal order based on fairness and objectivity. International law will only retain its credibility and usefulness as a set of international norms in the pursuit of peace if it is applied fairly, objectively, reasonably and with full regard to both context and historic realities.

2. Israel and International Law

2.1 Binding principles or rules of international law operate as a limitation of state sovereignty, which remains the core principle of international law. For that reason, the body of international law is relatively limited. According to Article 38 of the Statute of the ICJ, there are only four sources of international law: obligations contained in treaties; international custom (evidence of general practice accepted as law); general principles recognized by civilized nations; and judicial decisions and writings of highly qualified publicists. In addition to these, nowadays decisions of international organizations are recognized as source of international law.

2.2 Statements of law must be distinguished from statements of policy or morality. The former are binding as a matter of law, while the latter are not. A treaty, for example, may contain provisions that are intended to be binding by their terms ("hard law"). Many of the resolutions and declarations referred to in Resolution 2334 and the 2004 Wall Advisory Opinion are only statements of intention or policy ("soft law").

2.3 The principle of the sovereign equality of states is the bedrock of the Westphalian system of international law. This principle means that: (a) all states are equal under the law—there should be no discrimination in the way law is interpreted or applied to states; (b) all states enjoy the rights inherent in full sovereignty; (c) all states have the right to political independence and territorial integrity; and (d) all states are under the same duty to comply with international law. Israel is a state, and as such enjoys all of these rights and duties in the same way and to the same extent as other states.

2.4 Israel is a UN Member State, and thus bound by the terms of the UN Charter, in the same way that all other UN Member States are bound by it. It is, however, not bound by the numerous, generally condemnatory, UN resolutions adopted by UN institutions in respect of Israel. Under the UN Charter, the General Assembly and its subsidiary organ, the UN Human Rights Council, have no power to adopt binding resolutions with external effect. The same is true for Security Council resolutions, unless they are made under Chapter VII of the UN Charter. Statements of law contained in UN General Assembly or UN Security Council resolutions may, in some cases, be evidence of *opinion juris*, but they do not—in and of themselves—constitute definitive statements of law. Accordingly, neither UN institutions nor UN Member States are entitled to treat such resolutions as definitive or binding. On the contrary, they are obliged to form an independent view on the relevant legal issues and their application to the factual situation under consideration.

2.5 The ICJ has the jurisdiction (power) to give a binding judgment in a contentious case only when the states concerned consent to it doing so. The ICJ may also issue an advisory opinion on a legal matter when asked to do so by another UN institution. By their nature, such opinions may contain important statements, but they are advisory only—not binding by their terms. The 2004 Wall Advisory Opinion is therefore not binding on the State of Israel, nor is it binding on other states.

2.6 Since the early 1970's, especially after the Yom Kippur War (October 1973), the UN system has been "used" by certain blocks of states to isolate and delegitimize the State of Israel. The notion that "Zionism is Racism" once expressed in a UN General Assembly resolution, epitomizes their approach. There are a number of reasons for this. One of them is the influence of the Organization of Islamic Cooperation (OIC) and the League of Arab States (the Arab League), which, as a matter of policy, deny the legitimacy of the Jewish State of Israel, and promote the creation of an independent Arab/Islamic State of Palestine. Another is the role of the European nations, which in the early 1970's, adopted a policy to support the creation of a state of Palestine. This is a policy that has subsequently become known and received recognition as "the two-state solution." The UN system has also been increasingly influenced by non-governmental organizations (NGOs), many of which have an "anti-Israel" agenda. In addition, the UN has created several institutions dealing with "Palestinian" issues that are consistently condemning Israel for breaches of international law. No other state has been subjected, and continues to be subjected, so intensively and consistently to such scrutiny and condemnation.

2.7 The discriminatory activities of other states to isolate Israel disproportionally constitutes a fundamental infringement of Israel's right to sovereign equality. These outcomes are often made possible by the voting behavior of numerous countries, often themselves human rights violators, that form voting blocs that protect and support each other and simultaneously condemn the State of Israel for violations of international law. Human rights law in particular is used instrumentally by UN Member States as a weapon that results in "the rule of some groups over others by and through the law, rather than a community united under the rule of law."

2.8 There are many procedural and substantive problems with the 2004 Wall Advisory Opinion of the ICJ, which undermine its authoritativeness. In particular:

- The ICJ was, in fact, purporting to determine a conflict—which it had no jurisdiction to do, as Israel did not consent to the court's jurisdiction;
- By relying on very limited information, the ICJ failed to take adequate account of the historical, political and military/strategic complexities of the Israel/Palestine conflict;
- Because the court only received arguments put forth by certain parties, most of which are hostile towards Israel, its Advisory Opinion is in many respects poorly reasoned and fails to take adequate account of the legal significance of the relevant instruments and events prior to 1948, such as the Mandate for Palestine, resulting in unbalanced findings on the status of the disputed territories and of the Jewish settlements therein;
- The ICJ virtually denied Israel's right to self-defense against terrorist attacks originating from the disputed territories.

2.9 This instrumental and discriminatory use of international law and the UN system in order to achieve a political outcome (namely undermining the validity of the Jewish State of Israel and promoting the creation of a "state of Palestine" based on certain boundaries that have no legal significance as borders) is called *lawfare*. *Lawfare* is problematic for several reasons: It ignores the rights and interests of the State of Israel under international law; it does not take satisfactory account of the status of the relevant territories pursuant to the law applicable to territorial sovereignty, and it conflicts with the purposes and principles of the UN Charter. In particular:

- The discriminatory application of international law to Israel breaches the principle of the sovereign equality of states;
- The continual support for the Palestinian cause without, when necessary, condemning the use of terror against Israeli citizens, and in many cases supporting the use of terror, breaches the principle that all UN Member States must respect and protect the territorial integrity of other UN Member States;
- Imposing conditions on Israel for the resolution of its dispute with its neighbors, that are not imposed on other states, conflicts with the object of establishing "conditions under which justice and respect for the obligations arising from treaties and other sources of international law can be maintained";

- Failing to condemn the use of terror against innocent citizens breaches the object of "[practicing] tolerance and [living] together in peace with one another as good neighbors"; and "[ensuring] by the acceptance of principles and the institution of methods, that armed force shall not be used, save in the common interest."

2.10 Finally, *lawfare* devalues and undermines the international legal order itself, by selectively using the terms of certain instruments while ignoring other obligations and sources of international law. When the law is no longer strictly followed and applied but instead instrumentally used to achieve political ends, the stability, certainty and predictability of the legal system are threatened.

3. The State of Israel

3.1 In terms of modern international law, the State of Israel can be seen as an expression of the self-determination of the Jewish people. The very long history of this people sharing a common religion, culture and language, as well as its continuing relationship to the territory in the Middle East, which as a result of the Roman occupation became known as Palestine, is substantiated by an overwhelming body of evidence. In addition, it has become clear that the ambition to establish an independent Jewish political entity in the territory was clearly expressed by the Zionist movement as from the end of the 19th century. This ambition was recognized by the British government in the Balfour Declaration of 1917 and confirmed by the agreement of the Allied Powers, who had the obligation (and power) to decide on the future of the territories of the Ottoman Empire after World War I, in the San Remo Resolution of 1920. Finally, it was recognized in the Mandate for Palestine, adopted by the Council of the League of Nations in 1922. This instrument explicitly recognized the historical connection between the Jewish people and Palestine and the grounds for reconstituting their national home there.

3.2 The Mandate for Palestine is unique in comparison to all the other mandates created by the League of Nations in that its primary beneficiaries were not only the Jewish inhabitants at that time living in Palestine, but the Jewish people as a whole, the majority of which was still living outside the territory. The mandatory power (Great Britain) had the obligation to secure for them the establishment of a Jewish national home (Article 2). Therefore, the Mandate for Palestine also included the duty to facilitate the immigration of Jews and their "close settlement" in the Mandate territory (Article 6). In addition to the duty to implement the political rights of the Jewish people, the Mandate for Palestine included an obligation to safeguard the civil and religious rights of all its inhabitants (including Arabs). We have shown that—unfortunately—the Mandatory Power did not live up to its obligations. More and more, Britain ignored the unique character of the Mandate for Palestine, restricting Jewish immigration and settlement. Eventually, Britain decided to resign its commission and withdraw from Palestine. It withdrew from Palestine on 15 May 1948. Already two years earlier, the League of Nations was dissolved. Notwithstanding all these facts, the Mandate for Palestine still has legal relevance; based on Article 80 of the UN Charter, the rights of all peoples under the Mandate system should be respected.

3.3 This history has implications for the legal relationship of Israel to the whole territory subject to the former Mandate. The Gaza Strip and Judea/Samaria (the West Bank including East Jerusalem) are not ordinary occupied territories, while the Jewish settlers in those areas are, in principle, entitled to be there having regard to Article 6 of the Mandate.

3.4 The day before Britain left Palestine, 14 May 1948, the State of Israel was proclaimed in Tel Aviv. The State of Israel immediately came into being because, at that moment, it fulfilled all of the criteria for statehood under international law. Israel became a full member of the UN in August 1949. Israel has all the rights of UN Member States, which all other Member States are obliged to respect. In particular:

a. Israel is entitled to be treated equally under international law; and,
b. Israel has the same rights to territorial integrity, political independence and security as all other states.

3.5 In the Declaration on the Establishment of the State of Israel we find the contours of Israel as a Jewish and democratic state. It is Jewish, because the majority of its population is Jewish. Its Jewishness is expressed in its official symbols, national anthem and official holidays. Its legal system is, to a large extent, secular, but Jewish law plays a role. The Law of Return enables Jews to become Israeli nationals. Against those who qualify the Jewish character of the state as "racist" or consider Israel to be an "apartheid" state, we have underlined that under international law the right to self-determination includes the right to opt for a specific cultural identity, including the right to offer citizenship to Jews from all over the world.

3.6 The fact that Israel qualifies itself as a Jewish state does not mean that it is not democratic. In fact, it has a clearly democratic character, with a parliamentary democracy that respects the rule of law. It is in that respect the exception in the Middle East.

4. Territorial Sovereignty and Boundaries

4.1 The State of Israel emerged out of, and came into being as a result of, the San Remo resolution of the Principal Allied Powers (1920) and the Mandate for Palestine (1922), which implemented the Balfour Declaration (1917). The core purpose of the Balfour Declaration, the San Remo Resolution and the Mandate for Palestine was the creation of a "Jewish national home" in Palestine. That homeland was to be created by means of enabling the immigration of Jews into Palestine from the diaspora, and their "close settlement" of the land. The Jewish homeland was to ensure the protection of the civil and religious rights of non-Jews in Palestine.

4.2 It is arguable that the San Remo Resolution was effective in transferring to the Jewish people sovereign title to the territory known as Palestine, and that the State of Israel (as an expression of the right of the Jewish people to self-determination) inherited those rights upon its creation in May 1948.

4.3 The whole of the territory that is today considered part of "Israel proper," as well as the so-called "Occupied Palestinian Territories" (East Jerusalem, the West Bank, and Gaza) were all an integral and inseparable part of the Mandate for Palestine, which was created pursuant to the decisions of the Principle Allied Powers after WWI, and subsequently implemented by the League of Nations (in 1922).

4.4 The Mandate for Palestine was equivalent to a treaty that was (and arguably remains) binding on all the states that were members of the League of Nations.

4.5 The area of Transjordan, which subsequently became the Hashemite Kingdom of Transjordan in 1946, was part of the Mandate for Palestine as was determined by the League of Nations. On the unilateral determination by Great Britain, with the approval of the League, administration of Transjordan was subsequently (in 1921) separated from administration of the western part of the Mandate territory in order to accommodate the interests of the Arab Palestinians. In a very real sense, therefore, Jordan was intended to be, and in fact became, an Arab Palestinian state.

4.6 There are strong arguments to support the view that the borders of the State of Israel are determined by the principle of *uti possidetis* *juris*. This general principle of international law essentially means that the administrative borders of the relevant Mandate at the time the state emerges, become the borders of that state. The principle of *uti possidetis juris* has been applied to all other states emerging from Mandates, such as Syria and Iraq. Pursuant to the sovereign equality of states, the same principle should be applied to Israel. Application of the principle of *uti possidetis juris* to Israel means that the administrative boundaries of the Mandate for Palestine, as they were applied on 14 May 1948, became the borders of the new State of Israel when it came into existence on that date. This included all of "modern Israel" as well as the Gaza Strip and the West Bank (including East Jerusalem).

4.7 It is important to note that the so-called "Partition Plan" adopted by the UN General Assembly in November 1947 never came into effect and therefore has no legal relevance. Given the fact that it was Arab rejection of the Partition Plan that prevented it from coming into effect, it is disingenuous, inappropriate and misleading for Arab states and the Palestine Liberation Organization (PLO) to refer to this resolution as having any legal relevance whatsoever.

4.8 Resolution 2334 of the Security Council and many other UN resolutions assert that the so-called "1967 lines" should be treated as *de jure* border of the State of Israel. The UN and its Member States have no jurisdiction to determine the borders between the State of Israel and its neighbors. In any event, the 1949 Armistice Lines (often referred to as the "the 1967 lines," "the 1967 borders," "the 4 June lines," or "the Green Line") have never acquired the status of international borders under international law. They therefore should not be, directly or indirectly, referred to as the borders of the State of Israel or any prospective State of Palestine. Nothing since 1948 has altered or affected the legal status of these territories or the borders of Israel as at 14 May 1948.

4.9 The right of the State of Israel to territorial integrity means that the State of Israel is entitled to claim and protect governance of the territories belonging properly to the State of Israel upon its creation. It also means that the State of Israel has the right to defend itself against acts of aggression against that territory, or citizens located in that territory.

4.10 UN Security Council Resolutions 242 and 338 are non-binding resolutions. However, they do refer to important principles of international law that are binding on Israel and other states.

4.10.1 One of those principles is the principle of "the inadmissibility of the acquisition of territory by war"—a foundational principle of international law which prohibits the acquisition of territory by acts of aggression. That principle is often (explicitly or implicitly) used to criticize Israel's control of East Jerusalem and the West Bank. In fact, Israel has never undertaken acts of aggression in order to, or with the result of, acquire or acquiring territory. The Six-Day War was, from Israel's perspective, a defensive war. Application of the principle of "the inadmissibility of the acquisition of territory by war" means that territorial gains of Egypt (Gaza) and Jordan (West Bank) in 1947-1949, which resulted in the 1949 Armistice Lines, were illegal. The principle of *ex iniuria ius non oritur* (or the "clean hands" principle) means that unjust acts cannot create law. The application of that principle to the nations that attacked Israel in 1948-1949 (Jordan, Syria, Lebanon, Egypt, and Iraq) means that they are not now entitled to claim any benefit from those acts of aggression. The leadership of the Arab Palestinians, under Grand Mufti Husseini, also publicly supported and actively participated in those acts of aggression. To the extent the PLO is the heir of that leadership, it too is prohibited from benefitting from those acts of aggression. This principle defeats their claims to territorial sovereignty over East Jerusalem and the West Bank.

4.10.2 The second principle referred to in UN Security Council resolution 242 is "the withdrawal of Israeli armed forces from territories occupied in the recent conflict." This formulation was purposefully and carefully drafted to ensure that it did not imply that Israel was required to withdraw all of its armed forces from all of the relevant territories. It therefore supports the view, as stated above, that, because of Israel's legitimate claims of territorial sovereignty, Israel was entitled to retain military control over the territories of which it gained control in the Six-Day War until such time as a peace treaty is reached.

4.10.3 In any event, it is strongly arguable that Israel has complied with the recommendation of the Security Council in Resolutions 242 and 338 to withdraw its forces from territories. Israel handed over the Sinai to Egypt in 1979 and withdrew from Gaza in 2005. Further, it has withdrawn its armed forces from Areas A and B in the West Bank.

4.11 The law of belligerent occupation is often used to imply that Israel is illegally controlling or possessing East Jerusalem and the West Bank. Much confusion has arisen over this issue, in part perhaps because Israel itself has not clearly asserted its sovereign rights and has elected (voluntarily) to apply the law of occupation to these territories (*de facto*, but not *de jure*) to the West Bank. This is implicit in the term "Occupied Palestinian Territories" that is now common parlance in UN literature.

4.11.1 In our view, it is strongly arguable that this body of law does not apply to these territories at all, as Israel did not assume control of them (in 1967) from a prior sovereign state (Jordan having illegally occupied the West Bank between 1949 and 1967).

4.11.2 In any event, the law of belligerent occupation does not apply to Gaza and, arguably, also does not apply to Areas A and B in the West Bank, as Israel does not exercise actual authority on the ground in those territories.

4.11.3 Even if the law of belligerent occupation applies to these territories (which we doubt), that body of law does not affect the sovereign status of the territories. The law of belligerent occupation governs the conduct of states that gain control over territory previously controlled or governed by a neighboring state, until the parties have reached an agreement terminating their conflict. It is designed to both protect the citizens of the occupied territory, and preserve the interested of the "ousted sovereign." It does not render the occupation itself illegal, nor does it affect the question of whether the territory belongs to one or the other party.

4.12 It is often and repeatedly claimed (as in Resolution 2334) that Israel's "settlements policies since 1967" infringe on international law. That claim rests solely on article 49(6) of the Fourth Geneva Convention, which prohibits an occupying power from transferring or deporting its own population into the "occupied territories." In our view, Article 49(6) was intended to apply to large-scale forced transfers or deportations of population groups. It only applies where it can be proven that a citizen of Israel has been forcibly moved into the "occupied territories" (i.e., the West Bank including East Jerusalem) as a direct result of a policy or program of the government of the State of Israel. For many reasons explained in this book, most Israelis living in these territories have not been forced to but are doing so of their own volition. In any event, article 49(6) of the Fourth Geneva Convention only applies to states. It does not render the conduct of individual citizens of Israel illegal.

4.13 Israel and the PLO have chosen to negotiate the terms of Palestinian self-determination under the terms and conditions set out in the Oslo Agreements. Those agreements remain in force, and therefore provide the agreed framework within which the self-determination of the Palestinian people is to be determined. "Jerusalem" and "settlements" are amongst the issues which Israel and the PLO have agreed will be resolved in permanent status negotiations. Seeking "unilateral" recognition of Palestinian statehood arguably breaches the terms of the Oslo Agreements.

4.14 Israel has reunified the city of Jerusalem and administers the city (both "East" and "West" Jerusalem) as a single, unified city. It has also declared Jerusalem to be the undivided capital of the State of Israel. The "international community" refuses to accept either the effective annexation of Jerusalem since June 1967, or its claimed status as capital of the State of Israel. This position is unfounded. Jerusalem undeniably constituted part of the Mandate for Palestine, which did not make any separate provision for the city. Under the principle of *uti possidetis juris*, Jerusalem became an integral part of the State of Israel in 1948. As set out previously, the plans in the "Partition Plan" to make Jerusalem an international city never came into effect. By declaring undivided Jerusalem to be its capital, and by applying Israeli law and jurisdiction to the whole municipality of Jerusalem, Israel has clearly asserted its sovereign rights with respect to this territory. Accordingly, Israel, in our view, has every right to possess and control the whole of the city of Jerusalem.

5. **Israel and Human Rights**

5.1 Much of the criticism of Israel concerns its alleged infringement of human rights in general, and—more specifically—the rights of Palestinians.

5.2 Israel accepts the highest standards in this field, both in its national law and by the ratification of the major international human rights conventions. The enforcement of human rights within the national legal order in Israel is strengthened by the powers of judicial review of the Supreme Court of Israel, which is reputed for its high profile and critical attitude towards the executive branch of government.

5.3 A point of real concern is the human rights situation in the disputed territories. According to the ICJ, Israel is bound to comply with both the rules of international humanitarian law, as well as the rules of international human rights law. The Israeli government contends that both categories of law cannot be applied simultaneously but they are prepared to apply international humanitarian law *de facto* in the disputed territories. The Israel Supreme Court, on the other hand, is willing to apply international human rights law in respect of these territories. We acknowledge the intention to protect the rights and interests of all civilians, whether in times of peace or war. However, we find it difficult to understand how both categories of law can apply in their entirety simultaneously. In our submission, priority should be given to international humanitarian law as a *lex specialis* of human rights law.

Further, because of the fact that under the Interim Agreement certain powers are transferred to Palestinian authorities, Israel cannot be held liable for breaches of international humanitarian law in respect of powers exercised by those authorities in Areas A and B. However, the situation in which Israeli citizens living in the West Bank are given different treatment compared with non-Israeli civilians living there, should not continue indefinitely. A fair solution urgently needs to be found for the long term, in which all civilians living in the West Bank will have full civil, political, religious, economic, social and cultural rights, while allowing Israel to preserve its character as a Jewish State.

The situation in East Jerusalem is different. In East Jerusalem, Israel applies Israeli law and administration, and has offered all non-Israeli civilian residents the opportunity to become Israeli citizens. Israel cannot be held responsible for the fact that many of them have chosen not to accept this offer (and the consequent disadvantages that come with it).

5.4 Israel's respect for human rights is a prominent concern of UN monitoring mechanisms and organs. It has been submitted that Israel has been confronted over the years with an extraordinary and, at many times, extra-proportional criticism of its human rights record. While of course this record is—just as the record of other states—not always blameless, it can safely be assumed that within these mechanisms there has been, and still is, a strong bias against Israel. In that connection, we have pointed at the disproportionate number of resolutions on purported violations of human rights by Israel, as compared to the number of resolutions adopted against other states. In addition, it has been shown that the successive Special Rapporteurs on the question of the human rights in occupied Palestinian territory sometimes very explicitly displayed their anti-Israel bias. It has finally been noted that this question has been made by the UN Human Rights Council a fixed agenda item, a "privilege" granted only to Israel.

5.5 In the discussion of the substantive claims against Israel, we examined three common claims of breach of human rights:

5.5.1 First, the issue of discrimination. The malicious allegation that Zionism is to be equated to racism, and the related popular idea that Israel is an "apartheid state," have no basis in international law. These claims ignore the protections embedded in the Israeli legal system and overlook the significance of the Jewish right to self-determination. Israeli citizens of different backgrounds—Jews, Muslims and Christians—have equal civil and political rights. The allegations are arguably part of a campaign to delegitimize Israel as a Jewish state. The situation in the West Bank, while not a desirable situation in the long term, also cannot be considered racist. The decision of the State of Israel not to apply Israeli law to non-Israeli citizens in this territory is a legitimate decision. Nevertheless, we accept that the human rights of Palestinian Arabs in the West Bank demands changes to enable them to have full rights ensuring their fundamental freedoms and civil rights. International law does not, however, prescribe the way in which such improvement is to be achieved.

5.5.2 Secondly, the issue of the religious freedom in Israel was discussed, in light of the claim that Israel infringes on this freedom, in respect of its policies concerning the Temple Mount and other Islamic and Christian holy places. Under Israeli law, the religious freedom and the right to worship is guaranteed to all believers. Israel is, in that respect, the positive exception in the Middle East. In cases where, in practice, problems do arise, they can be and are addressed within the Israeli judicial system.

5.5.3 Finally, we elaborated on the claim that the measures taken by Israel to combat terrorism have infringed on Palestinian human rights. In this connection, it has been underlined that under international law Israel is obliged to combat terrorism. The aim of the fight against terrorism is, in itself, the protection of the most fundamental rights to life, personal integrity and health. It was observed that the international supervisory bodies have shown little or no understanding of Israel's need (and right) to balance the protection of human rights with its obligation to protect its own citizens.

6. "Palestine"

6.1 It is held by many that the "Palestinian people" is a people having a right to self-determination under international law. It is doubtful that this right did exist in the sense of the objective criterion of having a distinct historical, cultural, religious and linguistic identity in 1922, as Palestine was populated by groups representing various different peoples. In the succeeding decades, however, the non-Jewish Palestinian population increasingly developed a more or less coherent historical, cultural, religious and linguistic identity. It seems clear that from the 1960's onwards there has been a group of persons who identify themselves as Palestinian Arab people, and who have the political will to become an independent nation. This means that, on the basis of at least the subjective tests, it is arguable that there is today indeed a Palestinian people having a right to self-determination.

6.2 The territorial scope of the Palestinian-Arab claims to self-determination remains ambiguous. It would seem that the PLO and Arab states deliberately leave open the possibility of claims to territorial sovereignty over all of Palestine, including the pre-1967 territories. The Palestinian National Charter simply excludes the existence of the State of Israel in the Middle East. The popular view within the international community limits the territorial claims to the "occupied Palestinian territory"—which is also the starting point of the Oslo Agreements.

6.3 Assuming the Palestinian Arabs have such a right, the right to self-determination does not confer an automatic right to statehood. Self-determination may be implemented in several forms. Separate independent statehood is just one of these forms and, as such, is not imposed by international law. Recognition of the right to self-determination of a Palestinian people should, in any case, be accommodated with the right to self-determination of the Jewish people and the rights of the State of Israel to territorial integrity and political inviolability.

6.4 Notwithstanding the "accession" of Palestine to many international treaties (including the Statute of the International Criminal Court (ICC)), and its "recognition" by many other states, the "State of Palestine" does not yet exist as a matter of law, as it does not satisfy the criteria for statehood under international law. Further, admission of Palestine as a member of the UN requires demonstration that it is both able and willing—as a political entity—to comply with the most fundamental UN Charter principles. These include the obligation to respect other states, the prohibition of force and the requirement of friendly relations. At present, Palestine does not satisfy these requirements.

6.5 We have dwelled on the origins of the problem of Palestinian refugees, as well as on the comparable problem of the Jewish refugees, who had to flee Arab countries in the years 1947-1949. The legal aspects of the refugee issue are complex. First of all, the concept of a Palestinian refugee, used in the UNRWA practice, is totally different from the regular definition of a refugee, as included in the Convention on the Status of Refugees of 1951. Furthermore, there is the claim of a right of return, which is predominantly based on a non-binding General Assembly Resolution. There is arguably no "right of return" under international law. Moreover, an implementation of the right of return, as envisaged by Palestinian leaders, would mean the end of Israel as a Jewish State. Thus, we conclude that the parties concerned should negotiate the contours of another solution.

7. A State at War

7.1 Israel is a state at war. Israel has to contend daily with the application of international law designed to restrict the use of force. Its actions are continually scrutinized by the media while the actions of Israel's enemies generally receive less critical attention. Regarding the right to enter into war (*jus ad bellum),* the right to invoke and exercise the right of self-defense is an inherent right of states under international law.

7.2 Israel is entitled to invoke and exercise this right, also if non-state terrorist groups, such as Hezbollah and Hamas, attack it. The ICJ, in its Wall Advisory Opinion, in perhaps the most severely criticized part of its Opinion, has denied Israel this right in the case of attacks that are not imputable to another state, including attacks by terrorist groups. The ICJ has adopted an inaccurate interpretation of international law—more precisely, Article 51 of the UN Charter—on this point. It denies the State of Israel one of the most fundamental rights of a state—the right to defend itself and protect its citizens. It is difficult to understand how the ICJ could have come to this interpretation in an era where, generally speaking, warfare is between states and terrorist groups rather than inter-state.

7.3 Israel is also criticized regarding its application of international humanitarian law. There is ample evidence that Israel accepts, seeks to apply, and generally successfully applies the fundamental principles of distinction and proportionality. It is also important to realize that Israel is operating under incredibly difficult circumstances in defending itself against guerrilla warfare waged by its enemies, which include non-state actors such as Hezbollah and Hamas. This type of warfare involves the use of tactics that make it virtually impossible to make a clear distinction between combatants and non-combatants. The deliberate use of civilians and civilian buildings as shields, a practice employed by these militant groups, constitutes a violation of international humanitarian law.

7.4 In relation to possible violations of humanitarian law, the possibilities and impossibilities of bringing Israeli officials to trial before an international or a foreign tribunal has been discussed. It remains to be seen whether this is purely theoretical, having regard to the accession of Palestine to the ICC, which may bring changes in this respect. So far, prosecution before a foreign criminal court that applies the universality principle (or another principle establishing jurisdiction over foreigners) has not been successful. However, it is likely that those involved in *lawfare* against Israel will not give up easily. In principle, there is not a valid reason for the involvement of international or foreign courts. Israeli civil and military courts have proven to be well-equipped to deal with these matters.

Appendixes

Appendixes

Balfour Declaration, 2 November 1917

Foreign Office,
November 2nd, 1917.

Dear Lord Rothschild,

I have much pleasure in conveying to you, on behalf of His Majesty's Government, the following declaration of sympathy with Jewish Zionist aspirations which has been submitted to, and approved by, the Cabinet

"His Majesty's Government view with favour the establishment in Palestine of a national home for the Jewish people, and will use their best endeavours to facilitate the achievement of this object, it being clearly understood that nothing shall be done which may prejudice the civil and religious rights of existing non-Jewish communities in Palestine, or the rights and political status enjoyed by Jews in any other country"

I should be grateful if you would bring this declaration to the knowledge of the Zionist Federation.

Yours,
Arthur James Balfour

Agreement between Emir Feisal Ibn al-Hussein al-Hashemi, and the President of the World Zionist Organization, Dr. Chaim Weizmann, 3 January 1919

His Royal Highness the Emir Feisal, representing and acting on behalf of the Arab Kingdom of Hedjaz, and Dr. Chaim Weizmann, representing and acting on behalf of the Zionist Organization, mindful of the racial kinship and ancient bonds existing between the Arabs and the Jewish people, and realizing that the surest means of working out the consummation of their natural aspirations is through the closest possible collaboration in the development of the Arab State and Palestine, and being desirous further of confirming the good understanding which exists between them, have agreed upon the following:

Article I

The Arab State and Palestine in all their relations and undertakings shall be controlled by the most cordial goodwill and understanding, and to this end Arab and Jewish duly accredited agents shall be established and maintained in the respective territories.

Article II

Immediately following the completion of the deliberations of the Peace Conference, the definite boundaries between the Arab State and Palestine shall be determined by a Commission to be agreed upon by the parties hereto.

Article III

In the establishment of the Constitution and Administration of Palestine, all such measures shall be adopted as will afford the fullest guarantees for carrying into effect the British Government's Declaration of the 2nd of November, 1917.

Article IV

All necessary measures shall be taken to encourage and stimulate immigration of Jews into Palestine on a large scale, and as quickly as possible to settle Jewish immigrants upon the land through closer settlement and intensive cultivation of the soil. In taking such measures the Arab peasant and tenant farmers shall be protected in their rights and shall be assisted in forwarding their economic development.

Article V

No regulation or law shall be made prohibiting or interfering in any way with the free exercise of religion; and further, the free exercise and enjoyment of religious profession and worship, without discrimination or preference, shall forever be allowed. No religious test shall ever be required for the exercise of civil or political rights.

Article VI

The Mohammedan Holy Places shall be under Mohammedan control.

Article VII

The Zionist Organization proposes to send to Palestine a Commission of experts to make a survey of the economic possibilities of the country, and to report upon the best means for its development. The Zionist Organization will place the aforementioned Commission at the disposal of the Arab State for the purpose of a survey of the economic possibilities of the Arab State and to report upon the best means for its development. The Zionist Organization will use its best efforts to assist the Arab State in providing the means for developing the natural resources and economic possibilities thereof.

Article VIII

The parties hereto agree to act in complete accord and harmony on all matters embraced herein before the Peace Congress.

Article IX

Any matters of dispute which may arise between the contracting parties hall be referred to the British Government for arbitration.

Given under our hand at London, England, the third day of January, one thousand nine hundred and nineteen

Chaim Weizmann **Feisal Ibn-Hussein**

Reservation by the Emir Feisal

If the Arabs are established as I have asked in my manifesto of 4 January, addressed to the British Secretary of State for Foreign Affairs, I will carry out what is written in this agreement. If changes are made, I cannot be answerable for failing to carry out this agreement.

Articles 20 – 22 of the Covenant of the League of Nations, 28 June 1919

Article 20.

The Members of the League severally agree that this Covenant is accepted as abrogating all obligations or understandings inter se which are inconsistent with the terms thereof, and solemnly undertake that they will not hereafter enter into any engagements inconsistent with the terms thereof.

In case any Member of the League shall, before becoming a Member of the League, have undertaken any obligations inconsistent with the terms of this Covenant, it shall be the duty of such Member to take immediate steps to procure its release from such obligations.

Article 21.

Nothing in this Covenant shall be deemed to affect the validity of international engagements, such as treaties of arbitration or regional understandings like the Monroe doctrine, for securing the maintenance of peace.

Article 22.

To those colonies and territories which as a consequence of the late war have ceased to be under the sovereignty of the States which formerly governed them and which are inhabited by peoples not yet able to stand by themselves under the strenuous conditions of the modern world, there should be applied the principle that the well-being and development of such peoples form a sacred trust of civilisation and that securities for the performance of this trust should be embodied in this Covenant.

The best method of giving practical effect to this principle is that the tutelage of such peoples should be entrusted to advanced nations who by reason of their resources, their experience or their geographical position can best undertake this responsibility, and who are willing to accept it, and that this tutelage should be exercised by them as Mandatories on behalf of the League.

The character of the mandate must differ according to the stage of the development of the people, the geographical situation of the territory, its economic conditions and other similar circumstances.

Certain communities formerly belonging to the Turkish Empire have reached a stage of development where their existence as independent nations can be provisionally recognized subject to the rendering of administrative advice and assistance by a Mandatory until such time as they are able to stand alone. The wishes of these communities must be a principal consideration in the selection of the Mandatory.

Other peoples, especially those of Central Africa, are at such a stage that the Mandatory must be responsible for the administration of the territory under conditions which will guarantee freedom of conscience and religion, subject only to the maintenance of public order and morals, the prohibition of abuses such as the slave trade, the arms traffic and the liquor traffic, and the prevention of the establishment of fortifications or military and naval bases and of military training of the natives for other than police purposes and the defence of territory, and will also secure equal opportunities for the trade and commerce of other Members of the League.

There are territories, such as South-West Africa and certain of the South Pacific Islands, which, owing to the sparseness of their population, or their small size, or their remoteness from the centres of civilisation, or their geographical contiguity to the territory of the Mandatory, and other circumstances, can be best administered under the laws of the Mandatory as integral portions of its territory, subject to the safeguards above mentioned in the interests of the indigenous population.

In every case of mandate, the Mandatory shall render to the Council an annual report in reference to the territory committed to its charge.

The degree of authority, control, or administration to be exercised by the Mandatory shall, if not previously agreed upon by the Members of the League, be explicitly defined in each case by the Council.

A permanent Commission shall be constituted to receive and examine the annual reports of the Mandatories and to advise the Council on all matters relating to the observance of the mandates.

San Remo Resolution, 25 April 1920

It was agreed –

(a) To accept the terms of the Mandates Article as given below with reference to Palestine, on the understanding that there was inserted in the proces-verbal an undertaking by the Mandatory Power that this would not involve the surrender of the rights hitherto enjoyed by the non-Jewish communities in Palestine; this undertaking not to refer to the question of the religious protectorate of France, which had been settled earlier in the previous afternoon by the undertaking given by the French Government that they recognized this protectorate as being at an end.

(b) that the terms of the Mandates Article should be as follows:

The High Contracting Parties agree that Syria and Mesopotamia shall, in accordance with the fourth paragraph of Article 22, Part I (Covenant of the League of Nations), be provisionally recognized as independent States, subject to the rendering of administrative advice and assistance by a mandatory until such time as they are able to stand alone. The boundaries of the said States will be determined, and the selection of the Mandatories made, by the Principal Allied Powers.

The High Contracting Parties agree to entrust, by application of the provisions of Article 22, the administration of Palestine, within such boundaries as may be determined by the Principal Allied Powers, to a Mandatory, to be selected by the said Powers. The Mandatory will be responsible for putting into effect the declaration originally made on November 8, 1917, by the British Government, and adopted by the other Allied Powers, in favour of the establishment in Palestine of a national home for the Jewish people, it being clearly understood that nothing shall be done which may prejudice the civil and religious rights of existing non-Jewish communities in Palestine, or the rights and political status enjoyed by Jews in any other country.

Mandate for Palestine, 24 July 1922

LEAGUE OF NATIONS.

MANDATE FOR PALESTINE,

TOGETHER WITH A

NOTE BY THE SECRETARY-GENERAL RELATING TO ITS APPLICATION

TO THE

TERRITORY KNOWN AS TRANS-JORDAN, under the provisions of Article 25.

Presented to Parliament by Command of His Majesty, December, 1922

LONDON:
PUBLISHED BY HIS MAJESTY'S STATIONARY OFFICE.

The Council of the League of Nations:

Whereas the Principal Allied Powers have agreed, for the purpose of giving effect to the provisions of Article 22 of the Covenant of the League of Nations, to entrust to a Mandatory selected by the said Powers the administration of the territory of Palestine, which formerly belonged to the Turkish Empire, within such boundaries as may be fixed by them; and

Whereas the Principal Allied Powers have also agreed that the Mandatory should be responsible for putting into effect the declaration originally made on November 2nd, 1917, by the Government of His Britannic Majesty, and adopted by the said Powers, in favor of the establishment in Palestine of a national home for the Jewish people, it being clearly understood that nothing should be done which might prejudice the civil and religious rights of existing non-Jewish communities in Palestine, or the rights and political status enjoyed by Jews in any other country; and

Whereas recognition has thereby been given to the historical connection of the Jewish people with Palestine and to the grounds for reconstituting their national home in that country; and

Whereas the Principal Allied Powers have selected His Britannic Majesty as the Mandatory for Palestine; and

Whereas the mandate in respect of Palestine has been formulated in the following terms and submitted to the Council of the League for approval; and

Whereas His Britannic Majesty has accepted the mandate in respect of Palestine and undertaken to exercise it on behalf of the League of Nations in conformity with the following provisions; and

Whereas by the afore-mentioned Article 22 (paragraph 8), it is provided that the degree of authority, control or administration to be exercised by the Mandatory, not having been previously agreed upon by the Members of the League, shall be explicitly defined by the Council of the League Of Nations;

confirming the said Mandate, defines its terms as follows:

Article 1.

The Mandatory shall have full powers of legislation and of administration, save as they may be limited by the terms of this mandate.

Article 2.

The Mandatory shall be responsible for placing the country under such political, administrative and economic conditions as will secure the establishment of the Jewish national home, as laid down in the preamble, and the development of self-governing institutions, and also for safeguarding the civil and religious rights of all the inhabitants of Palestine, irrespective of race and religion.

Article 3.

The Mandatory shall, so far as circumstances permit, encourage local autonomy.

Article 4.

An appropriate Jewish agency shall be recognised as a public body for the purpose of advising and co-operating with the Administration of Palestine in such economic, social and other matters as may affect the establishment of the Jewish national home and the interests of the Jewish population in Palestine, and, subject always to the control of the Administration to assist and take part in the development of the country.

The Zionist organization, so long as its organization and constitution are in the opinion of the Mandatory appropriate, shall be recognised as such agency. It shall take steps in consultation with His Britannic Majesty's Government to secure the co-operation of all Jews who are willing to assist in the establishment of the Jewish national home.

Article 5.

The Mandatory shall be responsible for seeing that no Palestine territory shall be ceded or leased to, or in any way placed under the control of the Government of any foreign Power.

Article 6.

The Administration of Palestine, while ensuring that the rights and position of other sections of the population are not prejudiced, shall facilitate Jewish immigration under suitable conditions and shall encourage, in co-operation with the Jewish agency referred to in Article 4, close settlement by Jews on the land, including State lands and waste lands not required for public purposes.

Article 7.

The Administration of Palestine shall be responsible for enacting a nationality law. There shall be included in this law provisions framed so as to facilitate the acquisition of Palestinian citizenship by Jews who take up their permanent residence in Palestine.

Article 8.

The privileges and immunities of foreigners, including the benefits of consular jurisdiction and protection as formerly enjoyed by Capitulation or usage in the Ottoman Empire, shall not be applicable in Palestine.

Unless the Powers whose nationals enjoyed the afore-mentioned privileges and immunities on August 1st, 1914, shall have previously renounced the right to their re-establishment, or shall have agreed to their non-application for a specified period, these privileges and immunities shall, at the expiration of the mandate, be immediately re-established in their entirety or with such modifications as may have been agreed upon between the Powers concerned.

Article 9.

The Mandatory shall be responsible for seeing that the judicial system established in Palestine shall assure to foreigners, as well as to natives, a complete guarantee of their rights.

Respect for the personal status of the various peoples and communities and for their religious interests shall be fully guaranteed. In particular, the control and administration of Wakfs shall be exercised in accordance with religious law and the dispositions of the founders.

Article 10.

Pending the making of special extradition agreements relating to Palestine, the extradition treaties in force between the Mandatory and other foreign Powers shall apply to Palestine.

Article 11.

The Administration of Palestine shall take all necessary measures to safeguard the interests of the community in connection with the development of the country, and, subject to any international obligations accepted by the Mandatory, shall have full power to provide for public ownership or control of any of the natural resources of the country or of the public works, services and utilities established or to be established therein. It shall introduce a land system appropriate to the needs of the country, having regard, among other things, to the desirability of promoting the close settlement and intensive cultivation of the land.

The Administration may arrange with the Jewish agency mentioned in Article 4 to construct or operate, upon fair and equitable terms, any public works, services and utilities, and to develop any of the natural resources of the country, in so far as these matters are not directly undertaken by the Administration. Any such arrangements shall provide that no profits distributed by such agency, directly or indirectly, shall exceed a reasonable rate of interest on the capital, and any further profits shall be utilised by it for the benefit of the country in a manner approved by the Administration.

Article 12.

The Mandatory shall be entrusted with the control of the foreign relations of Palestine and the right to issue exequaturs to consuls appointed by foreign Powers. He shall also be entitled to afford diplomatic and consular protection to citizens of Palestine when outside its territorial limits.

Article 13.

All responsibility in connection with the Holy Places and religious buildings or sites in Palestine, including that of preserving existing rights and of securing free access to the Holy Places, religious buildings and sites and the free exercise of worship, while ensuring the requirements of public order and decorum, is assumed by the Mandatory, who shall be responsible solely to the League of Nations in all matters connected herewith, provided that nothing in this article shall prevent the Mandatory from entering into such arrangements as he may deem reasonable with the Administration for the purpose of carrying the provisions of this article into effect; and provided also that nothing in this mandate shall be construed as conferring upon the Mandatory authority to interfere with the fabric or the management of purely Moslem sacred shrines, the immunities of which are guaranteed.

Article 14.

A special commission shall be appointed by the Mandatory to study, define and determine the rights and claims in connection with the Holy Places and the rights and claims relating to the different religious communities in Palestine. The method of nomination, the composition and the functions of this Commission shall be submitted to the Council of the League for its approval, and the Commission shall not be appointed or enter upon its functions without the approval of the Council.

Article 15.

The Mandatory shall see that complete freedom of conscience and the free exercise of all forms of worship, subject only to the maintenance of public order and morals, are ensured to all. No discrimination of any kind shall be made between the inhabitants of Palestine on the ground of race, religion or language. No person shall be excluded from Palestine on the sole ground of his religious belief.

The right of each community to maintain its own schools for the education of its own members in its own language, while conforming to such educational requirements of a general nature as the Administration may impose, shall not be denied or impaired.

Article 16.

The Mandatory shall be responsible for exercising such supervision over religious or eleemosynary bodies of all faiths in Palestine as may be required for the maintenance of public order and good government. Subject to such supervision, no measures shall be taken in Palestine to obstruct or interfere with the enterprise of such bodies or to discriminate against any representative or member of them on the ground of his religion or nationality.

Article 17.

The Administration of Palestine may organist on a voluntary basis the forces necessary for the preservation of peace and order, and also for the defence of the country, subject, however, to the supervision of the Mandatory, but shall not use them for purposes other than those above specified save with the consent of the Mandatory. Except for such purposes, no military, naval or air forces shall be raised or maintained by the Administration of Palestine.

Nothing in this article shall preclude the Administration of Palestine from contributing to the cost of the maintenance of the forces of the Mandatory in Palestine.

The Mandatory shall be entitled at all times to use the roads, railways and ports of Palestine for the movement of armed forces and the carriage of fuel and supplies.

Article 18.

The Mandatory shall see that there is no discrimination in Palestine against the nationals of any State Member of the League of Nations (including companies incorporated under its laws) as compared with those of the Mandatory or of any foreign State in matters concerning taxation, commerce or navigation, the exercise of industries or professions, or in the treatment of merchant vessels or civil aircraft. Similarly, there shall be no discrimination in Palestine against goods originating in or destined for any of the said States, and there shall be freedom of transit under equitable conditions across the mandated area.

Subject as aforesaid and to the other provisions of this mandate, the Administration of Palestine may, on the advice of the Mandatory, impose such taxes and customs duties as it may consider necessary, and take such steps as it may think best to promote the development of the natural resources of the country and to safeguard the interests of the population. It may also, on the advice of the Mandatory, conclude a special customs agreement with any State the territory of which in 1914 was wholly included in Asiatic Turkey or Arabia.

Article 19.

The Mandatory shall adhere on behalf of the Administration of Palestine to any general international conventions already existing, or which may be concluded hereafter with the approval of the League of Nations, respecting the slave traffic, the traffic in arms and ammunition, or the traffic in drugs, or relating to commercial equality, freedom of transit and navigation, aerial navigation and postal, telegraphic and wireless communication or literary, artistic or industrial property.

Article 20.

The Mandatory shall co-operate on behalf of the Administration of Palestine, so far as religious, social and other conditions may permit, in the execution of any common policy adopted by the League of Nations for preventing and combating disease, including diseases of plants and animals.

Article 21.

The Mandatory shall secure the enactment within twelve months from this date, and shall ensure the execution of a Law of Antiquities based on the following rules. This law shall ensure equality of treatment in the matter of excavations and archaeological research to the nationals of all States Members of the League of Nations.

(1) "Antiquity" means any construction or any product of human activity earlier than the year 1700 A. D.

(2) The law for the protection of antiquities shall proceed by encouragement rather than by threat.
Any person who, having discovered an antiquity without being furnished with the

authorization referred to in paragraph 5, reports the same to an official of the competent Department, shall be rewarded according to the value of the discovery.

(3) No antiquity may be disposed of except to the competent Department, unless this Department renounces the acquisition of any such antiquity.

No antiquity may leave the country without an export licence from the said Department.

(4) Any person who maliciously or negligently destroys or damages an antiquity shall be liable to a penalty to be fixed.

(5) No clearing of ground or digging with the object of finding antiquities shall be permitted, under penalty of fine, except to persons authorised by the competent Department.

(6) Equitable terms shall be fixed for expropriation, temporary or permanent, of lands which might be of historical or archaeological interest.

(7) Authorization to excavate shall only be granted to persons who show sufficient guarantees of archaeological experience. The Administration of Palestine shall not, in granting these authorizations, act in such a way as to exclude scholars of any nation without good grounds.

(8)The proceeds of excavations may be divided between the excavator and the competent Department in a proportion fixed by that Department. If division seems impossible for scientific reasons, the excavator shall receive a fair indemnity in lieu of a part of the find.

Article 22.

English, Arabic and Hebrew shall be the official languages of Palestine. Any statement or inscription in Arabic on stamps or money in Palestine shall be repeated in Hebrew and any statement or inscription in Hebrew shall be repeated in Arabic.

Article 23.

The Administration of Palestine shall recognise the holy days of the respective communities in Palestine as legal days of rest for the members of such communities.

Article 24.

The Mandatory shall make to the Council of the League of Nations an annual report to the satisfaction of the Council as to the measures taken during the year to carry out the provisions of the mandate. Copies of all laws and regulations promulgated or issued during the year shall be communicated with the report.

Article 25.

In the territories lying between the Jordan and the eastern boundary of Palestine as ultimately determined, the Mandatory shall be entitled, with the consent of the Council of the League of Nations, to postpone or withhold application of such provisions of this mandate as he may consider inapplicable to the existing local conditions, and to make such provision for the administration of the territories as he may consider suitable to those conditions, provided that no action shall be taken which is inconsistent with the provisions of Articles 15, 16 and 18.

Article 26.

The Mandatory agrees that, if any dispute whatever should arise between the Mandatory and another member of the League of Nations relating to the interpretation or the application of the provisions of the mandate, such dispute, if it cannot be settled by negotiation, shall be submitted to the Permanent Court of International Justice provided for by Article 14 of the Covenant of the League of Nations.

Article 27.

The consent of the Council of the League of Nations is required for any modification of the terms of this mandate.

Article 28.

In the event of the termination of the mandate hereby conferred upon the Mandatory, the Council of the League of Nations shall make such arrangements as may be deemed necessary for safeguarding in perpetuity, under guarantee of the League, the rights secured by Articles 13 and 14, and shall use its influence for securing, under the guarantee of the League, that the Government of Palestine will fully honour the financial obligations legitimately incurred by the Administration of Palestine during the period of the mandate, including the rights of public servants to pensions or gratuities.

The present instrument shall be deposited in original in the archives of the League of Nations and certified copies shall be forwarded by the Secretary-General of the League of Nations to all members of the League. Done at London the twenty-fourth day of July, one thousand nine hundred and twenty-two.

Charter of the United Nations, 26 June 1945 (Extract)

WE THE PEOPLES OF THE UNITED NATIONS DETERMINED

- to save succeeding generations from the scourge of war, which twice in our lifetime has brought untold sorrow to mankind, and
- to reaffirm faith in fundamental human rights, in the dignity and worth of the human person, in the equal rights of men and women and of nations large and small, and
- to establish conditions under which justice and respect for the obligations arising from treaties and other sources of international law can be maintained, and
- to promote social progress and better standards of life in larger freedom,

AND FOR THESE ENDS

- to practice tolerance and live together in peace with one another as good neighbours, and
- to unite our strength to maintain international peace and security, and
- to ensure, by the acceptance of principles and the institution of methods, that armed force shall not be used, save in the common interest, and
- to employ international machinery for the promotion of the economic and social advancement of all peoples,

HAVE RESOLVED TO COMBINE OUR EFFORTS TO ACCOMPLISH THESE AIMS

Accordingly, our respective Governments, through representatives assembled in the city of San Francisco, who have exhibited their full powers found to be in good and due form, have agreed to the present Charter of the United Nations and do hereby establish an international organization to be known as the United Nations.

CHAPTER I: PURPOSES AND PRINCIPLES

Article 1

The Purposes of the United Nations are:

- To maintain international peace and security, and to that end: to take effective collective measures for the prevention and removal of threats to the peace, and for the suppression of acts of aggression or other breaches of the peace, and to bring about by peaceful means, and in conformity with the principles of justice and international law, adjustment or settlement of international disputes or situations which might lead to a breach of the peace;
- To develop friendly relations among nations based on respect for the principle of equal rights and self-determination of peoples, and to take other appropriate measures to strengthen universal peace;
- To achieve international co-operation in solving international problems of an economic, social, cultural, or humanitarian character, and in promoting and encouraging respect for human rights and for fundamental freedoms for all without distinction as to race, sex, language, or religion; and

- To be a centre for harmonizing the actions of nations in the attainment of these common ends.

Article 2

The Organization and its Members, in pursuit of the Purposes stated in Article 1, shall act in accordance with the following Principles.

1. The Organization is based on the principle of the sovereign equality of all its Members.
2. All Members, in order to ensure to all of them the rights and benefits resulting from membership, shall fulfill in good faith the obligations assumed by them in accordance with the present Charter.
3. All Members shall settle their international disputes by peaceful means in such a manner that international peace and security, and justice, are not endangered.
4. All Members shall refrain in their international relations from the threat or use of force against the territorial integrity or political independence of any state, or in any other manner inconsistent with the Purposes of the United Nations.
5. All Members shall give the United Nations every assistance in any action it takes in accordance with the present Charter, and shall refrain from giving assistance to any state against which the United Nations is taking preventive or enforcement action.
6. The Organization shall ensure that states which are not Members of the United Nations act in accordance with these Principles so far as may be necessary for the maintenance of international peace and security.
7. Nothing contained in the present Charter shall authorize the United Nations to intervene in matters which are essentially within the domestic jurisdiction of any state or shall require the Members to submit such matters to settlement under the present Charter; but this principle shall not prejudice the application of enforcement measures under Chapter VII.

Article 51

Nothing in the present Charter shall impair the inherent right of individual or collective self-defence if an armed attack occurs against a Member of the United Nations, until the Security Council has taken measures necessary to maintain international peace and security. Measures taken by Members in the exercise of this right of self-defence shall be immediately reported to the Security Council and shall not in any way affect the authority and responsibility of the Security Council under the present Charter to take at any time such action as it deems necessary in order to maintain or restore international peace and security.

Article 80

Except as may be agreed upon in individual trusteeship agreements, made under Articles 77, 79, and 81, placing each territory under the trusteeship system, and until such agreements have been concluded, nothing in this Chapter shall be construed in or of itself to alter in any manner the rights whatsoever of any states or any peoples or the terms of existing international instruments to which Members of the United Nations may respectively be parties.

Paragraph 1 of this Article shall not be interpreted as giving grounds for delay or postponement of the negotiation and conclusion of agreements for placing mandated and other territories under the trusteeship system as provided for in Article 77.

Article 96

a. The General Assembly or the Security Council may request the International Court of Justice to give an advisory opinion on any legal question.

b. Other organs of the United Nations and specialized agencies, which may at any time be so authorized by the General Assembly, may also request advisory opinions of the Court on legal questions arising within the scope of their activities.

General Assembly Resolution 181 (II), 29 November 1947

Resolution 181 (II). Future government of Palestine

The General Assembly,

Having met in special session at the request of the mandatory Power to constitute and instruct a special committee to prepare for the consideration of the question of the future government of Palestine at the second regular session;

Having constituted a Special Committee and instructed it to investigate all questions and issues relevant to the problem of Palestine, and to prepare proposals for the solution of the problem, and

Having received and examined the report of the Special Committee (document A/364) 1/ including a number of unanimous recommendations and a plan of partition with economic union approved by the majority of the Special Committee,

Considers that the present situation in Palestine is one which is likely to impair the general welfare and friendly relations among nations;

Takes note of the declaration by the mandatory Power that it plans to complete its evacuation of Palestine by 1 August 1948;

Recommends to the United Kingdom, as the mandatory Power for Palestine, and to all other Members of the United Nations the adoption and implementation, with regard to the future government of Palestine, of the Plan of Partition with Economic Union set out below;

Requests that

(a) The Security Council take the necessary measures as provided for in the plan for its implementation;

(b) The Security Council consider, if circumstances during the transitional period require such consideration, whether the situation in Palestine constitutes a threat to the peace. If it decides that such a threat exists, and in order to maintain international peace and security, the Security Council should supplement the authorization of the General Assembly by taking measures, under Articles 39 and 41 of the Charter, to empower the United Nations Commission, as provided in this resolution, to exercise in Palestine the functions which are assigned to it by this resolution;

(c) The Security Council determine as a threat to the peace, breach of the peace or act of aggression, in accordance with Article 39 of the Charter, any attempt to alter by force the settlement envisaged by this resolution;

(d) The Trusteeship Council be informed of the responsibilities envisaged for it in this plan;

Calls upon the inhabitants of Palestine to take such steps as may be necessary on their part to put this plan into effect;

Appeals to all Governments and all peoples to refrain from taking action which might hamper or delay the carrying out of these recommendations, and

Authorizes the Secretary-General to reimburse travel and subsistence expenses of the members of the Commission referred to in Part I, Section B, paragraph 1 below, on such basis and in such form as he may determine most appropriate in the circumstances, and to provide the Commission with the necessary staff to assist in carrying out the functions assigned to the Commission by the General Assembly.

B2

The General Assembly

Authorizes the Secretary-General to draw from the Working Capital Fund a sum not to exceed $2,000,000 for the purposes set forth in the last paragraph of the resolution on the future government of Palestine.

Hundred and twenty-eighth plenary meeting
29 November 1947

[At its hundred and twenty-eighth plenary meeting on 29 November 1947 the General Assembly, in accordance with the terms of the above resolution [181 A], elected the following members of the United Nations Commission on Palestine: Bolivia, Czechoslovakia, Denmark, Panama and Philippines.]

PLAN OF PARTITION WITH ECONOMIC UNION

PART I

Future constitution and government of Palestine

A. TERMINATION OF MANDATE, PARTITION AND INDEPENDENCE

1. The Mandate for Palestine shall terminate as soon as possible but in any case not later than 1 August 1948.

2. The armed forces of the mandatory Power shall be progressively withdrawn from Palestine, the withdrawal to be completed as soon as possible but in any case not later than 1 August 1948.

The mandatory Power shall advise the Commission, as far in advance as possible, of its intention to terminate the Mandate and to evacuate each area.

The mandatory Power shall use its best endeavours to ensure than an area situated in the territory of the Jewish State, including a seaport and hinterland adequate to provide facilities for a substantial immigration, shall be evacuated at the earliest possible date and in any event not later than 1 February 1948.

3. Independent Arab and Jewish States and the Special International Regime for the City of Jerusalem, set forth in part III of this plan, shall come into existence in Palestine two months after the evacuation of the armed forces of the mandatory Power has been completed but in any case not later than 1 October 1948. The boundaries of the Arab State, the Jewish State, and the City of Jerusalem shall be as described in parts II and III below.

4. The period between the adoption by the General Assembly of its recommendation on the question of Palestine and the establishment of the independence of the Arab and Jewish States shall be a transitional period.

B. STEPS PREPARATORY TO INDEPENDENCE

1. A Commission shall be set up consisting of one representative of each of five Member States. The Members represented on the Commission shall be elected by the General Assembly on as broad a basis, geographically and otherwise, as possible.

2. The administration of Palestine shall, as the mandatory Power withdraws its armed forces, be progressively turned over to the Commission; which shall act in conformity with the recommendations of the General Assembly, under the guidance of the Security Council. The mandatory Power shall to the fullest possible extent co-ordinate its plans for withdrawal with the plans of the Commission to take over and administer areas which have been evacuated.

In the discharge of this administrative responsibility the Commission shall have authority to issue necessary regulations and take other measures as required.

The mandatory Power shall not take any action to prevent, obstruct or delay the implementation by the Commission of the measures recommended by the General Assembly.

3. On its arrival in Palestine the Commission shall proceed to carry out measures for the establishment of the frontiers of the Arab and Jewish States and the City of Jerusalem in accordance with the general lines of the recommendations of the General Assembly on the partition of Palestine. Nevertheless, the boundaries as described in part II of this plan are to be modified in such a way that village areas as a rule will not be divided by state boundaries unless pressing reasons make that necessary.

4. The Commission, after consultation with the democratic parties and other public organizations of The Arab and Jewish States, shall select and establish in each State as rapidly as possible a Provisional Council of Government. The activities of both the Arab and Jewish Provisional Councils of Government shall be carried out under the general direction of the Commission.

If by 1 April 1948 a Provisional Council of Government cannot be selected for either of the States, or, if selected, cannot carry out its functions, the Commission shall communicate that fact to the Security Council for such action with respect to that State as the Security Council may deem proper, and to the Secretary-General for communication to the Members of the United Nations.

5. Subject to the provisions of these recommendations, during the transitional period the Provisional Councils of Government, acting under the Commission, shall have full authority in the areas under their control, including authority over matters of immigration and land regulation.

6. The Provisional Council of Government of each State acting under the Commission, shall progressively receive from the Commission full responsibility for the administration of that State in the period between the termination of the Mandate and the establishment of the State's independence.

7. The Commission shall instruct the Provisional Councils of Government of both the Arab and Jewish States, after their formation, to proceed to the establishment of administrative organs of government, central and local.

8. The Provisional Council of Government of each State shall, within the shortest time possible, recruit an armed militia from the residents of that State, sufficient in number to maintain internal order and to prevent frontier clashes.

This armed militia in each State shall, for operational purposes, be under the command of Jewish or Arab officers resident in that State, but general political and military control, including the choice of the militia's High Command, shall be exercised by the Commission.

9. The Provisional Council of Government of each State shall, not later than two months after the withdrawal of the armed forces of the mandatory Power, hold elections to the Constituent Assembly which shall be conducted on democratic lines.

The election regulations in each State shall be drawn up by the Provisional Council of Government and approved by the Commission. Qualified voters for each State for this election shall be persons over eighteen years of age who are: (a) Palestinian citizens residing in that State and (b) Arabs and Jews residing in the State, although not Palestinian citizens, who, before voting, have signed a notice of intention to become citizens of such State.

Arabs and Jews residing in the City of Jerusalem who have signed a notice of intention to become citizens, the Arabs of the Arab State and the Jews of the Jewish State, shall be entitled to vote in the Arab and Jewish States respectively.

Women may vote and be elected to the Constituent Assemblies.

During the transitional period no Jew shall be permitted to establish residence in the area of the proposed Arab State, and no Arab shall be permitted to establish residence in the area of the proposed Jewish State, except by special leave of the Commission.

10. The Constituent Assembly of each State shall draft a democratic constitution for its State and choose a provisional government to succeed the Provisional Council of Government appointed by the Commission. The constitutions of the States shall embody chapters 1 and 2 of the Declaration provided for in section C below and include inter alia provisions for:

a. Establishing in each State a legislative body elected by universal suffrage and by secret ballot on the basis of proportional representation, and an executive body responsible to the legislature;
b. Settling all international disputes in which the State may be involved by peaceful means in such a manner that international peace and security, and justice, are not endangered;
c. Accepting the obligation of the State to refrain in its international relations from the threat or use of force against the territorial integrity of political independence of any State, or in any other manner inconsistent with the purposes of the United Nations;
d. Guaranteeing to all persons equal and non-discriminatory rights in civil, political, economic and religious matters and the enjoyment of human rights and fundamental freedoms, including freedom of religion, language, speech and publication, education, assembly and association;
e. Preserving freedom of transit and visit for all residents and citizens of the other State in Palestine and the City of Jerusalem, subject to considerations of national security, provided that each State shall control residence within its borders.

11. The Commission shall appoint a preparatory economic commission of three members to make whatever arrangements are possible for economic co-operation, with a view to establishing, as soon as practicable, the Economic Union and the Joint Economic Board, as provided in section D below.

12. During the period between the adoption of the recommendations on the question of Palestine by the General Assembly and the termination of the Mandate, the mandatory Power in Palestine shall maintain full responsibility for administration in areas from which it has not withdrawn its armed forces. The Commission shall assist the mandatory Power in the carrying out of these functions. Similarly the mandatory Power shall co-operate with the Commission in the execution of its functions.

13. With a view to ensuring that there shall be continuity in the functioning of administrative services and that, on the withdrawal of the armed forces of the mandatory Power, the whole administration shall be in the charge of the Provisional Councils and the Joint Economic Board, respectively, acting under the Commission, there shall be a progressive transfer, from the mandatory Power to the Commission, of responsibility for all the functions of government, including that of maintaining law and order in the areas from which the forces of the mandatory Power have been withdrawn.

14. The Commission shall be guided in its activities by the recommendations of the General Assembly and by such instructions as the Security Council may consider necessary to issue.

The measures taken by the Commission, within the recommendations of the General Assembly, shall become immediately effective unless the Commission has previously received contrary instructions from the Security Council.

The Commission shall render periodic monthly progress reports, or more frequently if desirable, to the Security Council.

15. The Commission shall make its final report to the next regular session of the General Assembly and to the Security Council simultaneously.

C. DECLARATION

A declaration shall be made to the United Nations by the provisional government of each proposed State before independence. It shall contain inter alia the following clauses:

General Provision

The stipulations contained in the declaration are recognized as fundamental laws of the State and no law, regulation or official action shall conflict or interfere with these stipulations, nor shall any law, regulation or official action prevail over them.

Chapter 1

Holy Places, religious buildings and sites

1. Existing rights in respect of Holy Places and religious buildings or sites shall not be denied or impaired.

2. In so far as Holy Places are concerned, the liberty of access, visit and transit shall be guaranteed, in conformity with existing rights, to all residents and citizens of the other State and of the City of Jerusalem, as well as to aliens, without distinction as to nationality, subject to requirements of national security, public order and decorum.

Similarly, freedom of worship shall be guaranteed in conformity with existing rights, subject to the maintenance of public order and decorum.

3. Holy Places and religious buildings or sites shall be preserved. No act shall be permitted which may in any way impair their sacred character. If at any time it appears to the Government that any particular Holy Place, religious building or site is in need of urgent repair, the Government may call upon the community or communities concerned to carry out such repair. The Government may carry it out itself at the expense of the community or communities concerned if no action is taken within a reasonable time.

4. No taxation shall be levied in respect of any Holy Place, religious building or site which was exempt from taxation on the date of the creation of the State.

No change in the incidence of such taxation shall be made which would either discriminate between the owners or occupiers of Holy Places, religious buildings or sites, or would place such owners or occupiers in a position less favourable in relation to the general incidence of taxation than existed at the time of the adoption of the Assembly's recommendations.

5. The Governor of the City of Jerusalem shall have the right to determine whether the provisions of the Constitution of the State in relation to Holy

Places, religious buildings and sites within the borders of the State and the religious rights appertaining thereto, are being properly applied and respected, and to make decisions on the basis of existing rights in cases of disputes which may arise between the different religious communities or the rites of a religious community with respect to such places, buildings and sites. He shall receive full co-operation and such privileges and immunities as are necessary for the exercise of his functions in the State.

Chapter 2
Religious and Minority Rights

1. Freedom of conscience and the free exercise of all forms of worship, subject only to the maintenance of public order and morals, shall be ensured to all.

2. No discrimination of any kind shall be made between the inhabitants on the ground of race, religion, language or sex.

3. All persons within the jurisdiction of the State shall be entitled to equal protection of the laws.

4. The family law and personal status of the various minorities and their religious interests, including endowments, shall be respected.

5. Except as may be required for the maintenance of public order and good government, no measure shall be taken to obstruct or interfere with the enterprise of religious or charitable bodies of all faiths or to discriminate against any representative or member of these bodies on the ground of his religion or nationality.

6. The State shall ensure adequate primary and secondary education for the Arab and Jewish minority, respectively, in its own language and its cultural traditions.

The right of each community to maintain its own schools for the education of its own members in its own language, while conforming to such educational requirements of a general nature as the State may impose, shall not be denied or impaired. Foreign educational establishments shall continue their activity on the basis of their existing rights.

7. No restriction shall be imposed on the free use by any citizen of the State of any language in private intercourse, in commerce, in religion, in the Press or in publications of any kind, or at public meetings.

8. No expropriation of land owned by an Arab in the Jewish State (by a Jew in the Arab State) shall be allowed except for public purposes. In all cases of expropriation full compensation as fixed by the Supreme Court shall be paid previous to dispossession.

Chapter 3

Citizenship, international conventions and financial obligations

1. Citizenship. Palestinian citizens residing in Palestine outside the City of Jerusalem, as well as Arabs and Jews who, not holding Palestinian citizenship, reside in Palestine outside the City of Jerusalem shall, upon the recognition of independence, become citizens of the State in which they are resident and enjoy full civil and political rights. Persons over the age of eighteen years may opt, within one year from the date of recognition of independence of the State in which they reside, for citizenship of the other State, providing that no Arab residing in the area of the proposed Arab State shall have the right to opt for citizenship in the proposed Jewish State and no Jew residing in the proposed Jewish State shall have the right to opt for citizenship in the proposed Arab State. The exercise of this right of option will be taken to include the wives and children under eighteen years of age of persons so opting.

Arabs residing in the area of the proposed Jewish State and Jews residing in the area of the proposed Arab State who have signed a notice of intention to opt for citizenship of the other State shall be eligible to vote in the elections to the Constituent Assembly of that State, but not in the elections to the Constituent Assembly of the State in which they reside.

2. International conventions.

(a) The State shall be bound by all the international agreements and conventions, both general and special, to which Palestine has become a party. Subject to any right of denunciation provided for therein, such agreements and conventions shall be respected by the State throughout the period for which they were concluded.

(b) Any dispute about the applicability and continued validity of international conventions or treaties signed or adhered to by the mandatory Power on behalf of Palestine shall be referred to the International Court of Justice in accordance with the provisions of the Statute of the Court.

3. Financial obligations.

(a) The State shall respect and fulfil all financial obligations of whatever nature assumed on behalf of Palestine by the mandatory Power during the exercise of the Mandate and recognized by the State. This provision includes the right of public servants to pensions, compensation or gratuities.

(b) These obligations shall be fulfilled through participation in the Joint economic Board in respect of those obligations applicable to Palestine as a whole, and individually in respect of those applicable to, and fairly apportionable between, the States.

(c) A Court of Claims, affiliated with the Joint Economic Board, and composed of one member appointed by the United Nations, one representative of the United Kingdom and one representative of the State concerned, should be established. Any dispute between the United Kingdom and the State respecting claims not recognized by the latter should be referred to that Court.

(d) Commercial concessions granted in respect of any part of Palestine prior to the adoption of the resolution by the General Assembly shall continue to be valid according to their terms, unless modified by agreement between the concession-holder and the State.

Chapter 4

Miscellaneous Provisions

1. The provisions of chapters 1 and 2 of the declaration shall be under the guarantee of the United Nations, and no modifications shall be made in them without the assent of the General Assembly of the United nations. Any Member of the United Nations shall have the right to bring to the attention of the General Assembly any infraction or danger of infraction of any of these stipulations, and the General Assembly may thereupon make such recommendations as it may deem proper in the circumstances.

2. Any dispute relating to the application or the interpretation of this declaration shall be referred, at the request of either party, to the International Court of Justice, unless the parties agree to another mode of settlement.

D. ECONOMIC UNION AND TRANSIT

1. The Provisional Council of Government of each State shall enter into an undertaking with respect to economic union and transit. This undertaking shall be drafted by the commission provided for in section B, paragraph 1, utilizing to the greatest possible extent the advice and co-operation of representative organizations and bodies from each of the proposed States. It shall contain provisions to establish the Economic Union of Palestine and provide for other matters of common interest. If by 1 April 1948 the Provisional Councils of Government have not entered into the undertaking, the undertaking shall be put into force by the Commission.

The Economic Union of Palestine

2. The objectives of the Economic Union of Palestine shall be:
a. A customs union;
b. A joint currency system providing for a single foreign exchange rate;
c. Operation in the common interest on a non-discriminatory basis of railways; inter-State highways; postal, telephone and telegraphic services, and port and airports involved in international trade and commerce;
d. Joint economic development, especially in respect of irrigation, land reclamation and soil conservation;
e. Access for both States and for the City of Jerusalem on a non-discriminatory basis to water and power facilities.

3. There shall be established a Joint Economic Board, which shall consist of three representatives of each of the two States and three foreign members appointed by the Economic and Social Council of the United Nations. The

foreign members shall be appointed in the first instance for a term of three years; they shall serve as individuals and not as representatives of States.

4. The functions of the Joint Economic Board shall be to implement either directly or by delegation the measures necessary to realize the objectives of the Economic Union. It shall have all powers of organization and administration necessary to fulfil its functions.

5. The States shall bind themselves to put into effect the decisions of the Joint Economic Board. The Board's decisions shall be taken by a majority vote.

6. In the event of failure of a State to take the necessary action the Board may, by a vote of six members, decide to withhold an appropriate portion of that part of the customs revenue to which the State in question is entitled under the Economic Union. Should the State persist in its failure to co-operate, the Board may decide by a simple majority vote upon such further sanctions, including disposition of funds which it has withheld, as it may deem appropriate.

7. In relation to economic development, the functions of the Board shall be the planning, investigation and encouragement of joint development projects, but it shall not undertake such projects except with the assent of both States and the City of Jerusalem, in the event that Jerusalem is directly involved in the development project.

8. In regard to the joint currency system the currencies circulating in the two States and the City of Jerusalem shall be issued under the authority of the Joint Economic Board, which shall be the sole issuing authority and which shall determine the reserves to be held against such currencies.

9. So far as is consistent with paragraph 2 (b) above, each State may operate its own central bank, control its own fiscal and credit policy, its foreign exchange receipts and expenditures, the grant of import licenses, and may conduct international financial operations on its own faith and credit. During the first two years after the termination of the Mandate, the Joint Economic Board shall have the authority to take such measures as may be necessary to ensure that--to the extent that the total foreign exchange revenues of the two States from the export of goods and services permit, and provided that each State takes appropriate measures to conserve its own foreign exchange resources--each State shall have available, in any twelve months' period, foreign exchange sufficient to assure the supply of quantities of imported goods and services for consumption in its territory equivalent to the quantities of such goods and services consumed in that territory in the twelve months' period ending 31 December 1947.

10. All economic authority not specifically vested in the Joint Economic Board is reserved to each State.

11. There shall be a common customs tariff with complete freedom of trade between the States, and between the States and the City of Jerusalem.

12. The tariff schedules shall be drawn up by a Tariff Commission, consisting

of representatives of each of the States in equal numbers, and shall be submitted to the Joint Economic Board for approval by a majority vote. In case of disagreement in the Tariff Commission, the Joint Economic Board shall arbitrate the points of difference. In the event that the Tariff Commission fails to draw up any schedule by a date to be fixed, the Joint Economic Board shall determine the tariff schedule.

13. The following items shall be a first charge on the customs and other common revenue of the Joint Economic Board:

(a) The expenses of the customs service and of the operation of the joint services;
(b) The administrative expenses of the Joint Economic Board;
(c) The financial obligations of the Administration of Palestine consisting of:
  (i) The service of the outstanding public debt;
  (ii) The cost of superannuation benefits, now being paid or falling due in the future, in accordance with the rules and to the extent established by paragraph 3 of chapter 3 above.

14. After these obligations have been met in full, the surplus revenue from the customs and other common services shall be divided in the following manner: not less than 5 per cent and not more than 10 per cent to the City of Jerusalem; the residue shall be allocated to each State by the Joint Economic Board equitably, with the objective of maintaining a sufficient and suitable level of government and social services in each State, except that the share of either State shall not exceed the amount of that State's contribution to the revenues of the Economic Union by more than approximately four million pounds in any year. The amount granted may be adjusted by the Board according to the price level in relation to the prices prevailing at the time of the establishment of the Union. After five years, the principles of the distribution of the joint revenues may be revised by the Joint Economic Board on a basis of equity.

15. All international conventions and treaties affecting customs tariff rates, and those communications services under the jurisdiction of the Joint Economic Board, shall be entered into by both States. In these matters, the two States shall be bound to act in accordance with the majority vote of the Joint Economic Board.

16. The Joint Economic Board shall endeavour to secure for Palestine's export fair and equal access to world markets.

17. All enterprises operated by the Joint Economic Board shall pay fair wages on a uniform basis.

Freedom of transit and visit

18. The undertaking shall contain provisions preserving freedom of transit and visit for all residents or citizens of both States and of the City of Jerusalem, subject to security considerations; provided that each state and the City shall control residence within its borders.

Termination, modification and interpretation of the undertaking

19. The undertaking and any treaty issuing therefrom shall remain in force for a period of ten years. It shall continue in force until notice of termination, to take effect two years thereafter, is given by either of the parties.

20. During the initial ten-year period, the undertaking and any treaty issuing therefrom may not be modified except by consent of both parties and with the approval of the General Assembly.

21. Any dispute relating to the application or the interpretation of the undertaking and any treaty issuing therefrom shall be referred, at the request of either party, to the international Court of Justice, unless the parties agree to another mode of settlement.

E. ASSETS

1. The movable assets of the Administration of Palestine shall be allocated to the Arab and Jewish States and the City of Jerusalem on an equitable basis. Allocations should be made by the United Nations Commission referred to in section B, paragraph 1, above. Immovable assets shall become the property of the government of the territory in which they are situated.

2. During the period between the appointment of the United Nations Commission and the termination of the Mandate, the mandatory Power shall, except in respect of ordinary operations, consult with the Commission on any measure which it may contemplate involving the liquidation, disposal or encumbering of the assets of the Palestine Government, such as the accumulated treasury surplus, the proceeds of Government bond issues, State lands or any other asset.

F. ADMISSION TO MEMBERSHIP IN THE UNITED NATIONS

When the independence of either the Arab or the Jewish State as envisaged in this plan has become effective and the declaration and undertaking, as envisaged in this plan, have been signed by either of them, sympathetic consideration should be given to its application for admission to membership in the United Nations in accordance with Article 4 of the Charter of the United Nations.

The Declaration on the establishment of the State of Israel, 14 May 1948

ERETZ-ISRAEL [(Hebrew) - the Land of Israel, Palestine] was the birthplace of the Jewish people. Here their spiritual, religious and political identity was shaped. Here they first attained to statehood, created cultural values of national and universal significance and gave to the world the eternal Book of Books.

After being forcibly exiled from their land, the people kept faith with it throughout their Dispersion and never ceased to pray and hope for their return to it and for the restoration in it of their political freedom.

Impelled by this historic and traditional attachment, Jews strove in every successive generation to re-establish themselves in their ancient homeland. In recent decades they returned in their masses. Pioneers, ma'pilim [(Hebrew) - immigrants coming to Eretz-Israel in defiance of restrictive legislation] and defenders, they made deserts bloom, revived the Hebrew language, built villages and towns, and created a thriving community controlling its own economy and culture, loving peace but knowing how to defend itself, bringing the blessings of progress to all the country's inhabitants, and aspiring towards independent nationhood.

In the year 5657 (1897), at the summons of the spiritual father of the Jewish State, Theodore Herzl, the First Zionist Congress convened and proclaimed the right of the Jewish people to national rebirth in its own country.

This right was recognized in the Balfour Declaration of the 2nd November, 1917, and re-affirmed in the Mandate of the League of Nations which, in particular, gave international sanction to the historic connection between the Jewish people and Eretz-Israel and to the right of the Jewish people to rebuild its National Home.

The catastrophe which recently befell the Jewish people - the massacre of millions of Jews in Europe - was another clear demonstration of the urgency of solving the problem of its homelessness by re-establishing in Eretz-Israel the Jewish State, which would open the gates of the homeland wide to every Jew and confer upon the Jewish people the status of a fully privileged member of the comity of nations.

Survivors of the Nazi holocaust in Europe, as well as Jews from other parts of the world, continued to migrate to Eretz-Israel, undaunted by difficulties, restrictions and dangers, and never ceased to assert their right to a life of dignity, freedom and honest toil in their national homeland.

In the Second World War, the Jewish community of this country contributed its full share to the struggle of the freedom- and peace-loving nations against the forces of Nazi wickedness and, by the blood of its soldiers and its war effort, gained the right to be reckoned among the peoples who founded the United Nations.

On the 29th November, 1947, the United Nations General Assembly passed a resolution calling for the establishment of a Jewish State in Eretz-Israel; the General Assembly required the inhabitants of Eretz-Israel to take such steps as were necessary on their part for the implementation of that resolution. This recognition by the United Nations of the right of the Jewish people to establish their State is irrevocable.

This right is the natural right of the Jewish people to be masters of their own fate, like all other nations, in their own sovereign State.

ACCORDINGLY WE, MEMBERS OF THE PEOPLE'S COUNCIL, REPRESENTATIVES OF THE JEWISH COMMUNITY OF ERETZ-ISRAEL AND OF THE ZIONIST MOVEMENT, ARE HERE ASSEMBLED ON THE DAY OF THE TERMINATION OF THE BRITISH MANDATE OVER ERETZ-ISRAEL AND, BY VIRTUE OF OUR NATURAL AND HISTORIC RIGHT AND ON THE STRENGTH OF THE RESOLUTION OF THE UNITED NATIONS GENERAL ASSEMBLY, HEREBY DECLARE THE ESTABLISHMENT OF A JEWISH STATE IN ERETZ-ISRAEL, TO BE KNOWN AS THE STATE OF ISRAEL.

WE DECLARE that, with effect from the moment of the termination of the Mandate being tonight, the eve of Sabbath, the 6th Iyar, 5708 (15th May, 1948), until the establishment of the elected, regular authorities of the State in accordance with the Constitution which shall be adopted by the Elected Constituent Assembly not later than the 1st October 1948, the People's Council shall act as a Provisional Council of State, and its executive organ, the People's Administration, shall be the Provisional Government of the Jewish State, to be called "Israel".

THE STATE OF ISRAEL will be open for Jewish immigration and for the Ingathering of the Exiles; it will foster the development of the country for the benefit of all its inhabitants; it will be based on freedom, justice and peace as envisaged by the prophets of Israel; it will ensure complete equality of social and political rights to all its inhabitants irrespective of religion, race or sex; it will guarantee freedom of religion, conscience, language, education and culture; it will safeguard the Holy Places of all religions; and it will be faithful to the principles of the Charter of the United Nations.

THE STATE OF ISRAEL is prepared to cooperate with the agencies and representatives of the United Nations in implementing the resolution of the General Assembly of the 29th November, 1947, and will take steps to bring about the economic union of the whole of Eretz-Israel.

WE APPEAL to the United Nations to assist the Jewish people in the building-up of its State and to receive the State of Israel into the comity of nations.

WE APPEAL - in the very midst of the onslaught launched against us now for months - to the Arab inhabitants of the State of Israel to preserve peace and participate in the upbuilding of the State on the basis of full and equal citizenship and due representation in all its provisional and permanent institutions.

WE EXTEND our hand to all neighbouring states and their peoples in an offer of peace and good neighbourliness, and appeal to them to establish bonds of cooperation and mutual help with the sovereign Jewish people settled in its own land. The State of Israel is prepared to do its share in a common effort for the advancement of the entire Middle East.

WE APPEAL to the Jewish people throughout the Diaspora to rally round the Jews of Eretz-Israel in the tasks of immigration and upbuilding and to stand by them in the great struggle for the realization of the age-old dream - the redemption of Israel.

PLACING OUR TRUST IN THE "ROCK OF ISRAEL", WE AFFIX OUR SIGNATURES TO THIS PROCLAMATION AT THIS SESSION OF THE PROVISIONAL COUNCIL OF STATE, ON THE SOIL OF THE HOMELAND, IN THE CITY OF TEL-AVIV, ON THIS SABBATH EVE, THE 5TH DAY OF IYAR, 5708 (14TH MAY,1948).

David Ben-Gurion

Daniel Auster
Mordekhai Bentov
Yitzchak Ben Zvi
Eliyahu Berligne
Fritz Bernstein
Rabbi Wolf Gold
Meir Grabovsky
Yitzchak Gruenbaum
Dr. Abraham Granovsky
Eliyahu Dobkin
Meir Wilner-Kovner
Zerach Wahrhaftig
Herzl Vardi

Rachel Cohen
Rabbi Kalman Kahana
Saadia Kobashi
Rabbi Yitzchak Meir Levin
Meir David Loewenstein
Zvi Luria
Golda Myerson
Nachum Nir
Zvi Segal
Rabbi Yehuda Leib Hacohen Fishman

David Zvi Pinkas
Aharon Zisling
Moshe Kolodny
Eliezer Kaplan
Abraham Katznelson
Felix Rosenblueth
David Remez
Berl Repetur
Mordekhai Shattner
Ben Zion Sternberg
Bekhor Shitreet
Moshe Shapira
Moshe Shertok

*** Published in the Official Gazette, No. 1 of the 5th, Iyar, 5708 (14th May, 1948).**

Israel-(Trans-)Jordan Armistice Agreement, 3 April 1949

Preamble

The Parties to the present Agreement,

Responding to the Security Council resolution of 16 November 1948, calling upon them, as a further provisional measure under Article 40 of the Charter of the United Nations and in order to facilitate the transition from the present truce to permanent peace in Palestine, to negotiate an armistice;

Having decided to enter into negotiations under United Nations chairmanship concerning the implementation of the Security Council resolution of 16 November 1948; and having appointed representatives empowered to negotiate and conclude an Armistice Agreement;

The undersigned representatives of their respective Governments, having exchanged their full powers found to be in good and proper form, have agreed upon the following provisions:

Article I

With a view to promoting the return of permanent peace in Palestine and in recognition of the importance in this regard of mutual assurances concerning the future military operations of the Parties, the following principles, which shall be fully observed by both Parties during the armistice, are hereby affirmed:

1. The injunction of the Security Council against resort to military force in the settlement of the Palestine question shall henceforth be scrupulously respected by both Parties;
2. No aggressive action by the armed forces - land, sea, or air - of either Party shall be undertaken, planned, or threatened against the people or the armed forces of the other; it being understood that the use of the term planned in this context has no bearing on normal staff planning as generally practised in military organisations;
3. The right of each Party to its security and freedom from fear of attack by the armed forces of the other shall be fully respected;
4. The establishment of an armistice between the armed forces of the two Parties is accepted as an indispensable step toward the liquidation of armed conflict and the restoration of peace in Palestine.

Article II

With a specific view to the implementation of the resolution of the Security Council of 16 November 1948, the following principles and purposes are affirmed:

1. The principle that no military or political advantage should be gained under the truce ordered by the Security Council is recognised;
2. It is also recognised that no provision of this Agreement shall in any way prejudice the rights, claims and positions of either Party hereto in the ultimate peaceful settlement of the Palestine question, the provisions of this Agreement being dictated exclusively by military considerations.

Article III

1. In pursuance of the foregoing principles and of the resolution of the Security Council of 16 November 1948, a general armistice between the armed forces of the two Parties - land, sea and air - is hereby established.

2. No element of the land, sea or air military or para-military forces of either Party, including non-regular forces, shall commit any warlike or hostile act against the military or para-military forces of the other Party, or against civilians in territory under the control of that Party; or shall advance beyond or pass over for any purpose whatsoever the Armistice Demarcation Lines set forth in articles V and VI of this Agreement; or enter into or pass through the air space of the other Party.

3. No warlike act or act of hostility shall be conducted from territory controlled by one of the Parties to this Agreement against the other Party.

Article IV

1. The lines described in articles V and VI of this Agreement shall be designated as the Armistice Demarcation Lines and are delineated in pursuance of the purpose and intent of the resolution of the Security Council of 16 November 1948.

2. The basic purpose of the Armistice Demarcation Lines is to delineate the lines beyond which the armed forces of the respective Parties shall not move.

3. Rules and regulations of the armed forces of the Parties, which prohibit civilians from crossing the fighting lines or entering the area between the lines, shall remain in effect after the signing of this Agreement with application to the Armistice Demarcation Lines defined in articles V and VI.

Article 49 Geneva Convention (IV) relative to the Protection of Civilian Persons in Time of War, Geneva, 12 August 1949

Article 49 - Deportations, transfers, evacuations

1. Individual or mass forcible transfers, as well as deportations of protected persons from occupied territory to the territory of the Occupying Power or to that of any other country, occupied or not, are prohibited, regardless of their motive.
2. Nevertheless, the Occupying Power may undertake total or partial evacuation of a given area if the security of the population or imperative military reasons so demand. Such evacuations may not involve the displacement of protected persons outside the bounds of the occupied territory except when for material reasons it is impossible to avoid such displacement. Persons thus evacuated shall be transferred back to their homes as soon as hostilities in the area in question have ceased.
3. The Occupying Power undertaking such transfers or evacuations shall ensure, to the greatest practicable extent, that proper accommodation is provided to receive the protected persons, that the removals are effected in satisfactory conditions of hygiene, health, safety and nutrition, and that members of the same family are not separated.
4. The Protecting Power shall be informed of any transfers and evacuations as soon as they have taken place.
5. The Occupying Power shall not detain protected persons in an area particularly exposed to the dangers of war unless the security of the population or imperative military reasons so demand.
6. The Occupying Power shall not deport or transfer parts of its own civilian population into the territory it occupies.

General Assembly Resolution 2253 (ES-V), 4 July 1967

Adopted unanimously at the 1382nd meeting.

2253 (ES-V). Measures taken by Israel to change
the status of the City of Jerusalem

The General Assembly,

Deeply concerned at the situation prevailing in Jerusalem as a result of the measures taken by Israel to change the status of the City,

1. Considers that these measures are invalid;

2. Calls upon Israel to rescind all measures already taken and to desist forthwith from taking any action which would alter the status of Jerusalem;

3. Requests the Secretary-General to report to the General Assembly and the Security Council on the situation and on the implementation of the present resolution not later than one week from its adoption.

The Karthoum Resolution of 1 September 1967 issued at the conclusion of the 1967 Arab League Summit in Karthoum, Sudan

1. The conference has affirmed the unity of Arab states, the unity of joint action and the need for coordination and for the elimination of all differences. The Kings, Presidents and representatives of the other Arab Heads of State at the conference have affirmed their countries' stand by an implementation of the Arab Solidarity Charter which was signed at the third Arab summit conference in Casablanca.
2. The conference has agreed on the need to consolidate all efforts to eliminate the effects of the aggression on the basis that the occupied lands are Arab lands and that the burden of regaining these lands falls on all the Arab States.
3. The Arab Heads of State have agreed to unite their political efforts at the international and diplomatic level to eliminate the effects of the aggression and to ensure the withdrawal of the aggressive Israeli forces from the Arab lands which have been occupied since the aggression of 5 June. This will be done within the framework of the main principles by which the Arab States abide, namely, no peace with Israel, no recognition of Israel, no negotiations with it, and insistence on the rights of the Palestinian people in their own country.
4. The conference of Arab Ministers of Finance, Economy and Oil recommended that suspension of oil pumping be used as a weapon in the battle. However, after thoroughly studying the matter, the summit conference has come to the conclusion that the oil pumping can itself be used as a positive weapon, since oil is an Arab resource which can be used to strengthen the economy of the Arab States directly affected by the aggression, so that these States will be able to stand firm in the battle. The conference has, therefore, decided to resume the pumping of oil, since oil is a positive Arab resource that can be used in the service of Arab goals. It can contribute to the efforts to enable those Arab States which were exposed to the aggression and thereby lost economic resources to stand firm and eliminate the effects of the aggression. The oil-producing States have, in fact, participated in the efforts to enable the States affected by the aggression to stand firm in the face of any economic pressure.
5. The participants in the conference have approved the plan proposed by Kuwait to set up an Arab Economic and Social Development Fund on the basis of the recommendation of the Baghdad conference of Arab Ministers of Finance, Economy and Oil.
6. The participants have agreed on the need to adopt the necessary measures to strengthen military preparation to face all eventualities.
7. The conference has decided to expedite the elimination of foreign bases in the Arab States.

Security Council Resolution 242 (1967), 22 November 1967

Resolution 242 (1967)
of 22 November 1967

The Security Council,

Expressing its continuing concern with the grave situation in the Middle East,

Emphasizing the inadmissibility of the acquisition of territory by war and the need to work for a just and lasting peace in which every State in the area can live in security,

Emphasizing further that all Member States in their acceptance of the Charter of the United Nations have undertaken a commitment to act in accordance with Article 2 of the Charter,

1. Affirms that the fulfilment of Charter principles requires the establishment of a just and lasting peace in the Middle East which should include the application of both the following principles:
(i) Withdrawal of Israel armed forces from territories occupied in the recent conflict;
(ii) Termination of all claims or states of belligerency and respect for and acknowledgment of the sovereignty, territorial integrity and political independence of every State in the area and their right to live in peace within secure and recognized boundaries free from threats or acts of force;

2. *Affirms further the necessity*
(a) For guaranteeing freedom of navigation through international waterways in the area;
(b) For achieving a just settlement of the refugee problem;
(c) For guaranteeing the territorial inviolability and political independence of every State in the area, through measures including the establishment of demilitarized zones;

3. *Requests* the Secretary-General to designate a Special Representative to proceed to the Middle East to establish and maintain contacts with the States concerned in order to promote agreement and assist efforts to achieve a peaceful and accepted settlement in accordance with the provisions and principles in this resolution;

4. *Requests* the Secretary-General to report to the Security Council on the progress of the efforts of the Special Representative as soon as possible.

Palestine National Charter, 1968 version

Article 1:

Palestine is the homeland of the Arab Palestinian people; it is an indivisible part of the Arab homeland, and the Palestinian people are an integral part of the Arab nation.

Article 2:

Palestine, with the boundaries it had during the British Mandate, is an indivisible territorial unit.

Article 3:

The Palestinian Arab people possess the legal right to their homeland and have the right to determine their destiny after achieving the liberation of their country in accordance with their wishes and entirely of their own accord and will.

Article 4:

The Palestinian identity is a genuine, essential, and inherent characteristic; it is transmitted from parents to children. The Zionist occupation and the dispersal of the Palestinian Arab people, through the disasters which befell them, do not make them lose their Palestinian identity and their membership in the Palestinian community, nor do they negate them.

Article 5:

The Palestinians are those Arab nationals who, until 1947, normally resided in Palestine regardless of whether they were evicted from it or have stayed there. Anyone born, after that date, of a Palestinian father - whether inside Palestine or outside it - is also a Palestinian.

Article 6:

The Jews who had normally resided in Palestine until the beginning of the Zionist invasion will be considered Palestinians.

Article 7:

That there is a Palestinian community and that it has material, spiritual, and historical connection with Palestine are indisputable facts. It is a national duty to bring up individual Palestinians in an Arab revolutionary manner. All means of information and education must be adopted in order to acquaint the Palestinian with his country in the most profound manner, both spiritual and material, that is possible. He must be prepared for the armed struggle and ready to sacrifice his wealth and his life in order to win back his homeland and bring about its liberation.

Article 8:

The phase in their history, through which the Palestinian people are now living, is that of national (watani) struggle for the liberation of Palestine. Thus the conflicts among the Palestinian national forces are secondary, and should be ended for the sake of the basic conflict that exists between the forces of Zionism and of imperialism on the one hand, and the Palestinian Arab people on the other. On this basis the Palestinian masses, regardless of whether they are residing in the national homeland or in diaspora (mahajir) constitute - both their organizations and the individuals - one national front working for the retrieval of Palestine and its liberation through armed struggle.

Article 9:

Armed struggle is the only way to liberate Palestine. This it is the overall strategy, not merely a tactical phase. The Palestinian Arab people assert their absolute determination and firm resolution to continue their armed struggle and to work for an armed popular revolution for the liberation of their country and their return to it . They also assert their right to normal life in Palestine and to exercise their right to self-determination and sovereignty over it.

Article 10:

Commando action constitutes the nucleus of the Palestinian popular liberation war. This requires its escalation, comprehensiveness, and the mobilization of all the Palestinian popular and educational efforts and their organization and involvement in the armed Palestinian revolution. It also requires the achieving of unity for the national (watani) struggle among the different groupings of the Palestinian people, and between the Palestinian people and the Arab masses, so as to secure the continuation of the revolution, its escalation, and victory.

Article 11:

The Palestinians will have three mottoes: national (wataniyya) unity, national (qawmiyya) mobilization, and liberation.

Article 12:

The Palestinian people believe in Arab unity. In order to contribute their share toward the attainment of that objective, however, they must, at the present stage of their struggle, safeguard their Palestinian identity and develop their consciousness of that identity, and oppose any plan that may dissolve or impair it.

Article 13:

Arab unity and the liberation of Palestine are two complementary objectives, the attainment of either of which facilitates the attainment of the other. Thus, Arab unity leads to the liberation of Palestine, the liberation of Palestine leads to Arab unity; and work toward the realization of one objective proceeds side by side with work toward the realization of the other.

Article 14:

The destiny of the Arab nation, and indeed Arab existence itself, depend upon the destiny of the Palestine cause. From this interdependence springs the Arab nation's pursuit of, and striving for, the liberation of Palestine. The people of Palestine play the role of the vanguard in the realization of this sacred (qawmi) goal.

Article 15:

The liberation of Palestine, from an Arab viewpoint, is a national (qawmi) duty and it attempts to repel the Zionist and imperialist aggression against the Arab homeland, and aims at the elimination of Zionism in Palestine. Absolute responsibility for this falls upon the Arab nation - peoples and governments - with the Arab people of Palestine in the vanguard. Accordingly, the Arab nation must mobilize all its military, human, moral, and spiritual capabilities to participate actively with the Palestinian people in the liberation of Palestine. It must, particularly in the phase of the armed Palestinian revolution, offer and furnish the Palestinian people with all possible help, and material and human support, and make available to them the means and opportunities that will enable them to continue to carry out their leading role in the armed revolution, until they liberate their homeland.

Article 16:

The liberation of Palestine, from a spiritual point of view, will provide the Holy Land with an atmosphere of safety and tranquility, which in turn will safeguard the country's religious sanctuaries and guarantee freedom of worship and of visit to all, without discrimination of race, color, language, or religion. Accordingly, the people of Palestine look to all spiritual forces in the world for support.

Article 17:

The liberation of Palestine, from a human point of view, will restore to the Palestinian individual his dignity, pride, and freedom. Accordingly the Palestinian Arab people look forward to the support of all those who believe in the dignity of man and his freedom in the world.

Article 18:

The liberation of Palestine, from an international point of view, is a defensive action necessitated by the demands of self-defense. Accordingly the Palestinian people, desirous as they are of the friendship of all people, look to freedom-loving, and peace-loving states for support in order to restore their legitimate rights in Palestine, to re-establish peace and security in the country, and to enable its people to exercise national sovereignty and freedom.

Article 19:

The partition of Palestine in 1947 and the establishment of the state of Israel are entirely illegal, regardless of the passage of time, because they were contrary to the will of the Palestinian people and to their natural right in their homeland, and inconsistent with the principles embodied in the Charter of the United Nations; particularly the right to self-determination.

Article 20:

The Balfour Declaration, the Mandate for Palestine, and everything that has been based upon them, are deemed null and void. Claims of historical or religious ties of Jews with Palestine are incompatible with the facts of history and the true conception of what constitutes statehood. Judaism, being a religion, is not an independent nationality. Nor do Jews constitute a single nation with an identity of its own; they are citizens of the states to which they belong.

Article 21:

The Arab Palestinian people, expressing themselves by the armed Palestinian revolution, reject all solutions which are substitutes for the total liberation of Palestine and reject all proposals aiming at the liquidation of the Palestinian problem, or its internationalization.

Article 22:

Zionism is a political movement organically associated with international imperialism and antagonistic to all action for liberation and to progressive movements in the world. It is racist and fanatic in its nature, aggressive, expansionist, and colonial in its aims, and fascist in its methods. Israel is the instrument of the Zionist movement, and geographical base for world imperialism placed strategically in the midst of the Arab homeland to combat the hopes of the Arab nation for liberation, unity, and progress. Israel is a constant source of threat vis-a-vis peace in the Middle East and the whole world. Since the liberation of Palestine will destroy the Zionist and imperialist presence and will contribute to the establishment of peace in the Middle East, the Palestinian people look for the support of all the progressive and peaceful forces and urge them all, irrespective of their affiliations and beliefs, to offer the Palestinian people all aid and support in their just struggle for the liberation of their homeland.

Article 23:

The demand of security and peace, as well as the demand of right and justice, require all states to consider Zionism an illegitimate movement, to outlaw its existence, and to ban its operations, in order that friendly relations among peoples may be preserved, and the loyalty of citizens to their respective homelands safeguarded.

Article 24:

The Palestinian people believe in the principles of justice, freedom, sovereignty, self-determination, human dignity, and in the right of all peoples to exercise them.

Article 25:

For the realization of the goals of this Charter and its principles, the Palestine Liberation Organization will perform its role in the liberation of Palestine in accordance with the Constitution of this Organization.

Article 26:

The Palestine Liberation Organization, representative of the Palestinian revolutionary forces, is responsible for the Palestinian Arab people's movement in its struggle - to retrieve its homeland, liberate and return to it and exercise the right to self-determination in it - in all military, political, and financial fields and also for whatever may be required by the Palestine case on the inter-Arab and international levels.

Article 27:

The Palestine Liberation Organization shall cooperate with all Arab states, each according to its potentialities; and will adopt a neutral policy among them in the light of the requirements of the war of liberation; and on this basis it shall not interfere in the internal affairs of any Arab state.

Article 28:

The Palestinian Arab people assert the genuineness and independence of their national (wataniyya) revolution and reject all forms of intervention, trusteeship, and subordination.

Article 29:

The Palestinian people possess the fundamental and genuine legal right to liberate and retrieve their homeland. The Palestinian people determine their attitude toward all states and forces on the basis of the stands they adopt vis-a-vis to the Palestinian revolution to fulfill the aims of the Palestinian people.

Article 30:

Fighters and carriers of arms in the war of liberation are the nucleus of the popular army which will be the protective force for the gains of the Palestinian Arab people.

Article 31:

The Organization shall have a flag, an oath of allegiance, and an anthem. All this shall be decided upon in accordance with a special regulation.

Article 32:

Regulations, which shall be known as the Constitution of the Palestinian Liberation Organization, shall be annexed to this Charter. It will lay down the manner in which the Organization, and its organs and institutions, shall be constituted; the respective competence of each; and the requirements of its obligation under the Charter.

Article 33:

This Charter shall not be amended save by [vote of] a majority of two-thirds of the total membership of the National Congress of the Palestine Liberation Organization [taken] at a special session convened for that purpose.

Security Council Resolution 476 (1980), 30 June 1980

Resolution 476 (1980)

Adopted by the Security Council at its 2242nd meeting on 30 June 1980

The Security Council,

Having considered the letter of 28 May 1980 from the representative of Pakistan, the current Chairman of the Organization of the Islamic Conference, as contained in document S/13966 of 28 May 1980,

Reaffirming that acquisition of territory by force is inadmissible,

Bearing in mind the specific status of Jerusalem and, in particular, the need for protection and preservation of the unique spiritual and religious dimension of the Holy Places in the city,

Reaffirming its resolutions relevant to the character and status of the Holy City of Jerusalem, in particular resolutions 252 (1968) of 21 May 1968, 267 (1969) of 3 July 1969, 271 (1969) of 15 September 1969, 298 (1971) of 25 September 1971 and 465 (1980) of 1 March 1980,

Recalling the Fourth Geneva Convention of 12 August 1949 relative to the Protection of Civilian Persons in Time of War,

Deploring the persistence of Israel, in changing the physical character, demographic composition, institutional structure and the status of the Holy City of Jerusalem,

Gravely concerned over the legislative steps initiated in the Israeli Knesset with the aim of changing the character and status of the Holy City of Jerusalem,

1. *Reaffirms* the overriding necessity to end the prolonged occupation of Arab territories occupied by Israel since 1967, including Jerusalem;
2. *Strongly* deplores the continued refusal of Israel, the occupying Power, to comply with the relevant resolutions of the Security Council and the General Assembly;

3. *Reconfirms* that all legislative and administrative measures and actions taken by Israel, the occupying Power, which purport to alter the character and status of the Holy City of Jerusalem have no legal validity and constitute a flagrant violation of the Fourth Geneva Convention relative to the Protection of Civilian Persons in Time of War and also constitute a serious obstruction to achieving a comprehensive, just and lasting peace in the Middle East;

4. *Reiterates* that all such measures which have altered the geographic, demographic and historical character and status of the Holy City of Jerusalem are null and void and must be rescinded in compliance with the relevant resolutions of the Security Council;

5. *Urgently* calls on Israel, the occupying Power, to abide by this and previous Security Council resolutions and to desist forthwith from persisting in the policy and measures affecting the character and status of the Holy city of Jerusalem;

6. *Reaffirms* its determination in the event of non-compliance by Israel with this resolution, to examine practical ways and means in accordance with relevant provisions of the Charter of the United Nations to secure the full implementation of this resolution.

Basic Law: Jerusalem the Capital of Israel (5740-1980)

(Unofficial translation)

1. Jerusalem, complete and united, is the capital of Israel.

2. Jerusalem is the seat of the President of the State, the Knesset, the Government and the Supreme Court.

3. The Holy Places shall be protected from desecration and any other violation and from anything likely to violate the freedom of access of the members of the different religions to the places sacred to them or their feelings towards those places.

4. (a) The Government shall provide for the development and prosperity of Jerusalem and the well-being of its inhabitants by allocating special funds, including a special annual grant to the Municipality of Jerusalem (Capital City Grant) with the approval of the Finance Committee of the Knesset.

(b) Jerusalem shall be given special priority in the activities of the authorities of the State so as to further its development in economic and other matters.

(c) The Government shall set up a special body or special bodies for the implementation of this section.

Area of the jurisdiction of Jerusalem (Amendment no. 1)

5. The jurisdiction of Jerusalem includes, as pertaining to this basic law, among others, all of the area that is described in the appendix of the proclamation expanding the borders of municipal Jerusalem beginning the 20th of Sivan 5727 (June 28, 1967), as was given according to the Cities' Ordinance.

Prohibition of the transfer of authority (Amendment no. 1)

6. No authority that is stipulated in the law of the State of Israel or of the Jerusalem Municipality may be transferred either permanently or for an allotted period of time to a foreign body, whether political, governmental or to any other similar type of foreign body.

Entrenchment (Amendment no. 1)

7. Clauses 5 and 6 shall not be modified except by a Basic Law passed by a majority of the members of the Knesset.

MENAHEM BEGIN
Prime Minister

YITZCHAK NAVON
President of the State

* Passed by the Knesset on the 17th Av, 5740 (30th July, 1980) and published in Sefer Ha-Chukkim No. 980 of the 23rd Av, 5740 (5th August, 1980), p. 186; the Bill and an Explanatory Note were published in Hatza'ot Chok No. 1464 of 5740, p. 287.

Amendment no. 1 was passed by the Knesset on the 29th Heshvan 5761 (27th November 2000) and published in Sefer Ha-Chukkim No. 5762, p. 28.

(https://www.knesset.gov.il/laws/special/eng/basic10_eng.htm)

Amendment of Article 7 adopted 2 January 2018. Unofficial translation:

In Article 7 of the Basic Law: Jerusalem, Capital of Israel, before the words "Clauses 5 and 6 shall not be modified" will come the words "Despite what was mentioned in any other law". Also, "Clauses 5 and 6" will be replaced with "Clauses 5, 6 and 7" and "by a majority of the members of the Knesset" will be replaced with "by a majority of 80 Knesset members".

(www.alhaq.org/en/wp-content/uploads/2018/02/P-20-4346.pdf)

Security Council Resolution 478 (1980), 20 August 1980

Resolution 478 (1980)
of 20 August 1980

The Security Council,

Recalling its resolution 476 (1980),

Reaffirming again that the acquisition of territory by force is inadmissible,

Deeply concerned over the enactment of a "basic law" in the Israeli Knesset proclaiming a change in the character and status of the Holy City of Jerusalem, with its implications for peace and security,

Noting that Israel has not complied with resolution 476 (1980),

Reaffirming its determination to examine practical ways and means, in accordance with the relevant provisions of the Charter of the United Nations, to secure the full implementation of its resolution 476 (1980), in the event of non-compliance by Israel,

1. Censures in the strongest terms the enactment by Israel of the "basic law" on Jerusalem and the refusal to comply with relevant Security Council resolutions;

2. Affirms that the enactment of the "basic law" by Israel constitutes a violation of international law and does not affect the continued application of the Geneva Convention relative to the Protection of Civilian Persons in Time of War, of 12 August 1949, in the Palestinian and other Arab territories occupied since June 1967, including Jerusalem;

3. Determines that all legislative and administrative measures and actions taken by Israel, the occupying Power, which have altered or purport to alter the character and status of the Holy City of Jerusalem, and in particular the recent "basic law" on Jerusalem, are null and void and must be rescinded forthwith;

4. Affirms also that this action constitutes a serious obstruction to achieving a comprehensive, just and lasting peace in the Middle East;

5. Decides not to recognize the "basic law" and such other actions by Israel that, as a result of this law, seek to alter the character and status of Jerusalem and calls upon:
(a) All Member States to accept this decision;
(b) Those States that have established diplomatic missions at Jerusalem to withdraw such missions from the Holy City;

6. Requests the Secretary-General to report to the Security Council on the implementation of the present resolution before 15 November 1980;

7. Decides to remain seized of this serious situation.

Adopted at the 2245th meeting by 14 votes to none, with 1 abstention (United States of America).

Hamas Covenant, 1988

The Covenant
of the
Islamic Resistance Movement

18 August 1988

In The Name Of The Most Merciful Allah

"Ye are the best nation that hath been raised up unto mankind: ye command that which is just, and ye forbid that which is unjust, and ye believe in Allah. And if they who have received the scriptures had believed, it had surely been the better for them: there are believers among them, but the greater part of them are transgressors. They shall not hurt you, unless with a slight hurt; and if they fight against you, they shall turn their backs to you, and they shall not be helped. They are smitten with vileness wheresoever they are found; unless they obtain security by entering into a treaty with Allah, and a treaty with men; and they draw on themselves indignation from Allah, and they are afflicted with poverty. This they suffer, because they disbelieved the signs of Allah, and slew the prophets unjustly; this, because they were rebellious, and transgressed." (Al-Imran - verses 109-111).

Israel will exist and will continue to exist until Islam will obliterate it, just as it obliterated others before it" (The Martyr, Imam Hassan al-Banna, of blessed memory).

"The Islamic world is on fire. Each of us should pour some water, no matter how little, to extinguish whatever one can without waiting for the others." (Sheikh Amjad al-Zahawi, of blessed memory).

In The Name Of The Most Merciful Allah

Introduction

Praise be unto Allah, to whom we resort for help, and whose forgiveness, guidance and support we seek; Allah bless the Prophet and grant him salvation, his companions and supporters, and to those who carried out his message and adopted his laws - everlasting prayers and salvation as long as the earth and heaven will last. Hereafter:

O People:

Out of the midst of troubles and the sea of suffering, out of the palpitations of faithful hearts and cleansed arms; out of the sense of duty, and in response to Allah's command, the call has gone out rallying people together and making them follow the ways of Allah, leading them to have determined will in order to fulfill their role in life, to overcome all obstacles, and surmount the difficulties on the way. Constant preparation has continued and so has the readiness to sacrifice life and all that is precious for the sake of Allah.

Thus it was that the nucleus (of the movement) was formed and started to pave its way through the tempestuous sea of hopes and expectations, of wishes and yearnings, of troubles and obstacles, of pain and challenges, both inside and outside.

When the idea was ripe, the seed grew and the plant struck root in the soil of reality, away from passing emotions, and hateful haste. The Islamic Resistance Movement emerged to carry out its role through striving for the sake of its Creator, its arms intertwined with those of all the fighters for the liberation of Palestine. The spirits of its fighters meet with the spirits of all the fighters who have sacrificed their lives on the soil of Palestine, ever since it was conquered by the companions of the Prophet, Allah bless him and grant him salvation, and until this day.

This Covenant of the Islamic Resistance Movement (HAMAS), clarifies its picture, reveals its identity, outlines its stand, explains its aims, speaks about its hopes, and calls for its support, adoption and joining its ranks. Our struggle against the Jews is very great and very serious. It needs all sincere efforts. It is a step that inevitably should be followed by other steps. The Movement is but one squadron that should be supported by more and more squadrons from this vast Arab and Islamic world, until the enemy is vanquished and Allah's victory is realised.

Thus we see them coming on the horizon "and you shall learn about it hereafter" "Allah hath written, Verily I will prevail, and my apostles: for Allah is strong and mighty." (The Dispute - verse 21).

"Say to them, This is my way: I invite you to Allah, by an evident demonstration; both I and he who followeth me; and, praise be unto Allah! I am not an idolator." (Joseph - verse 107).

Hamas (means) strength and bravery -(according to) Al-Mua'jam al-Wasit: c1.

Definition of the Movement

Ideological Starting-Points

Article One:

The Islamic Resistance Movement: The Movement's programme is Islam. From it, it draws its ideas, ways of thinking and understanding of the universe, life and man. It resorts to it for judgement in all its conduct, and it is inspired by it for guidance of its steps.

The Islamic Resistance Movement's Relation With the Moslem Brotherhood Group:

Article Two:

The Islamic Resistance Movement is one of the wings of Moslem Brotherhood in Palestine. Moslem Brotherhood Movement is a universal organization which constitutes the largest Islamic movement in modern times. It is characterised by its deep understanding, accurate comprehension and its complete embrace of all Islamic concepts of all aspects of life, culture, creed, politics, economics, education, society, justice and judgement, the spreading of Islam, education, art, information, science of the occult and conversion to Islam.

Structure and Formation

Article Three:

The basic structure of the Islamic Resistance Movement consists of Moslems who have given their allegiance to Allah whom they truly worship, - "I have created the jinn and humans only for the purpose of worshipping" - who know their duty towards themselves, their families and country. In all that, they fear Allah and raise the banner of Jihad in the face of the oppressors, so that they would rid the land and the people of their uncleanliness, vileness and evils.

"But we will oppose truth to vanity, and it shall confound the same; and behold, it shall vanish away." (Prophets - verse 18).

Article Four:

The Islamic Resistance Movement welcomes every Moslem who embraces its faith, ideology, follows its programme, keeps its secrets, and wants to belong to its ranks and carry out the duty. Allah will certainly reward such one.

Time and Place Extent of the Islamic Resistance Movement:

Article Five:

Time extent of the Islamic Resistance Movement: By adopting Islam as its way of life, the Movement goes back to the time of the birth of the Islamic message, of the righteous ancestor, for Allah is its target, the Prophet is its example and the Koran is its constitution. Its extent in place is anywhere that there are Moslems who embrace Islam as their way of life everywhere in the globe. This being so, it extends to the depth of the earth and reaches out to the heaven.

"Dost thou not see how Allah putteth forth a parable; representing a good word, as a good tree, whose root is firmly fixed in the earth, and whose branches reach unto heaven; which bringeth forth its fruit in all seasons, by the will of its Lord? Allah propoundeth parables unto men, that they may be instructed." (Abraham - verses 24-25).

Characteristics and Independence:

Article Six:

The Islamic Resistance Movement is a distinguished Palestinian movement, whose allegiance is to Allah, and whose way of life is Islam. It strives to raise the banner of Allah over every inch of Palestine, for under the wing of Islam followers of all religions can coexist in security and safety where their lives, possessions and rights are concerned. In the absence of Islam, strife will be rife, oppression spreads, evil prevails and schisms and wars will break out.

How excellent was the Moslem poet, Mohamed Ikbal, when he wrote:

"If faith is lost, there is no security and there is no life for him who does not adhere to religion. He who accepts life without religion, has taken annihilation as his companion for life."

The Universality of the Islamic Resistance Movement:

Article Seven:

As a result of the fact that those Moslems who adhere to the ways of the Islamic Resistance Movement spread all over the world, rally support for it and its stands, strive towards enhancing its struggle, the Movement is a universal one. It is well-equipped for that because of the clarity of its ideology, the nobility of its aim and the loftiness of its objectives.

On this basis, the Movement should be viewed and evaluated, and its role be recognised. He who denies its right, evades supporting it and turns a blind eye to facts, whether intentionally or unintentionally, would awaken to see that events have overtaken him and with no logic to justify his attitude. One should certainly learn from past examples.

The injustice of next-of-kin is harder to bear than the smite of the Indian sword.

"We have also sent down unto thee the book of the Koran with truth, confirming that scripture which was revealed before it; and preserving the same safe from corruption. Judge therefore between them according to that which Allah hath revealed; and follow not their desires, by swerving from the truth which hath come unto thee. Unto every of you have we given a law, and an open path; and if Allah had pleased, he had surely made you one people; but he hath thought it fit to give you different laws, that he might try you in that which he hath given you respectively. Therefore strive to excel each other in good works; unto Allah shall ye all return, and then will he declare unto you that concerning which ye have disagreed." (The Table, verse 48).

The Islamic Resistance Movement is one of the links in the chain of the struggle against the Zionist invaders. It goes back to 1939, to the emergence of the martyr Izz al-Din al Kissam and his brethren the fighters, members of Moslem Brotherhood. It goes on to reach out and become one with another chain that includes the struggle of the Palestinians and Moslem Brotherhood in the 1948 war and the Jihad operations of the Moslem Brotherhood in 1968 and after.

Moreover, if the links have been distant from each other and if obstacles, placed by those who are the lackeys of Zionism in the way of the fighters obstructed the continuation of the struggle, the Islamic Resistance Movement aspires to the realisation of Allah's promise, no matter how long that should take. The Prophet, Allah bless him and grant him salvation, has said:

"The Day of Judgement will not come about until Moslems fight the Jews (killing the Jews), when the Jew will hide behind stones and trees. The stones and trees will say O Moslems, O Abdulla, there is a Jew behind me, come and kill him. Only the Gharkad tree, (evidently a certain kind of tree) would not do that because it is one of the trees of the Jews." (related by al-Bukhari and Moslem).

The Slogan of the Islamic Resistance Movement:

Article Eight:

Allah is its target, the Prophet is its model, the Koran its constitution: Jihad is its path and death for the sake of Allah is the loftiest of its wishes.

Objectives

Incentives and Objectives:

Article Nine:

The Islamic Resistance Movement found itself at a time when Islam has disappeared from life. Thus rules shook, concepts were upset, values changed and evil people took control, oppression and darkness prevailed, cowards became like tigers: homelands were usurped, people were scattered and were caused to wander all over the world, the state of justice disappeared and the state of falsehood replaced it. Nothing remained in its right place. Thus, when Islam is absent from the arena, everything changes. From this state of affairs the incentives are drawn.

As for the objectives: They are the fighting against the false, defeating it and vanquishing it so that justice could prevail, homelands be retrieved and from its mosques would the voice of the mu'azen emerge declaring the establishment of the state of Islam, so that people and things would return each to their right places and Allah is our helper.

"...and if Allah had not prevented men, the one by the other, verily the earth had been corrupted: but Allah is beneficient towards his creatures." (The Cow - verse 251).

Article Ten:

As the Islamic Resistance Movement paves its way, it will back the oppressed and support the wronged with all its might. It will spare no effort to bring about justice and defeat injustice, in word and deed, in this place and everywhere it can reach and have influence therein.

Strategies and Methods

Strategies of the Islamic Resistance Movement: Palestine Is Islamic aqf:

Article Eleven:

The Islamic Resistance Movement believes that the land of Palestine is an Islamic Waqf consecrated for future Moslem generations until Judgement Day. It, or any part of it, should not be squandered: it, or any part of it, should not be given up. Neither a single Arab country nor all Arab countries, neither any king or president, nor all the kings and presidents, neither any organization nor all of them, be they Palestinian or Arab, possess the right to do that. Palestine is an Islamic Waqf land consecrated for Moslem generations until Judgement Day. This being so, who could claim to have the right to represent Moslem generations till Judgement Day?

This is the law governing the land of Palestine in the Islamic Sharia (law) and the same goes for any land the Moslems have conquered by force, because during the times of (Islamic) conquests, the Moslems consecrated these lands to Moslem generations till the Day of Judgement.

It happened like this: When the leaders of the Islamic armies conquered Syria and Iraq, they sent to the Caliph of the Moslems, Umar bin-el-Khatab, asking for his advice concerning the conquered land - whether they should divide it among the soldiers, or leave it for its owners, or what? After consultations and discussions between the Caliph of the Moslems, Omar bin-el-Khatab and companions of the Prophet, Allah bless him and grant him salvation, it was decided that the land should be left with its owners who could benefit by its fruit. As for the real ownership of the land and the land itself, it should be consecrated for Moslem generations till Judgement Day. Those who are on the land, are there only to benefit from its fruit. This Waqf remains as long as earth and heaven remain. Any procedure in contradiction to Islamic Sharia, where Palestine is concerned, is null and void.

"Verily, this is a certain truth. Wherefore praise the name of thy Lord, the great Allah." (The Inevitable - verse 95).

Homeland and Nationalism from the Point of View of the Islamic Resistance Movement in Palestine:

Article Twelve:

Nationalism, from the point of view of the Islamic Resistance Movement, is part of the religious creed. Nothing in nationalism is more significant or deeper than in the case when an enemy should tread Moslem land. Resisting and quelling the enemy become the individual duty of every Moslem, male or female. A woman can go out to fight the enemy without her husband's permission, and so does the slave: without his master's permission.

Nothing of the sort is to be found in any other regime. This is an undisputed fact. If other nationalist movements are connected with materialistic, human or regional causes, nationalism of the Islamic Resistance Movement has all these elements as well as the more important elements that give it soul and life. It is connected to the source of spirit and the granter of life, hoisting in the sky of the homeland the heavenly banner that joins earth and heaven with a strong bond.

If Moses comes and throws his staff, both witch and magic are annulled.

"Now is the right direction manifestly distinguished from deceit: whoever therefore shall deny Tagut, and believe in Allah, he shall surely take hold with a strong handle, which shall not be broken; Allah is he who heareth and seeth." (The Cow - Verse 256).

Peaceful Solutions, Initiatives and International Conferences:

Article Thirteen:

Initiatives, and so-called peaceful solutions and international conferences, are in contradiction to the principles of the Islamic Resistance Movement. Abusing any part of Palestine is abuse directed against part of religion. Nationalism of the Islamic Resistance Movement is part of its religion. Its members have been fed on that. For the sake of hoisting the banner of Allah over their homeland they fight. "Allah will be prominent, but most people do not know."

Now and then the call goes out for the convening of an international conference to look for ways of solving the (Palestinian) question. Some accept, others reject the idea, for this or other reason, with one stipulation or more for consent to convening the conference and participating in it. Knowing the parties constituting the conference, their past and present attitudes towards Moslem problems, the

Islamic Resistance Movement does not consider these conferences capable of realising the demands, restoring the rights or doing justice to the oppressed. These conferences are only ways of setting the infidels in the land of the Moslems as arbitraters. When did the infidels do justice to the believers?

"But the Jews will not be pleased with thee, neither the Christians, until thou follow their religion; say, The direction of Allah is the true direction. And verily if thou follow their desires, after the knowledge which hath been given thee, thou shalt find no patron or protector against Allah." (The Cow - verse 120).

There is no solution for the Palestinian question except through Jihad. Initiatives, proposals and international conferences are all a waste of time and vain endeavors. The Palestinian people know better than to consent to having their future, rights and fate toyed with. As in said in the honourable Hadith:

"The people of Syria are Allah's lash in His land. He wreaks His vengeance through them against whomsoever He wishes among His slaves It is unthinkable that those who are double-faced among them should prosper over the faithful. They will certainly die out of grief and desperation."

The Three Circles:

Article Fourteen:

The question of the liberation of Palestine is bound to three circles: the Palestinian circle, the Arab circle and the Islamic circle. Each of these circles has its role in the struggle against Zionism. Each has its duties, and it is a horrible mistake and a sign of deep ignorance to overlook any of these circles. Palestine is an Islamic land which has the first of the two kiblahs (direction to which Moslems turn in praying), the third of the holy (Islamic) sanctuaries, and the point of departure for Mohamed's midnight journey to the seven heavens (i.e. Jerusalem).

"Praise be unto him who transported his servant by night, from the sacred temple of Mecca to the farther temple of Jerusalem, the circuit of which we have blessed, that we might show him some of our signs; for Allah is he who heareth, and seeth." (The Night-Journey - verse 1).

Since this is the case, liberation of Palestine is then an individual duty for very Moslem wherever he may be. On this basis, the problem should be viewed. This should be realised by every Moslem.

The day the problem is dealt with on this basis, when the three circles mobilize their capabilities, the present state of affairs will change and the day of liberation will come nearer.

"Verily ye are stronger than they, by reason of the terror cast into their breasts from Allah. This, because they are not people of prudence." (The Emigration - verse 13).

The Jihad for the Liberation of Palestine is an Individual Duty:

Article Fifteen:

The day that enemies usurp part of Moslem land, Jihad becomes the individual duty of every Moslem. In face of the Jews' usurpation of Palestine, it is compulsory that the banner of Jihad be raised. To do this requires the diffusion of Islamic consciousness among the masses, both on the regional, Arab and Islamic levels. It is necessary to instill the spirit of Jihad in the heart of the nation so that they would confront the enemies and join the ranks of the fighters.

It is necessary that scientists, educators and teachers, information and media people, as well as the educated masses, especially the youth and sheikhs of the Islamic movements, should take part in the operation of awakening (the masses). It is important that basic changes be made in the school curriculum, to cleanse it of the traces of ideological invasion that affected it as a result of the orientalists and missionaries who infiltrated the region following the defeat of the Crusaders at the hands of Salah el-Din (Saladin). The Crusaders realised that it was impossible to defeat the Moslems without first having ideological invasion pave the way by upsetting their thoughts, disfiguring their heritage and violating their ideals. Only then could they invade with soldiers. This, in its turn, paved the way for the imperialistic invasion that made Allenby declare on entering Jerusalem: "Only now have the Crusades ended." General Guru stood at Salah el-Din's grave and said: "We have returned, O Salah el-Din." Imperialism has helped towards the strengthening of ideological invasion, deepening, and still does, its roots. All this has paved the way towards the loss of Palestine.

It is necessary to instill in the minds of the Moslem generations that the Palestinian problem is a religious problem, and should be dealt with on this basis. Palestine contains Islamic holy sites. In it there is al- Aqsa Mosque which is bound to the great Mosque in Mecca in an inseparable bond as long as heaven and earth speak of Isra` (Mohammed's midnight journey to the seven heavens) and Mi'raj (Mohammed's ascension to the seven heavens from Jerusalem).

"The bond of one day for the sake of Allah is better than the world and whatever there is on it. The place of one's whip in Paradise is far better than the world and whatever there is on it. A worshipper's going and coming in the service of Allah is better than the world and whatever there is on it." (As related by al-Bukhari, Moslem, al-Tarmdhi and Ibn Maja).

"I swear by the holder of Mohammed's soul that I would like to invade and be killed for the sake of Allah, then invade and be killed, and then invade again and be killed." (As related by al-Bukhari and Moslem).

The Education of the Generations:

Article Sixteen:

It is necessary to follow Islamic orientation in educating the Islamic generations in our region by teaching the religious duties, comprehensive study of the Koran, the study of the Prophet's Sunna (his sayings and doings), and learning about Islamic history and heritage from their authentic sources. This should be done by specialised and learned people, using a curriculum that would healthily form the thoughts and faith of the Moslem student. Side by side with this, a comprehensive study of the enemy, his human and financial capabilities, learning about his points of weakness and strength, and getting to know the forces supporting and helping him, should also be included. Also, it is important to be acquainted with the current events, to follow what is new and to study the analysis and commentaries made of these events. Planning for the present and future, studying every trend appearing, is a must so that the fighting Moslem would live knowing his aim, objective and his way in the midst of what is going on around him.

"O my son, verily every matter, whether good or bad, though it be the weight of a grain of mustard-seed, and be hidden in a rock, or in the heavens, or in the earth, Allah will bring the same to light; for Allah is clear-sighted and knowing. O my son, be constant at prayer, and command that which is just, and forbid that which is evil: and be patient under the afflictions which shall befall thee; for this is a duty absolutely incumbent on all men. Distort not thy face out of contempt to men, neither walk in the earth with insolence; for Allah loveth no arrogant, vain-glorious person." (Lokman - verses 16-18).

The Role of the Moslem Woman:

Article Seventeen:

The Moslem woman has a role no less important than that of the moslem man in the battle of liberation. She is the maker of men. Her role in guiding and educating the new generations is great. The enemies have realised the importance of her role. They consider that if they are able to direct and bring her up they way they wish, far from Islam, they would have won the battle. That is why you find them giving these attempts constant attention through information campaigns, films, and the school curriculum, using for that purpose their lackeys who are infiltrated through Zionist organizations under various names and shapes, such as Freemasons, Rotary Clubs, espionage groups and others, which are all nothing more than cells of subversion and saboteurs. These organizations have ample resources that enable them to play their role in societies for the purpose of achieving the Zionist targets and to deepen the concepts that would serve the enemy. These organizations operate in the absence of Islam and its estrangement among its people. The Islamic peoples should perform their role in confronting the conspiracies of these saboteurs. The day Islam is in control of guiding the affairs of life, these organ izations, hostile to humanity and Islam, will be obliterated.

Article Eighteen:

Woman in the home of the fighting family, whether she is a mother or a sister, plays the most important role in looking after the family, rearing the children and embuing them with moral values and thoughts derived from Islam. She has to teach them to perform the religious duties in preparation for the role of fighting awaiting them. That is why it is necessary to pay great attention to schools and the curriculum followed in educating Moslem girls, so that they would grow up to be good mothers, aware of their role in the battle of liberation.

She has to be of sufficient knowledge and understanding where the performance of housekeeping matters are concerned, because economy and avoidance of waste of the family budget, is one of the requirements for the ability to continue moving forward in the difficult conditions surrounding us. She should put before her eyes the fact that the money available to her is just like blood which should never flow except through the veins so that both children and grown-ups could continue to live.

"Verily, the Moslems of either sex, and the true believers of either sex, and the devout men, and the devout women, and the men of veracity, and the women of veracity, and the patient men, and the patient women, and the humble men, and the humble women, and the alms-givers of either sex who remember Allah frequently; for them hath Allah prepared forgiveness and a great reward." (The Confederates - verse 25).

The Role of Islamic Art in the Battle of Liberation:

Article Nineteen:

Art has regulations and measures by which it can be determined whether it is Islamic or pre-Islamic (Jahili) art. The issues of Islamic liberation are in need of Islamic art that would take the spirit high, without raising one side of human nature above the other, but rather raise all of them harmoniously an in equilibrium.

Man is a unique and wonderful creature, made out of a handful of clay and a breath from Allah. Islamic art addresses man on this basis, while pre-Islamic art addresses the body giving preference to the clay component in it.

The book, the article, the bulletin, the sermon, the thesis, the popular poem, the poetic ode, the song, the play and others, contain the characteristics of Islamic art, then these are among the requirements of ideological mobilization, renewed food for the journey and recreation for the soul. The road is long and suffering is plenty. The soul will be bored, but Islamic art renews the energies, resurrects the movement, arousing in them lofty meanings and proper conduct. "Nothing can improve the self if it is in retreat except shifting from one mood to another."

All this is utterly serious and no jest, for those who are fighters do not jest.

Social Mutual Responsibility:

Article Twenty:

Moslem society is a mutually responsible society. The Prophet, prayers and greetings be unto him, said: "Blessed are the generous, whether they were in town or on a journey, who have collected all that they had and shared it equally among themselves."

The Islamic spirit is what should prevail in every Moslem society. The society that confronts a vicious enemy which acts in a way similar to Nazism, making no differentiation between man and woman, between children and old people - such a society is entitled to this Islamic spirit. Our enemy relies on the methods of collective punishment. He has deprived people of their homeland and properties, pursued them in their places of exile and gathering, breaking bones, shooting at women, children and old people, with or without a reason. The enemy has opened detention camps where thousands and thousands of people are thrown and kept under sub-human conditions. Added to this, are the demolition of houses, rendering children orphans, meting cruel sentences against thousands of young people, and causing them to spend the best years of their lives in the dungeons of prisons.

In their Nazi treatment, the Jews made no exception for women or children. Their policy of striking fear in the heart is meant for all. They attack people where their breadwinning is concerned, extorting their money and threatening their honour. They deal with people as if they were the worst war criminals. Deportation from the homeland is a kind of murder.

To counter these deeds, it is necessary that social mutual responsibility should prevail among the people. The enemy should be faced by the people as a single body which if one member of it should complain, the rest of the body would respond by feeling the same pains.

Article Twenty-One:

Mutual social responsibility means extending assistance, financial or moral, to all those who are in need and joining in the execution of some of the work. Members of the Islamic Resistance Movement should consider the interests of the masses as their own personal interests. They must spare no effort in achieving and preserving them. They must prevent any foul play with the future of the upcoming generations and anything that could cause loss to society. The masses are part of them and they are part of the masses. Their strength is theirs, and their future is theirs. Members of the Islamic Resistance Movement should share the people's joy and grief, adopt the demands of the public and whatever means by which they could be realised. The day that such a spirit prevails, brotherliness would deepen, cooperation, sympathy and unity will be enhanced and the ranks will be solidified to confront the enemies.

Supportive Forces Behind the Enemy:

Article Twenty-Two:

For a long time, the enemies have been planning, skillfully and with precision, for the achievement of what they have attained. They took into consideration the causes affecting the current of events. They strived to amass great and substantive material wealth which they devoted to the realisation of their dream. With their money, they took control of the world media, news agencies, the press, publishing houses, broadcasting stations, and others. With their money they stirred revolutions in various parts of the world with the purpose of achieving their interests and reaping the fruit therein. They were behind the French Revolution, the Communist revolution and most of the revolutions we heard and hear about, here and there. With their money they formed secret societies, such as Freemasons, Rotary Clubs, the Lions and others in different parts of the world for the purpose of sabotaging societies and achieving Zionist interests. With their money they were able to control imperialistic countries and instigate them to colonize many countries in order to enable them to exploit their resources and spread corruption there.

You may speak as much as you want about regional and world wars. They were behind World War I, when they were able to destroy the Islamic Caliphate, making financial gains and controlling resources. They obtained the Balfour Declaration, formed the League of Nations through which they could rule the world. They were behind World War II, through which they made huge financial gains by trading in armaments, and paved the way for the establishment of their state. It was they who instigated the replacement of the League of Nations with the United Nations and the Security Council to enable them to rule the world through them. There is no war going on anywhere, without having their finger in it.

"So often as they shall kindle a fire for war, Allah shall extinguish it; and they shall set their minds to act corruptly in the earth, but Allah loveth not the corrupt doers." (The Table - verse 64).

The imperialistic forces in the Capitalist West and Communist East, support the enemy with all their might, in money and in men. These forces take turns in doing that. The day Islam appears, the forces of infidelity would unite to challenge it, for the infidels are of one nation.

"O true believers, contract not an intimate friendship with any besides yourselves: they will not fail to corrupt you. They wish for that which may cause you to perish: their hatred hath already appeared from out of their mouths; but what their breasts conceal is yet more inveterate. We have already shown you signs of their ill will towards you, if ye understand." (The Family of Imran - verse 118).

It is not in vain that the verse is ended with Allah's words "if ye understand."

Our Attitudes Towards:

A. Islamic Movements:

Article Twenty-Three:

The Islamic Resistance Movement views other Islamic movements with respect and appreciation. If it were at variance with them on one point or opinion, it is in agreement with them on other points and understandings. It considers these movements, if they reveal good intentions and dedication to Allah, that they fall into the category of those who are trying hard since they act within the Islamic circle. Each active person has his share.

The Islamic Resistance Movement considers all these movements as a fund for itself. It prays to Allah for guidance and directions for all and it spares no effort to keep the banner of unity raised, ever striving for its realisation in accordance with the Koran and the Prophet's directives.

"And cleave all of you unto the covenant of Allah, and depart not from it, and remember the favour of Allah towards you: since ye were enemies, and he reconciled your hearts, and ye became companions and brethren by his favour: and ye were on the brink of a pit of fire, and he delivered you thence. Allah declareth unto you his signs, that ye may be directed." (The Family of Imran - Verse 102).

Article Twenty-Four:

The Islamic Resistance Movement does not allow slandering or speaking ill of individuals or groups, for the believer does not indulge in such malpractices. It is necessary to differentiate between this behaviour and the stands taken by certain individuals and groups. Whenever those stands are erroneous, the Islamic Resistance Movement preserves the right to expound the error and to warn against it. It will strive to show the right path and to judge the case in question with objectivity. Wise conduct is indeed the target of the believer who follows it wherever he discerns it.

"Allah loveth not the speaking ill of anyone in public, unless he who is injured call for assistance; and Allah heareth and knoweth: whether ye publish a good action, or conceal it, or forgive evil, verily Allah is gracious and powerful." (Women - verses 147-148).

B. Nationalist Movements in the Palestinian Arena:

Article Twenty-Five:

The Islamic Resistance Movement respects these movements and appreciates their circumstances and the conditions surrounding and affecting them. It encourages them as long as they do not give their allegiance to the Communist East or the Crusading West. It confirms to all those who are integrated in it, or sympathetic towards it, that the Islamic Resistance Movement is a fighting movement that has a moral and enlightened look of life and the way it should cooperate with the other (movements). It detests opportunism and desires only the good of people, individuals and groups alike. It does not seek material gains, personal fame, nor does it look for a reward from others. It works with its own resources and whatever is at its disposal "and prepare for them whatever force you can", for the fulfilment of the duty, and the earning of Allah's favour. It has no other desire than that.

The Movement assures all the nationalist trends operating in the Palestinian arena for the liberation of Palestine, that it is there for their support and assistance. It will never be more than that, both in words and deeds, now and in the future. It is there to bring together and not to divide, to preserve and not to squander, to unify and not to throw asunder. It evaluates every good word, sincere effort and good offices. It closes the door in the face of side disagreements and does not lend an ear to rumours and slanders, while at the same time fully realising the right for self-defence.

Anything contrary or contradictory to these trends, is a lie disseminated by enemies or their lackeys for the purpose of sowing confusion, disrupting the ranks and occupy them with side issues.

"O true believers, if a wicked man come unto you with a tale, inquire strictly into the truth thereof; lest ye hurt people through ignorance, and afterwards repent of what ye have done." (The Inner Apartments - verse 6).

Article Twenty-Six:

In viewing the Palestinian nationalist movements that give allegiance neither to the East nor the West, in this positive way, the Islamic Resistance Movement does not refrain from discussing new situations on the regional or international levels where the Palestinian question is concerned. It does that in such an objective manner revealing the extent of how much it is in harmony or contradiction with the national interests in the light of the Islamic point of view.

C. The Palestinian Liberation Organization:

Article Twenty-Seven:

The Palestinian Liberation Organisation is the closest to the heart of the Islamic Resistance Movement. It contains the father and the brother, the next of kin and the friend. The Moslem does not estrange himself from his father, brother, next of kin or friend. Our homeland is one, our situation is one, our fate is one and the enemy is a joint enemy to all of us.

Because of the situations surrounding the formation of the Organization, of the ideological confusion prevailing in the Arab world as a result of the ideological invasion under whose influence the Arab world has fallen since the defeat of the Crusaders and which was, and still is, intensified through orientalists, missionaries and imperialists, the Organization adopted the idea of the secular state. And that it how we view it.

Secularism completely contradicts religious ideology. Attitudes, conduct and decisions stem from ideologies.

That is why, with all our appreciation for the Palestinian Liberation Organisation - and what it can develop into - and without belittling its role in the Arab-Israeli conflict, we are unable to exchange the present or future Islamic Palestine with the secular idea. The Islamic nature of Palestine is part of our religion and whoever takes his religion lightly is a loser.

"Who will be adverse to the religion of Abraham, but he whose mind is infatuated? (The Cow - verse 130).

The day the Palestinian Liberation Organisation adopts Islam as its way of life, we will become its soldiers, and fuel for its fire that will burn the enemies.

Until such a day, and we pray to Allah that it will be soon, the Islamic Resistance Movement's stand towards the PLO is that of the son towards his father, the brother towards his brother, and the relative to relative, suffers his pain and supports him in confronting the enemies, wishing him to be wise and well-guided.

"Stand by your brother, for he who is brotherless is like the fighter who goes to battle without arms. One's cousin is the wing one flies with - could the bird fly without wings?"

D. Arab and Islamic Countries:

Article Twenty-Eight:

The Zionist invasion is a vicious invasion. It does not refrain from resorting to all methods, using all evil and contemptible ways to achieve its end. It relies greatly in its infiltration and espionage operations on the secret organizations it gave rise to, such as the Freemasons, The Rotary and Lions clubs, and other sabotage groups. All these organizations, whether secret or open, work in the interest of Zionism and according to its instructions. They aim at undermining societies, destroying values, corrupting consciences, deteriorating character and annihilating Islam. It is behind the drug trade and alcoholism in all its kinds so as to facilitate its control and expansion.

Arab countries surrounding Israel are asked to open their borders before the fighters from among the Arab and Islamic nations so that they could consolidate their efforts with those of their Moslem brethren in Palestine.

As for the other Arab and Islamic countries, they are asked to facilitate the movement of the fighters from and to it, and this is the least thing they could do.

We should not forget to remind every Moslem that when the Jews conquered the Holy City in 1967, they stood on the threshold of the Aqsa Mosque and proclaimed that "Mohammed is dead, and his descendants are all women."

Israel, Judaism and Jews challenge Islam and the Moslem people. "May the cowards never sleep."

E. Nationalist and Religious Groupings, Institutions, Intellectuals, The Arab and Islamic World:

The Islamic Resistance Movement hopes that all these groupings will side with it in all spheres, would support it, adopt its stand and solidify its activities and moves, work towards rallying support for it so that the Islamic people will be a base and a stay for it, supplying it with strategic depth an all human material and informative spheres, in time and in place. This should be done through the convening of solidarity conferences, the issuing of explanatory bulletins, favourable articles and booklets, enlightening the masses regarding the Palestinian issue, clarifying what confronts it and the conspiracies woven around it. They should mobilize the Islamic nations, ideologically, educationally and culturally, so that these peoples would be equipped to perform their role in the decisive battle of liberation, just as they did when they vanquished the Crusaders and the Tatars and saved human civilization. Indeed, that is not difficult for Allah.

“Allah hath written, Verily I will prevail, and my apostles: for Allah is strong and mighty.” (The Dispute - verse 21).

Article Thirty:

Writers, intellectuals, media people, orators, educaters and teachers, and all the various sectors in the Arab and Islamic world - all of them are called upon to perform their role, and to fulfill their duty, because of the ferocity of the Zionist offensive and the Zionist influence in many countries exercised through financial and media control, as well as the consequences that all this lead to in the greater part of the world.

Jihad is not confined to the carrying of arms and the confrontation of the enemy. The effective word, the good article, the useful book, support and solidarity - together with the presence of sincere purpose for the hoisting of Allah’s banner higher and higher - all these are elements of the Jihad for Allah’s sake.

“Whosoever mobilises a fighter for the sake of Allah is himself a fighter. Whosoever supports the relatives of a fighter, he himself is a fighter.” (related by al-Bukhari, Moslem, Abu-Dawood and al-Tarmadhi).

F. Followers of Other Religions: The Islamic Resistance Movement Is A Humanistic Movement:

Article Thirty-One:

The Islamic Resistance Movement is a humanistic movement. It takes care of human rights and is guided by Islamic tolerance when dealing with the followers of other religions. It does not antagonize anyone of them except if it is antagonized by it or stands in its way to hamper its moves and waste its efforts.

Under the wing of Islam, it is possible for the followers of the three religions - Islam, Christianity and Judaism - to coexist in peace and quiet with each other. Peace and quiet would not be possible except under the wing of Islam. Past and present history are the best witness to that.

It is the duty of the followers of other religions to stop disputing the sovereignty of Islam in this region, because the day these followers should take over there will be nothing but carnage, displacement and terror. Everyone of them is at variance with his fellow-religionists, not to speak about followers of other religionists. Past and present history are full of examples to prove this fact.

"They will not fight against you in a body, except in fenced towns, or from behind walls. Their strength in war among themselves is great: thou thinkest them to be united; but their hearts are divided. This, because they are people who do not understand." (The Emigration - verse 14).

Islam confers upon everyone his legitimate rights. Islam prevents the incursion on other people's rights. The Zionist Nazi activities against our people will not last for long. "For the state of injustice lasts but one day, while the state of justice lasts till Doomsday."

"As to those who have not borne arms against you on account of religion, nor turned you out of your dwellings, Allah forbiddeth you not to deal kindly with them, and to behave justly towards them; for Allah loveth those who act justly." (The Tried - verse 8).

The Attempt to Isolate the Palestinian People:

Article Thirty-Two:

World Zionism, together with imperialistic powers, try through a studied plan and an intelligent strategy to remove one Arab state after another from the circle of struggle against Zionism, in order to have it finally face the Palestinian people only. Egypt was, to a great extent, removed from the circle of the struggle, through the treacherous Camp David Agreement. They are trying to draw other Arab countries into similar agreements and to bring them outside the circle of struggle.

The Islamic Resistance Movement calls on Arab and Islamic nations to take up the line of serious and persevering action to prevent the success of this horrendous plan, to warn the people of the danger eminating from leaving the circle of struggle against Zionism. Today it is Palestine, tomorrow it will be one country or another. The Zionist plan is limitless. After Palestine, the Zionists aspire to expand from the Nile to the Euphrates. When they will have digested the region they overtook, they will aspire to further expansion, and so on. Their plan is embodied in the "Protocols of the Elders of Zion", and their present conduct is the best proof of what we are saying.

Leaving the circle of struggle with Zionism is high treason, and cursed be he who does that. "for whoso shall turn his back unto them on that day, unless he turneth aside to fight, or retreateth to another party of the faithful, shall draw on himself the indignation of Allah, and his abode shall be hell; an ill journey shall it be thither." (The Spoils - verse 16). There is no way out except by concentrating all powers and energies to face this Nazi, vicious Tatar invasion. The alternative is loss of one's country, the dispersion of citizens, the spread of vice on earth and the destruction of religious values. Let every person know that he is responsible before Allah, for "the doer of the slightest good deed is rewarded in like, and the does of the slightest evil deed is also rewarded in like."

The Islamic Resistance Movement consider itself to be the spearhead of the circle of struggle with world Zionism and a step on the road. The Movement adds its efforts to the efforts of all those who are active in the Palestinian arena. Arab and Islamic Peoples should augment by further steps on their part; Islamic groupings all over the Arab world should also do the same, since all of these are the best-equipped for the future role in the fight with the warmongering Jews.

"..and we have put enmity and hatred between them, until the day of resurrection. So often as they shall kindle a fire of war, Allah shall extinguish it; and they shall set their minds to act corruptly in the earth, but Allah loveth not the corrupt doers." (The Table - verse 64).

Article Thirty-Three:

The Islamic Resistance Movement, being based on the common coordinated and interdependent conceptions of the laws of the universe, and flowing in the stream of destiny in confronting and fighting the enemies in defence of the Moslems and Islamic civilization and sacred sites, the first among which is the Aqsa Mosque, urges the Arab and Islamic peoples, their governments, popular and official groupings, to fear Allah where their view of the Islamic Resistance Movement and their dealings with it are concerned. They should back and support it, as Allah wants them to, extending to it more and more funds till Allah's purpose is achieved when ranks will close up, fighters join other fighters and masses everywhere in the Islamic world will come forward in response to the call of duty while loudly proclaiming: Hail to Jihad. Their cry will reach the heavens and will go on being resounded until liberation is achieved, the invaders vanquished and Allah's victory comes about.

"And Allah will certainly assist him who shall be on his side: for Allah is strong and mighty." (The Pilgrimage - verse 40).

The Testimony of History

Across History in Confronting the Invaders:

Article Thirty-Four:

Palestine is the navel of the globe and the crossroad of the continents. Since the dawn of history, it has been the target of expansionists. The Prophet, Allah bless him and grant him salvation, had himself pointed to this fact in the noble Hadith in which he called on his honourable companion, Ma'adh ben-Jabal, saying: O Ma'ath, Allah throw open before you, when I am gone, Syria, from Al-Arish to the Euphrates. Its men, women and slaves will stay firmly there till the Day of Judgement. Whoever of you should choose one of the Syrian shores, or the Holy Land, he will be in constant struggle till the Day of Judgement."

Expansionists have more than once put their eye on Palestine which they attacked with their armies to fulfill their designs on it. Thus it was that the Crusaders came with their armies, bringing with them their creed and carrying their Cross. They were able to defeat the Moslems for a while, but the Moslems were able to retrieve the land only when they stood under the wing of their religious banner, united their word, hallowed the name of Allah and surged out fighting under the leadership of Salah ed-Din al-Ayyubi. They fought for almost twenty years and at the end the Crusaders were defeated and Palestine was liberated.

"Say unto those who believe not, Ye shall be overcome, and thrown together into hell; an unhappy couch it shall be." (The Family of Imran - verse 12).

This is the only way to liberate Palestine. There is no doubt about the testimony of history. It is one of the laws of the universe and one of the rules of existence. Nothing can overcome iron except iron. Their false futile creed can only be defeated by the righteous Islamic creed. A creed could not be fought except by a creed, and in the last analysis, victory is for the just, for justice is certainly victorious.

"Our word hath formerly been given unto our servants the apostles; that they should certainly be assisted against the infidels, and that our armies should surely be the conquerors." (Those Who Rank Themselves - verses 171-172).

Article Thirty-Five:

The Islamic Resistance Movement views seriously the defeat of the Crusaders at the hands of Salah ed-Din al-Ayyubi and the rescuing of Palestine from their hands, as well as the defeat of the Tatars at Ein Galot, breaking their power at the hands of Qataz and Al-Dhaher Bivers and saving the Arab world from the Tatar onslaught which aimed at the destruction of every meaning of human civilization. The Movement draws lessons and examples from all this. The present Zionist onslaught has also been preceded by Crusading raids from the West and other Tatar raids from the East. Just as the Moslems faced those raids and planned fighting and defeating them, they should be able to confront the Zionist invasion and defeat it. This is indeed no problem for the Almighty Allah, provided that the intentions are pure, the determination is true and that Moslems have benefited from past experiences, rid themselves of the effects of ideological invasion and followed the customs of their ancestors.

The Islamic Resistance Movement is Composed of Soldiers:

Article Thirty-Six:

While paving its way, the Islamic Resistance Movement, emphasizes time and again to all the sons of our people, to the Arab and Islamic nations, that it does not seek personal fame, material gain, or social prominence. It does not aim to compete against any one from among our people, or take his place. Nothing of the sort at all. It will not act against any of the sons of Moslems or those who are peaceful towards it from among non-Moslems, be they here or anywhere else. It will only serve as a support for all groupings and organizations operating against the Zionist enemy and its lackeys.

The Islamic Resistance Movement adopts Islam as its way of life. Islam is its creed and religion. Whoever takes Islam as his way of life, be it an organization, a grouping, a country or any other body, the Islamic Resistance Movement considers itself as their soldiers and nothing more.

We ask Allah to show us the right course, to make us an example to others and to judge between us and our people with truth. "O Lord, do thou judge between us and our nation with truth; for thou art the best judge." (Al Araf - Verse 89).

The last of our prayers will be praise to Allah, the Master of the Universe.

Palestinian Declaration of Independence

15 November 1988

In the name of God, the Compassionate, the Merciful

Palestine, the land of the three monotheistic faiths, is where the Palestinian Arab people was born, on which it grew, developed and excelled. Thus the Palestinian Arab people ensured for itself an everlasting union between itself, its land, and its history.

Resolute throughout that history, the Palestinian Arab people forged its national identity, rising even to unimagined levels in its defense, as invasion, the design of others, and the appeal special to Palestine's ancient and luminous place on the eminence where powers and civilizations are joined. All this intervened thereby to deprive the people of its political independence. Yet the undying connection between Palestine and its people secured for the land its character, and for the people its national genius.

Nourished by an unfolding series of civilizations and cultures, inspired by a heritage rich in variety and kind, the Palestinian Arab people added to its stature by consolidating a union between itself and its patrimonial Land. The call went out from Temple, Church, and Mosque that to praise the Creator, to celebrate compassion and peace was indeed the message of Palestine. And in generation after generation, the Palestinian Arab people gave of itself unsparingly in the valiant battle for liberation and homeland. For what has been the unbroken chain of our people's rebellions but the heroic embodiment of our will for national independence. And so the people was sustained in the struggle to stay and to prevail.

When in the course of modern times a new order of values was declared with norms and values fair for all, it was the Palestinian Arab people that had been excluded from the destiny of all other peoples by a hostile array of local and foreign powers. Yet again had unaided justice been revealed as insufficient to drive the world's history along its preferred course.

And it was the Palestinian people, already wounded in its body, that was submitted to yet another type of occupation over which floated that falsehood that "Palestine was a land without people." This notion was foisted upon some in the world, whereas in Article 22 of the Covenant of the League of Nations (1919) and in the Treaty of Lausanne (1923), the community of nations had recognized that all the Arab territories, including Palestine, of the formerly Ottoman provinces, were to have granted to them their freedom as provisionally independent nations.

Despite the historical injustice inflicted on the Palestinian Arab people resulting in their dispersion and depriving them of their right to self-determination, following upon U.N. General Assembly Resolution 181 (1947), which partitioned Palestine into two states, one Arab, one Jewish, yet it is this Resolution that still provides those conditions of international legitimacy that ensure the right of the Palestinian Arab people to sovereignty.

By stages, the occupation of Palestine and parts of other Arab territories by Israeli forces, the willed dispossession and expulsion from their ancestral homes of the majority of Palestine's civilian inhabitants, was achieved by organized terror; those Palestinians who remained, as a vestige subjugated in its homeland, were persecuted and forced to endure the destruction of their national life.

Thus were principles of international legitimacy violated. Thus were the Charter of the United Nations and its Resolutions disfigured, for they had recognized the Palestinian Arab people's national rights, including the right of Return, the right to independence, the right to sovereignty over territory and homeland.

In Palestine and on its perimeters, in exile distant and near, the Palestinian Arab people never faltered and never abandoned its conviction in its rights of Return and independence. Occupation, massacres and dispersion achieved no gain in the unabated Palestinian consciousness of self and political identity, as Palestinians went forward with their destiny, undeterred and unbowed. And from out of the long years of trial in ever-mounting struggle, the Palestinian political identity emerged further consolidated and confirmed. And the collective Palestinian national will forged for itself a political embodiment, the Palestine Liberation Organization, its sole, legitimate representative recognized by the world community as a whole, as well as by related regional and international institutions. Standing on the very rock of conviction in the Palestinian people's inalienable rights, and on the ground of Arab national consensus and of international legitimacy, the PLO led the campaigns of its great people, molded into unity and powerful resolve, one and indivisible in its triumphs, even as it suffered massacres and confinement within and without its home. And so Palestinian resistance was clarified and raised into the forefront of Arab and world awareness, as the struggle of the Palestinian Arab people achieved unique prominence among the world's liberation movements in the modern era.

The massive national uprising, the intifada, now intensifying in cumulative scope and power on occupied Palestinian territories, as well as the unflinching resistance of the refugee camps outside the homeland, have elevated awareness of the Palestinian truth and right into still higher realms of comprehension and actuality. Now at last the curtain has been dropped around a whole epoch of prevarication and negation. The intifada has set siege to the mind of official Israel, which has for too long relied exclusively upon myth and terror to deny Palestinian existence altogether. Because of the intifada and its revolutionary irreversible impulse, the history of Palestine has therefore arrived at a decisive juncture.

Whereas the Palestinian people reaffirms most definitively its inalienable rights in the land of its patrimony:

Now by virtue of natural, historical and legal rights, and the sacrifices of successive generations who gave of themselves in defense of the freedom and independence of their homeland;

In pursuance of Resolutions adopted by Arab Summit Conferences and relying on the authority bestowed by international legitimacy as embodied in the Resolutions of the United Nations Organization since 1947;

And in exercise by the Palestinian Arab people of its rights to self-determination, political independence and sovereignty over its territory,

The Palestine National Council, in the name of God, and in the name of the Palestinian Arab people, hereby proclaims the establishment of the State of Palestine on our Palestinian territory with its capital Jerusalem (Al-Quds Ash-Sharif).

The State of Palestine is the state of Palestinians wherever they may be. The state is for them to enjoy in it their collective national and cultural identity, theirs to pursue in it a complete equality of rights. In it will be safeguarded their political and religious convictions and their human dignity by means of a parliamentary democratic system of governance, itself based on freedom of expression and the freedom to form parties. The rights of minorities will duly be respected by the majority, as minorities must abide by decisions of the majority. Governance will be based on principles of social justice, equality and non-discrimination in public rights of men or women, on grounds of race, religion, color or sex, and the aegis of a constitution which ensures the rule of law and an independent judiciary. Thus shall these principles allow no departure from Palestine's age-old spiritual and civilizational heritage of tolerance and religious coexistence.

The State of Palestine is an Arab state, an integral and indivisible part of the Arab nation, at one with that nation in heritage and civilization, with it also in its aspiration for liberation, progress, democracy and unity. The State of Palestine affirms its obligation to abide by the Charter of the League of Arab States, whereby the coordination of the Arab states with each other shall be strengthened. It calls upon Arab compatriots to consolidate and enhance the reality of state, to mobilize potential, and to intensify efforts whose goal is to end Israeli occupation.

The State of Palestine proclaims its commitment to the principles and purposes of the United Nations, and to the Universal Declaration of Human Rights. It proclaims its commitment as well to the principles and policies of the Non-Aligned Movement.

It further announces itself to be a peace-loving State, in adherence to the principles of peaceful co-existence. It will join with all states and peoples in order to assure a permanent peace based upon justice and the respect of rights so that humanity's potential for well-being may be assured, an earnest competition for excellence may be maintained, and in which confidence in the future will eliminate fear for those who are just and for whom justice is the only recourse.

In the context of its struggle for peace in the land of Love and Peace, the State of Palestine calls upon the United Nations to bear special responsibility for the Palestinian Arab people and its homeland. It calls upon all peace-and freedom-loving peoples and states to assist it in the attainment of its objectives, to provide it with security, to alleviate the tragedy of its people, and to help it terminate Israel's occupation of the Palestinian territories.

The State of Palestine herewith declares that it believes in the settlement of regional and international disputes by peaceful means, in accordance with the U.N. Charter and resolutions. With prejudice to its natural right to defend its territorial integrity and independence, it therefore rejects the threat or use of force, violence and terrorism against its territorial integrity or political independence, as it also rejects their use against territorial integrity of other states.

Therefore, on this day unlike all others, November 15, 1988, as we stand at the threshold of a new dawn, in all honor and modesty we humbly bow to the sacred spirits of our fallen ones, Palestinian and Arab, by the purity of whose sacrifice for the homeland our sky has been illuminated and our Land given life. Our hearts are lifted up and irradiated by the light emanating from the much blessed intifada, from those who have endured and have fought the fight of the camps, of dispersion, of exile, from those who have borne the standard for freedom, our children, our aged, our youth, our prisoners, detainees and wounded, all those ties to our sacred soil are confirmed in camp, village, and town. We render special tribute to that brave Palestinian Woman, guardian of sustenance and Life, keeper of our people's perennial flame. To the souls of our sainted martyrs, the whole of our Palestinian Arab people that our struggle shall be continued until the occupation ends, and the foundation of our sovereignty and independence shall be fortified accordingly.

Therefore, we call upon our great people to rally to the banner of Palestine, to cherish and defend it, so that it may forever be the symbol of our freedom and dignity in that homeland, which is a homeland for the free, now and always.

In the name of God, the Compassionate, the Merciful: "Say: 'O God, Master of the Kingdom, Thou givest the Kingdom to whom Thou wilt, and seizes the Kingdom from whom Thou wilt, Thou exalted whom Thou wilt, and Thou abasest whom Thou wilt; in Thy hand is the good; Thou are powerful over everything."

Oslo I - Declaration of Principles on Interim Self-Government Arrangements, 13 September 1993

The Government of the State of Israel and the PLO team (in the Jordanian-Palestinian delegation to the Middle East Peace Conference) (the "Palestinian Delegation"), representing the Palestinian people, agree that it is time to put an end to decades of confrontation and conflict, recognise their mutual legitimate and political rights, and strive to live in peaceful coexistence and mutual dignity and security and achieve a just, lasting and comprehensive peace settlement and historic reconciliation through the agreed political process. Accordingly, the two sides agree to the following principles:

Article I - Aim of negotiations:

The aim of the Israeli-Palestinian negotiations within the current Middle East peace process is, among other things, to establish a Palestinian Interim SelfGovernment Authority, the elected Council (the "Council"), for the Palestinian people in the West Bank and the Gaza Strip, for a transitional period not exceeding five years, leading to a permanent settlement based on Security Council resolutions 242 (1967) and 338 (1973). It is understood that the interim arrangements are an integral part of the whole peace process and that the negotiations on the permanent status will lead to the implementation of Security Council resolutions 242 (1967) and 338 (1973).

Article II -Framework for the interim period:

The agreed framework for the interim period is set forth in this Declaration of Principles.

Article III - Elections:

1. In order that the Palestinian people in the West Bank and Gaza Strip may govern themselves according to democratic principles, direct, free and general political elections will be held for the Council under agreed supervision and international observation, while the Palestinian police will ensure public order.

2. An agreement will be concluded on the exact mode and conditions of the elections in accordance with the protocol attached as Annex I, with the goal of holding the elections not later than nine months after the entry into force of this Declaration of Principles.

3. These elections will constitute a significant interim preparatory step toward the realisation of the legitimate rights of the Palestinian people and their just requirements.

Article IV -Jurisdiction:

Jurisdiction of the Council will cover West Bank and Gaza Strip territory, except for issues that will be negotiated in the permanent status negotiations. The two sides view the West Bank and the Gaza Strip as a single territorial unit, whose integrity will be preserved during the interim period.

Article V - Transitional period and permanent status negotiations:

1. The five-year transitional period will begin upon the withdrawal from the Gaza Strip and Jericho area.

2. Permanent status negotiations will commence as soon as possible, but not later than the beginning of the third year of the interim period, between the Government of Israel and the Palestinian people's representatives.

3. It is understood that these negotiations shall cover remaining issues, including: Jerusalem, refugees, settlements, security arrangements, borders, relations and co-operation with other neighbours, and other issues of common interest.

4. The two parties agree that the outcome of the permanent status negotiations should not be prejudiced or pre-empted by agreements reached for the interim period.

Article VI - Preparatory transfer of powers and responsibilities:

1. Upon the entry into force of this Declaration of Principles and the withdrawal from the Gaza Strip and the Jericho area, a transfer of authority from the Israeli military government and its Civil Administration to the authorised Palestinians for this task, as detailed herein, will commence. This transfer of authority will be of a preparatory nature until the inauguration of the Council.

2. Immediately after the entry into force of this Declaration of Principles and the withdrawal from the Gaza Strip and Jericho area, with the view to promoting economic development in the West Bank and Gaza Strip, authority will be transferred to the Palestinians in the following spheres: education and culture, health, social welfare, direct taxation and tourism. The Palestinian side will commence in building the Palestinian police force, as agreed upon. Pending the inauguration of the Council, the two parties may negotiate the transfer of additional powers and responsibilities, as agreed upon.

Article VII - Interim agreement:

1. The Israeli and Palestinian delegations will negotiate an agreement on the interim period (the "Interim Agreement").

2. The Interim Agreement shall specify, among other things, the structure of the Council, the number of its members, and the transfer of powers and responsibilities from the Israeli military government and its Civil Administration to the Council. The Interim Agreement shall also specify the Council's executive authority, legislative authority in accordance with Article IX below, and the independent Palestinian judicial organs.

3. The Interim Agreement shall include arrangements, to be implemented upon the inauguration of the Council, for the assumption by the Council of all of the powers and responsibilities transferred previously in accordance with Article VI above.

4. In order to enable the Council to promote economic growth, upon its inauguration, the Council will establish, among other things, a Palestinian Electricity Authority, a Gaza Sea Port Authority, a Palestinian Development Bank, a Palestinian Export Promotion Board, a Palestinian Environmental Authority, a Palestinian Land Authority and a Palestinian Water Administration Authority and any other Authorities agreed upon, in accordance with the Interim Agreement, that will specify their

powers and responsibilities.

5. After the inauguration of the Council, the Civil Administration will be dissolved, and the Israeli military government will be withdrawn.

Article VIII - Public order and security:

In order to guarantee public order and internal security for the Palestinians of the West Bank and the Gaza Strip, the Council will establish a strong police force, while Israel will continue to carry the responsibility for defending against external threats, as well as the responsibility for overall security of Israelis for the purpose of safeguarding their internal security and public order.

Article IX - Laws and military orders:

1. The Council will be empowered to legislate, in accordance with the Interim Agreement, within all authorities transferred to it.

2. Both parties will review jointly laws and military orders presently in force in remaining spheres

Article X: Joint Israeli-Palestinian liaison committee:

In order to provide for a smooth implementation of this Declaration of Principles and any subsequent agreements pertaining to the interim period, upon the entry into force of this Declaration of Principles, a Joint Israeli-Palestinian Liaison Committee will be established in order to deal with issues requiring coordination, other issues of common interest and disputes.

Article XI:

Israeli-Palestinian cooperation in economic fields: Recognising the mutual benefit of co-operation in promoting the development of the West Bank, the Gaza Strip and Israel, upon the entry into force of this Declaration of Principles, an Israeli-Palestinian Economic Co-operation Committee will be established in order to develop and implement in a cooperative manner the programmes identified in the protocols attached as Annex III and Annex IV.

Article XII:

Liaison and co-operation with Jordan and Egypt: The two parties will invite the Governments of Jordan and Egypt to participate in establishing further liaison and co-operation arrangements between the Government of Israel and the Palestinian representatives, on the one hand, and the Governments of Jordan and Egypt, on the other hand, to promote cooperation between them.

These arrangements will include the constitution of a Continuing Committee that will decide by agreement on the modalities of admission of persons displaced from the West Bank and Gaza Strip in 1967, together with necessary measures to prevent disruption and disorder. Other matters of common concern will be dealt with by this Committee.

Article XIII - Redeployment of Israeli forces:

1. After the entry into force of this Declaration of Principles, and not later than the eve of elections for the Council, a redeployment of Israeli military forces in

the West Bank and the Gaza Strip will take place, in addition to withdrawal of Israeli forces carried out in accordance with Article XIV.

2. In redeploying its military forces, Israel will be guided by the principle that its military forces should be redeployed outside populated areas.

3. Further redeployments to specified locations will be gradually implemented commensurate with the assumption of responsibility for public order and internal security by the Palestinian police force pursuant to Article VIII above.

Article XIV:

Israeli withdrawal from the Gaza strip and Jericho area: Israel will withdraw from the Gaza Strip and Jericho area, as detailed in the protocol attached as Annex II.

Article XV - Resolution of disputes:

1. Disputes arising out of the application or interpretation of this Declaration of Principles, or any subsequent agreements pertaining to the interim period, shall be resolved by negotiations through the Joint Liaison Committee to be established pursuant to Article X above.

2. Disputes which cannot be settled by negotiations may be resolved by a mechanism of conciliation to be agreed upon by the parties.

3. The parties may agree to submit to arbitration disputes relating to the interim period, which cannot be settled through conciliation. To this end, upon the agreement of both parties, the parties will establish an arbitration committee.

Article XVI:

Israeli-Palestinian cooperation concerning regional programmes: Both parties view the multilateral working groups as an appropriate instrument for promoting a “Marshall Plan”, the regional programmes and other programmes, including special programmes for the West Bank and Gaza Strip, as indicated in the protocol attached as Annex IV.

Article XVII - Miscellaneous provisions:

1. This Declaration of Principles will enter into force one month after its signing.

2. All protocols annexed to this Declaration of Principles and agreed minutes pertaining thereto shall be regarded as an integral part hereof. Done in Washington, DC. this thirteenth day of September 1993.

For the Government of Israel: (Signed) Shimon Peres **For the PLO:** (Signed) Mahmud Abbas **Witnessed by:** The United States of America (Signed) Warren Christopher and The Russian Federation (Signed) Andrei V Kozyrev

Treaty of Peace between the State of Israel and the Hashemite Kingdom of Jordan, 26 October 1994

TREATY OF PEACE BETWEEN THE STATE OF ISRAEL AND THE HASHEMITE KINGDOM OF JORDAN

PREAMBLE

The Government of the State of Israel and the Government of the Hashemite Kingdom of Jordan:

Bearing in mind the Washington Declaration , signed by them on 25th July, 1994, and which they are both committed to honour;

Aiming at the achievement of a just, lasting and comprehensive peace in the Middle East based on Security Council resolutions 242 and 338 in all their aspects;

Bearing in mind the importance of maintaining and strengthening peace based on freedom, equality, justice and respect for fundamental human rights, thereby overcoming psychological barriers and promoting human dignity;

Reaffirming their faith in the purposes and principles of the Charter of the United Nations and recognising their right and obligation to live in peace with each other as well as with all states, within secure and recognised boundaries;

Desiring to develop friendly relations and co-operation between them in accordance with the principles of international law governing international relations in time of peace;

Desiring as well to ensure lasting security for both their States and in particular to avoid threats and the use of force between them;

Bearing in mind that in their Washington Declaration of 25th July, 1994, they declared the termination of the state of belligerency between them;

Deciding to establish peace between them in accordance with this Treaty of Peace;

Have agreed as follows:

ARTICLE 1

ESTABLISHMENT OF PEACE

Peace is hereby established between the State of Israel and the Hashemite Kingdom of Jordan (the "Parties") effective from the exchange of the instruments of ratification of this Treaty.

ARTICLE 2

GENERAL PRINCIPLES

1. The Parties will apply between them the provisions of the Charter of the United Nations and the principles of international law governing relations among states in times of peace. In particular:

2. They recognise and will respect each other's sovereignty, territorial integrity and political independence;
3. They recognise and will respect each other's right to live in peace within secure and recognised boundaries;
4. They will develop good neighbourly relations of co-operation between them to ensure lasting security, will refrain from the threat or use of force against each other and will settle all disputes between them by peaceful means;
5. They respect and recognise the sovereignty, territorial integrity and political independence of every state in the region;
6. They respect and recognise the pivotal role of human development and dignity in regional and bilateral relationships;
7. They further believe that within their control, involuntary movements of persons in such a way as to adversely prejudice the security of either Party should not be permitted.

ARTICLE 3

INTERNATIONAL BOUNDARY

1. The international boundary between Israel and Jordan is delimited with reference to the boundary definition under the Mandate as is shown in Annex I (a), on the mapping materials attached thereto and co-ordinates specified therein.
2. The boundary, as set out in Annex I (a), is the permanent, secure and recognised international boundary between Israel and Jordan, without prejudice to the status of any territories that came under Israeli military government control in 1967.
3. The parties recognise the international boundary, as well as each other's territory, territorial waters and airspace, as inviolable, and will respect and comply with them.
4. The demarcation of the boundary will take place as set forth in Appendix (I) to Annex I and will be concluded not later than nine months after the signing of the Treaty.
5. It is agreed that where the boundary follows a river, in the event of natural changes in the course of the flow of the river as described in Annex I (a), the boundary shall follow the new course of the flow. In the event of any other changes the boundary shall not be affected unless otherwise agreed.
6. Immediately upon the exchange of the instruments of ratification of this Treaty, each Party will deploy on its side of the international boundary as defined in Annex I (a).
7. The Parties shall, upon the signature of the Treaty, enter into negotiations to conclude, within 9 months, an agreement on the delimitation of their maritime boundary in the Gulf of Aqaba.
8. Taking into account the special circumstances of the Naharayim/Baqura area, which is under Jordanian sovereignty, with Israeli private ownership rights, the Parties agreed to apply the provisions set out in Annex I (b).

With respect to the Zofar/Al-Ghamr area, the provisions set out in Annex I (c) will apply.

Oslo II - Israeli-Palestinian Interim Agreement on the West Bank and the Gaza Strip

Washington, D.C., September 28, 1995

The Government of the State of Israel and the Palestine Liberation Organization (hereinafter "the PLO"), the representative of the Palestinian people;

PREAMBLE

WITHIN the framework of the Middle East peace process initiated at Madrid in October 1991;

REAFFIRMING their determination to put an end to decades of confrontation and to live in peaceful coexistence, mutual dignity and security, while recognizing their mutual legitimate and political rights;

REAFFIRMING their desire to achieve a just, lasting and comprehensive peace settlement and historic reconciliation through the agreed political process;

RECOGNIZING that the peace process and the new era that it has created, as well as the new relationship established between the two Parties as described above, are irreversible, and the determination of the two Parties to maintain, sustain and continue the peace process;

RECOGNIZING that the aim of the Israeli-Palestinian negotiations within the current Middle East peace process is, among other things, to establish a Palestinian Interim Self-Government Authority, i.e. the elected Council (hereinafter "the Council" or "the Palestinian Council"), and the elected Ra'ees of the Executive Authority, for the Palestinian people in the West Bank and the Gaza Strip, for a transitional period not exceeding five years from the date of signing the Agreement on the Gaza Strip and the Jericho Area (hereinafter "the Gaza-Jericho Agreement") on May 4, 1994, leading to a permanent settlement based on Security Council Resolutions 242 and 338;

REAFFIRMING their understanding that the interim self-government arrangements contained in this Agreement are an integral part of the whole peace process, that the negotiations on the permanent status, that will start as soon as possible but not later than May 4, 1996, will lead to the implementation of Security Council Resolutions 242 and 338, and that the Interim Agreement shall settle all the issues of the interim period and that no such issues will be deferred to the agenda of the permanent status negotiations;

REAFFIRMING their adherence to the mutual recognition and commitments expressed in the letters dated September 9, 1993, signed by and exchanged between the Prime Minister of Israel and the Chairman of the PLO;

DESIROUS of putting into effect the Declaration of Principles on Interim Self-Government Arrangements signed at Washington, D.C. on September 13, 1993, and the Agreed Minutes thereto (hereinafter "the DOP") and in particular Article III and Annex I concerning the holding of direct, free and general political elections for the Council and the Ra'ees of the Executive Authority in order that the Palestinian people in the West Bank, Jerusalem and the Gaza Strip may democratically elect accountable representatives;

RECOGNIZING that these elections will constitute a significant interim preparatory step toward the realization of the legitimate rights of the Palestinian people and their just requirements and will provide a democratic basis for the establishment of Palestinian institutions;

REAFFIRMING their mutual commitment to act, in accordance with this Agreement, immediately, efficiently and effectively against acts or threats of terrorism, violence or incitement, whether committed by Palestinians or Israelis;

FOLLOWING the Gaza-Jericho Agreement; the Agreement on Preparatory Transfer of Powers and Responsibilities signed at Erez on August 29, 1994 (hereinafter "the Preparatory Transfer Agreement"); and the Protocol on Further Transfer of Powers and Responsibilities signed at Cairo on August 27, 1995 (hereinafter "the Further Transfer Protocol"); which three agreements will be superseded by this Agreement;

HEREBY AGREE as follows:

CHAPTER I - THE COUNCIL

ARTICLE I
Transfer of Authority

1. Israel shall transfer powers and responsibilities as specified in this Agreement from the Israeli military government and its Civil Administration to the Council in accordance with this Agreement. Israel shall continue to exercise powers and responsibilities not so transferred.

2. Pending the inauguration of the Council, the powers and responsibilities transferred to the Council shall be exercised by the Palestinian Authority established in accordance with the Gaza-Jericho Agreement, which shall also have all the rights, liabilities and obligations to be assumed by the Council in this regard. Accordingly, the term "Council" throughout this Agreement shall, pending the inauguration of the Council, be construed as meaning the Palestinian Authority.

3. The transfer of powers and responsibilities to the police force established by the Palestinian Council in accordance with Article XIV below (hereinafter "the Palestinian Police") shall be accomplished in a phased manner, as detailed in this Agreement and in the Protocol concerning Redeployment and Security Arrangements attached as Annex I to this Agreement (hereinafter "Annex I").

4. As regards the transfer and assumption of authority in civil spheres, powers and responsibilities shall be transferred and assumed as set out in the Protocol Concerning Civil Affairs attached as Annex III to this Agreement (hereinafter "Annex III").

5. After the inauguration of the Council, the Civil Administration in the West Bank will be dissolved, and the Israeli military government shall be withdrawn. The withdrawal of the military government shall not prevent it from exercising the powers and responsibilities not transferred to the Council.

6. A Joint Civil Affairs Coordination and Cooperation Committee (hereinafter "the CAC"), Joint Regional Civil Affairs Subcommittees, one for the Gaza Strip and the other for the West Bank, and District Civil Liaison Offices in the West Bank shall

be established in order to provide for coordination and cooperation in civil affairs between the Council and Israel, as detailed in Annex III.

7. The offices of the Council, and the offices of its Ra'ees and its Executive Authority and other committees, shall be located in areas under Palestinian territorial jurisdiction in the West Bank and the Gaza Strip.

ARTICLE II
Elections

1. In order that the Palestinian people of the West Bank and the Gaza Strip may govern themselves according to democratic principles, direct, free and general political elections will be held for the Council and the Ra'ees of the Executive Authority of the Council in accordance with the provisions set out in the Protocol concerning Elections attached as Annex II to this Agreement (hereinafter "Annex II").

2. These elections will constitute a significant interim preparatory step towards the realization of the legitimate rights of the Palestinian people and their just requirements and will provide a democratic basis for the establishment of Palestinian institutions.

3. Palestinians of Jerusalem who live there may participate in the election process in accordance with the provisions contained in this Article and in Article VI of Annex II (Election Arrangements concerning Jerusalem).

4. The elections shall be called by the Chairman of the Palestinian Authority immediately following the signing of this Agreement to take place at the earliest practicable date following the redeployment of Israeli forces in accordance with Annex I, and consistent with the requirements of the election timetable as provided in Annex II, the Election Law and the Election Regulations, as defined in Article I of Annex II.

ARTICLE III
Structure of the Palestinian Council

1. The Palestinian Council and the Ra'ees of the Executive Authority of the Council constitute the Palestinian Interim Self-Government Authority, which will be elected by the Palestinian people of the West Bank, Jerusalem and the Gaza Strip for the transitional period agreed in Article I of the DOP.

2. The Council shall possess both legislative power and executive power, in accordance with Articles VII and IX of the DOP. The Council shall carry out and be responsible for all the legislative and executive powers and responsibilities transferred to it under this Agreement. The exercise of legislative powers shall be in accordance with Article XVIII of this Agreement (Legislative Powers of the Council).

3. The Council and the Ra'ees of the Executive Authority of the Council shall be directly and simultaneously elected by the Palestinian people of the West Bank, Jerusalem and the Gaza Strip, in accordance with the provisions of this Agreement and the Election Law and Regulations, which shall not be contrary to the provisions of this Agreement.

4. The Council and the Ra'ees of the Executive Authority of the Council shall be elected for a transitional period not exceeding five years from the signing of the Gaza-Jericho Agreement on May 4, 1994.

5. Immediately upon its inauguration, the Council will elect from among its members a Speaker. The Speaker will preside over the meetings of the Council, administer the Council and its committees, decide on the agenda of each meeting, and lay before the Council proposals for voting and declare their results.

6. The jurisdiction of the Council shall be as determined in Article XVII of this Agreement (Jurisdiction).

7. The organization, structure and functioning of the Council shall be in accordance with this Agreement and the Basic Law for the Palestinian Interim Self-government Authority, which Law shall be adopted by the Council. The Basic Law and any regulations made under it shall not be contrary to the provisions of this Agreement.

8. The Council shall be responsible under its executive powers for the offices, services and departments transferred to it and may establish, within its jurisdiction, ministries and subordinate bodies, as necessary for the fulfillment of its responsibilities.

9. The Speaker will present for the Council's approval proposed internal procedures that will regulate, among other things, the decision-making processes of the Council.

ARTICLE IV
Size of the Council

The Palestinian Council shall be composed of 82 representatives and the Ra'ees of the Executive Authority, who will be directly and simultaneously elected by the Palestinian people of the West Bank, Jerusalem and the Gaza Strip.

ARTICLE V
The Executive Authority of the Council

1. The Council will have a committee that will exercise the executive authority of the Council, formed in accordance with paragraph 4 below (hereinafter "the Executive Authority").

2. The Executive Authority shall be bestowed with the executive authority of the Council and will exercise it on behalf of the Council. It shall determine its own internal procedures and decision making processes.

3. The Council will publish the names of the members of the Executive Authority immediately upon their initial appointment and subsequent to any changes.

4. a. The Ra'ees of the Executive Authority shall be an ex officio member of the Executive Authority.

b. All of the other members of the Executive Authority, except as provided in subparagraph c. below, shall be members of the Council, chosen and proposed to the Council by the Ra'ees of the Executive Authority and approved by the Council.

c. The Ra'ees of the Executive Authority shall have the right to appoint some persons, in number not exceeding twenty percent of the total membership of the Executive Authority, who are not members of the Council, to exercise executive authority and participate in government tasks. Such appointed members may not vote in meetings of the Council.

d. Non-elected members of the Executive Authority must have a valid address in an area under the jurisdiction of the Council.

ARTICLE VI
Other Committees of the Council

1. The Council may form small committees to simplify the proceedings of the Council and to assist in controlling the activity of its Executive Authority.

2. Each committee shall establish its own decision-making processes within the general framework of the organization and structure of the Council.

ARTICLE VII
Open Government

1. All meetings of the Council and of its committees, other than the Executive Authority, shall be open to the public, except upon a resolution of the Council or the relevant committee on the grounds of security, or commercial or personal confidentiality.

2. Participation in the deliberations of the Council, its committees and the Executive Authority shall be limited to their respective members only. Experts may be invited to such meetings to address specific issues on an ad hoc basis.

ARTICLE VIII
Judicial Review

Any person or organization affected by any act or decision of the Ra'ees of the Executive Authority of the Council or of any member of the Executive Authority, who believes that such act or decision exceeds the authority of the Ra'ees or of such member, or is otherwise incorrect in law or procedure, may apply to the relevant Palestinian Court of Justice for a review of such activity or decision.

ARTICLE IX
Powers and Responsibilities of the Council

1. Subject to the provisions of this Agreement, the Council will, within its jurisdiction, have legislative powers as set out in Article XVIII of this Agreement, as well as executive powers.

2. The executive power of the Palestinian Council shall extend to all matters within its jurisdiction under this Agreement or any future agreement that may be reached between the two Parties during the interim period. It shall include the power to formulate and conduct Palestinian policies and to supervise their implementation, to issue any rule or regulation under powers given in approved legislation and administrative decisions necessary for the realization of Palestinian self-government, the power to employ staff, sue and be sued and conclude contracts, and the power to keep and administer registers and records of the population, and issue certificates, licenses and documents.

3. The Palestinian Council's executive decisions and acts shall be consistent with the provisions of this Agreement.

4. The Palestinian Council may adopt all necessary measures in order to enforce the law and any of its decisions, and bring proceedings before the Palestinian courts and tribunals.

5. a. In accordance with the DOP, the Council will not have powers and responsibilities in the sphere of foreign relations, which sphere includes

the establishment abroad of embassies, consulates or other types of foreign missions and posts or permitting their establishment in the West Bank or the Gaza Strip, the appointment of or admission of diplomatic and consular staff, and the exercise of diplomatic functions.

b. Notwithstanding the provisions of this paragraph, the PLO may conduct negotiations and sign agreements with states or international organizations for the benefit of the Council in the following cases only:

1. economic agreements, as specifically provided in Annex V of this Agreement:
2. agreements with donor countries for the purpose of implementing arrangements for the provision of assistance to the Council,
3. agreements for the purpose of implementing the regional development plans detailed in Annex IV of the DOP or in agreements entered into in the framework of the multilateral negotiations, and
4. cultural, scientific and educational agreements. Dealings between the Council and representatives of foreign states and international organizations, as well as the establishment in the West Bank and the Gaza Strip of representative offices other than those described in subparagraph 5.a above, for the purpose of implementing the agreements referred to in subparagraph 5.b above, shall not be considered foreign relations.

6. Subject to the provisions of this Agreement, the Council shall, within its jurisdiction, have an independent judicial system composed of independent Palestinian courts and tribunals.

CHAPTER 2 - REDEPLOYMENT AND SECURITY ARRANGEMENTS

ARTICLE X
Redeployment of Israeli Military Forces

1. The first phase of the Israeli military forces redeployment will cover populated areas in the West Bank - cities, towns, villages, refugee camps and hamlets - as set out in Annex I, and will be completed prior to the eve of the Palestinian elections, i. e., 22 days before the day of the elections.

2. Further redeployments of Israeli military forces to specified military locations will commence after the inauguration of the Council and will be gradually implemented commensurate with the assumption of responsibility for public order and internal security by the Palestinian Police, to be completed within 18 months from the date of the inauguration of the Council as detailed in Articles XI (Land) and XIII (Security), below and in Annex I.

3. The Palestinian Police shall be deployed and shall assume responsibility for public order and internal security for Palestinians in a phased manner in accordance with XIII (Security) below and Annex I.

4. Israel shall continue to carry the responsibility for external security, as well as the responsibility for overall security of Israelis for the purpose of safeguarding their internal security and public order.

5. For the purpose of this Agreement, “Israeli military forces” includes Israel Police and other Israeli security forces.

ARTICLE XI
Land

1. The two sides view the West Bank and the Gaza Strip as a single territorial unit, the integrity and status of which will be preserved during the interim period.

2. The two sides agree that West Bank and Gaza Strip territory, except for issues that will be negotiated in the permanent status negotiations, will come under the jurisdiction of the Palestinian Council in a phased manner, to be completed within 18 months from the date of the inauguration of the Council, as specified below:

a. Land in populated areas (Areas A and B), including government and Al Waqf land, will come under the jurisdiction of the Council during the first phase of redeployment.

b. All civil powers and responsibilities, including planning and zoning, in Areas A and B, set out in Annex III, will be transferred to and assumed by the Council during the first phase of redeployment.

c. In Area C, during the first phase of redeployment Israel will transfer to the Council civil powers and responsibilities not relating to territory, as set out in Annex III.

d. The further redeployments of Israeli military forces to specified military locations will be gradually implemented in accordance with the DOP in three phases, each to take place after an interval of six months, after the inauguration of the Council, to be completed within 18 months from the date of the inauguration of the Council.

e. During the further redeployment phases to be completed within 18 months from the date of the inauguration of the Council, powers and responsibilities relating to territory will be transferred gradually to Palestinian jurisdiction that will cover West Bank and Gaza Strip territory, except for the issues that will be negotiated in the permanent status negotiations.

f. The specified military locations referred to in Article X, paragraph 2 above will be determined in the further redeployment phases, within the specified time-frame ending not later than 18 months from the date of the inauguration of the Council, and will be negotiated in the permanent status negotiations.

3. For the purpose of this Agreement and until the completion of the first phase of the further redeployments:

a. "Area A" means the populated areas delineated by a red line and shaded in brown on attached map No. 1;

b. "Area B" means the populated areas delineated by a red line and shaded in yellow on attached map No. 1, and the built-up area of the hamlets listed in Appendix 6 to Annex I, and

c. "Area C" means areas of the West Bank outside Areas A and B, which, except for the issues that will be negotiated in the permanent status negotiations, will be gradually transferred to Palestinian jurisdiction in accordance with this Agreement.

ARTICLE XII

Arrangements for Security and Public Order

1. In order to guarantee public order and internal security for the Palestinians of the West Bank and the Gaza Strip, the Council shall establish a strong police force as set out in Article XIV below. Israel shall continue to carry the responsibility for defense against external threats, including the responsibility for protecting the Egyptian and Jordanian borders, and for defense against external threats from the sea and from the air, as well as the responsibility for overall security of Israelis and Settlements, for the purpose of safeguarding their internal security and public order, and will have all the powers to take the steps necessary to meet this responsibility.

2. Agreed security arrangements and coordination mechanisms are specified in Annex I.

3. A Joint Coordination and Cooperation Committee for Mutual Security Purposes (hereinafter "the JSC"), as well as Joint Regional Security Committees (hereinafter "RSCs") and Joint District Coordination Offices (hereinafter "DCOs"), are hereby established as provided for in Annex I.

4. The security arrangements provided for in this Agreement and in Annex I may be reviewed at the request of either Party and may be amended by mutual agreement of the Parties. Specific review arrangements are included in Annex I.

5. For the purpose of this Agreement, "the Settlements" means, in the West Bank the settlements in Area C; and in the Gaza Strip - the Gush Katif and Erez settlement areas, as well as the other settlements in the Gaza Strip, as shown on attached map No. 2.

ARTICLE XIII

Security

I. The Council will, upon completion of the redeployment of Israeli military forces in each district, as set out in Appendix 1 to Annex I, assume the powers and responsibilities for internal security and public order in Area A in that district.

2. a. There will be a complete redeployment of Israeli military forces from Area B. Israel will transfer to the Council and the Council will assume responsibility for public order for Palestinians. Israel shall have the overriding responsibility for security for the purpose of protecting Israelis and confronting the threat of terrorism.

   b. In Area B the Palestinian Police shall assume the responsibility for public order for Palestinians and shall be deployed in order to accommodate the Palestinian needs and requirements in the following manner:

   1. The Palestinian Police shall establish 25 police stations and posts in towns, villages, and other places listed in Appendix 2 to Annex I and as delineated on map No. 3. The West Bank RSC may agree on the establishment of additional police stations and posts, if required.
   2. The Palestinian Police shall be responsible for handling public order incidents in which only Palestinians are involved.
   3. The Palestinian Police shall operate freely in populated places where

police stations and posts are located, as set out in paragraph b(1) above.

4. While the movement of uniformed Palestinian policemen in Area B outside places where there is a Palestinian police station or post will be carried out after coordination and confirmation through the relevant DCO, three months after the completion of redeployment from Area B, the DCOs may decide that movement of Palestinian policemen from the police stations in Area B to Palestinian towns and villages in Area B on roads that are used only by Palestinian traffic will take place after notifying the DCO.
5. The coordination of such planned movement prior to confirmation through the relevant DCO shall include a scheduled plan, including the number of policemen, as well as the type and number of weapons and vehicles intended to take part. It shall also include details of arrangements for ensuring continued coordination through appropriate communication links, the exact schedule of movement to the area of the planned operation, including the destination and routes thereto, its proposed duration and the schedule for returning to the police station or post. The Israeli side of the DCO will provide the Palestinian side with its response, following a request for movement of policemen in accordance with this paragraph, in normal or routine cases within one day and in emergency cases no later than 2 hours.
6. The Palestinian Police and the Israeli military forces will conduct joint security activities on the main roads as set out in Annex I.
7. The Palestinian Police will notify the West Bank RSC of the names of the policemen, number plates of police vehicles and serial numbers of weapons, with respect to each police station and post in Area B.
8. Further redeployments from Area C and transfer of internal security responsibility to the Palestinian Police in Areas B and C will be carried out in three phases, each to take place after an interval of six months, to be completed 18 months after the inauguration of the Council, except for the issues of permanent status negotiations and of Israel's overall responsibility for Israelis and borders.
9. The procedures detailed in this paragraph will be reviewed within six months of the completion of the first phase of redeployment.

ARTICLE XIV
The Palestinian Police

1. The Council shall establish a strong police force. The duties, functions, structure, deployment and composition of the Palestinian Police, together with provisions regarding its equipment and operation, as well as rules of conduct, are set out in Annex I.

2. The Palestinian police force established under the Gaza-Jericho Agreement will be fully integrated into the Palestinian Police and will be subject to the provisions of this Agreement.

3. Except for the Palestinian Police and the Israeli military forces, no other armed forces shall be established or operate in the West Bank and the Gaza Strip.

4. Except for the arms, ammunition and equipment of the Palestinian Police

described in Annex I, and those of the Israeli military forces, no organization, group or individual in the West Bank and the Gaza Strip shall manufacture, sell, acquire, possess, import or otherwise introduce into the West Bank or the Gaza Strip any firearms, ammunition, weapons, explosives, gunpowder or any related equipment, unless otherwise provided for in Annex I.

ARTICLE XV
Prevention of Hostile Acts

1. Both sides shall take all measures necessary in order to prevent acts of terrorism, crime and hostilities directed against each other, against individuals falling under the other's authority and against their property and shall take legal measures against offenders.
2. Specific provisions for the implementation of this Article are set out in Annex I.

ARTICLE XVI
Confidence Building Measures

With a view to fostering a positive and supportive public atmosphere to accompany the implementation of this Agreement, to establish a solid basis of mutual trust and good faith, and in order to facilitate the anticipated cooperation and new relations between the two peoples, both Parties agree to carry out confidence building measures as detailed herewith:

1. 1. Israel will release or turn over to the Palestinian side, Palestinian detainees and prisoners, residents of the West Bank and the Gaza Strip. The first stage of release of these prisoners and detainees will take place on the signing of this Agreement and the second stage will take place prior to the date of the elections. There will be a third stage of release of detainees and prisoners. Detainees and prisoners will be released from among categories detailed in Annex VII (Release of Palestinian Prisoners and Detainees). Those released will be free to return to their homes in the West Bank and the Gaza Strip.
2. 2. Palestinians who have maintained contact with the Israeli authorities will not be subjected to acts of harassment, violence, retribution or prosecution. Appropriate ongoing measures will be taken, in coordination with Israel, in order to ensure their protection.
3. 3. Palestinians from abroad whose entry into the West Bank and the Gaza Strip is approved pursuant to this Agreement, and to whom the provisions of this Article are applicable, will not be prosecuted for offenses committed prior to September 13, 1993.

CHAPTER 3 - LEGAL AFFAIRS

ARTICLE XVII
Jurisdiction

1. In accordance with the DOP, the jurisdiction of the Council will cover West Bank and Gaza Strip territory as a single territorial unit, except for:

   d. issues that will be negotiated in the permanent status negotiations: Jerusalem, settlements, specified military locations, Palestinian refugees, borders, foreign relations and Israelis; and

e. powers and responsibilities not transferred to the Council.

2. Accordingly, the authority of the Council encompasses all matters that fall within its territorial, functional and personal jurisdiction, as follows:

a. The territorial jurisdiction of the Council shall encompass Gaza Strip territory, except for the Settlements and the Military Installation Area shown on map No. 2, and West Bank territory, except for Area C which, except for the issues that will be negotiated in the permanent status negotiations, will be gradually transferred to Palestinian jurisdiction in three phases, each to take place after an interval of six months, to be completed 18 months after the inauguration of the Council. At this time, the jurisdiction of the Council will cover West Bank and Gaza Strip territory, except for the issues that will be negotiated in the permanent status negotiations.

Territorial jurisdiction includes land, subsoil and territorial waters, in accordance with the provisions of this Agreement.

b. The functional jurisdiction of the Council extends to all powers and responsibilities transferred to the Council, as specified in this Agreement or in any future agreements that may be reached between the Parties during the interim period.

c. The territorial and functional jurisdiction of the Council will apply to all persons, except for Israelis, unless otherwise provided in this Agreement.

d. Notwithstanding subparagraph a. above, the Council shall have functional jurisdiction in Area C, as detailed in Article IV of Annex III.

3. The Council has, within its authority, legislative, executive and judicial powers and responsibilities, as provided for in this Agreement.

4. a. Israel, through its military government, has the authority over areas that are not under the territorial jurisdiction of the Council, powers and responsibilities not transferred to the Council and Israelis.

b. To this end, the Israeli military government shall retain the necessary legislative, judicial and executive powers and responsibilities, in accordance with international law. This provision shall not derogate from Israel's applicable legislation over Israelis in personam.

5. The exercise of authority with regard to the electromagnetic sphere and air space shall be in accordance with the provisions of this Agreement.

6. Without derogating from the provisions of this Article, legal arrangements detailed in the Protocol Concerning Legal Matters attached as Annex IV to this Agreement (hereinafter "Annex IV") shall be observed. Israel and the Council may negotiate further legal arrangements.

7. Israel and the Council shall cooperate on matters of legal assistance in criminal and civil matters through a legal committee (hereinafter "the Legal Committee"), hereby established.

8. The Council's jurisdiction will extend gradually to cover West Bank and Gaza Strip territory, except for the issues to be negotiated in the permanent status negotiations, through a series of redeployments of the Israeli military forces. The first phase of the redeployment of Israeli military forces will cover populated areas

in the West Bank - cities, towns, refugee camps and hamlets, as set out in Annex I - and will be completed prior to the eve of the Palestinian elections, i.e. 22 days before the day of the elections. Further redeployments of Israeli military forces to specified military locations will commence immediately upon the inauguration of the Council and will be effected in three phases, each to take place after an interval of six months, to be concluded no later than eighteen months from the date of the inauguration of the Council.

ARTICLE XVIII
Legislative Powers of the Council

1. For the purposes of this Article, legislation shall mean any primary and secondary legislation, including basic laws, laws, regulations and other legislative acts.

2. The Council has the power, within its jurisdiction as defined in Article XVII of this Agreement, to adopt legislation.

3. While the primary legislative power shall lie in the hands of the Council as a whole, the Ra'ees of the Executive Authority of the Council shall have the following legislative powers

   a. the power to initiate legislation or to present proposed legislation to the Council;

   b. the power to promulgate legislation adopted by the Council; and

   c. the power to issue secondary legislation, including regulations, relating to any matters specified and within the scope laid down in any primary legislation adopted by the Council.

4. a. Legislation, including legislation which amends or abrogates existing laws or military orders, which exceeds the jurisdiction of the Council or which is otherwise inconsistent with the provisions of the DOP, this Agreement, or of any other agreement that may be reached between the two sides during the interim period, shall have no effect and shall be void ab initio.
   b. The Ra'ees of the Executive Authority of the Council shall not promulgate legislation adopted by the Council if such legislation falls under the provisions of this paragraph.

5. All legislation shall be communicated to the Israeli side of the Legal Committee.

6. Without derogating from the provisions of paragraph 4 above, the Israeli side of the Legal Committee may refer for the attention of the Committee any legislation regarding which Israel considers the provisions of paragraph 4 apply, in order to discuss issues arising from such legislation. The Legal Committee will consider the legislation referred to it at the earliest opportunity.

ARTICLE XIX
Human Rights and the Rule of Law

Israel and the Council shall exercise their powers and responsibilities pursuant to this Agreement with due regard to internationally-accepted norms and principles of human rights and the rule of law.

ARTICLE XX
Rights, Liabilities and Obligations

1. a. The transfer of powers and responsibilities from the Israeli military government and its civil administration to the Council, as detailed in Annex III, includes all related rights, liabilities and obligations arising with regard to acts or omissions which occurred prior to such transfer. Israel will cease to bear any financial responsibility regarding such acts or omissions and the Council will bear all financial responsibility for these and for its own functioning.

   b. Any financial claim made in this regard against Israel will be referred to the Council.

   c. Israel shall provide the Council with the information it has regarding pending and anticipated claims brought before any court or tribunal against Israel in this regard.

   d. Where legal proceedings are brought in respect of such a claim, Israel will notify the Council and enable it to participate in defending the claim and raise any arguments on its behalf.

   e. In the event that an award is made against Israel by any court or tribunal in respect of such a claim, the Council shall immediately reimburse Israel the full amount of the award.

   f. Without prejudice to the above, where a court or tribunal hearing such a claim finds that liability rests solely with an employee or agent who acted beyond the scope of the powers assigned to him or her, unlawfully or with willful malfeasance, the Council shall not bear financial responsibility.

2. a. Notwithstanding the provisions of paragraphs l.d through l.f above, each side may take the necessary measures, including promulgation of legislation, in order to ensure that such claims by Palestinians including pending claims in which the hearing of evidence has not yet begun, are brought only before Palestinian courts or tribunals in the West Bank and the Gaza Strip, and are not brought before or heard by Israeli courts or tribunals.

   b. Where a new claim has been brought before a Palestinian court or tribunal subsequent to the dismissal of the claim pursuant to subparagraph a. above, the Council shall defend it and, in accordance with subparagraph l.a above, in the event that an award is made for the plaintiff, shall pay the amount of the award.

   c. The Legal Committee shall agree on arrangements for the transfer of all materials and information needed to enable the Palestinian courts or tribunals to hear such claims as referred to in subparagraph b. above, and, when necessary, for the provision of legal assistance by Israel to the Council in defending such claims.

3. The transfer of authority in itself shall not affect rights, liabilities and obligations of any person or legal entity, in existence at the date of signing of this Agreement.

4. The Council, upon its inauguration, will assume all the rights, liabilities and obligations of the Palestinian Authority.

5. For the purpose of this Agreement, "Israelis" also includes Israeli statutory agencies and corporations registered in Israel.

ARTICLE XXI

Settlement of Differences and Disputes

Any difference relating to the application of this Agreement shall be referred to the appropriate coordination and cooperation mechanism established under this Agreement. The provisions of Article XV of the DOP shall apply to any such difference which is not settled through the appropriate coordination and cooperation mechanism, namely:

1. Disputes arising out of the application or interpretation of this Agreement or any related agreements pertaining to the interim period shall be settled through the Liaison Committee.
2. Disputes which cannot be settled by negotiations may be settled by a mechanism of conciliation to be agreed between the Parties.
3. The Parties may agree to submit to arbitration disputes relating to the interim period, which cannot be settled through conciliation. To this end, upon the agreement of both Parties, the Parties will establish an Arbitration Committee.

CHAPTER 4 - COOPERATION

ARTICLE XXII

Relations between Israel and the Council

1. Israel and the Council shall seek to foster mutual understanding and tolerance and shall accordingly abstain from incitement, including hostile propaganda, against each other and, without derogating from the principle of freedom of expression, shall take legal measures to prevent such incitement by any organizations, groups or individuals within their jurisdiction.

2. Israel and the Council will ensure that their respective educational systems contribute to the peace between the Israeli and Palestinian peoples and to peace in the entire region, and will refrain from the introduction of any motifs that could adversely affect the process of reconciliation.

3. Without derogating from the other provisions of this Agreement, Israel and the Council shall cooperate in combating criminal activity which may affect both sides, including offenses related to trafficking in illegal drugs and psychotropic substances, smuggling, and offenses against property, including offenses related to vehicles.

ARTICLE XXIII

Cooperation with Regard to Transfer of Powers and Responsibilities

In order to ensure a smooth, peaceful and orderly transfer of powers and responsibilities, the two sides will cooperate with regard to the transfer of security powers and responsibilities in accordance with the provisions of Annex I, and the transfer of civil powers and responsibilities in accordance with the provisions of Annex III.

ARTICLE XXIV
Economic Relations

The economic relations between the two sides are set out in the Protocol on Economic Relations signed in Paris on April 29, 1994, and the Appendices thereto, and the Supplement to the Protocol on Economic Relations all attached as Annex V, and will be governed by the relevant provisions of this Agreement and its Annexes.

ARTICLE XXV
Cooperation Programs

1. The Parties agree to establish a mechanism to develop programs of cooperation between them. Details of such cooperation are set out in Annex VI.

2. A Standing Cooperation Committee to deal with issues arising in the context of this cooperation is hereby established as provided for in Annex VI.

ARTICLE XXVI
The Joint Israeli-Palestinian Liaison Committee

1. The Liaison Committee established pursuant to Article X of the DOP shall ensure the smooth implementation of this Agreement. It shall deal with issues requiring coordination, other issues of common interest and disputes.

2. The Liaison Committee shall be composed of an equal number of members from each Party. It may add other technicians and experts as necessary.

3. The Liaison Committee shall adopt its rules of procedures, including the frequency and place or places of its meetings.

4. The Liaison Committee shall reach its decisions by agreement.

5. The Liaison Committee shall establish a subcommittee that will monitor and steer the implementation of this Agreement (hereinafter "the Monitoring and Steering Committee"). It will function as follows:

d. The Monitoring and Steering Committee will, on an ongoing basis, monitor the implementation of this Agreement, with a view to enhancing the cooperation and fostering the peaceful relations between the two sides.

e. The Monitoring and Steering Committee will steer the activities of the various joint committees established in this Agreement (the JSC, the CAC, the Legal Committee, the Joint Economic Committee and the Standing Cooperation Committee) concerning the ongoing implementation of the Agreement, and will report to the Liaison Committee.

f. The Monitoring and Steering Committee will be composed of the heads of the various committees mentioned above.

g. The two heads of the Monitoring and Steering Committee will establish its rules of procedures, including the frequency and places of its meetings.

ARTICLE XXVII
Liaison and Cooperation with Jordan and Egypt

1. Pursuant to Article XII of the DOP, the two Parties have invited the Governments of Jordan and Egypt to participate in establishing further liaison and cooperation arrangements between the Government of Israel and the Palestinian representatives on the one hand, and the Governments of Jordan and Egypt on the other hand, to

promote cooperation between them. As part of these arrangements a Continuing Committee has been constituted and has commenced its deliberations.

2. The Continuing Committee shall decide by agreement on the modalities of admission of persons displaced from the West Bank and the Gaza Strip in 1967, together with necessary measures to prevent disruption and disorder.

3. The Continuing Committee shall also deal with other matters of common concern.

ARTICLE XXVIII
Missing Persons

1. Israel and the Council shall cooperate by providing each other with all necessary assistance in the conduct of searches for missing persons and bodies of persons which have not been recovered, as well as by providing information about missing persons.

2. The PLO undertakes to cooperate with Israel and to assist it in its efforts to locate and to return to Israel Israeli soldiers who are missing in action and the bodies of soldiers which have not been recovered.

CHAPTER 5 - MISCELLANEOUS PROVISIONS

ARTICLE XXIX
Safe Passage between the West Bank and the Gaza Strip

Arrangements for safe passage of persons and transportation between the West Bank and the Gaza Strip are set out in Annex I.

ARTICLE XXX
Passages

Arrangements for coordination between Israel and the Council regarding passage to and from Egypt and Jordan, as well as any other agreed international crossings, are set out in Annex I.

ARTICLE XXXI
Final Clauses

1. This Agreement shall enter into force on the date of its signing.

2. The Gaza-Jericho Agreement, except for Article XX (Confidence-Building Measures), the Preparatory Transfer Agreement and the Further Transfer Protocol will be superseded by this Agreement.

3. The Council, upon its inauguration, shall replace the Palestinian Authority and shall assume all the undertakings and obligations of the Palestinian Authority under the Gaza-Jericho Agreement, the Preparatory Transfer Agreement, and the Further Transfer Protocol.

4. The two sides shall pass all necessary legislation to implement this Agreement.

5. Permanent status negotiations will commence as soon as possible, but not later than May 4, 1996, between the Parties. It is understood that these negotiations shall cover remaining issues, including: Jerusalem, refugees, settlements, security arrangements, borders, relations and cooperation with other neighbors, and other issues of common interest.

6. Nothing in this Agreement shall prejudice or preempt the outcome of the negotiations on the permanent status to be conducted pursuant to the DOP. Neither Party shall be deemed, by virtue of having entered into this Agreement, to have renounced or waived any of its existing rights, claims or positions.

7. Neither side shall initiate or take any step that will change the status of the West Bank and the Gaza Strip pending the outcome of the permanent status negotiations.

8. The two Parties view the West Bank and the Gaza Strip as a single territorial unit, the integrity and status of which will be preserved during the interim period.

9. The PLO undertakes that, within two months of the date of the inauguration of the Council, the Palestinian National Council will convene and formally approve the necessary changes in regard to the Palestinian Covenant, as undertaken in the letters signed by the Chairman of the PLO and addressed to the Prime Minister of Israel, dated September 9, 1993 and May 4, 1994.

10. Pursuant to Annex I, Article IX of this Agreement, Israel confirms that the permanent checkpoints on the roads leading to and from the Jericho Area (except those related to the access road leading from Mousa Alami to the Allenby Bridge) will be removed upon the completion of the first phase of redeployment.

11. Prisoners who, pursuant to the Gaza-Jericho Agreement, were turned over to the Palestinian Authority on the condition that they remain in the Jericho Area for the remainder of their sentence, will be free to return to their homes in the West Bank and the Gaza Strip upon the completion of the first phase of redeployment.

12. As regards relations between Israel and the PLO, and without derogating from the commitments contained in the letters signed by and exchanged between the Prime Minister of Israel and the Chairman of the PLO, dated September 9, 1993 and May 4, 1994, the two sides will apply between them the provisions contained in Article XXII, paragraph 1, with the necessary changes.

13. a. The Preamble to this Agreement, and all Annexes, Appendices and maps attached hereto, shall constitute an integral part hereof.
    b. The Parties agree that the maps attached to the Gaza-Jericho Agreement as:
        a. map No. 1 (The Gaza Strip), an exact copy of which is attached to this Agreement as map No. (in this Agreement "map No. 2");
        b. map No. 4 (Deployment of Palestinian Police in the Gaza Strip), an exact copy of which is attached to this Agreement as map No. 5 (in this Agreement "map No. 5"); and
        c. map No. 6 (Maritime Activity Zones), an exact copy of which is attached to this Agreement as map No. 8 (in this Agreement "map No. 8"; are an integral part hereof and will remain in effect for the duration of this Agreement.

14. While the Jeftlik area will come under the functional and personal jurisdiction of the Council in the first phase of redeployment, the area's transfer to the territorial jurisdiction of the Council will be considered by the Israeli side in the first phase of the further redeployment phases.

Done at Washington DC, this 28th day of September, 1995.

Article 8 Rome Statute of the International Criminal Court, 1 July 2002

1. The Court shall have jurisdiction in respect of war crimes in particular when committed as part of a plan or policy or as part of a large-scale commission of such crimes.
2. For the purpose of this Statute, "war crimes" means:
   a. Grave breaches of the Geneva Conventions of 12 August 1949, namely, any of the following acts against persons or property protected under the provisions of the relevant Geneva Convention:
      i. Wilful killing;
      ii. Torture or inhuman treatment, including biological experiments;
      iii. Wilfully causing great suffering, or serious injury to body or health;
      iv. Extensive destruction and appropriation of property, not justified by military necessity and carried out unlawfully and wantonly;
      v. Compelling a prisoner of war or other protected person to serve in the forces of a hostile Power;
      vi. Wilfully depriving a prisoner of war or other protected person of the rights of fair and regular trial;
      vii. Unlawful deportation or transfer or unlawful confinement;
      viii. Taking of hostages.

   b. Other serious violations of the laws and customs applicable in international armed conflict, within the established framework of international law, namely, any of the following acts:
      i. Intentionally directing attacks against the civilian population as such or against individual civilians not taking direct part in hostilities;
      ii. Intentionally directing attacks against civilian objects, that is, objects which are not military objectives;
      iii. Intentionally directing attacks against personnel, installations, material, units or vehicles involved in a humanitarian assistance or peacekeeping mission in accordance with the Charter of the United Nations, as long as they are entitled to the protection given to civilians or civilian objects under the international law of armed conflict;
      iv. Intentionally launching an attack in the knowledge that such attack will cause incidental loss of life or injury to civilians or damage to civilian objects or widespread, long-term and severe damage to the natural environment which would be clearly excessive in relation to the concrete and direct overall military advantage anticipated;
      v. Attacking or bombarding, by whatever means, towns, villages, dwellings or buildings which are undefended and which are not military objectives;
      vi. Killing or wounding a combatant who, having laid down his arms or having no longer means of defence, has surrendered at discretion;
      vii. Making improper use of a flag of truce, of the flag or of the military

insignia and uniform of the enemy or of the United Nations, as well as of the distinctive emblems of the Geneva Conventions, resulting in death or serious personal injury;

viii. The transfer, directly or indirectly, by the Occupying Power of parts of its own civilian population into the territory it occupies, or the deportation or transfer of all or parts of the population of the occupied territory within or outside this territory;

ix. Intentionally directing attacks against buildings dedicated to religion, education, art, science or charitable purposes, historic monuments, hospitals and places where the sick and wounded are collected, provided they are not military objectives;

x. Subjecting persons who are in the power of an adverse party to physical mutilation or to medical or scientific experiments of any kind which are neither justified by the medical, dental or hospital treatment of the person concerned nor carried out in his or her interest, and which cause death to or seriously endanger the health of such person or persons;

xi. Killing or wounding treacherously individuals belonging to the hostile nation or army;

xii. Declaring that no quarter will be given;

xiii. Destroying or seizing the enemy's property unless such destruction or seizure be imperatively demanded by the necessities of war;

xiv. Declaring abolished, suspended or inadmissible in a court of law the rights and actions of the nationals of the hostile party;

xv. Compelling the nationals of the hostile party to take part in the operations of war directed against their own country, even if they were in the belligerent's service before the commencement of the war;

xvi. Pillaging a town or place, even when taken by assault;

xvii. Employing poison or poisoned weapons;

xviii. Employing asphyxiating, poisonous or other gases, and all analogous liquids, materials or devices;

xix. Employing bullets which expand or flatten easily in the human body, such as bullets with a hard envelope which does not entirely cover the core or is pierced with incisions;

xx. Employing weapons, projectiles and material and methods of warfare which are of a nature to cause superfluous injury or unnecessary suffering or which are inherently indiscriminate in violation of the international law of armed conflict, provided that such weapons, projectiles and material and methods of warfare are the subject of a comprehensive prohibition and are included in an annex to this Statute, by an amendment in accordance with the relevant provisions set forth in articles 121 and 123;

xxi. Committing outrages upon personal dignity, in particular humiliating and degrading treatment;

xxii. Committing rape, sexual slavery, enforced prostitution, forced pregnancy, as defined in article 7, paragraph 2 (f), enforced sterilization, or any other form of sexual violence also constituting a grave breach of the Geneva Conventions;

xxiii. Utilizing the presence of a civilian or other protected person to render certain points, areas or military forces immune from military operations;

xxiv. Intentionally directing attacks against buildings, material, medical units and transport, and personnel using the distinctive emblems of the Geneva Conventions in conformity with international law;

xxv. Intentionally using starvation of civilians as a method of warfare by depriving them of objects indispensable to their survival, including wilfully impeding relief supplies as provided for under the Geneva Conventions;

xxvi. Conscripting or enlisting children under the age of fifteen years into the national armed forces or using them to participate actively in hostilities.

c. In the case of an armed conflict not of an international character, serious violations of article 3 common to the four Geneva Conventions of 12 August 1949, namely, any of the following acts committed against persons taking no active part in the hostilities, including members of armed forces who have laid down their arms and those placed hors de combat by sickness, wounds, detention or any other cause:

   i. Violence to life and person, in particular murder of all kinds, mutilation, cruel treatment and torture;

   ii. Committing outrages upon personal dignity, in particular humiliating and degrading treatment;

   iii. Taking of hostages;

   iv. The passing of sentences and the carrying out of executions without previous judgement pronounced by a regularly constituted court, affording all judicial guarantees which are generally recognized as indispensable.

d. Paragraph 2 (c) applies to armed conflicts not of an international character and thus does not apply to situations of internal disturbances and tensions, such as riots, isolated and sporadic acts of violence or other acts of a similar nature.

e. Other serious violations of the laws and customs applicable in armed conflicts not of an international character, within the established framework of international law, namely, any of the following acts:

   i. Intentionally directing attacks against the civilian population as such or against individual civilians not taking direct part in hostilities;

   ii. Intentionally directing attacks against buildings, material, medical units and transport, and personnel using the distinctive emblems of the Geneva Conventions in conformity with international law;

   iii. Intentionally directing attacks against personnel, installations, material, units or vehicles involved in a humanitarian assistance or peacekeeping mission in accordance with the Charter of the United Nations, as long as they are entitled to the protection given to civilians or civilian objects under the international law of armed conflict;

iv. Intentionally directing attacks against buildings dedicated to religion, education, art, science or charitable purposes, historic monuments, hospitals and places where the sick and wounded are collected, provided they are not military objectives;

v. Pillaging a town or place, even when taken by assault;

vi. Committing rape, sexual slavery, enforced prostitution, forced pregnancy, as defined in article 7, paragraph 2 (f), enforced sterilization, and any other form of sexual violence also constituting a serious violation of article 3 common to the four Geneva Conventions;

vii. Conscripting or enlisting children under the age of fifteen years into armed forces or groups or using them to participate actively in hostilities;

viii. Ordering the displacement of the civilian population for reasons related to the conflict, unless the security of the civilians involved or imperative military reasons so demand;

ix. Killing or wounding treacherously a combatant adversary;

x. Declaring that no quarter will be given;

xi. Subjecting persons who are in the power of another party to the conflict to physical mutilation or to medical or scientific experiments of any kind which are neither justified by the medical, dental or hospital treatment of the person concerned nor carried out in his or her interest, and which cause death to or seriously endanger the health of such person or persons;

xii. Destroying or seizing the property of an adversary unless such destruction or seizure be imperatively demanded by the necessities of the conflict;

f. Paragraph 2 (e) applies to armed conflicts not of an international character and thus does not apply to situations of internal disturbances and tensions, such as riots, isolated and sporadic acts of violence or other acts of a similar nature. It applies to armed conflicts that take place in the territory of a State when there is protracted armed conflict between governmental authorities and organized armed groups or between such groups.

3. Nothing in paragraph 2 (c) and (e) shall affect the responsibility of a Government to maintain or re-establish law and order in the State or to defend the unity and territorial integrity of the State, by all legitimate means.

General Assembly Resolution 67/19, 4 December 2012

67/19. Status of Palestine in the United Nations

The General Assembly,

Guided by the purposes and principles of the Charter of the United Nations, and stressing in this regard the principle of equal rights and self-determination of peoples,

Recalling its resolution 2625 (XXV) of 24 October 1970, by which it affirmed, inter alia, the duty of every State to promote, through joint and separate action, realization of the principle of equal rights and self-determination of peoples,

Stressing the importance of maintaining and strengthening international peace founded upon freedom, equality, justice and respect for fundamental human rights,

Recalling its resolution 181 (II) of 29 November 1947,

Reaffirming the principle, set out in the Charter, of the inadmissibility of the acquisition of territory by force,

Reaffirming also relevant Security Council resolutions, including resolutions 242 (1967) of 22 November 1967, 338 (1973) of 22 October 1973, 446 (1979) of 22 March 1979, 478 (1980) of 20 August 1980, 1397 (2002) of 12 March 2002, 1515 (2003) of 19 November 2003 and 1850 (2008) of 16 December 2008,

Reaffirming further the applicability of the Geneva Convention relative to the Protection of Civilian Persons in Time of War, of 12 August 1949, to the Occupied Palestinian Territory, including East Jerusalem, including with regard to the matter of prisoners,

Reaffirming its resolution 3236 (XXIX) of 22 November 1974 and all relevant resolutions, including resolution 66/146 of 19 December 2011, reaffirming the right of the Palestinian people to self-determination, including the right to their independent State of Palestine,

Reaffirming also its resolutions 43/176 of 15 December 1988 and 66/17 of 30 November 2011 and all relevant resolutions regarding the peaceful settlement of the question of Palestine, which, inter alia, stress the need for the withdrawal of Israel from the Palestinian territory occupied since 1967, including East Jerusalem, the realization of the inalienable rights of the Palestinian people, primarily the right to self-determination and the right to their independent State, a just resolution of the problem of the Palestine refugees in conformity with resolution 194 (III) of 11 December 1948 and the complete cessation of all Israeli settlement activities in the Occupied Palestinian Territory, including East Jerusalem,

Reaffirming further its resolution 66/18 of 30 November 2011 and all relevant resolutions regarding the status of Jerusalem, bearing in mind that the annexation of East Jerusalem is not recognized by the international community, and emphasizing the need for a way to be found through negotiations to resolve the status of Jerusalem as the capital of two States,

Recalling the advisory opinion of the International Court of Justice of 9 July 2004,

Reaffirming its resolution 58/292 of 6 May 2004 affirming, inter alia, that the status of the Palestinian territory occupied since 1967, including East Jerusalem, remains one of military occupation and that, in accordance with international law and relevant United Nations resolutions, the Palestinian people have the right to self-determination and to sovereignty over their territory,

Recalling its resolutions 3210 (XXIX) of 14 October 1974 and 3237 (XXIX) of 22 November 1974, by which, respectively, the Palestine Liberation Organization was invited to participate in the deliberations of the General Assembly as the representative of the Palestinian people and was granted observer status,

Recalling also its resolution 43/177 of 15 December 1988, by which it, inter alia, acknowledged the proclamation of the State of Palestine by the Palestine National Council on 15 November 1988 and decided that the designation "Palestine" should be used in place of the designation "Palestine Liberation Organization" in the United Nations system, without prejudice to the observer status and functions of the Palestine Liberation Organization within the United Nations system,

Taking into consideration that the Executive Committee of the Palestine Liberation Organization, in accordance with a decision by the Palestine National Council, is entrusted with the powers and responsibilities of the Provisional Government of the State of Palestine,

Recalling its resolution 52/250 of 7 July 1998, by which additional rights and privileges were accorded to Palestine in its capacity as observer,

Recalling also the Arab Peace Initiative adopted in March 2002 by the Council of the League of Arab States,

Reaffirming its commitment, in accordance with international law, to the two-State solution of an independent, sovereign, democratic, viable and contiguous State of Palestine living side by side with Israel in peace and security on the basis of the pre-1967 borders,

Bearing in mind the mutual recognition of 9 September 1993 between the Government of the State of Israel and the Palestine Liberation Organization, the representative of the Palestinian people,

Affirming the right of all States in the region to live in peace within secure and internationally recognized borders,

Commending the Palestinian National Authority's 2009 plan for constructing the institutions of an independent Palestinian State within a two-year period, and welcoming the positive assessments in this regard about readiness for statehood by the World Bank, the United Nations and the International Monetary Fund and as reflected in the Ad Hoc Liaison Committee Chair conclusions of April 2011 and subsequent Chair conclusions, which determined that the Palestinian Authority is above the threshold for a functioning State in key sectors studied,

Recognizing that full membership is enjoyed by Palestine in the United Nations Educational, Scientific and Cultural Organization, the Economic and Social Commission for Western Asia and the Group of Asia-Pacific States and that Palestine is also a full member of the League of Arab States, the Movement of NonAligned Countries, the Organization of Islamic Cooperation and the Group of 77 and China,

Recognizing also that, to date, 132 States Members of the United Nations have accorded recognition to the State of Palestine,

Taking note of the 11 November 2011 report of the Security Council Committee on the Admission of New Members,

Stressing the permanent responsibility of the United Nations towards the question of Palestine until it is satisfactorily resolved in all its aspects,

Reaffirming the principle of universality of membership of the United Nations,

1. Reaffirms the right of the Palestinian people to self-determination and to independence in their State of Palestine on the Palestinian territory occupied since 1967;
2. Decides to accord to Palestine non-member observer State status in the United Nations, without prejudice to the acquired rights, privileges and role of the Palestine Liberation Organization in the United Nations as the representative of the Palestinian people, in accordance with the relevant resolutions and practice;
3. Expresses the hope that the Security Council will consider favourably the application submitted on 23 September 2011 by the State of Palestine for admission to full membership in the United Nations;
4. Affirms its determination to contribute to the achievement of the inalienable rights of the Palestinian people and the attainment of a peaceful settlement in the Middle East that ends the occupation that began in 1967 and fulfils the vision of two States: an independent, sovereign, democratic, contiguous and viable State of Palestine living side by side in peace and security with Israel on the basis of the pre-1967 borders;
5. Expresses the urgent need for the resumption and acceleration of negotiations within the Middle East peace process based on the relevant United Nations resolutions, the terms of reference of the Madrid Conference, including the principle of land for peace, the Arab Peace Initiative5 and the Quartet road map to a permanent two-State solution to the Israeli-Palestinian conflict for the achievement of a just, lasting and comprehensive peace settlement between the Palestinian and Israeli sides that resolves all outstanding core issues, namely the Palestine refugees, Jerusalem, settlements, borders, security and water;
6. Urges all States and the specialized agencies and organizations of the United Nations system to continue to support and assist the Palestinian people in the early realization of their right to self-determination, independence and freedom;
7. Requests the Secretary-General to take the necessary measures to implement the present resolution and to report to the General Assembly within three months on progress made in this regard.

EU Council Conclusions on the Middle East Peace process, 18 January 2016

1 The Council is deeply concerned that the continuing cycle of violence has led to a serious loss of human life in Israel and the Palestinian territory in recent months. The EU firmly condemns the terror attacks and violence from all sides and in any circumstances, including the death of children. The EU calls on political leaders to work together through visible actions to contribute to calm and address the underlying causes of the tensions. The EU recalls the special significance of the holy sites, and calls for upholding the status quo put in place in 1967 for the Temple Mount / al-Haram al-Sharif in line with previous understandings and with respect to Jordan's special role.

2. The EU urges all parties to refrain from any action that would worsen the situation by way of incitement or provocation and calls on the parties to condemn attacks when they occur and adhere strictly to the principles of necessity and proportionality in the use of force. It commends both sides for upholding security coordination in the light of an extremely challenging situation. The EU welcomes progress on the Duma investigation and calls for Israel to hold all perpetrators of settler violence to account. The EU also calls on both sides to jointly and resolutely fight incitement and hate speech, for instance by establishing a mechanism to consult on incitement along the lines of their previous commitments.

3. The EU is convinced that only the reestablishment of a political horizon and the resumption of dialogue can stop the violence. Security measures alone cannot stop the cycle of violence. The underlying causes of the conflict need to be addressed. The EU reaffirms its support to the Quartet calls for significant transformative steps to be taken, consistent with the transition envisaged by prior agreements, in order to restore confidence and rebuild trust. The EU urges both sides to implement these measures at the earliest juncture possible. A fundamental change of policy by Israel with regard to the occupied Palestinian territory, particularly in Area C, will significantly increase economic opportunities, empower Palestinian institutions and enhance stability and security for both Israelis and Palestinians.

4. The EU is united in its commitment to achieving a two-state solution - based on parameters set out in the Council Conclusions of July 2014 - that meets Israeli and Palestinian security needs and Palestinian aspirations for statehood and sovereignty, ends the occupation that began in 1967, and resolves all permanent status issues in order to end the conflict. It strongly opposes all actions that undermine the viability of the two state solution and urges both sides to demonstrate, through policies and actions, a genuine commitment to a two-state solution in order to rebuild trust and create a path back to meaningful negotiations. To this end, the EU will continue to closely monitor developments on the ground and their broader implications and will consider further action in order to protect the viability of the two-state solution, which is constantly eroded by new facts on the ground.

5. Securing a just and lasting peace, ending all claims, will require an increased common international effort. The EU, including through the action of its Special Representative, will work actively with all relevant stakeholders, including partners in the Quartet, notably the United States, in the region and in the United Nations Security Council, towards a renewed multilateral approach to the peace process. Recalling the spirit of dialogue and cooperation that presided over the Madrid Conference 25 years ago, the establishment of an International Support Group and a further international conference are both possible ways to contribute to this end. The EU recalls its willingness to engage further with regional partners on the basis of the Arab Peace Initiative which provides key elements for the settlement of the Arab-Israeli conflict as well as the opportunity for building a regional security framework.

6. The EU recalls that compliance with international humanitarian law and international human rights law by states and non-state actors, including accountability, is a cornerstone for peace and security in the region. The EU calls for the protection of children, including ensuring the right to education in a safe and secure school environment. The Council highlights the importance of unhindered work of civil society both in Israel and the occupied Palestinian territory and follows recent developments in this regard with concern.

7. Recalling that settlements are illegal under international law, constitute an obstacle to peace and threaten to make a two state solution impossible, the EU reiterates its strong opposition to Israel's settlement policy and actions taken in this context, such as building the separation barrier beyond the 1967 line, demolitions and confiscation - including of EU funded projects - evictions, forced transfers including of Bedouins, illegal outposts and restrictions of movement and access. It urges Israel to end all settlement activity and to dismantle the outposts erected since March 2001, in line with prior obligations. Settlement activity in East Jerusalem seriously jeopardizes the possibility of Jerusalem serving as the future capital of both States.

8. The EU and its Member States are committed to ensure continued, full and effective implementation of existing EU legislation and bilateral arrangements applicable to settlements products. The EU expresses its commitment to ensure that - in line with international law - all agreements between the State of Israel and the EU must unequivocally and explicitly indicate their inapplicability to the territories occupied by Israel in 1967. This does not constitute a boycott of Israel which the EU strongly opposes.

9. The EU urges all Palestinian factions to engage in good faith in the reconciliation process which is an important element for reaching the two state solution. The EU will continue its support to Palestinian aspirations for Statehood. It is of the utmost importance that the positive results of the past are not lost and Palestinian institutions must continue to grow stronger, more transparent, more accountable and more democratic. The EU calls upon the government to work towards genuine and democratic elections for all Palestinians. Strong, inclusive and democratic institutions, based on respect of the rule of law and human rights, are crucial in view of the establishment of a viable and sovereign Palestinian State. To this

end, the EU calls on all Palestinian factions to find common ground and to work together to address the needs of the Palestinian population.

10. The EU calls for all parties to take swift steps to produce a fundamental change to the political, security and economic situation in the Gaza Strip, including the end of the closure and a full opening of the crossing points, while addressing Israel's legitimate security concerns. Recent rocket fire by militant groups is unacceptable and underlines again the danger of escalation. All stakeholders must commit to non-violence and peace. The EU urges the Palestinian sides to make the reconstruction of Gaza an overarching national priority especially as regards to health, energy and access to water. The Palestinian Authority must fully resume its governmental functions in Gaza, as it is an integral part of a future Palestinian state. The EU welcomes the steps that Israel has taken to ease some restrictions on Gaza. However the lifting of restriction on movement of people, services and goods - particularly those designated as 'dual-use items' - is needed to allow reconstruction efforts and basic service delivery. The EU calls all parties, state and non-state actors to guarantee unimpeded humanitarian access to Gaza, as foreseen by international humanitarian law, for national, local and international humanitarian organizations, including EU bodies and Member States. The EU remains ready to engage with the parties and relevant stakeholders towards resolving the situation and calls on the international community to swiftly honour its pledges.

11. The EU reiterates its offer to both parties of a package of European political, economic and security support and of a Special Privileged Partnership with the EU, which offers substantial benefits to both parties, in the event of a final peace agreement. The EU underlines that the future development of the relations between the EU and both the Israeli and Palestinian partners will also depend on their engagement towards a lasting peace based on a two-state solution.

Security Council Resolution 2334 (2016), 23 December 2016

Resolution 2334 (2016)

Adopted by the Security Council at its 7853rd meeting, on 23 December 2016

The Security Council,

Reaffirming its relevant resolutions, including resolutions 242 (1967), 338

(1973), 446 (1979), 452 (1979), 465 (1980), 476 (1980), 478 (1980), 1397 (2002), 1515 (2003), and 1850 (2008),

Guided by the purposes and principles of the Charter of the United Nations, and reaffirming, inter alia, the inadmissibility of the acquisition of territory by force,

Reaffirming the obligation of Israel, the occupying Power, to abide scrupulously by its legal obligations and responsibilities under the Fourth Geneva Convention relative to the Protection of Civilian Persons in Time of War, of 12 August 1949, and recalling the advisory opinion rendered on 9 July 2004 by the International Court of Justice,

Condemning all measures aimed at altering the demographic composition, character and status of the Palestinian Territory occupied since 1967, including East Jerusalem, including, inter alia, the construction and expansion of settlements, transfer of Israeli settlers, confiscation of land, demolition of homes and displacement of Palestinian civilians, in violation of international humanitarian law and relevant resolutions,

Expressing grave concern that continuing Israeli settlement activities are dangerously imperilling the viability of the two-State solution based on the 1967 lines,

Recalling the obligation under the Quartet Roadmap, endorsed by its resolution 1515 (2003), for a freeze by Israel of all settlement activity, including “natural growth”, and the dismantlement of all settlement outposts erected since March 2001,

Recalling also the obligation under the Quartet roadmap for the Palestinian Authority Security Forces to maintain effective operations aimed at confronting all those engaged in terror and dismantling terrorist capabilities, including the confiscation of illegal weapons,

Condemning all acts of violence against civilians, including acts of terror, as well as all acts of provocation, incitement and destruction,

Reiterating its vision of a region where two democratic States, Israel and Palestine, live side by side in peace within secure and recognized borders,

Stressing that the status quo is not sustainable and that significant steps, consistent with the transition contemplated by prior agreements, are urgently needed in order to (i) stabilize the situation and to reverse negative trends on the ground, which are steadily eroding the two-State solution and entrenching a one-State reality, and (ii) to create the conditions for successful final status negotiations and for advancing the two-State solution through those negotiations and on the ground,

1. *Reaffirms* that the establishment by Israel of settlements in the Palestinian territory occupied since 1967, including East Jerusalem, has no legal validity and constitutes a flagrant violation under international law and a major obstacle to the achievement of the two-State solution and a just, lasting and comprehensive peace;
2. *Reiterates* its demand that Israel immediately and completely cease all settlement activities in the occupied Palestinian territory, including East Jerusalem, and that it fully respect all of its legal obligations in this regard;
3. *Underlines* that it will not recognize any changes to the 4 June 1967 lines, including with regard to Jerusalem, other than those agreed by the parties through negotiations;
4. *Stresses* that the cessation of all Israeli settlement activities is essential for salvaging the two-State solution, and calls for affirmative steps to be taken immediately to reverse the negative trends on the ground that are imperilling the two-State solution;
5. *Calls* upon all States, bearing in mind paragraph 1 of this resolution, to distinguish, in their relevant dealings, between the territory of the State of Israel and the territories occupied since 1967;
6. *Calls* for immediate steps to prevent all acts of violence against civilians, including acts of terror, as well as all acts of provocation and destruction, calls for accountability in this regard, and calls for compliance with obligations under international law for the strengthening of ongoing efforts to combat terrorism, including through existing security coordination, and to clearly condemn all acts of terrorism;
7. *Calls* upon both parties to act on the basis of international law, including international humanitarian law, and their previous agreements and obligations, to observe calm and restraint, and to refrain from provocative actions, incitement and inflammatory rhetoric, with the aim, inter alia, of de-escalating the situation on the ground, rebuilding trust and confidence, demonstrating through policies and actions a genuine commitment to the two-State solution, and creating the conditions necessary for promoting peace;
8. *Calls* upon all parties to continue, in the interest of the promotion of peace and security, to exert collective efforts to launch credible negotiations on all final status issues in the Middle East peace process and within the time frame specified by the Quartet in its statement of 21 September 2010;
9. *Urges* in this regard the intensification and acceleration of international and regional diplomatic efforts and support aimed at achieving, without delay a comprehensive, just and lasting peace in the Middle East on the basis of the relevant United Nations resolutions, the Madrid terms of reference, including the principle of land for peace, the Arab Peace Initiative and the Quartet Roadmap and an end to the Israeli occupation that began in 1967; and underscores in this regard the importance of the ongoing efforts to advance the Arab Peace Initiative, the initiative of France for the convening of an international peace conference, the recent efforts of the Quartet, as well as the efforts of Egypt and the Russian Federation;

10. *Confirms* its determination to support the parties throughout the negotiations and in the implementation of an agreement;
11. *Reaffirms* its determination to examine practical ways and means to secure the full implementation of its relevant resolutions;
12. *Requests* the Secretary-General to report to the Council every three months on the implementation of the provisions of the present resolution;
13. *Decides* to remain seized of the matter.

Middle East Peace Conference Joint Declaration, Paris, 15 January 2017

I) Following the Ministerial meeting held in Paris on 3 June 2016, the Participants met in Paris on 15 January 2017 to reaffirm their support for a just, lasting and comprehensive resolution of the Israeli-Palestinian conflict. They reaffirmed that a negotiated solution with two states, Israel and Palestine, living side by side in peace and security, is the only way to achieve enduring peace.

They emphasized the importance for the parties to restate their commitment to this solution, to take urgent steps in order to reverse the current negative trends on the ground, including continued acts of violence and ongoing settlement activity, and to start meaningful direct negotiations.

They reiterated that a negotiated two-state solution should meet the legitimate aspirations of both sides, including the Palestinians' right to statehood and sovereignty, fully end the occupation that begin in 1967, satisfy Israel's security needs and resolve all permanent status issues on the basis of United Nations Security Council resolutions 242 (1967) and 338 (1973), and also recalled relevant Security Council resolutions.

They underscored the importance of the Arab Peace Initiative of 2002 as a comprehensive framework for the resolution of the Arab-Israeli conflict, thus contributing to regional peace and security.

They welcomed international efforts to advance Middle East peace, including the adoption of United Nations Security Council resolution 2334 on 23 December 2016, which clearly condemned settlement activity, incitement and all acts of violence and terror, and called on both sides to take steps to advance the two-state solution on the ground; the recommendations of the Quartet on 1 July 2016; and the United States Secretary of State's principle on the two-state solution on 28 December 2016.

They noted the importance of addressing the dire humanitarian and security situation in the Gaza Strip and called for swift steps to improve the situation.

They emphasized the importance for Israelis and Palestinians to comply with international law, including international humanitarian law and human rights law.

II) The Participants highlighted the potential for security, stability and prosperity for both parties that could result from a peace agreement. They expressed their readiness to exert necessary efforts toward the achievement of the two-state solution and to contribute substantially to arrangements for ensuring the sustainability of a negotiated peace agreement, in particular in the areas of political and economic incentives, the consolidation of Palestinian state capacities, and civil society dialogue. Those could include, inter alia:

- a European privileged partnership; other political and economic incentives and increased private sector involvement; support to further efforts by the parties to improve economic cooperation; continued financial support to the Palestinian Authority in building the infrastructure for a viable Palestinian economy;

- supporting and strengthening Palestinian steps to exercise their responsibilities of statehood through consolidating their institutions and institutional capacities, including for service delivery;
- convening Israeli and Palestinian civil society fora, in order to enhance dialogue between the parties, rekindle the public debate and strengthen the role of civil society on both sides.

III) Looking ahead, the Participants;

- call upon both sides to officially restate their commitment to the two-state solution, thus disassociating themselves from voices that reject this solution;
- call on each side to independently demonstrate, through policies and actions, a genuine commitment to the two-state solutions and refrain from unilateral steps that prejudge the outcome of negotiations on final status issues, including, inter alia, on Jerusalem, borders, security, refugees and which they will not recognize;
- welcome the prospect of closer cooperation between the Quartet and Arab League members and other relevant actors to further the objectives of this Declaration.

As follow-up to the Conference, interested Participants, expressing their readiness to review progress, resolved to meet again before the end of the year in order to support both sides in advancing the two-state solution through negotiations.

France will inform the parties about the international community's collective support and concrete contribution to the two-state solution contained in this joint declaration.

Hamas Charter, May 2017

Praise be to Allah, the Lord of all worlds. May the peace and blessings of Allah be upon Muhammad, the Master of Messengers and the Leader of the mujahidin, and upon his household and all his companions.

Preamble

Palestine is the land of the Arab Palestinian people, from it they originate, to it they adhere and belong, and about it they reach out and communicate.

Palestine is a land whose status has been elevated by Islam, a faith that holds it in high esteem, that breathes through it its spirit and just values and that lays the foundation for the doctrine of defending and protecting it.

Palestine is the cause of a people who have been let down by a world that fails to secure their rights and restore to them what has been usurped from them, a people whose land continues to suffer one of the worst types of occupation in this world.

Palestine is a land that was seized by a racist, anti-human and colonial Zionist project that was founded on a false promise (the Balfour Declaration), on recognition of a usurping entity and on imposing a fait accompli by force.

Palestine symbolises the resistance that shall continue until liberation is accomplished, until the return is fulfilled and until a fully sovereign state is established with Jerusalem as its capital.

Palestine is the true partnership among Palestinians of all affiliations for the sublime objective of liberation.

Palestine is the spirit of the Ummah and its central cause; it is the soul of humanity and its living conscience.

This document is the product of deep deliberations that led us to a strong consensus. As a movement, we agree about both the theory and the practice of the vision that is outlined in the pages that follow. It is a vision that stands on solid grounds and on well-established principles. This document unveils the goals, the milestones and the way in which national unity can be enforced. It also establishes our common understanding of the Palestinian cause, the working principles which we use to further it, and the limits of flexibility used to interpret it.

The movement

1. The Islamic Resistance Movement “Hamas” is a Palestinian Islamic national liberation and resistance movement. Its goal is to liberate Palestine and confront the Zionist project. Its frame of reference is Islam, which determines its principles, objectives and means.

The Land of Palestine

2. Palestine, which extends from the River Jordan in the east to the Mediterranean in the west and from Ras al-Naqurah in the north to Umm al-Rashrash in the south, is an integral territorial unit. It is the land and the home of the Palestinian people. The expulsion and banishment of the Palestinian people from their land

and the establishment of the Zionist entity therein do not annul the right of the Palestinian people to their entire land and do not entrench any rights therein for the usurping Zionist entity.

3. Palestine is an Arab Islamic land. It is a blessed sacred land that has a special place in the heart of every Arab and every Muslim.

The Palestinian people

4. The Palestinians are the Arabs who lived in Palestine until 1947, irrespective of whether they were expelled from it, or stayed in it; and every person that was born to an Arab Palestinian father after that date, whether inside or outside Palestine, is a Palestinian.

5. The Palestinian identity is authentic and timeless; it is passed from generation to generation. The catastrophes that have befallen the Palestinian people, as a consequence of the Zionist occupation and its policy of displacement, cannot erase the identity of the Palestinian people nor can they negate it. A Palestinian shall not lose his or her national identity or rights by acquiring a second nationality.

6. The Palestinian people are one people, made up of all Palestinians, inside and outside of Palestine, irrespective of their religion, culture or political affiliation.

Islam and Palestine

7. Palestine is at the heart of the Arab and Islamic Ummah and enjoys a special status. Within Palestine there exists Jerusalem, whose precincts are blessed by Allah. Palestine is the Holy Land, which Allah has blessed for humanity. It is the Muslims' first Qiblah and the destination of the journey performed at night by Prophet Muhammad, peace be upon him. It is the location from where he ascended to the upper heavens. It is the birthplace of Jesus Christ, peace be upon him. Its soil contains the remains of thousands of prophets, companions and mujahidin. It is the land of people who are determined to defend the truth – within Jerusalem and its surroundings – who are not deterred or intimidated by those who oppose them and by those who betray them, and they will continue their mission until the Promise of Allah is fulfilled.

8. By virtue of its justly balanced middle way and moderate spirit, Islam – for Hamas - provides a comprehensive way of life and an order that is fit for purpose at all times and in all places. Islam is a religion of peace and tolerance. It provides an umbrella for the followers of other creeds and religions who can practice their beliefs in security and safety. Hamas also believes that Palestine has always been and will always be a model of coexistence, tolerance and civilizational innovation.

9. Hamas believes that the message of Islam upholds the values of truth, justice, freedom and dignity and prohibits all forms of injustice and incriminates oppressors irrespective of their religion, race, gender or nationality. Islam is against all forms of religious, ethnic or sectarian extremism and bigotry. It is the religion that inculcates in its followers the value of standing up to aggression and of supporting the oppressed; it motivates them to give generously and make sacrifices in defence of their dignity, their land, their peoples and their holy places.

Jerusalem

10. Jerusalem is the capital of Palestine. Its religious, historic and civilisational status is fundamental to the Arabs, Muslims and the world at large. Its Islamic and Christian holy places belong exclusively to the Palestinian people and to the Arab and Islamic Ummah. Not one stone of Jerusalem can be surrendered or relinquished. The measures undertaken by the occupiers in Jerusalem, such as Judaisation, settlement building, and establishing facts on the ground are fundamentally null and void.

11. The blessed al-Aqsa Mosque belongs exclusively to our people and our Ummah, and the occupation has no right to it whatsoever. The occupation's plots, measures and attempts to judaize al-Aqsa and divide it are null, void and illegitimate.

Refugees and right of return

12. The Palestinian cause in its essence is a cause of an occupied land and a displaced people. The right of the Palestinian refugees and the displaced to return to their homes from which they were banished or were banned from returning to – whether in the lands occupied in 1948 or in 1967 (that is the whole of Palestine), is a natural right, both individual and collective. This right is confirmed by all divine laws as well as by the basic principles of human rights and international law. It is an inalienable right and cannot be dispensed with by any party, whether Palestinian, Arab or international.

13. Hamas rejects all attempts to erase the rights of the refugees, including the attempts to settle them outside Palestine and through the projects of the alternative homeland. Compensation to the Palestinian refugees for the harm they have suffered as a consequence of banishing them and occupying their land is an absolute right that goes hand in hand with their right to return. They are to receive compensation upon their return and this does not negate or diminish their right to return.

The Zionist project

14. The Zionist project is a racist, aggressive, colonial and expansionist project based on seizing the properties of others; it is hostile to the Palestinian people and to their aspiration for freedom, liberation, return and self-determination. The Israeli entity is the plaything of the Zionist project and its base of aggression.

15. The Zionist project does not target the Palestinian people alone; it is the enemy of the Arab and Islamic Ummah posing a grave threat to its security and interests. It is also hostile to the Ummah's aspirations for unity, renaissance and liberation and has been the major source of its troubles. The Zionist project also poses a danger to international security and peace and to mankind and its interests and stability.

16. Hamas affirms that its conflict is with the Zionist project not with the Jews because of their religion. Hamas does not wage a struggle against the Jews because they are Jewish but wages a struggle against the Zionists who occupy Palestine. Yet, it is the Zionists who constantly identify Judaism and the Jews with their own colonial project and illegal entity.

17. Hamas rejects the persecution of any human being or the undermining of his or her rights on nationalist, religious or sectarian grounds. Hamas is of the view that the Jewish problem, anti-Semitism and the persecution of the Jews are phenomena fundamentally linked to European history and not to the history of the Arabs and the Muslims or to their heritage. The Zionist movement, which was able with the help of Western powers to occupy Palestine, is the most dangerous form of settlement occupation which has already disappeared from much of the world and must disappear from Palestine.

The position toward Occupation and political solutions

18. The following are considered null and void: the Balfour Declaration, the British Mandate Document, the UN Palestine Partition Resolution, and whatever resolutions and measures that derive from them or are similar to them. The establishment of "Israel" is entirely illegal and contravenes the inalienable rights of the Palestinian people and goes against their will and the will of the Ummah; it is also in violation of human rights that are guaranteed by international conventions, foremost among them is the right to self-determination.

19. There shall be no recognition of the legitimacy of the Zionist entity. Whatever has befallen the land of Palestine in terms of occupation, settlement building, judaisation or changes to its features or falsification of facts is illegitimate. Rights never lapse.

20. Hamas believes that no part of the land of Palestine shall be compromised or conceded, irrespective of the causes, the circumstances and the pressures and no matter how long the occupation lasts. Hamas rejects any alternative to the full and complete liberation of Palestine, from the river to the sea. However, without compromising its rejection of the Zionist entity and without relinquishing any Palestinian rights, Hamas considers the establishment of a fully sovereign and independent Palestinian state, with Jerusalem as its capital along the lines of the 4th of June 1967, with the return of the refugees and the displaced to their homes from which they were expelled, to be a formula of national consensus.

21. Hamas affirms that the Oslo Accords and their addenda contravene the governing rules of international law in that they generate commitments that violate the inalienable rights of the Palestinian people. Therefore, the Movement rejects these agreements and all that flows from them, such as the obligations that are detrimental to the interests of our people, especially security coordination (collaboration).

22. Hamas rejects all the agreements, initiatives and settlement projects that are aimed at undermining the Palestinian cause and the rights of our Palestinian people. In this regard, any stance, initiative or political programme must not in any way violate these rights and should not contravene them or contradict them.

23. Hamas stresses that transgression against the Palestinian people, usurping their land and banishing them from their homeland cannot be called peace. Any settlements reached on this basis will not lead to peace. Resistance and jihad for the liberation of Palestine will remain a legitimate right, a duty and an honour for all the sons and daughters of our people and our Ummah.

Resistance and Liberation

24. The liberation of Palestine is the duty of the Palestinian people in particular and the duty of the Arab and Islamic Ummah in general. It is also a humanitarian obligation as necessitated by the dictates of truth and justice. The agencies working for Palestine, whether national, Arab, Islamic or humanitarian, complement each other and are harmonious and not in conflict with each other.

25. Resisting the occupation with all means and methods is a legitimate right guaranteed by divine laws and by international norms and laws. At the heart of these lies armed resistance, which is regarded as the strategic choice for protecting the principles and the rights of the Palestinian people.

26. Hamas rejects any attempt to undermine the resistance and its arms. It also affirms the right of our people to develop the means and mechanisms of resistance. Managing resistance, in terms of escalation or de-escalation, or in terms of diversifying the means and methods, is an integral part of the process of managing the conflict and should not be at the expense of the principle of resistance.

The Palestinian political system

27. A real state of Palestine is a state that has been liberated. There is no alternative to a fully sovereign Palestinian State on the entire national Palestinian soil, with Jerusalem as its capital.

28. Hamas believes in, and adheres to, managing its Palestinian relations on the basis of pluralism, democracy, national partnership, acceptance of the other and the adoption of dialogue. The aim is to bolster the unity of ranks and joint action for the purpose of accomplishing national goals and fulfilling the aspirations of the Palestinian people.

29. The PLO is a national framework for the Palestinian people inside and outside of Palestine. It should therefore be preserved, developed and rebuilt on democratic foundations so as to secure the participation of all the constituents and forces of the Palestinian people, in a manner that safeguards Palestinian rights.

30. Hamas stresses the necessity of building Palestinian national institutions on sound democratic principles, foremost among them are free and fair elections. Such process should be on the basis of national partnership and in accordance with a clear programme and a clear strategy that adhere to the rights, including the right of resistance, and which fulfil the aspirations of the Palestinian people.

31. Hamas affirms that the role of the Palestinian Authority should be to serve the Palestinian people and safeguard their security, their rights and their national project.

32. Hamas stresses the necessity of maintaining the independence of Palestinian national decision-making. Outside forces should not be allowed to intervene. At the same time, Hamas affirms the responsibility of the Arabs and the Muslims and their duty and role in the liberation of Palestine from Zionist occupation.

33. Palestinian society is enriched by its prominent personalities, figures, dignitaries,

civil society institutions, and youth, students, trade unionist and women's groups who together work for the achievement of national goals and societal building, pursue resistance, and achieve liberation.

34. The role of Palestinian women is fundamental in the process of building the present and the future, just as it has always been in the process of making Palestinian history. It is a pivotal role in the project of resistance, liberation and building the political system.

The Arab and Islamic Ummah

35. Hamas believes that the Palestinian issue is the central cause for the Arab and Islamic Ummah.

36. Hamas believes in the unity of the Ummah with all its diverse constituents and is aware of the need to avoid anything that could fragment the Ummah and undermine its unity.

37. Hamas believes in cooperating with all states that support the rights of the Palestinian people. It opposes intervention in the internal affairs of any country. It also refuses to be drawn into disputes and conflicts that take place among different countries. Hamas adopts the policy of opening up to different states in the world, especially the Arab and Islamic states. It endeavours to establish balanced relations on the basis of combining the requirements of the Palestinian cause and the Palestinian people's interests on the one hand with the interests of the Ummah, its renaissance and its security on the other.

The Humanitarian and international aspect

38. The Palestinian issue is one that has major humanitarian and international dimensions. Supporting and backing this cause is a humanitarian and civilisational task that is required by the prerequisites of truth, justice and common humanitarian values.

39. From a legal and humanitarian perspective, the liberation of Palestine is a legitimate activity, it is an act of self-defence, and it is the expression of the natural right of all peoples to self-determination.

40. In its relations with world nations and peoples, Hamas believes in the values of cooperation, justice, freedom and respect of the will of the people.

41. Hamas welcomes the stances of states, organisations and institutions that support the rights of the Palestinian people. It salutes the free peoples of the world who support the Palestinian cause. At the same time, it denounces the support granted by any party to the Zionist entity or the attempts to cover up its crimes and aggression against the Palestinians and calls for the prosecution of Zionist war criminals.

42. Hamas rejects the attempts to impose hegemony on the Arab and Islamic Ummah just as it rejects the attempts to impose hegemony on the rest of the world's nations and peoples. Hamas also condemns all forms of colonialism, occupation, discrimination, oppression and aggression in the world.

Bibliography

Bibliography

Abbott, Kenneth W., and Duncan Snidal (2000), 'Hard and Soft Law in International Governance', International Organization, Vol. 54, No. 3, Summer 2000, pp. 421-456.

Advisory Council on International Affairs (2013), Between words and deeds. Prospects for a sustainable peace in the Middle East, No.83, March 2013.

Agt, Dries van (2009), Een schreeuw om recht [A cry for justice], Amsterdam: De Bezige Bij, 2009.

Albeck, Pliya (1985), 'Lands in Judea and Samaria' (in Hebrew), lecture at Bet Hapraklit on 28 May 1985, Israel Bar Association.

Altschul, Mark J. (2002), 'Israel's Law of Return and the Debate of Altering, Repealing, or Maintaining its Present Language', University of Illinois Law Review, Vol. 2002, No. 5, pp. 1354-1371.

Andrews, Fannie Fern (1931), The Holy Land under Mandate, Vol. 1, Boston: Houghton Mifflin and Company, 1931.

Antonius, George (1938), The Arab Awakening. The Story of the Arab National Movement, London: H. Hamilton, 1938.

Arian, Asher, and Ayala Keissar-Sugarmen (2012), A Portrait of Israeli Jews. Beliefs, Observance, and Values of Israeli Jews, 2009,The Israeli Democracy Institute / AVI CHAI Israel Foundation, The Israeli Democracy Institute Publications, 2012.

Asseburg, Muriel (2017), 'The Fatah-Hamas Reconciliation Agreement of October 2017: An Opportunity to End Gaza's Humanitarian Crisis and Permanently Overcome the Blockade', SWP Comment C 44, November 2017, (SWP = Stiftung Wissenschaft und Politik [German Institute of International and Security Affairs]).

Auerbach, Jerold (2012), 'How Benzion Netanyahu Helped Put in the UN Charter A Clause That Could Yet Save the Jewish State', Special to The Sun (New York), 2 May 2012.

Avinoam, Sharon (2009), Why is Israel's Presence in the Territories still called 'Occupation'?, Jerusalem Center for Public Affairs, 2009.

Avnery, Arieh L. (1982), The Claim of Dispossession: Jewish Land-Settlement and the Arabs, 1878-1948, New Brunswick, New Jersey: Transaction Books, 1982.

Baker, Alan (ed.) (2011 a), Israel's Rights as a Nation-State in International Diplomacy, Jerusalem Center for Public Affairs - World Jewish Congress, 2011.

Baker, Alan (2011 b), 'Israel's Rights Regarding Territories and the Settlements in the Eyes of the International Community', in: Alan Baker (ed.), Israel's Rights as a Nation-State in International Diplomacy, Jerusalem Center for Public Affairs - World Jewish Congress, 2011, pp. 65-74.

Baker, Alan (2011 c), The Settlements Issue: Distorting the Geneva Convention and the Oslo Accords, Jerusalem Center for Public Affairs, 5 January 2011 (http://jcpa.org/article/the-settlements-issuedistorting-the-geneva-convention-and-the-oslo-accords).

Baker, Alan (2014), 'The Changing Historical Narrative: Saeb Erekat's New Spin', Jerusalem Center for Public Affairs, Institute for Contemporary Affairs, Vol. 14, No. 8, 23 March 2014.

Bar-Yaacov, Nissim (1990), 'The Applicability of the Laws of War to Judea and Samaria (The West Bank) and to the Gaza Strip', Israel Law Review, Vol. 24, Nos 3-4, Autumn 1990, pp. 485-506.

Barak, Aharon (2002), 'Some Reflections on the Israeli Legal System and its Judiciary', Electronic Journal of Comparative Law (EJCL), Vol. 6, No. 1, April 2002 (http://www.ejcl.org/61-1.html).

Barghouti, Omar (2011 a), BDS: Boycott Divestment Sanctions; the Global Struggle for Palestinian Rights, Chicago, Illinois: Haymarket Books, 2011.

Barghouti, Omar (2011 b), 'Our South Africa Moment has arrived', in: Omar Barghouti, BDS: Boycott Divestment Sanctions; the Global Struggle for Palestinian Rights, Chicago, Illinois: Haymarket Books, 2011, pp. 191-204.

Baruch, Pnina Sharvit (2014), 'Operation Protective Edge: The Legal Angle', in: Anat Kurz & Shlomo Brom (eds.), The Lessons of Operation Protective Edge, Tel Aviv: Institute for National Security Studies, 30 September 2014, pp. 65-72.

Bassiouni, M. Cherif (1971), 'Self-determination and the Palestinians', Proceedings of the American Society of International Law, Vol. 65, No. 4, 1971, Strategies for World Order, pp. 31-40.

Bat Ye'or (2005), Eurabia – the Euro-Arab Axis, Vancouver: Fairleigh Dickinson University Press, 2005.

Bat Ye'or (2011), Europe, Globalization and the Coming Universal Caliphate, Vancouver: Fairleigh Dickinson University Press, 2011.

Bayefsky, Anne (2002), 'Ending Bias in the Human Rights System', The New York Times, 22 May 2002.

Becker, Tal (1998), 'Self-Determination in Perspective: Palestinian Claims to Statehood and the Relativity of the Right to Self-Determination', Israel Law Review, Vol. 32, No. 2, 1998, pp. 301-354.

Begin, Menachem (1977), The Revolt, Jerusalem/Tel Aviv/Haifa: Steimatzky's Agency Ltd., 1977.

Bell, Abraham (2011), 'A Critique of the Goldstone Report and its Treatment of International Humanitarian Law', in: Gerald M. Steinberg & Anne Herzberg (eds.), The Goldstone Report 'Reconsidered': A critical analysis, Jerusalem Center for Public Affairs, Jerusalem: NGO Monitor, 2011, pp. 265-275.

Bell, Abraham and Eugene Kontorovich (2016), 'Palestine, Uti Possidetis Juris, and the borders of Israel', Arizona Law Review, Vol. 58, 2016, pp. 633-692.

Ben-Gurion, David (1972), Israel. A Personal History, Tel Aviv: Sabra Books, 1972.

Benjamin, David (Lt. Col. res.) (2014), 'Israel, Gaza and Humanitarian Law: Efforts to Limit Civilian Casualties', in: Hirsh Goodman & Dore Gold (eds.), The Gaza War 2014: The War Israel Did Not Want and the Disaster It Averted, Jerusalem Center for Public Affairs, 2014, pp. 45-60.

Benoniel, Daniel (2011), 'Israel, Turkey and the Gaza Blockade', University of Pennsylvania Journal of International Law, Vol. 33, No. 2, Winter 2011, pp. 615-662.

Bentwich, Norman (1921-1922), 'Mandated territories: Palestine and Mesopotamia (Iraq)', British Yearbook of International Law, 1921-22, pp. 48-56.

Benvenisti, Eyal (1993), The International Law of Occupation, 2nd ed., Oxford: Oxford University Press, 1993.

Berkovitz, Peter (2011 a), 'The Goldstone Report and International Law', in: Gerald M. Steinberg & Anne Herzberg (eds.), The Goldstone Report 'Reconsidered': A critical analysis, Jerusalem Center for Public Affairs, Jerusalem: NGO Monitor, 2011, pp. 182-202.

Berkowitz, Peter (2011 b), 'The Gaza Flotilla and International Law', Policy Review (Hoover Institution), No. 168, 1 August 2011 (https://www.hoover.org/research/gaza-flotilla-and-international-law).

Biger, Gideon (2004), The Boundaries of Modern Palestine 1840-1947, London/New York: Routledge Curzon, 2004.

Blank, Laurie (2011), 'The Application of IHL in the Goldstone Report: A Critical Commentary', in: Gerald M. Steinberg & Anne Herzberg (eds.), The Goldstone Report 'Reconsidered': A critical analysis, Jerusalem Center for Public Affairs, Jerusalem: NGO Monitor, 2011, pp. 203-264.

Blois, Matthijs de (2010), Israël: een staat ter discussie? Over de internationaalrechtelijke positie van Israël, Heerenveen: Jongbloed/Groen, 2010.

Blois, Matthijs de (2011), 'Jewish family law and secular legal orders: the example of get refusal', in: Jane Mair & Esin Őrűcű (eds.), The Place of Religion in Family Law: A Comparative Research, Cambridge/Antwerp/Portland: Intersentia, 2011, pp. 207-233.

Blois, Matthijs de (2015), 'Bad Law and Hard Case? The Impact of the Wall Advisory Opinion of the ICJ', in: Cedric Ryngaert, Erik J. Molenaar & Sarah M.H. Nouwen (eds.), What's Wrong with International Law? (Liber Amicorum A.H.A. Soons), Leiden/Boston: Koninklijke Brill/ Nijhoff, 2015, pp. 93-113.

Blois, Matthijs de (2016), 'The Unique Character of the Mandate for Palestine', Israel Law Review, Vol. 49, No. 3, 2016, pp. 365-389.

Blum, Yehuda Z. (1968), 'The Missing Reversioner: Reflections on the Status of Judea and Samaria', Israel Law Review, Vol. 3, No. 2, 1968, pp. 279-301.

Blum, Yehuda Z. (1975), 'Reflections on the Changing Concept of Self-Determination', Israel Law Review, Vol. 10, No. 4, 1975, pp. 509-514.

Blum, Yehuda Z. (1998), 'Israel and the United Nations: A Retrospective Overview', in: Alfred Kellerman et al. (eds.), Israel Among the Nations, The Hague: Kluwer Law International, 1998, pp. 69-77.

Bocco, Riccardo (2009), 'UNRWA and the Palestinian Refugees: a History within History', Refugee Survey Quarterly, Vol. 28, Nos. 2 & 3, 2009, pp. 229-252.

Bourrinet, Jacques (ed.) (1979), Le Dialogue Euro-Arabe, Paris: Economica, 1979.

Bowker, Robert P.G. (2003), Palestinian Refugees: Mythology, Identity, and the Search for Peace, Boulder, Colorado: Lynne Rienner Publishers, 2003.

Brierly, James (1963), The Law of Nations, an introduction to the international law of peace, 6th ed., Oxford: Clarendon Press, 1963.

Brownlie, Ian (1988), 'The Rights of Peoples in Modern International Law', in: James Crawford (ed.); The Rights of Peoples, Vol.1, Oxford: Clarendon Press, 1988.

Brownlie, Ian (1990), Principles of Public International Law, 4th ed., Oxford: Clarendon Press, 1990.

Brownlie, Ian (2001), Principles of Public International Law, 5th ed., Oxford: Oxford University Press, 2001.

Bruce, Frederick Fyvie (1963), Israel and the Nations, Exeter: Paternoster Press, 1963.

B'Tselem (2002), The Israeli Information Center for Human Rights in the Occupied Territories, Land Grab: Israel's Settlement Policy in the West Bank, May 2002.

Caplan, Robert (2005), 'Mending the "Fence": How Treatment of the Israeli-Palestinian Conflict by the International Court of Justice at The Hague has Redefined the Doctrine of Self-Defense', Florida Law Review, Vol. 57, 2005, pp. 717-769.

Carol, Steven (2015), Understanding the Volatile and Dangerous Middle East: A Comprehensive Analysis, Bloomington, Indiana: iUniverse Publishing, 2015.

Carter, Jimmy (2006), Palestine: Peace Not Apartheid, New York: Simon & Schuster Paperbacks, 2006.

Cassese, Antonio (1993), 'The Israel-PLO Agreement and Self-Determination', European Journal of International Law, Vol. 4, 1993, pp. 564-571.

Cassese, Antonio (1995), Self-determination of Peoples. A Legal Appraisal, Cambridge: Cambridge University Press, 1995.

Cassese, Antonio (2005), International Law, 2nd ed., Oxford: Oxford University Press, 2005.

Cassin, René (1971), 'From the Ten Commandments to the Rights of Men', in: Shlomo Shoham (ed.), Of Law and Man. Essays in Honor of Haim H. Cohn, New York/Tel Aviv: Sabra Books, 1971.

Cattan, Henry (1976), Palestine and International Law: The Legal Aspects of the Arab-Israeli Conflict, London: Longman, 1976.

Chomsky, Noam (2012), Making the Future: Occupations, Interventions, Empire and Resistance, San Francisco, California: City Lights Bookstore, 2012.

Church of Scotland (2013), Abraham's inheritance, 2013.

CIDI (2014), Israël en de Palestijnse gebieden. Feiten en cijfers [Israel and the Palestinian Territories. Facts and Figures], CIDI Informatiereeks, Soesterberg: Uitgeverij Aspekt, 2014.

Cohen, Yinon, Yitchak Haberfled, and Irena Kogan (2011), 'Who went there? Jewish immigration from the Former Soviet Union to Israel, the USA and Germany, 1990-2000', Israel Affairs, Vol. 17, No. 1, January 2011, pp. 7-20.

Cotler, Irwin (2009), Global Anti-Semitism: Assault on Human Rights, Working Paper, Manhattan, New York: Institute for the Study of Global Antisemitism and Policy (ISGAP), 2009.

Cotran, Eugene, and Chibli Mallat (eds.) (1996), The Arab-Israeli Accords: Legal Perspectives, London/The Hague/Boston: Kluwer Law International, 1996.

Crawford, James (1977), 'The Criteria for Statehood in International Law', British Yearbook of International Law, Vol. 48, No. 1, January 1977, pp. 93-182.

Crawford, James (1979), The Creation of States in International Law, 2nd ed., Oxford: Clarendon Press, 1979.

Crawford, James (ed.) (1988), The Rights of Peoples, Vol.1, Oxford: Clarendon Press, 1988.

Crawford, James (1990), 'The Creation of the State of Palestine: Too Much Too Soon', European Journal of International Law, Vol. 1, 1990, pp. 307-313.

Crawford, James (2006), The Creation of States in International Law, 2nd ed., Oxford: Oxford University Press, 2006.

Crawford, James (2011), The Creation of States in International Law, 2nd ed., Oxford: Clarendon Press, 2011.

Cryer, Robert (2005), Prosecuting International Crimes: Selectivity and the International Criminal Law Regime, Cambridge: Cambridge University Press, 2005.

Cuykens, Hanne (2015), Revisiting the Law of Belligerent Occupation, Boston/Leiden: Brill/Nijhoff, 2015.

Czapliński, Wladyslaw (2006), 'Jus Cogens and the Law of Treaties', in: Christian Tomuschat & Jean-Marc Thouvenin (eds.), The Fundamental Rules of the International Legal Order, Leiden: Brill, 2006, pp. 83-97.

Dajani, Omar M. (1997-1998), 'Stalled between Seasons: The International Status of Palestine During the Interim Period', Denver Journal of International Law and Policy, Vol. 26, 1997-1998, pp. 27-92.

Dershowitz, Alan (2003), The Case for Israel, Hoboken, New Jersey: John Wiley & Sons, Inc., 2003.

Dershowitz, Alan (2010), 'Israel obeyed international law: Legally, the Gaza flotilla conflict is an open-and-shut case', The New York Daily News, 2 June 2010.

Dershowitz, Alan (2014), 'The Case Against the Goldstone Report. A Study in Evidentiary Bias', in: Gerald M. Steinberg & Anne Herzberg (eds.), The Goldstone Report 'Reconsidered': A critical analysis, Jerusalem Center for Public Affairs, Jerusalem: NGO Monitor, 2014, pp. 101-152.

Dershowitz, Alan (2015), 'The Case Against the International Criminal Court Investigating Israel', the Algemeiner, e-paper, 23 January 2015.

Dinstein, Yoram (2009), The International Law of Belligerent Occupation, Cambridge: Cambridge University Press, 2009.

Dixon, Martin, and Robert McCorquodale (2000), Cases & Materials on International Law, London: Blackstone Press Limited, 2000.

Dugard, John (2013), 'Palestine and the International Criminal Court', Journal of International Criminal Justice, Vol. 11, No. 3, July 2013, pp. 563-570.

Dugard, John and John Reynolds (2013), 'Apartheid, International Law and the Occupied Palestinian Territory', European Journal of International Law, Vol. 24, No. 3, 2013, pp. 867-913.

Dunlop, Charles (2001), 'Law and Military Interventions: Preserving Humanitarian Values in 21st century Conflicts'; Prepared for the 'Humanitarian Challenges in Military Intervention Conference', Carr Center for Human Rights Policy, Kennedy School of Government, Harvard University, Washington, D.C., 29 November 2001.

Dunlop, Charles (2011), 'Lawfare Today... and Tomorrow', in: Raul A. Pedroso & Saria P. Wollschlaeger (eds.), International Law and the Changing Character of War, US Naval War College International Law Studies, Vol. 87, Newport (Rhode Island), 2011, pp. 315-325.

Eban, Abba (1968), My people, The story of the Jews, New York: Behrman House/Random House, 1968.

Edwards, Steven (2002), 'UN Backs Palestinian Violence', Christian Action for Israel, 16 April 2002.

Einhorn, Talia (2011), 'Israel', in: Dinah Shelton (ed.), International Law and Domestic Legal Systems, Oxford: Oxford University Press, 2011, pp. 288-327.

Eisenberg, Josy (1970), Une histoire des Juifs, Paris: Culture, Art, Literature, 1970.

El Ouali, Abdelhamid (2012), Territorial Integrity in a Globalizing World: International Law and States' Quest for Survival, Berlin/Heidelberg: Springer-Verlag, 2012.

Encyclopedia of Public International Law (1987), Elsevier Science Publishers, 1987.

Ernst, Dan (2009), 'The Meaning and Liberal Justifications of Israel's Law of Return', Israel Law Review, Vol. 42, No. 3, 2009, pp. 564-602.

Falk, Richard (2007), 'Slouching Toward a Palestinian Holocaust', Counter Currents Org., 7 July 2007.

Farrant, James (2013), 'The Gaza Flotilla Incident and the Modern Law of Blockade', Naval War College Review, Vol. 66, No. 3, Summer 2013, pp. 81-98.

Feinäugle, Clemens A. (ed.) (2016), The Rule of Law and its Application to the United Nations (Studies of the Max Planck Institute Luxembourg for International, European and Regulatory Procedural Law, nr. 6), Haywards Heath, UK: Nomos/Hart, 2016.

Feinberg, Nathan (1974 a), 'The Recognition of the Jewish People in International Law', in: John Norton Moore (ed.), The Arab-Israeli Conflict, Vol. 1, Princeton, NJ: Princeton University Press, 1974, pp. 59-87.

Feinberg, Nathan (1974 b), 'The Arab-Israeli Conflict in International Law', in: John Norton Moore (ed.), The Arab-Israeli Conflict, Vol. 1, Princeton, NJ: Princeton University Press, 1974, pp. 386-488.

Feinstein, Barry (2005), 'The Applicability of the Regime of Human Rights in Times of Armed Conflict and Particularly to Occupied Territories': The Case of Israel's Security Barrier', Northwestern Journal of International Human Rights, Vol. 4, No. 2, Winter 2005, pp. 238-302.

Fendel, Hillel (2007), 'Chief Doesn't Like Message, Threatens Messenger', Arutz Sheva, 28 March 2007.

Finkelstein, Norman (1995), Image and Reality of the Israel-Palestine Conflict, Brooklyn, New York: Verso Books, 1995.

Fishman, Joel (2011), ' "A Disaster of Another Kind": Zionism=Racism, Its Beginning, and the War of Delegitimization against Israel', Israel Journal of Foreign Affairs, Vol. 3, No. 5, 2011, pp. 75-92.

Fitzmaurice, Gerald (1953), 'The Law and Procedure of the International Court of Justice, 1951–54: General Principles and Sources of Law', British Yearbook of International Law, Vol. 30, 1953, pp. 1-71.

Friedell, Steven F. (2009), 'Some Observations About Jewish Law in Israel's Supreme Court', Washington University Global Studies Law Review, Vol. 8, No. 4, 2009, pp. 659-700.

Friedländer, Saul (1998), Nazi Germany and the Jews; Volume I: The Years of Persecution, 1933-1939, New York: Harper Collins Publishers, 1998.

Gauthier, Jacques Paul (2007), Sovereignty over the Old City of Jerusalem: A Study of the Historical, Religious, Political and Legal Aspects of the Old City, Geneva: Institut universitaire des hautes études internationales, 2007.

Gavison, Ruth (1996), 'Legal Systems and Public Attitudes during Negotiations towards Transition from Conflict to Reconciliation: The Middle East, 1992-1994', in: Eugene Cotran & Chibli Mallat (eds.), The Arab-Israeli Accords: Legal Perspectives, London/The Hague/Boston: Kluwer Law International, 1996, pp. 21-44.

Gavison, Ruth (2010), The Law of Return at Sixty Years: History, Ideology, Justification (translated from Hebrew), Position paper, Jerusalem: The Metzilah Center for Zionist, Jewish, Liberal and Humanist Thought, 2010.

Gerloff, Johannes (2016), The Palestinians: Myths and Martyrs, Solingen-Wald: Azar Gbr Trostberg, 2016.

Gil, Moshe (1992), A History of Palestine, 634-1099, Cambridge: Cambridge University Press, 1992.

Gilbert, Martin (1978), Exile and Return. The Emergence of Jewish Statehood, Jerusalem/Tel Aviv/Haifa: Steimatzky's Agency Ltd., 1978.

Gilbert, Martin (1996), Jerusalem in the Twentieth Century, New York: John Wiley & Sons, Inc., 1996.

Gilbert, Martin (1999), Israel a History, London: Black Swan, 1999.

Gilbert, Martin (2002), The Routledge Atlas of the Arab-Israeli Conflict. The Complete History of the Struggle and the Efforts to Resolve It, 7th ed., Abingdon: Routledge, 2002.

Gilbert, Martin (2005), The Arab-Israeli Conflict: Its History in Maps, 8th ed., Abingdon: Routledge, 2005.

Gilbert, Martin (2007), Churchill & The Jews: A Lifelong Friendship, London: Simon & Schuster, 2007.

Glaser, Daryl J. (2003), 'Zionism and Apartheid: a moral comparison', Ethnic and Racial Studies, Vol. 26, No. 3, May 2003, pp. 403-421.

Gold, Dore (2004), Tower of Babble – How the United Nations has Fueled Global Chaos, New York: Crown Forum, 2004.

Gold, Dore (2007), The Fight for Jerusalem: Radical Islam, the West and the Future of the Holy City, Washington D.C.: Regnery Publishing, Inc., 2007.

Goldstein, Brooke (n.d.), The Lawfare Project (http://www.thelawfareproject.org/what-is-lawfare.html).

Goodman, Hirsh, and Dore Gold (eds.) (2014), The Gaza War 2014: The War Israel Did Not Want and the Disaster It Averted, Jerusalem Center for Public Affairs, 2014.

Goodrich, Leland (ed.) (1970), Charter of the United Nations: Commentary and Documents, 3rd ed., New York: Columbia University Press, 1970.

Goodrich, Leland M. and Edvard I. Hambo (1946), Charter of the United Nations: Commentary and Documents, Boston: World Peace Foundation, 1946.

Goodwin-Gill, Guy S. (1983), The Refugee in International Law, Oxford: Clarendon Press, 1983.

Grief, Howard (2008), The Legal Foundation and Borders of Israel under International Law, Jerusalem: Mazo Publishers, 2008.

Grintz, Jehoshua M. (1966), 'The Treaty of Joshua with the Gibeonites', Journal of the American Oriental Society, Vol. 86, No. 2, 1966, pp. 113-126.

Groiss, Arnon, and Ronni Shaked (2017), Schoolbooks of the Palestinian Authority (PA): The Attitude to the Jews, to Israel and to Peace, Simon Wiesenthal Center, Middle East Forum, September 2017.

Grotius, Hugo (1925), The Law of War and Peace (translated by F.W. Kelsey et al.), Classics of International Law, 3 Volumes, Oxford/London: Clarendon Press/Milford, 1925.

Gruenberg, Justin (2009), 'An analysis of United Nations Security Council Resolutions: Are All Countries Treated Equally?', Case Western Reserve Journal of International Law, Vol. 41, No. 2, 2009, pp. 468-511.

Guilfoyle, Douglas (2011), 'The Mavi Marmara Incident and the Blockade in Armed Conflict', British Yearbook of International Law, Vol. 81, No. 1, January 2011, pp. 171-223.

Guzman, Andrew T., and Timothy I. Meyer (2010), 'International Soft Law', Journal of Legal Analysis, Vol. 2, No. 1, Spring 2010, pp. 171-225.

Hampson, Françoise J. (2008), 'The relationship between international humanitarian law and human rights law from the perspective of a human rights treaty body', International Review of the Red Cross, Vol. 90, No. 871, September 2008, pp. 549-572.

Hart, H.L.A. (1958), 'Positivism and the separation of laws and morals', Harvard Law Review, Vol. 71, No. 4, February 1958, pp. 593-629.

Hertz, Allen (2009), 'Jewish Aboriginal Rights to Israel: Do the Jewish people have legal "rights of entry, sojourn, and settlement" to the land of Israel?', Tablet, 2009 (www.allenhertz.com/2009/11/aboriginal-rights-to-israel.html).

Herzberg, Anne (2010), NGO 'Lawfare': Exploitation of the Courts in the Israeli-Arab Conflict, 2nd Expanded Edition: NGO Monitor, 2010.

Herzl, Theodor (1896), Der Judenstaat, Leipzig/Vienna: Max Breitensteins Verlagsbuchhandlung, 1896.

Higgins, Rosalyn (1963), The Development of International Law through the Political Organs of the UN, London/New York/Toronto: Oxford University Press, 1963.

Higgins, Rosalyn (1970), 'The Place of International Law in the Settlement of Disputes by the Security Council', American Journal of International Law, Vol. 64, No. 1, 1970, pp. 1-18.

Hilpold, Peter (2009), 'The Kosovo Case and International Law: Looking for Applicable Theories', Chinese Journal of International Law, Vol. 8, No. 1, 2009, pp. 47-61.

Holzgrefe, J.L., and Robert O. Keohane (eds.) (2003), Humanitarian Intervention. Ethical, Legal and Political Dilemmas, Cambridge: Cambridge University Press, 2003.

Horowitz, David (2015), 'Shame on you, Mary McGowan Davis', The Times of Israel, 23 June 2015.

Horowitz, Sigal (2011), 'Accountability of the Hamas under International Humanitarian Law', in: Hamas, the Gaza War and Accountability under International Law (Updated proceedings of an International Conference on 18 June 2009), Jerusalem Center for Public Affairs, 2011, pp. 29-44.

Ignatieff, Michael (2009), 'Israel, Apartheid Week and CUPE Ontario's anti-Israel Posturing Should be Condemned', National Post, 5 March 2009.

Jennings, Richard Y. (1963), The Acquisition of Territory in International Law, Manchester: Manchester University Press, 1963.

Kapitan, Tomis, and Raja Halwani (2008), The Israeli-Palestinian Conflict: Philosophical Essays on Self-Determination, Terrorism and the One-State Solution, London: Palgrave Macmillan, 2008.

Karsh, Efraim (2010), Palestine Betrayed, New Haven, Connecticut: Yale University Press, 2010.

Kattan, Victor (2004-2005), 'From Beirut to Brussels: Universal Jurisdiction: Statelessness and the Saba and Chatila Massacres', Yearbook of Islamic and Middle Eastern Law, Vol. 11, 2004-2005, pp. 32-82.

Keller, Werner (1966), Und wurden zerstreut unter alle Völker. Die nachbiblische Geschichte des jüdischen Volkes, München/Zürich: Droemer Knaur,1966.

Kellerman, Alfred, Kurt Siehr, and Talia Einhorn (eds.) (1998), Israel Among the Nations, The Hague: Kluwer Law International, 1998.

Kelsen, Hans (1967), Pure Theory of Law (transl. Max Knight), Berkeley: University of California Press, 1967.

Kelsen, Hans (2000), The Law of the United Nations: A Critical Analysis of Its Fundamental Problems, Clark, New Jersey: The Lawbook Exchange Ltd., 2000.

Khaled Al-Azm (1973), Memoirs, Part 1, Beirut, 1973.

Kiernan, Thomas (1978), The Arabs – their history, aims and challenge to the industrialized world, London: Abacus, 1978.

Kissinger, Henry (2014), World Order, New York: Penguin Press, 2014.

Kittrie, Orde F. (2016), Lawfare: Law as a Weapon of War, New York: Oxford University Press, 2016.

Kliot, Nurit (1995), 'The Evolution of the Egypt-Israel Boundary: From Colonial Foundations to Peaceful Borders', Boundary & Territory Briefing (University of Durham), Vol. 1, No. 8, 1995.

Kohn, Irit (2009), 'Averting Abuse of Universal Jurisdiction', Jerusalem Center For Public Affairs, Jerusalem Viewpoints, No. 570, 26 February 2009 (http://jcpa.org/article/averting-abuse-of-universal-jurisdiction/).

Kontorovich, Eugene (2017), 'Unsettled: A Global Study of Settlements in Occupied Territories', Northwestern University School of Law Public and Legal Theory Series, No. 16-20, Working draft. (published: 8 december 2017 in: Journal of Legal Analysis, https://doi.org/10.1093/jla/lax004).

Kooijmans, P.H. (1964), The Doctrine of the Legal Equality of States. An inquiry into the foundations of international law, Leiden: Sijthoff, 1964.

Kortenoeven, Wim (2007), Hamas. Portret en achtergrond [Hamas: Portrait and backgrounds], Soesterberg: Uitgeverij Aspekt, 2007.

Krieger, Hilary Keila (2006), 'Jews forced out of Arab countries seek repatriation', The Jerusalem Post, 23 October 2006.

Kurtz, Anat,and Shlomo Brom (eds.) (2014), The Lessons of Operation Protective Edge, Tel Aviv: Institute for National Security Studies, 2014.

Lacey, Ian (ed.) (2004), International Law and the Arab-Israeli Conflict: extracts from Israel and Palestine; Assaults on the law of nations by Julius Stone, 2nd ed., Bellevue, New South Wales, Australia: Jirlac Publications, 2004.

Landes, Richard (2011), 'Goldstone's Gaza Report: A Failure of Intelligence ', in: Gerald M. Steinberg & Anne Herzberg (eds.), The Goldstone Report 'Reconsidered': A critical analysis, Jerusalem Center for Public Affairs, Jerusalem: NGO Monitor, 2011, pp. 45-67.

Lapidoth, Ruth (1990), 'The Expulsion of Civilians from Areas which came under Israeli Control in 1967: Some Legal Issues', European Journal of International Law, Vol. 2, 1990, pp. 97-109.

Lapidoth, Ruth (1995), 'Jerusalem – Some Jurisprudential Aspects', Catholic University Law Review (Catholic University of America, Washington D.C.), Vol. 45, No. 3, 1995, pp. 661-686.

Lapidoth, Ruth (1996), 'Jerusalem: Past, Present and Future', Revue internationale de droit comparé, Vol. 48, No. 1, 1996, pp. 9-33.

Lapidoth, Ruth (2002), 'Legal Aspects of the Palestinian Refugee Question', Jerusalem letter / Viewpoints No. 485, 24 Elul 5762, 1 September 2002.

Lapidoth, Ruth (2011), 'The Misleading Interpretation of Security Council Resolution 242 (1967)', in: Alan Baker (ed.), Israel's Rights as a Nation-State in International Diplomacy, Jerusalem Centre for Public Affairs – World Jewish Congress, 2011, pp. 85-96.

Lapidoth, Ruth (2013), 'A Recent Agreement on the Holy Places in Jerusalem', Israel Journal of Foreign Affairs, Vol. 7, No. 3, 2013, pp. 61-70.

Laqueur, Walter (1978), A History of Zionism, New York: Shocken Books, 1978.

Laqueur, Walter, and Dan Schueftan (eds.) (2002), The Israeli-Arab reader: A Documentary History of the Middle East Conflict, New York: Ballantine Books, 2002.

Lauterpacht, Elihu (1968), Jerusalem and the Holy Places, London: The Anglo-Israel Association, 1968.

Lauterpacht, Elihu (ed.) (1977), International Law Collected Papers: The Law of Peace, Parts II-VI, Cambridge: Cambridge University Press, 1977.

Lauterpacht, Hersch (1946), 'The Grotian Tradition in International Law', British Yearbook of International Law, Vol. 23, No. 1, 1946, pp. 1-53.

Lauterpacht, Hersch (ed.) (1952), Oppenheim's International Law, 7th ed., London: Longmans, 1952.

Lauterpacht, Hersch (1977 a), 'The Mandate under International Law in the Covenant of the League of Nations', in: Elihu Lauterpacht (ed.), International Law Collected Papers: The Law of Peace, Parts II-VI, Cambridge: Cambridge University Press, 1977, 29-84.

Lauterpacht, Hersch (1977 b), 'Article 18 of the Mandate for Palestine and the Dissolution of the League of Nations', in: Elihu Lauterpacht (ed.), International Law Collected Papers: The Law of Peace, Parts II-VI, Cambridge: Cambridge University Press, 1977, pp. 101-112.

Lefkovitz, Edgar (2007), 'Expelled Jews hold deeds on Arab lands', The Jerusalem Post, 16 November 2007.

Lerner, Natan (2007), 'Religious Liberty in the State of Israel', Emory International Law Review, Vol. 21, 2007, pp. 239-276.

Lewis, Bernard (1995), The Middle East: 2000 years of history from the rise of Christianity to the present day, London: Weidenfeld & Nicolson, 1995.

Lloyd George, David (1938), The Truth about the Peace Treaties, Vol. 1, London: V. Gollancz, 1938.

Louis, William Roger (ed.) (2005), Yet More Adventures with Britannia: Personalities, Politics and Culture in Britain, London: I.B. Taurus, 2005.

Luke, Harry Charles, and Edward Keith-Roach (eds.) (1922), The Handbook of Palestine, London: MacMillan and Co., 1922.

Mair, Jane, and Esin Őrűcű (eds.) (2011), The Place of Religion in Family Law: A Comparative Research, Cambridge/Antwerp/Portland: Intersentia, 2011.

Makowski, Andrzej (2013), 'The Mavi Marmara Incident and the Modern Law of Armed Conflict at Sea', Israel Journal of Foreign Affairs, Vol. 7, No. 2, 2013, pp. 75-89.

Malanczuk, Peter (1996), 'Some Basic Aspects of the Agreements between Israel and the PLO from the Perspective of International Law', European Journal of International Law, Vol. 7, 1996, pp. 485-500.

Marxsen, Christian (2015), 'Territorial Integrity in International Law – Its Concept and Implications for Crimea', Zeitschrift fűr ausländisches Recht und Völkerrecht (Heidelberg Journal of International Law), Vol. 75, 2015, pp. 7-26.

Maurer, Peter (President of the ICRC) (2012), 'Challenges to international humanitarian law: Israel's occupation policy', International Review of the Red Cross, Vol. 94, No. 888, 2012, pp. 1503-1510.

McCarthy, Rory (2009), 'Israel annexing East Jerusalem, says EU', The Guardian, 7 March 2009.

McCorquodale, Robert (2016), 'The Rule of Law Internationally', in: Clemens A. Feinäugle (ed.), The Rule of Law and its Application to the United Nations, (Studies of the Max Planck Institute Luxembourg for International, European and Regulatory Procedural Law, nr. 6), Haywards Heath, UK: Nomos/Hart, 2016, pp. 51-74.

Meloni, Chantal, and Giani Tognoni (eds.) (2012), Is There a Court for Gaza?, The Hague: T.M.C. Asser Press, 2012.

Meron, Ya'akov (1995), 'Why Jews Fled the Arab Countries', The Middle East Quarterly, Vol. 2, No. 3, September 1995, pp. 47-55.

Meyerowitz-Katz, Daniel (2013), 'Israel refuses to participate in UN "human rights" farce', Australia/Israel & Jewish Affairs Council (AIJAC), 1 February 2013 (http://aijac.org.au/news/article/israel-refuses-to-participate-in-un-human-rights).

Miko, Samantha (2013), 'Al-Skeini v. United Kingdom and Extraterritorial Jurisdiction under the European Convention for Human Rights', Boston College International & Comparative Law Review, Vol. 35, No. 3, 2013, Electronic Supplement, pp. 63-79.

Miller, David Hunter (1928), The Drafting of the Covenant, New York: G.P. Putman's Sons, 1928.

Milman, Henry Hart (1939), The History of the Jews, 1830, Two Volumes: London: J.M. Dent & Sons Ltd. / E.P. Dutton & Co. Inc., 1939.

Moore, John Norton (ed.) (1974), The Arab-Israeli Conflict, Vol. 1, Princeton, NJ: Princeton University Press, 1974.

Morgan, Ed (2004), 'Slaughterhouse Six: Updating the Law of War', German Law Journal, Vol. 5, No. 5, May 2004, pp. 525-544.

Morris, Benny (2008), 1948: A History of the First Arab-Israeli War, New Haven/London: Yale University Press, 2008.

Murphy, Sean D. (2005), 'Self-Defense and the Israeli Wall Advisory Opinion: An Ipse Dixit from the ICJ?', American Journal of International Law, Vol. 99, No. 1, January 2005, pp. 62-76.

Nutting, Anthony (1972), Balfour and Palestine, a Legacy of Deceit, London: Council for the Advancement of Arab-British Understanding, 1972.

Őberg, Marko Divac (2005), 'The Legal Effects of Resolutions of the UN Security Council and General Assembly in the Jurisprudence of the ICJ', The European Journal of International Law, Vol. 16, No. 5, 2005, pp. 879-906.

O'Connell, D.P. (1970), International Law, 2nd ed., London: Stevens & Sons, 1970.

Ohlin, Jens David (2015), The Assault on International Law, Oxford: Oxford University Press, 2015.

Oren, Michael B. (2002), Six Days of War: June 1967 and the Making of the Modern Middle East, Oxford: Oxford University Press, 2002 (hardcover).

Oren, Michael B. (2003), Six Days of War: June 1967 and the Making of the Modern Middle East, New York: Presidio Press, Ballantine Books, 2003 (paperback).

Panàkovà, Jana (2011), 'Law and Politics of Universal Jurisdiction', Amsterdam Law Forum, Vol. 3, No. 3, Summer 2011, pp. 49-72.

Pappé, Ilan (2006), The Ethnic Cleansing of Palestine, Oxford: Oneworld Publications, 2006.

Pedroso, Raul A., and Daria P. Wollschlaeger (eds.) (2011), International Law and the Changing Character of War, US Naval War College International Law Studies, Vol. 87, Newport, Rhode Island, 2011.

Peters, Joan (1984), From Time Immemorial: The Origins of the Arab-Jewish Conflict over Palestine, JKAP Publications, 1984.

Pictet, Jean S. (ed.) (1960), The Geneva Conventions of 12 August 1949, Geneva: International Committee of the Red Cross (ICRC), 1960.

Posner, Richard A. (2010), 'Judicial Review, a Comparative Perspective: Israel, Canada, and the United States', Cardozo Law Review, Vol. 31, No. 6, 2010, pp. 2393-2456.

Prescott, Victor, and Gillian D. Triggs (2008), International Frontiers and Boundaries: Law, Politics and Geography, Leiden: Martinus Nijhoff Publishers, 2008.

Quigley, John (2005), The Case for Palestine: An International Law Perspective, Durham, North Carolina: Duke University Press, 2005.

Quigley, John (2012), 'The Palestine Declaration to the International Court: The Statehood Issue', in: Chantal Meloni & Giani Tognoni (eds.), Is There a Court for Gaza?, The Hague: T.M.C. Asser Press, 2012, pp. 429-440.

Ratner, Steven (1996), 'Drawing a better line: Uti Possidetis and the borders of new states', American Journal of International Law, Vol. 90, No. 4, October 1996, pp. 590-634.

Ravitch, Frank S. (2009), 'Religious Freedom and Israeli Law', Drake Law Review, Vol. 57, No. 4, 2009, pp. 879-895.

Reagan, David R. (n.d.), 'The Story Behind Israel's Flag. Prophetic symbol of Israel', McKinney, Texas: Lamb & Lion Ministries (http://www.Lamblion.com/articles/articles_jews9.php).

Rose, Greg (2011), 'Lawfare', Australia/Israel & Jewish Affairs Council (AIJAC), 29 March 2011 (http://www.aijac.org.au/news/article/essay-lawfare).

Rosenne, Shabtai (1971), 'On Multi-Lingual Interpretation', Israel Law Review, Vol. 6, 1971, pp. 360-365.

Ross, Dennis (2004), The Missing Peace: The Inside Story of the Fight for Middle East Peace, New York: Farrar, Straus and Giroux, 2004.

Rostow, Eugene W. (1975), 'Illegality of the Arab Attack on Israel of October 6, 1973', American Journal of International Law, Vol. 69, No. 2, 1975, pp. 272-289.

Rostow, Eugene W. (1991), 'Resolved: are the settlements legal?: Israeli West Bank policies', The New Republic, 21 October 1991.

Rostow, Eugene W. (1993), 'The Future of Palestine', National Defense University, MacNair paper 24, November 1993 (https://www.files.ethz.ch/isn/23476/mcnair24.pdf)

Roth, Cecil and Geoffrey Wigoder (Editors-in-Chief) (1975), The New Standard Jewish Encyclopedia, Jerusalem: Massada Press, 1975.

Ryngaert, Cedric and Christine Griffioen (2009), 'The Relevance of the Right to Self-Determination in the Kosovo Matter: In partial response to the Agora Papers', Chinese Journal of International Law, Vol. 8, No. 3, November 2009, pp. 573-587.

Ryngaert, Cedric, Erik J. Molenaar and Sarah Nouwen (eds.) (2015), What's Wrong with International Law? (Liber Amicorum A.H.A. Soons), Leiden/Boston: Koninklijke Brill/Nijhoff, 2015.

Sabel, Ronnie (2009), 'The Campaign to Delegitimize Israel with the False Charge of Apartheid', Jewish Political Chronicle (Jerusalem Center for Public Affairs), Vol. 14, No. 2, Winter 2009, pp. 18-31.

Sacks, Rabbi Jonathan (2009), The Koren Siddur (Introduction, Translation and Commentary), Jerusalem: Koren Publishers, 2009.

Salahi, Reem (2008), 'Reinterpreting Article 1D: seeking Viable Solutions to the Palestinian Refugee Anomaly', Berkeley Journal of Middle Eastern & Islamic Law, Vol. 1, 2008, article 3, pp. 127-161.

Samson, Elizabeth (2010), 'Is Gaza Occupied?: Redefining the Status of Gaza Under International Law', American University International Law Review, Vol. 25, No. 5, 2010, pp. 915-967.

Sands, Philippe (2016), East West Street: On the Origins of Genocide and Crimes Against Humanity, New York: Alfred A. Knopf, 2016.

Schneer, Jonathan (2010), The Balfour Declaration. The Origins of the Arab-Israeli Conflict, London etc.: Bloomsbury, 2010.

Schwartz, Adi (2008), 'All I Wanted Was Justice', Haaretz, 3 January 2008.

Schwebel, Stephen M. (1994), Justice in International Law. Selected Writings of Judge Stephen M. Schwebel, Cambridge: Cambridge University Press, 1994.

Seligson, Susan (2010), 'Noam Chomsky Rails Against Israel Again', BU Today, 3 March 2010.

Shabas, William A. (2007), 'Lex Specialis? Belt and suspenders? The Parallel Operation of Human Rights Law and the Law of Armed Conflict and the Conundrum of Jus ad Bellum', Israel Law Review, Vol. 40, No. 2, 2007, pp. 592-613.

Shamir, Ilana, and Shlomo Shavit (eds.) (1987), Encyclopedie van de Joodse Geschiedenis [Encyclopedia of Jewish History], Kampen: Uitgeversmaatschappij Kok / Turnhout: Uitgeverij Brepols, 1987.

Shapira, Amos (1971), 'The Six-Day War and the Right to Self-Defense', Israel Law Review, Vol. 6, No. 1, 1971, pp. 65-80.

Shapira, Amos (2004), 'The Six-Day War and the Right of Self Defence, in: John Norton Moore (ed.), The Arab-Israeli Conflict, Vol. II, Princeton: Princeton University Press, 1974, pp. 203-220.

Shaw, Malcolm N. (1986), International Law, 2th ed., Cambridge: Grotius Publications Ltd., 1986.

Shaw, Malcolm N. (1997), 'The Heritage of States. The Principle of Uti Possidetis Today', British Yearbook of International Law, Vol. 67, No. 1, January 1997, pp. 75-154.

Shaw, Malcolm N. (2003), International Law, 5th ed., Cambridge: Cambridge University Press, 2003.

Shaw, Malcolm N. (2008), International Law, 6th ed., Cambridge: Cambridge University Press, 2008.

Shaw, Malcolm N. (2014), International Law, 7th ed., Cambridge: Cambridge University Press, 2014.

Shelton, Dinah (2000), Commitment and Compliance: The Role of Non-binding Norms in the International Legal System, Oxford: Oxford University Press, ed. 2000.

Shelton, Dinah (ed.) (2011), International Law and Domestic Legal Systems, Oxford: Oxford University Press, 2011.

Shetreet, Shimon (n.d.), 'Human Rights in Israel: Freedom of Religion', Jewish Virtual Library, a project of the American Israel Cooperation Enterprise (AICI), Chevy Chase, Maryland (http://www.jewishvirtuallibrary.org/freedom-of-religion-in-israel).

Shlaim, Avi (2005), 'The Balfour Declaration And its Consequences', in: William Roger Louis (ed.), Yet More Adventures with Britannia: Personalities, Politics and Culture in Britain, London: I.B. Taurus, 2005, pp. 251-270.

Shoham, Shlomo (ed.) (1971), Of Law and Man. Essays in Honor of Haim H. Cohn, New York/Tel Aviv: Sabra Books, 1971.

Simma, Bruno et al. (2002), The Charter of the United Nations: A Commentary, 2nd ed., New York: Columbia University Press, 2002.

Simmons, Shraga (2012), David & Goliath: The explosive inside story of media bias in the Israeli-Palestinian conflict, New York/Jerusalem: Emesphere Productions, 2012.

Singer, Joel (1994), 'Aspects of Foreign Relations Under the Israeli-Palestinian Agreements on Interim Self-Government Arrangements for the West Bank and Gaza', Israel Law Review, Vol. 28, Nos. 2-3, 1994, pp. 268-293.

Singer, Joel (1995), 'The West Bank and Gaza Strip: Phase Two', Justice (Magazine of the International Association of Jewish Lawyers and Jurists), Magazine No. 7, December 1995, pp. 5-17.

Sloan, James, and Christian J. Tams. (2013), The Development of International Law by the International Court of Justice, Oxford: Oxford University Press, 2013.

Slonim, Schlomo (1984), 'The United States and the Status of Jerusalem 1947-1984', Israel Law Review, Vol. 19, No. 2, 1984, pp. 179-252.

Smelik, Klaas A.D. (2014), Tussen hoop en catastrophe. Tikva of Nakba [Between hope and catastrophy. Tikva or Nakba], Soesterberg: Uitgeverij Aspekt, 2014.

Sokolov, Nahum (1919), History of Zionism, 2 Volumes, London: Longmans, Green, and Co., 1919.

Stahn, Carsten (2008), The Law and Practice of International Territorial Administration, Cambridge: Cambridge University Press, 2008.

Stahn-Don, Karen (2017), The British Mandate – Defining the Legality of Jewish Sovereignty over Judea and Samaria under International Law, Jerusalem: Israel Sovereignty Institute, 2017.

Steinberg, Gerald M. (2006), 'The centrality of NGOs in the Durban strategy', Yale Israel Journal, July 2006, pp. 3-20 (http://www.ngo-monitor.org/article/_the_centrality_of_ngos_in_the_durban_strategy_)

Steinberg, Gerald M., and Anne Herzberg (2011), The Goldstone Report 'Reconsidered': A critical analysis, Jerusalem Center for Public Affairs, Jerusalem: NGO Monitor, 2011.

Stoyanovsky, Jacob (1928), The Mandate for Palestine: a Contribution to the Theory and Practice of International Mandates, London/New York/Toronto: Longmans, Green and Co., 1928.

Summers, James (2013), Peoples and International Law: How Nationalism and Self-Determination Shape a Contemporary Law of Nations, Leiden/Boston: Martinus Nijhoff Publishers, 2013.

Susskind, Lawrence J. (2010), 'Lawfare', The American Thinker, 7 February 2010.

Tamanaha, Brian Z. (2007), 'How an Instrumental View of Law Corrodes the Rule of Law', DePaul Law Review (Special issue on the Symposium: Is the Rule of Law Waning in America?), Vol. 56, No. 2, Winter 2007, pp. 469-505.

The Times of Israel (Staff of) (2018), 'Palestinian reconciliation deal dying a slow death', The Times of Israel, 2 February 2018.

Tomuschat, Christian, and Jean-Marc Thouvenin (eds.) (2006), The Fundamental Rules of the International Legal Order, Leiden: Brill, 2006.

Trigano, Shmuel (2009), La fin du judaïsme en terres de l'Islam, Paris : Editions Denoël, 2009.

Tuchmann, Barbara W. (1982), Bible and Sword. How the British came to Palestine, London: MacMillan, 1982.

Turnberg, Leslie (2017), Beyond the Balfour Declaration: The 100-Year Quest for Israeli–Palestinian Peace, London: Biteback Publishing, 2017.

Tutu, Desmond (2014), 'Israel is guilty of apartheid in treatment of Palestinians', **The Jerusalem Post**, 10 March 2014.

United States Department of State (2014), International Religious Freedom Report for 2013, Report of 28 July 2014: 'Israel and the Occupied Territories', Section I, Religious Demography, US Dept. of State: Bureau of Democracy, Human Rights and Labor, Report, 2014.

Veerman, Gert Jan (1977), Het zelfbeschikkingsrecht der naties en de rechten van de mens [Self-determination of nations and human rights], Amsterdam: Academische Pers, 1977.

Verdross, Alfred, and Bruno Simma (1984), Universelles Völkerrecht: Theorie und Praxis, 3rd ed., Berlin/Munich: Duncker & Humblot, 1984.

Verrijn Stuart, H. (2009), 'We zullen disproportioneel geweld gebruiken. De plaats van het recht naast politiek en oorlog' [We will use disproportionate force. The role of law in politics and war], Nederlands Juristenblad [Dutch Lawyers Journal], 30 January 2009, pp. 243-250.

Waldock, Claud Humphrey M. (1952), 'The Regulation of the Use of Force by Individual States in International Law', Academie de Droit Int.l Des Cours, Vol. 81, 1952, pp. 451-517.

Waldock, Claud Humphrey M. (1962), 'General Course on Public International Law', Recueil des cours, Vol. 106, No. 11, 1962, pp. 1-251.

Wallace, Cynthia D. (2012), Foundations of the International Legal Rights of the Jewish People and the State of Israel and the Implications for the Proposed New Palestinian State, Lake Mary, Florida: Creation House, 2012.

Walzer, Michael (2009 a), 'On Proportionality: How Much is Too Much in War?', The New Republic, 8 January 2009.

Walzer, Michael (2009 b), 'Responsibility and Proportionality in State and Nonstate Wars, Parameters, Spring 2009, pp. 40-52.

Watts, Sir Arthur (1993), 'The International Rule of Law', German Yearbook of International Law, Vol. 36, 1993, pp. 15-45.

Wedgwood, Ruth (2005), 'The ICJ Advisory Opinion on the Israeli Security Force and the Limits of Self-Defense', American Journal of International Law, Vol. 99, No. 1, January 2005, pp. 52-61.

Weiner, Justus R. (1997), 'The Palestinian Refugees' "Right to Return" and the Peace Process', Boston College International and Comparative Law Review, Vol. 2, No. 1, 1997, pp. 1-53.

Weiner, Justus R. (2005), 'The NGOs, demolition of illegal building in Jerusalem, and international law', Jerusalem Center for Public Affairs (JCPA), (www.jcpa.org), Jewish Political Studies Review , Vol. 17, No. 1-2, Spring 2005.

Weiner, Justus R., and Abraham Bell (2008), 'International Law and the Fighting in Gaza', Jerusalem Center for Public Affairs (JCPA), paper, 2008.

Weizmann, Chaim (1983), The Letters and Papers of Chaim Weizmann: August 1898 – July 1931, Jerusalem: Israel University Press, 1983.

Whiston, William (1987) (translation), The Works of Flavius Josephus, Peabody, Massachusetts: Hendrickson Publishers, 1987.

Wilde, Ralph (2008), International Territorial Administration: How Trusteeship and the Civilizing Mission Never Went Away, Oxford: Oxford University Press, 2008.

Williams, Phil (2008), 'Violent non-State Actors and National and International Security', International Relations and Security Network (ISN), 2008 (http://www.isn.ethz.ch/Digital-Library/Publications/Detail?id=93880)

Wistrich, Robert S. (2010), A Lethal Obsession. Anti-Semitism from Antiquity to Global Jihad, New York: Random House, 2010.

Wood, Michael (n.d.), 'Territorial Integrity', in: Encyclopedia Princeoniensis (The Princeton Encyclopedia of Self-Determination), Princeton, New Jersey.

Yakobson, Alexander (2010), 'Joining the Jewish People: Non-Jewish Immigrants from the Former USSR, Israeli Identity and Jewish Peoplehood', Israel Law Review, Vol. 43, No. 3, 2010, pp. 218-239.

Zemanek, Karl (1997), The Legal Foundations of the International System, The Hague: Martinus Nijhoff, 1997.

Ziri, Danielle (2016), 'Ban Ki-moon Recognizes Bias against Israel in last Security Council speech', in: The Jerusalem Post, 16 December 2016.

Zoher, Zion (ed.) (2005), Sephardic and Mizrahi Jewry. From the Golden Age of Spain to Modern Times, New York: New York University Press, 2005.

Biographies

Dr. Matthijs de Blois (Bussum, 1953) studied law at Utrecht University, graduating in 1977 with a Master of Laws. After 1977, he worked in the Law Faculty of Leiden University, in the Department of International Law, where he received his PhD. Since 1990, he has been an assistant professor at Utrecht University's Institute of Legal Theory of the Law Faculty. His academic focus is the philosophical and historical aspects of the law, specifically the relationship between law and religion.

Matthijs is a senior fellow of The Hague Initiative for International Cooperation (*thinc.*). He writes about the position of the State of Israel under international law, which, after his departure from the Law Faculty in August 2017, has become the main focus of his research within the framework of *thinc.*. His recent publications in this field include:

Israël: een staat ter discussie? Over de internationaalrechtelijke positie van Israël ["Israel: A State under Discussion"] Jongbloed/Groen, Heerenveen 2010, 112 pp.; "Bad Law and a Hard Case? The Impact of the *Wall* Advisory Opinion of the ICJ," in Cedric Ryngaert, Erik Molenaar and Sarah Nouwen, *What's Wrong with International Law? Liber Amicorum Alfred H.A. Soons,* Leiden, Brill/Nijhoff, 2015, pp. 94-113; "The Unique Character of the Mandate for Palestine" in *Israel Law Review* 49(3) 2016, pp. 365-389.

Andrew Tucker BA/LLB BCL (Canberra, 1963) studied law in Australia, UK and The Netherlands, and has worked since 1988 as an adviser and consultant to private companies, governments and (semi-)public entities in various fields of international law.

Andrew was a Fellow of the Law Faculty of the University of Melbourne from 1994 to 2001, and Research Associate at the TMC Asser Institute from 1996-1998. Based in The Netherlands, he is Principal of Tucker & Associates, and Legal Counsel to the European Coalition for Israel—a Brussels-based NGO advocating the position and interests of the Jewish people and the State of Israel within the European Union and the United Nations.

Andrew is a Director of the Hague Initiative for International Cooperation (*thinc.*). His publications in the area of international law include:

"The Energy Charter Treaty and 'Compulsory' International State/ Investor Arbitration", Leiden Journal of International Law, Vol. 11 (1998), pp. 513-526.